First Workshop on Scholarly Document Processing (SDP 2020)

Online
19 November 2020

ISBN: 978-1-7138-1987-5

EMNLP 2020

First Workshop on Scholarly Document Processing

Proceedings of the Workshop

November 19, 2020
Online

Introduction

Welcome to the First Workshop on Scholarly Document Processing (SDP) at EMNLP 2020.

Next to keeping up with the growing literature in their own and related fields, scholars increasingly also need to rebut pseudo-science and disinformation. To address this challenge, computational work on enhancing search, summarization, and analysis of scholarly documents has flourished. However, the various strands of research on scholarly document processing remain fragmented. To reach to the broader NLP and AI/ML community, pool distributed efforts and enable shared access to published research, we held the 1st Workshop on Scholarly Document Processing at EMNLP20. The SDP workshop consisted of a research track and three Shared Tasks, geared towards easier access to scientific methods and results.
`https://ornlcda.github.io/SDProc/`

Organizers:

Muthu Kumar Chandrasekaran, Amazon, Seattle, USA Anita de Waard, Elsevier, USA Guy Feigenblat, IBM Research AI, Haifa Research Lab, Israel Dayne Freitag, SRI International, San Diego, USA Tirthankar Ghosal, Indian Institute of Technology Patna, India Eduard Hovy, Research Professor, LTI, Carnegie Melon University, USA Petr Knoth, Open University, UK David Konopnicki, IBM Research AI, Haifa Research Lab, Israel Philipp Mayr, GESIS – Leibniz Institute for the Social Sciences, Germany Robert M. Patton, Oak Ridge National Laboratory, USA Michal Shmueli-Scheuer, IBM Research AI, Haifa Research Lab, Israel

Program Committee:

Please find our programme committee in the following webpage:
`https://ornlcda.github.io/SDProc/programcommittee.html`

Invited Speaker:

Kuansan Wang, Managing Director, MSR Outreach Academic Services, USA Steinn Sigurðsson, Scientific Director of arXiv, Professor in the Department of Astronomy & Astrophysics at The Pennsylvania State University

Table of Contents

Conference Program

Research Track Session 3

DeepPaperComposer: A Simple Solution for Training Data Preparation for Parsing Research Papers
Meng Ling and Jian Chen

Improved Local Citation Recommendation Based on Context Enhanced with Global Information
Zoran Medić and Jan Snajder

Poster Session

On the effectiveness of small, discriminatively pre-trained language representation models for biomedical text mining
Ibrahim Burak Ozyurt

SciWING– A Software Toolkit for Scientific Document Processing
Abhinav Ramesh Kashyap and Min-Yen Kan

Multi-task Peer-Review Score Prediction
Jiyi Li, Ayaka Sato, Kazuya Shimura and Fumiyo Fukumoto

ERLKG: Entity Representation Learning and Knowledge Graph based association analysis of COVID-19 through mining of unstructured biomedical corpora
Sayantan Basu, Sinchani Chakraborty, Atif Hassan, Sana Siddique and Ashish Anand

Towards Grounding of Formulae
Takuto Asakura, André Greiner-Petter, Akiko Aizawa and Yusuke Miyao

SChuBERT: Scholarly Document Chunks with BERT-encoding boost Citation Count Prediction.
Thomas van Dongen, Gideon Maillette de Buy Wenniger and Lambert Schomaker

Structure-Tags Improve Text Classification for Scholarly Document Quality Prediction
Gideon Maillette de Buy Wenniger, Thomas van Dongen, Eleri Aedmaa, Herbert Teun Kruitbosch, Edwin A. Valentijn and Lambert Schomaker

Cydex: Neural Search Infrastructure for the Scholarly Literature
Shane Ding, Edwin Zhang and Jimmy Lin

Overview of the First Workshop on Scholarly Document Processing (SDP)

Muthu Kumar Chandrasekaran
Amazon, USA
cmkumar087@gmail.com

Guy Feigenblat
IBM Research AI, Israel
guyf@il.ibm.com

Dayne Freitag
SRI International, USA
daynefreitag@sri.com

Tirthankar Ghosal
Indian Institute of Technology Patna, India
tirthankar.pcs16@iitp.ac.in

Eduard Hovy
Carnegie Melon University, USA
hovy@cmu.edu

Philipp Mayr
GESIS – Leibniz Institute for
the Social Sciences, Germany
philipp.mayr@gesis.org

Michal Shmueli-Scheuer
IBM Research AI, Israel
shmueli@il.ibm.com

Anita de Waard
Elsevier, USA
a.dewaard@elsevier.com

Abstract

Next to keeping up with the growing literature in their own and related fields, scholars increasingly also need to rebut pseudo-science and disinformation. To address these challenges, computational work on enhancing search, summarization, and analysis of scholarly documents has flourished. However, the various strands of research on scholarly document processing remain fragmented. To reach to the broader NLP and AI/ML community, pool distributed efforts and enable shared access to published research, we held the 1st Workshop on Scholarly Document Processing at EMNLP 2020 as a virtual event. The SDP workshop consisted of a research track (including a poster session), two invited talks and three Shared Tasks (CL-SciSumm, LaySumm and LongSumm), geared towards easier access to scientific methods and results. **Website**: https://ornlcda.github.io/SDProc

1 Workshop description

Over the past several years and at various venues, the Joint Workshop on Bibliometric-enhanced IR and NLP for Digital Libraries (**BIRNDL**[1]) (Cabanac et al., 2020; Mayr et al., 2018), the **CL-SciSumm** Shared Task (Chandrasekaran et al., 2019), and the International Workshop on Mining Scientific Publications (**WOSP**[2]) have established themselves as the principal venues for scholarly document processing (SDP) research. However, as these venues are collocated with conferences that are not focused on NLP, current solutions in this domain lag behind modern techniques generated by the greater NLP community.

---

[1] https://philippmayr.github.io/BIRNDL-WS/

[2] https://wosp.core.ac.uk/

The goal of SDP 2020 was to help foster cross-fertilization of ideas by bringing together people from different communities to leverage work on scientific literature and data. In doing so, we hope to create a premier meeting point to facilitate discussions converging towards solutions to open problems in SDP.

We believe that ACL events are the most appropriate venue for the SDP workshop for two reasons. First, ACL events are the premier venues for the confluence of NLP and ML and most of the cornerstone tasks in processing scholarly documents are NLP tasks. Improving machine understanding of scholarly semantics embedded in research papers is essential to further many tasks and applications in scholarly document processing. ACL events would, therefore, help integrate the broader NLP and AI/ML community with the distributed efforts in scholarly IR and Data Mining such that this field can progress as a more unified community. From our previous foray with IR and Data Mining we are convinced that delving into the language model of scholarly artefacts and improving machine understanding of scholarly semantics embedded in research papers is essential to further many tasks and applications in scholarly document processing. Second, we seek to bring together researchers and practitioners from various backgrounds focusing on different aspects of scholarly document processing. We believe the interdisciplinary nature of ACL venues would greatly assist in encouraging submissions from a diverse set of fields.

Topics. The topics of interest to SDP encompass all approaches to mining scholarly data and encourage submissions from all relevant communities, including:

1

Proceedings of the First Workshop on Scholarly Document Processing, pages 1–6
Online, November 19, 2020. ©2020 Association for Computational Linguistics
https://doi.org/10.18653/v1/P17

1. Information extraction, text mining and parsing of scholarly literature;

2. Reproducibility and peer review;

3. Lay Summarization (i.e., summaries created for non-experts) of individual and collections of scholarly documents;

4. Discourse modeling and argument mining;

5. Summarization and question-answering for scholarly documents;

6. Semantic and network-based indexing, search and navigation in structured text;

7. Graph analysis/mining including citation and co-authorship networks;

8. New scholarly language resources and evaluation;

9. Connecting and interlinking publications, data, tweets, blogs or their parts;

10. Disambiguation, metadata extraction, enrichment, and data quality assurance for scholarly documents;

11. Bibliometrics, scientometrics, and altmetrics approaches and applications;

12. Other aspects of scientific workflows including open access/science, and research assessment;

13. Infrastructures for accessing scientific publications and/or research data;

14. Results and research questions on the COVID-19 Open Research Dataset (CORD-19).

Workshop agenda. The SDP 2020 workshop[3] consisted of:

Two keynote talks, a Research Track (including a poster session) and a Shared Task Track with 3 separate shared tasks.

Keynotes. (1) **Kuansan Wang**, Managing Director, Microsoft Research Outreach Academic Services gave the first keynote titled: "Mitigating scholarly corpus biases with citations: A case study on CORD-19". *Abstract*: With the broad adoption of evidence based decision making processes, recent years have witnessed more frequent examples where biases in the datasets or the analytical algorithms lead to unfortunate and sometimes harmful outcomes. Being mindful of potential biases and actively taking measures to mitigate them have become a necessary second nature for scholars and decision makers alike. Citations in scholarly publications have long been known to represent the crowd-sourced collective judgments on scholarly communications and can be a valuable source of information in analyzing scholarly documents. This study describes a methodology that uses citations to identify biases in such corpus, using as an example the COVID-19 Open Research Dataset, or CORD-19, a corpus created to advance the development of intelligent technologies that can assist scientists in navigating through the voluminous literature of COVID-19. By expanding to articles in the citation networks seeded by CORD-19 with three distinct algorithms, it can be shown that CORD-19 has a strong tilt in favor of recent articles and uneven coverages in the topical fields and the publication venues. Using CORD-19 to identify critical knowledge and assess the journal importance, for example, will lead to different conclusions from the analyses based on the three expanded datasets, of which results largely agree with one another. CORD-19, however, does not appear to exhibit biases in describing research collaborations in terms of team sizes or geolocations. Currently, the three citation network traversal algorithms only utilize bibliographic records. How improvements can be made to them, such as through more sophisticated uses of citation contexts, will also be discussed.

(2) **Steinn Sigurðsson**, Scientific Director of arXiv, Professor in the Department of Astronomy & Astrophysics at The Pennsylvania State University gave the second keynote titled: "The future of arXiv and knowledge discovery in open science"[4]. *Abstract*: arXiv, the preprint server for the physical and mathematical sciences, is in its third decade of operation. As the flow of new, open access research increases inexorably, the challenges to keep up with and discover research content also become greater. I will discuss the status and future of arXiv, and possibilities and plans to make more effective use of the research database to enhance ongoing research efforts.

---

[3] The full program is available via `https://ornlcda.github.io/SDProc/program.html`.

[4] See the keynote paper in the SDP proceedings.

2   Research Track

In total, we received 34 papers for the research track. We accepted 9 papers for oral presentation (7 as full papers and 2 as short papers). We rejected 14 research paper submissions. In order to include a broader variety of contributions, we decided to invite all research papers with borderline scores as poster papers, leading us to accept 11 posters, which were presented in a separate virtual poster slot.

This year, the EMNLP organizers added a new resource, the "Findings of EMNLP"[5]. 520 EMNLP papers were accepted to Findings of EMNLP. Some of the authors of these Findings papers choose the SDP workshop as primary presentation venue. We accommodated and invited 3 "Findings" papers for oral presentation and 1 as a poster.

One demo paper was accepted as technical contribution in addition to the scientific program.

In the following, we list all contributions which were presented in some form at the workshop.

Oral presentations (full papers):
- Wu et al.: *Acknowledgement Entity Recognition in CORD-19 Papers.*

- Bhambhoria et al.: *A Smart System to Generate and Validate Question Answer Pairs for COVID-19 Literature.*

- Zhang et al.: *Covidex: Neural Ranking Models and Keyword Search Infrastructure for the COVID-19 Open Research Dataset.*

- Satish et al.: *The impact of preprint servers in the formation of novel ideas.*

- Berger et al.: *Effective Distributed Representations for Academic Expert Search.*

- Kim et al.: *Learning CNF Blocking for Large-scale Author Name Disambiguation.*

- Müller et al.: *Reconstructing Manual Information Extraction with DB-to-Document Backprojection: Experiments in the Life Science Domain.*

Oral presentations (short papers):

- Ling & Chen: *DeepPaperComposer: A Simple Solution for Training Data Preparation for Parsing Research Papers.*

- Medić & Snajder: *Improved Local Citation Recommendation Based on Context Enhanced with Global Information.*

Poster presentations:
- Ozyurt: *On the effectiveness of small, discriminatively pre-trained language representation models for biomedical text mining.*

- Kashyap & Kan: *SciWING – A Software Toolkit for Scientific Document Processing.*

- Li et al.: *Multi-task Peer-Review Score Prediction.*

- Basu et al.: *ERLKG: Entity Representation Learning and Knowledge Graph based association analysis of COVID-19 through mining of unstructured biomedical corpora.*

- Asakura et al.: *Towards Grounding of Formulae.*

- van Dongen et al.: *SChuBERT: Scholarly Document Chunks with BERT-encoding boost Citation Count Prediction.*

- de Buy Wenniger et al.: *Structure-Tags Improve Text Classification for Scholarly Document Quality Prediction.*

- Ding et al.: *Cydex: Neural Search Infrastructure for the Scholarly Literature.*

- Patel et al.: *On the Use of Web Search to Improve Scientific Collections.*

- Goldfarb-Tarrant et al.: *Scaling Systematic Literature Reviews with Machine Learning Pipelines.*

- Kang et al.: *Document-Level Definition Detection in Scholarly Documents: Existing Models, Error Analyses, and Future Directions.*

Poster (demo paper):
- Fadaee et al.[6]: *A New Neural Search and Insights Platform for Navigating and Organizing AI Research.*

---

[5] https://2020.emnlp.org/blog/
2020-04-19-findings-of-emnlp

[6]This paper was accepted as technical demo beside the research program.

EMNLP 2020 Findings papers: Cao et al., Noh & Kavuluru, Subramanian et al. were presented as short papers; Kobs et al. was presented as a poster.

- Cao et al.: *Will This Idea Spread Beyond Academia? Understanding Knowledge Transfer of Scientific Concepts across Text Corpora.*

- Noh & Kavuluru: *Literature Retrieval for Precision Medicine with Neural Matching and Faceted Summarization.*

- Subramanian et al.: *MedICaT: A Dataset of Medical Images, Captions, and Textual References.*

- Kobs et al.: *Where to Submit? Helping Researchers to Choose the Right Venue.*

3 Shared Task Track

In addition to the research track, SDP hosted three Shared Tasks. Details of the task, results and overview are provided in a companion paper, '*Overview and Insights from the First Workshop on from Scholarly Document Processing: Shared Tasks: CL-SciSumm, LaySumm and LongSumm*' (Chandrasekaran et al., Forthcoming). We added these since summarization is an important and challenging effort within scholarly document processing, as the number and complexity of scientific papers increases exponentially, and making them accessible to both a lay and professional audience becomes increasingly important.

3.1 CL-SciSumm

CL-SciSumm is the first medium-scale shared task on scientific document summarization in the computational linguistics domain with over 500 documents annotated for their citation and citation targets and over a 1000 more documents with human annotated summaries inherited and integrated from SciSummNet (Yasunaga et al., 2019). Last year's CL-SciSumm shared task introduced large scale training datasets, both annotated from ScisummNet and auto-annotated. For this year's task, systems were provided with a Reference Paper (RP) and 10 or more Citing Papers (CPs) that all contain citations to the RP, which they used to summarise the RP. This was evaluated against abstract, citation-based summaries and human-written summaries with ROUGE. The shared task attracted 50+ registrations and 11 final system submissions. Importantly, we have now released the gold standard labels for our hitherto blind test set[7] which can serve as a public benchmark for evaluations on the CL-SciSumm corpus.

3.2 LaySumm

The **LaySumm** summarization task considers automating the generation of a Lay Summary: a text of about 70–100 words intended for a non-technical audience that explains, succinctly and without using technical jargon, the overall scope, goal, and potential impact expressed in a scientific paper. The corpus for this task comprised 572 full-text papers with lay summaries, in a variety of domains, including archaeology, hematology, and engineering, made available by *Elsevier*

The Lay summaries had to be representative of the content, comprehensible, and interesting to a lay audience. The intrinsic evaluation was done by ROUGE, through the CodaLabs Platform[8] In addition, a subset of randomly selected summaries underwent human evaluation by a team of science journalists and communicators for comprehensiveness, legibility, and interest. Authors were also asked to provide an automatically generated lay summary of their own paper together with their contribution.

3.3 LongSumm

The **LongSumm** task aims at creating long summaries of around 600 words. Often, for researchers, short summaries (e.g., abstract) are not detailed enough. Thus, longer summaries are mainly intended for helping researchers understand the gist of a paper without the need to read it entirely. The corpus for this task includes a training set that consists of 1705 extractive summaries, and 531 abstractive summaries of NLP and Machine Learning scientific papers. The extractive summaries are based on video talks from associated conferences (Lev et al., 2019) while the abstractive summaries are based on blog posts created by NLP and ML researchers. The test set consists of 22 abstractive summaries for evaluating the submissions. In total, 9 systems participated in the task, with a total of 100 submissions. The

---

[7] https://github.com/WING-NUS/
scisumm-corpus/tree/master/data/
Test-Set-2018-Gold
[8] https://competitions.codalab.org/
competitions/25516#learn_the_details

evaluation was conducted using the ROUGE measure (Lin, 2004) and executed on a public leaderboard[9]. In addition, a subset of randomly selected summaries, of the top ranked systems, was evaluated by experts

4 Workshop Overview and Outlook

The organizers were gratified by both the size and breadth of the response to the inaugural edition of SDP. The subjects of accepted papers and posters ranged from end uses of the scholarly literature (such as search, recommendation, or literature curation) to challenges associated with automated understanding (such as entity recognition and disambiguation or formula grounding), to adaptations of recent successes in the broader field of NLP (such as generation or question answering). It is apparent that automated processing of the scholarly literature is a problem that meets with substantial interest. And it seems likely that we are observing the beginnings of a research community with a narrow enough focus to make rapid progress, but a broad enough set of concerns to offer ample opportunities for cross-pollination.

To a first approximation, we regard SDP as a confluence of three communities: NLP, information retrieval, and scientometrics. Given our co-location with EMNLP, it is perhaps not surprising that the majority of our submissions emphasized NLP. Certainly, our shared tasks all share a research focus, summarization, that is a traditional NLP problem area. As we consider future iterations of the workshop, we are discussing ways to increase its subject diversity. We have begun by identifying a more varied set of shared tasks, each highlighting challenges unique to the automated processing of the scholarly literature. As we proceed with planning and advertising, a key objective will be to elicit high-quality submissions from researchers interested in the uses and metalinguistic aspects of scholarly communication.

5 Organising and Steering Committees

A formal Organizing Committee and a Steering Committee helped guide the successful organisation first SDP. We thank all members for their help in reviewing all submissions, submitting the workshop proposal, and planning the final program: C. Lee Giles, Pennsylvania State University, USA;

Min-Yen Kan, National University of Singapore; Petr Knoth, Open University, UK; Robert Patton, Oak Ridge National Laboratory, USA; Dragomir Radev, Yale University, USA; Jie Tang, Tsinghua University, China; Kuansan Wang, MSR Outreach Academic Services, USA; Bonnie Webber, University of Edinburgh, UK.

6 Conclusion

The scholarly literature has long served as a rich source of interesting and challenging problems for computer science. Recent events regarding misinterpretation of scholarly information accentuate the importance of better approaches to the automated processing of scholarly literature.

We hope that this event helps to connect these challenges to use cases, fostering solutions that ultimately improve the practice of scholarship and serve society.

References

Guillaume Cabanac, Ingo Frommholz, and Philipp Mayr. 2020. Bibliometric-Enhanced Information Retrieval 10th Anniversary Workshop Edition. In Joemon M. Jose, Emine Yilmaz, João Magalhães, Pablo Castells, Nicola Ferro, Mário J. Silva, and Flávio Martins, editors, *Advances in Information Retrieval*, volume 12036, pages 641–647. Springer International Publishing, Cham.

M. K. Chandrasekaran, G. Feigenblat, Hovy. E., A. Ravichander, M. Shmueli-Scheuer, and A De Waard. Forthcoming. Overview and insights from scientific document summarization shared tasks 2020: CL-SciSumm, LaySumm and LongSumm. In *Proceedings of the First Workshop on Scholarly Document Processing (SDP 2020)*.

Muthu Kumar Chandrasekaran, Michihiro Yasunaga, Dragomir Radev, Dayne Freitag, and Min-Yen Kan. 2019. Overview and results: Cl-scisumm shared task 2019. *arXiv preprint arXiv:1907.09854*.

Guy Lev, Michal Shmueli-Scheuer, Jonathan Herzig, Achiya Jerbi, and David Konopnicki. 2019. Talksumm: A dataset and scalable annotation method for scientific paper summarization based on conference talks. *arXiv preprint arXiv:1906.01351*.

Chin-Yew Lin. 2004. Rouge: A package for automatic evaluation of summaries. In *Text summarization branches out: Proceedings of the ACL-04 workshop*, volume 8. Barcelona, Spain.

Philipp Mayr, Ingo Frommholz, Guillaume Cabanac, Muthu Kumar Chandrasekaran, Kokil Jaidka, Min-Yen Kan, and Dietmar Wolfram. 2018. Introduction

---

to the Special Issue on Bibliometric-Enhanced Information Retrieval and Natural Language Processing for Digital Libraries (BIRNDL). *International Journal on Digital Libraries*, 19(2-3):107–111.

Michihiro Yasunaga, Jungo Kasai, Rui Zhang, Alexander R Fabbri Irene Li Dan, and Friedman Dragomir R Radev. 2019. Scisummnet: A large annotated corpus and content-impact models for scientific paper summarization with citation networks.

The future of arXiv and knowledge discovery in open science

Steinn Sigurdsson
arXiv, Cornell Tech
ss3783@cornell.edu
& Pennsylvania State University
University Park, PA 16803

Abstract

arχiv, the preprint server for the physical and mathematical sciences, is in its third decade of operation. As the flow of new, open access research increases inexorably, the challenges to keep up with and discover research content also become greater. I will discuss the status and future of arχiv, and possibilities and plans to make more effective use of the research database to enhance ongoing research efforts.

1 Introduction

arχiv as of the time of writing contains $1,777,731$ e–prints across 158 categories in 8 different subject areas. The e–prints are distributed under license, and archived, free to the author and free to the reader. Distribution is fast, by daily e–mail blasts by category, RSS feeds, and direct web access. arχiv gets approximately a quarter of a million hits per hour, and currently receives about 15,000 new submissions per month. Each submission, upon acceptance, is assigned a unique arXiv:###.#####v# ID which is stable and maintains version control for revisions.

The average category has about five new primary submissions per day, but the larger categories have many dozens of new e–prints per day, and keeping up with the literature is accurately likened to trying to drink from a firehose. Finding the research you want and need seems to become harder as the tools to access the literature improve. Curating the flow of information and enabling discovery are critical tasks and expediting knowledge discovery will likely enable more rapid progress across a wide range of fields.

A peculiarity of the arχiv category system is that the submissions, each day, are ordered by time of submission, with the breakpoint being 2 pm eastern time each day. The e–prints submitted first after the 2 pm switch show up first, both in emails to subscribers and in web page listings. This leads to a well known effect that the e–prints first in this rank order are disproportionately cited compared to later ranked e–prints (Haque and Ginsparg, 2009, 2010). While this provides a form of knowledge discovery, and one that undoubtedly correlates with some attributes of the researchers who wrote and submitted the e–print, it is not an optimal technique for efficient discovery.

Additional discovery is enabled by the sorting of e–prints into *categories* within their *subject* areas. While this is primarily done by authors at the time of submission, the ultimate choice of categorization is done by arχiv moderators, with the assistance of automated tools. arχiv reserves the right to set the primary category in which the submissions appear, and to assign or remove secondary categories or later cross listings.

Moderation of Categories: The moderation process within arχiv currently occurs in three primary stages. On submission the e–print is processed and checked for a number of technical issues. Approximately 10% of e–prints have some error and are referred back to the author (not counting minor errors which are generally fixed during submission). The median time from a submitting author logging into the system and a submission being complete is 34 minutes.

During submission an automatic classification system scans the paper and recommends a choice of categories. For most submissions the choice of primary category matches that of the author, in other cases the system may recommend a different category. The author may choose to accept the new recommended category, or add it as a secondary category in which to list the submission, or they may proceed with their original category and ignore the system recommendation.

Proceedings of the First Workshop on Scholarly Document Processing, pages 7–9
Online, November 19, 2020. ©2020 Association for Computational Linguistics
https://doi.org/10.18653/v1/P17

Each category has an assigned moderator, with 194 voluntary moderators covering the range of subject categories. Some categories have two or more moderators, generally the high volume categories. At any given time there are gaps in moderation, sometimes covered on an *ad hoc* basis by volunteer super–moderators, who may have responsibility for multiple categories. The moderators are generally senior PhD researchers who are active in the field they are moderating. The ideal moderator is someone who was checking the distribution in "their" category every morning anyway, someone who wants to see first what is new.

The moderators have primary responsibility for the choice of categories, and whether a submission is released, held for further checks, or rejected. A small fraction of submissions get held for an extended period (currently about 0.5% are on hold for two or more weeks). Extended holds mostly occur due to coordination issues between moderators, including moderators who are out of action, disagreements on choice of categories, or policy questions. Submissions may be rejected for being out of scope, not being the type of content arχiv accepts, or not meeting the threshold for standard of acceptance in that subject and category. arχiv makes substantial effort to maintain consistent standards across categories and subject areas, but there are some differences in approach and style across academic fields, and where these cross is often where papers are put on hold or rejected. arχiv is a curated collection, it is not a general repository. arχiv is not the internet. In order to remain useful to its community of users arχiv curates content for relevance and interest, while trying to avoid gatekeeping and active refereeing of content. This means there are always borderline cases. The borderline cases are generally not important in the aggregate, but they are important to the individual authors, and there is a strong motivation not to exclude original or innovative approaches through overly strong filtering. However, there is always some border between accepting and rejecting, and wherever that border is, there are always edge cases which end up being judgement calls. Moving the border does not resolve the issue, it merely moves which submissions are borderline.

2   Classification

Papers submitted to arχiv are run through a natural language processing classifier (Ginsparg et al., 2010). Currently three classifiers are operational: the original full text classifier from Ginsparg; a beta version of a more general broad classification package, including full text, run asynchronously; and a new fast metadata classifier developed by Papers with Code. Note that arχiv submissions come with very sparse metadata. Demanding large amounts of metadata provided by the author puts a burden on the author during submission and discourages use of arχiv for rapid distribution of research.

Moderators see the classifier score, and a paper with a high score in a particular category not selected by the author may be queued up for consideration by the moderators of that category, for selection either as a primary category or as a secondary choice of category. A few percent of submissions typically get some category changes, often the addition of one or more secondary categories for listing.

Category changes also lead to significant fraction of holds of submissions, both when a moderator deems a submission unsuitable for the choice of category, or when moderators disagree amongst themselves about the choice of category. Orphaned submissions, those rejected from all choices of primary categories, may be rejected as out of scope. Moderators will often recommend alternative possible choices of primary, or recommend secondary categories for submission.

The classifiers are imperfect, in particular when trying to determine a fit for the smaller categories, even after balancing, and some broad categories are treated as exception cases. Training the classifier is an iterative process, and more work is needed.

3   Knowledge Discovery

Ultimately researchers and other readers want to discover the latest research that is relevant to their interests, and to find other relevant results, novel methods, complementary insights or other useful or interesting knowledge. A lot of discovery comes from finding your lane and staying in it, the categories provide useful silos for a significant fraction of researchers and push most of the directly relevant science to that community. Beyond the silo, searches of the literature are useful for discovery, but are often constrained by what can be indexed for searching and how the search algorithm keys in on search terms. Improved search algorithms and federated cross platform searches generally improve prospects for discovery.

arχiv currently has formal relations with several

entities to expedite cross platform discovery, including INSPIRE, ADS, DBLP, Semantic Scholar and Google Scholar. We are working to improve discovery including author disambiguation. Author ID services such as ORCID and Institutional Identifiers like ROR also expedite searches. An ambition of arχiv is to provide custom delivery of new submissions beyond the current categories, to include among other options, author selection, types of content, and inclusion and exclusion by keywords and relevance.

Balancing this impetus is the danger of loss of discovery by browsing, the serendipitous discovery that came when browsing a physical journal and finding a surprise article adjacent to the one you were seeking, or a topical book you were not aware of shelved next to those you browsed. Refined and narrow searches limit surprises. Sometimes what you are looking for is not the "known unknowns" but rather the "unknown unknowns". It is tempting to consider providing a small fraction of random or semi-random search results in searches in the hope of triggering the rare discovery of an unknown.

A more formal process may be more efficient and likelier to succeed, and arχiv is interested in pursuing knowledge discovery techniques, including knowledge graphs and novel techniques for finding relevant results that are not adjacent to the research area being searched. There are very large benefits to finding an existing solution to an experimental problem, a new computational technique making your modeling tractable, a statistical or mathematical method making your problem solvable, or the novel theoretical insight from a different subfield.

More broadly we want to find emerging new directions of research, even before those doing the research realize there is an emergent effort which is headed in a new direction, to see disparate subfields converge into new synergistic research opportunities, and adjacent subfields diverge to nucleate new areas of research. These are hard problems, but exciting and with very high potential for discovery and speeding up research.

arχiv core functionality is to get the paper to the reader, but quantity has a quality all of its own (Clement et al., 2019). Bulk downloads of content for natural language processing, machine learning and other aggregate exploration has been enabled for some time through Amazon's S3, with the user paying. arχiv has now partnered with kaggle to provide bulk access to arχiv contents, providing both aggregate metadata, and access to processing full text. The kaggle dataset is updated periodically and is free to use. Text retrieval of any particular paper still goes through arxiv.org.

4 arχiv Labs

arχiv has set up a framework for us to work on a range of issues with external partners through arχiv Labs, https://labs.arxiv.org. Currently arχiv Labs includes the arχiv Bibliographic Explorer, a new collaboration with Papers with Code to link papers and code (https://paperswithcode.com), and the CORE Recommender (Knoth et al., 2017) (https://core.ac.uk).

arχiv Labs is committed to open source, and partners working through the framework are expected to abide by the general arχiv principles. We are interested in working with individuals or groups on third party services, as well as more structured services that could be brought in–house and run from the arχiv side as services to our users, or even part of our core operations. We are in discussion about several other projects.

References

Colin B. Clement, Matthew Bierbaum, Kevin P. O'Keeffe, and Alexander A. Alemi. 2019. On the use of arxiv as a dataset. *Computing Research Repository*, arXiv:1905.00075.

Paul Ginsparg, Paul Houle, Thorsten Joachims, and Jae-Hoon Sul. 2010. Last but not least: Additional positional effects on citation and readership in arxiv. *Computing Research Repository*, arXiv:1010.2757.

Asif-ul Haque and Paul Ginsparg. 2009. Positional effects on citation and readership in arxiv. *Computing Research Repository*, arXiv:0907.4740.

Asif-ul Haque and Paul Ginsparg. 2010. Last but not least: Additional positional effects on citation and readership in arxiv. *Computing Research Repository*, arXiv:1010.2757.

Petr Knoth, Lucas Anastasiou, Aristotelis Charalampous, Mattero Cancellieri, Samuel Pearce, Nancy Pontika, and Vaclav Bayer. 2017. Towards effective research recommender systems for repositories. *Computing Research Repository*, arXiv:1705.00578.

Acknowledgement Entity Recognition in CORD-19 Papers

Jian Wu
Computer Science
Old Dominion University
Norfolk, VA, USA
jwu@cs.odu.edu

Pei Wang, Xin Wei
Computer Science
Old Dominion University
Norfolk, VA, USA
{pwang001,xwei001}@odu.edu

Sarah Michele Rajtmajer, C. Lee Giles
Information Sciences and Technology
Pennsylvania State University
University Park, PA, USA

Christopher Griffin
Applied Research Laboratory
Pennsylvania State University
University Park, PA, USA

Abstract

Acknowledgements are ubiquitous in scholarly papers. Existing acknowledgement entity recognition methods assume all named entities are acknowledged. Here, we examine the nuances between acknowledged and named entities by analyzing sentence structure. We develop an acknowledgement extraction system, ACKEXTRACT based on open-source text mining software and evaluate our method using manually labeled data. ACKEXTRACT uses the PDF of a scholarly paper as input and outputs acknowledgement entities. Results show an overall performance of $F_1 = 0.92$. We built a supplementary database by linking CORD-19 papers with acknowledgement entities extracted by ACKEXTRACT including persons and organizations and find that only up to 50–60% of named entities are actually acknowledged. We further analyze chronological trends of acknowledgement entities in CORD-19 papers. All codes and labeled data are publicly available at https://github.com/lamps-lab/ackextract.

1 Introduction

Acknowledgements have been an institutionalized part of research publications for some time (Blaise, 2001). Acknowledgement statements show the authors' public gratitude and recognition to individuals, organizations, and grants for various contributions. Acknowledged individuals and organizations have been under-presented in author ranking and citation impact analysis mostly due to their presumed sub-authorship contribution. A recent survey found that discipline, academic rank, and gender have a significant effect on coauthorship disagreement rate (Smith et al., 2019), leading to non-author collaborators receiving less attention. Recently, the presence of non-author collaborators in the biomedical and social sciences (Paul-Hus et al., 2017) showed that non-author collaborators are not rare and their presence varies significantly by disciplines.

Acknowledgements can be classified depending on the nature of the contribution. Song et al. (2020) classified sentences in acknowledgement sections into 6 categories: declaration, financial, peer interactive communication and technical support, presentation, general acknowledgement, and general statement. They can also be classified based on the type of entities such as individual, organization, and grant. Since 2008, funding acknowledgements have been indexed by Web of Science. However, there is still no dedicated software to accurately recognize acknowledged *people* and *organizations* and generate a centralized acknowledgement database. Early works on acknowledgements were based on datasets manually extracted from specific journals, which was not scalable. Building such a large database can support further study of acknowledgements at a larger scale.

There are several scenarios that make the acknowledgement entity recognition (AER) task challenging. The upper panel of Figure 1 shows examples of sentences appearing in an isolated acknowledgement section. The "Utrecht University" is mentioned but should not be counted as an acknowledgement entity because it is just the affiliation of "Arno van Vliet" who is acknowledged. Acknowledgement statements can also appear at footnotes (Figure 1 *Bottom*), mixed with other footnote and/or body text. Author names may also appear in the statements, such as "Andreoni" in this example, and should be excluded.

Existing works on AER leverage off-the-shelf named entity recognition (NER) packages, such

10

Proceedings of the First Workshop on Scholarly Document Processing, pages 10–19
Online, November 19, 2020. ©2020 Association for Computational Linguistics
https://doi.org/10.18653/v1/P17

The figure box (Figure 1) reproduces two acknowledgement statements:

ACKNOWLEDGMENTS

We thank Raoul de Groot and Arno van Vliet (Utrecht University) for providing the virus isolates and helpful advice and Polly Roy (London School of Hygiene and Tropical Medicine) for ED cells.

This work was supported by Wellcome Trust grant 106207 and European Research Council grant 646891 to A.E.F., as well as NWO-CW ECHO grant 711.014.004 from the Netherlands Organization for Scientific Research to E.J.S.

Andreoni would like to thank the National Science Foundation (SES-1024683), and the Science of Generousity Initiative for financial support. This research was approved by the UCSD IRB. We would also like to thank Mark Isaac, James Walker, two anonymous referees, Christopher Cotton, Jennifer Coats, Joseph Falkinger, Rosemarie Nagel, David Scmidtz, Jeff Zabel, and participants at the ESA and BABEEW conferences for their helpful comments.

Figure 1: *Upper:* Acknowledgement statements appear in an isolated section (Stewart et al., 2018). *Bottom:* acknowledgement statements appear in a footnote (Andreoni and Gee, 2015).

as the Natural Language Toolkits (NLTK) (Bird, 2006) e.g., Khabsa et al. (2012); Paul-Hus et al. (2020), followed by simple semi-manual data cleansing, resulting in a fraction of entities that are *mentioned* but *not actually acknowledged*. In this paper, we design an automatic AER system called ACKEXTRACT that further classifies extraction results from open source NER packages that recognize *people* and *organizations* and distinguish entities that are *actually acknowledged*. The extractor finds acknowledgement statements from isolated sections and other locations such as footnotes, which is common for papers in social and behavioral sciences. Our contributions are:

1. Develop ACKEXTRACT as open-source software to automatically extract acknowledgement entities from research papers.

2. Apply ACKEXTRACT on the CORD-19 dataset and supplement the dataset with a corpus of classified acknowledgement entities for further studies.

3. Use the CORD-19 dataset as a case study to demonstrate that acknowledgement studies without classifying named entities, can significantly overestimate the number of entities that are actually acknowledged because many people and organizations are mentioned but not explicitly acknowledged.

2 Related Works

Early work on acknowledgement extraction was manually applied, which was labor-intensive. Cronin et al. (1993) extracted a total of 9561 peer interactive communication (PIC) names from a total of 4200 research sociology articles, most were persons' names. They also defined the following six categories of acknowledgement: moral support, financial support, editorial support, presentational support, instrumental/technical support, and conceptual support, or PIC (Cronin et al., 1992).

Councill et al. (2005) used a hybrid method for automatic AER from research papers and automatically created an acknowledgement index(Giles and Councill, 2004). The algorithm first used a heuristic method for identifying acknowledgement passages. It then uses an SVM model for identifying lines containing acknowledgement sentences outside labeled acknowledgement sections. A regular expression was used to extract entity names from acknowledging text. This method achieved an overall precision of about 0.785 and a recall of 0.896 on CiteSeer papers (Giles et al., 1998). The algorithm does not distinguish entity types.

Khabsa et al. (2012) leveraged OpenCalais[1] and AlchemyAPI[2], free services at that time, to extract named entities from acknowledgement sections and built ACKSEER, a search engine for acknowledgement entities. They merged outputs of both NER APIs and generated a list and disambiguated entity mentions using the longest common subsequence (LCS) algorithm. The ground truth contains 200 top-cited CiteSeerX papers in which 130 had acknowledgement sections. They achieved 92.3% and 91.6% precision and recall for acknowledgement section extraction but did not evaluate entity extraction.

Recent studies of acknowledgements tend to use results from off-the-shelf NER packages with simple filters, assuming that *named entities* were *acknowledged entities*. For example, Paul-Hus et al. (2020) uses the Stanford NER module in NLTK to extract persons. Song et al. (2020) also directly use people and organizations recognized by the Stanford CoreNLP (Manning et al., 2014). These works achieved a high recall by recognizing most name entities in the acknowledgements but ignored their relations to the papers where they appear, resulting in a fraction of entities that are mentioned but not actually acknowledged. Song et al. (2020) consider grammar structure such as verb tense and voice and sentence patterns when labeling sentences to their six categories. For example, "was funded" is followed by an "organization". However, they only label sentences and do not annotate them down to

<hr>

[1] https://web.archive.org/web/20081023021111/http://opencalais.com/calaisAPI#

[2] https://web.archive.org/web/20090921044923/http://www.alchemyapi.com/

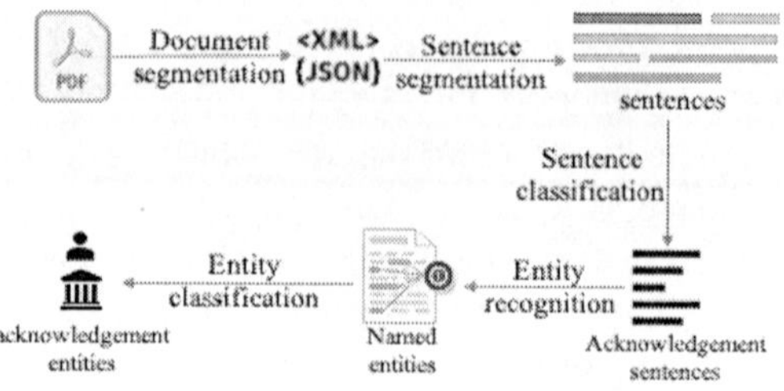

Figure 2: Architecture of ACKEXTRACT.

the entity level. Our system examines the relationship between entities and the current work, with the purpose of discriminating *acknowledgement entities* from *named entities*. In this system, we focus on *people* and *organizations*.

Recently, Dai et al. (2019) proposed GrantExtractor, a pipeline system to extract grant support information from scientific papers. A model combining BiLSTM-CRF and pattern matching was used to extract entities of grant numbers and agencies from funding sentences, which are identified using heuristic methods. The system achieves a micro-F_1 up to 0.90 in extracting grant pairs (agency, number).

Kayal et al. (2019) proposed an *ensemble* approach called FUNDINGFINDER for extracting funding information from text. The authors construct feature vectors for candidate entities using whether the entities are recognized by four NER implementation: Stanford (Conditional Random Field model), LingPipe (Hidden Markov model), OpenNLP (Maximum Entropy model), and Elsevier's Fingerprint Engine. The F_1-measure for funding body is only 0.68 ± 0.3.

Our method is different from existing methods in threefold. (1) It is built on top of state-of-the-art neural NER methods, which results in a relatively high recall. (2) It uses a heuristic method to filter out entities that are just mentioned but not acknowledged. (3) It extracts both organizations and people.

3 Dataset

On March 16th, 2020, Allen Institute of Artificial Intelligence, released the first version of the COVID-19 Open Research Dataset (CORD-19) (Wang et al., 2020), in collaboration with several other institutions. The dataset contains metadata and segmented full text of research articles selected by searching a list of keywords about coronavirus, SARS-CoV, MERS, and other related terms from four digital libraries including WHO, PubMed Central, BioRxiv, and MedRxiv. The initial dataset contained about 28k papers and was updated weekly with papers from new sources and the latest publication. We used the dataset released on April 10, 2020 containing over 59,312 metadata records, among which 54,756 have the full text in JSON format. The CORD-19 papers were generated by processing PDFs using the S2ORD pipeline (Lo et al., 2019), in which GROBID (Lopez, 2009) was employed for document segmentation and metadata extraction.

The full text in JSON files is directly used for sentence segmentation. However, we observe that GROBID extraction results are not perfect. In particular, we estimate the fraction of acknowledgement sections omitted. We also estimate the number of acknowledgement entities omitted in the data release due to the extraction error of GROBID. To do this, we downloaded 45,916 full-text PDF papers collected by the Internet Archive (IA) because the CORD-19 dataset does not include PDF files[3]. We found 13,103 CORD-19 papers in the IA dataset.

4 Acknowledgement Extraction

4.1 Overview

The architecture of our acknowledgement entity extraction system is depicted in Figure 2. The system can be divided into the following modules.

1. **Document segmentation.** CORD-19 provides full text as JSON files, but in general, most research articles are published in PDF, so our first step is converting a PDF document to text and segment it into sections. We use GROBID that has shown superior performance over many other document extraction methods (Lipinski et al., 2013). The output is an XML file in TEI schema.

2. **Sentence segmentation.** Paragraphs are segmented into sentences. We compare several sentence segmentation software packages and choose Stanza (Qi et al., 2020) because of its relatively high accuracy.

3. **Sentence classification.** Sentences are classified into acknowledgement and non-acknowledgement statements. The result is a set of acknowledgement statements inside or outside the acknowledgement sections.

[3]https://archive.org/download/covid19_fatcat_20200410

4. **Entity recognition.** Named entities are extracted from acknowledgement statements. We compare four commonly used NER software packages and choose Stanza because of its relatively high performance. In this work, we focus on *person* and *organization*.

5. **Entity classification.** In this module we classify named entities by analyzing sentence structures, aiming at discriminating named entities that are actually acknowledged, rather than just mentioned. We demonstrate that triple extraction packages such as REVERB and OLLIE fail to handle acknowledgement statements with multiple entities in objects in our dataset. The results are acknowledgement entities including *people* or *organizations*.

4.2 Document Segmentation

The majority of scholarly papers are published in PDF format, which are not readily readable by text processors. Several attempts have been made to convert PDF into text (Bast and Korzen, 2017) and segment the document into section and sub-section levels. GROBID is a machine learning library for extracting, parsing, and re-structuring raw documents into TEI encoded documents. Other similar methods have been recently developed such as OCR++ (Singh et al., 2016) and Science Parse[4]. Lipinski et al. (2013) compared 7 metadata extraction methods and found that GROBID (version 0.4.0) achieved superior performance over the others. GROBID trained a cascading of conditional random field (CRF) models on PubMed and computer science papers. The recent version (0.6.0) has a set of powerful functionalities such as extracting and parsing headers and segmenting full-text extraction. GROBID supports a batch mode and an API service mode, the latter enables large scale document processing on multi-core servers such as in CiteSeerX (Wu et al., 2015). A benchmarking result for version 0.6.0 shows that the section title parsing achieves and $F_1 = 0.70$ under the strict matching criteria and $F_1 = 0.75$ under the soft matching criteria[5]. Singh et al. (2016) claims OCR++ achieves better performance than GROBID in several fields evaluated on computer science papers. However, the lack of a service mode API and multi-domain adaptability limits its usability. Science-Parse only extracts key metadata such as

title, authors, year, and venue. Therefore, we adopt GROBID to convert PDF documents into XML files.

Depending on the structure and provenance of PDFs, GROBID may miss acknowledgements in certain papers. To estimate the fraction of papers in which acknowledgements were missed by GROBID, we visually inspected a random sample of 200 papers from the CORD-19 dataset, and found that only 146 papers (73%) contain acknowledgement statements, out of which GROBID successfully extracted all acknowledgement statements from 120 papers (82%). For the remaining 26 papers that GROBID failed to parse, 17 papers are in sections, 9 papers are in footnotes. We developed a heuristic method that can extract acknowledgement statements from all 120 papers with acknowledgement statements output by GROBID.

4.3 Sentence Segmentation

The acknowledgement sections or statements extracted above are paragraphs, which needs to be segmented (or tokenized) into sentences. we compared four software packages for sentence segmentation including NLTK (Bird, 2006), Stanza (Qi et al., 2020), Gensim (Řehůřek and Sojka, 2010), and the Pragmatic Segmenter[6].

NLTK includes a sentence tokenization method `sent_tokenize()`, which uses an unsupervised algorithm to build a model for abbreviated words, collocations, and words that start sentences; and then uses that model to find sentence boundaries. **Stanza** is a Python natural language analysis package developed by the Stanford NLP group. Sentence segmentation is modeled as a tagging problem over character sequences, where the neural model predicts whether a given character is the end of a sentence. The `split_sentences()` function in **Gensim** package splits a text and returns list of sentences from a given text string using unsupervised pattern recognition. The **Pragmatic Segmenter** is a rule-based sentence boundary detection gem that works out-of-the-box across many languages.

To compare the above methods, we created a ground truth corpus by randomly selecting acknowledgment sections or statements from 47 papers and manually segmenting them, resulting in 100 sentences. Table 1 shows the comparison results for four methods. The precision is calculated

---

[4] https://github.com/allenai/spv2

[5] https://grobid.readthedocs.io/en/latest/Benchmarking-pmc/

[6] https://github.com/diasks2/pragmatic_segmenter

Method	Precision	Recall	F_1
Gensim	0.65	0.64	0.65
NLTK	0.72	0.69	0.70
Pragmatic	0.86	0.76	0.81
Stanza	**0.81**	**0.88**	**0.84**

Table 1: Sentence segmentation performance.

Method	Entity	Precision	Recall	F_1
NLTK	Person	0.45	0.68	0.55
	Org.	0.59	0.77	0.67
spaCy	Person	0.74	0.88	0.80
	Org.	0.63	0.74	0.68
Stanford-CoreNLP	Person	0.88	0.87	0.87
	Org.	0.68	0.80	0.73
Stanza	Person	**0.89**	**0.93**	**0.91**
	Org.	**0.60**	**0.89**	**0.72**

Table 2: Comparison of NER software package.

by dividing the number of correctly segmented sentences by the total number of sentences segmented. The recall is calculated by dividing the number of correctly segmented sentences by the total number of manually segmented sentences. Stanza outperforms the other three, achieving an $F_1 = 0.84$.

4.4 Sentence Classification

Not all sentences in acknowledgement sections express acknowledgement, such as the following sentence, `The funders played no role in the study or preparation of the manuscript` Song et al. (2020). In this module, we classify sentences into acknowledgement and non-acknowledgement statements. We developed a set of regular expressions that match both verbs (e.g., thank, gratitude to, indebted to), adjectives (e.g., grateful to), and nouns (e.g., helpful comments, useful feedback) to cover as many cases as possible. To evaluate this method, we manually selected 100 sentences, including 50 positive and negative samples from the sentences obtained in Section 4.3. Our results show that 96 out of 100 sentences were classified correctly, resulting accuracy of 0.96.

4.5 Entity Recognition

In this step, named entities are extracted using state-of-the-art NER software packages, including NLTK Bird (2006), Stanford CoreNLP Manning et al. (2014), spaCy Honnibal and Montani (2017), and Stanza (Qi et al., 2020). Stanza is a Python library offering fully neural pre-trained models that provide state-of-the-art performance on many raw text processing tasks when it was released. The NER model adopted the contextualized sequence tagger in Akbik et al. (2018). The architecture includes a Bi-LSTM character-level language model, followed by a one-layer Bi-LSTM sequence tagger with a conditional random field (CRF) encoder. Although Stanza was developed based on Stanford CoreNLP, they exhibit differential performances in our NER task.

The ground truth is built by randomly selecting 100 acknowledgement paragraphs from sections, footnotes, and body text, and manually annotating *person* and *organization* entities, without discriminating whether they are acknowledged or not. This results in 146 *person* and 209 *organization* entities. The comparison results indicate that overall Stanza outperforms the other three, achieving $F_1 = 0.91$ for *person* and $F_1 = 0.72$ for *organization*. Especially, the recall of Stanza is 9% higher than Stanford CoreNLP (Table 2).

4.6 Entity Classification

As we showed, not all named entities are acknowledged, such as the "'Utrecht University" in Figure 1. Therefore, it is necessary to build a classifier to discriminate acknowledgement entities – entities that are thanked by the paper or the authors, from named entities.

The majority of acknowledgement statements in academic articles have a relatively standard subject-predicate-object (SPO) structure. They use a limited number of words or phrases, such as "thank", "acknowledge", "are grateful", "is supported", and "is funded" as predicates. However, the object can contain multiple named entities, some of which are used as attributes of the others. In rare cases, certain sentences may not have subjects and predicates, such as the first sentence in Figure 4.

Our approach can be divided into three steps. Two representative examples are illustrated in Figure 3. The pseudo-code is shown in Algorithm 1.

Step 1: We resolve the type of voice (active or passive), subject, and predicate of a sentence using dependency parsing by Stanza. This is because named entities can appear as subjective or objective parts. We then locate all named entities. The semantic meaning of a predicate and its type of voice can be used to determine whether entities acknowledged are in the objective part or subjective part. In most cases the target entities are objects.

Step 2: A sentence with multiple entities in the objective part is split into shorter sentences, called "subsentences", so that each subsentence is associated with only up to one named entity. This is done by first splitting the sentence by "and". For each subsentence, if the subject and predicate are missing, we fill them up using the subject and predicate of the original sentence. The object in each subsentence does not necessarily contain an entity. For example, in the right panel of Figure 3, because "expertise" is not a named entity, it is replaced by "none" in the subsentence. The SPO relations that do not contain named entities are removed.

There are two scenarios. In the first scenario, a sentence or a subsentence may contain a list of entities, with only the first being acknowledged. In the third example of Figure 4, the named entities are `['Qi Yang', 'Morehouse School of Medicine', 'Atlanta', 'GA']` but only the first entity is acknowledged. The rest entities, which are recognized as *organizations* or *locations*, are used for supplementing more information. In this scenario, only the first named entity is extracted.

Step 3: In the second scenario, acknowledged entities are connected by commas or "and", such as in `We thank `Shirley Hauta, Yurij Popowych, Elaine van Moorlehem `and` Yan Zhou `for help in the virus production.` In this scenario, entities in this structure have the same type, indicating that they play similar roles. This parallel pattern can be captured by regular expressions. The entities resolved in Step 2 and 3 will be merged to form the final set.

The method to find the parallel structure is as follows. First, check each entity whether its type is *person*. If so, the entities are substituted with integer indexes. The sentence becomes `The authors would like to thank 0, 1 and 2, and the kind support of Bayer Animal Health GmbH and Virbac Group.` If there are 3 or more consecutive numbers in this form, this is the parallel pattern, which is captured by regular expressions. The pattern also allows text between names (Figure 5). Next, the numbers in this part will be extracted and mapped to corresponding entities. In the example above, the numbers `[0,1,2]` correspond to the index of the entities `[Norbert Mencke, Lourdes Mottier, David McGahieand]`. Similar pattern recognition are performed for *organization*. The process is depicted in Figure 5.

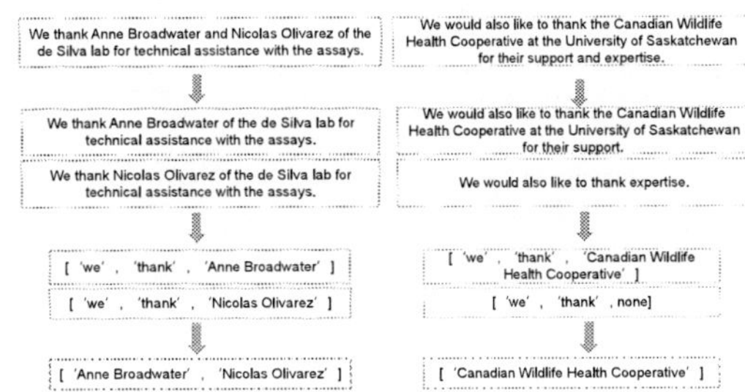

Figure 3: Process mapping multiple subject-predicate-object relations to acknowledgement entities with two representative examples. "None" means the object does not contain named entities.

Method	Precision	Recall	F_1
Stanza	0.57	0.91	0.70
RB(without step 3)	0.94	0.78	0.85
RB	**0.94**	**0.90**	**0.92**

Table 3: Performance of Stanza and our relation-based (RB) classifier. Precision and recall show overall results by combining *person* and *organization*.

We investigated open information extraction methods such as REVERB (Fader et al., 2011) and OLLIE (Mausam et al., 2012). We found that they only work for sentences with relatively simple structures such as `The authors wish to thank Ming-Wei Guo for reagents and technical assistance,` but fail with more complicated sentences with long objective part or parallel subsentences (Figure 4). We also investigated the semantic role labeling (SRL) library in AllenNLP toolkit (Shi and Lin, 2019). For the third sentence in Figure 4, the AllenNLP SRL library resolves the entire string after "thank" as an argument, but fails to distinguish entity types. Our method can handle all statements in Figure 4.

As a baseline, we use Stanza to extract all named entities and compare its performance with our relation-based (RB) classifier. The ground truth is compiled using the same corpus described in Section 4.5 except that only acknowledgement entities (as opposed to all named entities) are labeled positive. The results (Table 3) show that Stanza achieves high recall but poor precision, indicating that a significant fraction ($\sim 40\%$) of named entities are not acknowledged. In contrast, our classifier (RB) achieves a precision of 0.94, with a small loss of recall, achieving an $F_1 = 0.92$.

One limitation of the RB classifier is that it relies on text quality. Sentences are expected to follow

To <u>Aulio Costa Zambenedetti</u>, for the art work, <u>Nilson Fidêncio</u>, <u>Silvio Marques</u>, <u>Tania Schepainski</u> and <u>Sibelli Tanjoni de Souza</u>, for technical assistance.

The authors also thank <u>the Program for Technological Development in Tools</u> for Health-PDTIS FIOCRUZ, for the use of its facilities (Platform RPT09H -Real Time PCR -Instituto Carlos Chagas/Fiocruz-PR).

The authors wish to thank Ms. <u>Qi Yang</u>, DNA sequencing lab, Morehouse School of Medicine, Atlanta, GA, and the <u>Research Cores at Morehouse School of Medicine</u> supported through the Research Centers at Minority Institutions (RCMI) Program, NIH/NCRR/RCMI Grant G12-RR03034.

Figure 4: Sentence examples, from which REVERB or OLLIE failed to extract acknowledgement entities underlined, which can be identified by our method.

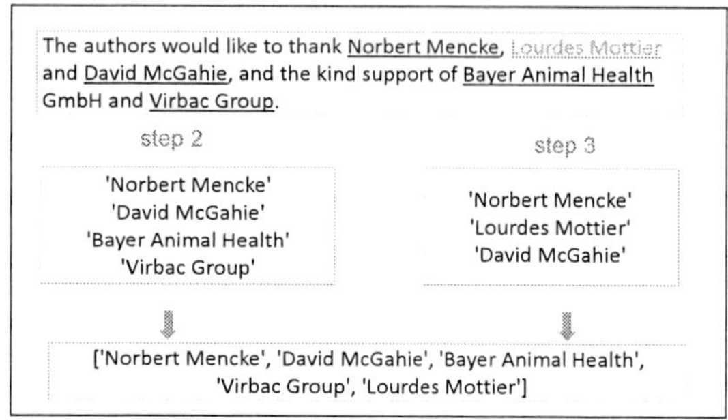

Figure 5: Merge the results given by step 2 and step 3 and obtain the final results.

the editorial convention, such that entity names are clearly segmented by period. If two sentences are not properly delimited, e.g., missing a period, the classifier may make incorrect predictions.

5 Data Analysis

The CORD-19 dataset contains PMC and PDF folders. We found that almost all papers in the PMC folders are included in the PDF folders. For consistency, we only work on papers in the PDF folders, containing 37,612 unique PDF papers[7]. Using ACKEXTRACT, we extracted a total of 102,965 named entities from 21,469 CORD-19 papers. The fraction of papers with named entities ($21469/37612 \approx 57\%$) is roughly consistent with the fraction obtained from the 200 samples ($120/200 \approx 60\%$ in Section 4.2). Among all named entities, 58,742 are acknowledgement entities. These numbers suggest that using our model, only about 50% of named entities are acknowledged. Using only named entities, acknowledgement studies could significantly overestimate the

---

[7]We excluded 2003 duplicate papers with exactly the same SHA1 values.

Algorithm 1: Relation-Based Classifier

```
 1  Function find_entity():
 2      pre-process with punctuation and format
 3      find candidate entities entity_list by Stanza
 4      for x ∈ entity_list do
 5          if x ∈
               subject part (differs based on predicate)
               then
 6              └ x = none
 7      entity_list.remove(none)
 8      return entity_list

 9  Input: sentence
10  Output: entity_list_all
11  find subject part, predicate and the object part
12  if "predicate value" ∈ reg expression 1 then
13      if "and" ∈ sentence then
14          split into subsentences by 'and'
15          for each subsentence do
16              entity_list
                  ← find_entity(subsentence)
17              if entity_list ≠ none then
18                  entity_list_all
                      ← append.entity_list[0]

19      else if "and" ∉ sentence then
20          entity_list ← find_entity(subsentence)
21          entity_list_all ← entity_list[0]

22  else if "predicate value" ∈ reg expression 2 then
23      do the same in if part but focus on entities in
        subject

24  for x ∈ candidate list by Stanza do
25      if x ∈ sentence&x.type = type then
26          orig_list ← append x
27          sent ← replace x by index(x)
28      if reg format ∈ sent then
29          temp ← find reg expression in sent
30          numlist ← find numbers in temp
31          list ← index orig_list by numlist

32  combine list and entity_list_all
```

number of acknowledgement entities by relying on entities recognized by NER software packages without further classification. Here, we analyze our results and study some trends of acknowledgement entities in the CORD-19 dataset.

The top 10 acknowledged organizations (Table 4) are all funding agencies. Overall NIH (NIAID is an institute of NIH) is acknowledged the most, but funding agencies in other countries are also acknowledged a lot in CORD-19 papers.

Figure 6 shows the numbers of CORD-19 papers with vs. without acknowledgement (*person* or *organization*) recognized from 1970 to 2020. The huge leap around 2002 was due to the wave of coronavirus studies during the SARS period. The small drop-down in 2020 was due to data incompleteness. The plot indicates that the fraction of

Organization	Count
National Institutes of Health or NIH	1414
National Natural Science Foundation of China or NSFC	615
National Institute of Allergy & Infectious Diseases or NIAID	209
National Science Foundation or NSF	183
Ministry of Health	160
Wellcome Trust	146
Deutsche Forschungsgemeinschaft	119
Ministry of Education	119
National Science Council	104
Public Health Service	85

Table 4: Top 10 acknowledged organizations identified in our CORD-19 dataset.

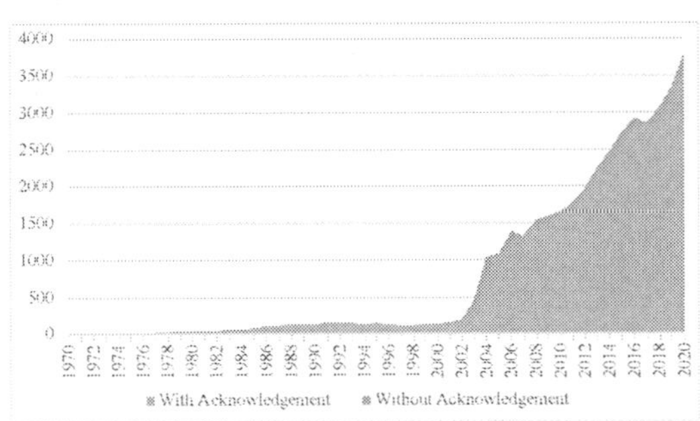

Figure 6: Numbers of CORD-19 papers with vs. without acknowledgement recognized from 1970 to 2020.

papers with acknowledgement has been increasing gradually over the last 20 years. Figure 7 shows the numbers of the top 10 acknowledged organizations from 1983 to 2020. The figure indicates that the number of acknowledgements to NIH has been gradually decreasing over the past 10 years while the acknowledgements to NSF is roughly constant. In contrast, the number has been gradually increasing from NSFC (a Chinese funding agency). Note that the distribution of acknowledged organizations has a long tail and organizations behind the top 10 actually dominate the total number. However, the top 10 organizations are the biggest research agencies and the trend to some extent reflects strategic shifts of funding support.

6 Conclusion and Future Work

Here, we extended the work of Khabsa et al. (2012) and built an acknowledgement extraction framework denoted as ACKEXTRACT for research articles. ACKEXTRACT is based on heuristic methods and state-of-the-art text mining libraries (e.g., GROBID and Stanza) but features a classifier that discriminates acknowledgement entities from named entities by analyzing the multiple subject-predicate-object relations in a sentence. Our ap-

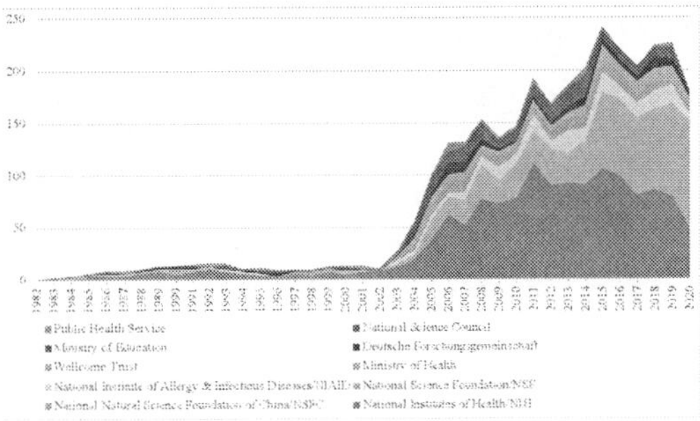

Figure 7: Trend of acknowledged organizations of top 10 organizations from 1983 to 2020.

proach successfully recognizes acknowledgement entities that cannot be recognized by OIE packages such as REVERB, OLLIE, and the AllenNLP SRL library.

This method is applied to the CORD-19 dataset released on April 10, 2020, processing one PDF document in 5 seconds on average. Our results indicate that only 50–60% named entities are acknowledged. The rest are mentioned to provide additional information (e.g., affiliation or location) about acknowledgement entities. Working on clean data, our method achieves an overall $F_1 = 0.92$ for *person* and *organization* entities. The trend analysis of the CORD-19 papers verifies that more and more papers include acknowledgement entities since 2002, when the SARS outbreak happened. The trend also reveals that the overall number of acknowledgements to NIH is gradually decreasing over the past 10 years, while more papers acknowledge NSFC, a Chinese funding agency. One caveat of our method is that organizations in different countries are not distinguished. For example, many countries have agencies called "Ministry of Health". In the future, we plan to build learning-based models for sentence classification and entity classification. The code and data of this project have been released on GitHub at: https://github.com/lamps-lab/ackextract.

Acknowledgments

This work was partially supported by the Defense Advanced Research Projects Agency (DARPA). under cooperative agreement No. W911NF-19-2-0272. The content of the information does not necessarily reflect the position or the policy of the Government, and no official endorsement should be inferred.

References

Alan Akbik, Duncan Blythe, and Roland Vollgraf. 2018. Contextual string embeddings for sequence labeling. In *Proceedings of the 27th International Conference on Computational Linguistics*, pages 1638–1649, Santa Fe, New Mexico, USA. Association for Computational Linguistics.

James Andreoni and Laura K. Gee. 2015. Gunning for efficiency with third party enforcement in threshold public goods. *Experimental Economics*, 18(1):154–171.

Hannah Bast and Claudius Korzen. 2017. A benchmark and evaluation for text extraction from PDF. In *2017 ACM/IEEE Joint Conference on Digital Libraries, JCDL 2017, Toronto, ON, Canada, June 19-23, 2017*, pages 99–108. IEEE Computer Society.

Steven Bird. 2006. NLTK: the natural language toolkit. In *ACL 2006, 21st International Conference on Computational Linguistics and 44th Annual Meeting of the Association for Computational Linguistics, Proceedings of the Conference, Sydney, Australia, 17-21 July 2006*. The Association for Computer Linguistics.

Cronin Blaise. 2001. Acknowledgement trends in the research literature of information science. 57(3):427–433.

Isaac G. Councill, C. Lee Giles, Hui Han, and Eren Manavoglu. 2005. Automatic acknowledgement indexing: Expanding the semantics of contribution in the citeseer digital library. In *Proceedings of the 3rd International Conference on Knowledge Capture*, K-CAP '05, pages 19–26, New York, NY, USA. ACM.

Blaise Cronin, Gail McKenzie, Lourdes Rubio, and Sherrill Weaver-Wozniak. 1993. Accounting for influence: Acknowledgments in contemporary sociology. *Journal of the American Society for Information Science*, 44(7):406–412.

Blaise Cronin, Gail McKenzie, and Michael Stiffler. 1992. Patterns of acknowledgement. *Journal of Documentation*.

S. Dai, Y. Ding, Z. Zhang, W. Zuo, X. Huang, and S. Zhu. 2019. Grantextractor: Accurate grant support information extraction from biomedical fulltext based on bi-lstm-crf. *IEEE/ACM Transactions on Computational Biology and Bioinformatics*, pages 1–1.

Anthony Fader, Stephen Soderland, and Oren Etzioni. 2011. Identifying relations for open information extraction. In *Proceedings of the 2011 Conference on Empirical Methods in Natural Language Processing, EMNLP 2011, 27-31 July 2011, John McIntyre Conference Centre, Edinburgh, UK, A meeting of SIGDAT, a Special Interest Group of the ACL*, pages 1535–1545.

C. Lee Giles, Kurt D. Bollacker, and Steve Lawrence. 1998. CiteSeer: An automatic citation indexing system. In *Proceedings of the 3rd ACM International Conference on Digital Libraries, June 23-26, 1998, Pittsburgh, PA, USA*, pages 89–98.

C Lee Giles and Isaac G Councill. 2004. Who gets acknowledged: Measuring scientific contributions through automatic acknowledgment indexing. *Proceedings of the National Academy of Sciences*, 101(51):17599–17604.

Matthew Honnibal and Ines Montani. 2017. spaCy 2: Natural language understanding with Bloom embeddings, convolutional neural networks and incremental parsing. To appear.

Subhradeep Kayal, Zubair Afzal, George Tsatsaronis, Marius Doornenbal, Sophia Katrenko, and Michelle Gregory. 2019. A framework to automatically extract funding information from text. In *Machine Learning, Optimization, and Data Science*, pages 317–328, Cham. Springer International Publishing.

Madian Khabsa, Pucktada Treeratpituk, and C. Lee Giles. 2012. Ackseer: a repository and search engine for automatically extracted acknowledgments from digital libraries. In *Proceedings of the 12th ACM/IEEE-CS Joint Conference on Digital Libraries, JCDL '12, Washington, DC, USA, June 10-14, 2012*, pages 185–194. ACM.

Mario Lipinski, Kevin Yao, Corinna Breitinger, Joeran Beel, and Bela Gipp. 2013. Evaluation of header metadata extraction approaches and tools for scientific pdf documents. In *Proceedings of the 13th ACM/IEEE-CS Joint Conference on Digital Libraries*, JCDL '13, pages 385–386, New York, NY, USA. ACM.

Kyle Lo, Lucy Lu Wang, Mark Neumann, Rodney Kinney, and Dan S. Weld. 2019. S2orc: The semantic scholar open research corpus.

Patrice Lopez. 2009. Grobid: Combining automatic bibliographic data recognition and term extraction for scholarship publications. In *Proceedings of the 13th European Conference on Research and Advanced Technology for Digital Libraries*, ECDL'09, pages 473–474, Berlin, Heidelberg. Springer-Verlag.

Christopher D. Manning, Mihai Surdeanu, John Bauer, Jenny Finkel, Steven J. Bethard, and David McClosky. 2014. The Stanford CoreNLP natural language processing toolkit. In *Association for Computational Linguistics (ACL) System Demonstrations*, pages 55–60.

Mausam, Michael Schmitz, Robert Bart, Stephen Soderland, and Oren Etzioni. 2012. Open language learning for information extraction. In *Proceedings of the 2012 Joint Conference on Empirical Methods in Natural Language Processing and Computational Natural Language Learning*, EMNLP-CoNLL '12, pages 523–534, Stroudsburg, PA, USA. Association for Computational Linguistics.

Adèle Paul-Hus, Adrián A. Díaz-Faes, Maxime Sainte-Marie, Nadine Desrochers, Rodrigo Costas, and Vincent Larivière. 2017. Beyond funding: Acknowledgement patterns in biomedical, natural and social sciences. *PLOS ONE*, 12(10):1–14.

Adèle Paul-Hus, Philippe Mongeon, Maxime Sainte-Marie, and Vincent Larivière. 2020. Who are the acknowledgees? an analysis of gender and academic status. *Quantitative Science Studies*, 0(0):1–17.

Peng Qi, Yuhao Zhang, Yuhui Zhang, Jason Bolton, and Christopher D. Manning. 2020. Stanza: A python natural language processing toolkit for many human languages. *CoRR*, abs/2003.07082.

Radim Řehůřek and Petr Sojka. 2010. Software Framework for Topic Modelling with Large Corpora. In *Proceedings of the LREC 2010 Workshop on New Challenges for NLP Frameworks*, pages 45–50, Valletta, Malta. ELRA. http://is.muni.cz/publication/884893/en.

Peng Shi and Jimmy Lin. 2019. Simple BERT models for relation extraction and semantic role labeling. *CoRR*, abs/1904.05255.

Mayank Singh, Barnopriyo Barua, Priyank Palod, Manvi Garg, Sidhartha Satapathy, Samuel Bushi, Kumar Ayush, Krishna Sai Rohith, Tulasi Gamidi, Pawan Goyal, and Animesh Mukherjee. 2016. OCR++: A robust framework for information extraction from scholarly articles. In *COLING 2016, 26th International Conference on Computational Linguistics, Proceedings of the Conference: Technical Papers, December 11-16, 2016, Osaka, Japan*, pages 3390–3400. ACL.

E. Smith, B. Williams-Jones, Z. Master, V. Larivière, C. R. Sugimoto, A. Paul-Hus, M. Shi, and D. B. Resnik. 2019. Misconduct and misbehavior related to authorship disagreements in collaborative science. *Sci Eng Ethics*.

Min Song, Keun Young Kang, Tatsawan Timakum, and Xinyuan Zhang. 2020. Examining influential factors for acknowledgements classification using supervised learning. *PLOS ONE*, 15(2):1–21.

H. Stewart, K. Brown, A. M. Dinan, N. Irigoyen, E. J. Snijder, and A. E. Firth. 2018. Transcriptional and translational landscape of equine torovirus. *J Virol*, 92(17).

Lucy Lu Wang, Kyle Lo, Yoganand Chandrasekhar, Russell Reas, Jiangjiang Yang, Darrin Eide, Kathryn Funk, Rodney Kinney, Ziyang Liu, William Merrill, Paul Mooney, Dewey Murdick, Devvret Rishi, Jerry Sheehan, Zhihong Shen, Brandon Stilson, Alex D. Wade, Kuansan Wang, Chris Wilhelm, Boya Xie, Douglas Raymond, Daniel S. Weld, Oren Etzioni, and Sebastian Kohlmeier. 2020. CORD-19: the covid-19 open research dataset. *CoRR*, abs/2004.10706.

Jian Wu, Jason Killian, Huaiyu Yang, Kyle Williams, Sagnik Ray Choudhury, Suppawong Tuarob, Cornelia Caragea, and C. Lee Giles. 2015. Pdfmef: A multi-entity knowledge extraction framework for scholarly documents and semantic search. In *Proceedings of the 8th International Conference on Knowledge Capture*, K-CAP 2015, pages 13:1–13:8, New York, NY, USA. ACM.

A Smart System to Generate and Validate Question Answer Pairs for COVID-19 Literature

Rohan Bhambhoria[*†], **Luna Feng**[*‡], **Dawn Sepehr**[*‡], **John Chen**[§¶], **Conner Cowling**[‡],
Sedef Akinli Kocak[¶], **Elham Dolatabadi**[§¶]

Queen's University[†], Thomson Reuters[‡], University of Toronto[§], Vector Institute[¶]

r.bhambhoria@queensu.ca, johnc@cs.toronto.edu,

{luna.feng,dawn.sepehr,conner.cowling}@thomsonreuters.com,

{sedef.kocak, elham.dolatabadi}@vectorinstitute.ai

Abstract

Automatically generating question answer (QA) pairs from the rapidly growing coronavirus-related literature is of great value to the medical community. Creating high quality QA pairs would allow researchers to build models to address scientific queries for answers which are not readily available in support of the ongoing fight against the pandemic. QA pair generation is, however, a very tedious and time consuming task requiring domain expertise for annotation and evaluation. In this paper we present our contribution in addressing some of the challenges of building a QA system without gold data. We first present a method to create QA pairs from a large semi-structured dataset through the use of transformer and rule-based models. Next, we propose a means of engaging subject matter experts (SMEs) for annotating the QA pairs through the usage of a web application. Finally, we demonstrate some experiments showcasing the effectiveness of leveraging active learning in designing a high performing model with a substantially lower annotation effort from the domain experts.

1 Introduction

Building a QA system is a complex process requiring advanced text mining approaches (Jothi et al., 2015) and domain expertise for model evaluation. Accordingly, automatically generating question-answer pairs using recent advances in natural language processing (NLP) models has gained much attention from researchers and has achieved impressive results on various publicly available datasets. (Yang et al., 2018; Rajpurkar et al., 2016). In this work, we explore the COVID-19 Open Research Dataset (CORD-19) (Wang et al., 2020) first in-

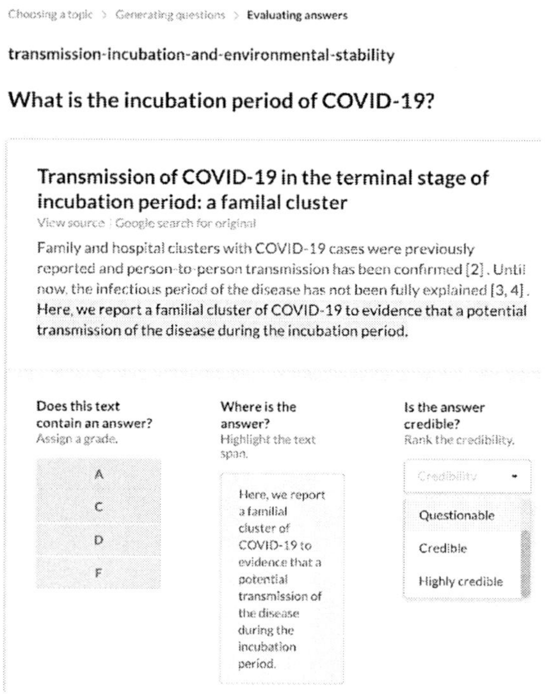

Figure 1: User Engagement App: SMEs are provided with information including the question, the title of the article, and some context from the article to grade the answer, highlight the exact answer, and rate the credibility of the source.

troduced in a Kaggle Competition[1]. The competition has been launched as a call to action for machine learning researchers to assist the medical community in developing answers to high-priority scientific questions related to COVID-19. A major challenge in dealing with a large semi-structured dataset (i.e., scholarly articles) is the lack of gold data which we aim to address in this work.

---

[*]Equal contributions, listed alphabetically

[1]https://www.kaggle.com/
allen-institute-for-ai/
CORD-19-research-challenge

Proceedings of the First Workshop on Scholarly Document Processing, pages 20–30
Online, November 19, 2020. ©2020 Association for Computational Linguistics
https://doi.org/10.18653/v1/P17

Existing methods developed by different groups in the Kaggle competition have mainly used clustering approaches (Kanungo et al., 2002) coupled with statistical methods (Blei et al., 2003) in order to group articles together and discover keywords from the resulting representation of the scholarly articles, respectively. Other researchers made use of transformer-based QA models and BERTserini (Yang et al., 2019) to retrieve relevant answers to keywords extracted from a question, after which resulting solutions were ranked by unsupervised embedding methods (Cer et al., 2018). Finally, top-ranking results were combined and summarized (Chipman et al., 2010). Other QA models made use of BERT (Devlin and Toutanova, 2019), adapted variations of BERT models (Huang et al., 2019; Beltagy et al., 2019), and BERT-like models (Lan et al., 2020) to produce semantically meaningful sentence embeddings from abstracts to answer important questions raised by the healthcare community. Developing QA systems for COVID-19 was not limited to the Kaggle competition; in (Oniani and Wang, 2020), a hybrid approach based on GPT-2 (Radford et al., 2019) was proposed to generate responses for different COVID-19 related questions. In general, developing QA generation has achieved promising progress recently. However, answering a question in specific domains such as health domain is still challenging, due to the requirement of expert knowledge and lack of high-quality training data. For example, Walonoski et al. (Walonoski et al., 2018) focused on generation of dataset from the state transition of patient records. Recently, Shen at al. (Shen et al., 2020) introduced structure information of QA pairs generation in medical domain. They proposed an unsupervised detector to automatically explore external materials for the validity of generated QA pairs. Despite all these attempts and solutions by various researchers, lack of annotated data for the CORD-19 dataset presents a challenge to automatically verify the correctness of the created QA pairs and also prevents us from leveraging supervised techniques.

To help address the shortcomings of previous approaches, we aim to create gold data related to COVID-19 which in turn can serve the purpose of training and evaluating supervised models. We employ transformer and rule-based methods to automatically generate a set of QA pairs, which we call Silver QA, and then leverage various active learning selection strategies to present samples to SMEs for annotation. To the best of our knowledge, this is the first work which explores the potential use of generative models to create QA pairs for quality verification by SMEs. Our proposed approach can serve as a practical foundation for the creation of a QA system for any complex semi-structured dataset requiring the employment of domain knowledge experts to maintain the standard of the generated QA pairs.

To provide a better user experience during the annotation process, we build a web application, which we call the User Engagement App (UEA), shown in Figure 1. The UEA presents a batch of QA pairs once the SMEs select their expertise of a specific domain and topics of interest (e.g., vaccines and therapeutics, virus genetics, origin, and evolution). It also allows the SMEs to grade the QA pairs, select exact answers, and rank the credibility of the source. While developing the web application, we engaged two medical students to obtain their feedback. We summarize their feedback into two major issues when annotating the QA pairs, details of which are outlined in Section 2. From these sets of feedback, we may firstly conclude that the SMEs require several hours to review a small batch of QA pairs due to the scientific complexity of the questions, and secondly, a high degree of domain-specific knowledge (e.g., virology, molecular genetics) is required to answer these scientific questions. We address the first feedback from the SMEs by introducing an active learning strategy which provides a method on how to select a limited number of samples. This in turn reduces the annotation efforts required to develop a practical QA system. In the future work section, we also provide some directions for the second feedback based on the results obtained from the QA pairs that we have generated.

Figure 2 illustrates the overview of how we integrate these different strategies to create the QA pairs and obtain gold data provided by the SMEs via the web application. We explain these steps in more details in Sections 2 and 3 and also provide the experimental results in Section 4.

2 Datasets

In this section, we introduce the publicly available biomedical datasets that we use for our experiments. We also describe various methods conducted in this work to generate QAs specifically but not limited to COVID-19.

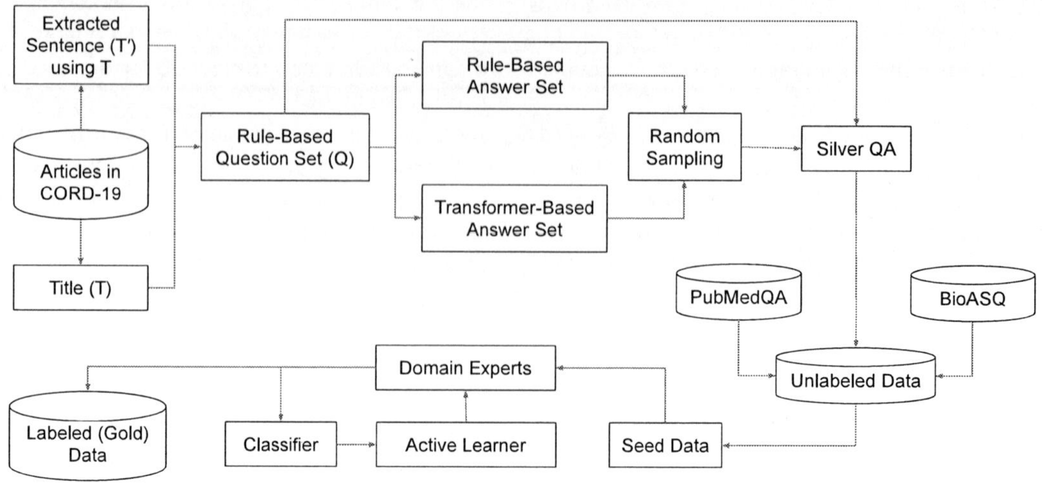

Figure 2: Generation of the Silver QA Data and the Process of Obtaining Gold Data using Active Learning

2.1 Existing Biomedical Datasets

We use three existing biomedical datasets:

- PubMedQA (Jin et al., 2019): a biomedical QA dataset collected from the abstracts of PubMed articles. PubMedQA has 1k expert-annotated, 61.2k unlabeled and 211.3k artificially generated QA instances.

- BioASQ (Tsatsaronis et al., 2015): a biomedical QA dataset consisting of 2,747 questions in the "Training 7b" dataset and 500 questions in the "7b golden enriched" test dataset. The questions are provided with their relevant articles, snippets, concepts and Resource Description Framework (RDF) triples, "exact" and "ideal" answers.

- CORD-19 (Wang et al., 2020): a resource of over 158K scholarly articles (released on April 16th, 2020), including over 75K with full text, about COVID-19, SARS-CoV-2, and related coronaviruses collected by the White House and a coalition of leading research groups and it was released along the Kaggle Competition.

2.2 Generating the Silver QA Dataset

We limit our question generation procedure to transformer and rule-based methods, refraining from the usage of other neural question generation methods such as (Du et al., 2017; Krishna and Iyyer, 2019) in order to create simple baselines for the comparison and evaluation of subsequent sections.

We recognize the importance of exploring neural methods to further assess the quality of the generated QA pairs and leave this exploration to the future work. The details of the steps taken to create the Silver QA are explained in this section and are also illustrated at the top part of Figure 2. In order to engage the SMEs effectively, we use two approaches. In our first approach, we create "QA-pre" by considering only the titles of the CORD-19 dataset starting with "Do/Does" and "Is/Are", i.e., titles with these prepended keywords, in order to be consistent with the schema of PubMedQA in which questions can be answered by "yes/no/maybe". However, this would result in a very small dataset. We therefore also include questions prefixed with "Wh". Including all the three question types our dataset contained only 553 titles with these prefixes which can serve as questions. To further generate a larger dataset, we consider all titles with verbs and incorporate the usage of a POS-tagger to formulate questions from titles. The resulting titles are grammatically incorrect in several instances and a potential direction would be to solely prepend "Do/Does" and "Is/Are" to titles containing verbs to formulate questions. This would require the SMEs to correct questions if they do not match the potential answer based on the choices available to them. Due to the limited size of "QA-pre", we introduce our second approach using a siamese BERT structure (SBERT) (Reimers and Gurevych, 2019).

To create a structured dataset which is practical for the SMEs to provide annotations, we follow a procedure of creating valid QA pairs using:

1. Titles of CORD-19 scholarly articles which we consider, for n articles in the CORD-19 dataset as the set $\{t_1, t_2, ...t_n\} \in T$ where T contains all titles obtained from the scholarly articles, $\{d_1, d_2, ...d_n\} \in D$ where d_i represents a single article from which a corresponding title, t_i is obtained.

2. Sentences with high cosine similarity to the titles of CORD-19 scholarly articles taken from the abstracts and conclusions from CORD-19 represented by $\{t_1', t_2', ..., t_n'\} \in T'$, obtained using SBERT as the encoder.

Sentences from T and T' are used as inputs for generating a set of questions $\{q_1, q_2, ...q_n\} \in Q$ and answers $\{a_1, a_1', a_2, a_2', ..., a_n', a_n\} \in A$. The set of questions, Q, is generated from these sentences solely using rule-based methods which make use of a syntactic parser to refactor them into questions by prepending "Wh" interrogative words to T and T' (Heilman and Smith, 2009). Similarly, the answers, $a_i \in A$, are generated based on rule-based methods, also making use of a syntactic parser for matching or refactoring sentences to a specific structure, maintaining an answer-like format. The subset of answers, $a_i' \in A$ are generated from the recently released Text-to-Text Transfer Transformer model, T5 (Raffel et al., 2019). This becomes possible as T and T' contains sufficient context for any given scholarly article in D. At the time of writing this paper, T5 is the highest ranking encoder-decoder structured model on a wide variety of NLP tasks, including the GLUE benchmark (Wang et al., 2018), and the extractive, context-based question answering task (Rajpurkar et al., 2016). Moreover, T5 also shows good performance on *closed-book question answering*, a question answering task that involves generating answers to questions when no context is supplied (Roberts et al., 2020).

The generation of $a_i' \in A$ involves finetuning of a pre-trained "large" configuration of the T5 model (770M parameters) on a mixture of three datasets: the TriviaQA dataset (Joshi et al., 2017), the Natural Questions dataset (ignoring the available context) (Kwiatkowski et al., 2019), and finally a domain specific COVID-19 dataset[2] with human-annotated answers. The model is finetuned for 25,000 steps and greedy decoding is performed.

[2]https://github.com/xhlulu/covid-qa

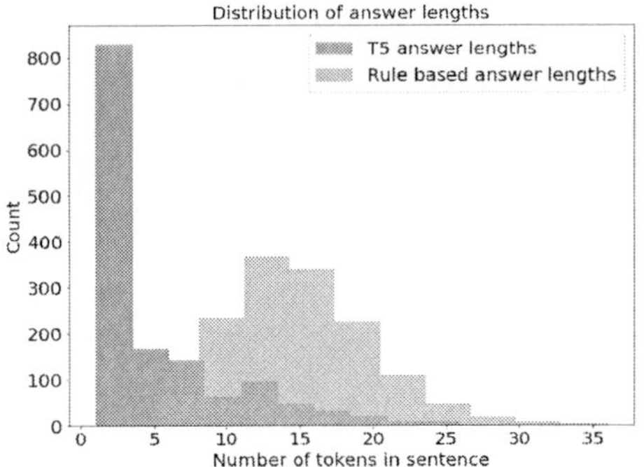

Figure 3: T5 answers are generally composed of fewer tokens than those generated via the rule-based approach.

As titles may not be written in the form of natural sentences, we add an additional layer of validation by asking four individuals without domain-specific expertise to provide manual annotations. The purpose of this validation step is to filter out grammatically incorrect questions generated by the rule-based methods. We measure the inter-annotator agreement of these annotations using the Cohen's kappa coefficient (McHugh, 2012) on 100 unique questions from T' and summarize these statistics in Table 1. In general higher values of this coefficient confirms a higher level of agreement between the annotators (Landis and Koch, 1977). We observe that the inter-annotator agreement scores for these annotations are low and we suspect this is due to the lack of detailed instructions for the annotation process. We would like to address this issue by setting up comprehensive instructions in the future work. As T' contains a natural sentence structure in contrast to T, QA pairs formulated from these sentences are directly taken into consideration without the extra validation step for filtering.

Annotator ID	1	2	3	4
1	1	0.21	0.35	0.16
2	0.21	1	0.53	0.52
3	0.35	0.53	1	0.4
4	0.16	0.52	0.4	1

Table 1: Inter-annotator agreement scores calculated based on Cohen's kappa coefficient

The resulting dataset, which we denote as Silver QA, contains all questions from Q and randomly sampled answers from A. The reason for random sampling of answers which are generated by transformer and rule-based methods is to avoid bias which may be introduced by either method on producing answers. A subset of the samples in the Silver QA dataset are shown in Table 2. We find that the two approaches generally do not produce similar answers: neither method produces the exact same answer for any given input question. The rule-based method, which extracts chunks of text, produces longer answers, while the T5 model, which generates answers token by token via greedy decoding, produces more terse responses as seen in Figure 3. When looking at fuzzy matches (as computed by the fuzzywuzzy[3] Python package), the answers have a fuzzy match score (Levenshtein distance similarity ratio) (Levenshtein, 1966) of 0.196, indicating on average that a large number of edits are required to transform one answer to another. Finally, they also share a low average cosine similarity of 0.07 on a simple bag-of-words encoding.

3 An Active Learning Strategy for Data Selection

Active learning (AL) strategies are shown to be effective in reducing the number of samples a machine learning model requires to achieve comparable performance to the case where a large amount of data is annotated (Aggarwal et al., 2014). Here, the main idea is to ask the SMEs to annotate strategically picked samples in small batches to minimize their efforts while encouraging the creation of a successful QA system.

At a high level, we start by randomly choosing a small subset of the samples from the unlabeled pool, details are in the next section, as the seed data to be annotated by the SMEs. Using the annotated seed data, we train a binary classifier to differentiate between different samples. The next step is to choose which unlabeled data points should be sent to the SMEs in the next iteration. After obtaining the annotations, the labeled samples are added to the pool of labeled data and further used to retrain the classifier. This iterative process, as illustrated at the bottom part of Figure 2, is repeated until either the annotation budget runs out or all the samples in the unlabeled pool have been annotated. In the following subsections, we explain how we formulate this problem as a binary classification task and introduce the different sampling strategies we have implemented.

---

[3]https://github.com/seatgeek/fuzzywuzzy

3.1 Problem Formulation

To show the effectiveness of the AL strategies, we consider the following human-annotated QA pairs from the datasets introduced in Section 2: 1) the questions and long answers from the PubMedQA expert-annotated dataset considering only the yes/no answers; and 2) the questions and ideal answers from the BioASQ dataset. We label these QA pairs as "valid" since the answers are the expected results for the questions. We also consider the QA pairs created in the Silver QA as valid. However, to differentiate between the valid QA pairs already annotated by the SMEs and the ones for which we would like to get the SMEs feedback using the UEA, we assign different weights to these samples in the AL strategy. We explain the details of these strategies in Section 3.2. It is noteworthy that we consider the PubMedQA and BioASQ datasets in our experiments since our models can benefit from these larger publicly available structured datasets in the biomedical domain which is similar to the domain of the COVID-19.

Furthermore, to create the set of QA pairs labeled as "invalid", for each question in the valid QA pairs, we randomly select a text snippet from the articles in the CORD-19 dataset and use it as the answer assuming that there is a small chance that the text snippet actually answers the question. Following this procedure, we build a dataset with 23,208 valid and invalid QA pairs with a 50% split between the two classes. We keep nearly 5% of the samples which results in 1,000 samples in each of the validation and test datasets with an equal split between the two classes and use the rest for training.

At this point, we can utilize a binary classifier to distinguish between the valid and invalid QA pairs to pick which samples should be sent to the SMEs. This trained binary classifier can be further used in our QA system to retrieve answers that are more likely to be labeled as correct by the SMEs, thus, reducing the cost of the annotation process even further. We choose XGBoost (Chen and Guestrin, 2016) as the classifier due to its efficiency in speed and performance in the AL experiments. Furthermore, we use sentence embeddings produced by transformer-based models (Vaswani et al., 2017) such as BERT (Devlin and Toutanova, 2019), and BioBERT (Lee et al., 2019) as the features for each QA pair. Specifically, we concatenate each question and answer separated by a blank space and

Question	Answer (Rule-Based)	Answer (Transformer-Based)
What has played a significant role in controlling measles in China?	The live-attenuated measles virus vaccine based on the Hu191 strain has played a significant role in controlling measles in China	the chinese government has taken proactive steps to reduce the spread of the disease
What are respiratory and enteric bovine coronavirus strains distinctive in?	It is unclear whether respiratory and enteric bovine coronavirus strains are distinctive in biological, antigenic and genetic characteristics	they are not conspecific
What is Pneumonia an inflammatory disease of?	Pneumonia is an inflammatory disease of the lung, responsible for high morbidity and mortality worldwide	lungs
what causes lower respiratory tract infections?	Background: Human metapneumovirus causes lower respiratory tract infections, particularly in young children and the elderly	bacteria, viruses, and protozoa
What mediates viral entry into host cells?	The filovirus surface glycoprotein mediates viral entry into host cells	a complex interaction between the virus and host cell membranes

Table 2: Qualitative Assessment of QA Pairs. The first column contains Questions from the set Q, the second and third columns contain generated rule-based and transformer-based answers from the set A respectively.

then obtain its embedding. More details of these experiments are reported in Section 4.

3.2 Design of the Sampling Strategies

We propose leveraging different AL strategies to sample unlabeled QA pairs from the pool of valid and invalid QA pairs to be annotated by the SMEs. A baseline strategy in comparison with any AL approach is choosing the samples randomly according to a uniform probability distribution and we also use this baseline to compare the performance of our proposed methods.

The first AL strategy that we implement, denoted by AL-Uncertainty, is based on the uncertainty of the classifier. In this case, the probability of the labels predicted by the classifier is used as a measure of uncertainty and the samples for which the binary classifier is the least certain about their labels are selected for annotation. Despite its simplicity, this technique has been successfully used in many different applications and has been one of the ubiquitous AL strategies to select the most informative samples for a model to be annotated by the SMEs (Fu et al., 2013; Aggarwal et al., 2014; Konyushkova et al., 2017). One can formulate this strategy as follows

$$x^* = \arg\min_{x_i \in \mathcal{U}} P(y_i = y \mid x_i) \qquad (1)$$

where $P(y_i = y \mid x_i)$ is the probability of the predicted class y for sample x_i, $\mathcal{U}$ is the pool of unlabeled samples, and x^* is the sample picked for annotation. In our simulations, in order to differentiate between the already human-annotated QA pairs and the samples in the Silver QA dataset, we consider different weights for different data sources. Indeed, we rank the samples after considering their class predicted probability based on the weight of their data source. Thus, we can write the following

$$R(x_i) = w_i \, r_{\mathrm{P}}(x_i) \qquad (2)$$

where $R(x_i)$ is the final rank of sample x_i, w_i is the weight assigned to the source of x_i, and $r_{\mathrm{P}}(x_i)$ is the rank of x_i using the probability P over all samples in $\mathcal{U}$. The AL-Uncertainty strategy picks a number of samples equal to the batch size which have the lowest final rank R, thus, samples with a lower source weight have a higher chance of being selected for annotation.

As our second AL strategy, we propose promoting sample diversity to the uncertainty approach in order to improve the performance of the AL-Uncertainty as explained in (Fu et al., 2013). Inspired by (Shuyang et al., 2018) and denoted by AL-Clustering, this strategy is based on clustering the samples. This method clusters the samples, represented by the features obtained from the embeddings of the QA pair, and then picks one sample within each cluster for which the classifier is the least confident about its predicted label. We can formulate this strategy as follows

$$x^* = \arg \min_{x_i \in \mathcal{U}_{c_i}} P(y_i = y \mid x_i) \qquad (3)$$

where $\mathcal{U}_{c_i}$ is the cluster that x_i belongs to in the pool of unlabeled samples, and x^* is the sample picked for annotation in cluster c_i. We would like to emphasize that unlike the method in (Shuyang et al., 2018), we perform the clustering in each iteration to rearrange the samples in different clusters as we get more annotated samples. We set the number of clusters in each iteration equal to the batch size and also employ the same weighting scheme described for the AL-Uncertainty strategy which results in

$$R^{c_i}(x_i) = w_i\, r_P^{c_i}(x_i) \qquad (4)$$

where $R^{c_i}(x_i)$ is the final rank of sample x_i in its cluster c_i, w_i is the weight assigned to the source of x_i, and $r_P^{c_i}(x_i)$ is the rank of x_i using the probability P over all samples in $\mathcal{U}$ which belong to cluster c_i. The AL-Clustering strategy picks one sample in each cluster which has the lowest final rank R, thus, similar to the AL-Uncertainty strategy, samples with a lower source weight have a higher chance of being selected for annotation.

4 Experiments and Results

We evaluate the performance of the different AL strategies by reporting both the accuracy and F1 score on the test dataset. To have a fair assessment of the performance of each method, we run the experiments 5 times using different random seeds and average the results as illustrated in Figure 4. We discuss the details of the implementation and setup for all of these experiments in Section 4.1 and discuss the details of the results in Section 4.2

4.1 Experimental Setup

We randomly choose 20 QA pairs from the unlabeled pool of the training set as the initial seed data. The batch size of the samples to be selected per iteration is 5 and the total number of iterations is set to 50 which amounts to 1.2% of the entire training dataset. As aforementioned, we use the XGBoost classifier to predict whether a QA pair is valid or not. The sentence embedding of each QA pair is employed as its input features. We experiment with two settings of embeddings that are produced by the pre-trained "bert-base-cased"[4] and "biobert-base v1.1"[5] transformer-based models. For both of these models, the output of the network for the [CLS] token is used to represent the input sentence.

For the weights of data sources utilized in the AL-Uncertainty and AL-Clustering strategies, we follow this scheme: X weights to the samples from PubMedQA and BioASQ, $3X$ weights to the samples from Silver QA, and $2X$ weights to the samples from CORD-19. The intuition behind this setting is that, at this point, the samples in Silver QA and CORD-19 have not been validated by the SMEs yet. However, in the real world scenario when we use the UEA, reversing the setting of the weights (i.e., lower values given to QA pairs from Silver QA and CORD-19) would result in a higher probability for selection of the QA pairs for which the model is unable to make a clear judgment about their labels. Also, due to the fact that the QA pairs from PubMedQA and BioASQ have already been annotated, we can filter them out in the UEA if they are selected by the active learner.

4.2 Results and Discussion

We empirically compare the performance of the three selection strategies described in Section 3.2. We also compare the achievable performance of the two XGBoost-based models with "DistilBERT-base-cased"[4], a BERT-based classifier, when trained on the entire dataset, as reported in Table 3. We observe that the DistilBERT model (Sanh et al.,

Model	F1 Score
BERT + XGBoost	0.85
BioBERT + XGBoost	0.87
DistilBERT	0.98

Table 3: F1 Score for three models trained on the entire dataset

2019) outperforms the XGBoost-based models substantially due to its more advanced architecture in which the embedding layers of the network are also updated during the training whereas the sentence embeddings used in the XGBoost-based models are static. However, incorporating the DistilBERT model in our experiments is both time and resource intensive since DistilBERT runs 36 times slower than XGBoost per AL iteration on a K80 GPU. Therefore, in this work, we only experiment with

---

[4]https://huggingface.co/
[5]https://github.com/dmis-lab/biobert

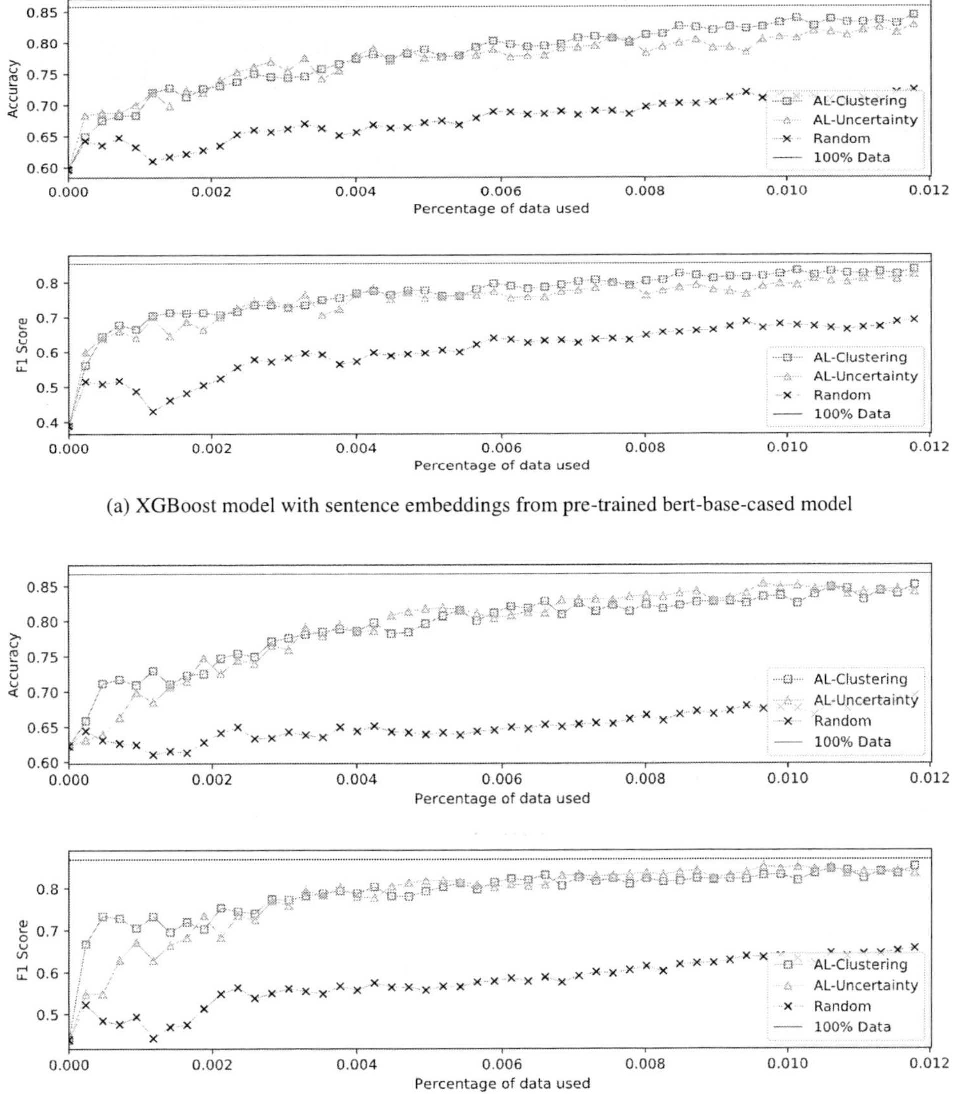

(a) XGBoost model with sentence embeddings from pre-trained bert-base-cased model

(b) XGBoost model with sentence embeddings from pre-trained biobert-base v1.1 model

Figure 4: Evaluation of the different AL strategies using accuracy and F1 score measures

the two XGBoost-based models, yet we would like to include the BERT-based classifiers in the experiments for our future work to compare the performance. Also, the XGBoost model with sentence embeddings produced by BioBERT improves the F1 score by 2% compared with the one using BERT since BioBERT is pre-trained on biomedical articles which aligns with the domain of our experiment dataset.

The curves in Figures 4(a)-(b) clearly show that the AL selection strategies outperform the random baseline for both sentence embedding settings. Indeed, we observe that the random strategy using 1.2% of the data achieves a similar performance compared to the AL strategies using less than 0.2% of the data which is a significant improvement since the AL strategies use much less annotated data. We also observe that both of the AL strategies achieve 99% of the achievable performance of the model using only 1.2% of the training dataset. Thus, one can clearly deduce that compared with the random strategy, AL-Uncertainty and AL-Clustering can achieve better performance with much less labeling effort, therefore, justifying our proposed method to obtain the gold data for the CORD-19 dataset using the UEA.

5 Conclusions and Future Work

In this work, we propose a novel strategy consisting of transformer and rule-based methods to generate QA pairs from scientific literature gathered in the CORD-19, while making use of a validation procedure to maintain the quality. We engage SMEs from the medical community and develop a web application to serve the purpose of providing an efficient user interface for annotating the QA pairs generated by our designed system. We also leverage active learning strategies to significantly reduce the required annotation effort from the SMEs.

This work paves the way for several interesting areas which can be explored further in the future. We believe that the engagement app, which will be released to the public soon, would enable the medical community to use it to its full extent as it can incorporate several subjective opinions from different SMEs and researchers. With the foundation laid by this work, we can also investigate better ways to explore the generation process of accurate questions by diving deeper into the task of question generation which is gaining attention in the field of NLP. In order to further benefit from our proposed method to improve the generalizability of the model using only a small annotated dataset, we can provide higher quality QA pairs by removing redundant questions using methods which are proven to work for graphical structures. These methods treat each scholarly article as a node which results in reducing the number of highly interlinked questions. Another plausible direction to explore is the incorporation of tasks such as extreme multi-label classification which would allow us to categorize scholarly articles under areas which may be better suited for annotations and align with the expertise of SMEs. Lastly, as explained earlier, generation of QA pairs in this work was limited to transformer and rule-based methods. We would like to explore the integration of successful neural based methods in our proposed approach.

Acknowledgments

The authors would like to thank all the organizers of the COVID-19 Open Research Dataset Kaggle Challenge. We would like to thank Vector Institute for making this collaboration possible and providing academic infrastructure and computing support during all phases of this work. We would also like to thank Richard Pito from Thomson Reuters for his invaluable feedback and support throughout this project. Last but not least, special thanks to Dr. Frank Rudzicz and Dr. Xiaodan Zhu for their academic supervision and insights.

References

Charu C. Aggarwal, Xiangnan Kong, Quanquan Gu, Jiawei Han, and Philip S. Yu. 2014. *Active learning: A survey*, pages 571–605. CRC Press.

Iz Beltagy, Kyle Lo, and Arman Cohan. 2019. Scibert: A pretrained language model for scientific text. In *Proceedings of the 2019 Conference on Empirical Methods in Natural Language Processing and the 9th International Joint Conference on Natural Language Processing (EMNLP-IJCNLP)*, pages 3606–3611.

David M. Blei, Andrew Y. Ng, and Michael I. Jordan. 2003. Latent dirichlet allocation. *J. Mach. Learn. Res.*, 3(null):993–1022.

Daniel Cer, Yinfei Yang, Sheng yi Kong, Nan Hua, Nicole Limtiaco, Rhomni St. John, Noah Constant, Mario Guajardo-Cespedes, Steve Yuan, Chris Tar, Yun-Hsuan Sung, Brian Strope, and Ray Kurzweil. 2018. Universal sentence encoder.

Tianqi Chen and Carlos Guestrin. 2016. XGBoost: A scalable tree boosting system. In *Proceedings of the 22nd ACM SIGKDD International Conference on Knowledge Discovery and Data Mining*, KDD '16, pages 785–794, New York, NY, USA. ACM.

Hugh A. Chipman, Edward I. George, and Robert E. McCulloch. 2010. Bart: Bayesian additive regression trees. *The Annals of Applied Statistics*, 4(1):266–298.

Lee Devlin, Chang and Toutanova. 2019. Bert: Pre-training of deep bidirectional transformers for language understanding. *arXiv preprint arXiv:1810.04805*.

Xinya Du, Junru Shao, and Claire Cardie. 2017. Learning to ask: Neural question generation for reading comprehension. *CoRR*, abs/1705.00106.

Yifan Fu, Xingquan Zhu, and Bin Li. 2013. A survey on instance selection for active learning. *Knowledge and information systems*, 35(2):249–283.

Michael Heilman and Noah A. Smith. 2009. Question generation via overgenerating transformations and ranking.

Kexin Huang, Jaan Altosaar, and Rajesh Ranganath. 2019. Clinicalbert: Modeling clinical notes and predicting hospital readmission.

Qiao Jin, Bhuwan Dhingra, Zhengping Liu, William Cohen, and Xinghua Lu. 2019. Pubmedqa: A dataset for biomedical research question answering. In *Proceedings of the 2019 Conference on Empirical*

Methods in Natural Language Processing and the 9th International Joint Conference on Natural Language Processing (EMNLP-IJCNLP), pages 2567–2577.

Mandar Joshi, Eunsol Choi, Daniel Weld, and Luke Zettlemoyer. 2017. TriviaQA: A large scale distantly supervised challenge dataset for reading comprehension. In *Proceedings of the 55th Annual Meeting of the Association for Computational Linguistics (Volume 1: Long Papers)*, pages 1601–1611, Vancouver, Canada. Association for Computational Linguistics.

Neesha Jothi, Nur'Aini Abdul Rashid, and Wahidah Husain. 2015. Data mining in healthcare – a review. *Procedia Computer Science*, 72:306 – 313. The Third Information Systems International Conference 2015.

T. Kanungo, D. M. Mount, N. S. Netanyahu, C. D. Piatko, R. Silverman, and A. Y. Wu. 2002. An efficient k-means clustering algorithm: analysis and implementation. *IEEE Transactions on Pattern Analysis and Machine Intelligence*, 24(7):881–892.

Ksenia Konyushkova, Raphael Sznitman, and Pascal Fua. 2017. Learning active learning from data. In I. Guyon, U. V. Luxburg, S. Bengio, H. Wallach, R. Fergus, S. Vishwanathan, and R. Garnett, editors, *Advances in Neural Information Processing Systems 30*, pages 4225–4235. Curran Associates, Inc.

Kalpesh Krishna and Mohit Iyyer. 2019. Generating question-answer hierarchies. *CoRR*, abs/1906.02622.

Tom Kwiatkowski, Jennimaria Palomaki, Olivia Redfield, Michael Collins, Ankur Parikh, Chris Alberti, Danielle Epstein, Illia Polosukhin, Matthew Kelcey, Jacob Devlin, Kenton Lee, Kristina N. Toutanova, Llion Jones, Ming-Wei Chang, Andrew Dai, Jakob Uszkoreit, Quoc Le, and Slav Petrov. 2019. Natural questions: a benchmark for question answering research. *Transactions of the Association of Computational Linguistics*.

Zhenzhong Lan, Mingda Chen, Sebastian Goodman, Kevin Gimpel, Piyush Sharma, and Radu Soricut. 2020. Albert: A lite bert for self-supervised learning of language representations. In *International Conference on Learning Representations*.

J. Richard Landis and Gary G. Koch. 1977. The measurement of observer agreement for categorical data. *Biometrics*, 33(1):159–174.

Jinhyuk Lee, Wonjin Yoon, Sungdong Kim, Donghyeon Kim, Sunkyu Kim, Chan Ho So, and Jaewoo Kang. 2019. BioBERT: a pretrained biomedical language representation model for biomedical text mining. *Bioinformatics*, 36(4):1234–1240.

VI Levenshtein. 1966. Binary Codes Capable of Correcting Deletions, Insertions and Reversals. *Soviet Physics Doklady*, 10:707.

Mary L McHugh. 2012. Interrater reliability: the kappa statistic. *Biochemia medica*, 22(3):276–282.

David Oniani and Yanshan Wang. 2020. A qualitative evaluation of language models on automatic question-answering for covid-19.

Alec Radford, Jeff Wu, Rewon Child, David Luan, Dario Amodei, and Ilya Sutskever. 2019. Language models are unsupervised multitask learners.

Colin Raffel, Noam Shazeer, Adam Roberts, Katherine Lee, Sharan Narang, Michael Matena, Yanqi Zhou, Wei Li, and Peter J. Liu. 2019. Exploring the limits of transfer learning with a unified text-to-text transformer.

Pranav Rajpurkar, Jian Zhang, Konstantin Lopyrev, and Percy Liang. 2016. Squad: 100,000+ questions for machine comprehension of text.

Reimers and Gurevych. 2019. Sentence-bert: Sentence embeddings using siamese bert-networks. *arXiv preprint arXiv:1908.10084*.

Adam Roberts, Colin Raffel, and Noam Shazeer. 2020. How much knowledge can you pack into the parameters of a language model? *arXiv preprint arXiv:2002.08910*.

Victor Sanh, Lysandre Debut, Julien Chaumond, and Thomas Wolf. 2019. Distilbert, a distilled version of bert: smaller, faster, cheaper and lighter.

Sheng Shen, Yaliang Li, Nan Du, Xian Wu, Yusheng Xie, Shen Ge, Tao Yang, Kai Wang, Xingzheng Liang, and Wei Fan. 2020. On the generation of medical question-answer pairs. In *AAAI*, pages 8822–8829.

Z. Shuyang, T. Heittola, and T. Virtanen. 2018. An active learning method using clustering and committee-based sample selection for sound event classification. In *2018 16th International Workshop on Acoustic Signal Enhancement (IWAENC)*, pages 116–120.

George Tsatsaronis, Georgios Balikas, Prodromos Malakasiotis, Ioannis Partalas, Matthias Zschunke, Michael R Alvers, Dirk Weissenborn, Anastasia Krithara, Sergios Petridis, Dimitris Polychronopoulos, Yannis Almirantis, John Pavlopoulos, Nicolas Baskiotis, Patrick Gallinari, Thierry Artieres, Axel Ngonga, Norman Heino, Eric Gaussier, Liliana Barrio-Alvers, Michael Schroeder, Ion Androutsopoulos, and Georgios Paliouras. 2015. An overview of the bioasq large-scale biomedical semantic indexing and question answering competition. *BMC Bioinformatics*, 16:138.

Ashish Vaswani, Noam Shazeer, Niki Parmar, Jakob Uszkoreit, Llion Jones, Aidan N Gomez, Łukasz Kaiser, and Illia Polosukhin. 2017. Attention is all you need. In *Advances in neural information processing systems*, pages 5998–6008.

Jason Walonoski, Mark Kramer, Joseph Nichols, Andre Quina, Chris Moesel, Dylan Hall, Carlton Duffett, Kudakwashe Dube, Thomas Gallagher, and Scott McLachlan. 2018. Synthea: An approach, method, and software mechanism for generating synthetic patients and the synthetic electronic health care record. *Journal of the American Medical Informatics Association*, 25(3):230–238.

Alex Wang, Amanpreet Singh, Julian Michael, Felix Hill, Omer Levy, and Samuel Bowman. 2018. GLUE: A multi-task benchmark and analysis platform for natural language understanding. In *Proceedings of the 2018 EMNLP Workshop BlackboxNLP: Analyzing and Interpreting Neural Networks for NLP*, pages 353–355, Brussels, Belgium. Association for Computational Linguistics.

Lucy Lu Wang, Kyle Lo, Yoganand Chandrasekhar, Russell Reas, Jiangjiang Yang, Darrin Eide, Kathryn Funk, Rodney Kinney, Ziyang Liu, William Merrill, Paul Mooney, Dewey Murdick, Devvret Rishi, Jerry Sheehan, Zhihong Shen, Brandon Stilson, Alex D. Wade, Kuansan Wang, Chris Wilhelm, Boya Xie, Douglas Raymond, Daniel S. Weld, Oren Etzioni, and Sebastian Kohlmeier. 2020. Cord-19: The covid-19 open research dataset.

Wei Yang, Yuqing Xie, Aileen Lin, Xingyu Li, Luchen Tan, Kun Xiong, Ming Li, and Jimmy Lin. 2019. End-to-end open-domain question answering with bertserini. *CoRR*, abs/1902.01718.

Zhilin Yang, Peng Qi, Saizheng Zhang, Yoshua Bengio, William Cohen, Ruslan Salakhutdinov, and Christopher D. Manning. 2018. HotpotQA: A dataset for diverse, explainable multi-hop question answering. In *Proceedings of the 2018 Conference on Empirical Methods in Natural Language Processing*, pages 2369–2380, Brussels, Belgium. Association for Computational Linguistics.

Covidex: Neural Ranking Models and Keyword Search Infrastructure for the COVID-19 Open Research Dataset

Edwin Zhang,[1] Nikhil Gupta,[1] Raphael Tang,[1] Xiao Han,[1] Ronak Pradeep,[1] Kuang Lu,[2]
Yue Zhang,[2] Rodrigo Nogueira,[1] Kyunghyun Cho,[3,4] Hui Fang,[2] and Jimmy Lin[1]

[1] University of Waterloo   [2] University of Delaware
[3] New York University   [4] CIFAR Associate Fellow

Abstract

We present Covidex, a search engine that exploits the latest neural ranking models to provide information access to the COVID-19 Open Research Dataset curated by the Allen Institute for AI. Our system has been online and serving users since late March 2020. The Covidex is the user application component of our three-pronged strategy to develop technologies for helping domain experts tackle the ongoing global pandemic. In addition, we provide robust and easy-to-use keyword search infrastructure that exploits mature fusion-based methods as well as standalone neural ranking models that can be incorporated into other applications. These techniques have been evaluated in the multi-round TREC-COVID challenge: Our infrastructure and baselines have been adopted by many participants, including some of the best systems. In round 3, we submitted the highest-scoring run that took advantage of previous training data and the second-highest fully automatic run. In rounds 4 and 5, we submitted the highest-scoring fully automatic runs.

1 Introduction

As a response to the worldwide COVID-19 pandemic, on March 13, 2020, the Allen Institute for AI (AI2) released the COVID-19 Open Research Dataset (CORD-19) (Wang et al., 2020). With regular updates since the initial release (first weekly, then daily), the corpus contains around 300,000 scientific articles (as of October, 2020), including most with full text, about COVID-19 and coronavirus-related research more broadly (for example, SARS and MERS). These articles are gathered from a variety of sources, including PubMed, a curated list of articles from the WHO, as well as preprints from arXiv, bioRxiv, and medRxiv. The goal of the effort is "to mobilize researchers to apply recent advances in natural language processing to generate new insights in support of the fight against this infectious disease." We responded to this call to arms.

As motivation, we believe that information access capabilities (search, question answering, etc.) can be applied to provide users with high-quality information from the scientific literature, to inform evidence-based decision making and to support insight generation. Examples include public health officials assessing the efficacy of wearing face masks, clinicians conducting meta-analyses to update care guidelines based on emerging studies, and virologist probing the genetic structure of COVID-19 in search of vaccines. We hope to contribute to these efforts via a three-pronged strategy:

1. Despite significant advances in the application of neural architectures to text ranking, keyword search (e.g., with "bag of words" queries) remains an important core technology. Building on top of our Anserini IR toolkit (Yang et al., 2018), we have released robust and easy-to-use open-source keyword search infrastructure that the broader community can build on.

2. Leveraging our own infrastructure, we explored the use of sequence-to-sequence transformer models for document expansion and candidate reranking, combined with a simple classification-based feedback approach to exploit existing relevance judgments. We have also open sourced all these models, which can be integrated into other systems.

3. Finally, we package the previous two components into Covidex, an end-to-end search engine and browsing interface deployed at covidex.ai, initially described in Zhang et al. (2020a).

All three efforts have been successful. In the TREC-COVID challenge, our infrastructure and baselines have been adopted by many teams, which in some

Proceedings of the First Workshop on Scholarly Document Processing, pages 31–41
Online, November 19, 2020. ©2020 Association for Computational Linguistics
https://doi.org/10.18653/v1/P17

cases have submitted runs that scored higher than our own submissions. This illustrates the success of our infrastructure-building efforts (1). In round 3, we submitted the highest-scoring run that took advantage of previous training data and the second-highest fully automatic run. In rounds 4 and 5, we submitted the highest-scoring fully automatic runs. These results affirm the quality of our own ranking models (2). Finally, usage statistics offer some evidence for the success of our deployed Covidex search engine (3).

2 Ranking Components

Multi-stage search architectures represent the most common design for modern search engines, with work in academia dating back over a decade (Matveeva et al., 2006; Wang et al., 2011; Asadi and Lin, 2013). Known production deployments of this design include the Bing web search engine (Pedersen, 2010) as well as Alibaba's e-commerce search engine (Liu et al., 2017).

The idea behind multi-stage ranking is straightforward: instead of a monolithic ranker, ranking is decomposed into a series of stages. Typically, the pipeline begins with an initial retrieval stage, most often using bag-of-words queries against an inverted index. One or more subsequent stages reranks and refines the candidate set successively until the final results are presented to the user. The multi-stage design provides a clean interface between keyword search, neural reranking models, and the user application.

This section details individual components in our architecture. We describe later how these building blocks are assembled in the deployed system (Section 3) and for TREC-COVID (Section 4.2).

2.1 Keyword Search

In our design, initial retrieval is performed by the Anserini IR toolkit (Yang et al., 2017, 2018),[1] which we have been developing for several years and powers a number of our previous systems that incorporate various neural architectures (Yang et al., 2019; Yilmaz et al., 2019). Anserini represents an effort to better align real-world search applications with academic information retrieval research: under the covers, it builds on the popular and widely-deployed open-source Lucene search library, on top of which we provide a number of

missing features for conducting research on modern IR test collections.

Anserini provides an abstraction for document collections, and comes with a variety of adaptors for different corpora and formats: web pages in WARC containers, XML documents in tarballs, JSON objects in text files, etc. Providing keyword search capabilities over CORD-19 required only writing an adaptor for the corpus that allows Anserini to ingest the documents.

An issue that immediately arose with CORD-19 concerned the granularity of indexing, i.e., what should we consider to be a "document" as the "atomic unit" of indexing and retrieval? One complication is that the corpus contains a mix of articles that vary widely in length, not only in terms of natural variations (scientific articles of varying lengths, book chapters, etc.), but also because the full text is not available for some articles. It is well known in the IR literature, dating back several decades (e.g., Singhal et al. 1996), that length normalization plays an important role in retrieval effectiveness.

Guided by previous work on searching full-text articles (Lin, 2009), we explored three separate indexing schemes:

- An index comprised of only titles and abstracts.

- An index comprised of each full-text article as a single, individual document; articles without full text contained only titles and abstracts.

- A paragraph-level index structured as follows: each full-text article was segmented into paragraphs and for *each* paragraph, we created a "document" comprising the title, abstract, and that paragraph. The title and abstract alone comprised an additional "document". Thus, a full-text article with n paragraphs yielded $n + 1$ separate retrieval units in the index.

To be consistent with standard IR parlance, we call each of these retrieval units a "document", in a generic sense, despite their composite structure.

In addition to the above indexing schemes, we considered three more based on our doc2query document expansion technique (Nogueira et al., 2019b; Nogueira and Lin, 2019). The idea behind using document expansion is to enhance each document with (synthetic) queries for which the document may be relevant, to alleviate the vocabulary mismatch problem by increasing the likelihood that query terms and document terms match. We used

---

[1] http://anserini.io/

the T5-base doc2query model trained on the MS MARCO passage dataset (Bajaj et al., 2018) provided by Nogueira and Lin (2019). Due to limited computational resources, we only generated expansions from the article abstracts. However, even the abstracts alone often exceeded the model's input length restriction of 512 tokens. To address this issue, we first segmented each document into passages by applying a sliding window of ten sentences with a stride of five. These passages were then prepended with the title of the article. Inference was performed on these passages using a top-k sampling decoder that generated 40 queries (i.e., expansions) per abstract passage. Finally, for each of the index conditions above, we expanded the documents by appending all the expansion queries to form three more doc2query-enhanced indexes. Note that when applying inference with neural networks during the reranking stage, we used the original abstracts (i.e., without expansions).

In all cases (both the original indexes and doc2query-enhanced indexes), documents were initially retrieved using the popular BM25 scoring function (Robertson et al., 1994).

With the paragraph index, a query is likely to retrieve multiple paragraphs from the same underlying article; since the final task is to rank articles, we took the highest-scoring paragraph of an article as its score. Articles were then ranked according to their scores. Furthermore, we combined results from these different indexing schemes to capture different ranking signals using fusion techniques, which further improved effectiveness; see Section 4.2 for details.

Since Anserini is built on top of Lucene, which is implemented in Java, it is designed to run on the Java Virtual Machine (JVM). However, TensorFlow (Abadi et al., 2016) and PyTorch (Paszke et al., 2019), the two most popular neural network toolkits today, use Python as their main language. More broadly, with its diverse and mature ecosystem, Python has emerged as the language of choice for most data scientists today. Anticipating this gap, we have been working on Pyserini,[2] Python bindings for Anserini, since late 2019 (Yilmaz et al., 2020). Pyserini is released as a well-documented, easy-to-use Python module distributed via PyPI and easily installable via `pip`.[3]

Putting everything together, we provide the com-

munity keyword search infrastructure by sharing code, indexes, as well as baseline runs. First, all our code is available open source. Second, we share pre-built versions of CORD-19 indexes, so that users can replicate our results with minimal effort. Finally, we provide baseline runs for TREC-COVID that can be directly incorporated into other participants' submissions.

2.2 Rerankers

In our infrastructure, the output of Pyserini is fed to rerankers that aim to improve ranking quality. We describe three different approaches: two are based on neural architectures, and the third exploits relevance judgments in a feedback setting using a classification approach.

monoT5. Despite the success of BERT for document ranking (Dai and Callan, 2019; MacAvaney et al., 2019; Yilmaz et al., 2019), there is evidence that ranking with sequence-to-sequence models can achieve even better effectiveness, particularly in zero-shot and other settings with limited training data (Nogueira et al., 2020a,b), such as for TREC-COVID. Our "base" reranker, called monoT5, is based on T5 (Raffel et al., 2020).

Given a query q and a set of candidate documents D from Pyserini, for each $d \in D$ we construct the following input sequence to feed into our model:

$$\text{Query: } q \text{ Document: } d \text{ Relevant:} \qquad (1)$$

The model is fine-tuned to produce either "true" or "false" depending on whether the document is relevant or not to the query. That is, "true" and "false" are the ground truth predictions in the sequence-to-sequence task, what we call the "target tokens".

At inference time, to compute probabilities for each query–document pair, we apply softmax only to the logits of the "true" and "false" tokens. We rerank the candidate documents according to the probabilities assigned to the "true" token. See Nogueira et al. (2020a,b) for additional details about this logit normalization trick and the effects of different target tokens.

Since in the beginning we did not have training data specific to COVID-19, we fine-tuned our model on the MS MARCO passage dataset (Bajaj et al., 2018), which comprises 8.8M passages obtained from the top 10 results retrieved by the Bing search engine (based on around 1M queries). The training set contains approximately 500K pairs of query and relevant documents, where each query

---

[2] http://pyserini.io/
[3] https://pypi.org/project/pyserini/

has one relevant passage on average; non-relevant documents for training are also provided as part of the training data. Nogueira et al. (2020a,b) and Yilmaz et al. (2019) have previously demonstrated that models trained on MS MARCO can be effectively applied to other document ranking tasks in a zero-shot manner.

We fine-tuned our monoT5 model with a constant learning rate of 10^{-3} for 10K iterations with class-balanced batches of size 128. We used a maximum of 512 input tokens and two output tokens (one for the target token, either "true" or "false", and another for the end-of-sequence token). In the MS MARCO passage dataset, none of the inputs required truncation when using this length limit. Training model variants based on T5-base and T5-3B took approximately 4 and 40 hours, respectively, on a single Google TPU v3-8.

At inference time, since output from Pyserini is usually longer than the length restrictions of the model, it is not possible to feed the *entire* text of the document into our model at once. To address this issue, we first segmented each document into passages by applying a sliding window of ten sentences with a stride of five. We obtained a probability of relevance for each passage by performing inference on it independently, and then selected the highest probability among the passages as the relevance score of the document.

duoT5. A pairwise reranker estimates the probability $s_{i,j}$ that candidate d_i is more relevant than d_j for query q, where $i \neq j$. Nogueira et al. (2019a) demonstrated that a pairwise BERT reranker running on the output of a pointwise BERT reranker in a multi-stage ranking pipeline yielded statistically significant improvements in output quality. We applied the same intuition to T5 to build a pairwise reranker called duoT5, which takes as input the following sequence:

Query: q Document0: d_i Document1: d_j Relevant:

where d_i and d_j are unique pairs of candidates from the set D. The model is fine-tuned to predict "true" if candidate d_i is more relevant than d_j to query q and "false" otherwise. We fine-tuned duoT5 using the same hyperparameters as monoT5.

At inference time, we used the top 50 highest-scoring documents according to monoT5 as our candidate set $\{d_i\}$. We then obtained probabilities $p_{i,j}$ of d_i being more relevant than d_j for all unique candidate pairs $\{d_i, d_j\}, \forall i \neq j$. Finally, we computed a single score s_i for candidate d_i as follows:

$$s_i = \sum_{j \in J_i} (p_{i,j} + (1 - p_{j,i})) \qquad (2)$$

where $J_i = \{0 \leq j < 50, j \neq i\}$. Based on exploratory studies on the MS MARCO passage dataset, this setting led to the most stable and effective rankings.

Relevance Feedback. The setup of TREC-COVID (see Section 4.1) provided a feedback setting where systems can exploit a limited number of relevance judgments on a per-query basis. How do we take advantage of such training data? Despite work on fine-tuning transformers in a few-shot setting (Zhang et al., 2020b; Lee et al., 2020), we were wary of the dangers of overfitting on limited data, particularly since there is little guidance on relevance feedback using transformers in the literature. Instead, we implemented a robust approach that treats relevance feedback as a document classification problem using simple linear classifiers, described in Yu et al. (2019) and Lin (2019).

The approach is conceptually simple: for each query, we trained a linear classifier (logistic regression) that attempts to distinguish relevant from non-relevant documents *for that query*. The classifier operated on sparse bag-of-words representations using tf–idf term weighting. At inference time, each candidate document was fed to the classifier, and the classifier score was then linearly interpolated with the original candidate document score to produce a final score. We describe the input source documents in Section 4.2.

All components above have also been open sourced. The two neural reranking modules are available in PyGaggle,[4] which is our recently developed neural ranking library designed to work with Pyserini. Our classification-based approach to feedback is implemented in Pyserini directly. These components are available for integration into any system.

3   The Covidex

Beyond sharing our keyword search infrastructure and reranking models, we've built the Covidex as an operational search engine to demonstrate our capabilities to domain experts who are not interested in individual components. As deployed, we use the paragraph index and monoT5-base as the

---

[4]`http://pygaggle.ai/`

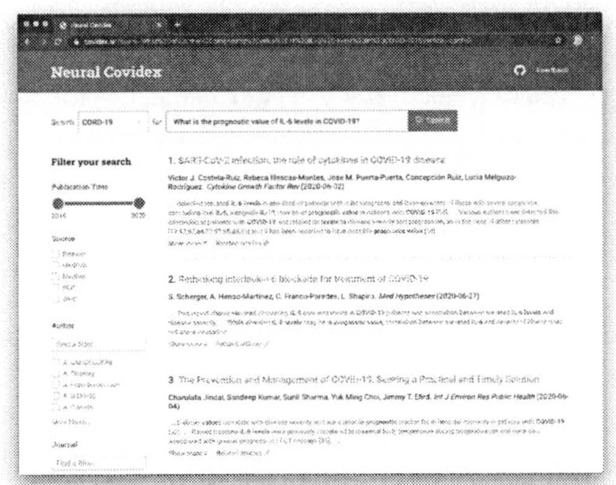

Figure 1: Screenshot of the Covidex.

reranker. An additional highlighting module based on BioBERT was described in Zhang et al. (2020a). To decrease end-to-end latency, we rerank only the top 96 documents per query and truncate reranker input to a maximum of 256 tokens.

The Covidex was built using the FastAPI Python web framework, where all incoming API requests are handled by a service that performs searching, reranking, and text highlighting. Search is performed with Pyserini (Section 2.1), and the results are then reranked with PyGaggle (Section 2.2). The frontend (which is also open source) was built with the React JavaScript library to support the use of modular, declarative components, taking advantage of its vast ecosystem.

A screenshot of our system is shown in Figure 1. Covidex provides standard search capabilities, either based on keyword queries or natural-language input. Users can click "Show more" to reveal the abstract as well as excerpts from the full text, where potentially relevant passages are highlighted. Clicking on the title brings the user to the article's source on the publisher's site. In addition, we have implemented a faceted browsing feature. From CORD-19, we were able to easily expose facets corresponding to dates, authors, journals, and sources. Navigating by year, for example, allows a user to focus on older coronavirus research (e.g., on SARS) or the latest research on COVID-19, and a combination of the journal and source facets allows a user to differentiate between preprints and the peer-reviewed literature, and between venues with different reputations.

The system is currently deployed across a small cluster of servers, each with two NVIDIA V100 GPUs, as our pipeline requires neural network inference at query time. Each server runs the complete software stack in a simple replicated setup (no partitioning). On top of this, we leverage Cloudflare as a simple load balancer, which uses a round robin scheme to dispatch requests across the different servers. The end-to-end latency for a typical query is around two seconds.

The first implementation of our system was deployed in late March, and we have been incrementally adding features since. Based on Cloudflare statistics, our site receives around two hundred unique visitors per day and the site serves more than one thousand requests each day. Of course, usage statistics were (up to several times) higher when we first launched due to publicity on social media. However, the figures cited above represent a "steady state" that has held up over the past few months, in the absence of any deliberate promotion.

4 TREC-COVID

Reliable, large-scale evaluations of text retrieval methods are a costly endeavor, typically beyond the resources of individual research groups. Fortunately, the community-wide TREC-COVID challenge sponsored by the U.S. National Institute for Standards and Technology (NIST) provided a forum for evaluating our techniques.

4.1 Evaluation Overview

The TREC-COVID challenge, which ran from mid-April to late-August 2020, provided an opportunity for researchers to study methods for quickly standing up information access systems, both in response to the current pandemic and to prepare for similar future events (Voorhees et al., 2020; Roberts et al., 2020). The challenge was open to everyone.

Both out of logistic necessity in evaluation design and because the body of scientific literature is rapidly expanding, TREC-COVID was organized into a series of "rounds" (five in total), each of which used the CORD-19 collection at a snapshot in time. For a particular round, participating teams developed systems that return results for a number of information needs, called "topics"—one example is "serological tests that detect antibodies of COVID-19". These results comprise a run or a submission. Each team could submit up to three runs per round (increased to eight in the final round). NIST then gathered and evaluated these runs using a standard pooling methodology (Voorhees, 2002).

The product of each round was a collection of relevance judgments, which are annotations by domain experts about the relevance of documents with respect to topics. On average, there were around 300 judgments (both positive and negative) *per topic* from each round. These relevance judgments were used to evaluate the effectiveness of systems (populating a leaderboard) and could also be used to train machine-learning models in future rounds. Runs that took advantage of these relevance judgments were known as "feedback" runs, in contrast to "automatic" runs that did not. A third category, "manual" runs, could involve human input, but we did not submit any such runs.

The TREC-COVID challenge spanned a total of five rounds. Each round contained a number of topics that were persistent (i.e., carried over from previous rounds) as well as new topics. To avoid retrieving duplicate documents, the evaluation adopted a residual collection methodology, where judged documents (either relevant or not) from previous rounds were automatically removed from consideration. Thus, for each topic, future rounds only evaluated documents that had not been examined before (either newly published articles or articles that had never been retrieved). It is worth emphasizing that due to the evaluation methodology, scores across rounds *are not* comparable.

The official evaluation metric was nDCG, at rank cutoff 10 for the first three rounds, increased to 20 for rounds 4 and 5. NIST also reported a few other metrics, including precision at a fixed ranked cutoff and average precision (AP) to the standard rank depth of 1000.

4.2 Results

A selection of results from TREC-COVID is shown in Table 1, where we report standard metrics computed by NIST. We submitted runs under team "covidex" (for neural models) and team "anserini" (for our bag-of-words baselines). In our narrative below, when we refer to rank positions (e.g., the second-best run), we disregard multiple runs from the same team. For complete details of all results, we refer readers to the official NIST site[5] or a mirror of the results in an easily comparable format that we have compiled.[6]

In **Round 1**, there were 143 runs from 56 teams. Our best run T5R1 (1c) used BM25 for first-stage

retrieval using the paragraph index followed by our monoT5-3B reranker, trained on MS MARCO (as described in Section 2.2). The best automatic neural run was run2 (1b) from team GUIR_S2 (MacAvaney et al., 2020), which was built on Anserini. This run placed second behind the best automatic run, sabir.meta.docs (1a), which interestingly was based on the vector-space model.

While we did make meaningful infrastructure contributions (e.g., Anserini provided the keyword search results that fed the neural ranking models of team GUIR_S2), our own run T5R1 (1c) was substantially behind the top-scoring runs. A post-hoc experiment with round 1 relevance judgments showed that using the paragraph index did not turn out to be the best choice: simply replacing with the abstract index (but retaining the monoT5-3B reranker) improved nDCG@10 from 0.5223 to 0.5702.[7]

We learned two important lessons from the results of round 1:

1. The effectiveness of simple rank fusion techniques that can exploit diverse ranking signals by combining multiple ranked lists. Many teams adopted such techniques (including the top-scoring run), which proved both robust and effective. This is not a new observation in information retrieval, but is once again affirmed by TREC-COVID.

2. The importance of building the "right" query representations for keyword search. Each TREC-COVID topic contains three fields: query, question, and narrative. The query field describes the information need using a few keywords, similar to what a user would type into a web search engine. The question field phrases the information need as a well-formed natural language question, and the narrative field contains additional details in a short paragraph. The query field may be missing important keywords, but the other two fields often contain too many "noisy" terms unrelated to the information need.

Thus, it makes sense to leverage information from multiple fields in constructing keyword queries, but to do so selectively. Based on results from round 1, the following query genera-

[5]https://ir.nist.gov/covidSubmit/
[6]https://github.com/castorini/TREC-COVID

---

[7]Despite this finding, we suspected that there may have been evaluation artifacts at play, because our impressions from the deployed system suggested that results from the paragraph index were better. Thus, the deployed Covidex still uses paragraph indexes.

	Team	Run	Type	nDCG@10	P@5	AP
Round 1: 30 topics						
(1a)	sabir	`sabir.meta.docs`	automatic	0.6080	0.7800	0.3128
(1b)	GUIR_S2	`run2`[†]	automatic	0.6032	0.6867	0.2601
(1c)	covidex	`T5R1` (= monoT5)	automatic	0.5223	0.6467	0.2838
Round 2: 35 topics						
(2a)	mpiid5	`mpiid5_run3`[†]	manual	0.6893	0.8514	0.3380
(2b)	CMT	`SparseDenseSciBert`[†]	feedback	0.6772	0.7600	0.3115
(2c)	UIowaS	`UIowaS_Run3`	feedback	0.6382	0.7657	0.2845
(2d)	GUIR_S2	`GUIR_S2_run1`[†]	automatic	0.6251	0.7486	0.2842
(2e)	covidex	`covidex.t5` (= monoT5)	automatic	0.6250	0.7314	0.2880
(2f)	anserini	`r2.fusion2`	automatic	0.5553	0.6800	0.2725
(2g)	anserini	`r2.fusion1`	automatic	0.4827	0.6114	0.2418
Round 3: 40 topics						
(3a)	covidex	`r3.t5_lr` (= monoT5 + LR)	feedback	0.7740	0.8600	0.3333
(3b)	BioinformaticsUA	`BioInfo-run1`	feedback	0.7715	0.8650	0.3188
(3c)	SFDC	`SFDC-fus12-enc23-tf3`[†]	automatic	0.6867	0.7800	0.3160
(3d)	covidex	`r3.duot5` (= monoT5 + duoT5)	automatic	0.6626	0.7700	0.2676
(3e)	covidex	`r3.monot5` (= monoT5)	automatic	0.6596	0.7800	0.2635
(3f)	anserini	`r3.fusion2`	automatic	0.6100	0.7150	0.2641
(3g)	anserini	`r3.fusion1`	automatic	0.5359	0.6100	0.2293

	Team	Run	Type	nDCG@20	P@20	AP
Round 4: 45 topics						
(4a)	unique_ptr	`UPrrf38rrf3-r4`[†]	feedback	0.7843	0.8211	0.4681
(4b)	covidex	`covidex.r4.duot5.lr` (= expando + monoT5 + duoT5 + LR)	feedback	0.7745	0.7967	0.3846
(4c)	covidex	`covidex.r4.d2q.duot5` (= expando + monoT5 + duoT5)	automatic	0.7219	0.7267	0.3122
(4d)	covidex	`covidex.r4.duot5` (= monoT5 + duoT5)	automatic	0.6877	0.6922	0.3283
(4e)	uogTr	`uogTrDPH_QE_SCB1`	automatic	0.6820	0.7144	0.3457
(4f)	anserini	`r4.fusion2`	automatic	0.6089	0.6589	0.3088
(4g)	anserini	`r4.fusion1`	automatic	0.5244	0.5611	0.2666
Round 5: 50 topics						
(5a)	unique_ptr	`UPrrf93-wt-r5`[†]	feedback	0.8496	0.8760	0.4718
(5b)	covidex	`covidex.r5.2s.lr` (= monoT5 + duoT5 + LR)	feedback	0.8311	0.8460	0.3922
(5c)	covidex	`covidex.r5.d2q.2s.lr` (= expando + monoT5 + duoT5 + LR)	feedback	0.8304	0.8380	0.3875
(5d)	covidex	`covidex.r5.d2q.2s` (= expando + monoT5 + duoT5)	automatic	0.7539	0.7700	0.3227
(5e)	covidex	`covidex.r5.2s` (= monoT5 + duoT5)	automatic	0.7457	0.7610	0.3212
(5f)	uogTr	`uogTrDPH_QE_SB_CB`	automatic	0.7427	0.7910	0.3305
(5g)	covidex	`covidex.r5.d2q.1s` (= expando + monoT5)	automatic	0.7121	0.7320	0.3150
(5h)	anserini	`r5.fusion2`	automatic	0.6007	0.6440	0.2734
(5i)	anserini	`r5.fusion1`	automatic	0.5313	0.5840	0.2314

Table 1: Selected TREC-COVID results. Our submissions are under teams "covidex" and "anserini". All runs notated with [†] incorporate our infrastructure components in some way. Note that the metrics used in the first three rounds are different from those used in the final two rounds.

tion technique proved to be effective: when constructing the keyword query for a given topic, we take the non-stopwords from the query field and further expand them with terms belonging to named entities extracted from the question field using ScispaCy (Neumann et al., 2019).

We saw these two lessons as an opportunity to further contribute community infrastructure, and starting in round 2 we made two fusion runs from Anserini freely available: `fusion1` and `fusion2`. In both runs, we combined rankings from the abstract, full-text, and paragraph indexes via reciprocal rank fusion (RRF) (Cormack et al., 2009). The runs differed in their treatment of the query representation. The run `fusion1` simply took the query field from the topics as the basis for keyword search, while run `fusion2` incorporated the query generator described above to augment the query representation with key phrases. These runs were made available *before* the deadline of subsequent rounds so that other teams could use them, and indeed many took advantage of this resource.

In **Round 2**, there were 136 runs from 51 teams. Our two Anserini baseline fusion runs are shown as `r2.fusion1` (2g) and `r2.fusion2` (2f) in Table 1. Comparing these two fusion baselines, we see that our query generation approach yields a large gain in effectiveness. Ablation studies further confirmed that ranking signals from the different indexes do contribute to the overall higher effectiveness of the rank fusion runs. That is, the effectiveness of the fusion results is higher than results from any of the individual indexes.

Our `covidex.t5` (2e) run took `r2.fusion1` (2g) and `r2.fusion2` (2f), reranked both with monoT5-3B, and then combined their outputs with reciprocal rank fusion. The monoT5-3B model was fine-tuned on MS MARCO and then fine-tuned (again) on a medical subset of MS MARCO (MacAvaney et al., 2020). This run essentially tied for the best automatic run `GUIR_S2_run1` (2d), which scored just 0.0001 higher.

As additional context, Table 1 shows the best manual and feedback runs from round 2, `mpiid5_run3` (2a) and `SparseDenseSciBert` (2b), respectively, which were also the top two runs overall. These results show that manual and feedback techniques can achieve quite a bit of gain over fully automatic techniques. Both of these runs and four out of the five top teams in round 2 took advantage of the fusion baselines we provided, which

demonstrated our impact not only in developing effective ranking models, but also our service to the community in providing infrastructure.

As another point of comparison, `UIowaSRun3` (2c) represented a fusion of two traditional (i.e., term-based) relevance feedback runs, and did not use any neural networks. Interestingly, its effectiveness is not very far behind `SparseDenseSciBert` (2b), the best run in the feedback category (which does take advantage of BERT). It seems that BERT-based methods for exploiting relevance judgments yielded only modest improvements, likely due to the paucity of relevance judgments, as we discussed in Section 2.2.

In **Round 3**, there were 79 runs from 31 teams. Our Anserini fusion baselines, `r3.fusion1` (3g) and `r3.fusion2` (3f), remained the same from the previous round and continued to provide strong baselines, both for our team's own submissions and other participants as well.

Our run `r3.duot5` (3d) was the first deployment of our monoT5 and duoT5 multi-stage ranking pipeline (see Section 2.2), which was a fusion of the fusion runs as the first-stage candidates, reranked by monoT5 and then duoT5. From Table 1, we see that duoT5 did indeed improve over just using monoT5, run `r3.monot5` (3e), albeit the gains were small (but we found that the duoT5 run had more unjudged documents). The run `r3.duot5` (3d) ranked second among all teams under the automatic condition, and we were about two points in nDCG@10 behind team SFDC (3c), who submitted the best run. According to Esteva et al. (2020), their general approach incorporated Anserini fusion runs, which bolsters our case that we provided valuable infrastructure for the community.

Our own feedback run `r3.t5_lr` (3a) implemented the classification-based feedback technique (see Section 2.2) with monoT5 results as the input source document (with a mixing weight of 0.5 to combine monoT5 scores with classifier scores). This was the highest-scoring run across all submissions (all categories), just a bit ahead of `BioInfo-run1` (3b).

In **Round 4**, there were 72 runs from 27 participating teams. Our Anserini fusion baselines, `r4.fusion1` (4g) and `r4.fusion2` (4f), remained exactly the same as before.

This round saw the first deployment of our doc2query document expansion technique. The run `covidex.r4.d2q.duot5` (4c) was essentially the same as `r3.duot5` from round 3, except with doc2query-enhanced indexes; in Table 1 we denote this as "expando". This run was the best automatic run submitted, about four points ahead in terms of nDCG@20 of the second-best automatic run, from team uogTr (4e). Our run `covidex.r4.duot5` (4d) adopted the same approach as `r3.duot5` from round 3 and thus provided an ablation that shows the impact of document expansion. We see from these results that doc2query contributed nearly four points in terms of nDCG@20.

Our feedback run, `covidex.r4.duot5.lr` (4b) used the same relevance classification approach as our run `r3.t5_lr` (3a) from round 3, but with doc2query-enhanced indexes. This was the second-best feedback run, about a point in nDCG@20 behind the best run from team unique_ptr (4a), which was an ensemble of more than 100 runs (Bendersky et al., 2020).

In **Round 5**, there were 126 runs from 28 participating teams. For this final round, NIST increased the number of runs that each team was allowed to submit, up to eight in total. Our Anserini fusion baselines, `r5.fusion1` (5i) and `r5.fusion2` (5h), remained exactly as before.

We used this final round as an opportunity to consolidate and refactor our codebase; no new techniques were introduced. In terms of rankings, little changed from round 4: we reported the best automatic run (5d), slightly ahead of a run from team uogTr (5f), and the second-best feedback run (5b), behind a run from team unique_ptr (5a), as shown in Table 1.

The ability to submit more runs also allowed us to conduct ablation analyses. The runs (5b) and (5c) quantified the effect of document expansion in the feedback setting. We see, quite interestingly, that document expansion has minimal effect, and in fact the run *without* document expansion achieved a slightly higher nDCG@20 (but likely just noise). Similarly, runs (5d) and (5e) quantified the effects of document expansion in the automatic setting. Contrary to what we observed in round 4, the benefits were relatively modest. Runs (5d) and (5g) quantified the effects of the pairwise reranker, with document expansion. Unlike round 3, here we see that two-stage reranking (monoT5 + duoT5) brought considerable improvement over single-stage reranking (monoT5).

For cases where we saw less improvement than expected, one possible explanation is that the topics

had become "too easy", at least given the standards of relevance assessment and the evaluation metrics. This can be seen in the high absolute values of the scores. If we examine, say, precision at rank cutoff 10, most of the high-scoring runs attained scores above 0.9; that is, nine of the top ten results were relevant on average! It may be the case that the evaluation had lost discriminative power to separate runs that were all "pretty good".

5 Conclusions

Our project has three goals: build community infrastructure, advance the state of the art in neural ranking, and provide a useful application. We believe that we have succeeded in all three goals. Beyond COVID-19, the capabilities we've developed can be applied to analyzing the scientific literature more broadly.

Acknowledgments

This research was supported in part by the Canada First Research Excellence Fund, the Natural Sciences and Engineering Research Council (NSERC) of Canada, CIFAR AI & COVID-19 Catalyst Funding 2019–2020, and Microsoft AI for Good COVID-19 Grant. We'd like to thank Kyle Lo from AI2 for helpful discussions and Colin Raffel from Google for his assistance with T5.

References

Martín Abadi, Paul Barham, Jianmin Chen, Zhifeng Chen, Andy Davis, Jeffrey Dean, Matthieu Devin, Sanjay Ghemawat, Geoffrey Irving, Michael Isard, Manjunath Kudlur, Josh Levenberg, Rajat Monga, Sherry Moore, Derek G. Murray, Benoit Steiner, Paul Tucker, Vijay Vasudevan, Pete Warden, Martin Wicke, Yuan Yu, and Xiaoqiang Zheng. 2016. TensorFlow: A system for large-scale machine learning. In *12th USENIX Symposium on Operating Systems Design and Implementation (OSDI '16)*, pages 265–283.

Nima Asadi and Jimmy Lin. 2013. Effectiveness/efficiency tradeoffs for candidate generation in multi-stage retrieval architectures. In *Proceedings of the 36th Annual International ACM SIGIR Conference on Research and Development in Information Retrieval (SIGIR 2013)*, pages 997–1000, Dublin, Ireland.

Payal Bajaj, Daniel Campos, Nick Craswell, Li Deng, Jianfeng Gao, Xiaodong Liu, Rangan Majumder, Andrew McNamara, Bhaskar Mitra, Tri Nguyen,

Mir Rosenberg, Xia Song, Alina Stoica, Saurabh Tiwary, and Tong Wang. 2018. MS MARCO: A Human Generated MAchine Reading COmprehension Dataset. *arXiv:1611.09268v3*.

Michael Bendersky, Honglei Zhuang, Ji Ma, Shuguang Han, Keith Hall, and Ryan McDonald. 2020. RRF102: Meeting the TREC-COVID challenge with a 100+ runs ensemble. *arXiv:2010.00200*.

Gordon V. Cormack, Charles L. A. Clarke, and Stefan Büttcher. 2009. Reciprocal rank fusion outperforms Condorcet and individual rank learning methods. In *Proceedings of the 32nd Annual International ACM SIGIR Conference on Research and Development in Information Retrieval (SIGIR 2009)*, pages 758–759, Boston, Massachusetts.

Zhuyun Dai and Jamie Callan. 2019. Deeper text understanding for IR with contextual neural language modeling. In *Proceedings of the 42nd Annual International ACM SIGIR Conference on Research and Development in Information Retrieval (SIGIR 2019)*, pages 985–988, Paris, France.

Andre Esteva, Anuprit Kale, Romain Paulus, Kazuma Hashimoto, Wenpeng Yin, Dragomir Radev, and Richard Socher. 2020. CO-Search: COVID-19 information retrieval with semantic search, question answering, and abstractive summarization. *arXiv:2006.09595*.

Cheolhyoung Lee, Kyunghyun Cho, and Wanmo Kang. 2020. Mixout: Effective regularization to finetune large-scale pretrained language models. In *Proceedings of the 8th International Conference on Learning Representations (ICLR 2020)*.

Jimmy Lin. 2009. Is searching full text more effective than searching abstracts? *BMC Bioinformatics*, 10:46.

Jimmy Lin. 2019. The simplest thing that can possibly work: pseudo-relevance feedback using text classification. *arXiv:1904.08861*.

Shichen Liu, Fei Xiao, Wenwu Ou, and Luo Si. 2017. Cascade ranking for operational e-commerce search. In *Proceedings of the 23rd ACM SIGKDD International Conference on Knowledge Discovery and Data Mining (SIGKDD 2017)*, pages 1557–1565, Halifax, Nova Scotia, Canada.

Sean MacAvaney, Arman Cohan, and Nazli Goharian. 2020. SLEDGE: A simple yet effective baseline for coronavirus scientific knowledge search. *arXiv:2005.02365*.

Sean MacAvaney, Andrew Yates, Arman Cohan, and Nazli Goharian. 2019. CEDR: Contextualized embeddings for document ranking. In *Proceedings of the 42nd Annual International ACM SIGIR Conference on Research and Development in Information Retrieval (SIGIR 2019)*, pages 1101–1104, Paris, France.

Irina Matveeva, Chris Burges, Timo Burkard, Andy Laucius, and Leon Wong. 2006. High accuracy retrieval with multiple nested ranker. In *Proceedings of the 29th Annual International ACM SIGIR Conference on Research and Development in Information Retrieval (SIGIR 2006)*, pages 437–444, Seattle, Washington.

Mark Neumann, Daniel King, Iz Beltagy, and Waleed Ammar. 2019. ScispaCy: Fast and robust models for biomedical natural language processing. *arXiv:1902.07669*.

Rodrigo Nogueira, Zhiying Jiang, and Jimmy Lin. 2020a. Document ranking with a pretrained sequence-to-sequence model. *arXiv:2003.06713*.

Rodrigo Nogueira, Zhiying Jiang, Ronak Pradeep, and Jimmy Lin. 2020b. Document ranking with a pretrained sequence-to-sequence model. In *Findings of EMNLP*.

Rodrigo Nogueira and Jimmy Lin. 2019. From doc2query to docTTTTTquery.

Rodrigo Nogueira, Wei Yang, Kyunghyun Cho, and Jimmy Lin. 2019a. Multi-stage document ranking with BERT. *arXiv:1910.14424*.

Rodrigo Nogueira, Wei Yang, Jimmy Lin, and Kyunghyun Cho. 2019b. Document expansion by query prediction. *arXiv:1904.08375*.

Adam Paszke, Sam Gross, Francisco Massa, Adam Lerer, James Bradbury, Gregory Chanan, Trevor Killeen, Zeming Lin, Natalia Gimelshein, Luca Antiga, Alban Desmaison, Andreas Köpf, Edward Yang, Zach DeVito, Martin Raison, Alykhan Tejani, Sasank Chilamkurthy, Benoit Steiner, Lu Fang, Junjie Bai, and Soumith Chintala. 2019. PyTorch: An imperative style, high-performance deep learning library. In *Advances in Neural Information Processing Systems*, pages 8024–8035.

Jan Pedersen. 2010. Query understanding at Bing. In *Industry Track Keynote at the 33rd Annual International ACM SIGIR Conference on Research and Development in Information Retrieval (SIGIR 2010)*, Geneva, Switzerland.

Colin Raffel, Noam Shazeer, Adam Roberts, Katherine Lee, Sharan Narang, Michael Matena, Yanqi Zhou, Wei Li, and Peter J. Liu. 2020. Exploring the limits of transfer learning with a unified text-to-text transformer. *Journal of Machine Learning Research*, 21:1–67.

Kirk Roberts, Tasmeer Alam, Steven Bedrick, Dina Demner-Fushman, Kyle Lo, Ian Soboroff, Ellen Voorhees, Lucy Lu Wang, and William R. Hersh. 2020. TREC-COVID: Rationale and structure of an information retrieval shared task for COVID-19. *Journal of the American Medical Informatics Association*.

Stephen E. Robertson, Steve Walker, Susan Jones, Micheline Hancock-Beaulieu, and Mike Gatford. 1994. Okapi at TREC-3. In *Proceedings of the 3rd Text REtrieval Conference (TREC-3)*, pages 109–126, Gaithersburg, Maryland.

Amit Singhal, Chris Buckley, and Mandar Mitra. 1996. Pivoted document length normalization. In *Proceedings of the 19th Annual International ACM SIGIR Conference on Research and Development in Information Retrieval (SIGIR 1996)*, pages 21–29, Zürich, Switzerland.

Ellen Voorhees. 2002. The philosophy of information retrieval evaluation. In *Evaluation of Cross-Language Information Retrieval Systems: Second Workshop of the Cross-Language Evaluation Forum, Lecture Notes in Computer Science Volume 2406*, pages 355–370.

Ellen Voorhees, Tasmeer Alam, Steven Bedrick, Dina Demner-Fushman, William R. Hersh, Kyle Lo, Kirk Roberts, Ian Soboroff, and Lucy Lu Wang. 2020. TREC-COVID: Constructing a pandemic information retrieval test collection. *SIGIR Forum*, 54(1):1–12.

Lidan Wang, Jimmy Lin, and Donald Metzler. 2011. A cascade ranking model for efficient ranked retrieval. In *Proceedings of the 34th Annual International ACM SIGIR Conference on Research and Development in Information Retrieval (SIGIR 2011)*, pages 105–114, Beijing, China.

Lucy Lu Wang, Kyle Lo, Yoganand Chandrasekhar, Russell Reas, Jiangjiang Yang, Doug Burdick, Darrin Eide, Kathryn Funk, Yannis Katsis, Rodney Kinney, Yunyao Li, Ziyang Liu, William Merrill, Paul Mooney, Dewey Murdick, Devvret Rishi, Jerry Sheehan, Zhihong Shen, Brandon Stilson, Alex Wade, Kuansan Wang, Nancy Xin Ru Wang, Chris Wilhelm, Boya Xie, Douglas Raymond, Daniel S. Weld, Oren Etzioni, and Sebastian Kohlmeier. 2020. CORD-19: The COVID-19 Open Research Dataset. *arXiv:2004.10706*.

Peilin Yang, Hui Fang, and Jimmy Lin. 2017. Anserini: enabling the use of Lucene for information retrieval research. In *Proceedings of the 40th Annual International ACM SIGIR Conference on Research and Development in Information Retrieval (SIGIR 2017)*, pages 1253–1256, Tokyo, Japan.

Peilin Yang, Hui Fang, and Jimmy Lin. 2018. Anserini: reproducible ranking baselines using Lucene. *Journal of Data and Information Quality*, 10(4):Article 16.

Wei Yang, Yuqing Xie, Aileen Lin, Xingyu Li, Luchen Tan, Kun Xiong, Ming Li, and Jimmy Lin. 2019. End-to-end open-domain question answering with BERTserini. In *Proceedings of the 2019 Conference of the North American Chapter of the Association for Computational Linguistics (Demonstrations)*, pages 72–77, Minneapolis, Minnesota.

Zeynep Akkalyoncu Yilmaz, Charles L. A. Clarke, and Jimmy Lin. 2020. A lightweight environment for learning experimental IR research practices. In *Proceedings of the 43rd Annual International ACM SIGIR Conference on Research and Development in Information Retrieval (SIGIR 2020)*.

Zeynep Akkalyoncu Yilmaz, Wei Yang, Haotian Zhang, and Jimmy Lin. 2019. Cross-domain modeling of sentence-level evidence for document retrieval. In *Proceedings of the 2019 Conference on Empirical Methods in Natural Language Processing and the 9th International Joint Conference on Natural Language Processing (EMNLP-IJCNLP)*, pages 3481–3487, Hong Kong, China.

Ruifan Yu, Yuhao Xie, and Jimmy Lin. 2019. Simple techniques for cross-collection relevance feedback. In *Proceedings of the 41th European Conference on Information Retrieval, Part I (ECIR 2019)*, pages 397–409, Cologne, Germany.

Edwin Zhang, Nikhil Gupta, Rodrigo Nogueira, Kyunghyun Cho, and Jimmy Lin. 2020a. Rapidly deploying a neural search engine for the COVID-19 Open Research Dataset: Preliminary thoughts and lessons learned. *arXiv:2004.05125*.

Tianyi Zhang, Felix Wu, Arzoo Katiyar, Kilian Q. Weinberger, and Yoav Artzi. 2020b. Revisiting few-sample BERT fine-tuning. *arXiv:2006.05987*.

The impact of preprint servers in the formation of novel ideas

Swarup Satish[*]
University of Massachussetts, Amherst
`ssatish@cs.umass.edu`

Zonghai Yao[*]
University of Massachussetts, Amherst
`zonghaiyao@cs.umass.edu`

Andrew Drozdov
University of Massachussetts, Amherst
`adrozdov@cs.umass.edu`

Boris Veytsman
Chan Zuckerverg Initiative
George Mason University
`bveytsman@chanzuckerberg.com`

Abstract

We study whether novel ideas in biomedical literature appear first in preprints or traditional journals. We develop a Bayesian method to estimate the time of appearance for a phrase in the literature, and apply it to a number of phrases, both automatically extracted and suggested by experts. We see that presently most phrases appear first in the traditional journals, but there is a number of phrases with the first appearance on preprint servers. A comparison of the general composition of texts from bioRxiv and traditional journals shows a growing trend of bioRxiv being predictive of traditional journals. We discuss the application of the method for related problems.

1 Introduction

A paper submitted to a journal goes through several stages: peer review, editorial work, copyediting, publication. This leads to a long waiting time between submission and the final publication (Powell, 2016). The situation is especially bad in the life sciences, where the waiting time between submission and publication approaches the duration of a traditional PhD study, creating serious difficulties for young scientists (Vale, 2015). While this is frustrating for scientists whose recognition and promotion often depend on the publication record, it is also bad for science itself, significantly slowing down its progress (Qunaj et al., 2018).

Preprint servers were offered as a means of accelerating science (Berg et al., 2016; Desjardins-Proulx et al., 2013; Sarabipour et al., 2019; Schloss, 2017; Lauer et al., 2015; Peiperl, 2018), especially in the wake of COVID-19 epidemics (Krumholz et al., 2020). The discussion about the benefits (and dangers) of preprint is no longer confined to the scientific literature, coming to the pages of popular newspapers (Eisen and Tibshirani, 2020).

The benefits of preprints for accelerating science are often raised in the discussions between regulatory agencies, funders, scientists and publishers. Thus a method to objectively assess them is important. One way to do this assessment is to look at a new important idea and to measure whether it first appears in a traditional journal or on a preprint server.

An implementation of this approach requires one to define what is an important idea, and how to find the time of appearance for it. This is the goal of our work.

The definition of novelty in science and the methods to determine and predict novelty have a long history discussed in the next section. In this work we use a very simple approach (Garfield, 1967; Latour and Woolgar, 1986): new ideas correspond to new terms. Thus if we find new words and phrases in scientific papers, we can surmise the appearance of new ideas.

The definition of the time of appearance for a new idea is not trivial. It is not enough to register the first mention of a term. First, some hits might be erroneous, and give us false positives. On the other hand, we might miss some mentions of a term due to the incompleteness of the corpus. Therefore a more subtle method to determine the time of appearance is needed. In this work we offer a Bayesian approach to this problem.

Based on our definitions of novelty and the time of appearance for novel ideas we compare the time of appearance for several novel ideas in the papers published in bioRxiv/medRxiv `https://www.biorxiv.org/` and PubMed Central full text collection `https://www.ncbi.nlm.nih.gov/pmc/`.

2 Related Works

Novel ideas and breakthroughs are among the central concepts for the science of science. A number

[*]Equal contribution.

Proceedings of the First Workshop on Scholarly Document Processing, pages 42–55
Online, November 19, 2020. ©2020 Association for Computational Linguistics
https://doi.org/10.18653/v1/P17

of studies propose different ideas to quantify originality in science and technology (Cozzens et al., 2010; Alexander et al., 2013; Rzhetsky et al., 2015; Rotolo et al., 2015; Wang et al., 2016; Wang and Chai, 2018; Shibayama and Wang, 2020) or their impact on the other works (Shi et al., 2010; Shahaf et al., 2012; Sinatra et al., 2016; Hutchins et al., 2016; Wesley-Smith et al., 2016; Herrmannova et al., 2018b,a; Zhao et al., 2019; Bornmann et al., 2019; Small et al., 2019). The prediction of breakthroughs, scientific impact and citation counts is a well developed area (Schubert and Schubert, 1997; Garfield et al., 2002; Dietz et al., 2007; Lokker et al., 2008; Shi et al., 2010; Uzzi et al., 2013; Alexander, 2013; Klimek et al., 2016; Tahamtan et al., 2016; McKeown et al., 2016; Clauset et al., 2017; Peoples et al., 2017; Salatino et al., 2018; Dong et al., 2018; Iacopini et al., 2018; Feldman et al., 2018; van den Besselaar and Sandström, 2018; Klavans et al., 2020). However, the question asked in these works is different from the one we ask. Most of the researchers tried to determine what makes a work original or impactful, and how to predict originality or impact. Our question is the following: suppose we know a certain idea is novel (or impactful). Can we pinpoint a moment in time when this idea appeared, and where did it appear?

Sentence level novelty detection was a topic of novelty tracks of Text Retrieval Conferences (TREC) from 2002 to 2004 (Soboroff and Harman, 2003; Harman, 2002; Clarke et al., 2004; Soboroff and Harman, 2005). The goal of these tracks was to highlight the relevant sentences that contain novel information, given a topic and an ordered list of relevant documents. At the document level, Karkali et al. (2013) computed novelty score based on the inverse document frequency scoring function. Another work by Verheij et al. (2012) presents a comparison study of different novelty detection methods evaluated on news articles where language model based methods perform better than the cosine similarity based ones. Dasgupta and Dey (2016) conducted experiments with information entropy measure to calculate novelty of a document. Again, the work that we present here significantly differs from the existing novelty detection methods since we use the novelty detection as a starting point rather than a goal. We first get candidate phrases from the documents with the most appropriate key phrases extraction method, and then determine the appearance timing of these phrases.

Another field that is relevant to our research is the detection of change points in a stream of events. Change point detection (or CPD) detects abrupt shifts in time series trends that can be easily identified via the human eye, but are harder to pinpoint using traditional statistical approaches. The research in CPD is applicable across an array of industries, including finance, manufacturing quality control, energy, medical diagnostics, and human activity analysis. There are many representative methods of CPD. Binary segmentation (Bai, 1997) is a sequential approach: first, one change point is detected in the complete input signal, then series is split around this change point, then the operation is repeated on the two resulting sub-signals. As opposite to binary segmentation, which is a greedy procedure, bottom-up segmentation (Fryzlewicz, 2007) is generous: it starts with many change points and successively deletes the less significant ones. First, the signal is divided in many sub-signals along a regular grid. Then contiguous segments are successively merged according to a measure of how similar they are. Because the enumeration of all possible partitions is impossible, Pelt (Killick et al., 2012) relies on a pruning rule. Many indexes are discarded, greatly reducing the computational cost while retaining the ability to find the optimal segmentation. Window-based change point detection (Aminikhanghahi and Cook, 2016) uses two windows which slide along the data stream. Dynamic programming was also used for this task (Truong et al., 2020). In this work we propose a simple Bayesian approach to the detection of change points, which seems to give intuitively reasonable results for our purpose.

3 Bayesian Approach to Novelty Detection

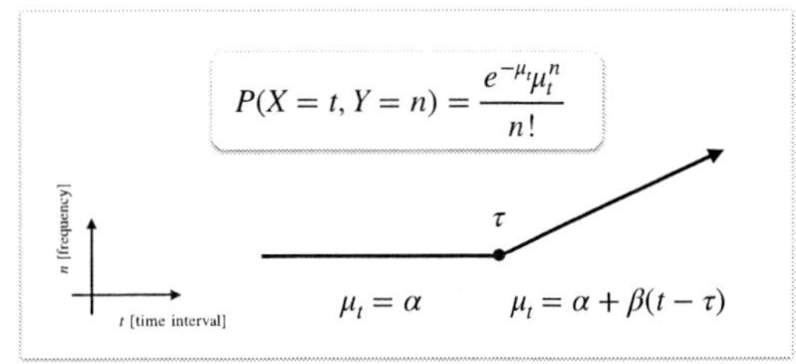

Figure 1: Our Bayesian Approach to Novelty Detection (BAND). The goal is to find the inflection point τ that indicates the earliest point attributed to the rapid research growth associated with a novel idea.

Our proposed Bayesian Approach to Novelty Detection (BAND) finds the time interval τ that maximizes the observed series of publication frequency for a phrase (Figure 1). Paper publications are events, so it is reasonable to assume that the number of publications n in a unit interval at the time t containing the given phrase z follows a Poisson distribution. The joint density function for publication frequency is given by the equation

$$P(X = t, Y = n) = \frac{e^{-\mu_t}\mu_t^n}{n!}, \qquad (1)$$

where μ_t is modeled by a piecewise linear function of t:

$$\mu_t = \begin{cases} \alpha & t < \tau, \\ \alpha + \beta(t - \tau) & t \geq \tau. \end{cases} \qquad (2)$$

Prior to τ, we expect the number of publications containing the given phrase to be small, ideally zero. The parameter $\alpha > 0$ controls for the noise (misattributed papers, improper or ambiguous usage of the phrase, etc.). After the moment τ, we expect the steady grow of phrase popularity with the rate β. In other words, τ is the point in time ehen the phrase begins to be adopted.

We consider each phrase independently and use Bayesian modeling to find the most probable parameters α, β, and τ given the observed data using the standard Bayesian approach

$$P(\alpha, \beta, \tau | X, Y) \propto$$
$$P(\alpha, \beta, \tau)P(X, Y | \alpha, \beta, \tau). \qquad (3)$$

We use a flat uniformative prior with

$$P(\alpha, \beta, \tau) = \text{const.} \qquad (4)$$

Our motivation for finding τ using BAND is to compare the impact of different publication venues (i.e. preprint servers and peer-reviewed journals) that cover overlapping research topics. For a single phrase z, we use the observed data from two sources and estimate the posterior probability $P(\alpha, \beta, \tau)$ for each source separately. Then we run a simulation to find the 95% confidence interval of τ using the following procedure:

1. For a single data source, compute $P(\alpha, \beta, \tau)$ for all possible configurations on a grid.

2. Sample a large number of triplets (α, β, τ) from the posterior computed in Step 1.

3. Remove 2.5% of the triples with the highest value of τ, and 2.5% of triplets with the lowest value of τ. The probability for τ to lie in the remaining interval can be estimated as 95%.

In order to compare two sources, we create two sets of tuples, one for each source. Then we randomly draw a tuple from the first set and a tuple from the second one. For each pair i we compute δ_i, the expected difference between the two sources where $\tau_i^{(s)}$ is the i-th sample in source s:

$$\delta_i = \tau_i^{(s_0)} - \tau_i^{(s_1)}. \qquad (5)$$

The conclusion about the priority is based on distribution of δ around zero. If $\delta > 0$ for the majority of the pairs, then the phrase gains traction first on source s_0. Otherwise the second source wins.

4 Experimental Setup

In this section we describe our data collection procedure and background on methods of text processing and assessing data quality. Our code for running experiments is publicly available.[1]

4.1 Data Sources (Publication Venues)

We consider two types of publication venues: peer-reviewed journals and preprint servers. There are now many preprint servers for various areas of science, including arXiv, bioRxiv, medRxiv, PsyArXiv, SocArXiv, ChemRxiv, AgriRXiv, and others. To compare a preprint server to a traditional venue one needs a large open access collection of traditionally published papers. In biomedical sciences there is a huge Pubmed Central Open Access Dataset described below, which drove our choice for bioRxiv/medRxiv as a comparison venue. Another reason for this choice of data sources is that one of our organizations, Chan Zuckerberg Initiative, has a special interest in biomedical sciences in general and bioRxiv & medRxiv in particular.

PubMed is a central repository for biomedical papers published in peer-reviewed journals. It contains over 26 million journal publications. Abstracts are publicly available for all papers, and for a subset (the PubMed Central Open Access Dataset with over 1.6 million papers) full texts are available.[2]

---

[1] `https://github.com/seasonyao/BiorXivImpact`

[2] A minute percentage of titles are missing from the PubMed data. This is attributed to noisy data entry rather than some data being closed or open.

In contrast to PubMed, bioRxiv is a preprint server for the biological sciences. Papers published there are not required to pass a strict and lengthy review process. BioRxiv hosts over 70,000 full text articles, each open to the public. Recently medical papers were separated into a special server medRxiv. Since the search engine provided by bioRxiv can search both servers, below we use the term "bioRxiv" for the longer, but more correct term "the union of bioRxiv and medRxiv papers".

PubMed and bioRxiv cover the two representative categories of publication venue. We also include data sources using information from COVID-19 Open Research Dataset Challenge (Wang et al., 2020).

4.2 Text Processing and Data Collection

In our experiments and analysis we leverage a large collection of phrases collected in an unsupervised way using TextRank (Mihalcea and Tarau, 2004; Nathan, 2016). The procedure to extract the phrase is the following:

1. First we extract all candidate phrases from bioRxiv abstracts using TextRank. This results in 1,587,408 phrases.

2. We filter the phrases from Step 1 to the 239,608 phrases by eliminating phrases that were detected by TextRank only once.

3. For each phrase from Step 2 we generate monthly time series data for both PMC and bioRxiv using full text.[3]

We use this data collection procedure and recommendations from CZI biomedical curators to create three groups of phrases:

(a) Common phrases: 20 banal phrases manually selected that are also extracted by TextRank (includes 'medical history', 'heart disease', 'x-ray', etc.).

(b) Novel phrases: 20 phrases selected by experts (includes 'mass cytometry', 'gene editing', 'fluorescence activated cell sorting', etc.).

(c) Top extracted phrases: The top 7000 phrases extracted by TextRank determined by average importance score.

All common and novel phrases, and a subset of the top ranking phrases are shown in Appendices A.2, A.1.2, and A.1.1.

4.3 Baselines for finding τ

To assess the effectiveness of BAND for finding τ we include a strong baseline in our experiments. In our analysis (Section 5.2), we compare these methods to BAND not only for finding the first clear inflection point, but also how relevant τ is for the end goal of novelty detection and comparing research impact.

The baseline we include is Window-based Change Point Detection (see Section 2). It works by maximizing the discrepancy measuring function

$$d(x_a, x_b) = c(x_a, x_b) - c(x_a, \tau) - c(\tau, x_b), \quad (6)$$

which is large when the left segment $c(x_a, \tau)$ is dissimilar from the right segment $c(\tau, x_b)$.

Window-based Changepoint Detection (WCPD) is flexible and has been successful when applied to many tasks. However, for a number of novel phrases (see the first two examples on Figure 3) it gives intuitively unsatisfactory results for the detection of the idea onset. The reason is, WCPD tries to find the point where the publication frequency significantly changes, which often corresponds to the moment the idea is widely adopted. Our task, on the other hand, is to find the point when the idea appears, which is a different problem. Therefore one may expect BAND to work better for the cause of the novelty detection because its model of growth starting from zero might be more suitable to describe the publication frequency than the generic model of WCPD.

We found necessary to run WCPD using the finite difference approximation of the publication frequency gradient to obtain reasonable predictions.

We use the implementation of WCPD provided in ruptures (Truong et al., 2020) with an L^2-cost function (c), window size of 10, penalty of 1, and no specification on how many changepoints to return.[4] In our figures we display all changepoints from WCPD to illustrate these changepoints do not solely identify the point before rapid growth in idea adaptation. On the other hand our method

---

[3]For computing time series, we simply count if a phrase occurred in a document independent of its importance score from TextRank. This approach scales easily to large corpora such as full text from PubMed papers.

[4]A simple heuristic to get one changepoint is to use the first one, although this does not work universally well. Constraining WCPD to return a single changepoint (e.g. highest discrepancy) similarly does not consistently return the most desirable changepoints.

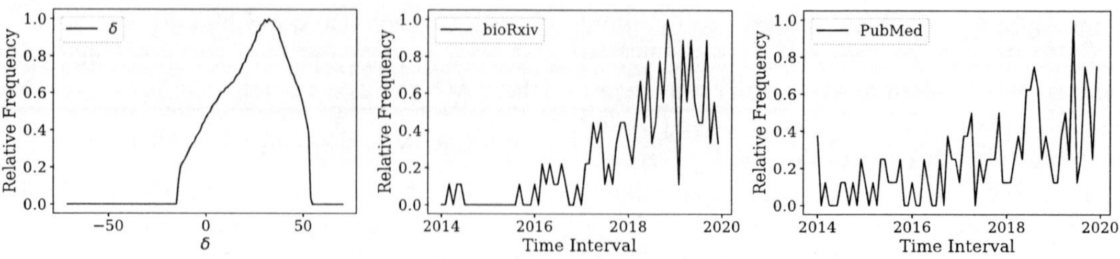

(a) CEL-Seq. Across simulations, δ is typically positive indicating relevant papers appeared first on bioRxiv.

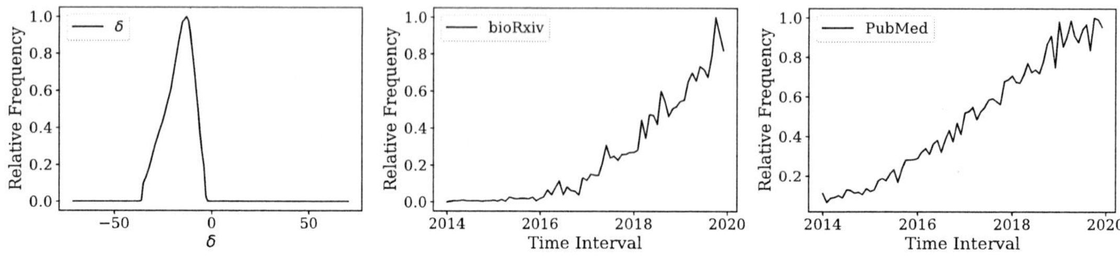

(b) CRISPR. Across simulations, δ is typically negative indicating relevant papers appeared first on PubMed.

Figure 2: The distribution of δ (left column), publication frequency on bioRxiv (center), and publication frequency on PubMed (right) for two phrases

(BAND) consistently finds changepoints that match this criterion.

5 Results and Analysis

In this section we discuss the following hypotheses and research questions:

- Can we find the point τ in time when a phrase is determined novel using our Bayesian Approach to Novelty Detection (BAND)?

- Is the value of τ effective for comparing the impact of two publication venues?

- Do our findings verify that preprint servers are having a positive impact on the development of novel ideas?

- How effective is publication frequency for distinguishing from novel and banal phrases?

Below we answer each of these questions.

5.1 Are pre-print servers accelerating research?

The common wisdom is the preprint servers have positive impact on research, by making research available openly and quickly. We attempt to verify that ideas develop faster on bioRxiv rather than on PubMed. Our results indicate that this might be true in some, but not all, cases. For some phrases δ leans

positive (see Figure 2 top), indicating the relevant phrase and presumably the novel idea appeared first on bioRxiv. However, the opposite is true more often than not (see Figure 2, bottom).

Why is PubMed frequently the first place that novel ideas appear? One reason might be that bioRxiv is relatively new, did not gain enough traction yet, and its benefits are not widely appreciated. One can even say it is surprising and encouraging that *some* novel ideas appear first on bioRxiv despite the it being a relative newcomer. Thus one interpretation of our finding is that while preprint servers are already having a positive impact on research, there is still a potential for the growth. In this case we expect that in the future novel ideas will appear first on bioRxiv at a higher rate. We further check this assumption in Section 5.3.

5.2 Is BAND effective at determining τ?

We assume that curves of publication frequency of novel ideas follow a particular shape—they are relatively flat followed by a growth period. This assumption is built in the design of BAND. To verify BAND's effectiveness, we use a set of novel phrases provided by the team of biomedical curators at Chan Zuckerberg Initiative (CZI), extract their publication frequency data from PubMed, and calculate τ using BAND. Qualitatively, we see in Figure 3 that BAND results agree with the intuition

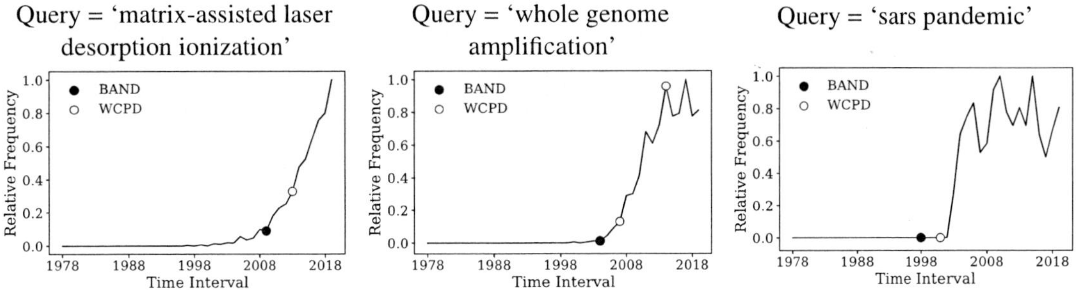

Figure 3: BAND often finds a more desirable point of inflection than WCPD (left). In addition, WCPD may return multiple points (center). However, in cases when the evolution of a term does not follow our model, WCPD is more effective (right).

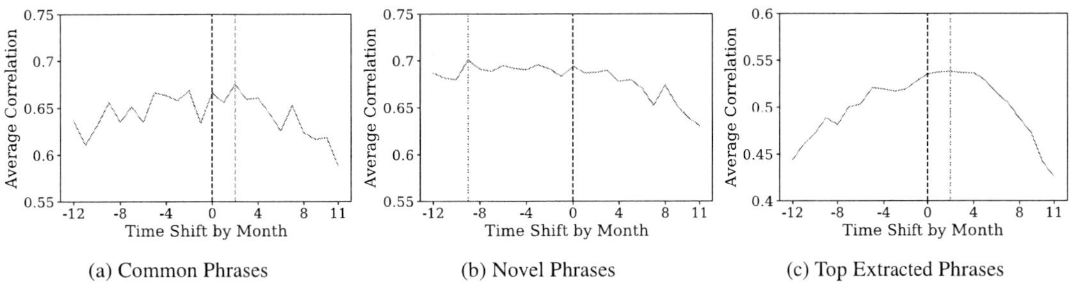

(a) Common Phrases   (b) Novel Phrases   (c) Top Extracted Phrases

Figure 4: **Coarse-grained correlation analysis.** We report average correlation between PubMed and bioRxiv for publication frequency in a 6-year window. We shift the window for bioRxiv one month at a time, where positive values on the x-axis correspond to shifts back in time and negative values indicate shifts forward in time. If at the highest value (indicated by the dotted red line) the offset is positive bioRxiv is a predictor of PubMed's content. If the offset is negative, the opposite is true. We perform this analysis for 3 subsets of terms: common phrases (a), novel phrases (b), and phrases from TextRank (c) starting in January 2014.

about the novelty onset.

As discussed in Section 4.3, WCPD is another technique for finding points of inflection. WCPD is a useful method because it finds inflection points without requiring any prior model of the data. As expected, if the evolution of data follows our model of growth, BAND gives a better estimate for the novelty onset (Figure 3, left and center). On the other hand, if the data do not follow BAND model, BAND is not supposed to work well, and assumption-free models like WCPD might work better. An example is shown on (Figure 3, right), where a period of growth is followed by a plateau rather than the growth assumed by BAND model.

5.3 Are pre-print servers mature?

A potentially confounding variable in our experimental setup is the relative recency in the establishment of bioRxiv (2013) compared to PubMed (1996). This motivates us to measure the correlation between the publication frequency of these two data sources. We proceed by looking at three groups of phrases: (a) common phrases found in medical terminology, (b) novel phrases provided by experts, and (c) highest scoring phrases according to TextRank.

First, we aggregated the last 6 years of data. We found the similarity between PubMed and bioRxiv for common phrases and phrases extracted from TextRank most similar when comparing the early snapshot of bioRxiv with the later snapshot of PubMed (Figure 4). Thus for these phrases bioRxiv is predictive of PubMed. On the other hand, phrases selected by experts (Section 5.2) tend to appear on PubMed first (Figure 4, center).

Taking into account that bioRxiv is still evolving, we performed a more fine-grained analysis where results are only aggregated across 2 years instead of 6. This also allowed us to study how the content alignment between PubMed and bioRxiv has changed over time. The result is shown on Figure 5. According to this figure, as bioRxiv matures, it becomes a better leading indicator of PubMed. Perhaps more critically, it also shows that the con-

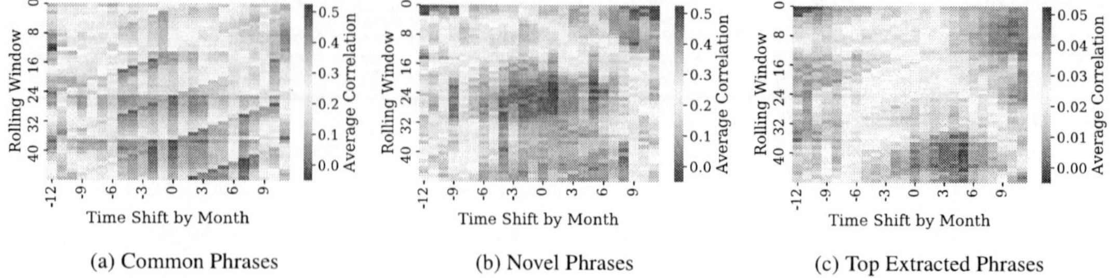

(a) Common Phrases   (b) Novel Phrases   (c) Top Extracted Phrases

Figure 5: **Fine-grained correlation analysis.** We perform the same analysis as in Figure 4, except with a smaller window (two years) and shifting both bioRxiv (x-axis) and the starting month (y-axis). If $x = 1$ and $y = 3$, then the start month is April 2014 for PubMed and March 2014 for bioRxiv. The data are shown on a grid with darker red indicate high correlation and dark blue indicating low or inverse correlation. In general, we see higher correlation between bioRxiv and PubMed as bioRxiv matures.

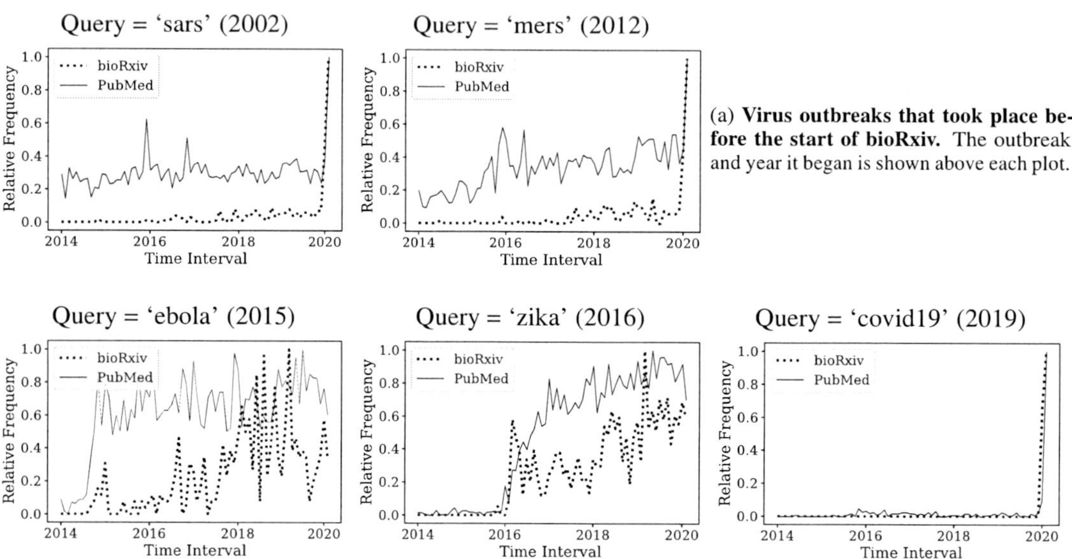

(a) **Virus outbreaks that took place before the start of bioRxiv.** The outbreak and year it began is shown above each plot.

(b) **Virus outbreaks that took place after the start of bioRxiv.** The outbreak and year it began is shown above each plot.

Figure 6: Outbreaks that occurred before bioRxiv became widespread (top row, a) with publishing activity plateaued in recent years v. outbreaks occurring after bioRxiv was founded (bottom row, b) with recent growth in research activity.

tent alignment is indeed changing.

The analysis we provide in this work at best is a glimpse into the relationship between pre-print servers and peer-reviewed journals. It will likely change as bioRxiv continues to mature.

5.4 Qualitative analysis for the spread of ideas during virus outbreaks

During natural disasters such as virus outbreaks, scientific progress towards understanding diseases and their cures is critical, warranting fast dissemination of ideas and results of research. Pre-print servers are particularly well suited to this end. Thus we compare bioRxiv to PubMed for five recent virus outbreaks, some of which took place prior to the founding of bioRxiv.

Each virus outbreak was analyzed using a composite of publication frequency of multiple related phrases. For example, values for 'sars-cov2' and 'covid-19' are aggregated in the COVID-19 plot. The five relevant outbreaks are listed below:

- Prior to bioRxiv establishment (before November 2013, Figure 6, top): MERS and SARS.

- After bioRxiv establishment (Figure 6, bottom): Zika, Ebola, and COVID-19.

48

The first group of outbreaks exhibits the expected behavior: bioRxiv activity is fairly minimal given that the growth of research on those topics had begun to saturate by the time bioRxiv was formed. But the second group exhibits a different behavior. For Ebola outbreak, which took place in 2015, the activity in bioRxiv is fairly low compared to PMC. For Zika (2017) and Covid-19 (2019) bioRxiv has an early activity spike.

Through this analysis we can see that bioRxiv has become increasingly important in emergency situations during recent years.

6 Future Directions

Our work serves as a first attempt for discovering research impact of publication venues using full text analysis. One notable assumption we make is that all phrase mentions are treated equally. In the future, we may want to distinguish how a phrase is being used. For example, if the phrase of interest is z, then a research paper may write about works extending z, but alternatively it may simply discuss techniques similar to z. Similar analysis has provided useful for citations (Jurgens et al., 2018).

Furthermore, our approach leverages TextRank to find many relevant phrases, but we do not cluster phrases, so two or more phrases with similar meaning will be treated separately (i.e. FACS and Fluorescence Activated Cell Sorting). A simple alias table or string similarity extension (Tam et al., 2019) would be a clear improvement. Leveraging high precision concept extraction systems (King et al., 2020) might improve clustering even more.

Another approach would be to use a better proxy for ideas than textual phrase, like concepts or topics extracted from the corpus.

7 Conclusions

We introduce a Bayesian model for novelty detection (BAND), and use this model to investigate how quickly new ideas form on pre-print servers compared to peer-reviewed journals. Our findings indicate that novel phrases, which we use as a proxy for new ideas, in most cases appear on pre-print servers and in peer reviewed journals. In some cases, novel phrases appear on pre-print servers first. In many cases the content of preprints is a predictor of the content of peer reviewed journals. As the preprint servers mature, this feature becomes more prominent. When a fast review time is in high demand (such as during epidemic outbreaks), pre-print servers have a high utility, and the related novel phrases appear on pre-print servers first.

Acknowledgments

The authors are grateful to Bill Burkholder (Chan Zuckerberg Biohub) who suggested this research, and to Barbara Vidal & Michaela Torkar (Chan Zuckerberg Initiative) for their expert help in selecting the phrases for comparison.

This research was initiated at the University of Massachusetts Amherst Industry Mentorship Program.

References

J. Alexander, K. Bache, J. Chase, C. Freyman, J. D. Roessner, and P. Smyth. 2013. An exploratory study of interdisciplinarity and breakthrough ideas. In *2013 Proceedings of PICMET '13: Technology Management in the IT-Driven Services (PICMET)*.

Jeffrey Alexander. 2013. A reasoning-based framework for the computation of technical emergence. GTM 2013-Atlanta, GA.

Samaneh Aminikhanghahi and Diane J. Cook. 2016. A survey of methods for time series change point detection. *Knowledge and Information Systems*, 51(2):339–367.

Jushan Bai. 1997. Estimating multiple breaks one at a time. *Econometric Theory*, 13(3):315–352.

Jeremy M. Berg, Needhi Bhalla, Philip E. Bourne, Martin Chalfie, David G. Drubin, James S. Fraser, Carol W. Greider, Michael Hendricks, Chonnettia Jones, Robert Kiley, Susan King, Marc W. Kirschner, Harlan M. Krumholz, Ruth Lehmann, Maria Leptin, Bernd Pulverer, Brooke Rosenzweig, John E. Spiro, Michael Stebbins, Carly Strasser, Sowmya Swaminathan, Paul Turner, Ronald D. Vale, K. VijayRaghavan, and Cynthia Wolberger. 2016. Preprints for the life sciences. *Science*, 352(6288).

Peter van den Besselaar and Ulf Sandström. 2018. Measuring researcher independence using bibliometric data: A proposal for a new performance indicator. Technical report, Cold Spring Harbor Laboratory.

Lutz Bornmann, K. Brad Wray, and Robin Haunschild. 2019. Citation concept analysis (CCA): a new form of citation analysis revealing the usefulness of concepts for other researchers illustrated by exemplary case studies including classic books by thomas s. kuhn and karl r. popper. *Scientometrics*, 122(2):1051–1074.

Charles LA Clarke, Nick Craswell, and Ian Soboroff. 2004. Overview of the TREC 2004 terabyte track. In *TREC*, volume 4.

Aaron Clauset, Daniel B. Larremore, and Roberta Sinatra. 2017. Data-driven predictions in the science of science. *Science*, 355(6324):477–480.

Susan E. Cozzens, Sonia Gatchair, Jongseok Kang, Kyung-Sup Kim, Hyuck Jai Lee, Gonzalo R. Ordóñez, and Alan L. Porter. 2010. Emerging technologies: quantitative identification and measurement. *Techn. Analysis & Strat. Manag.*, 22.

Tirthankar Dasgupta and Lipika Dey. 2016. Automatic scoring for innovativeness of textual ideas. In *Workshops at the Thirtieth AAAI Conference on Artificial Intelligence*.

Philippe Desjardins-Proulx, Ethan P. White, Joel J. Adamson, Karthik Ram, Timothée Poisot, and Dominique Gravel. 2013. The case for open preprints in biology. *PLOS Biology*, 11(5).

Laura Dietz, Steffen Bickel, and Tobias Scheffer. 2007. Unsupervised prediction of citation influences. In *Proceedings of the 24th international conference on Machine learning - ICML'07*. ACM Press.

Y. Dong, H. Ma, J. Tang, and K. Wang. 2018. Collaboration Diversity and Scientific Impact. *ArXiv e-prints*.

Michael B. Eisen and Robert Tibshirani. 2020. How to identify flawed research before it becomes dangerous. *New York Times*. July 20.

Sergey Feldman, Kyle Lo, and Waleed Ammar. 2018. Citation count analysis for papers with preprints. *ArXiv*, abs/1805.05238.

Piotr Fryzlewicz. 2007. Unbalanced haar technique for nonparametric function estimation. *Journal of the American Statistical Association*, 102(480):1318–1327.

Eugene Garfield. 1967. Primordial concepts, citation indexing, and historio-bibliography. *The Journal of library history*, 2(3):235–249.

Eugene Garfield, A. I. Pudovkin, and V. S. Istomin. 2002. Algorithmic citation-linked historiography——mapping the literature of science. *Proceedings of the American Society for Information Science and Technology*, 39(1):14–24.

Donna Harman. 2002. Overview of the TREC 2002 novelty track. In *Proceedings of the Eleventh Text Retrieval Conference (TREC 2002), NIST Special Publication 500-251*. Citeseer.

Drahomira Herrmannova, Petr Knoth, and Robert M. Patton. 2018a. Analyzing citation-distance networks for evaluating publication impact. In *LREC*.

Drahomira Herrmannova, Petr Knoth, Christopher Stahl, Robert Patton, and Jack Wells. 2018b. Text and graph based approach for analyzing patterns of research collaboration: An analysis of the TrueImpactDataset. In *Proceedings of the Eleventh International Conference on Language Resources and Evaluation (LREC 2018)*, Paris, France. European Language Resources Association (ELRA).

B. Ian Hutchins, Xin Yuan, James M. Anderson, and George M. Santangelo. 2016. Relative citation ratio (RCR): A new metric that uses citation rates to measure influence at the article level. *PLOS Biology*, 14(9).

Iacopo Iacopini, Staša Milojević, and Vito Latora. 2018. Network dynamics of innovation processes. *Phys. Rev. Lett.*, 120.

David Jurgens, Srijan Kumar, Raine Hoover, Dan McFarland, and Dan Jurafsky. 2018. Measuring the evolution of a scientific field through citation frames. *Transactions of the Association for Computational Linguistics*, 6:391–406.

Margarita Karkali, François Rousseau, Alexandros Ntoulas, and Michalis Vazirgiannis. 2013. Efficient online novelty detection in news streams. In *Lecture Notes in Computer Science*, pages 57–71. Springer Berlin Heidelberg.

R. Killick, P. Fearnhead, and I. A. Eckley. 2012. Optimal detection of changepoints with a linear computational cost. *Journal of the American Statistical Association*, 107(500):1590–1598.

Daniel King, Doug Downey, and Daniel S. Weld. 2020. High-Precision Extraction of Emerging Concepts from Sientific Literature. In *Proceedings of the 43rd International ACM SIGIR Conference on Research and Development in Information Retrieval (SIGIR '20)*, Virtual Event, China. ACM.

Richard Klavans, Kevin W. Boyack, and Dewey A. Murdick. 2020. A novel approach to predicting exceptional growth in research. *arXiv e-prints*, page arXiv:2004.13159.

Peter Klimek, Aleksandar S. Jovanovic, Rainer Egloff, and Reto Schneider. 2016. Successful fish go with the flow: citation impact prediction based on centrality measures for term–document networks. *Scientometrics*, 107(3):1265–1282.

Harlan M. Krumholz, Theodora Bloom, and Joseph S. Ross. 2020. Preprints can fill a void in times of rapidly changing science. *StatNews*.

Bruno Latour and Steve Woolgar. 1986. *Laboratory Life: The Construction of Scientific Facts*. Princeton University Press, Princeton, NJ.

Michael S Lauer, Harlan M Krumholz, and Eric J Topol. 2015. Time for a prepublication culture in clinical research? *Lancet*, 386:2447–2449.

Cynthia Lokker, K Ann McKibbon, R James McKinlay, Nancy L Wilczynski, and R Brian Haynes. 2008. Prediction of citation counts for clinical articles at two years using data available within three weeks of publication: retrospective cohort study. *BMJ*, 336(7645):655–657.

Kathy McKeown, Hal Daume, Snigdha Chaturvedi, John Paparrizos, Kapil Thadani, Pablo Barrio, Or Biran, Suvarna Bothe, Michael Collins, Kenneth R. Fleischmann, Luis Gravano, Rahul Jha, Ben King, Kevin McInerney, Taesun Moon, Arvind Neelakantan, Diarmuid O'Seaghdha, Dragomir Radev, Clay Templeton, and Simone Teufel. 2016. Predicting the impact of scientific concepts using full-text features. *Journal of the Association for Information Science and Technology*, 67(11):2684–2696.

Rada Mihalcea and Paul Tarau. 2004. Textrank: Bringing order into text. In *Proceedings of the 2004 conference on empirical methods in natural language processing*.

Paco Nathan. 2016. Pytextrank, a python implementation of textrank for phrase extraction and summarization of text documents. https://github.com/DerwenAI/pytextrank/.

Larry Peiperl. 2018. Preprints in medical research: Progress and principles. *PLOS Medicine*, 15(4).

Brandon K. Peoples, Stephen R. Midway, Dana Sackett, Abigail Lynch, and Patrick B. Cooney. 2017. Twitter predicts citation rates of ecological research. *PLoS ONE*, 11.

Kendall Powell. 2016. Does it take too long to publish research? *Nature*, 530.

Lindor Qunaj, Raina H. Jain, Coral L. Atoria, Renee L. Gennarelli, Jennifer E. Miller, and Peter B. Bach. 2018. Delays in the publication of important clinical trial findings in oncology. *JAMA Oncology*, 4(7).

Daniele Rotolo, Diana Hicks, and Ben Martin. 2015. What is an emerging technology? *SSRN Electronic Journal*.

Andrey Rzhetsky, Jacob G. Foster, Ian T. Foster, and James A. Evans. 2015. Choosing experiments to accelerate collective discovery. *Proceedings of the National Academy of Sciences*, 112(47):14569–14574.

Angelo A. Salatino, Francesco Osborne, and Enrico Motta. 2018. AUGUR. In *Proceedings of the 18th ACM/IEEE on Joint Conference on Digital Libraries*. ACM.

Sarvenaz Sarabipour, Humberto J. Debat, Edward Emmott, Steven J. Burgess, Benjamin Schwessinger, and Zach Hensel. 2019. On the value of preprints: An early career researcher perspective. *PLOS Biology*, 17(2).

Patrick D. Schloss. 2017. Preprinting microbiology. *mBio*, 8(3).

András P. Schubert and Gábor A. Schubert. 1997. Inorganica Chimica Acta: its publications, references and citations. an update for 1995–1996. *Inorganica Chimica Acta*, 266(2):125 – 133.

Dafna Shahaf, Carlos Guestrin, and Eric Horvitz. 2012. Metro maps of science. In *Proceedings of the 18th ACM SIGKDD International Conference on Knowledge Discovery and Data Mining*, KDD '12, New York, NY, USA. ACM.

Xiaolin Shi, Jure Leskovec, and Daniel A. McFarland. 2010. Citing for high impact. *CoRR*, abs/1004.3351.

Sotaro Shibayama and Jian Wang. 2020. Measuring originality in science. *Scientometrics*, 122.

R. Sinatra, D. Wang, P. Deville, C. Song, and A.-L. Barabasi. 2016. Quantifying the evolution of individual scientific impact. *Science*, 354(6312):aaf5239–aaf5239.

Henry Small, Kevin W. Boyack, and Richard Klavans. 2019. Citations and certainty: a new interpretation of citation counts. *Scientometrics*, 118(3):1079–1092.

Ian Soboroff and Donna Harman. 2003. Overview of the TREC 2003 novelty track. In *TREC*. Citeseer.

Ian Soboroff and Donna Harman. 2005. Novelty detection: the TREC experience. In *Proceedings of the conference on Human Language Technology and Empirical Methods in Natural Language Processing*. Association for Computational Linguistics.

Iman Tahamtan, Askar Safipour Afshar, and Khadijeh Ahamdzadeh. 2016. Factors affecting number of citations: a comprehensive review of the literature. *Scientometrics*, 107(3):1195–1225.

Derek Tam, Nicholas Monath, Ari Kobren, Aaron Traylor, Rajarshi Das, and Andrew McCallum. 2019. Optimal transport-based alignment of learned character representations for string similarity. In *Proceedings of the 57th Annual Meeting of the Association for Computational Linguistics*, pages 5907–5917, Florence, Italy. Association for Computational Linguistics.

Charles Truong, Laurent Oudre, and Nicolas Vayatis. 2020. Selective review of offline change point detection methods. *Signal Processing*, 167:107299.

Brian Uzzi, Satyam Mukherjee, Michael Stringer, and Ben Jones. 2013. Atypical combinations and scientific impact. *Science*, 342(6157):468–472.

Ronald D. Vale. 2015. Accelerating scientific publication in biology. *Proceedings of the National Academy of Sciences*, 112(44).

Arnout Verheij, Allard Kleijn, Flavius Frasincar, and Frederik Hogenboom. 2012. A comparison study for novelty control mechanisms applied to web news stories. In *2012 IEEE/WIC/ACM International Conferences on Web Intelligence and Intelligent Agent Technology*. IEEE.

Jian Wang, Reinhilde Veugelers, and Paula Stephan. 2016. Bias against novelty in science: A cautionary tale for users of bibliometric indicators. Technical report, National Bureau of Economic Research.

Lucy Lu Wang, Kyle Lo, Yoganand Chandrasekhar, Russell Reas, Jiangjiang Yang, Darrin Eide, Kathryn Funk, Rodney Kinney, Ziyang Liu, William Merrill, Paul Mooney, Dewey Murdick, Devvret Rishi, Jerry Sheehan, Zhihong Shen, Brandon Stilson, Alex D. Wade, Kuansan Wang, Chris Wilhelm, Boya Xie, Douglas Raymond, Daniel S. Weld, Oren Etzioni, and Sebastian Kohlmeier. 2020. CORD-19: The Covid-19 open research dataset. *arXiv e-prints*, page arXiv:2004.10706.

Mengyang Wang and Lihe Chai. 2018. Three new bibliometric indicators/approaches derived from keyword analysis. Technical Report 2, Springer Science and Business Media LLC.

Ian Wesley-Smith, Carl T. Bergstrom, and Jevin D. West. 2016. Static ranking of scholarly papers using article-level eigenfactor (alef). *ArXiv*, abs/1606.08534.

Fen Zhao, Yi Zhang, Jianguo Lu, and Ofer Shai. 2019. Measuring academic influence using heterogeneous author-citation networks. *Scientometrics*, 118(3):1119–1140.

A Appendices

A.1 Summary of phrases found in data sources

In our experiments and analysis we primarily consider two data sources: bioRxiv (representative of pre-print servers) and PubMed (representative of peer-reviewed journals). We extract phrases using TextRank as described in Section 4.2. In this section of the appendix, we summarize the phrases considered in the experiments.

A.1.1 Phrases from TextRank

TextRank extracted 1,587,408 phrases from bioRxiv abstracts. We further filter this list to 239,608 by only including phrases that were detected by TextRank more than once. This does not necessarily mean that the phrases that were filtered only occur in the bioRxiv abstracts a single time but that TextRank only found it to be a key phrase once. The distribution of phrase lengths is shown in Figure 7. A sample of phrases is listed in Table 3.

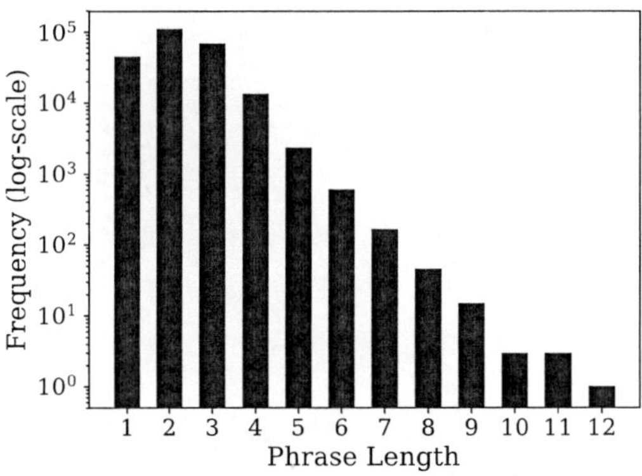

Figure 7: Frequency of various phrase lengths that were extracted from our corpus using TextRank.

A.1.2 Phrases from Experts

To validate the effectiveness of BAND, we use a small set of curated phrases provided by experts at CZI. Those results are discussed in detail in Section 5.2. The complete list of phrases is shown in Table 1.

A.2 Common phrases used in bio-medicine

In conducting the correlation study, explained in Section 5.3, we used a set of phrases that can be considered to be commonly used in biomedical literature. The complete list can be found in the Table 2.

A.2.1 Phrases for Crises

Pre-print servers are especially useful during crises such as pandemics. We chose 5 recent virus outbreaks to study their response which is discussed in Section 5.4: SARS, MERS, Ebola, Zika, and Covid-19. We made one compound time series curve for each virus's frequency based occurrence in PubMed and bioRxiv. Table 4 shows two lists. The phrases are obtained using all ordered combinations of entries from column 2 and column 3. For example we can combine "SARS-Cov" and "epidemic" to form "SARS-Cov epidemic". Each epidemic is associated with a set of phrases to form one compound set of phrases.

10X Genomics	ELISA
chromosome conformation	enzyme linked immunosorbent assay
CRISPR	Exome
CyTOF	FACS
electrospray ionization	Fluorescence Activated Cell Sorting
Mass Spectroscopy	Matrix-assisted laser desorption ionization
Proximity Extension Assay	scATAC-seq
Whole Genome Amplification	MALDI
gene editing	Mass cytometry
laser capture microdissection	Microfluidics
LINNAEUS	Translating Ribosome Affinity Purification

Table 1: The list of phrases used in Section 5.2. These phrases were provided by experts at CZI.

antibiotic	compound fracture
medicine	anti-inflammatory
physical therapy	trauma care
chemotherapy	medical history
kidney dialysis	intensive care unit
organ transplant	nervous system
X-Ray	digestive system
MRI	digestive tract
general practitioner	urinary tract
scar tissue	heart disease

Table 2: The list of common phrases used in our correlation analysis in Section 5.3. These phrases are phrases that can be considered common in medical literature

brain age estimation	e2 ubiquitin conjugating enzymes
te loads	acoustic droplet ejection
cell cycle stages	trauma care
cancer stem cell plasticity	age prediction models
marker selection methods	co-functioning genes
serum uric acid	structural mri images
drug structural information	anti-sense transcripts
hand performance	recursive splicing
repetition effects	partial gene trees
vigorous physical activity	published phylogenetic trees
cell isolation	iron distribution
x-chromosome dosage compensation	dna mixtures
terminal cell differentiation	place cell responses
trophic niche breadth	fossil age uncertainty
npy neurons	context reinstatement

Table 3: The list of top ranked phrases from TextRank used in our correlation analysis Section 5.3.

Outbreak	Phrase component
SARS	SARS
	SARS-cov
	Severe Acute Respiratory Syndrome
MERS	MERS
	MERS-Cov
	Middle Eastern Respiratory Syndrome
Ebola	Ebola
	Ebov
	Ebolavirus
Zika	Zika
	ZIKV
	Zika Virus
COVID-19	COVID2019
	2019-nCov
	novel coronavirus
	coronavirus
	COVID-19
	nCov

(a) First component

Phrase component
epidemic
forecasting
model
modeling
spreading
outbreak

(b) Second component

Table 4: A reference table for constructing phrases used in 5.4. For each virus outbreak, the list of phrases consists of all combinations of the first component concatenated with the second component. For instance, 'SARS epidemic' or 'COVID-19 forecasting'.

Effective Distributed Representations for Academic Expert Search

Mark Berger
University of Amsterdam
Amsterdam, The Netherlands
mark@maberger.nl

Jakub Zavrel
Zeta Alpha Vector
Amsterdam, The Netherlands
zavrel@zeta-alpha.com

Paul Groth
University of Amsterdam
Amsterdam, The Netherlands
p.groth@uva.nl

Abstract

Expert search aims to find and rank experts based on a user's query. In academia, retrieving experts is an efficient way to navigate through a large amount of academic knowledge. Here, we study how different distributed representations of academic papers (i.e. embeddings) impact academic expert retrieval. We use the Microsoft Academic Graph dataset and experiment with different configurations of a document-centric voting model for retrieval. In particular, we explore the impact of the use of contextualized embeddings on search performance. We also present results for paper embeddings that incorporate citation information through retrofitting. Additionally, experiments are conducted using different techniques for assigning author weights based on author order. We observe that using contextual embeddings produced by a transformer model trained for sentence similarity tasks produces the most effective paper representations for document-centric expert retrieval. However, retrofitting the paper embeddings and using elaborate author contribution weighting strategies did not improve retrieval performance.

1 Introduction

To help navigate a large body of academic knowledge, it can be useful to identify expert individuals. Identifying such individuals may be useful to find collaborators (Zhan et al., 2011; Schleyer et al., 2012; Sziklai, 2018), to find paper reviewers (Silva, 2014; Price and Flach, 2017), to find supervisors (Alarfaj et al., 2012a), or to investigate literature in a certain domain. This process of identifying experts given a particular topic is called expert finding (Balog et al., 2009), expertise retrieval (Gonçalves and Dorneles, 2019), or expert search. Expert search systems are information retrieval systems that can automatically rank candidate experts based on their expertise on a certain subject (Husain et al., 2019). In this study, we target the domain of retrieving academic experts based on papers they authored.

Given the central role of papers to defining expertise in this domain, we focus on document-centric expert search systems (Balog et al., 2006). These systems largely rely on statistical language modeling, topic modeling, or term frequency-based approaches to represent documents (Gonçalves and Dorneles, 2019; Husain et al., 2019). Surprisingly, given the rapid advances in the field of contextualized text embeddings (Wang et al., 2020b), little work has been done in applying these approaches to document representation for this task. We hypothesize that considering single words, which is common in the bag-of-words and probabilistic term-based approaches, may significantly reduce the system's "understanding" of the underlying academic documents. To achieve a potentially deeper understanding of these papers, contextualized text embeddings could be used.

Thus, in this paper, we explore the impact of contextualized text embeddings on the performance of the expert search. Specifically, we make the following contributions:

- a comparison of expert search performance using token-based (i.e. BERT (Devlin et al., 2018)) and sentence-based (Sentence-BERT (Reimers and Gurevych, 2019)) contextualized embeddings, non-contextualized embeddings (e.g. GloVe (Pennington et al., 2014)) and classic term frequency representations;

- measurement of the impact on performance when incorporating citation information into contextualized representations through *retrofitting* (Faruqui et al., 2015); and (Zhang, 2019).

Proceedings of the First Workshop on Scholarly Document Processing, pages 56–71
Online, November 19, 2020. ©2020 Association for Computational Linguistics
https://doi.org/10.18653/v1/P17

- a comparison of two different *strategies* for combining embeddings of the title and abstract of papers.

Additionally, all experiments are conducted using different techniques for assigning author weightings based on author order. Overall, this paper provides evidence for the efficacy of contextualized embeddings for the task of academic expert search. Note that this paper primarily focuses on investigating the performance of various contextualized embeddings and expert ranking aggregation methods within expert retrieval, and not on the entire retrieval process. Therefore, some aspects of neural information retrieval systems such as query understanding, query expansion, or re-ranking are out of the scope of this study.

Source code for the methods and data processing used in this paper can be found at `https://github.com/mabergerx/SDP500_expert_search`. The processed data used by our methods is available at (Berger, 2020).

The rest of this paper is organized as follows. We begin with a discussion of related work. Afterwards, the data used in this study is described. This is followed by a description of the various embeddings used and our approach to author ranking. Section 6 defines the evaluation and Section 7 details its results. We, then, briefly describe a prototype implementation using these representations. Finally, we discuss the limitations of the work, potential future work and conclude.

2   Related work

In this section, we introduce the primary paradigm for expert search. We then discuss work on voting models, document representations, and the use of text embedding techniques within expert search.

Probabilistic models   A driving force behind expertise retrieval research was the launch of the TREC Enterprise Track in 2005 (Craswell et al., 2005). This evaluation campaign led to the emergence of probabilistic models, in particular in the form of language models, as the primary paradigm for expertise retrieval. The core idea behind these approaches is to estimate a language model for each document and then rank the documents by the likelihood of the user query according to the language models (Balog et al., 2009).

Voting models   We can see documents authored by experts as evidence for their expertise. A partic-

ular type of models, based on *data fusion* methods that aggregate document scores into expert rankings, are called voting models (Husain et al., 2019; Balog et al., 2012).

Given a query, the retrieved documents are assumed to provide evidence about a possible ranking of the authors. This aggregation of the final author list can then be modelled as a voting process, where the document scores are aggregated into author scores (Macdonald, 2009; Macdonald and Ounis, 2008, 2006b,a).

Paper embeddings   Document-centric expert search systems rely on the documents to aggregate an expert ranking. However, effectively embedding longer documents is still an open research problem (Beltagy et al., 2020; Zhang et al., 2016; Liu and Lapata, 2017).

Unsupervised document embedding techniques include Sent2Vec (Pagliardini et al., 2018) and Doc2VecC (Chen, 2017), while supervised document embedding techniques include the Universal Sentence Encoder (Cer et al., 2018) and InferSent (Conneau et al., 2018). Recently, the Longformer (Beltagy et al., 2020) was proposed to embed even longer sequences of text than sentences. One research proposed evaluating various sentence encoding techniques in re-ranking of BM25-based research paper recommendations and found that the sentence encoding could be a beneficial method in addition to the BM25 retrieval, but not on its own (Hassan et al., 2019). Adding the BERT [CLS] token embedding into other ranking model's signal has been proposed and is shown to improve the underlying neural ranking architecture (MacAvaney et al., 2019).

As for the embedding of academic papers, most of the research focuses on learning the paper embeddings using linkage information and considers this a graph problem (Wang et al., 2016; Zhang et al., 2019; Mai et al., 2018).

Embedding expertise   Given the amount of research on document embedding techniques, there has been surprisingly little attention given to the application of contextualized embedding techniques in the field of expertise retrieval. Three recent surveys and reviews on the field of expertise retrieval (Gonçalves and Dorneles, 2019; Husain et al., 2019; Lin et al., 2017) contained little to no information about the application of embedding techniques.

One of the first works to introduce this concept into expertise retrieval was Author2Vec (J et al., 2016), which uses two models, the *content-info model* and the *link-info model* within the context of the co-authorship network. In the context-info model, the text of the written papers is represented using Paragraph2Vec (Le and Mikolov, 2014).

As briefly mentioned in the introduction, authors that cite each other can be considered having similar interests (Tho et al., 2007; Shibata et al., 2008). Zhang (Zhang, 2019) suggested using retrofitting in the domain of academic papers as a means of introducing this network information into the representation of a paper. Retrofitting is a concept introduced by Faruqui et al. (Faruqui et al., 2015) which proposes the incorporation of the information from semantic lexicons such as WordNet into word embeddings.

3   Data description

The Microsoft Academic Graph (MAG) (Wang et al., 2020a) was used at the primary data source. The data consists of over 200 million papers (titles & abstracts) as well as a variety of metadata. We accessed the November 2018 snapshot of the MAG data through the Open Academic Graph initiative[1], in particular the OAG v2 release.

Due to the very large size of the MAG, we created a custom subset of the data that mainly consisted of Computer Science (CS) related papers. This domain allows us to interpret results better than other science domains.

Our approach in extracting Computer Science (CS) related papers was to take the 113.864 paper titles obtained from arXiv[2] - a widely used preprint server - and do an exhaustive title matching on the full MAG dataset. This search resulted in 29.237 exact title matches, which corresponds to 26,6% of the arXiv data. This set provided us with a substantial initial seed of papers to extract more CS papers from the MAG data.

To allow retrofitting later in the process and create a larger dataset, we expanded this set with the references of all the 29.237 papers, which resulted in a set of 221.347 papers. These references were retrieved by accessing the *references* field of each of the 29.237 paper in the MAG data. Note that these references are not necessarily always complete: some cited articles may not be present in

our data due to incompleteness of the source MAG data.

From these 221.347 papers, we then performed bounded stratified sampling for the authors to retrieve a subset of 5.000 authors who are representative of both highly-, medium- and less prolific author populations. The full sampling method is described in Algorithm 5 in the Algorithms appendix.

This set of 5.000 authors served as a starting point for a second, final round of data retrieval. For these authors, we retrieved all their papers and references, resulting in a set of 127.716 papers, which included authors of the referenced papers. For all these new authors, we collected the metadata from the MAG authors dataset and aggregated this information into a single final authors dataset. The reason for expanding the set of authors beyond the 5.000 sampled authors is that a larger pool of papers is beneficial for the retrieval due to the larger search space.

For all titles and abstracts in our dataset, we performed data cleaning. Specifically, (corpus-specific) stopwords were removed, redundant whitespace and Unicode characters were both normalized. URLs and e-mails were removed.

4   Paper embedding methodology

In this section, we describe the paper embedding techniques employed and discuss our approach to embedding indexing and search, as well as retrofitting embeddings.

4.1   Embedding techniques

Various approaches have been used to embed the papers. We divide our approaches into the custom contextual approach and the baseline approaches. In all our baseline approaches, we use the concatenation of the title and the abstract to represent the paper.

Custom contextual approach   We use the title and the abstract as representative texts for a paper. Although the title and abstract of a paper are both relevant representations, they may contain information that differs in importance and granularity. In order to capture the possible semantic weight differences between the title and the abstract, we deploy two different embedding combination strategies: the **merge strategy** and the **separate strategy**.

In the merge strategy, we assume that the semantic weights of the title sentence and the abstract sentences are equal. That means that we want to

---

[1]https://www.openacademic.ai/oag/
[2]https://arxiv.org

take the average over the title- and abstract sentence embeddings without assigning any extra weight to neither. A detailed specification is given in the Algorithm 1 in the appendix.

In the separate strategy, we do want to differentiate between the title and the abstract. In particular, we want to assign more weight to the title than to the individual abstract sentences. We achieve this by first computing the average abstract embedding and then taking the average between that and the title embedding. A detailed specification is given in the Algorithm 3 in the appendix.

We refer to the actual text embedding model as the *embedder*. The *embedder* of choice is Sentence-BERT (Reimers and Gurevych, 2019), which is specifically designed for producing meaningful sentence-level embeddings, suited for Semantic Textual Similarity (STS). Specifically, we make use of the RoBERTa-base model fine-tuned on the combination of NLI datasets, and then further fine-tuned on the STS benchmark training set [3].

Baseline approach: Latent Semantic Indexing (LSI) (Deerwester et al., 1990) TF-IDF vectors with applied singular value decomposition. For our experiments, we chose to set the LSI vector's dimensionality to 768 dimensions, the same as the Sentence-BERT embedding dimensionality.

Baseline approach: BERT- and GloVe pooling To provide a comparison between specifically tuned for document-level representations Sentence-BERT and conventional pooling document embedding techniques, we produced paper embeddings by averaging both BERT and GloVe token embeddings. In both averaging operations, we perform double pooling: first, all tokens within each sentence are embedded and averaged into a single sentence embedding, and then these sentence embeddings are once again averaged into a single paper embedding. The details of this embedding process are shown in Algorithm 2 in the appendix and is identical for both BERT and GloVe embeddings. For both BERT (*bert-base-uncased*) and GloVe embedding calculations, we used the *Flair* (Akbik et al., 2018) Python library.

4.2 Retrofitting

Authors that cite each other can be considered as having similar interests. In the context of having a semantic representation of expertise, it could be helpful to "expand" a paper embedding to broaden the expertise scope of the author beyond a particular paper. To achieve this broadening, we use a technique called retrofitting, which introduces network information into the embeddings.

Inspired by (Zhang, 2019), we adapt the original implementation[4] of retrofitting (Faruqui et al., 2015) to work with academic papers that have been contextually embedded. The retrofitting process is performed for ten iterations. Algorithm 4 in the appendix shows the details about the algorithm.

4.3 Embedding storage and search

We chose the FAISS (Johnson et al., 2017) library by Facebook for our indexing purposes. It is optimized for memory usage and speed and can handle a large number of vectors.

For our embeddings, we chose the *IndexHN-SWFlat* index [5]. We use cosine similarity as the measure of similarity between the query embedding $\vec{Q}$ and any of the indexed embeddings $\vec{V}$.

5 Author ranking via voting

From the FAISS index we can, given a query, retrieve top N similar papers. To produce a final author ranking, we adopt a *voting model* based approach.

We can consider the retrieved paper results as the "expertise evidence" for the authors of these papers. A range of different voting approaches based on data fusion techniques has been proposed (Macdonald and Ounis, 2008; Afzal and Maurer, 2011; Alarfaj et al., 2012b) to produce an author ranking given the documents.

Each retrieved document d from the set of retrieved documents $R(Q)$ has an associated similarity score $s(d, Q)$ to it, with regard to the query Q. We can then combine these document scores into aggregated author scores using the *ExpCombSUM (eCS)* data fusion function (Macdonald, 2009):

$$eCS(C, Q) = \sum_{d \in R(Q) \cap D_C} e^{(s(d,Q)))} \quad (1)$$

where C is a candidate expert, D_C is the set of documents associated with candidate C.

This algorithm (Macdonald and Ounis, 2008; Macdonald, 2009), assumes that each document produces a static score per related author. In the case of academic papers, that is not the case, as most papers have multiple authors. These authors mostly have a different level of involvement in a particular paper and, therefore, may have a different vote produced by the document, depending on their authorship role. Recent research has shown that because the research is increasingly more inter-disciplinary, evaluating authors based on their rank within the order of authors is becoming increasingly difficult (Júnior et al., 2017). Therefore, it could be valuable to assign different weights to different authors of the same document. To the best of our knowledge, no previous work has been done on exactly defining weights on the authorship scores within a voting model. We define four different weighting strategies:

1. **Binary weighting**. Each author gets the full score for a document. This strategy assumes that each author contributed equally.

2. **Uniform weighting**. Each author gets $\frac{fullScore}{\#\ authors}$ for a document. This strategy assumes that each author contributed equally but does normalize the score by the number of authors.

3. **Descending weighting**. The first author gets the full document score. Each following author gets $fullScore * decayFactor$, where $decayFactor$ starts at 0.8 and decreases with 0.2 for each consecutive author. This strategy assumes that the authors are listed in descending involvement order.

4. **Parabolic weighting**. The first and last author get the full document score. All authors in between follow the **descending weighting**. This strategy assumes that the first author is similar to the descending weighting, but also takes the possible importance of the last author as the project supervisor.

Using these data fusion approaches, a fairness problem may occur: highly prolific authors, that may be associated with many documents (for instance, because they are the head of a lab) may receive an unfairly large number of votes, which does not necessarily indicate their expertise. Candidate length normalization is proposed to deal with this unfairness, just as document length normalization is often performed in document retrieval systems (Macdonald, 2009).

The use of a classical document normalization technique based on the *Divergence From Randomness framework* (Amati, 2003) is proposed (Macdonald, 2009), and has the following formula:

$$s_N(C, Q) = s(C, Q) \cdot log_2(1 + \alpha \cdot \frac{aL}{lP}) \quad (2)$$

where α is a hyperparameter controlling the amount of normalization, aL is the average amount of publications, and lP is the length of the profile of the candidate C. The lower the α parameter is, the more less prolific authors are boosted, and the more highly prolific authors are suppressed.

In practice, we discovered that because of the nature of our dataset, if we apply the above normalization technique, many authors from the long tail are retrieved, even when we use high α values. Therefore, we experimented with introducing another term to the equation: β, which serves as a profile length "booster":

$$s_N(C, Q) = s(C, Q) \cdot log_2(1 + \alpha \cdot \frac{aL}{lP + \beta}) \quad (3)$$

While it does introduce bias and eases the normalization, in our case, it provided an extra parameter to tune and resulted in a better mix of well- and lesser-known authors.

6 Evaluation methods

To evaluate the different retrieval strategies, we developed a method which uses the *field of work* tags present in the MAG dataset for the authors as a proxy for evaluating the relevance of an author. Because we use a document-centric retrieval strategy which uses strictly only the embeddings of the paper's title and abstract, the *field of work* tags are not used in the retrieval process, allowing us to use these tags in the evaluation process.

The query test set for our research was selected from the full distribution of author tags. The final query test set contained a hundred Computer Science related queries. The set is available in Table 3 in the appendix.

6.1 Relevance metrics

Before we can use any of the existing binary information retrieval metrics, we need to define a notion of *relevance* of an author given a query.

Based on the *field of work* tags, we define two relevance checks:

1. **Exact topic query evaluation (Brochier et al., 2018).** This approach takes a description of a topic and uses it directly as a query. The experts associated with that topic are then the ground truth list of candidates to be retrieved. In our case, the *field of work* tags of the authors are used as queries, and the retrieved authors are labelled relevant if they have that tag.

2. **Approximate topic query evaluation.** Sometimes, a query retrieves authors who have an incomplete *field of work* tag list or have tags which are very similar to the query but do not exactly match it. For instance, author A may have *"automatic summarization"* in their tags list, while the query was *"automatic text summarization"*. This author is clearly highly relevant to the query but would be labelled as irrelevant by the exact topic query evaluation method. Therefore, we introduce a fuzzy relevance checking method which, given a query, calculates the cosine similarity between the query embedding and each of the author's tags. If any of the similarities are higher than a chosen threshold, then we deem the author relevant.

Once we can label each retrieved author as relevant or not relevant, we can use different evaluation metrics. We evaluate our system by using three binary relevance metrics, all measured @N and using both the exact and approximate topic query evaluation: **Mean Reciprocal Rank** ($MRR@N_{exact}$, $MRR@N_{approx}$), **Mean Precision @ N** ($MP@N_{exact}$, $MP@N_{approx}$), and **Mean Average Precision** ($MAP@N_{exact}$, $MAP@N_{approx}$)

Some authors are more relevant than others. To incorporate this into our evaluation, we also use the **Normalized discounted cumulative gain** (nDCG@N) score, which is sensitive to the position of the relevant items in the produced ranking.

To produce the nDCG scores, we first need to have the score for the ideal ranking given a query, IDCG. To calculate the IDCG scores, for each query in our test set, we created a mapping between the query and the corresponding top authors.

Each author in such mapping got a relevance label in relation to the query. In our implementation of the author's relevance, we use the citations of the relevant papers of an author as a proxy for the expertise. Although any expertise measure of an author is not fully objective, and many factors seem to have effect on the citation activity (Yan et al., 2011), we chose the citation counts of the papers as a proxy for expertise for the following reasons:

- This measure is explainable.

- It prevents highly prolific but rarely cited authors to be labeled as highly relevant for multiple topics just based on their output

Given this final query-to-expert mapping, we precalculated the IDCG@10 score for each of the test queries in our dataset, so we could later calculate the nDCG@10 score per query. Once we calculated all the scores for our test set, we can take the average of those scores to have a single nDCG@10 score for our current system.

7 Results

In this section, first the overall quantitative evaluation results are discussed and then we zoom in on the performance of retrofitting and author contribution weighting.

7.1 Voting model results

The results of the voting model approach are presented in Table 1. Here we only present the exact topic query evaluation results, as we observe that approximate topic query evaluation results correspond to the exact results but are overall higher. In particular, for MRR, the approximate results are 0.06 higher on average; for MAP, the approximate results are 0.16 higher; for MP@10 the approximate results are 0.15 higher; and finally the MP@5 approximate results are, again, 0.15 higher. The full results table with the approximate query evaluation results included, are presented in Table 2 in the Appendix.

We can observe that the LSI baseline produces strong results, outperforming both embedding pooling baselines. From the four used author contribution weighting schemes, the binary score weighting is the best performing weighting. However, the overall performance difference between the weightings is quite small.

PAPER EMBEDDING KIND	DATA FUSION TECHNIQUE	MRR@10 EXACT	MAP@10 EXACT	MP@10 EXACT	MP@5 EXACT	NDCG @10	NDCG @5
LSI	$expCombSUM_{uniform}$	0.75	0.399	0.462	0.496	0.39	0.42
	$expCombSUM_{binary}$	0.753	0.428	0.491	0.512	0.41	0.44
	$expCombSUM_{descending}$	0.755	0.411	0.476	0.484	0.39	0.42
	$expCombSUM_{parabolic}$	0.763	0.392	0.457	0.482	0.39	0.42
Average pooled BERT	$expCombSUM_{uniform}$	0.554	0.117	0.198	0.206	0.1	0.11
	$expCombSUM_{binary}$	0.558	0.12	0.203	0.222	0.12	0.13
	$expCombSUM_{descending}$	0.556	0.117	0.2	0.208	0.11	0.12
	$expCombSUM_{parabolic}$	0.56	0.107	0.18	0.218	0.1	0.12
Average pooled GloVe	$expCombSUM_{uniform}$	0.626	0.272	0.369	0.398	0.27	0.29
	$expCombSUM_{binary}$	0.672	0.304	0.402	0.414	0.3	0.31
	$expCombSUM_{descending}$	0.661	0.286	0.383	0.398	0.28	0.3
	$expCombSUM_{parabolic}$	0.676	0.254	0.33	0.392	0.25	0.28
Merged Sentence-BERT	$expCombSUM_{uniform}$	0.834	0.419	0.491	0.528	0.43	0.47
	$expCombSUM_{binary}$	0.83	0.437	0.509	0.546	0.42	0.46
	$expCombSUM_{descending}$	0.818	0.419	0.493	0.526	0.41	0.46
	$expCombSUM_{parabolic}$	0.812	0.4	0.484	0.508	0.41	0.45
Separate Sentence-BERT	$expCombSUM_{uniform}$	0.838	0.495	0.572	0.616	0.53	0.58
	expCombSUM$_{binary}$	0.837	0.518	**0.59**	**0.626**	**0.54**	**0.6**
	$Norm(expCombSUM_{binary})$ $\beta = 0$ and $\alpha = 1$	0.619	0.174	0.282	0.272	0.15	0.14
	$Norm(expCombSUM_{binary})$ $\beta = 0$ and $\alpha = 1000$	0.694	0.218	0.318	0.324	0.16	0.17
	$Norm(expCombSUM_{binary})$ $\beta = 10$ and $\alpha = 1000$	0.777	0.293	0.381	0.406	0.22	0.25
	$Norm(expCombSUM_{binary})$ $\beta = 50$ and $\alpha = 1000$	0.769	0.362	0.455	0.466	0.31	0.33
	$Norm(expCombSUM_{binary})$ $\beta = 1000$ and $\alpha = 1000$	0.813	0.404	0.491	0.52	0.37	0.4
	$expCombSUM_{descending}$	0.839	0.501	0.581	0.612	0.52	0.58
	$expCombSUM_{parabolic}$	0.819	0.486	0.565	0.592	0.52	0.56
Retrofitted merged Sentence-BERT	$expCombSUM_{uniform}$	0.792	0.384	0.45	0.482	0.38	0.42
	$expCombSUM_{binary}$	0.83	0.404	0.467	0.496	0.39	0.44
	$expCombSUM_{descending}$	0.813	0.39	0.454	0.486	0.38	0.42
	$expCombSUM_{parabolic}$	0.775	0.38	0.445	0.474	0.38	0.4
Retrofitted separate Sentence-BERT	$expCombSUM_{uniform}$	0.821	0.51	0.577	0.606	0.5	0.54
	$expCombSUM_{binary}$	**0.841**	**0.519**	0.584	0.616	0.51	0.54
	$expCombSUM_{descending}$	0.831	0.505	0.569	0.61	0.49	0.54
	$expCombSUM_{parabolic}$	0.808	0.509	0.583	0.596	0.5	0.53

Table 1: Results for the voting model author retrieval strategy. The best results are formatted in bold.

The best performing configuration is the separate embedding strategy with the binary distributed paper scores. We see that normalizing the *expCombSUM* function with a low α and $\beta = 0$ leads to steep decrease in performance. With higher α and β, the performance goes up but can be explained by "cancelling out" the normalization effect. One of the reasons for this bad performance could be that the dataset contains many authors from the long tail; some of the authors naturally may have worse metadata resulting in missing expertise tags. Moreover, for lesser-known authors in the MAG, we have encountered a problem that the profiles get deleted or get different author ids, which also corrupts the metadata and the results.

Retrofitting the embeddings did not improve the results, except for two evaluation metrics: $MRR@10_{exact}$ and $MAP@10_{exact}$ in case of the retrofitted separate embeddings.

7.2 Performance of retrofitting

Retrofitting the embeddings did not improve our retrieval performance with the exception of two metrics. One of the explanations could be that the relatively small size of our dataset can hurt the retrofitting process. Combined with the variance in the number of neighbours per paper, some of the resulting retrofitted embeddings might be driven away too much from the original embedding, while other embeddings are not modified "enough".

7.3 Effect of different author contribution weightings

Throughout the experiment, we observed that the binary author contribution weighting performs the best. Therefore, we can conclude that, for our voting model configuration, introducing elaborate author contribution combinations does not improve the retrieval performance.

8 Prototype implementation

We implemented our model int a prototype, which consists of a REST API, where the users can, given a search query, look for N most relevant experts. Each individual expert representation is contained within a JSON object which contains not only the author's name and MAG id, but also the authors affiliation information (retrieved using GRID [6]), the list of papers which voted for the author and their corresponding document scores in relation to the query, and additional author information from WikiData (Vrandečić and Krötzsch, 2014).

9 Discussion & Future work

This study faced multiple challenges regarding data quality, data freshness, embedding strategy considerations, and the retrieval base on embeddings. In this section, we discuss these issues.

Data completeness and variability. The *field-of-work* tags used in the evaluation are not always complete and are subject to the specific format used by the MAG. In addition, for some authors, no tags are present in our snapshot of the MAG data. This has an effect on the evaluation performance by introducing both false positives and -negatives into the relevancy determining process. Overall, our system would profit significantly from a larger pool of papers and authors.

Shifting expertise. Many authors have varying interests during their academic career. Our system is inherently a snapshot of their academic activity: we only search and aggregate within a bounded set of papers. Introducing temporal aspect into the author search, which would intelligently account for shifting expertise could improve the retrieval results.

Representing expertise domains. Many authors are not experts in just one niche field, but rather are knowledgeable about a pretty broad field of science, with more in-depth knowledge about a few specific sub-fields. Clustering within the author expertise to find expertise sub-clusters might help to create more nuanced author representations by taking the cluster centroids as the individual author embeddings. This approach, while interesting, requires more data, as clustering within the papers of one author requires having a significant amount of papers per author.

---

[6] https://www.grid.ac/

Performance of individual retrieval strategies. Different types of embeddings may perform well in different scenarios. For example, retrofitting of the paper embeddings leads to the "widening" of the semantic representation of a paper into the direction of its neighbours. For example, retrofitted embeddings may perform better for more broad/general queries and worse on more specific queries. The same applies for normalization in the voting model: retrieving less prolific authors may be beneficial for some user's needs, while it technically hurts the quantitative performance of the system.

Document pooling strategies. In the two paper embedding strategies, we perform pooling over multiple sentence embeddings. While these strategies seem to work well to represent the papers for our task, it would still be interesting to use new, state-of-the-art approaches for embedding longer texts, such as the Longformer (Beltagy et al., 2020), to avoid using any pooling strategies and loosing semantic value. Techniques like the recently introduced SPECTER (Cohan et al., 2020) could also be used to produce better citation-informed document embeddings. Finally, we could employ the SciBERT (Beltagy et al., 2019) model in our baseline pooling strategies or even fine-tune a SciBERT model on longer sequences, similarly to Sentence-BERT, as it is better suited for academic texts.

Graph embeddings. In our approach, we used retrofitting to introduce citation network information into our initial paper embeddings. However, we could also go a step further and use graph embedding techniques to create native graph-based embeddings for our papers (Mai et al., 2018; Wang et al., 2016; Zhang et al., 2019).

10 Conclusion

In this study, we investigated different approaches for embedding academic papers and using the embeddings in an expert search task.

Overall, we found that Transformer-based contextual text embeddings work well on the domain of academic papers. By using the Sentence-BERT model trained on NLI and SNS tasks, we outperformed the strong LSI baseline often employed in information retrieval systems on all ten evaluation metrics. We also outperformed the baseline strategies of average pooled BERT and GloVe embeddings.

Employing a weighted embedding combination strategy to represent a paper can however be valuable, as we found that using a separate embedding combination strategy outperformed the "default" merged strategy on nine out of ten metrics.

We hypothesized that enriching the paper embeddings with citation information, in a process called retrofitting, could improve improve retrieval performance. Our experiments did not confirm this hypothesis, as non-retrofitted embeddings performed better in our task on all but two evaluation metrics.

Finally, we employed various data fusion techniques to convert the top N retrieved papers given a query into a ranking of authors. A voting model was used, where each document served as evidence for the corresponding author's expertise. We investigated whether using author contribution weighting strategies within the voting process would improve expertise retrieval. We observed no performance gain over the "default" binary strategy.

Given the direction of this study, we think that the most suitable application areas for the methodology we proposed are reviewer finding, supervisor finding and investigating literature on a topic. The reasoning behind this is that finding a collaborator may require and involve more sophisticated information about the institution, availability and current field of interest of the found experts. The proposed three areas, however, allow for less specificity and can better benefit from the improved retrieval.

While research in the field of expertise retrieval is not as active in the second half of the 2010s as it was in the first half, the area of text representations and retrieval has seen dramatic improvements. This study was an effort to apply these new techniques into the field of expertise retrieval and has shown that substantial improvements can be made over the existing retrieval algorithms. We hope that this study can contribute to a new research wave within the field of (academic) expertise retrieval.

Acknowledgements

We would like to thank the reviewers for their insightful commentary. Additionally, we would like to thank dr. Wouter Weerkamp from Zeta Alpha for his valuable feedback and assessment of the work.

References

Muhammad Tanvir Afzal and Hermann A Maurer. 2011. Expertise recommender system for scientific community. *J. UCS*, 17(11):1529–1549.

Alan Akbik, Duncan Blythe, and Roland Vollgraf. 2018. Contextual string embeddings for sequence labeling. In *COLING 2018, 27th International Conference on Computational Linguistics*, pages 1638–1649.

Fawaz Alarfaj, Udo Kruschwitz, David Hunter, and Chris Fox. 2012a. Finding the right supervisor: Expert-finding in a university domain. In *Proceedings of the NAACL HLT 2012 Student Research Workshop*, pages 1–6, Montréal, Canada. Association for Computational Linguistics.

Fawaz Alarfaj, Udo Kruschwitz, David Hunter, and Chris Fox. 2012b. Finding the right supervisor: Expert-finding in a university domain. In *Proceedings of the 2012 Conference of the North American Chapter of the Association for Computational Linguistics: Human Language Technologies: Student Research Workshop*, NAACL HLT '12, page 1–6, USA. Association for Computational Linguistics.

G Amati. 2003. *Probabilistic Models for Information Retrieval based on Divergence from Randomness. University of Glasgow, UK*. Ph.D. thesis, PhD Thesis.

Krisztian Balog, Leif Azzopardi, and Maarten De Rijke. 2006. Formal models for expert finding in enterprise corpora. *Proceedings of the Twenty-Ninth Annual International ACM SIGIR Conference on Research and Development in Information Retrieval*, 2006:43–50.

Krisztian Balog, Leif Azzopardi, and Maarten de Rijke. 2009. A language modeling framework for expert finding. *Information Processing and Management*, 45(1):1–19.

Krisztian Balog, Yi Fang, Maarten De Rijke, Pavel Serdyukov, and Luo Si. 2012. Expertise retrieval. *Foundations and Trends in Information Retrieval*, 6(2-3):127–256.

Iz Beltagy, Kyle Lo, and Arman Cohan. 2019. Scibert: Pretrained language model for scientific text. In *EMNLP*.

Iz Beltagy, Matthew E. Peters, and Arman Cohan. 2020. Longformer: The long-document transformer.

Mark Berger. 2020. Datasets for effective distributed representations for academic expert search.

Robin Brochier, Adrien Guille, Benjamin Rothan, and Julien Velcin. 2018. Impact of the query set on the evaluation of expert finding systems. *CEUR Workshop Proceedings*, 2132:32–45.

Daniel Cer, Yinfei Yang, Sheng-yi Kong, Nan Hua, Nicole Limtiaco, Rhomni St John, Noah Constant, Mario Guajardo-Céspedes, Steve Yuan, Chris Tar, Yun-Hsuan Sung, Brian Strope, and Ray Kurzweil Google Research Mountain View. 2018. Universal Sentence Encoder.

Minmin Chen. 2017. Efficient vector representation for documents through corruption. *CoRR*, abs/1707.02377.

Arman Cohan, Sergey Feldman, Iz Beltagy, Doug Downey, and Daniel Weld. 2020. Specter: Document-level representation learning using citation-informed transformers. pages 2270–2282.

Alexis Conneau, Douwe Kiela, Holger Schwenk, Loïc Barrault, and Antoine Bordes. 2018. Supervised Learning of Universal Sentence Representations from Natural Language Inference Data.

Nick Craswell, Arjen P. de Vries, and Ian Soboroff. 2005. Overview of the trec 2005 enterprise track. In *TREC*.

Scott Deerwester, Susan T Dumais, George W Furnas, Thomas K Landauer, and Richard Harshman. 1990. Indexing by latent semantic analysis. *Journal of the American society for information science*, 41(6):391–407.

Jacob Devlin, Ming-Wei Chang, Kenton Lee, and Kristina Toutanova. 2018. BERT: Pre-training of Deep Bidirectional Transformers for Language Understanding.

Manaal Faruqui, Jesse Dodge, Sujay K. Jauhar, Chris Dyer, Eduard Hovy, and Noah A. Smith. 2015. Retrofitting word vectors to semantic lexicons. *NAACL HLT 2015 - 2015 Conference of the North American Chapter of the Association for Computational Linguistics: Human Language Technologies, Proceedings of the Conference*, (i):1606–1615.

Rodrigo Gonçalves and Carina Friedrich Dorneles. 2019. Automated expertise retrieval: A taxonomy-based survey and open issues. *ACM Comput. Surv.*, 52(5).

Hebatallah A Mohamed Hassan, Giuseppe Sansonetti, Fabio Gasparetti, Alessandro Micarelli, and Joeran Beel. 2019. BERT, ELMo, USE and InferSent Sentence Encoders: The Panacea for Research-Paper Recommendation?

Omayma Husain, Naomie Salim, Rose Alinda Alias, Samah Abdelsalam, and Alzubair Hassan. 2019. Expert finding systems: A systematic review. *Applied Sciences (Switzerland)*, 9(20):1–32.

Ganesh J, Soumyajit Ganguly, Manish Gupta, Vasudeva Varma, and Vikram Pudi. 2016. Author2vec: Learning author representations by combining content and link information. In *Proceedings of the 25th International Conference Companion on World Wide Web*, WWW '16 Companion, page 49–50, Republic and Canton of Geneva, CHE. International World Wide Web Conferences Steering Committee.

Jeff Johnson, Matthijs Douze, and Hervé Jégou. 2017. Billion-scale similarity search with gpus. *CoRR*, abs/1702.08734.

E. A. C. Júnior, F. N. Silva, L. Costa, and Diego R. Amancio. 2017. Patterns of authors contribution in scientific manuscripts. *ArXiv*, abs/1609.05545.

Quoc V. Le and Tomas Mikolov. 2014. Distributed Representations of Sentences and Documents.

Shuyi Lin, Wenxing Hong, Dingding Wang, and Tao Li. 2017. A survey on expert finding techniques. *Journal of Intelligent Information Systems*, 49(2):255–279.

Yang Liu and Mirella Lapata. 2017. Learning structured text representations. *CoRR*, abs/1705.09207.

Sean MacAvaney, Andrew Yates, Arman Cohan, and Nazli Goharian. 2019. Cedr: Contextualized embeddings for document ranking. In *Proceedings of the 42nd International ACM SIGIR Conference on Research and Development in Information Retrieval*, SIGIR'19, page 1101–1104, New York, NY, USA. Association for Computing Machinery.

Craig Macdonald. 2009. *The voting model for people search*. Ph.D. thesis, University of Glasgow.

Craig Macdonald and Iadh Ounis. 2006a. A Belief Network Model for Expert Search. *Computing*.

Craig Macdonald and Iadh Ounis. 2006b. Voting for candidates. In *Proceedings of the 15th ACM international conference on Information and knowledge management - CIKM '06*, page 387, New York, New York, USA. ACM Press.

Craig Macdonald and Iadh Ounis. 2008. Voting techniques for expert search. *Knowl Inf Syst*, 16:259–280.

Gengchen Mai, Krzysztof Janowicz, and Bo Yan. 2018. Combining text embedding and knowledge graph embedding techniques for academic search engines. In *Joint proceedings of the 4th Workshop on Semantic Deep Learning (SemDeep-4) and NLIWoD4: Natural Language Interfaces for the Web of Data (NLIWOD-4) and 9th Question Answering over Linked Data challenge (QALD-9) co-located with 17th International Semantic Web Conference (ISWC 2018), Monterey, California, United States of America, October 8th - 9th, 2018*, volume 2241 of *CEUR Workshop Proceedings*, pages 77–88. CEUR-WS.org.

Matteo Pagliardini, Prakhar Gupta, and Martin Jaggi. 2018. Unsupervised learning of sentence embeddings using compositional n-gram features. In *Proceedings of the 2018 Conference of the North American Chapter of the Association for Computational Linguistics: Human Language Technologies, Volume 1 (Long Papers)*, pages 528–540, New Orleans, Louisiana. Association for Computational Linguistics.

Jeffrey Pennington, Richard Socher, and Christopher Manning. 2014. GloVe: Global vectors for word representation. In *Proceedings of the 2014 Conference on Empirical Methods in Natural Language Processing (EMNLP)*, pages 1532–1543, Doha, Qatar. Association for Computational Linguistics.

Simon Price and Peter A Flach. 2017. Computational support for academic peer review: A perspective from artificial intelligence. *Communications of the ACM*, 60(3):70–79.

Nils Reimers and Iryna Gurevych. 2019. Sentence-BERT: Sentence embeddings using Siamese BERT-networks. In *Proceedings of the 2019 Conference on Empirical Methods in Natural Language Processing and the 9th International Joint Conference on Natural Language Processing (EMNLP-IJCNLP)*, pages 3982–3992, Hong Kong, China. Association for Computational Linguistics.

Titus Schleyer, Brian S. Butler, Mei Song, and Heiko Spallek. 2012. Conceptualizing and advancing research networking systems. *ACM Trans. Comput.-Hum. Interact.*, 19(1).

Naoki Shibata, Yuya Kajikawa, Yoshiyuki Takeda, and Katsumori Matsushima. 2008. Detecting emerging research fronts based on topological measures in citation networks of scientific publications. *Technovation*, 28(11):758 – 775.

Attulugamage Thushari Priyangika Silva. 2014. *A research analytics framework for expert recommendation in research social networks*. Ph.D. thesis, City University of Hong Kong.

Balázs Sziklai. 2018. How to identify experts in a community? *International Journal of Game Theory*, 47:155–173.

Quan Thanh Tho, S.C. Hui, and A.C.M. Fong. 2007. A citation-based document retrieval system for finding research expertise. *Information Processing & Management*, 43(1):248 – 264.

Denny Vrandečić and Markus Krötzsch. 2014. Wikidata: A free collaborative knowledgebase. *Commun. ACM*, 57(10):78–85.

Kuansan Wang, Zhihong Shen, Chiyuan Huang, Chieh-Han Wu, Yuxiao Dong, and Anshul Kanakia. 2020a. Microsoft academic graph: When experts are not enough. *Quantitative Science Studies*, 1(1):396–413.

Suhang Wang, Jiliang Tang, Charu Aggarwal, and Huan Liu. 2016. Linked document embedding for classification. In *Proceedings of the 25th ACM International on Conference on Information and Knowledge Management*, CIKM '16, page 115–124, New York, NY, USA. Association for Computing Machinery.

Yuxuan Wang, Yutai Hou, Wanxiang Che, and Ting Liu. 2020b. From static to dynamic word representations: a survey. *International Journal of Machine Learning and Cybernetics*.

Rui Yan, Jie Tang, Xiaobing Liu, Dongdong Shan, and Xiaoming Li. 2011. Citation count prediction: Learning to estimate future citations for literature. In *Proceedings of the 20th ACM International Conference on Information and Knowledge Management*, CIKM '11, page 1247–1252, New York, NY, USA. Association for Computing Machinery.

Zhenjiang Zhan, Lichun Yang, Shenghua Bao, Dingyi Han, Zhong Su, and Yong Yu. 2011. Finding appropriate experts for collaboration. In *Proceedings of the 12th International Conference on Web-Age Information Management*, WAIM'11, page 327–339, Berlin, Heidelberg. Springer-Verlag.

Ye Zhang, Md Mustafizur Rahman, Alex Braylan, Brandon Dang, Heng-Lu Chang, Henna Kim, Quinten McNamara, Aaron Angert, Edward Banner, Vivek Khetan, Tyler McDonnell, An Thanh Nguyen, Dan Xu, Byron C. Wallace, and Matthew Lease. 2016. Neural Information Retrieval: A Literature Review. (November).

Yi Zhang. 2019. *Learning Embeddings for Academic Papers*. Ph.D. thesis.

Yi Zhang, Fen Zhao, and Jianguo Lu. 2019. P2V: large-scale academic paper embedding. *Scientometrics*, 121(1):399–432.

Algorithm 1: Paper embedding creation following the merge strategy.

Result: Paper embeddings ME following the **merge** strategy

Input: A set of paper titles T, a set of batches of abstract sentences A (with $|T| = |A|$) and an embedder model $Embedder$

---

mergedEmbeddings $\leftarrow []$
abstractEmbeddingBatches $\leftarrow []$
titleEmbeddings $\leftarrow Embedder.embed(T)$
for $aBatch \in A$ **do**
    batchEmbeddings $\leftarrow Embedder.embed(aBatch)$
    abstractEmbeddingBatches$.append$(batchEmbeddings)
end
assert $|titleEmbeddings| = |abstractEmbeddingBatches|$
for $tE \in titleEmbeddings, \quad aEB \in abstractEmbeddingBatches$ **do**
    $aEB.append$(tE)
    N $\leftarrow dim(aEB)$
    mergedEmbedding $\leftarrow \frac{1}{N} \sum_{i=1}^{N} (emb_i \in aEB)$ $\triangleright$ Take the element-wise average of all the embeddings, resulting in one embedding
    mergedEmbeddings$.append$(mergedEmbedding)
end
return mergedEmbeddings

Algorithm 2: Paper embedding creation following baseline BERT or GloVe strategy.

Result: Baseline paper embeddings ME created by either BERT or GloVe embedding model.

Input: A set of batches of abstract sentences A with elementwise appended corresponding paper titles T (with $|T| = |A|$) and an embedder model $Embedder$ (either BERT or GloVe)

---

embeddings $\leftarrow []$
abstractEmbeddingBatches $\leftarrow []$
for $aBatch \in A$ **do**
    batchEmbeddings $\leftarrow Embedder.embed(aBatch)$
    abstractEmbeddingBatches$.append$(batchEmbeddings)
end
for $aEB \in abstractEmbeddingBatches$ **do**
    N $\leftarrow dim(aEB)$
    pooledEmbedding $\leftarrow \frac{1}{N} \sum_{i=1}^{N} (emb_i \in aEB)$ $\triangleright$ Take the element-wise average of all the embeddings, resulting in one embedding
    embeddings$.append$(pooledEmbedding)
end
return embeddings

Algorithm 3: Paper embedding creation following the separate strategy.

Result: Paper embeddings ME following the **separate** strategy

Input: A set of paper titles T, a set of batches of abstract sentences A (with $|T| = |A|$) and an embedder model $Embedder$

mergedEmbeddings $\leftarrow$ []
abstractAverageEmbeddings $\leftarrow$ []
titleEmbeddings $\leftarrow Embedder.embed(T)$
for $aBatch \in A$ **do**
    batchEmbeddings $\leftarrow Embedder.embed(aBatch)$
    N $\leftarrow dim(batchEmbeddings)$
    averageBatchEmbedding $\leftarrow \frac{1}{N} \sum_{i=1}^{N} (emb_i \in batchEmbeddings)$ ▷ Create an average embedding for abstract sentences only.
    abstractAverageEmbeddings.$append$(averageBatchEmbedding)
end
assert $|titleEmbeddings| = |abstractAverageEmbeddings|$
for $tE \in titleEmbeddings, \ aE \in abstractAverageEmbeddings$ **do**
    separateArray $\leftarrow [tE, aE]$ ▷ Create a two item array consisting of the title embedding and the average abstract embedding.
    N $\leftarrow dim(separateArray)$
    separateEmbedding $\leftarrow \frac{1}{N} \sum_{i=1}^{N} (emb_i \in separateArray)$ ▷ Create an average embedding over just two embeddings.
    separateEmbeddings.$append$(separateEmbedding)
end
return separateEmbeddings

Algorithm 4: The retrofitting algorithm.

Result: Retrofitted paper embeddings

Data: A mapping between paper id's and their embeddings $\rightarrow C$ (corpus), the mapping between paper id's in lexicon and their references $\rightarrow L$ (lexicon), and the amount of algorithm iterations $\rightarrow$ **numIter**.

Retrofit $(C, L, numIter)$

  $newCorpus \leftarrow$ deepcopy (C) ▷ Deep copy the corpus into a new variable to alter

  $I \leftarrow newCorpus.$keys()   ▷ Extract all the keys (paper id's) from the corpus

  $corpusVocabulary \leftarrow$ set (I) ▷ Consider only the unique paper id's

  // Two lines below exist for the case where the paper id's in lexicon differ from paper id's in corpus, normally not the case in our environment. Otherwise, they have not effect.

  $LI \leftarrow L.$keys()   ▷ Extract all the keys (paper id's) from the lexicon

  $relevantVocabulary \leftarrow corpusVocabulary \cap$ set (LI) ▷ Consider only the overlapping id's from lexicon and corpus

  for $it \leftarrow 0$ *to* $numIter$ **do**

    foreach *paper* $\in$ *relevantVocabulary* **do**

      $paperNeighbours \leftarrow$ set $(L[word]) \cap corpusVocabulary$ ▷ Extract the set of neighbours of the current paper that actually have an embedding in our corpus

      $numNeighbours \leftarrow$ len $(paperNeighbours)$

      if $numNeighbours = 0$ **then**

        continue   ▷ If the paper has no neighbours, do not adjust the embedding and go to next paper

      end

      $newEmbedding \leftarrow numNeighbours * C[paper]$ ▷ Initialize the new embedding by weighing in the original embedding

      foreach *neighbour in paperNeighbours* **do**

        $newEmbedding \mathrel{+}= newCorpus[neighbour]$ ▷ Add the neighbour embedding with weight 1.

      end

      $newCorpus[paper] \leftarrow \dfrac{newEmbedding}{2*numNeighbours}$ ▷ Finalize the new embedding by dividing the current new embedding by (2 * number_neighbours), essentially putting the embedding back in the same space.

    end

  end

  return *newCorpus*

Algorithm 5: The author sampling strategy from the arXiv subset.

Result: A stratified sample of authors $randomAuthorSample$ of size $s = 5000$.

Input: A set of authors $authorsArxiv$ extracted from the the arXiv subset with the corresponding metadata and the final sample size $s = 5000$ (arbitrarily chosen).

1. Filter $authorsArxiv$ to only contain authors which, for their papers, have references in the data. That is needed to be able to do retrofitting later.

2. Given this new proper set of authors, $properA$, initialize four bins (strata) based on the amount of author publications:

   (a) 5 - 10 publications
   (b) 10 - 50 publications
   (c) 50 - 100 publications
   (d) 100+ publications

3. Calculate the bin size for each bin and also the total amount of authors in all the bins.

4. Perform proportionate allocation using a sampling fraction in each of the strata that is proportional to that of the total population. We went for a sample size of 5000 authors. For a single bin, the allocation process is as following:

   Bin 1 (5 - 10 publications) has 22.943 authors. The total population of authors in all the bins is 35.450 authors ($|properA|$). The share of Bin1 in the final 5.000 authors set is then

   Bin 1 $=>$ 22.943 * (5.000 / 35.450) = 3.235 authors

5. Proceed doing a simple random sampling from those pools of authors, resulting in $randomAuthorSample$.

---

return $randomAuthorSample$

PAPER EMBEDDING KIND	DATA FUSION TECHNIQUE	MRR@10 EXACT	MRR@10 APPRX	MAP@10 EXACT	MAP@10 APPRX	MP@10 EXACT	MP@10 APPRX	MP@5 EXACT	MP@5 APPRX	NDCG@10	NDCG@5
LSI	$expCombSUM_{uniform}$	0.75	0.864	0.399	0.603	0.462	0.662	0.496	0.696	0.39	0.42
	$expCombSUM_{binary}$	0.753	0.844	0.428	0.626	0.491	0.693	0.512	0.708	0.41	0.44
	$expCombSUM_{descending}$	0.755	0.857	0.411	0.603	0.476	0.668	0.484	0.684	0.39	0.42
	$expCombSUM_{parabolic}$	0.763	0.864	0.392	0.587	0.457	0.651	0.482	0.68	0.39	0.42
Average pooled BERT	$expCombSUM_{uniform}$	0.554	-	0.117	-	0.198	-	0.206	-	0.1	0.11
	$expCombSUM_{binary}$	0.558	-	0.12	-	0.203	-	0.222	-	0.12	0.13
	$expCombSUM_{descending}$	0.556	-	0.117	-	0.2	-	0.208	-	0.11	0.12
	$expCombSUM_{parabolic}$	0.56	-	0.107	-	0.18	-	0.218	-	0.1	0.12
Average pooled GloVe	$expCombSUM_{uniform}$	0.626	-	0.272	-	0.369	-	0.398	-	0.27	0.29
	$expCombSUM_{binary}$	0.672	-	0.304	-	0.402	-	0.414	-	0.3	0.31
	$expCombSUM_{descending}$	0.661	-	0.286	-	0.383	-	0.398	-	0.28	0.3
	$expCombSUM_{parabolic}$	0.676	-	0.254	-	0.33	-	0.392	-	0.25	0.28
Merged Sentence-BERT	$expCombSUM_{uniform}$	0.834	**0.903**	0.419	0.586	0.491	0.658	0.528	0.684	0.43	0.47
	$expCombSUM_{binary}$	0.83	0.893	0.437	0.606	0.509	0.677	0.546	0.708	0.42	0.46
	$expCombSUM_{descending}$	0.818	**0.903**	0.419	0.59	0.493	0.657	0.526	0.688	0.41	0.46
	$expCombSUM_{parabolic}$	0.812	0.869	0.4	0.555	0.484	0.634	0.508	0.666	0.41	0.45
Separate Sentence-BERT	$expCombSUM_{uniform}$	0.838	0.875	0.495	0.673	0.572	0.744	0.616	0.764	0.53	0.58
	expCombSUM$_{binary}$	0.837	0.892	0.518	**0.69**	**0.59**	**0.751**	**0.626**	**0.784**	**0.54**	**0.6**
	$Norm(expCombSUM_{binary})$ $\beta = 0$ and $\alpha = 1$	0.619	0.678	0.174	0.284	0.282	0.42	0.272	0.398	0.15	0.14
	$Norm(expCombSUM_{binary})$ $\beta = 0$ and $\alpha = 1000$	0.694	0.737	0.218	0.331	0.318	0.452	0.324	0.456	0.16	0.17
	$Norm(expCombSUM_{binary})$ $\beta = 10$ and $\alpha = 1000$	0.777	0.807	0.293	0.409	0.381	0.509	0.406	0.542	0.22	0.25
	$Norm(expCombSUM_{binary})$ $\beta = 50$ and $\alpha = 1000$	0.769	0.81	0.362	0.49	0.455	0.589	0.466	0.602	0.31	0.33
	$Norm(expCombSUM_{binary})$ $\beta = 1000$ and $\alpha = 1000$	0.813	0.853	0.404	0.548	0.491	0.638	0.52	0.658	0.37	0.4
	$expCombSUM_{descending}$	0.839	0.894	0.501	0.666	0.581	0.737	0.612	0.758	0.52	0.58
	$expCombSUM_{parabolic}$	0.819	0.878	0.486	0.654	0.565	0.729	0.592	0.742	0.52	0.56
Retrofitted merged Sentence-BERT	$expCombSUM_{uniform}$	0.792	0.839	0.384	0.551	0.45	0.61	0.482	0.638	0.38	0.42
	$expCombSUM_{binary}$	0.83	0.865	0.404	0.563	0.467	0.618	0.496	0.652	0.39	0.44
	$expCombSUM_{descending}$	0.813	0.843	0.39	0.551	0.454	0.609	0.486	0.644	0.38	0.42
	$expCombSUM_{parabolic}$	0.775	0.847	0.38	0.542	0.445	0.598	0.474	0.638	0.38	0.4
Retrofitted separate Sentence-BERT	$expCombSUM_{uniform}$	0.821	0.893	0.51	0.658	0.577	0.716	0.606	0.732	0.5	0.54
	$expCombSUM_{binary}$	**0.841**	0.893	**0.519**	0.661	0.584	0.718	0.616	0.75	0.51	0.54
	$expCombSUM_{descending}$	0.831	0.895	0.505	0.647	0.569	0.702	0.61	0.734	0.49	0.54
	$expCombSUM_{parabolic}$	0.808	0.863	0.509	0.658	0.583	0.724	0.596	0.732	0.5	0.53

Table 2: Results for the voting model author retrieval strategy. The best results are formatted in bold.

Queries			
'cluster analysis'	'Bayesian statistics'	'world wide web'	'Novelty detection'
'Image segmentation'	'kernel density estimation'	'gibbs sampling'	'semantic grid'
'Parallel algorithm'	'learning to rank'	'user interface'	'Knowledge extraction'
'Monte Carlo method'	'relational database'	'belief propagation'	'Computational biology'
'Convex optimization'	'activity recognition'	'interpolation'	'Web 2.0'
'Dimensionality reduction'	'wearable computer'	'wavelet transform'	'Network theory'
'Facial recognition system'	'ensemble learning'	'transfer of learning'	'Video denoising'
'k-nearest neighbors algorithm'	'wordnet'	'topic model'	'Quantum information science'
'Hierarchical clustering'	'medical imaging'	'clustering high-dimensional data'	'Color quantization'
'Automatic text summarization'	'deconvolution'	'game theory'	'social web'
'Dynamic programming'	'Latent Dirichlet allocation'	'biometrics'	'entity linking'
'Genetic algorithm'	'Euclidian distance'	'constraint satisfaction'	'information privacy'
'Human-computer interaction'	'web service'	'combinatorial optimization'	'random forest'
'Categorial grammar'	'multi-task learning'	'speech processing'	'cloud computing'
'Semantic Web'	'Linear separability'	'multi-agent system'	'Knapsack problem'
'fuzzy logic'	'OWL-S'	'mean field theory'	'Linear algebra'
'image restoration'	'Wireless sensor network'	'social network'	'batch processing'
'generative model'	'Semantic role labeling'	'lattice model'	'rule induction'
'search algorithm'	'Continuous-time Markov chain'	'automatic image annotation'	'Uncertainty quantification'
'sample size determination'	'Open Knowledge Base Connectivity'	'computational geometry'	'Computer architecture'
'anomaly detection'	'Propagation of uncertainty'	'Evolutionary algorithm'	'Best-first search'
'sentiment analysis'	'Fast Fourier transform'	'web search query'	'Gaussian random field'
'semantic similarity'	'Security token'	'eye tracking'	'Support vector machine'
'logic programming'	'machine translation'	'query optimization'	'ontology language'
'Hyperspectral imaging'	'middleware'	'Newton's method'	'big data'

Table 3: The full test queries set used for the system evaluation.

Learning CNF Blocking for Large-scale Author Name Disambiguation

Kunho Kim[†*], Athar Sefid[‡], C. Lee Giles[‡]
[†]Microsoft Corporation, Redmond, WA, USA
[‡] The Pennsylvania State University, University Park, PA, USA
kuki@microsoft.com, azs5955@psu.edu, clg20@psu.edu

Abstract

Author name disambiguation (AND) algorithms identify a unique author entity record from all similar or same publication records in scholarly or similar databases. Typically, a clustering method is used that requires calculation of similarities between each possible record pair. However, the total number of pairs grows quadratically with the size of the author database making such clustering difficult for millions of records. One remedy is a blocking function that reduces the number of pairwise similarity calculations. Here, we introduce a new way of learning blocking schemes by using a conjunctive normal form (CNF) in contrast to the disjunctive normal form (DNF). We demonstrate on PubMed author records that CNF blocking reduces more pairs while preserving high pairs completeness compared to the previous methods that use a DNF and that the computation time is significantly reduced. In addition, we also show how to ensure that the method produces disjoint blocks so that much of the AND algorithm can be efficiently paralleled. Our CNF blocking method is tested on the entire PubMed database of 80 million author mentions and efficiently removes 82.17% of all author record pairs in 10 minutes.

1 Introduction

Author name disambiguation (AND) refers to the problem of identifying each unique author entity record from all publication records in scholarly databases (Ferreira et al., 2012). It is also an important preprocessing step for a variety of problems. One example is processing author-related queries properly (e.g., identify all of a particular author's publications) in a digital library search engine. Another is to calculate author-related statistics such as an h-index, and collaboration relationships between authors.

Typically, a clustering method is used to calculate AND. Such clustering calculates pairwise similarities between each possible pairs of records that then determines whether each pair should be in the same cluster. Since the number of possible pairs in a database with the number of records n is $n(n-1)/2$, it grows as $O(n^2)$. Since n can be millions of authors in some databases such as PubMed, AND algorithms need methods that scale, such as a blocking function (Christen, 2012). The blocking function produces a reduced list of candidate pairs, and only the pairs on the list are considered for clustering.

Blocking usually consists of blocking predicates. Each predicate is a logical binary function with a combination of an attribute and a similarity criterion. One example can be exact match of the last name. A simple but effective way of blocking involves manually selecting the predicates, with respect to the data characteristics. Much recent work on large-scale AND uses a heuristic that is the *initial match of first name* and *exact match of last name* (Torvik and Smalheiser, 2009; Liu et al., 2014; Levin et al., 2012; Kim et al., 2016). Although this gives reasonable completeness, it can be problematic when the database is extremely large, such as the author mentions in CiteSeerX (10M publications, 32M authors), PubMed (24M publications, 88M authors), and Web of Science (45M publications, 163M authors)[1].

The blocking results on PubMed using this heuristic are shown in Table 1. Note that most of the block sizes are less than 100 names, but a few blocks are extremely large. Since the number

---

[*]Work done while the author was at Pennsylvania State University

A shorter preprint version of this paper was published at arXiv (Kim et al., 2017)

---

[1]Numbers were as of 2016.

Proceedings of the First Workshop on Scholarly Document Processing, pages 72–80
Online, November 19, 2020. ©2020 Association for Computational Linguistics
https://doi.org/10.18653/v1/P17

Table 1: Block Size Distribution of PubMed author mentions using the simple blocking heuristic.

Block Size	Frequency	Percentage
$2 \leq n < 10$	1,586,677	59.91%
$10 \leq n < 100$	910,272	34.37%
$100 \leq n < 1000$	144,361	5.45%
$1000 \leq n < 10000$	6,998	0.26%
$10000 \leq n < 50000$	184	0.01%
$n \geq 50000$	9	< 0.01%
Total	2,648,501	100.0 %

of pairs grows quadratically, those few blocks can dominate the computation time. This imbalance of the block size is due to the popularity of certain surnames, especially Asian names (Kim et al., 2016). To make matters worse, this problem increases in time, since the growth rates of publication records are rapidly increasing.

To improve the blocking, there has been work on learning the blocking (Bilenko et al., 2006; Michelson and Knoblock, 2006; Cao et al., 2011; Kejriwal and Miranker, 2013; Das Sarma et al., 2012; Fisher et al., 2015). These can be categorized into two different methods. One is a disjoint blocking, where each block is separated so each record belongs to a single block. Another is non-disjoint blocking, where some blocks have shared records. Each has advantages. Disjoint blocking can make the clustering step easily parallelized, while non-disjoint blocking often produces smaller blocks. and also has more degrees of freedom from which to select the similarity criterion.

Here, we propose to learn a non-disjoint blocking with a conjunctive normal form (CNF). Our main contributions are:

- Propose a CNF blocking, which reduces more pairs compared to DNF blocking, in order to achieve a large number of pairs completeness. This also reduces the processing time, which benefits various applications such as online disambiguation, author search, etc.

- Extend the method to produce disjoint blocks, so that the AND clustering step can be easily parallelized.

- Compare different gain functions, which are used to find the best blocking predicates for each step of learning.

Previous work is discussed in the next session. This is followed by problem definition. Next, we describe learning of CNF blocking and how to use it to ensure the production of disjoint blocks. Next, we evaluate our methods on the PubMed dataset. Finally, the last section consists of a summary work with possible future directions.

2   Related Work

Blocking has been widely studied for record linkage and entity disambiguation. Standard blocking is the simplest but most widely used method (Fellegi and Sunter, 1969). It is done by considering only pairs that meet all blocking predicates. Another is the sorted neighborhood approach (Hernández and Stolfo, 1995) which sorts the data by a certain blocking predicate, and forms blocks with pairs of those records within a certain window. Yan et al. (2007) further improved this method to adaptively select the size of the window. Aizawa and Oyama (2005) introduced a suffix array-based indexing method, which uses an inverted index of suffixes to generate candidate pairs. Canopy clustering (McCallum et al., 2000) generates blocks by clustering with a simple similarity measure and use loose & tight thresholds to generate overlapping clusters. Recent surveys (Christen, 2012; Papadakis et al., 2016, 2020) imply that there are no clear winners and proper parameter tuning is required for a specific task.

Much work optimized the blocking function for standard blocking. The blocking function is typically presented with a logical formula with blocking predicates. Two studies focused on learning a disjunctive normal form (DNF) blocking (Bilenko et al., 2006; Michelson and Knoblock, 2006) were published in the same year. Making use of manually labeled record pairs, they used a sequential covering algorithm to find the optimal blocking predicates in a greedy manner. Additional unlabeled data was used to estimate the reduction ratio of their cost function (Cao et al., 2011) while an unsupervised algorithm was used to automatically generate labeled pairs with rule-based heuristics used to learn DNF blocking (Kejriwal and Miranker, 2013).

All the work above proposed to learn non-disjoint blocking because of the logical *OR* terms in the DNF. However, other work learns the blocking function with a pure conjunction, to ensure the generation of disjoint blocks. Das et al. (2012) learns a conjunctive blocking tree, which has different blocking predicates for each branch of the tree. Fisher et al. (2015) produces blocks with respect to a size restriction, by generating candidate blocks with a list of predefined blocking predicates and then performs a merge and split to generate the block with the desired size.

Our work proposes a method for learning a non-disjoint blocking function in a conjunctive normal form (CNF). Our method is based on a previous CNF learner(Mooney, 1995), which uses the fact that a CNF can be a logical dual of a DNF.

3 Problem Definition

Our work tackles the same problem with baseline DNF blocking (Bilenko et al., 2006; Michelson and Knoblock, 2006), but in a different way to get the optimized blocking function. Let $R = \{r_1, r_2, \cdots, r_n\}$ be the set of records in the database, where n is the number of records. Each record r has k attributes, and A be the attribute set $A = \{a_1.a_2, \cdots, a_k\}$. A blocking predicate p is a combination of an attribute a and a similarity function s defined to a. An example of s is exact string match of a. A blocking predicate can be seen as a logical binary function applied to each pair of records, so $p(r_x, r_y) = \{0, 1\}$, where $r_x, r_y \in R$. A blocking function f is a boolean logic formula consisting with blocking predicates $p_1, p_2, \cdots, p_n$, and each predicate is connected with either conjunction $\wedge$ or disjunction $\vee$. An example is $f_{example} = (p_1 \wedge p_2) \vee p_3$. Since it is made up of blocking predicates, $f(r_x, r_y) = \{0, 1\}$ for all $r_x, r_y \in R$.

The goal is to find an optimal blocking function f^* that covers a minimum number of record pairs while missing up to a fraction ε of total number of matching record pairs. To formalize it,

$$f^* = \operatorname*{argmin}_{f} \sum_{(r_x, r_y) \in R} f(r_x, r_y) \tag{1}$$
$$\text{such that} \geq (1 - \varepsilon) \times |R^+|$$

where R^+ is set of matching record pairs.

4 Learning the Blocking Function

Here, we first briefly review DNF blocking and then introduce our CNF blocking function. This section describes the gain functions that select an optimal predicate term for each step in the CNF learner. Finally, we discuss an extension that ensures the production of disjunctive blocks.

Algorithm 1 DNF Blocking

1: **function** LEARNCONJTERMS(L, P, p, k)
2:     Let Pos be set of positive samples in L
3:     Let Neg be set of negative samples in L
4:     $Terms \leftarrow \{p\}$
5:     $CurTerm \leftarrow p$
6:     $i \leftarrow 1$
7:     **while** $i < k$ **do**
8:         Find $p_i \in P$ that maximizes gain function CALCGAIN($Pos, Neg, CurTerm \wedge p_i$)
9:         $CurTerm \leftarrow CurTerm \wedge p_i$
10:         Add $CurTerm$ to $Terms$
11:         $i \leftarrow i + 1$
12:     **end while**
13:     **return** $Terms$
14: **end function**
15:
16: **function** LEARNDNF(L, P, k)
17:     $CandTerms \leftarrow \phi$
18:     **for** $p \in P$ **do**
19:         $Terms \leftarrow$LEARNCONJ(L, P, p, k)
20:         $CandTerms \leftarrow CandTerms \cup Terms$
21:     **end for**
22:     Let Pos be set of positive samples in L
23:     Let Neg be set of negative samples in L
24:     $DNF \leftarrow \phi$
25:     **while** $|Pos| > \varepsilon \times |Pos|$ **do**
26:         Find $T \in CandTerms$ that maximizes gain function CALCGAIN(Pos, Neg, T)
27:         **if** CALCGAIN(Pos, Neg, t) > 0 **then**
28:             $DNF \leftarrow DNF \vee T$
29:             Let $PosCov$ be all $l \in Pos$ that satisfies T
30:             Let $NegCov$ be all $l \in Neg$ that satisfies T
31:             $Pos \leftarrow Pos - PosCov$
32:             $Neg \leftarrow Neg - NegCov$
33:         **else**
34:             break loop
35:         **end if**
36:     **end while**
37:     **return** DNF
38: **end function**

4.1 DNF Blocking

DNF blocking was originally proposed by (Bilenko et al., 2006; Michelson and Knoblock, 2006). Given labeled pairs, these methods attempt to learn the blocking function in the form of a DNF, the disjunction (logical *OR*) of conjunction (logical *AND*) terms. Learning DNFs is known to be a NP-hard problem (Bilenko et al., 2006). Thus, an approximation algorithm was used to learn k-DNF blocking by using a sequential covering algorithm. k-DNF means each conjunction term has, at most, k predicates. Algorithm 1 shows the process of DNF blocking. Function LEARNDNF in lines 16-38 is the main part of the algorithm. It has 3 inputs which are the L labeled sample pairs, P blocking predicates, and k parameters of maximum predicates considered for each conjunction term.

First, the algorithm selects a set of candidate conjunction terms with at most k predicates. For each predicate p, it generates k candidate conjunction terms with the highest gain function. Using the candidate terms, the algorithm learns the blocking function by using a sequential covering algorithm. It sequentially selects a conjunction term, from the set of candidates, that has the maximum gain value on the remaining samples, and attaches it with logical *OR* to the DNF term. In each step, all samples covered by the selected conjunction term are removed. This process repeats until it covers the desired minimum amount of positive samples, or there is no candidate term that can further be improved.

4.2 CNF Blocking

CNF blocking can be learned with a small modification to DNF blocking. CNF can be presented as the entire negation of a corresponding DNF and vice versa based on De Morgan's laws. Using this, Mooney proposed CNF learning (Mooney, 1995), which is a logical dual of DNF learning. This motivated our CNF blocking method.

Algorithm 2 illustrates the proposed CNF blocking and has a similar structure to algorithm 1. Instead of running a sequential covering algorithm to cover all positive samples, CNF blocking tries to cover all negative samples using negated blocking predicates. In other words, a DNF formula is learned that is consistent with a negated predicate, which we designate negated DNF ($NegDNF$). $NegP$ is the negation of each predicate p in P. LEARNCNF gets 3 inputs, where L are labeled

---

Algorithm 2 CNF Blocking

1: **function** LEARNNEGCONJTERMS($L, NegP, p, k$)
2:     Let Pos be set of positive samples in L
3:     Let Neg be set of negative samples in L
4:     $Terms \leftarrow \{p\}$
5:     $CurTerm \leftarrow p$
6:     $i \leftarrow 1$
7:     **while** $i < k$ **do**
8:         Find $p_i \in NegP$ that maximizes gain function CALCNEGGAIN($Pos, Neg, CurTerm \wedge p_i$)
9:         $CurTerm \leftarrow CurTerm \wedge p_i$
10:         Add $CurTerm$ to $Terms$
11:         $i \leftarrow i + 1$
12:     **end while**
13:     **return** $Terms$
14: **end function**
15:
16: **function** LEARNCNF(L, P, k)
17:     $CandTerms \leftarrow \phi$
18:     Let $NegP$ is negation of each $p \in P$
19:     **for** $p \in NegP$ **do**
20:         $Terms \leftarrow$ LEARNNEGCONJ($L, NegP, p, k$)
21:         $CandTerms \leftarrow CandTerms \cup Terms$
22:     **end for**
23:     Let Pos be set of positive samples in L
24:     Let Neg be set of negative samples in L
25:     $NegDNF \leftarrow \phi$
26:     **while** $|Pos| > (1 - \varepsilon) \times |Pos|$ **do**
27:         Find $T \in CandNegTerms$ that maximizes gain function CALCNEGGAIN($Pos, Neg, Term$)
28:         **if** CALCNEGGAIN(Pos, Neg, T) > 0 **then**
29:             $NegDNF \leftarrow NegDNF \vee T$
30:             Let $PosCov$ be all l in Pos that satisfies T
31:             Let $NegCov$ be all l in Neg that satisfies T
32:             $Pos \leftarrow Pos - PosCov$
33:             $Neg \leftarrow Neg - NegCov$
34:         **else**
35:             break loop
36:         **end if**
37:     **end while**
38:     $CNF \leftarrow \neg(NegDNF)$
39:     **return** CNF
40: **end function**

sample pairs, P are blocking predicates, and k is maximum number of predicates in each term.

The algorithm first generates a set of negated candidate conjunction term $Terms$ from all p in $NegP$ (line 19-22). A dual of the original gain function CALCNEGGAIN selects a predicate for generating a negated candidate conjunction. Then, as in DNF blocking, the sequential covering algorithm is used to learn the negated DNF formula (line 26-37), which iteratively adds a negated conjunction term until it covers the desired number of samples. We select a negated conjunction term with a gain function, CALCNEGGAIN. Also, note that the termination condition of the loop (line 26) is when ε of total positive samples are covered with the learned $NegDNF$. This ensures that we miss less than ε of the total number of positive samples in the final CNF formula. After getting the final $NegDNF$, it is negated to get the desired CNF.

4.3   Gain Function

The gain function estimates the benefit of adding a specific term to the learned formula. It is used in two different places in the algorithm - when choosing the conjunction candidates (line 8) and when choosing a term from the candidates for each iteration (line 27-28). Previous methods have proposed different gain functions. Here we describe each and compare the results in the experiments. P, N is the total number of positive and negative samples, and p, n is the number of remaining positive and negative samples covered by the term.

4.3.1   Information Gain

Originally from Mooney's CNF learner (1995), it is the dual of the information gain of a DNF learner

$$gain_{CNF} = n \times \left[\log\left(\frac{n}{n+p}\right) - \log\left(\frac{N}{N+P}\right) \right]. \tag{2}$$

4.3.2   Ratio Between Positive and Negative Samples Covered

Bilenko et al. (2006) used this for DNF blocking. It calculates the ratio between the number of positives and the number of negatives covered. For CNF learning, we use its dual

$$gain_{CNF} = \frac{n}{p}. \tag{3}$$

4.3.3   Reduction Ratio

Michaelson and Knoblock (2006) used terms with the maximum reduction ratio (RR). In addition,

---

Algorithm 3 Disjoint CNF Blocking

1: **function** DIS-JOINTCNF($L, P_{disjoint}, P_{full}, k$)
2:     $Conj \leftarrow$ LEARNCNF($L, P_{disjoint}, 1$)
3:     Let L' be set of $l \in L$ satisfies $Conj$
4:     $CNF \leftarrow$ LEARNCNF(L_{remain}, P_{full}, k)
5:     $Blocks \leftarrow$ Apply $Conj$ to whole data
6:     **for** $Block \in Blocks$ **do**
7:         Let L'' be $l \in Block$ that satisfies CNF
8:         Consider pairs in L'' only for clustering
9:     **end for**
10: **end function**

---

they filter out all terms with pairwise completeness (PC) below threshold t. We use the dual of the original function used as a CNF, which is now

$$gain_{CNF} = \begin{cases} \frac{p+n}{P+N} & \text{if } \frac{n}{N} > t \\ 0 & \text{otherwise.} \end{cases} \tag{4}$$

4.4   Learning Disjoint Blocks

Disjoint blocking functions generate blocks for each record that resides in a single block; thus such blocks are mutually exclusive. It has the advantage that parallelization can be performed efficiently after applying the blocking by running processes for each blocks separately. A blocking function is disjoint if and only if it satisfies the following conditions: 1) it only consists of pure conjunction (logical *AND*), 2) all predicates use non-relative similarity measures. That is, measures that compare the absolute value of blocking key, e.g. exact match of first n characters.

DNF and CNF blocking are both non-disjoint blocking due to the condition 1 above. We introduce a simple extension to ensure our CNF blocking can produce disjoint blocks. This is done by first producing two blocking functions. The first function learns a blocking function with only conjunctions based on our CNF blocking method using $k = 1$ and a limited set of predicates with non-relative similarity measures. Then, CNF blocking is learned with our k-CNF method with the whole set of predicates for pairs remaining after applying 1-CNF (conjunction of single attributes).

We first apply the 1-CNF to the whole database to produce disjoint blocks. Then for each block, we apply the second k-CNF blocking function to filter out pairs not satisfies the k-CNF function. This is similar to applying a filter as in Gu and Baxter

Table 2: Summary of PubMed Benchmark Dataset

# Authors	# Mentions	# Total Pairs	# Matched Pairs
214	3,964	7,854,666	51,052

(2004) and Khabsa et al. (2015). While they use a heuristic, our method automatically learns the optimal one. Note that this method still produces a CNF since it combines conjunction terms and k-CNF with logical *AND*.

5   Experiments

5.1   Benchmark Dataset

We use the PubMed to evaluate these methods. PubMed is a public large-scale scholarly database maintained by the National Center for Biotechnology Information (NCBI) at the National Library of Medicine (NLM). We use NIH principal investigator (PI) data for evaluation, which include PI IDs and corresponding publications. We randomly picked 10 names from the most frequent ones in the dataset and manually verified that all publications belong to each PI. The set of names include C* Lee, J* Chen, J* Smith, M* Johnson, M* Miller, R* Jones, S* Kim, X* Yang, Y* Li, Y* Wang, where C* means any name starts with C.

Table 2 shows the statistics of the dataset. Experiments are done with 5-fold cross validation.

5.2   Methodology

5.2.1   Evaluation Metrics

We evaluate our CNF blocking with reduction ratio (RR), pairs completeness (PC), and F-measure. These metrics are often used to evaluate blocking methods. Those metrics can be calculated as follows:

$$RR = 1 - \frac{p + n}{P + N}, \tag{5}$$

$$PC = \frac{p}{P}, \tag{6}$$

$$F = \frac{2 \times RR \times PC}{RR + PC}. \tag{7}$$

where P, N are the numbers of positive and negative samples, and p, n are the numbers of positive and negative samples covered with the blocking function. RR measures the efficiency of the blocking function, PC measures the quality of the blocking function. F is the harmonic mean of RR and PC.

Table 3: Blocking Predicates Used for Learning Non-Disjoint Blocking Function

Blocking Key	Similarity Criterion
First Name	$exact, first(n), last(n), compatible$
Last Name	$exact, first(n), last(n), compatible$
Middle Name	$exact, first(n), last(n), compatible$
Title	cos
Affiliation	$exact, cos, compatible$
Coauthor	cos
Order	$order$
Year	$exact, digit, diff$
Venue	$exact, cos$

5.2.2   Blocking Predicates Used

We first define the similarity criterion used for the experiments. We observed an important characteristic of the data: some attributes are empty (e.g. year: 7.8%, affiliation: 81.1%) or have only partial information (54.5% has only initials for the first name). To deal with this, we add *compatible* to those blocking keys. Below is brief explanation of each similarity criterion.

- *exact*: Exact match.

- $first(n), last(n)$:   First/Last n character match, where n is an integer. We check $\{1, 3, 5, 7\}$ for name attributes.

- *order*: Assigns $True$ if both records are first authors, last authors, or non-first and non-last authors.

- $digit(n)$:   First n digit match. We check $\{1, 2, 3\}$ for year.

- *compatible*: $True$ if at least one of the records are empty (Eq. 8). If the key is name, it also checks if the initial matches if one of the records has only initial.

$$compatible(A, B) = \begin{cases} True & \text{if at least one is empty} \\ exact(A, B) & \text{otherwise} \end{cases} \tag{8}$$

- *cos*:   Cosine distance of TF-IDF bag-of-words vector.   We check with threshold $\{0.2, 0.4, 0.6, 0.8\}$.

- $diff$: Year difference. We use the threshold $\{2, 5, 10\}$.

Using those similarity measures, We define two different sets of blocking predicates. Table 3 shows

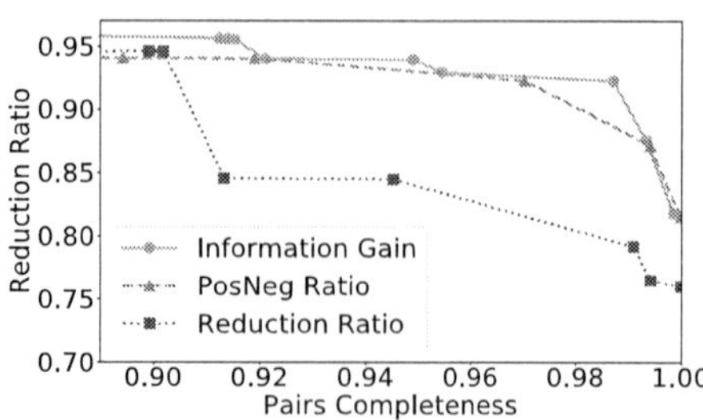

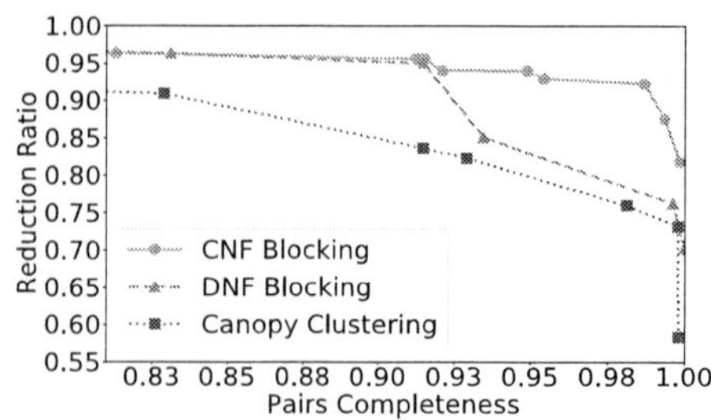

Figure 1: Gain Functions for PC–RR where PosNeg Ratio is the ratio between positive and negative samples covered.

Figure 2: PC–RR for non-disjoint blocking methods

blocking predicates used for non-disjoint blocking. Disjoint blocking requires the use of predicates with non-relative similarity measures to ensure blocks are mutually exclusive. For disjoint blocking, we use the set of blocking predicates excluding the ones with the relative similarity measures ($exact$, $compatible$, $diff$) in Table 3.

5.2.3 Parameter Setting

The parameter ε is used to vary the PC. We tested values in $[0, 1]$ to get the PC–RR curve. k is selected experimentally to calculate the maximum reachable F-measure. We use $k = 3$ for further experiments.

5.3 Experiments

5.3.1 Gain Function

Figure 1 shows the PC–RR curve tested on three different gain functions. Blocking usually requires a high PC, so that we do not lose matched pairs after it is applied. As such, we focused on experiments with high PC values. As we can see from the results, information gain has highest RR overall. Thus, we use it as the gain function for the rest of the experiments.

5.3.2 Non-disjoint CNF Blocking

We compare non-disjoint CNF blocking with the DNF blocking (Bilenko et al., 2006; Michelson and Knoblock, 2006) and canopy clustering (McCallum et al., 2000). We used the set of Jaro–Winkler distance attributes for canopy clustering. Figure 2 shows the PC–RR curve for each method. Both CNF and DNF were better than canopy clustering, as was shown in Bilenko et al. (2006). CNF and DNF results are comparable for lower PC values. However, for high PC (>0.9) values, CNF has a better RR. We also tested another dataset used

in (Khabsa et al., 2015). For PC=0.99, RR for CNF blocking was 0.882 while DNF blocking was 0.745.

We believe this is due to certain characteristics of scholarly databases. As discussed on the previous section, some attributes are empty for some records. DNF learns a blocking function by adding conjunction terms to gradually cover positive pairs. Although the proposed similarity criterion $compatible$ could catch positive pairs with empty attributes, it allows many negative pairs to pass the criterion, which makes the RR low. On the other hand, CNF learns a blocking function to cover (and filter out) negative pairs gradually. Negative pairs are much more obvious to define (pairs with different values), which makes the CNF more effective.

Another advantage of using CNF is the processing time. Fast processing time to apply blocking is important for some applications, one example is when we do a online disambiguation (Khabsa et al., 2015), another is to do an author search which requires to find the relevant cluster quickly (Kim et al., 2018). We measured the average processing time of applying each blocking method at high PC (PC=0.99), CNF blocking, DNF blocking, canopy clustering took 1.39s, 2.09s, 0.44s respectively. Canopy clustering was the fastest but generally we saw from the Figure 2 that its RR is much lower in high PC. CNF blocking has a faster processing time compared to DNF blocking. This is because CNF is composed with conjunctions, so it can quickly reject pairs that are not consistent with any terms. On the other hand, DNF consists of disjunction terms, so each pair should check all terms to make the decision. Learned CNF is also simpler than DNF. Learned CNF at this level is as below (fn, mn, ln is first, middle, last name respectively):

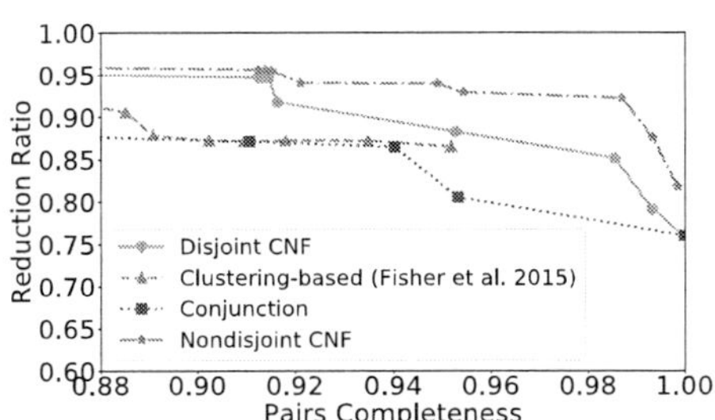

Figure 3: PC–RR for disjoint blocking methods

$\{(fn, first(5)) \vee (fn, compatible) \vee (coauth, cos(0.8))\}$
$\wedge \{(ln, exact)\}$
$\wedge \{(mn, compatible)\}$
$\wedge \{((fn, first(3)) \vee (fn, compatible))\}$

And learned DNF is:
$\{((coauth, cos(0.8)) \wedge (ln, exact) \wedge (mn, compatible))\}$
$\vee \{((venue, cos(0.4)) \wedge (mn, first(1)) \wedge (fn, compatible)\}$
$\vee \{(fn, compatible) \wedge (mn, first(1)) \wedge (ln, exact)\}$
$\vee \{((venue, cos(0.8)) \wedge (fn, exact)\}$

In addition, we observed that proposed *compatible* predicate was frequently used in our result. This shows the effectiveness of *compatible* in dealing with the empty value.

5.3.3 Extension to Disjoint CNF Blocking

We evaluate our extension to disjoint blocks with CNF blocking. We compare the blocking learned with a pure conjunction, our proposed method, and the method of Fisher et al. (2015).

Figure 3 shows the reduction ratio pair completion (RR–PC) curve for each method. We also plot the original non-disjoint CNF blocking for comparison. We see that our proposed disjoint CNF blocking is the best amongst all disjoint methods. Fisher's method produced nearly uniform-sized blocks, but had limitations in reaching a high PC and had a generally lower RR compared to our method. Disjoint CNF didn't perform as well when compared to non-disjoint CNF because it is forced to use a pure conjunction on its first step. However, this simple extension easily helps parallelize the clustering process, so that the algorithm scales better. Testing our method to all of PubMed, 82.17% of the pairs are created in 10.5 min with 24 threads. Parallelization is important for disambiguation algorithms to scale to PubMed size scholarly databases (Khabsa et al., 2014).

Processing time for disjoint CNF blocking

comparable to the original non-disjoint CNF blocking. The learned disjoint CNF is:
$\{(fn, first(1))\} \wedge \{(ln, exact)\} \wedge$
$\{(fn, compatible) \vee (coauth, cos(0.8))\} \wedge$
$\{(mn, compatible)\}$

First two terms are from 1-CNF, and others from 3-CNF learner. We also tested this function to the whole PubMed.

6 Conclusion

We show how to learn an efficient blocking function with a conjunctive normal form (CNF) of blocking predicates. Using CNF as a negation of the corresponding disjunctive normal form (DNF) of predi-cates (Mooney, 1995), our method is a logical dual of existing DNF blocking methods (Bilenko et al., 2006; Michelson and Knoblock, 2006). We find that our method reduces more pairs for a large number of target pairs completeness and has a faster run time. We devise an extension that ensures that our CNF blocking produces disjoint blocks. Thus, the clustering process can be efficiently parallelized.

Future work could use multiple levels of block-ing functions for processing each block (Das Sarma et al., 2012) and using linear programming to find an optimal CNF (Su et al., 2016).

7 Acknowledgement

We gratefully acknowledge partial support from the National Science Foundation and the National Bu-reau of Economic Research and useful discussions with Bruce Weinberg.

References

Akiko Aizawa and Keizo Oyama. 2005. A fast linkage detection scheme for multi-source information inte-gration. In *International Workshop on Challenges in Web Information Retrieval and Integration*, pages 30–39.

Mikhail Bilenko, Beena Kamath, and Raymond J. Mooney. 2006. Adaptive blocking: Learning to scale up record linkage. In *Proceedings of the 6th IEEE International Conference on Data Min-ing(ICDM'06)*, pages 87–96.

Yunbo Cao, Zhiyuan Chen, Jiamin Zhu, Pei Yue, Chin-Yew Lin, and Yong Yu. 2011. Leveraging unlabeled data to scale blocking for record linkage. In *Pro-ceedings of the International Joint Conference on Ar-tificial Intelligence (IJCAI)*, volume 22, page 2211.

Peter Christen. 2012. A survey of indexing techniques for scalable record linkage and deduplication. *IEEE Transactions on Knowledge and Data Engineering (TKDE)*, 24(9):1537–1555.

Anish Das Sarma, Ankur Jain, Ashwin Machanavajjhala, and Philip Bohannon. 2012. An automatic blocking mechanism for large-scale de-duplication tasks. In *Proceedings of the 21st ACM international conference on Information and knowledge management (CIKM)*, pages 1055–1064.

Ivan P Fellegi and Alan B Sunter. 1969. A theory for record linkage. *Journal of the American Statistical Association*, 64(328):1183–1210.

Anderson A. Ferreira, Marcos André Gonçalves, and Alberto H.F. Laender. 2012. A brief survey of automatic methods for author name disambiguation. *Acm Sigmod Record*, 41(2):15–26.

Jeffrey Fisher, Peter Christen, Qing Wang, and Erhard Rahm. 2015. A clustering-based framework to control block sizes for entity resolution. In *Proceedings of the 21th ACM SIGKDD International Conference on Knowledge Discovery and Data Mining*, pages 279–288.

Lifang Gu and Rohan Baxter. 2004. Adaptive filtering for efficient record linkage. In *Proceedings of the 2004 SIAM International Conference on Data Mining*, pages 477–481.

Mauricio A Hernández and Salvatore J Stolfo. 1995. The merge/purge problem for large databases. In *ACM Sigmod Record*, volume 24, pages 127–138.

Mayank Kejriwal and Daniel P Miranker. 2013. An unsupervised algorithm for learning blocking schemes. In *Proceedings of the IEEE 13th International Conference on Data Mining (ICDM)*, pages 340–349.

Madian Khabsa, Pucktada Treeratpituk, and C. Lee Giles. 2014. Large scale author name disambiguation in digital libraries. In *IEEE International Conference on Big Data*, pages 41–42.

Madian Khabsa, Pucktada Treeratpituk, and C. Lee Giles. 2015. Online person name disambiguation with constraints. In *Proceedings of the ACM/IEEE Joint Conference on Digital Libraries(JCDL'15)*, pages 37–46.

Kunho Kim, Madian Khabsa, and C. Lee Giles. 2016. Random forest dbscan clustering for uspto inventor name disambiguation and conflation. In *IJCAI-16 Workshop on Scholarly Big Data: AI Perspectives, Challenges, and Ideas*.

Kunho Kim, Athar Sefid, and C Lee Giles. 2017. Scaling author name disambiguation with cnf blocking. *arXiv preprint arXiv:1709.09657*.

Kunho Kim, Athar Sefid, and C. Lee Giles. 2018. A web service for author name disambiguation in scholarly databases. In *Proceedings of the IEEE International Conference on Web Services (ICWS)*, pages 265–273.

Michael Levin, Stefan Krawczyk, Steven Bethard, and Dan Jurafsky. 2012. Citation-based bootstrapping for large-scale author disambiguation. *Journal of the American Society for Information Science and Technology*, 63(5):1030–1047.

Wanli Liu, Rezarta Islamaj Doğan, Sun Kim, Donald C Comeau, Won Kim, Lana Yeganova, Zhiyong Lu, and W John Wilbur. 2014. Author name disambiguation for pubmed. *Journal of the Association for Information Science and Technology*, 65(4):765–781.

Andrew McCallum, Kamal Nigam, and Lyle H Ungar. 2000. Efficient clustering of high-dimensional data sets with application to reference matching. In *Proceedings of the sixth ACM SIGKDD international conference on Knowledge discovery and data mining*, pages 169–178.

Matthew Michelson and Craig A Knoblock. 2006. Learning blocking schemes for record linkage. In *Proceedings of the 21st AAAI Conference on Artificial Intelligence*, pages 440–445.

Raymond J Mooney. 1995. Encouraging experimental results on learning cnf. *Machine Learning*, 19(1):79–92.

George Papadakis, Dimitrios Skoutas, Emmanouil Thanos, and Themis Palpanas. 2020. Blocking and filtering techniques for entity resolution: A survey. *ACM Computing Surveys (CSUR)*, 53(2):1–42.

George Papadakis, Jonathan Svirsky, Avigdor Gal, and Themis Palpanas. 2016. Comparative analysis of approximate blocking techniques for entity resolution. *Proceedings of the VLDB Endowment*, 9(9):684–695.

Guolong Su, Dennis Wei, Kush R Varshney, and Dmitry M Malioutov. 2016. Learning sparse two-level boolean rules. In *Proceedings of the IEEE 26th International Workshop on Machine Learning for Signal Processing (MLSP)*, pages 1–6.

Vetle I Torvik and Neil R Smalheiser. 2009. Author name disambiguation in medline. *ACM Transactions on Knowledge Discovery from Data (TKDD)*, 3(3):11.

Su Yan, Dongwon Lee, Min-Yen Kan, and Lee C Giles. 2007. Adaptive sorted neighborhood methods for efficient record linkage. In *Proceedings of the 7th ACM/IEEE-CS joint conference on Digital libraries*, pages 185–194.

Reconstructing Manual Information Extraction with *DB-to-Document Backprojection*: Experiments in the Life Science Domain

Mark-Christoph Müller, Sucheta Ghosh, Maja Rey, Ulrike Wittig,
Wolfgang Müller and Michael Strube
Heidelberg Institute for Theoretical Studies gGmbH, Heidelberg, Germany
{mark-christoph.mueller,sucheta.ghosh,maja.rey,
ulrike.wittig,wolfgang.mueller,michael.strube}@h-its.org

Abstract

We introduce a novel scientific document processing task for making previously inaccessible information in printed paper documents available to automatic processing. We describe our data set of scanned documents and data records from the biological database SABIO-RK, provide a definition of the task, and report findings from preliminary experiments. Rigorous evaluation proved challenging due to lack of gold-standard data and a difficult notion of correctness. Qualitative inspection of results, however, showed the feasibility and usefulness of the task.

1 Introduction

Research results from the life sciences are mainly published in the form of written journal or conference papers, even though these results often take the form of measurements of experimental parameters, which would more appropriately be stored in a structured, machine-readable form. While there is some tendency towards directly publishing experimental data, e.g. on SourceData (Liechti et al., 2016) or (for environmental data) PANGAEA[1], this is not the norm yet, and does not help with the huge body of data already published in the conventional literature. It is common practice in the life sciences, therefore, to manually extract information (including measurements and the experimental conditions underlying them) from natural language documents, and to use it to populate biological databases. This process is called *biocuration* (International Society for Biocuration, 2018) and comprises, for every document, 1) identification and mark-up of curatable information, 2) data extraction, normalization, and consolidation, and 3) database insertion. Despite constant improvements in NLP technology, biocuration involves significant human labor (mostly reading) (Oughtred

et al., 2019; Huang et al., 2020; Wu et al., 2020; Abdelhakim et al., 2020), because data *quality* (i.e. correctness and integrity) has priority over *quantity* (i.e. more quickly available, but potentially less reliable, data), and the error rates of current NLP systems are still considered too high (Karp, 2016). For reasons of ergonomics and ease of handling (Buchanan and Loizides, 2007; Köpper et al., 2016; Clinton, 2019), the identification and mark-up step often involves paper printouts and highlighter pens,[2] like in the example page in Figure 1.

Figure 1: Page with mark-up (best viewed in color).

As mere intermediate products of the curation process, the manually highlighted printouts are only required until all data from the respective document has been curated, and they will normally be archived afterwards. We argue, however, that the printouts contain even *more* information which curation simply does not make full use of: First, some document sections, although containing highlighting, will *not* lead to the creation of a record in the biological database (see our results in Section 5.3). Yet, this highlighting can still be regarded as a kind of relevance annotation, produced by life science

---

[1]www.pangaea.de

[2]This is true for our own group, and has been corroborated in 2016 by an informal, unpublished survey among 21 curators from 15+ biological databases. The survey showed that a considerable number of curators rely on paper printouts for close reading and / or highlighting of important information.

Proceedings of the First Workshop on Scholarly Document Processing, pages 81–90
Online, November 19, 2020. ©2020 Association for Computational Linguistics
https://doi.org/10.18653/v1/P17

domain experts through attentive, task-oriented reading. Obviously, this information should be useful, e.g. for the analysis of how important information is dispersed over a scientific document. Second, for those database records that *are* created from highlighted document sections, the reference to that section is normally not preserved. Again, an obvious way to use this information is to allow users of the biological database to visually trace the record to its source in the document, including the original context.

In this paper, we describe our approach towards re-purposing scientific document printouts which were manually highlighted during biocuration. More precisely, our research question is: *Given records of curated information from the database and the original, scanned source document, (to what degree) can we recover the document section that a particular record was extracted from?* We consider this to be a novel scientific document processing task, and propose to refer to it as **DB-to-document backprojection**. The remainder of the paper is structured as follows. In Section 2 we describe the data basis of our work. Section 3 introduces the *highlighted text extraction* task, which we consider as self-contained and only loosely linked to the main task. Section 4 deals with the actual DB-to-document backprojection task, provides a precise definition, and describes our processing steps. Section 5 presents some preliminary experiments, results, and error analysis.Initially, this section will also discuss our approach to evaluation. In Section 6 we discuss some related work, and Section 7 contains our conclusions and directions for the future. Note that, although our data is from the life sciences, the task is relevant for all domains where manual information extraction is performed on natural language documents (like e.g. in Lipani et al. (2014), where information is extracted from IR research papers in the form of machine-readable 'nanopublications').

2 Data

The work in this paper is based on two related data sets, which have been collected in the SABIO-RK Biochemical Reaction Kinetics Database project[3]. SABIO-RK is a curated database containing structured information about biochemical reactions and their corresponding kinetics (Wittig et al., 2017, 2018). The **document data set** is an electronic

version of our archive of $6{,}000+$ manually highlighted printouts of documents from the life science domain, which have been curated in the 10+ years of our database's existence. Over the years, numerous different curators were involved in the manual mark-up. Different highlighter colors were used, sometimes even within the same document (see Figure 1). In case of equivalent information appearing repeatedly in the same document, curators generally attempted to be economical and to avoid redundancy by highlighting only the *most appropriate* appearance, which is often, but not always, the *first* appearance. While the mark-up was performed in a completely unrestricted manner (cf. below), in the vast majority of cases, highlighting was applied directly to words or lines (cf. Figure 1), which greatly helped in extracting the highlighted text (cf. Section 3). In some rare cases, curators selected whole sections by drawing a vertical line at the section's margin. Also, data in tables was sometimes highlighted on the cell level, while in other cases, only the column header, the table header, or even the table caption was highlighted. We created an electronic version of the document collection by scanning and OCR-processing all papers[4], which resulted in a sandwich PDF for each document with the (partially highlighted) background superimposed with the extracted text. OCR was performed with commercial software (Alaris Capture Pro), which was used out-of-the-box. The total number of tokens in the 98 documents is $630{,}153$, with $6{,}430$ tokens/document on average.

The second data set is the **record data set** which contains measurements of kinetic parameters that were extracted from individual documents from the document collection in the course of manual curation. Each of the $2{,}916$ records in this data set is linked to exactly one source document (via its PubMed ID), but no lower-level links (to pages or lines) exist. Each document, in turn, can be linked to an arbitrary number of records (29.76 records/document on average). It has to be noted that the above count of $2{,}916$ records contains a considerable number of *multiple counts*. This is true in particular for records of type *experimental condition* (cf. below), and is due to the fact that often, several measurements are performed under identical experimental conditions. For scoring and evaluation, however, this does not make a differ-

[3] http://sabio.h-its.org/

[4]For the experiments reported in this paper, we only use a subset of 98 documents.

ence, because we conflate semantically identical records before analysis. There are two main types of records, *experimental condition* and *parameter*. Each record consists of three to six attribute-value (a-v) pairs. Figures 2 and 3 show one example of each type of record.

```
conditionName: 'pH',
startValue    :  7.7,
buffer        : '0.10 M Tris-HCl,
                 100 mM KCl, 1 mM DTT,
                 4.0 mM MgCl2,
                 10% Glycerol'
```

Figure 2: Record of type *experimental condition* with three a-v pairs featuring one numeric, one atomic string, and one complex string value.

```
parameterName      : 'Km',
unitName           : 'µM',
startValue         :  123,
standardDeviation:   12,
associatedSpecies: 'Acetyl-CoA'
```

Figure 3: Record of type *parameter* with five a-v pairs, featuring two numeric and three atomic string values.

Note that we only consider a subset of all a-v pairs available for each record: Some attributes have unspecific values (e.g. `role:'Variable'`) which are not useful for searching. Also, most attributes have a variant with a *normalized* value, which does not appear in the text. With the exception of the experimental conditions' `buffer` attribute, all values are atomic. Therefore, the `buffer` attribute will be handled differently in the second phase of backprojection (see Section 4.2).

3   Highlighted Text Extraction

Highlighted text extraction comprises 1) extracting from each sandwich PDF both the searchable plain text and a background image for every page, 2) detecting highlighted areas in the background images, and 3) mapping the detected image areas to the extracted text. The workflow is shown in Figure 4. We use both `pdftohtml` and `pdftotext` from the Poppler[5] library to extract data from the scanned and OCR-processed sandwich PDF documents from our collection. The only task of `pdftohtml` is to extract, from each page, a PNG image with the non-textual background, which also includes the color-marked areas. These images were already generated during OCR processing and

consist of document pages from which pixels that were detected as belonging to text were removed by inpainting (see 'Page background image' in the lower left part of Figure 4). `pdftotext`, on the other hand, is used to extract the text that was previously recognized by OCR. It produces one XML file for the document, incl. bounding boxes on the token-level. These tokens reflect the original document layout, but come in correct reading order even for multi-column documents. The second step makes use of some simple image processing. As described above (Section 2), document highlighting can come in any color, so searching for areas of any *particular* color (like e.g. yellow) is not an option. Instead, our algorithm combines the facts that 1) highlighting is always *non-grey* and 2) shades of grey in the RGB color model are characterized by identical, or at least highly similar, values in the R, G, and B components.[6] We create a binarized version of each page by going over all pixels in a copy of the original image and setting each pixel to 'black' if the difference between the R, G, and B components is above a threshold of 50 (i.e. if the pixel is non-grey), and setting it to 'white' otherwise. The resulting image, then, contains regions with higher and lower density of black pixels (see 'Binarized page background image' in Figure 4). In the last step, text tokens are labelled as highlighted if their bounding boxes (from the XML file), when projected to the binarized image, cover an area that is at least 50% black. While this process is very simple, we found it to work surprisingly well, at least for the very frequent cases where the highlighting was applied directly to words or lines, yielding almost perfect extraction accuracy on most of the images we inspected. Of the $630,153$ tokens in our data set, only $39,071$ (6.2%) were detected as containing highlighting.

4   DB-to-Document Backprojection

4.1   Task Definition

DB-to-document backprojection attempts to reconstruct the manual information extraction performed during database curation, by recovering those document sections that the curated database records were extracted from. It works by matching database record values (as strings) to plain text from document sections. More precisely, we define the task as follows: Let $\mathbf{D}$ be the document data set, $\mathbf{R}$ the record data set, $\mathbf{R(d)}$ the set of

---

[5] https://poppler.freedesktop.org

[6] https://en.wikipedia.org/wiki/Grey

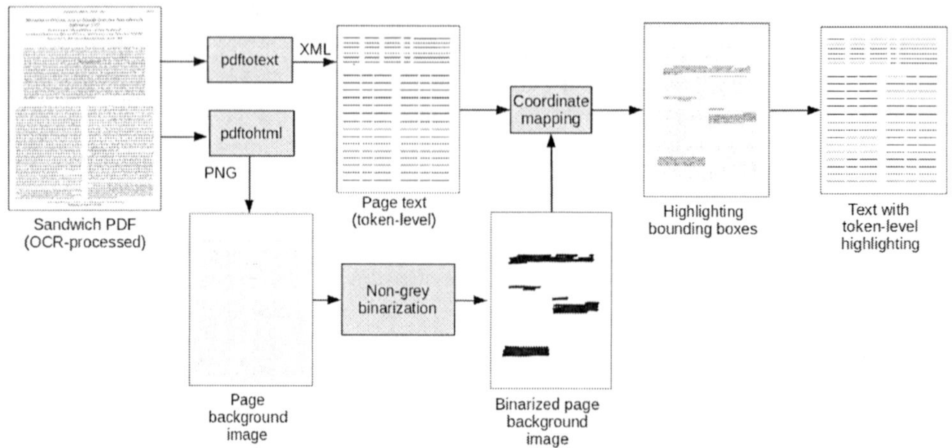

Figure 4: Highlighted text extraction workflow (best viewed in color).

records that were extracted from document $\mathbf{d} \in \mathbf{D}$, and $\mathbf{V(r)}$ the set of values belonging to record $\mathbf{r} \in \mathbf{R(d)}$. Also, let $\mathbf{SEC(d, sec\_size)}$ be the set of document sections of *sec_size* tokens into which document $\mathbf{d} \in \mathbf{D}$ can be segmented. Then, for every document $\mathbf{d} \in \mathbf{D}$, for every section $\mathbf{s} \in \mathbf{SEC(d, sec\_size)}$, and for every record $\mathbf{r} \in \mathbf{R(d)}$, a backprojection score between 0.0 and 1.0 is computed by counting how many of the values in $\mathbf{V(r)}$ can be matched to the tokens in $\mathbf{s}$, and normalizing by the total number of values in $\mathbf{V(r)}$. The result is a list of $< record, section, score >$ tuples for every document, from which the most *plausible* backprojections still needs to be selected (cf. Section 5.1).

The following is worth noting. First and foremost, the above definition reflects the fact that there is no simple notion of a *correct* backprojection of a database record to a document section, neither in our data sets nor, arguably, in reality. In part, this is because the same (or highly similar) information can appear in more than one section of a document. Second, the value of *sec_size* is important because, by specifying the number of tokens that are considered at the same time, it might penalize records with a comparably large number of values. At the same time, however, an excessively large *sec_size* will undermine the whole endeavour because it will be difficult to locate the actual matched values within the section. Also, with increasing *sec_size*, there is a growing risk of clustering values which are actually completely unrelated, creating spurious backprojection results. Finally, the role of automatically detected highlighting for DB-to-document backprojection is still unclear. Since obtaining this highlighting information was the prime reason for scanning the paper printouts in the first place, a rather strong contribution of this feature is desirable. One obvious role of highlighting is that of a filter for preventing *non*-highlighted tokens from being potential backprojection targets.

4.2   Processing Steps

The following two steps are performed for every document $\mathbf{d} \in \mathbf{D}$ and for every record $\mathbf{r} \in \mathbf{R(d)}$. In the first step, **search term creation**, the non-empty values in $\mathbf{V(r)}$ are converted into search terms. Initially, one search term list is created for each non-empty $\mathbf{v} \in \mathbf{V(r)}$. Thus, a record with three values will yield as many search term lists with *one* term each (an example is given below). These three lists are *complementary*, i.e. we try to match elements of as many of them as possible in a given document section. In order to improve matching and to capture variations introduced by spelling alternatives and / or OCR errors, we apply the following heuristics, which add *alternative* search terms to individual search term lists: For numerical values with a decimal point (e.g. '9.5') we add a term where that character is replaced by a comma. If OCR_OPTIMIZE=TRUE: For string values containing the μ character (e.g. 'μg/ml' or 'μM'), we add a term where that character is replaced by a 'p', which is a common OCR error / substitution. Likewise, for string values containing a lowercase 'm' character at the end (e.g. Km), we add several terms where that character is replaced by 'tn', 'ni', and a combination of commas, which are common OCR errors if the 'm' appears as a subscript. If

USE_SYNONYMS=TRUE: For string values representing chemical compound names, we consult a look-up table and add synonyms, spelling variants, or abbreviations as alternative terms.

For illustration, with OCR_OPTIMIZE=TRUE, the record of type *parameter* from Figure 3 above yields the following list of search term lists, with a range of possible matches from zero to five, corresponding to its number of values. Note the spelling variants for the first and second value. During term matching (cf. below), only *one* item per search term list needs to match in order for the value (first item in each list) to match.

```
[['Km', 'Ktn', 'Kni', 'K,,,'],
 ['μM', 'pM'],
 ['123'],
 ['12'],
 ['Acetyl-CoA']]
```

As mentioned in Section 2, the `buffer` attribute of records of type *experimental condition* is special because its value is a manually edited, comma-separated string containing several chemical substance names (see Figure 2). We split each value string into a list of individual substance names, and add each of these names as an *additional* search term list for that record.

Then, in the second step, the actual **term matching** is performed in the following way: For each document $\mathbf{d} \in \mathbf{D}$, we iterate over all tokens in $\mathbf{d}$ (extracted from the XML output of `pdftotext`, cf. Section 3), all records $\mathbf{r} \in \mathbf{R(d)}$, and all search term lists created for the respective $\mathbf{r}$ in the previous step. Then, we iterate over the terms in each search term list, trying to match each one in turn. Matching is done simply by using regular expressions. If a term can be matched to a token, we collect the matching record's ID and the matched value in the token's matchlist, and move on to the next search term list. This matching process is performed only once, and it is the same regardless of the value of *sec_size*.

Next, sections of different sizes are created by moving a window of size *sec_size* over all tokens in $\mathbf{d}$, one token at a time. These sections are the potential targets for backprojection. In our experiments, *sec_size* ranges from 3 to 39, in steps of 3, and the following steps are performed for each value of *sec_size*. If the first token in a potential section has a non-empty match list, a matching result for the entire section is computed in the following way: First, all record IDs with a match anywhere in the section are collected. Then, for each of these records, a

section score is computed by counting the *distinct* matches in the section and normalizing that with the maximum number of possible matches. The restriction to *distinct* values means that if a term matches more than one token in a section, it is only counted once *for each record*. Without this restriction, values appearing repeatedly in the same section (like e.g. unit names) would incorrectly boost the scores for the respective records. In most cases, a record will match several sections with different scores, but we only select the top scoring sections for each record. In the end, this results in a mapping of record IDs to the top score for these records and a list of sections with this score.

In addition, we introduce the following experimental parameters into the backprojection step: **HL_ROLE**: If HL_ROLE=IGNORE, highlighting information is not used, if HL_ROLE=ONLY, only highlighted tokens (as determined by highlighted text extraction (Section 3) will be considered for matching. **MIN_MATCHES**: The minimum number of values for a record that need to match in a section in order for that section to be considered. MIN_MATCHES < 2 will yield a lot of spurious matches. **REQUIRE_NUM_MATCH**: If REQUIRE_NUM_MATCH=TRUE, at least one of the matched record values in a section must be numeric. This is based on the rationale that numeric values are more distinctive than e.g. matches for parameter or unit names.

5   Experiments

5.1   A Note on Evaluation

As described in the task definition in the previous Section 4, the result of performing a DB-to-document backprojection run with a given set of parameters on a single document is a mapping of each record in the document to those section(s) that yielded the maximum score for that record (possibly none). While the *inspection* of this result (including visualisation, cf. below) is straightforward, an actual quantitative *evaluation* is more difficult. This evaluation would have to include the identification of true and false positives (i.e. records that are backprojected to correct resp. incorrect document sections) and false negatives (i.e. records that were *not* backprojected even though a document section with a sufficient fraction of the record's values exists). This form of evaluation is out of the scope of the present paper. The most obvious reason is that, at least at present, no annotated gold-level data is available which specifies, for each record, one or more document sections as the correct backprojection target. In addition, it will become clear in what follows that there not even is a simple notion of a *correct* backprojection.

5.2 Preliminary Experiments

We performed a couple of preliminary experiments, at first setting the parameters to HL_ROLE= IGNORE, REQUIRE_NUM_MATCH= TRUE, and MIN_MATCHES= 2. On the level of the individual document, inspection of experimental results is straightforward: Figure 5 contains a heatmap with the result for one document which shows, for each record[7] (rows) and different values of *sec_size* (columns), the maximum score (top of cell) and the number of sections with this score (bottom of cell). Cell values are only displayed if they change from column to column. The row headers contain the ID and the total number of values for each record (i.e. the size of $V(r)$), which is the maximum number of possible matches.

Figure 5 allows to make several observations: First, two records (269787 and 269763) could not be backprojected at all under the applied settings, which is visible in their score being 0.000 throughout the whole range of *sec_size* values. The overall highest score of 0.833 was reached by six records, each of which has six potentially matchable values, in precisely one section. However, for the first, third, and fifth record, the best match was found for *sec_size*=9, while for the fourth and sixth one, *sec_size* had to be as high as 24, and even 30 for the second one. In other words, while the six values of some of the records were found in close proximity to each other, for others, they were scattered over a range of more than twice resp. three times that size.

Next, we inspect the effect of *one possible way* of using automatically detected highlighting information, by re-running the previous experiment with HL_ROLE= ONLY, i.e. we require the presence of highlighting for a token to be part of a match. Ideally, this should improve backprojection *precision*, by eliminating spurious matches. Given the low incidence of highlighting in our data (only 6.2% of all tokens, cf. Section 3), this might drastically reduce the number of records that can be matched at all. What is more, given the unconstrained way

in which the highlighting was applied by the curators, care has to be taken that the presence (and, more importantly, the *absence*) of highlighting is not over-interpreted.

Figure 6 displays the result for the same document with HL_ROLE= ONLY. Some effects are clearly visible: Two records are no longer backprojected at all.[8] For two other records (163378193 and 269766), the maximum scores are reduced (from 0.833 to 0.500 and 0.333, respectively).

In summary, the above discussion shows that the heatmap visualisation provides a reasonable and reasonably compact representation of a complete DB-to-document backprojection result. It allows to identify record-to-section mappings with varying plausibility, on the basis of how widely scattered the values are in the target sections. This makes it useful for the comparison of different results, like the two results with HL_ROLE= IGNORE and ONLY. The actual verification and *qualitative* evaluation and error analysis, however, requires a more detailed approach (cf. Section 5.3).

5.3 Detailed Analysis

For detailed (error) analysis, records can visually be 'projected' to their automatically detected target sections. Figure 7 shows this for one page each from two documents. These results were created with OCR_OPTIMIZE and USE_SYNONYMS= TRUE, and HL_ROLE= IGNORE. Boxes on the right-hand side show (at the top) the record ID and the matching *sec_size* and score, followed by the section text as recognized by OCR, and all search terms, one search term list (cf. Section 4.2) per row. Unmatched values are given in bold red. The following points are interesting to note. For the first record on the top page, the system failed to identify the 'NaCL' token, which was caused by an OCR error which misread 'NaCL' as 'NaCI'. The bottom three records on the top page exemplify the positive effect of the OCR_OPTIMIZATION, since 'μM' was only matched because of the replacement 'pM' (the same is true for several records in the lower page). It is also instructive to see that, by setting HL_ROLE= IGNORE, two matches could be found in sections without any highlighting. In the lower page, we see the positive effect of USE_SYNONYMS= TRUE in the third and forth record, where the replacement 'NAD' was found

---

[7] For semantically identical records, only one, arbitrarily selected ID is provided, because all other records have exactly the same result.

[8] Both are actually false negatives, which were not highlighted but appeared as part of a table, which was highlighted on the title level.

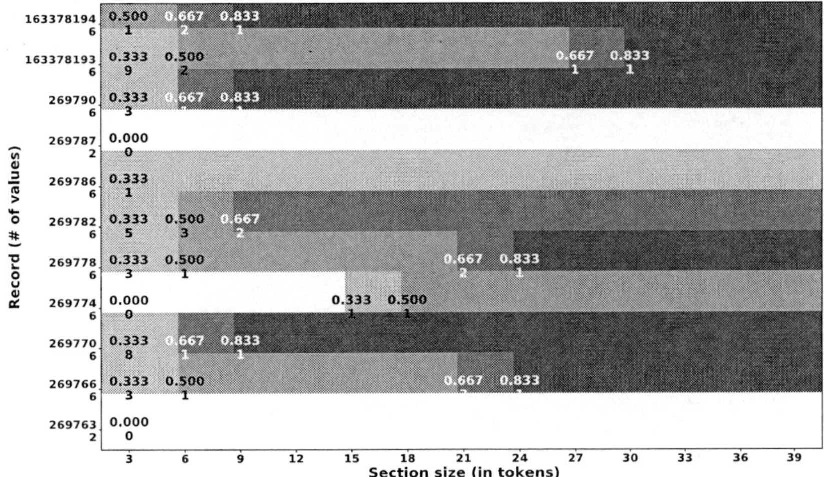

Figure 5: Single Document-level result, HL_ROLE=IGNORE

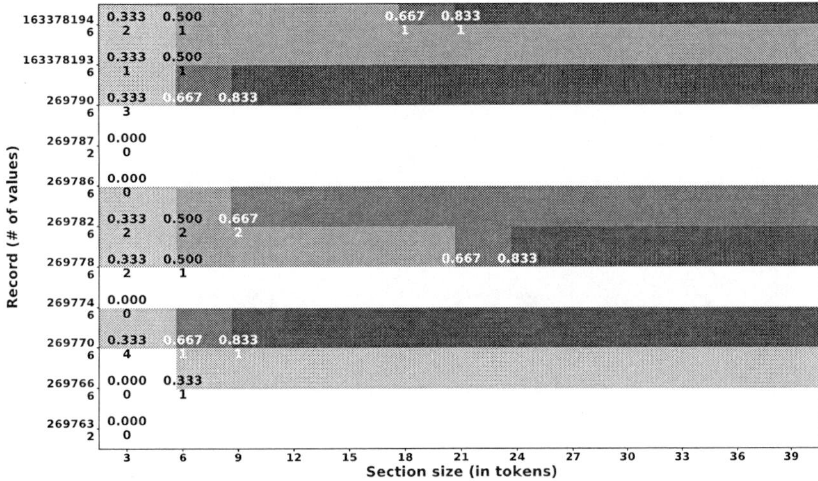

Figure 6: Single Document-level result, HL_ROLE=ONLY

instead of the originally required 'NAD+'. Finally, the lower page also shows that highlighting is not necessarily associated with extracted information.

6 Related Work

DB-to-document backprojection is related to several NLP and document processing tasks, but it is quite special in that it combines 1) OCR processing of scanned documents, 2) information extraction, 3) template matching, and 4) strictly string-based (as opposed to semantic) matching. Scanned paper documents are much less often subject of text or information extraction than born-digital documents like PDFs. *Robust reading*[9] is a common term under which several approaches are collected. A recent approach in this area is DeepReader (Vishwanath et al., 2018), which is a document understanding approach which seamlessly integrates low-level OCR with recognition of higher-level document structure and, to a certain extent, content. *Document Visual Question Answering* (Mathew et al., 2020), on the other hand, analyses scanned documents beyond mere OCR of text content, including manually applied highlighting, for answering questions about the documents' content. On the other hand, information extraction and semantic representation or modelling, especially from publications from the bio domain, is a very active field (Vahdati et al., 2019; Anteghini et al., 2020).

---

[9]https://rrc.cvc.uab.es/

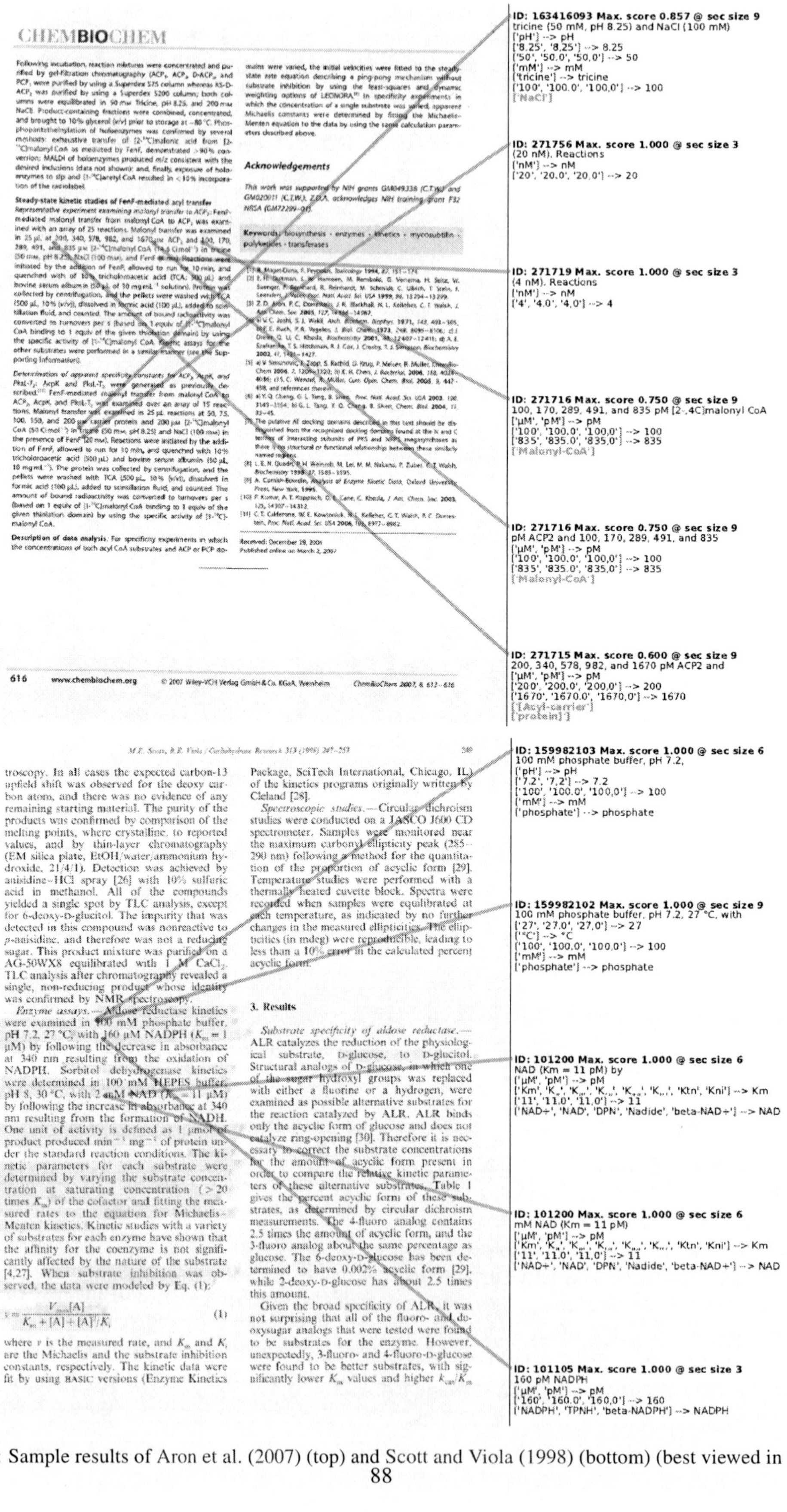

Figure 7: Sample results of Aron et al. (2007) (top) and Scott and Viola (1998) (bottom) (best viewed in color).

The difference, however, is that in these cases, previously *unknown* information is extracted, based on criteria that often take the form of templates in which potential slot fillers are defined in terms of semantic types (e.g. ENZYME) and (in the case of numerical values), ranges. In DB-to-document backprojection, in contrast, the expected information is explicitly known, fully specified, and 'only' needs to be located on the string level. Therefore, in contrast to a lot of the related work mentioned above, methods involving semantic similarity (like BioBERT (Lee et al., 2020)) are not necessarily superior to simple string matching when DB-to-document backprojection is concerned.

7 Conclusions & Future Work

In this paper, we introduced, defined, and performed some preliminary experiments with *DB-to-document backprojection*, a novel scientific document processing task. Our motivation for attempting this task comes from the requirements of a biocuration project, and from our idea to re-purpose previously unused (or rather *under*-used) data to advance biocuration methods. The focus of this initial paper was mostly on motivation, on a definition of the task and its functional parameters, and on the development of a better understanding of the effects and interactions of these parameters. For the latter, we performed some simple experiments and analysed the results. Rigorous evaluation, however, was not attempted, and, what is more, our results showed that defining what it means for a backprojection to be correct is difficult. While a quantitative evaluation remains difficult, a qualitative inspection of backprojection results clearly showed that the answer to our original research question is a positive one, which is the main result of this paper. Our findings regarding the role of color highlighting for backprojection, on the other hand, are somewhat mixed: While our system is able to detect highlighted tokens with high accuracy, appropriate ways to integrate this information into backprojection still need be be explored much further. The approach of *requiring* highlighting for matching, while not disproved yet, might be too strict, and alternative strategies will be evaluated in future work, for which our system and data sets provide a valuable basis. Additional future work includes the following: The optimization heuristics against OCR errors, although already shown to be effective in practice, are far from complete, and

should be improved by handling additional cases of OCR errors, and other spelling variants. Also, as suggested by one reviewer, XML versions of papers from e.g. PubMed could be used to inform the backprojection task, which might also include automatic correction of OCR errors. Future work will also include the creation of an annotated dataset by inspecting the automatic results and storing correct highlighting in the extracted XML. Ideally, this should be done with the help and feedback of domain experts. Finally, the system will be applied to our full data set of $6,000+$ documents, which will yield a stronger data basis for analysis.

Apart from the obvious use cases like quality assurance in biocuration (and other fields where information is manually extracted from documents), and support for users of biological databases, both by means of visualizations, we also envisage several other potential applications for DB-to-document backprojection. These include creation of multimodal training data for page-topology-based document understanding systems like Katti et al. (2018), creation of input for empirical studies on document structure (distribution of information in scientific documents), and others.

Acknowledgements

This work was done as part of the project DeepCurate, which is funded by the German Federal Ministry of Education and Research (BMBF) (No. 031L0204) and the Klaus Tschira Foundation, Heidelberg, Germany. We thank the anonymous reviewers for their helpful suggestions.

References

Marwa Abdelhakim, Eunice McMurray, Ali Raza Syed, Senay Kafkas, Allan Anthony Kamau, Paul N. Schofield, and Robert Hoehndorf. 2020. Ddiem: drug database for inborn errors of metabolism. *Orphanet Journal of Rare Diseases*, 15(1):146.

Marco Anteghini, Jennifer D'Souza, Vítor A. P. Martins dos Santos, and Sören Auer. 2020. Representing semantified biological assays in the open research knowledge graph. *CoRR*, abs/2009.07642.

Zachary D. Aron, Pascal D. Fortin, Christopher T. Calderone, and Christopher T. Walsh. 2007. Fenf: Servicing the mycosubtilin synthetase assembly line in trans. *ChemBioChem*, 8(6):613–616.

George Buchanan and Fernando Loizides. 2007. Investigating document triage on paper and electronic media. In *Research and Advanced Technology for Dig-*

ital Libraries, pages 416–427, Berlin, Heidelberg. Springer Berlin Heidelberg.

Virginia Clinton. 2019. Reading from paper compared to screens: A systematic review and meta-analysis. *Journal of Research in Reading*, 42(2):288–325.

Wei-Chih Huang, Hsin-Tzu Huang, Po-Yuan Chen, Wei-Chi Wang, Tai-Ming Ko, Sirjana Shrestha, Chi-Dung Yang, Chun-San Tai, Men-Yee Chiew, Yu-Pao Chou, Yu-Feng Hu, and Hsien-Da Huang. 2020. Svad: A genetic database curates non-ischemic sudden cardiac death-associated variants. *PLOS ONE*, 15(8):1–14.

International Society for Biocuration. 2018. Biocuration: Distilling data into knowledge. *PLOS Biology*, 16(4):1–8.

Peter Karp. 2016. Can we replace curation with information extraction software? *Database: The Journal of Biological Databases and Curation*, 2016.

Anoop R Katti, Christian Reisswig, Cordula Guder, Sebastian Brarda, Steffen Bickel, Johannes Höhne, and Jean Baptiste Faddoul. 2018. Chargrid: Towards understanding 2D documents. In *Proceedings of the 2018 Conference on Empirical Methods in Natural Language Processing*, pages 4459–4469, Brussels, Belgium. Association for Computational Linguistics.

Maja Köpper, Susanne Mayr, and Axel Buchner. 2016. Reading from computer screen versus reading from paper: does it still make a difference? *Ergonomics*, 59(5):615–632. PMID: 26736059.

Jinhyuk Lee, Wonjin Yoon, Sungdong Kim, Donghyeon Kim, Sunkyu Kim, Chan Ho So, and Jaewoo Kang. 2020. Biobert: a pre-trained biomedical language representation model for biomedical text mining. *Bioinform.*, 36(4):1234–1240.

Robin Liechti, Nancy George, Sara El-Gebali, Lou Götz, Isaac Crespo, Ioannis Xenarios, and Thomas Lemberger. 2016. Sourcedata - a semantic platform for curating and searching figures. *Nature Methods*, 14:1021–1022.

Aldo Lipani, Florina Piroi, Linda Andersson, and Allan Hanbury. 2014. Extracting nanopublications from IR papers. In *IRFC*, volume 8849 of *Lecture Notes in Computer Science*, pages 53–62. Springer.

Minesh Mathew, Dimosthenis Karatzas, R. Manmatha, and C. V. Jawahar. 2020. DocVQA: A dataset for vqa on document images.

Rose Oughtred, Chris Stark, Bobby-Joe Breitkreutz, Jennifer Rust, Lorrie Boucher, Christie Chang, Nadine Kolas, Lara O'Donnell, Genie Leung, Rochelle McAdam, Frederick Zhang, Sonam Dolma, Andrew Willems, Jasmin Coulombe-Huntington, Andrew Chatr-aryamontri, Kara Dolinski, and Mike Tyers. 2019. The BioGRID interaction database: 2019

update. *Nucleic Acids Research*, 47(D1):D529–D541.

Mary Ellen Scott and Ronald E. Viola. 1998. The use of fluoro- and deoxy-substrate analogs to examine binding specificity and catalysis in the enzymes of the sorbitol pathway. *Carbohydrate Research*, 313(3):247 – 253.

Sahar Vahdati, Said Fathalla, Sören Auer, Christoph Lange, and Maria-Esther Vidal. 2019. Semantic representation of scientific publications. In *TPDL*, volume 11799 of *Lecture Notes in Computer Science*, pages 375–379. Springer.

D Vishwanath, Rohit Rahul, Gunjan Sehgal, Swati, Arindam Chowdhury, Monika Sharma, Lovekesh Vig, Gautam M. Shroff, and Ashwin Srinivasan. 2018. Deep reader: Information extraction from document images via relation extraction and natural language. In *Computer Vision - ACCV 2018 Workshops - 14th Asian Conference on Computer Vision, Perth, Australia, December 2-6, 2018, Revised Selected Papers*, volume 11367 of *Lecture Notes in Computer Science*, pages 186–201. Springer.

Ulrike Wittig, Maja Rey, Andreas Weidemann, Renate Kania, and Wolfgang Müller. 2018. SABIO-RK: an updated resource for manually curated biochemical reaction kinetics. *Nucleic Acids Research*, 46(D1):D656–D660.

Ulrike Wittig, Maja Rey, Andreas Weidemann, and Wolfgang Müller. 2017. Data management and data enrichment for systems biology projects. *Journal of biotechnology.*, 261:229–237.

Wenyi Wu, Yan Wu, Dahui Hu, Yincong Zhou, Yanshi Hu, Yujie Chen, and Ming Chen. 2020. PncStress: a manually curated database of experimentally validated stress-responsive non-coding RNAs in plants. *Database*, 2020. Baaa001.

DeepPaperComposer: A Simple Solution for Training Data Preparation for Parsing Research Papers

Meng Ling and **Jian Chen**
The Ohio State University
{ling.253, chen.8028}@osu.edu

Abstract

We present *DeepPaperComposer*, a simple solution for preparing highly accurate (100%) training data without manual labeling to extract content from scholarly articles using convolutional neural networks (CNNs). We used our approach to generate data and trained CNNs to extract eight categories of both *textual* (titles, abstracts, authors, headers, figure and table captions, and body texts) and *non-textual* content (figures and tables) from 30 years of 2916 IEEE VIS conference papers, of which a third were scanned bitmap PDFs. We curated this dataset and named it VISpaper-3K. We then showed our initial benchmark performance using VISpaper-3K over CS-150 using YOLOv3 and Faster-RCNN. We have open-sourced DeepPaperComposer for training data generation[1] and have released the resulting annotation data VISpaper-3K[2] to promote reproducible research.

1 Introduction

Texts, figures, tables and their associated captions are used in leveraging key concepts, data, and inferences to improve accessibility of knowledge (Chaudhri et al., 2014), to offer succinct content summaries (Erera et al., 2019; Kupiec et al., 1995), to understand visual literacy, to tell data stories, and to improve research workflow, e.g., CiteSeerX (Caragea et al., 2014)[3], Microsoft Academic (Sinha et al., 2015)[4], Google Scholar (Dong et al., 2014)[5], Semantic Scholar (Lo et al., 2020)[6], and IBM Science summarizer (Choudhury et al., 2015)[7].

In these applications, extracting textual and non-textual content is often a necessary first step before any subsequent uses of these components are possible. However, the vast majority of published scholarly articles are available only in PDFs or scanned bitmaps. Even though recent deep-learning-based algorithms using convolutional neural networks (CNNs) provide considerably better performance (Xu et al., 2020; Kavasidis et al., 2019; Siegel et al., 2018; Schreiber et al., 2017; Gilani et al., 2017; Hao et al., 2016), the quality of the labeled training data often determines the success of these CNN-based algorithms. The lack of large-scale labeled document datasets has been recognized as a major hindrance in deep-learning research for structure analyses (Li et al., 2020; Qasim et al., 2019; Zhong et al., 2019).

Training data for the CNN-based algorithms are typically prepared manually by crowdsourcing (e.g., CS-150 (Clark and Divvala, 2015)) or by automated tag extraction in XML (e.g., CS-Large (Clark and Divvala, 2016)). Recently, Siegel et al. (2018) designed a most successful and least labor-intensive approach to align and modify LaTeX syntax-based documents to automatically extract labels of over 4-million pages and achieve training data label accuracy of up to 94%.

Inspired by these recent advances, we designed *DeepPaperComposer*, a simple data-preparation method to create 100% accurate training samples of any scale for content extraction in large numbers of scientific documents, by simply "rendering" papers to paste non-textual and textual content onto a white page to assemble the look of a real document. We introduce the workflow (Figure 1), the resulting real-world case study to construct a new annotated dataset *VISpaper-3K*, and two benchmark tests using this new dataset.

The main contributions of this work include:

1. *DeepPaperComposer*, a simple data-

---

[1] http://go.osu.edu/deeppapercomposer
[2] http://go.osu.edu/vispaper-3k.
[3] https://citeseerx.ist.psu.edu/
[4] https://academic.microsoft.com/
[5] https://scholar.google.com
[6] https://semanticscholar.org/
[7] https://dimsum.eu-gb.containers.appdomain.cloud

Proceedings of the First Workshop on Scholarly Document Processing, pages 91–96
Online, November 19, 2020. ©2020 Association for Computational Linguistics
https://doi.org/10.18653/v1/P17

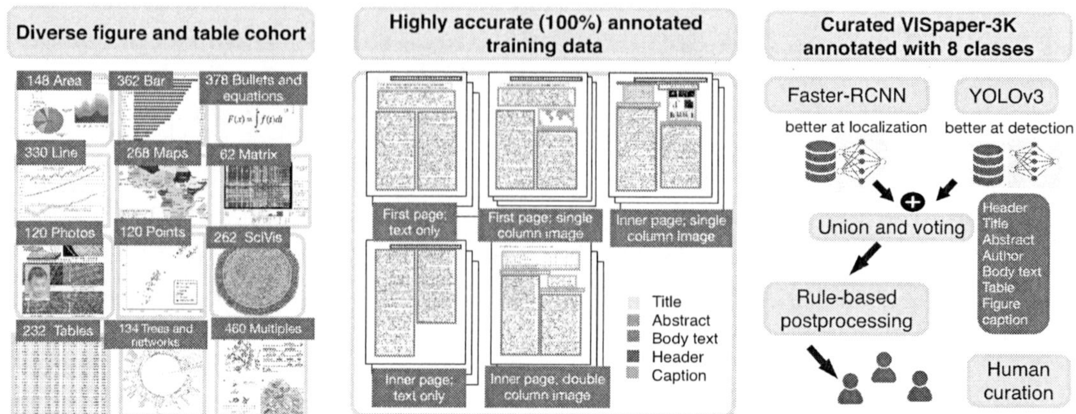

Figure 1: DeepPaperComposer is an end-to-end framework for reverse-engineering research papers by pasting image and text cohorts onto empty white pages, localizing textual and non-textual classes by combining the outputs from Faster-RCNN and YOLOv3, and further improving prediction accuracy by rule-based post-processing.

preparation method to synthesize dummy papers for generating accurate annotated labels, grounded upon scholarly articles' structural heuristics, without human intervention, in particular without manual labeling.

2. *VISpaper-3K*, a new scholarly dataset with eight categories of ground-truth annotation of 2916 IEEE-VIS conference papers (24,660 pages).

2 DeepPaperComposer: Our End-to-End Paper Parser

Our goal is to extract textual and non-textual content from research papers. The essence of our approach is to couple the new CNN-based solutions and the heuristic-based method: we use heuristics to produce the structures of dummy papers as the training set and then let CNNs perform classification tasks before feeding the results to post-processing (Figure 1).

2.1 Training Data: Dummy Paper Page Composer

We treat training data as a composition of individual document elements, where the goals are (1) to record bounding boxes for each of the labels/component parts in a PDF paper to produce high-quality labels, and (2) to synthesize appearance to reduce the differences between the training data and the real paper.

Composer workflow. We used our text corpus and figure and table corpus to automatically synthesize a large set of paper pages by inserting para-

graphs, figures, and tables using our Matlab-based rendering engine into pages (Figure 1). We first created a blank image with a default 1075×1400 pixel resolution. Depending on the page format, we inserted the randomly generated header, title, and abstract. We then 'pasted' a random number of images from our figure and table cohort, and added captions with random texts underneath figures and tables. Finally, we inserted body text in the white space and randomly broke the sentences into paragraphs. We recorded the accurate bounding-box locations in this process.

Textual and non-textual content. We assembled the textual content of a paper page (body text, document headers, paper titles, paper abstracts, and captions) using the context-free grammar in SCIgen (Stribling et al., 2005). We assembled a diverse set of figures and tables by repurposing images from the MASSVIS dataset collected by Borkin et al. (2013) and the spatial data collections by Li and Chen (2018).

Dummy paper pages. We generated 13,000 pages (10,000 for training and 3,000 for validation), each of dimensions of 1075×1400 pixels and labeled by up to 17 class tags shown in Table 1. All these tags have accurate ground-truth bounding box locations.

Compared to DeepFigures (Siegel et al., 2018), our approach does not depend on LaTeX syntax to obtain ground-truth bounding boxes. Theoretically, given an image cohort and classes, we can render any number of images with 100% accurate bounding boxes.

Textual content	**Five types:** body text; paper title; abstract, header; bullets and equations
Figures	**10 types:** area and circle charts; bar charts; line and curve charts; maps; matrix and parallel coordinates; multi-types; photos; points; scientific data visualizations; trees and networks
Tables	**One type:** tables with diverse layout and background colors
Captions	**One type:** figure and table caption

Table 1: Our Dummy Paper Page Composer can automatically compose 17 types of scholarly article content in four categories with accurate bounding box labels.

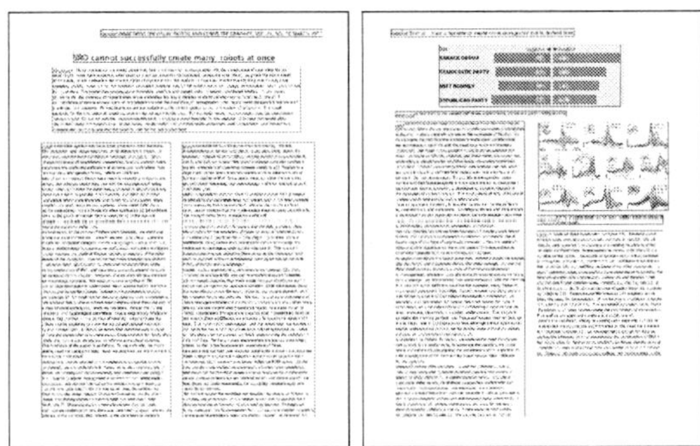

Figure 2: Sample dummy paper pages with automatically produced ground-truth labels.

2.2 Training and Voting on Two CNNs' Predictions

We trained two complementary CNN models, YOLOv3 (Redmon and Farhadi, 2018; Redmon et al., 2016) and Faster-RCNN (Ren et al., 2017), independently for subsequent figure extraction from the actual papers. Both YOLOv3 and Faster-RCNN returned the four coordinates of each bounding box, along with class labels. We chose these two CNN methods because we found during pilot studies that Faster-RCNN was a better localization method that provided more precise bounding boxes, while YOLOv3 was fast and improved recall compared to Faster-RCNN.

We combined the two models' labeling results by *union* and *voting*. We first union the detections captured by both Faster-RCNN (better localization) and YOLOv3 (better detection). The bounding boxes were taken by voting from the model with higher confidence. Annotations of the textual content labels are produced by heuristics (e.g., titles only appeared on the first page; author information is after the title and for IEEE VIS, abstracts and teaser images appear after author information). Figures can have several class labels since most figures in IEEE VIS contain multiple figure types.

2.3 Post-processing of Model Prediction

We then perform several post-processing steps:

1. tighten or expand labeled bounding boxes to acquire more accurate regions for each figure and table. In this process, *over-segmented tables* (Shafait and Smith, 2010) (different parts of the ground-truth tables were detected as separate tables) were often fixed especially for tables with boundaries.
2. remove redundant bounding boxes.
3. match captions to tables and figures by minimizing the total distance between them (Siegel et al., 2018).
4. compute author(s)' information assuming the author list is between title and abstract.

Textual content is computed after we obtain the ground-truth labels of figures, tables, and captions. We fill in the remaining spaces in between with text boxes, and tighten or expand them until fit.

3 Case Study: Curating the VISpaper-3K Dataset

We applied the proposed DeepPaperComposer framework to IEEE VIS publications over the past 30 years.

Training and validation data from dummy papers. In total, we used 13K dummy paper pages (10K for training and 3K for validation), each of dimensions 1075×1400 pixels and labeled by eight class tags (the five text content types, figure, table, and captions in Table 1). All these tags have accurate ground-truth bounding box locations.

DeepPaperComposer modeling process. The two CNN models are trained using the automated dummy paper generation. The output using DeepPaperComposer contains the annotated pages.

Preprocessing of test data. The collection consists of articles from a single narrow conference: IEEE VIS. The test dataset contains the 2916 full-paper PDFs for the years 1990–2019 (Isenberg

Training Data	Validation	Test Data	IoU	Precision	Recall	F1
10K dummy pages	3K dummy pages	IEEE VIS 24,660 pages	0.8	0.94	0.84	0.89

Table 2: Case study validation of our method against the 24,660 pages of the VISpaper-3K ground-truth data.

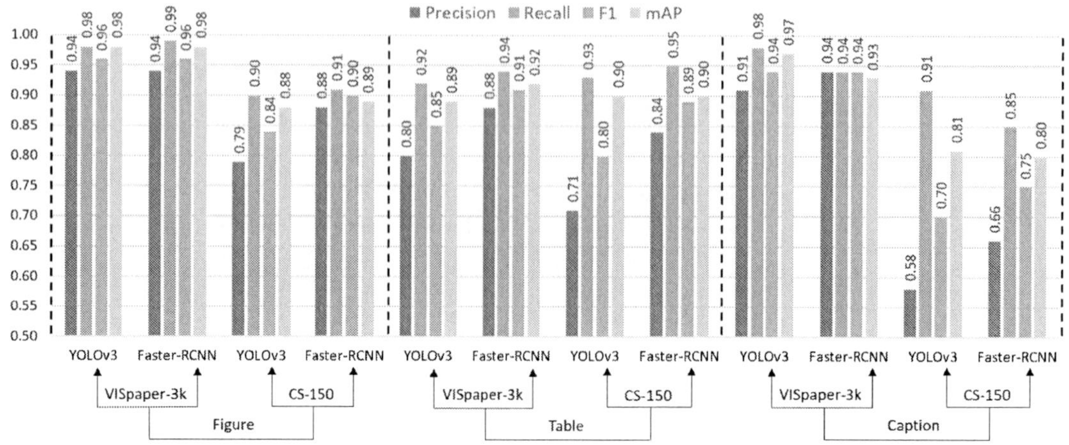

Figure 3: Benchmark performance of **VISpaper-3K** dataset for figure, table, and caption extraction. A total of 14,796 VISpaper-3K paper pages were used for training and 4932 pages for validation running 10 times for two popular CNN methods, YOLOv3 and Faster-RCNN. Models were tested using 4932 pages of VISpaper-3K and 1176 pages of the CS-150 benchmark data.

et al., 2016). We converted these PDFs to PNG images.

Validating DeepPaperComposer. Since we must have ground-truth in order to quantify the performance of our automatic pipeline using Deep-PaperComposer, we first curated the ground-truth data: 10 coders checked *figure* and *table* tags of 2916 papers. Given the groundtruth, we followed the evaluation metrics of Clark and Divvala (2016) to measure the overall performance obtained by our approach on VISpaper-3K. A predicted bounding box is compared to a ground truth based on the Jaccard index or intersection over union (IoU), and is considered correct when IoU exceeds 0.8. Extracted figures with identifiers that did not exist in the ground truth were considered incorrect. The results are in Table 2.

4   Quantitative Evaluation

To assess the utility of the VISpaper-3K dataset, we conducted two experiments aimed at understanding whether the dataset can be used to extract figures, tables, and captions.

Study settings. Both experiments used 60% (14,796 pages) and 20% (4932 pages) of VISpaper-3K for training and validation accordingly. Both

YOLOv3 and Faster-RCNN were used and tested on the remaining 20% (4932 pages) of VISpaper-3K and CS-150. We ran the models 10 times and tested the models using both our data and CS-150.

Results. We again followed the evaluation method of Clark and Divvala (2016) as described in Section 3. We show the main results in Figure 3. As we can see the four metric measures for tables are about the same for the two datasets but dropped considerably for figures and captions for the CS-150 dataset. Here the F1 score measures test accuracy; our F1 scores for figures in CS-150 (0.84 from YOLOv3 and 0.90 from Faster-RCNN) are slightly lower than that of PDFFigures 2.0 (0.97) (Clark and Divvala, 2016). The F1 scores for tables are also lower than PDFFigures 2.0 (0.97). One main reason could be that the structural content in CS-150 is different from IEEE-VIS papers and YOLOv3 and Faster-RCCN were trained with VISpaper-3K and tested on CS-150, indicating that the training set may not be diverse enough.

Analyses. The runtime performance computes the average time per page it takes to return the bounding boxes of the figures, tables, and captions. The current implementation of YOLOv3 takes 0.09 seconds and Faster-RCNN 0.23 seconds on average. YOLOv3 is considerably faster than Faster-RCNN.

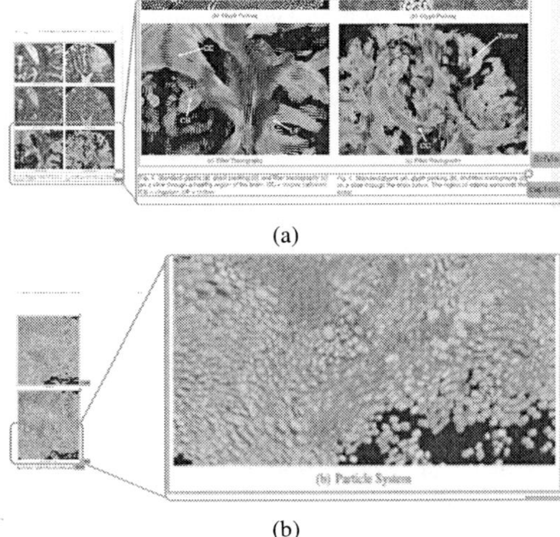

(a)

(b)

Figure 4: Sub-figure segmentation challenges. Multiple sub-figures with or without sub-captions are often combined by leaving gaps between these sub-figures. Neither YOLOv3 nor Faster-RCNN can simultaneously identify sub-figures and figures. Our algorithm sometimes (a) predicted a single figure and a single caption when there are two compound figures in two columns, and (b) included sub-captions in the predictions but not in other times; further, our algorithm did not couple these two sub-figures.

Evaluating algorithm performance is a challenging topic and different performance metrics have been used in the literature for evaluating figure- and table-detection algorithms. Consider the challenging cases with compound figures and captions shown in Figure 4. Using these metrics of precision, however, both subfigures in Figure 4(a) and (b) will be considered "correct" in classification tasks, although they still demand subsequent algorithmic or human corrections. Our future work will study metrics for detailed evaluation, as processing compound figures remains one of the leading challenges in document analyses (Davila et al., 2020).

5   Conclusion

We present in this short work-in-progress paper a new training data preparation approach to generate accurate ground-truth labels. Our preliminary results showed that our dummy paper composer could be a viable solution to train CNNs to extract several semantic and graphical entities. We have released our source code for training data generation online. We plan to diversify the structure and content our paper generator can compose and enable researchers to upload their own data to train

models and run the predictions.

Acknowledgments

We thank the anonymous reviewers for their constructive feedback. This work was supported in part by NSF-1945347 and by The Ohio State University (OSU) Translational Data Analytics Institute (TDAI). Any opinions, findings, and conclusions or recommendations expressed in this material are those of the authors and do not necessarily reflect the views of National Science Foundation.

References

Michelle A. Borkin, Azalea A. Vo, Zoya Bylinskii, Phillip Isola, Shashank Sunkavalli, Aude Oliva, and Hanspeter Pfister. 2013. What makes a visualization memorable? *IEEE Transactions on Visualization and Computer Graphics*, 19(12):2306–2315.

Cornelia Caragea, Jian Wu, Alina Ciobanu, Kyle Williams, Juan Fernández-Ramírez, Hung-Hsuan Chen, Zhaohui Wu, and Lee Giles. 2014. *CiteSeer^x*: A scholarly big dataset. In *European Conference on Information Retrieval*, pages 311–322.

Vinay K Chaudhri, Adam Overholtzer, and Aaron Spaulding. 2014. An intelligent textbook that answers questions. In *International Conference on Knowledge Engineering and Knowledge Management*, pages 131–135.

Sagnik Ray Choudhury, Prasenjit Mitra, and Clyde Lee Giles. 2015. Automatic extraction of figures from scholarly documents. In *Proceedings of the ACM Symposium on Document Engineering*, pages 47–50.

Christopher Clark and Santosh Divvala. 2015. Looking beyond text: Extracting figures, tables and captions from computer science papers. In *Workshops at the 29th AAAI Conference on Artificial Intelligence*.

Christopher Clark and Santosh Divvala. 2016. PDFFigures 2.0: Mining figures from research papers. In *Proceedings of IEEE/ACM Joint Conference on Digital Libraries*, pages 143–152.

Kenny Davila, Srirangaraj Setlur, David Doermann, Urala Kota Bhargava, and Venu Govindaraju. 2020. Chart mining: A survey of methods for automated chart analysis. *IEEE Transactions on Pattern Analysis and Machine Intelligence (pre-print)*.

Xin Dong, Evgeniy Gabrilovich, Geremy Heitz, Wilko Horn, Ni Lao, Kevin Murphy, Thomas Strohmann, Shaohua Sun, and Wei Zhang. 2014. Knowledge vault: A web-scale approach to probabilistic knowledge fusion. In *Proceedings of the 20th ACM SIGKDD International Conference on Knowledge Discovery and Data Mining*, pages 601–610.

Shai Erera, Michal Shmueli-Scheuer, Guy Feigenblat, Ora Peled Nakash, Odellia Boni, Haggai Roitman, Doron Cohen, Bar Weiner, Yosi Mass, Or Rivlin, et al. 2019. A summarization system for scientific documents. In *Proceedings of the Empirical Methods in Natural Language Processing (EMNLP) and 9th International Joint Conference on Natural Language Processing (IJCNLP)*, pages 211–216.

Azka Gilani, Shah Rukh Qasim, Imran Malik, and Faisal Shafait. 2017. Table detection using deep learning. In *14th IAPR International Conference on Document Analysis and Recognition (ICDAR)*, volume 1, pages 771–776.

Leipeng Hao, Liangcai Gao, Xiaohan Yi, and Zhi Tang. 2016. A table detection method for pdf documents based on convolutional neural networks. In *12th IAPR Workshop on Document Analysis Systems (DAS)*, pages 287–292.

Petra Isenberg, Florian Heimerl, Steffen Koch, Tobias Isenberg, Panpan Xu, Charles D Stolper, Michael Sedlmair, Jian Chen, Torsten Möller, and John Stasko. 2016. Vispubdata.org: A metadata collection about IEEE visualization (VIS) publications. *IEEE Transactions on Visualization and Computer Graphics*, 23(9):2199–2206.

Isaak Kavasidis, Carmelo Pino, Simone Palazzo, Francesco Rundo, Daniela Giordano, P Messina, and Concetto Spampinato. 2019. A saliency-based convolutional neural network for table and chart detection in digitized documents. In *International Conference on Image Analysis and Processing*, pages 292–302.

Julian Kupiec, Jan Pedersen, and Francine Chen. 1995. A trainable document summarizer. In *Proceedings of the 18th Annual International ACM SIGIR Conference on Research and Development in Information Retrieval*, pages 68–73.

Minghao Li, Yiheng Xu, Lei Cui, Shaohan Huang, Furu Wei, Zhoujun Li, and Ming Zhou. 2020. DocBank: A benchmark dataset for document layout analysis. *arXiv preprint 2006.01038*.

Rui Li and Jian Chen. 2018. Toward a deep understanding of what makes a scientific visualization memorable. In *Short Papers of IEEE Visualization/SciVis*, pages 26–31.

Kyle Lo, Lucy Lu Wang, Mark Neumann, Rodney Kinney, and Daniel S Weld. 2020. S2ORC: The semantic scholar open research corpus. In *Proceedings of the 58th Annual Meeting of the Association for Computational Linguistics*, pages 4969–4983.

Shah Rukh Qasim, Hassan Mahmood, and Faisal Shafait. 2019. Rethinking table recognition using graph neural networks. In *International Conference on Document Analysis and Recognition (ICDAR)*, pages 142–147.

Joseph Redmon, Santosh Divvala, Ross Girshick, and Ali Farhadi. 2016. You only look once: Unified, real-time object detection. In *IEEE Conference on Computer Vision and Pattern Recognition (CVPR)*, pages 779–788.

Joseph Redmon and Ali Farhadi. 2018. YOLOv3: An incremental improvement. 1804.02767.

Shaoqing Ren, Kaiming He, Ross Girshick, and Jian Sun. 2017. Faster R-CNN: Towards real-time object detection with region proposal networks. *IEEE Transactions on Pattern Analysis and Machine Intelligence*, 39(6):1137–1149.

Sebastian Schreiber, Stefan Agne, Ivo Wolf, Andreas Dengel, and Sheraz Ahmed. 2017. DeepDeSRT: Deep learning for detection and structure recognition of tables in document images. In *Proceedings of the 14th International Conference on Document Analysis and Recognition (ICDAR)*, volume 1, pages 1162–1167.

Faisal Shafait and Ray Smith. 2010. Table detection in heterogeneous documents. In *Proceedings of the 9th IAPR International Workshop on Document Analysis Systems*, pages 65–72.

Noah Siegel, Nicholas Lourie, Russell Power, and Waleed Ammar. 2018. Extracting scientific figures with distantly supervised neural networks. In *Proceedings of the 18th ACM/IEEE on Joint Conference on Digital Libraries*, pages 223–232.

Arnab Sinha, Zhihong Shen, Yang Song, Hao Ma, Darrin Eide, Bo-June Hsu, and Kuansan Wang. 2015. An overview of Microsoft Academic Service (MAS) and applications. In *Proceedings of the 24th International Conference on World Wide Web*, pages 243–246.

Jeremy Stribling, Max Krohn, and Dan Aguayo. 2005. SCIgen – An automatic CS paper generator. Online tool: https://pdos.csail.mit.edu/archive/scigen/.

Yiheng Xu, Minghao Li, Lei Cui, Shaohan Huang, Furu Wei, and Ming Zhou. 2020. LayoutLM: Pre-training of text and layout for document image understanding. In *Proceedings of the 26th ACM International Conference on Knowledge Discovery & Data Mining (SIGKDD)*, pages 1192—-1200.

Xu Zhong, Jianbin Tang, and Antonio Jimeno Yepes. 2019. PubLayNet: largest dataset ever for document layout analysis. In *IEEE International Conference on Document Analysis and Recognition (ICDAR)*, pages 1015–1022.

Improved Local Citation Recommendation Based on Context Enhanced with Global Information

Zoran Medić and **Jan Šnajder**
Text Analysis and Knowledge Engineering Lab
Faculty of Electrical Engineering and Computing, University of Zagreb
Unska 3, 10000 Zagreb, Croatia
`{zoran.medic, jan.snajder}@fer.hr`

Abstract

Local citation recommendation aims at finding articles relevant for given citation context. While most previous approaches represent context using solely text surrounding the citation, we propose enhancing context representation with global information. Specifically, we include citing article's title and abstract into context representation. We evaluate our model on datasets with different citation context sizes and demonstrate improvements with globally-enhanced context representations when citation contexts are smaller.

1 Introduction

The number of published scientific articles has been growing rapidly: it surpassed 50 million in 2009 (Jinha, 2010) and the global publication rate is still growing (Ware and Mabe, 2015). As a consequence, scholars are finding it increasingly difficult to keep up with relevant research. The problem can be alleviated by citation recommendation (CR) systems, which help researchers writing articles find published work that they might consider citing.

Approaches to CR come in two types: *global* (Bethard and Jurafsky, 2010; Ren et al., 2014; Guo et al., 2017; Bhagavatula et al., 2018) and *local* (He et al., 2010; Huang et al., 2012; Ebesu and Fang, 2017; Dai et al., 2019). Global CR models typically take the article's abstract or the entire text as input (the *citing* article) and output a list of relevant articles (the candidates for *cited* articles). In contrast, local CR models take an excerpt of the citing article (the citation context) as input and recommend articles that may be cited specifically in that context.[1] Although the cited article is already described by the citation context which the local CR

models use to find relevant articles, we hypothesize that these models could still benefit from global information on the citing article, which provides a broader context for specific citation. For instance, consider the following citation context:[2]

> *Other approaches include for example clustering-based algorithms, such as the one presented in* CITATION, *or techniques which rely on building a statistical language model to rank KPs, like the one presented in* CITATION.

Looking at the context alone, it is difficult to tell which articles were cited at CITATIONs. However, with global information (citing article's text) available, the model could narrow the search.

In this work, we address the task of local CR and experiment with enhancing the citation context with citing article's global information, more specifically with its title and abstract. We propose a model that produces the final recommendation score as a combination of semantic (based on the match between citing article's citation context and cited article's content) and bibliographic relevance (based on articles' popularity in the scientific community). Our evaluation on two datasets with different citation context sizes shows that enhancing citation context with global information helps when the citation context is smaller. We also show that inclusion of bibliographic relevance leads to better results compared to model with semantic relevance only. The contribution of our work is twofold: (1) we present a model that includes global information into local CR and obtains competitive results compared to previous work (Ebesu and Fang, 2017) and (2) we show that inclusion of global information besides citation context helps when citation contexts are smaller.

---

[1] Most work on local CR uses contexts from published articles with citations masked out. While this is a somewhat artificial setup as those articles are biased toward existing citations, local CR can nonetheless be used in this setup to recommend additional citations.

[2] Excerpt is from *Evaluating anaphora and coreference resolution to improve automatic keyphrase extraction* of Basaldella et al. (2016). The articles cited are *Clustering to find exemplar terms for keyphrase extraction* of Liu et al. (2009) and *A language model approach to keyphrase extraction* of Tomokiyo and Hurst (2003).

Proceedings of the First Workshop on Scholarly Document Processing, pages 97–103
Online, November 19, 2020. ©2020 Association for Computational Linguistics
https://doi.org/10.18653/v1/P17

2 Related Work

Compared to global CR, local CR has attracted less attention, presumably as there is fewer datasets with extracted citation contexts. A comprehensive overview of local CR is (Färber and Jatowt, 2020).

The task of local CR was introduced by He et al. (2010), who used TF-IDF representations of contexts and cited articles in a vector similarity based setup. He et al. (2011) proposed a model that detects contexts in an article's text and recommends citations using TF-IDF based matching with other contexts extracted from a corpus of articles. Huang et al. (2012) framed the task as statistical machine translation from context to cited article. Livne et al. (2014) built a system that provides recommendations while manuscript is being written. The system is based on a number of hand-crafted features extracted from both citation context and the rest of article's content.

Recently, deep learning models were proposed for the task. Huang et al. (2015) presented a neural probabilistic model that embeds words from the context and all the articles from the corpus into a shared embedding space. A neural module uses the so-obtained embeddings for determining the probability of citing an article in a given context. The model of Ebesu and Fang (2017) encodes citation context and decodes it into the title of cited article, using also the information about the authors of citing and cited articles. Dai et al. (2019) use stacked denoising autoencoders for representing cited articles and bidirectional LSTMs for citation context's embedding. Our approach extends on these models by enhancing the representation of citation context with global information. While there has been work that proposed adding global information to context representation (He et al., 2010; Livne et al., 2014), to the best of our knowledge, no such deep learning model has been proposed.

3 Model

The proposed model takes five inputs: (1) citation context text, (2) citing article's title and abstract (henceforth: citing article's text), (3) cited article title and abstract (henceforth: candidate article's text), (4) a list of cited article authors, and (5) the number of cited article citations per last y years, together with the total number of citations. The output of the model is a recommendation score indicating whether candidate article should be cited in input context.

Two modules make up the model: the semantic module and the bibliographic module. We depict the two modules in Figures 1 and 2. The final recommendation score is a weighted sum of the scores produced by the two modules. The intuition behind the weighted sum of the scores is that, depending on the context, the authors might prefer to cite articles that are influential in their research community (i.e., articles with high bibliographic score) or articles that pertain to the specifics of their work (e.g., a particular article their work builds on or a specific method they use). Intuitively, in the former case, the model should put more weight on the bibliographic score, while in the latter case a higher weight on semantic score would be expected.

Semantic module. Similarly to Dai et al. (2019), we use bidirectional long short-term memory (Bi-LSTM) cells (Hochreiter and Schmidhuber, 1997) to represent citation context, but also to represent both cited article and global information from the citing article. Text fed to the module is segmented and tokenized using spaCy.[3] Target citation and other citations are masked with TARGETCIT and OTHERCIT placeholders, respectively. All three textual inputs are passed through the same two layers: LSTM and attention layer.

Let n be the total number of tokens in the input sequence $s = (t_1, \ldots, t_n)$. Each token t_i is mapped to a d_e-dimensional embedding vector $\mathbf{x}_i \in \mathcal{R}^{d_e}$ to generate a sequence $\mathbf{x} = (\mathbf{x}_1, \ldots, \mathbf{x}_n)$; we use pretrained embeddings from (Bhagavatula et al., 2018). Sequence $\mathbf{x}$ is then passed through a Bi-LSTM layer with hidden state dimension of d_h, where output $\mathbf{h}_i$ at each step i is formed by concatenating backward and forward hidden states: $\mathbf{h}_i = [\overrightarrow{\mathbf{h}_i}; \overleftarrow{\mathbf{h}_i}]$, $\mathbf{h}_i \in \mathcal{R}^{2d_h}$. The hidden states of input sequence s are passed through an additive attention layer (Bahdanau et al., 2015) to produce the final sequence embedding $\mathbf{z}_s$. Given input query vector $\mathbf{q}$ and hidden state vector $\mathbf{h}_i$, attention score for each step i is:

$$a_i = \mathbf{v} \cdot \tanh(W \cdot [\mathbf{q}; \mathbf{h}_i]) \qquad (1)$$

where $\mathbf{v}$ and W are model parameters. Attention scores are normalized, applied to corresponding hidden states and summed to produce the final sequence embedding $\mathbf{z}_s$. A different query vector $\mathbf{q}$ is used depending on the input type. For citation context, we use the hidden state corresponding to

---

[3]https://spacy.io

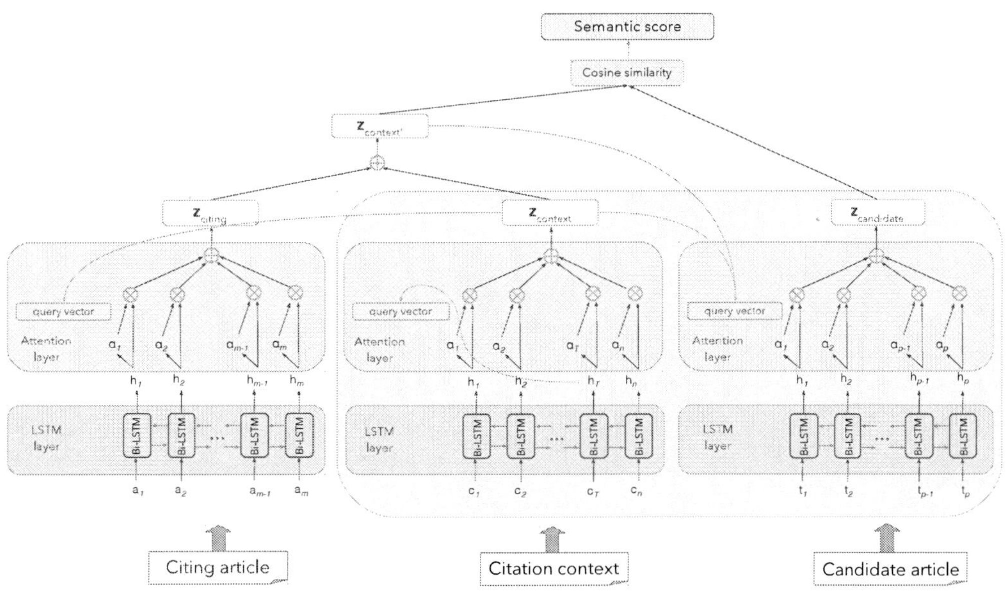

Figure 1: The semantic module of the local citation recommendation model. All text sequences pass through the same layers, with differences in attention query usage (indicated with arrows). The green oval corresponds to the *Con module variants, in which global information is not included.

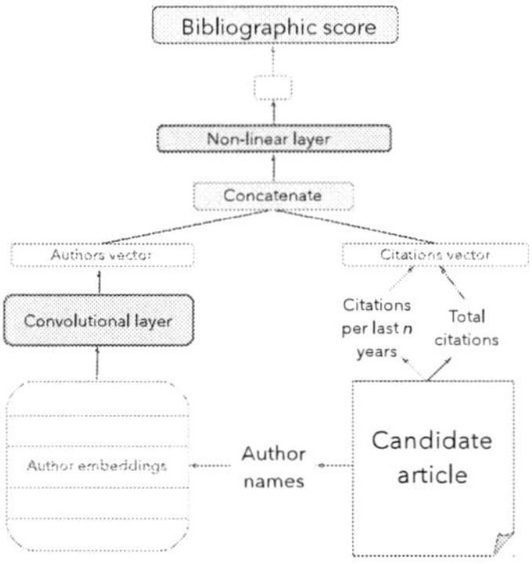

Figure 2: Architecture of the bibliographic module of the local citation recommendation model.

citation's placeholder ($\mathbf{h}_T$), so to focus context representation on the specific citation being predicted. For citing article's text, we use the final sequence embedding of the context ($\mathbf{z}_{\text{context}}$), while for candidate article's text we use the sum of citing article and context embeddings ($\mathbf{z}_{\text{citing}} + \mathbf{z}_{\text{context}}$). This allows the model to focus on context-specific information in both the citing and cited articles. More specifically, by using citation's placeholder hidden state as a query vector for calculating attention scores over citation context's tokens, we expect the model to focus on tokens in the context that are relevant for obtaining the embedding of the citation placeholder. Similarly, by using citation context embedding as a query for citing (or cited) article's text, the model focuses on tokens in the text that are relevant for given citation context, since article's text describes various aspects of an article and not all of them need to be equally relevant for the context at hand.

Given context c and candidate article p, semantic score scoring function $s_{\text{sem}}(c, p)$ is defined as cosine similarity between the enhanced context embedding and candidate article's embedding.

Bibliographic module. When the semantic context admits a number of citations, we assume the authors would prefer to cite articles that are well-known in the community. This is captured by the bibliographic module, which takes the authors' names and citation counts of candidate article p as input and produces a single bibliographic score.

Similarly to Ebesu and Fang (2017), we represent author names as embeddings. A sequence of author names $a = (a_1, \ldots, a_m)$ is first transformed into a sequence of author embeddings $\mathbf{a}_e = (\mathbf{a}_{e1}, \ldots, \mathbf{a}_{em})$. The sequence $\mathbf{a}_e$ is then passed through a convolutional layer followed by max-pooling and non-linear transformation to produce the final author embedding, which is then concatenated with article's total citation count and citation counts in last y years. Lastly, the entire vec-

Dataset	Train	Val	Test	Papers
ACL-ARC	30,390	9,381	9,585	19,711
RefSeer	3,521,582	124,911	126,593	624,957

Table 1: Dataset statistics (num. of contexts and papers)

tor is passed through non-linear layer to produce the bibliometric score $s_{\text{bib}}(p)$.

Final recommendation score. The final recommendation score $s_{\text{fin}}(c, p)$ is calculated as a weighted sum of the scores $s_{\text{sem}}(c, p)$ and $s_{\text{bib}}(p)$. Score weights are obtained by passing a context embedding $\mathbf{z}_{\text{context}}$ through a non-linear layer with two values at the output.

Loss function. We use the triplet loss to maximize recommendation score for true context-article pairs and minimize it for false pairs. The training set contains triplets (c, p_+, p_-), where c is the context, p_+ cited article, and p_- article not cited in the context. When sampling articles, we apply time-based filtering for choosing negative instances in triplets, i.e., we only consider articles published before the citing article. The loss function for a given scoring function $s(c, p_*)$ is defined as:

$$\mathcal{L}_s = \max(0, s(c, p_-) - s(c, p_+) + m) \quad (2)$$

where $s(c, p_*)$ is the recommendation score for article p_* and m is a margin used to enhance the difference between scores. We use the sum of three losses as the overall loss function, $\mathcal{L} = \mathcal{L}_{\text{sem}} + \mathcal{L}_{\text{bib}} + \mathcal{L}_{\text{fin}}$, where $\mathcal{L}_{\text{sem}}$, $\mathcal{L}_{\text{bib}}$, and $\mathcal{L}_{\text{fin}}$ correspond to semantic, bibliographic, and final recommendation score, respectively.[4]

4 Evaluation

We evaluate our model on two datasets: RefSeer (Huang et al., 2015) and ACL-ARC (Bird et al., 2008), both of which were used in work on local CR (Ebesu and Fang, 2017; Dai et al., 2019). Dataset statistics are given in Table 1. RefSeer dataset splits are subsets of those used in (Ebesu and Fang, 2017), while ACL-ARC splits are ours, as we were unable to obtain the version used in (Dai et al., 2019). Details on hyperparameters, pre-filtering, and training are given in the appendix.[5]

RefSeer.[6] This dataset comprises articles and citation contexts from various engineering domains. Citation contexts are excerpts of text spanning 200 characters before and after citation. We filter out about 230k articles whose title and abstract is shorter than 100 characters, presumably due to parsing errors. As for most articles the publication year is missing, we use only the total number of citations in the bibliographic module and do not apply time-based filtering for the triplet loss. We adopt the same data splits as in (Ebesu and Fang, 2017), however, due to filtering, our numbers differ.

ACL-ARC.[7] This dataset contains articles published at ACL venues. We use the version processed using ParsCit (Councill et al., 2008), with citation contexts of 600 characters before and after citation. To investigate the effect of different context sizes on model performance, we use two dataset variants: ACL-600 (citation context size of ± 600 characters) and ACL-200 (citation context size of ± 200 characters, i.e., the same as for RefSeer). As each article's ID contains a year of publication, we use this information for citations counts features and for time-based filtering when constructing triplets. We use time-based data splits: contexts from years 2009 to 2013 are in train, from 2014 in validation, and from 2015 in test set.

Results. We compare our model against BM25 (Robertson and Walker, 1994) on both datasets and Neural Citation Network (NCN) (Ebesu and Fang, 2017) on the RefSeer dataset.[8] We fine-tuned BM25 on validation part of the ACL-600 dataset by performing a grid search over a range of values for parameters b and k_1. We then trained the model on all three datasets with the best performing parameters. Details on BM25 fine-tuning are given in the Appendix.

In addition to the complete model, we also test four of its variants: (1) SemCon – only semantic score, with standard context representation (without citing article's text), (2) SemEnh – only semantic score, with enhanced context representation, (3) DualCon – both scores, without enhanced context, and (4) DualEnh – both scores, enhanced context.

---

[4]We tried taking only $\mathcal{L}_{\text{fin}}$ as the overall loss, but obtained worse results compared to the composite loss function.

[5]Both our code and dataset splits are publicly available: `https://github.com/zoranmedic/DualLCR`.

[6]`https://github.com/chbrown/refseer`

[7]`acl-arc.comp.nus.edu.sg`

[8]Unfortunately, we were not able to replicate the NCN results of Ebesu and Fang (2017) on the RefSeer dataset, so we include the result they reported (albeit on a slightly larger dataset of 148,927 contexts) and, consequently, do not apply NCN to ACL datasets. Färber et al. (2020) also reported they were unable to replicate the results of the NCN.

	ACL-600		ACL-200		RefSeer	
Model	R@10	MRR	R@10	MRR	R@10	MRR
BM25	.095	.049	.095	.049	.090	.050
NCN	–	–	–	–	*.291*	*.267*
SemCon	.568	.306	.537	.291	.340	.166
SemEnh	.553	.290	.546	.285	.445	.216
DualCon-s	.654	.322	.693	.340	.363	.185
DualCon-ws	.689	**.368****	.647	.335	.406	.206
DualEnh-s	.662	.315	**.716**	.341	.437	.230
DualEnh-ws	**.699**	.357	.703*	**.366***	**.534***	**.280***

Table 2: Results on RefSeer and two ACL-ARC dataset variants for baselines and variants of the proposed model with (*-ws*) and without (*-s*) final score weighting. ** and * indicate statistically significant difference between DualEnh-ws and DualCon-ws for p<0.05 and p<0.01, respectively (two-sided t-test for MRR and two-proportion z-test for R@10).

Additionally, we evaluate Dual model versions with and without weighting of the two scores in the final recommendation score. In line with most previous work (Ebesu and Fang, 2017; Dai et al., 2019), we report recall at 10 (R@10) and MRR (Voorhees et al., 1999) (calculated on top 10 recommendations) on test sets. Candidate articles were obtained as top n articles retrieved by BM25 (n=2048 for RefSeer as in Ebesu and Fang (2017), and n=2000 for ACL variants), with cited article included in top n articles, if not retrieved initially.

Results are given in Table 2. Overall, dual scoring models achieve the best results on all three datasets, while models with weighed sum scoring achieve better results than those without (except for R@10 on ACL-200). On RefSeer, the best results achieved with DualEnh model are better than those reported by Ebesu and Fang (2017) (although on a smaller test set and possibly different set of candidate papers). On two ACL-ARC variants, the Dual model performance varies. On ACL-600, R@10 is the highest with DualEnh, albeit without significant improvement compared to DualCon, while DualCon achieves the best MRR score. On the other hand, DualEnh models yield the best scores with both metrics on both ACL-200 and Refseer datasets. The differences with respect to context size are also observable with semantic models – SemCon outperforms SemEnh on ACL-600, on ACL-200 this gap is smaller, while on RefSeer SemEnh outperforms SemCon. Taken together, our results suggest that enhancing context representation with global information helps when citation contexts are smaller, but not when context are longer, as they seem to provide sufficient information for local CR.

5 Conclusion

We presented a model for local citation recommendation with citation contexts enhanced with global information, i.e., the text from citing article's title and abstract. Model shows improvements over a competitive model (Ebesu and Fang, 2017) on the RefSeer dataset and its variants on datasets with smaller citation context sizes. For future work, we plan to further investigate the differences in performance across different datasets.

Acknowledgments

The first author has been supported by a grant from the Croatian Science Foundation (HRZZ-DOK-2018-09).

References

Dzmitry Bahdanau, Kyunghyun Cho, and Yoshua Bengio. 2015. Neural Machine Translation by Jointly Learning to Align and Translate. In *3rd International Conference on Learning Representations, ICLR 2015, San Diego, CA, USA, May 7-9, 2015, Conference Track Proceedings*.

Steven Bethard and Dan Jurafsky. 2010. Who Should I Cite: Learning Literature Search Models from Citation Behavior. In *Proceedings of the 19th ACM International Conference on Information and Knowledge Management*, pages 609–618.

Chandra Bhagavatula, Sergey Feldman, Russell Power, and Waleed Ammar. 2018. Content-Based Citation Recommendation. In *Proceedings of the 2018 Conference of the North American Chapter of the Association for Computational Linguistics: Human Language Technologies, Volume 1 (Long Papers)*, pages 238–251.

Steven Bird, Robert Dale, Bonnie J Dorr, Bryan Gibson, Mark Thomas Joseph, Min-Yen Kan, Dongwon Lee, Brett Powley, Dragomir R Radev, and Yee Fan Tan. 2008. The ACL Anthology Reference Corpus: A Reference Dataset for Bibliographic Research in Computational Linguistics. In *Proceedings of the Sixth International Conference on Language Resources and Evaluation (LREC'08)*, pages 1755–1759. EUROPEAN LANGUAGE RESOURCES ASSOC-ELRA.

Isaac G Councill, C Lee Giles, and Min-Yen Kan. 2008. Parscit: an Open-source CRF Reference String Parsing Package. In *LREC*, volume 8, pages 661–667.

Tao Dai, Li Zhu, Yaxiong Wang, and Kathleen M Carley. 2019. Attentive Stacked Denoising Autoencoder with Bi-LSTM for Personalized Context-aware Citation Recommendation. *IEEE/ACM Transactions on Audio, Speech, and Language Processing*.

Travis Ebesu and Yi Fang. 2017. Neural Citation Network for Context-Aware Citation Recommendation. In *Proceedings of the 40th International ACM SIGIR conference on Research and Development in Information Retrieval*, pages 1093–1096.

Michael Färber, Timo Klein, and Joan Sigloch. 2020. Neural citation recommendation: A reproducibility study. In *Proceedings of the 10th International Workshop on Bibliometric-enhanced Information Retrieval*, pages 66–74.

Michael Färber and Adam Jatowt. 2020. Citation Recommendation: Approaches and Datasets. *International Journal on Digital Libraries*.

Lantian Guo, Xiaoyan Cai, Fei Hao, Dejun Mu, Changjian Fang, and Libin Yang. 2017. Exploiting Fine-grained Co-authorship for Personalized Citation Recommendation. *IEEE Access*, 5:12714–12725.

Qi He, Daniel Kifer, Jian Pei, Prasenjit Mitra, and C Lee Giles. 2011. Citation Recommendation without Author Supervision. In *Proceedings of the Forth International Conference on Web Search and Web Data Mining*, pages 755–764.

Qi He, Jian Pei, Daniel Kifer, Prasenjit Mitra, and Lee Giles. 2010. Context-aware Citation Recommendation. In *Proceedings of the 19th International Conference on World Wide Web*, pages 421–430.

Sepp Hochreiter and Jürgen Schmidhuber. 1997. Long Short-term Memory. *Neural Computation*, 9(8):1735–1780.

Wenyi Huang, Saurabh Kataria, Cornelia Caragea, Prasenjit Mitra, C Lee Giles, and Lior Rokach. 2012. Recommending Citations: Translating Papers into References. In *Proceedings of the 21st ACM International Conference on Information and Knowledge Management*, pages 1910–1914.

Wenyi Huang, Zhaohui Wu, Chen Liang, Prasenjit Mitra, and C Lee Giles. 2015. A Neural Probabilistic Model for Context Based Citation Recommendation. In *Proceedings of the Twenty-ninth AAAI Conference on Artificial Intelligence*, pages 2404–2410.

Arif E. Jinha. 2010. Article 50 million: an estimate of the number of scholarly articles in existence. *Learned Publishing*, 23(3):258–263.

Avishay Livne, Vivek Gokuladas, Jaime Teevan, Susan T Dumais, and Eytan Adar. 2014. Citesight: Supporting Contextual Citation Recommendation Using Differential Search. In *Proceedings of the 37th International ACM SIGIR Conference on Research & Development in Information Retrieval*, pages 807–816.

Xiang Ren, Jialu Liu, Xiao Yu, Urvashi Khandelwal, Quanquan Gu, Lidan Wang, and Jiawei Han. 2014. Cluscite: Effective Citation Recommendation by Information Network-based Clustering. In *Proceedings of the 20th ACM SIGKDD International Conference on Knowledge Discovery and Data Mining*, pages 821–830.

Stephen E Robertson and Steve Walker. 1994. Some Simple Effective Approximations to the 2-Poisson Model for Probabilistic Weighted Retrieval. In *SIGIR'94*, pages 232–241. Springer.

Ellen M Voorhees et al. 1999. The TREC-8 Question Answering Track Report. In *Proceedings of TREC-8*, pages 77–82.

Mark Ware and Michael Mabe. 2015. The STM Report: An overview of scientific and scholarly journal publishing.

A Model Training Details

Below we provide details on model training on both datasets. Model hyperparameters are given in Table 3.

Hyperparameter	ACL-ARC	RefSeer
LSTM hidden size	100	100
author embedding size	50	50
author embeddings number	4563	20000
$\mathbf{v}$ dimension	200	200
W dimension	400×400	400×400
non-linearity	sigmoid	sigmoid
cnn kernel sizes	$[1, 2]$	$[1, 2]$
cnn out channels	$[50, 50]$	$[50, 50]$
cnn non-linearity	ReLU	ReLU
n years features	4	n/a
title+abstract token cutoff	200	200
epochs	10	3
optimizer	Adam	Adam
learning rate	0.001	0.001
betas range	$(0.9, 0.999)$	$(0.9, 0.999)$
loss margin (m)	0.3	0.3
queries per batch	6	30
triplets per query	50	10
predict batch size	300	300
validation triplets per query	10	10

Table 3: Model's hyperparameter setting used for both datasets

Dataset construction. When constructing the ACL-ARC dataset variants, we match articles cited in citation context with the corresponding article in the collection by matching on lower-cased titles. When prefiltering authors, we keep those with more than 3 citations in the ACL-ARC dataset, and those with more than 5 citations in the RefSeer dataset.

Experiments environment. We run the ACL-ARC experiments on NVidia GeForce GTX 1080 GPU, with training time of approximately 5 hours. The RefSeer dataset experiments were run on NVidia GeForce RTX 2080 GPU, taking approximately 27 hours for the training.

Validation loss per model. To ensure reproducibility, we provide the best achieved validation loss for each model on all three datasets in Table 4.

Model	ACL-600	ACL-200	RefSeer
SemCon	0.01295	0.01853	0.00800
SemEnh	0.01239	0.01089	0.00400
DualCon-s	0.00279	0.00401	0.00512
DualCon-ws	0.04940	0.05080	0.12409
DualEnh-s	0.03469	0.00334	0.11590
DualEnh-ws	0.03635	0.03885	0.11578

Table 4: Best validation loss for each model and dataset

BM25 fine-tuning. For fine-tuning BM25 on ACL-600 dataset, we consider a range of values for parameters b and k_1. Parameter b was tested with in the following range: $[0.25, 0.5, 0.75]$, while k_1 was tested in the range: $[0.5, 1.5, 2.5]$. Table 5 contains results obtained on validation set for each combination of parameters.

Combination	R@10	MRR
$b = 0.25, k_1 = 0.5$	0.02878	0.01345
$b = 0.25, k_1 = 1.5$	0.02036	0.01036
$b = 0.25, k_1 = 2.5$	0.01418	0.00729
$b = 0.5, k_1 = 0.5$	0.06972	0.03557
$b = 0.5, k_1 = 1.5$	0.06407	0.03375
$b = 0.5, k_1 = 2.5$	0.04648	0.02545
$b = 0.75, k_1 = 0.5$	0.12824	0.06437
$b = 0.75, k_1 = 1.5$	**0.14721**	**0.07880**
$b = 0.75, k_1 = 2.5$	0.13570	0.07162

Table 5: BM25 grid search results on validation set of ACL-600 dataset.

On the effectiveness of small, discriminatively pre-trained language representation models for biomedical text mining

Ibrahim Burak Ozyurt

FDI Lab Dept. of Neuroscience
UCSD
La Jolla, USA
`iozyurt@ucsd.edu`

Abstract

Neural language representation models such as BERT (Devlin et al., 2019) have recently shown state of the art performance in downstream NLP tasks and bio-medical domain adaptation of BERT (Bio-BERT (Lee et al., 2019)) has shown same behavior on biomedical text mining tasks. However, due to their large model size and resulting increased computational need, practical application of models such as BERT is challenging making smaller models with comparable performance desirable for real word applications. Recently, a new language transformers based language representation model named ELECTRA (Clark et al., 2020) is introduced, that makes efficient usage of training data in a generative-discriminative neural model setting that shows performance gains over BERT. These gains are especially impressive for smaller models. Here, we introduce two small ELECTRA based model named Bio-ELECTRA and Bio-ELECTRA++ that are eight times smaller than BERT Base and Bio-BERT and achieves comparable or better performance on biomedical question answering, yes/no question answer classification, question answer candidate ranking and relation extraction tasks. Bio-ELECTRA is pre-trained from scratch on PubMed abstracts using a consumer grade GPU with only 8GB memory. Bio-ELECTRA++ is the further pre-trained version of Bio-ELECTRA trained on a corpus of open access full papers from PubMed Central. While, for biomedical named entity recognition, large BERT Base model outperforms Bio-ELECTRA++, Bio-ELECTRA and ELECTRA-Small++, with hyperparameter tuning Bio-ELECTRA++ achieves results comparable to BERT.

1 Introduction

Transformers based language representation learning methods such as Bidirectional Encoder Representations from Transformers (BERT) (Devlin et al., 2019) are becoming increasingly popular for downstream biomedical NLP tasks due to their performance advantages (Lee et al., 2019). The performance of these models comes at a steep increase in computation cost both at training and inference time. For example, we use a BERT based re-ranker as the final step in our biomedical question answering system (Ozyurt et al., 2020), where 60% of the question answering time latency is due to the BERT classifier with 110 million parameters. The increased size of the transformer models is correlated with the increased performance (Devlin et al., 2019). Since the computational cost involved at inference time for large models is a bottleneck in their practical applications in the real world especially for real time applications such as semantic search and question answering, new approaches to achieve similar performance on smaller models are getting increasingly popular. A popular approach on this end is distilling BERT to a smaller classifier such as DistillBERT (Sanh et al., 2019), TinyBERT (Jiao et al., 2019) and MobileBERT (Sun et al., 2020). However, a small and efficient model without going through the trouble of training a large model and mimicking it in a smaller model is more preferable.

BERT uses a masked language modeling (MLM) approach by masking 15% of the training sentences and learning to guess the masked tokens in a generative manner. This results BERT using only 15% of the training data. A recent approach called ELECTRA (Clark et al., 2020), introduced a new language modeling approach where a discriminative model is trained to detect whether each token in the corrupted input was replaced by a co-trained generator model sample or not. ELECTRA is computationally more efficient than BERT and outperforms BERT given the same model size, data and computation resources (Clark et al., 2020). The improvements over BERT is most impressive at

Proceedings of the First Workshop on Scholarly Document Processing, pages 104–112
Online, November 19, 2020. ©2020 Association for Computational Linguistics
https://doi.org/10.18653/v1/P17

small model sizes, which makes it an excellent candidate in pursuit of small and efficient language representation models for biomedical text mining.

In this paper, we introduce two small and efficient ELECTRA based domain-specific language representation models trained on PubMed abstracts and on PubMed Central (PMC) open-access full papers, respectively, with a domain specific vocabulary achieving comparable or (in some cases) better results on several biomedical text mining tasks to BERT Base model that have 8 times more parameters resulting in 8 times decrease in inference time. The models are trained on a modest consumer grade GPU with only 8GB RAM which is much lower bar for pre-training of domain-specific language representation models than for BERT and variants. The performance on biomedical named entity recognition (NER) of small ELECTRA models are not as impressive as in the question answering related tasks compared to BERT. However, Bio-ELECTRA++ NER performance can be significantly improved by hyperparameter tuning to achieve comparable performance to BERT.

2 Methods

2.1 Pre-training Bio-ELECTRA/Bio-ELECTRA++

Both ELECTRA and BERT are pre-trained on English Wikipedia and BooksCorpus as general purpose language models. They both also use WordPiece tokenization (Wu et al., 2016) which represents words as constructed from character n-grams of highest co-occurrence to allow out-of-vocabulary (OOV) words to be represented. Given a vocabulary size, the character n-grams (subwords) making up the vocabulary are determined from the corpus by using an objective similar to the compression algorithms to find the subwords that would generate each unique word in the corpus. OOV words are then generated by combination of subwords from the subwords vocabulary. Since the vocabulary of BERT and ELECTRA (Clark et al., 2020) are generated from general purpose corpora, a lot of biomedical domain specific words need to be composed from subwords that does not convey enough information by themselves. For example the gene BRCA1 in BERT/ELECTRA vocabulary represented as B##R##CA##1, mostly formed from single letter embedded representations. For Bio-ELECTRA, the vocabulary is generated using SentencePiece byte-pair-encoding (BPE)

model (Sennrich et al., 2016) from PubMed abstract texts from 2017. Using this domain-specific vocabulary BRCA1 is represented as BRCA##1. In this case, the composition from parts conveys more information since the learned vector embedding of BRCA subword is more likely to capture, for example, its breast cancer relatedness.

19.2 million most recent PubMed abstracts (having PMID greater than 10 million) as of March 2020 are used for Bio-ELECTRA pre-training. Sentences extracted from the paper title and abstract text are used to build the pre-training corpus of about 2.5 billion words. Using the PubMed abstract corpus and 2017 PubMed abstracts generated SentencePiece vocabulary a ELECTRA-Small model (14M trainable parameters) with a maximum sequence size of 256 and batch size of 64 is pre-trained from scratch on a RTX 2070 8GB GPU in four stages for 1.8 million steps lasting 24 days. Original ELECTRA Small was trained on a V100 32GB GPU in 4 days with a batch size of 128 for one million steps. However, the distributed ELECTRA Small++(Clark et al., 2020), which was used for our comparison experiments, was trained on the XLNet (Yang et al., 2019) corpus (about 33 billion subword corpus) with maximum sequence size of 512 for 4 million steps. Since the batch size of Bio-ELECTRA is half the size of the ELECTRA Small due to our GPUs memory size, two million steps are equivalent to one million ELECTRA training steps. ELECTRA Small++ is trained four times more than Bio-ELECTRA and trained on much larger corpus.

For the second stage of pre-training, full-text papers from open access subset of PubMed Central (PMC-OAI) as of May 2020 are used. Sentences extracted from all sections except the references section of the full-length papers are used to build a 12.3 billion words corpus. Bio-ELECTRA is further pre-trained for additional 1.8 million steps using this 12.3 billion words corpus on the same RTX 2070 8GB GPU for additional 24 days. The resulting pre-trained model is called Bio-ELECTRA++ analogous to ELECTRA Small++.

2.2 Fine-tuning for Biomedical Text Mining Tasks

The syntactic and semantic language modeling information latently captured in the pre-trained weights of transformer models combined with a classification layer were found to provide state-of-the-art results in many NLP tasks (Devlin et al., 2019; Clark et al., 2020). We fine-tune Bio-ELECTRA, Bio-ELECTRA++, ELECTRA Small++ and BERT Base for biomedical question answering, yes/no question answer classification, named entity recognition (NER), biomedical question answer candidate ranking and relation extraction tasks.

For biomedical question answering, we used BERT and ELECTRA architectures for SQuAD (Rajpurkar et al., 2016) for SQuAD v1.1. Similar to Wiese et al. and Lee et al. (Wiese et al., 2017; Lee et al., 2019), we have combined our BioASQ (Tsatsaronis et al., 2015) 8b training data generated factoid and list questions based training set with out-of-domain SQuAD v1.1 data set to increase performance over the smaller BioASQ data.

The biomedical yes/no question answer classification task is similar to sentiment (hedging for biomedical literature) detection where the polarity (positive/negative) of a candidate sentence needs to be detected in the context of a question. For ELECTRA and BERT, we have used their official codebase from GitHub slightly extended for our specific classification task.

Named entity recognition involves detection of names of biomedical entities in sentences and usually used for downstream tasks such as information extraction and question answering. For ELECTRA and Bio-ELECTRA/Bio-ELECTRA++, we have used the ELECTRA architecture for entity level tasks adapted for BIO annotation scheme. For BERT, we have used HuggingFace Transformers Python library single output layer entity classification architecture.

In biomedical question answering, after retrieving relevant documents, the sentences containing the answer need to be filtered and ranked for the end user. Given a set of answer candidate sentences per question, where the sentences answering the question are marked as relevant, the ranking problem can be cast as a 0/1 loss classification problem and the learned probability estimates can be used to rank the candidate sentences by relevance. Due to highly unbalanced nature of this data set (on average one positive example per 99 negative examples), we have also investigated a weighted loss function. This ranking approach is also compared to cosine distance based ranking on sentence embeddings generated by Sentence-BERT (Reimers

and Gurevych, 2019) with and without domain adaptation. For Sentence-BERT domain adaptation, we had further trained Sentence-BERT Siamese BERT classifier model with the training portion of our ranking data.

In biomedical relation extraction, a predetermined set of relations among two biomedical entities of interest are classified. For BERT and ELECTRA, relation extraction can be cast as a sentence classification task where the biomedical entities of interest are anonymized using pre-defined tokens to indicate to the classifier the identity of the named entities are not important compared to the context.

For each fine-tuning experiment, ten randomly initialized models are trained and average testing performances and standard deviations are reported. Default BERT and ELECTRA hyperparameters including the number of epochs (two for QA task and three for classification/NER tasks) are used for corresponding experiments. More performance can be squeezed out of the fine-tuned models by hyperparameter tuning. For data sets with an explicit development set, we have investigated the effect of the hyperparameter tuning. All of the ELECTRA based fine-tuning trainings are conducted on a GTX 1060 6GB GPU, while the eight times larger BERT models required training on our RTX 2070 8GB GPU. For BERT experiments, cased BERT Base model is used.

3 Results

3.1 Datasets

For biomedical question answering and yes/no answer classification tests, we have generated training and testing data sets from the publicly available 2020 BioASQ (Tsatsaronis et al., 2015) Task B (8b) training data set. BioASQ 8b training set consists of 3243 questions together with ideal and exact answers and gold standard snippets. The questions come in four categories (i.e. factoid, list, yes/no and summary). Factoid and list questions are usually answered by a word or phrase (multiple word/phrases for list questions) making them amendable for extractive answer span detection type exact question answering for which general purpose question answering data sets are available such as SQUAD (Rajpurkar et al., 2016). Snippets matching their corresponding exact answer(s) are selected for the bio-medical question answering labeled set generation. For about 30% of the factoid/list questions no snippet can be aligned with their corresponding ideal answers. We analyzed those cases and were able to recover additional 152 questions after manual inspection for synonyms and transliterations to include in our labeled data set. The labeled data set is split into 85%/15% training/testing data sets of size 9557 and 1809, respectively.

For yes/no answer classification, the ideal answer text of each BioASQ yes/no questions is used as the context and the exact answer (i.e. 'yes' or 'no') as label for binary classification. The ideal answers are cleaned up to remove the exact answer (yes or no) that sometimes occur at the beginning of the ideal answer. The labeled data is split into 85%/15% training/testing data sets of size 728 and 128, respectively. BioASQ yes/no questions are skewed towards yes answers where about 80% of the answers were 'yes'.

For named entity recognition tests, we have used publicly available datasets used by Crichton et. al (Crichton et al., 2017). Four common biomedical entity types are considered, namely disease, drug/chemical, gene/protein and species.

For our biomedical QA system, we have annotated up to 100 answer candidates per question as returned by the first answer ranker of our QA system as relevant or not (up to the first occurrence of a correct answer). The resulting annotated data set consists of a training set (44933 sentences for 492 questions) and a testing set (9064 sentences for 100 questions).

For biomedical relation extraction, we have used two datasets; GAD (Bravo et al., 2015) (a gene-disease relation dataset) and CHEMPROT (Krallinger et al., 2017) (a protein-chemical multi-relation dataset). For GAD, we have used the pre-processed version from Bio-BERT (Lee et al., 2019) Github repository. For CHEMPROT, we have adapted the pre-processed data from the Github repository of the relation extraction model described in (Lim and Kang, 2018) for our ELECTRA/Bio-ELECTRA/BERT experiments.

The datasets used in our experiments are summarized in Table 1. The datasets and source code are available on Github (https://github.com/SciCrunch/bio_electra). The Bio-ELECTRA models are available on Zenodo (https://doi.org/10.5281/zenodo.3971235).

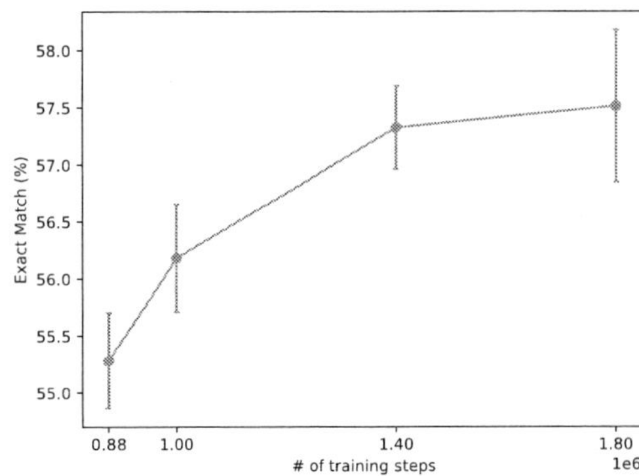

Figure 1: Change in the exact match performance for BioASQ question answering as a function of increased pre-training of Bio-ELECTRA

3.2 Effect of amount of pre-training on the Bio-ELECTRA performance

The effect of the increased number of training steps on the BioASQ question answering task is shown in Figure 1 on exact-match evaluation measure where the 95% confidence intervals are also shown, Even at 880K (or 440K in terms of ELECTRA Small++ pre-training with doubled batch size) training steps the performance of the Bio-ELECTRA is strong relative to BERT Base as shown in Table 2. Similar to what is observed in general purpose downstream question answering tasks (Devlin et al., 2019; Clark et al., 2020), more pre-training improves downstream performance in biomedical question answering.

3.3 Experimental Results

The biomedical factoid/list question answering results are shown in Table 2. We have used official SQUAD evaluation measures exact answer span match percentage and F_1 measure. While BERT Base model had slightly better performance, taken into account their 8 times smaller size and 45 times less training time (Clark et al., 2020), the performance of both Bio-ELECTRA and ELECTRA Small++ models are impressive. With one fourth of the training of ELECTRA Small++, Bio-ELECTRA has nearly same performance as the ELECTRA Small++. The best performance among ELECTRA models is observed for the Bio-ELECTRA++ model further decreasing already small performance gap between ELECTRA Small++ and BERT.

BioASQ yes/no question answer classification

Table 1: Bimedical text mining data sets

Biomedical Question Answering Dataset		
Dataset	**# training examples**	**# testing examples**
BioASQ 8b-factoid	9557	1809
Biomedical Yes/No Question Answer Classification Dataset		
Dataset	**# training examples**	**# testing examples**
BioASQ 8b-yes/no	728	128
Named Entity Recognition Datasets		
Dataset	**Entity Type**	**# training/dev/testing entities**
BC4CHEMD (Krallinger et al., 2015)	Drug/Chemical	29478/29486/25346
BC2GM (Smith et al., 2008)	Gene/Protein	15197/3061/6325
NCBI Disease (Doğan et al., 2014)	Disease	5134/787/960
LINNAEUS (Gerner et al., 2010)	Species	2119/711/1433
Biomedical Question Answer Candidate Ranking Dataset		
Dataset	**# training examples**	**# testing examples**
BioASQ 5b based	44933	9064
Relation Extraction Datasets		
Dataset	**Relation**	**# training/dev/testing examples**
GAD (Bravo et al., 2015)	Gene-disease	4796/-/534
CHEMPROT (Krallinger et al., 2017)	Protein-chemical	16521/10361/14396

Table 2: Biomedical Question Answering Test Results

Model	Exact Match	F_1
Bio-ELECTRA (1.8M)	57.51 (0.88)	66.87 (0.63)
Bio-ELECTRA++	57.93 (0.66)	67.48 (0.44)
ELECTRA Small++	57.78 (0.64)	67.10 (0.55)
BERT	**59.98** (0.66)	**70.25** (0.48)

task results are shown in Table 3. We have used the official BioASQ yes/no question evaluation measure of precision, recall and F_1 applied on both yes and no questions separately. While, both Bio-ELECTRA and Bio-ELECTRA++ outperforms BERT Base, BIO-ELECTRA++ is the clear winner due to its superior performance on questions with negative answer. The high standard deviations for Bio-ELECTRA and BERT Base are due to one random run in each case being stuck in a local minimum where the classifier always answers yes (since BioASQ yes/no questions are highly unbalanced towards the 'yes' answer (80% yes/20% no)).

The test results for biomedical NER experiments are shown in Table 4. Similar to BioBERT (Lee et al., 2019), we have used precision, recall and F_1 as evaluation measures. Here, the large BERT Base language representation model showed, the largest benefit over smaller models at the cost 8 times longer inference time. Bio-ELECTRA++ outperformed Bio-ELECTRA on all datasets and was better (in terms of mean F1 performance) than ELECTRA Small++ in three of the four NER entity types, while ELECTRA Small++ was slightly better than Bio-ELECTRA++ on the 'disease' entity type.

The test results for biomedical question answer candidate ranking experiments are shown in Table 5. We have used the mean reciprocal rank (MRR) to evaluate the ranking performance on the test set. Here, all of the ELECTRA models outperformed BERT, while Bio-ELECTRA++ being the best performing among them. Sentence-BERT sentence embeddings question-answer cosine similarity based approaches performed the worst.

The test results for biomedical relation extraction experiments are shown in Table 6. For the multi-relation dataset CHEMPROT, micro-averaged precision, recall and F_1 metrics are used. For GAD dataset, Bio-ELECTRA performed best closely followed by Bio-ELECTRA++. BERT showed best performance on the CHEMPROT dataset , followed by Bio-ELECTRA++.

Bio-ELECTRA++ outperformed Electra-SMALL++ in 8 out of 9 datasets spanning all five tasks. Against BERT, Bio-ELECTRA++ models showed, besides named entity recognition tasks, either competitive or better (in 3 out of 9 datasets) performance despite having only one eights of the BERT model's capacity (parameter size).

3.3.1 Effect of hyperparameter optimization on Bio-ELECTRA++

For all our BERT and ELECTRA experiments, we have used default parameters without any hyperparameter optimization. To investigate the effect of hyperparameter optimization on the test performance, we have selected the named entity datasets

Table 3: Biomedical Yes/No Question Answer Classification Test Results

Model	P (Yes)	R (Yes)	F_1 (Yes)	P (No)	R (No)	F_1 (No)
Bio-ELECTRA (1.8M)	87.99 (2.95)	**97.94** (1.35)	92.66 (1.56)	77.14 (26.47)	46.92 (16.39)	58.18 (19.91)
Bio-ELECTRA++	**91.24** (1.57)	95.29 (2.31)	**93.19** (0.75)	**78.91** (7.41)	**63.85** (7.92)	**69.84** (3.87)
ELECTRA Small++	88.18 (0.71)	94.31 (1.74)	91.14 (1.00)	69.92 (7.34)	50.38 (3.19)	58.40 (3.61)
BERT Base	87.02 (2.57)	95.49 (2.64)	90.99 (1.00)	65.15 (22.99)	43.46 (15.20)	51.71 (17.49)

Table 4: Biomedical Named Entity Recognition Test Results

Type	Dataset	Metrics	ELECTRA Small++	Bio-ELECTRA	Bio-ELECTRA++	BERT
Disease	NCBI disease	P	76.96 (0.80)	73.47 (0.92)	75.44 (1.06)	**85.43** (0.62)
		R	85.79 (0.64)	83.88 (0.64)	85.19 (0.77)	**87.08** (0.76)
		F_1	81.13 (0.69)	78.32 (0.52)	80.01 (0.68)	**86.24** (0.55)
Drug/chem.	BC4CHEMD	P	81.62 (0.53)	82.76 (0.42)	83.65 (0.18)	**91.36** (0.13)
		R	80.85 (0.47)	83.51 (0.46)	83.95 (0.27)	**89.46** (0.22)
		F_1	81.23 (0.15)	83.13 (0.18)	83.80 (0.19)	**90.40** (0.11)
Gene/protein	BC2GM	P	67.92 (0.40)	67.54 (0.48)	69.34 (0.43)	**83.95** (0.27)
		R	75.13 (0.29)	75.03 (0.16)	76.09 (0.28)	**84.30** (0.31)
		F_1	71.34 (0.27)	71.08 (0.23)	72.55 (0.30)	**84.13** (0.23)
Species	LINNAEUS	P	86.82 (1.16)	85.90 (1.53)	86.01 (1.55)	**96.01** (0.31)
		R	83.25 (1.42)	82.38 (0.72)	84.07 (0.92)	**93.90** (0.17)
		F_1	84.99 (1.02)	84.10 (0.79)	85.02 (0.59)	**94.94** (0.17)

Table 5: Biomedical Question Answer Candidate Reranking Test Results

Model	MRR
Electra Small++	0.281 (0.014)
Electra Small++ (weighted)	0.281 (0.008)
Bio-ELECTRA	0.325 (0.011)
Bio-ELECTRA (weighted)	0.332 (0.013)
Bio-ELECTRA++	**0.335** (0.017)
Bio-ELECTRA++ (weighted)	0.332 (0.013)
BERT Base	0.246 (0.007)
SBERT bert-base-nli-mean-tokens	0.181
SBERT domain-adaptation	0.163

and CHEMPROT relation extraction dataset, which have a development set to use for hyperparameter optimization. Using hyperopt (Bergstra et al., 2013) Python package, we searched for the optimum F_1 value on the corresponding development set of each dataset for the following hyperparameters; the learning rate among the values 1e-5, 5e-5, 1e-4 and 5e-4, number of epochs among the values 3, 5, 15 and 20 and batch size among the values 12, 24, 32 and 64. The best performing hyperparameter combination for each data set is then used to train ten randomly initialized Bio-ELECTRA++ based classifiers.

The test results of the effect of the hyperparameter optimization on Bio-ELECTRA++ are shown in Table 7. In all datasets, hyperparameter optimization resulted in substantial improvement over Bio-ELECTRA++ classifiers without hyper-

parameter optimization. For the NER datasets, the improved test performance caught up with the BERT test performance. Hyperpameter optimized bio-ELECTRA++ relation extraction classifier outperformed BERT. While BERT performance would also profit from hyperparameter optimization, BERT finetuning is more than an order of magnitude slower than Bio-ELECTRA++ finetuning impeding on its practicality.

4 Conclusion

In this paper, we have shown that small domain-specific language representation models that make more efficient use of pre-training data can achieve comparable or better (in some cases) downstream performance on several biomedical text mining tasks to BERT Base with eight times more parameters. Two domain-specific biomedical language representation models based on recently introduced ELECTRA architecture named Bio-ELECTRA and Bio-ELECTRA++ were pre-trained on a consumer grade GPU with only 8GB memory.

While, Bio-ELECTRA performance is highly competitive to BERT Base for question answering and classification tasks, its performance lags behing BERT Base for NER tasks. To further improve the performance of Bio-ELECTRA, we pre-trained it further with a second biomedical corpus of full papers from PMC open access initiative. The resulting biomedical language representation model,

Table 6: Biomedical Relation Extraction Test Results

Relation	Dataset	Metrics	ELECTRA Small++	Bio-ELECTRA	Bio-ELECTRA++	BERT
Gene-disease	GAD	P	71.06 (1.27)	72.99 (1.09)	72.48 (0.55)	**72.72** (1.08)
		R	91.35 (1.76)	92.70 (1.58)	**91.71** (1.17)	88.72 (2.12)
		F_1	79.92 (0.97)	81.66 (0.73)	**80.96** (0.35)	79.91 (1.07)
Protein-chemical	CHEMPROT	P	59.64 (2.41)	61.38 (1.90)	64.66 (1.63)	**69.75** (1.18)
		R	59.34 (2.09)	60.40 (3.12)	63.85 (2.35)	**69.87** (1.79)
		F_1	59.41 (0.88)	60.86 (2.22)	64.22 (1.40)	**69.80** (1.36)

Table 7: Effect of Hyperparameter Optimization on the Bio-ELECTRA++ Test Performance

Dataset	Metrics	Bio-ELECTRA++	Bio-ELECTRA++ opt	BERT
BC4CHEMD	P	83.65 (0.18)	88.45 (0.17)	**91.36** (0.13)
	R	83.95 (0.27)	87.44 (0.20)	**89.96** (0.22)
	F_1	83.80 (0.19)	87.94 (0.09)	**90.40** (0.11)
BC2GM	P	69.34 (0.43)	77.73 (0.38)	**83.95** (0.27)
	R	76.09 (0.28)	80.87 (0.34)	**84.30** (0.31)
	F_1	72.55 (0.30)	79.27 (0.31)	**84.13** (0.23)
NCBI disease	P	75.44 (1.06)	83.40 (0.79)	**85.43** (0.62)
	R	85.19 (0.77)	86.36 (0.65)	**87.08** (0.76)
	F_1	80.01 (0.68)	84.85 (0.65)	**86.24** (0.55)
LINNAEUS	P	86.01 (1.55)	93.77 (1.25)	**96.01** (0.31)
	R	84.07 (0.92)	**96.28** (0.65)	93.90 (0.17)
	F_1	85.02 (0.59)	**95.01** (0.84)	94.94 (0.17)
CHEMPROT	P	64.66 (1.63)	**73.23** (0.86)	69.75 (1.18)
	R	63.85 (2.35)	**71.46** (0.79)	69.87 (1.79)
	F_1	64.22 (1.40)	**72.33** (0.71)	69.80 (1.36)

Bio-ELECTRA++, outperformed Bio-ELECTRA in 8 out of 9 datasets. After hyperparameter fine-tuning, the performance lead of BERT Base over Bio-ELECTRA++ on NER tasks is drastically decreased making Bio-ELECTRA++ competitive or superior to BERT in all biomedical text mining tasks tested.

Acknowledgments

This work was supported by the NIDDK Information Network (dkNET; http://dknet.org) via NIHs National Institute of Diabetes and Digestive and Kidney Diseases (NIDDK) award U24DK097771.

References

J. Bergstra, D. Yamins, and D. D. Cox. 2013. Making a science of model search: Hyperparameter optimization in hundreds of dimensions for vision architectures. In *Proceedings of the 30th International Conference on International Conference on Machine Learning - Volume 28*, ICML13, page I115I123. JMLR.org.

Àlex Bravo, Janet Piñero, Núria Queralt-Rosinach, Michael Rautschka, and Laura I Furlong. 2015. Extraction of relations between genes and diseases from text and large-scale data analysis: implications for translational research. *BMC bioinformatics*, 16(1):55.

Kevin Clark, Minh-Thang Luong, Quoc V. Le, and Christopher D. Manning. 2020. Electra: Pre-training text encoders as discriminators rather than generators.

G. Crichton, S. Pyysalo, and Chiu. 2017. A neural network multi-task learning approach to biomedical named entity recognition. *BMC Bioinformatics*, 18(368).

Jacob Devlin, Ming-Wei Chang, Kenton Lee, and Kristina Toutanova. 2019. BERT: Pre-training of deep bidirectional transformers for language understanding. In *Proceedings of the 2019 Conference of the North American Chapter of the Association for Computational Linguistics: Human Language Technologies, Volume 1 (Long and Short Papers)*, pages 4171–4186, Minneapolis, Minnesota. Association for Computational Linguistics.

Rezarta Islamaj Doğan, Robert Leaman, and Zhiyong Lu. 2014. Ncbi disease corpus: a resource for disease name recognition and concept normalization. *Journal of biomedical informatics*, 47:1–10.

Martin Gerner, Goran Nenadic, and Casey M Bergman. 2010. Linnaeus: a species name identification system for biomedical literature. *BMC bioinformatics*, 11(1):85.

Xiaoqi Jiao, Yichun Yin, Lifeng Shang, Xin Jiang, Xiao Chen, Linlin Li, Fang Wang, and Qun Liu. 2019. Tinybert: Distilling bert for natural language understanding.

Martin Krallinger, Obdulia Rabal, Florian Leitner, Miguel Vazquez, David Salgado, Zhiyong Lu, Robert Leaman, Yanan Lu, Donghong Ji, Daniel M. Lowe, Roger A. Sayle, Riza Theresa Batista-Navarro, Rafal Rak, Torsten Huber, Tim Rocktäschel, Sérgio Matos, David Campos, Buzhou Tang, Hua Xu, Tsendsuren Munkhdalai, Keun Ho Ryu, SV Ramanan, Senthil Nathan, Slavko Žitnik, Marko Bajec, Lutz Weber, Matthias Irmer, Saber A. Akhondi, Jan A. Kors, Shuo Xu, Xin An, Utpal Kumar Sikdar, Asif Ekbal, Masaharu Yoshioka, Thaer M. Dieb, Miji Choi, Karin Verspoor, Madian Khabsa, C. Lee Giles, Hongfang Liu, Komandur Elayavilli Ravikumar, Andre Lamurias, Francisco M. Couto, Hong-Jie Dai, Richard Tzong-Han Tsai, Caglar Ata, Tolga Can, Anabel Usié, Rui Alves, Isabel Segura-Bedmar, Paloma Martínez, Julen Oyarzabal, and Alfonso Valencia. 2015. The chemdner corpus of chemicals and drugs and its annotation principles. *Journal of Cheminformatics*, 7(1).

Martin Krallinger et al. 2017. Overview of the BioCreative VI chemical-protein interaction track. In *Proceedings of the BioCreative VI Workshop*, pages 141–146, Bethesda, MD.

Jinhyuk Lee, Wonjin Yoon, Sungdong Kim, Donghyeon Kim, Sunkyu Kim, Chan Ho So, and Jaewoo Kang. 2019. BioBERT: a pretrained biomedical language representation model for biomedical text mining. *Bioinformatics*, 36(4):1234–1240.

Sangrak Lim and Jaewoo Kang. 2018. Chemical-gene relation extraction using recursive neural network. *Database*, 2018. Bay060.

Ibrahim Burak Ozyurt, Anita Bandrowski, and Jeffrey S Grethe. 2020. Bio-AnswerFinder: a system to find answers to questions from biomedical texts. *Database*, 2020. Baz137.

Pranav Rajpurkar, Jian Zhang, Konstantin Lopyrev, and Percy Liang. 2016. SQuAD: 100,000+ questions for machine comprehension of text. In *Proceedings of the 2016 Conference on Empirical Methods in Natural Language Processing*, pages 2383–2392, Austin, Texas. Association for Computational Linguistics.

Nils Reimers and Iryna Gurevych. 2019. Sentence-BERT: Sentence embeddings using Siamese BERT-networks. In *Proceedings of the 2019 Conference on Empirical Methods in Natural Language Processing and the 9th International Joint Conference on Natural Language Processing (EMNLP-IJCNLP)*, pages 3982–3992, Hong Kong, China. Association for Computational Linguistics.

Victor Sanh, Lysandre Debut, Julien Chaumond, and Thomas Wolf. 2019. Distilbert, a distilled version of bert: smaller, faster, cheaper and lighter.

Rico Sennrich, Barry Haddow, and Alexandra Birch. 2016. Neural machine translation of rare words with subword units. In *Proceedings of the 54th Annual Meeting of the Association for Computational Linguistics (Volume 1: Long Papers)*, pages 1715–1725, Berlin, Germany. Association for Computational Linguistics.

Larry Smith, Lorraine K. Tanabe, Rie Johnson nee Ando, Cheng-Ju Kuo, I-Fang Chung, Chun-Nan Hsu, Yu-Shi Lin, Roman Klinger, Christoph M. Friedrich, Kuzman Ganchev, Manabu Torii, Hongfang Liu, Barry Haddow, Craig A. Struble, Richard J. Povinelli, Andreas Vlachos, William A. Baumgartner, Lawrence Hunter, Bob Carpenter, Richard Tzong-Han Tsai, Hong-Jie Dai, Feng Liu, Yifei Chen, Chengjie Sun, Sophia Katrenko, Pieter Adriaans, Christian Blaschke, Rafael Torres, Mariana Neves, Preslav Nakov, Anna Divoli, Manuel Maña-López, Jacinto Mata, and W. John Wilbur. 2008. Overview of biocreative ii gene mention recognition. *Genome Biology*, 9(2).

Zhiqing Sun, Hongkun Yu, Xiaodan Song, Renjie Liu, Yiming Yang, and Denny Zhou. 2020. Mobilebert: a compact task-agnostic BERT for resource-limited devices. *CoRR*, abs/2004.02984.

George Tsatsaronis, Georgios Balikas, Prodromos Malakasiotis, Ioannis Partalas, Matthias Zschunke, Michael R Alvers, Dirk Weissenborn, Anastasia Krithara, Sergios Petridis, Dimitris Polychronopoulos, Yannis Almirantis, John Pavlopoulos, Nicolas Baskiotis, Patrick Gallinari, Thierry Artieres, Axel Ngonga, Norman Heino, Eric Gaussier, Liliana Barrio-Alvers, Michael Schroeder, Ion Androutsopoulos, and Georgios Paliouras. 2015. An overview of the bioasq large-scale biomedical semantic indexing and question answering competition. *BMC Bioinformatics*, 16:138.

Georg Wiese, Dirk Weissenborn, and Mariana Neves. 2017. Neural domain adaptation for biomedical question answering. In *Proceedings of the 21st Conference on Computational Natural Language Learning (CoNLL 2017)*, pages 281–289, Vancouver, Canada. Association for Computational Linguistics.

Yonghui Wu, Mike Schuster, Zhifeng Chen, Quoc V. Le, Mohammad Norouzi, Wolfgang Macherey, Maxim Krikun, Yuan Cao, Qin Gao, Klaus Macherey, Jeff Klingner, Apurva Shah, Melvin Johnson, Xiaobing Liu, ukasz Kaiser, Stephan Gouws, Yoshikiyo Kato, Taku Kudo, Hideto Kazawa, Keith Stevens, George Kurian, Nishant Patil, Wei Wang, Cliff Young, Jason Smith, Jason Riesa, Alex Rudnick, Oriol Vinyals, Greg Corrado, Macduff Hughes, and Jeffrey Dean. 2016. Google's neural machine translation system: Bridging the gap between human and machine translation.

Zhilin Yang, Zihang Dai, Yiming Yang, Jaime Carbonell, Russ R Salakhutdinov, and Quoc V Le. 2019. Xlnet: Generalized autoregressive pretraining for language understanding. In *Advances in Neural Information Processing Systems 32*, pages 5753–5763. Curran Associates, Inc.

SciWING – A Software Toolkit for Scientific Document Processing

Abhinav Ramesh Kashyap

National University of Singapore

abhinav@comp.nus.edu.sg

Min-Yen Kan

National University of Singapore

knmnyn@comp.nus.edu.sg

Abstract

We introduce SciWING, an open-source software toolkit which provides access to state-of-the-art pre-trained models for scientific document processing (SDP) tasks, such as citation string parsing, logical structure recovery and citation intent classification. Compared to other toolkits, SciWING follows a full neural pipeline and provides a Python interface for SDP. When needed, SciWING provides fine-grained control for rapid experimentation with different models by swapping and stacking different modules. Transfer learning from general and scientific documents specific pre-trained transformers (i.e., BERT, SciBERT, etc.) can be performed. SciWING incorporates ready-to-use web and terminal-based applications and demonstrations to aid adoption and development. The toolkit is available from http://sciwing.io and the demos are available at http://rebrand.ly/sciwing-demo[1].

1 Introduction

Automated scientific document processing (SDP) deploys natural language processing (NLP) on scholarly articles. As scholarly articles are long-form, complex documents with conventional structure and cross-reference to external resources, they require specialized treatment and have specialized tasks. Representative SDP tasks include parsing embedded reference strings (Prasad et al., 2018; Thai et al., 2020); identifying the importance, sentiment and provenance for citations (Cohan et al., 2019; Su et al., 2019); identifying logical sections and markup (Luong et al., 2012); parsing of equations, figures and tables (Clark and Divvala, 2016); and article summarization (Qazvinian and Radev, 2008; Qazvinian

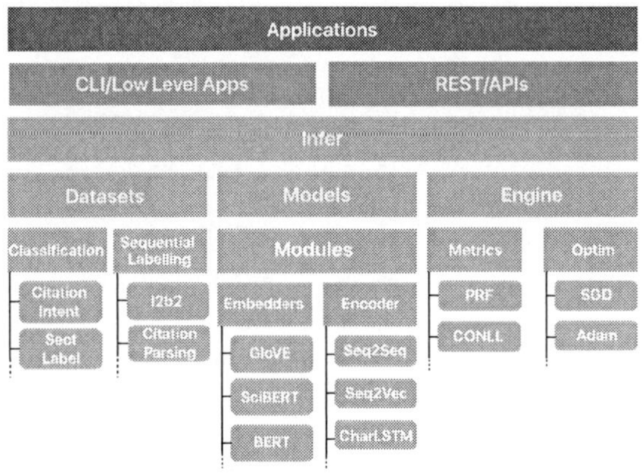

Figure 1: SciWING Components: Text classification and Sequence labelling **Datasets**, **Models** composed from low-level **Modules**, and **Engine** to train and record experiment parameters. **Infer** middleware does the inference and high-level functionality (e.g., developing APIs; low-level and web applications).

et al., 2013; Cohan and Goharian, 2015; Cohan et al., 2018; Cohan and Goharian, 2018). SDP tasks, in turn, help downstream systems and assist scholars in finding relevant documents and manage their knowledge discovery and utilization workflows. Next-generation introspective digital libraries such as Semantic Scholar (Ammar et al., 2018), Google Scholar and Microsoft Academic have begun to incorporate such services.

While NLP, in general, has seen tremendous progress with the introduction of neural network architectures and general toolkits and datasets to leverage them, their deployment for SDP is still limited. Over the past few years, many open-source software packages have accelerated the development of state-of-the-art (SOTA) NLP models. However, these frameworks have a few limitations concerning SDP. First, most are general purpose frameworks aimed at producing SOTA models for natural language understanding tasks or only for specific domains such as biomedicine.

---

[1] Watch our demo video at https://rebrand.ly/sciwing-video

Proceedings of the First Workshop on Scholarly Document Processing, pages 113–120
Online, November 19, 2020. ©2020 Association for Computational Linguistics
https://doi.org/10.18653/v1/P17

Framework	Pre-trained models	SOTA	Neural first	Extensible	Language/Framework
SciSpaCy	✔				Py
AllenNLP	✔		✔	✔	Py(Torch)
FLAIR	✔		✔	✔	Py(Torch)
Grobid	✔				Java
SciWING	✔	✔	✔	✔	Py(Torch)

Table 1: Comparison of SciWING with popular frameworks. **Pre-trained models**: availability of pretrained models. **SOTA**: state-of-the-art or comparably performing models for SDP. **Neural-Networks first**: supports end-to-end neural network development and training. **Extensible**: easily incorporates new datasets and architectures.

Second, they do not provide deployable, SOTA models for SDP. Most provide limited or no means for researchers to train models on their datasets, or experiment with model architectures.

A key barrier to entry is accessibility: a non-trivial level of expertise in NLP and machine learning is a prerequisite. Practitioners who wish to deploy SDP on their field's literature may lack knowledge and motivation to learn it for the sake of deployment. Thus, there is a clear need for a toolkit that unifies different efforts and provides access to pre-trained, SOTA models for SDP, while also allowing researchers to experiment with models rapidly to create deployable applications.

We introduce SciWING to address this need with respect to other frameworks (cf. Table 1). Built on top of PyTorch, it provides access to neural network models pre-trained for a growing number of SDP tasks which practitioners can easily deploy on their documents. For researchers, these models serve as baselines and SciWING encourage them to try architectural variations in a modular manner by swapping or composing modules in a declarative manner in a configuration file, without having to program or deal with complexities of generic tools like AllenNLP (Gardner et al., 2018).

SciWING is MIT licensed and comes with downloadabled pre-trained models and freely-available datasets. The package runs on Python 3.7 and can be easily installed from Python Packaging Index (PyPI) using `pip install sciwing`. For researchers aiming to further develop SciWING, we provide installation tools that set up the system, alongside documentation.

2 System Overview

Our view is that SDP-specific considerations are best embodied as an abstraction layer over exist-ing NLP frameworks. SciWING incorporates AllenNLP, the generic NLP pipeline (Gardner et al., 2018), developing models on top of it when necessary, while using the transformers package (Wolf et al., 2019) to enable transfer learning via its pre-trained general-purpose representations such as BERT (Devlin et al., 2019) and SDP-specific ones like SciBERT (Beltagy et al., 2019). Fig. 1 shows SciWING's Dataset, Model and Engine components facilitating flexible re-configuration. We now describe these components.

Datasets: There are many challenges for the researcher–practitioner to experiment with different SDP tasks. First, researchers must handle various data formats and datasets: for reference string parsing, the CoNLL format is most common; for text classification, CSV is most common. SciWING enables reading of dataset files in different formats and also facilitates the download of open datasets using command-line interfaces. For example, `sciwing download data --task scienceie` downloads the official, openly-available dataset for the ScienceIE task.

Current methods for pre-processing are cumbersome and error-prone. Processing can become complex when different models require different tokenisation and numericalisation methods. SciWING unifies these various input formats through a pipeline of pre-processing, tokenisation and numericalisation, via `Tokenisers` and `Numericalisers`. SciWING also handles batching and padding of examples.

Models: Paired Embedder–Encoder subcomponents combine to form a neural network model, themselves PyTorch classes.

Embedders: Modern NLP models represent natural language tokens as continuous vectors – embeddings. SciWING abstracts this concept via `Embedders`. Generic (non-SDP specific) embeddings such as GlovE (Pennington et al., 2014) are natively provided. Tokens in scientific documents can benefit from special attention, as most are missing from pre-trained embeddings. SciWING includes task-specific trained embeddings for reference strings (Prasad et al., 2018). SciWING also supports contextual word embeddings: ELMo (Peters et al., 2018), BERT (Devlin et al., 2019), SciBERT (Beltagy et al., 2019), etc. SOTA embedding models are built by concatenating multiple representations, via SciWING's `ConcatEmbedders` module. As an example, word and character embeddings are combined in NER models (Lample et al., 2016), and multiple contextual word embeddings are combined in various clinical and BioNLP tasks (Zhai et al., 2019).

Neural Network Encoders: SciWING ports commonly-used neural network components that can be composed to form neural architectures for different tasks. For example in text classification, encoding input sentence as a vector using an LSTM is a common task (SciWING's `seq2vecencoder`). Another common operation is obtaining a sequence of hidden states for a set of tokens, often used in sequence labelling tasks and SciWING's `Lstm2seq` achieves this. Further, it also includes attention based modules.

SciWING builds in generic linear classification and sequence labelling with CRF heads that can be attached to the encoders to build production models. It provides pretrained SOTA models for particular SDP tasks that work out-of-the-box or further fine-tuned.

Engine: SciWING handles all the boilerplate code to train the model, monitor the loss and metrics, check-pointing parameters at different stages of training, validation and testing. It helps researchers adopt best practices, such as clipping gradient-norms, as well as saving and deploying best performing models. Users can customize the following:

Optimisers: SciWING supports all the optimisers supported by PyTorch, and various learning rate schedulers that dynamically manage learning rates based on validation performance.

Experiment Logging: SciWING adopts current best practices in leveraging logging tools to monitor and manage experiments. SciWING writes logs for every experiment run and facilitates cloud-based experiment logging and corresponding charting of relevant metrics via the third-party API service of *Weights and Biases*[2], with the integration of alternative logging services on the way.

Metrics: Different SDP tasks require their respective metrics. SciWING abstracts a separate `Metrics` module to select appropriate metrics for each task. SciWING includes `PrecisionRecallFMeasure` suitable for text classification tasks, `TokenClassificationAccuracy`, and the official CONLL2003 shared task evaluation metric suitable for sequence labelling.

With these components given, SciWING's **Inference** middleware provides clear abstractions to perform inference once models are trained. The layer runs predictions on the test dataset, user inputs and files. Such abstractions also act as an interface for the development of upstream REST APIs and command-line applications.

2.1 Configuration using TOML

SciWING's flexible architecture is encapsulated by its use of declarative TOML configuration files. TOML was chosen as it is a widely-used, unambiguous, and human-readable configuration file format. This enables users to declare dataset, model architectures and experiment hyper-parameters in a single place. SciWING parses the TOML file and creates appropriate instances of the dataset, model and engine to run experiments.

A simple configuration file for reference string parsing along with its equivalent model declaration in Python is shown in the listings below. The class declaration and configuration file have a one-to-one correspondence. As deep learning models are made of multiple modules, SciWING automatically instantiates these submodules as needed. SciWING constructs a Directed Acyclic Graph (DAG) from the model definition to achieve this. The DAG's topological ordering instantiates the different submodules to form the final model.

```
[model]
    class="SimpleClassifier"
    encoding_dimension=300
    num_classes=23
```

[2]www.wandb.com.

```
 5      classification_layer_bias=true
 6      [model.encoder]
 7          emb_dim=300
 8          class="BOW_Encoder"
 9          dropout_value=0.5
10          aggregation_type="sum"
11          [[model.encoder.embedder]]
12          class="VanillaEmbedder"
13          embed="word_vocab"
14          freeze=False
```

```
1  class SimpleClassifier(nn.Module):
2      def __init__(
3      self,
4      encoder: nn.Module,
5      encoding_dim: int,
6      num_classes: int,
7      classification_layer_bias: bool)
```

2.2 Command Line Interface

Qualitatively analyzing the results of the model by drilling down to certain training and development instances can be telling and help to diagnose performance issues. SciWING facilitates this by providing an interactive inspection of the model through a command-line interface (CLI). Consider the task of reference string parsing: the confusion matrix for the different classes can be displayed through the provided CLI utility, which also allows finer-grained introspection of (Precision, Recall, F-measure) metrics and the viewing of error instances where one class is confused for another. For example, `sciwing interact neural-parscit` provides introspection utilities for the pre-trained reference string parsing model. Such introspection utilities are also available for other pre-trained models.

SciWING provides commands to run experiments from the configuration file, aiding replication. For example, experiments declared in a file named `experiment.toml`, can be run with the command `sciwing run experiment.toml`. SciWING then saves the best model. `sciwing test experiment.toml` invokes inference which deploys the best model against the test dataset and displays the resultant metrics.

2.3 End User Interfaces

SciWING's API service enables the development of various graphical user interfaces. SciWING uses its *Infer* layer and exposes APIs for various tasks including reference string parsing, citation intent classification, extracting abstracts and logical sections of articles, identifying entities in

Task	SciWING	Best
Reference String Parsing	**88.44**	—
ScienceIE	**49.9**	48.01
Logical Structure Recovery	**73.2**	—
Citation Intent Classification	82.16	82.6
I2B2 NER	85.83	86.23

Table 2: SciWING's SDP task performance, compared against other comparable models. Bolded values indicate state-of-the-art or comparable performance (without attention). Scores are macro F_1.

clinical notes, using `fastapi`[3]. The API enables the following application families downstream:

- **Web Demonstrations**: To provide quick access to predictions from state-of-the-art models, fulfilling one key aim of SciWING, we have developed an interactive demo using streamlit[4]: `http://rebrand.ly/sciwing-demo`. Pre-specified data or user data can be processed using the distributed models (Figure 2). Both API services and demos can also be run by installing SciWING locally.

- **Programmatic Interfaces** in SciWING provisions advanced use. Users can make predictions for documents stored as .pdf or text files. For example, to parse a text file's citations, SciWING provides a `NeuralParscit` class that has methods to parse all the strings in a file, storing them in a new file. Such a programmatic interface helps the practitioner make predictions easily.

3 Tasks

SciWING prepackages models for various SDP tasks. The examples demonstrate how to use the framework effectively. These models have performance close or comparable to state-of-the-art models (Table 2). They are production-ready, but also can be used as baselines for further research.

- **Reference String Parsing** assigns one of 13 classes to tokens of a reference string that correspond with a in-document citation: *author, journal* and *year* of publication, among them. Neural sequence labelling models, combining a bidirectional LSTM with CRF currently yield top results (Prasad et al., 2018). The model included in Sci-

---

[3] https://fastapi.tiangolo.com/
[4] http://www.streamlit.io

116

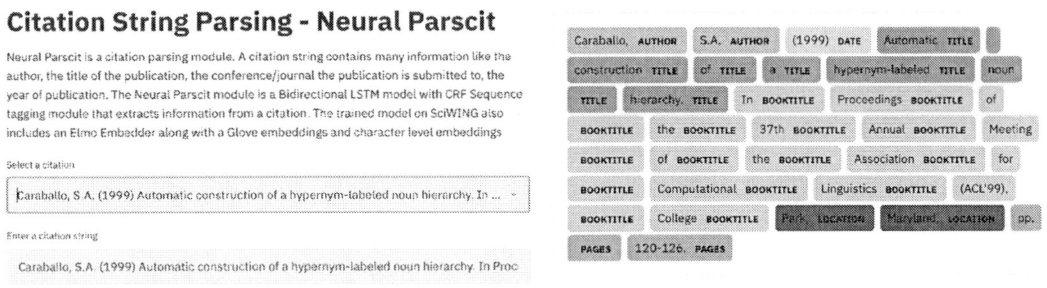

Figure 2: Sample SciWING's demonstration (`https://rebrand.ly/sciwing-demo`) for reference string parsing model, where input (l) is then classified into 13 output classes (r). We utilize the displaCy visualization toolkit (www.spacy.io) and streamlit (www.streamlit.io).

WING implements the same model architecture, but adds ELMo embeddings. Unfortunately, due to the high training expense of their 10-fold cross validation, we are not able to obtain directly comparable results to their model's performance.

- **ScienceIE** identifies typed keyphrases, originally from chemical documents: *Task* keyphrases that denote the end task or goal, *Material* keyphrases indicate any chemical, and *Dataset* that is being used by the scientific work and the process includes any scientific model or algorithm. The state-of-the-art system from 2017 includes a word and character embeddings and a bidirectional LSTM with CRF and uses language model (LM) embeddings (Ammar et al., 2017). SciWING includes a reference implementation without using LM embeddings and the results are comparable. We use the same dataset used by (Luong et al., 2012) for training the neural networks.

- **Logical Structure Recovery** identifies the logical sections of a document: introduction, related work, methodology, and experiments. This drives the relevant, targeted text to downstream tasks such as summarization, citation intent classification, among others. Currently, there are no neural network methods for this task, so SciWING's models can serve as strong baselines.

- **Citation Intent Classification** identifies the purpose of a citation. Some citations refer to another work for *background* knowledge, a few to a related work's *results* and others to *compare and contrast* their methods or results. Such citation intents get used in Semantic Scholar[5]. We train a bi-LSTM with ELMo on the Scicite dataset and achieve an F-score of 82.16. (Cohan et al., 2019) use Bi-LSTM with attention At the time of writing, SciWING does not include attention models,

and as such results are not strictly comparable. We plan to include attention-based models in future iterations of the package.

- **I2B2 Named Entity Recognition** identifies three kinds of entities from clinical notes; problems (e.g., a disease), treatments (e.g., a drug) and tests (e.g., diagnostic procedures). We use a similar model of Bi-LSTM CRF with ELMo embeddings, achieving 85.83 F_1.

4   Use Cases

SciWING caters to both use cases of practitioners looking to deploy pre-trained models as well as researchers looking to refine model architectures and perform fine-tuning domain adaptation on top of state-of-the-art contextual word embedding models. We now examine both use cases.

4.1   Using Pre-trained Reference String Parser

SciWING provisions out-of-the-box access to pre-trained models for direct deployment. Citation string parsing can be deployed with just a few lines of code as shown below.

```
from sciwing.models.neural_parscit
    import NeuralParscit

# instantiate the best model for
    reference string parsing.
neural_parscit = NeuralParscit()

# predict for some reference
neural_parscit.predict_for_text("
    reference")

# predict for a file containing one
    reference per line
neural_parscit.predict_for_file(/
    path/to/file)
```

[5]www.semanticscholar.org

4.2 Building a Reference String Parser from Scratch

State-of-the-art models can be built by stacking up multiple components. We illustrate how to construct such SciWING models, building up to such SOTA model by simple modifications. Such step-by-step model creation also facilitates ablation studies, a common part of empirical studies.

1. Bi-LSTM tagger: Our base model is a bi-LSTM with a GLoVE embedder. Every input token is classified into one of 13 different classes.

```
1   # initialize a word embedder
2   word_embedder = WordEmbedder(
3       embedding_type = "glove_6B_100")
4
5   # initialize a LSTM2Seq encoder
6   lstm2seqencoder = LSTM2SeqEncoder(
7       embedder = word_embedder,
8       hidden_dim = 100,
9       bidirectional = True)
10
11  # initialize a tagger without CRF
12  model = SimpleTagger(
13      rnn2seqencoder = lstm2seqencoder
        , encoding_dim = 200)
```

2. Bi-LSTM Tagger with CRF: We then make a single modification to the above code, swapping the simple tagger with one that uses a CRF.

```
1   ...
2
3   # an RNN tagger with CRF on top
4   model = RnnSeqCrfTagger(
5       rnn2seqencoder = lstm2seqencoder
        , encoding_dim = 200
6   )
```

3. Bi-LSTM tagger with character and ELMo Embeddings: We modify the code to include a bidirectional LSTM character embedder. We use the ConcatEmbedders module to create the final word embeddings (Line 16), which concatenates the character embeddings with those from the previous word embedding and a pretrained ELMo contextual word embedding. This final model is the provisioned model for the reference string parsing task provided in SciWING.

```
1   ...
2   word_embedder = WordEmbedder(
3       embedding_type = "glove_6B_100"
4   )
5
6   # LSTM character embedder
7   char_embedder = CharEmbedder(
8       char_embedding_dimension = 10,
9       hidden_dimension = 25,
10  )
11
```

```
12  # ELMo embedder
13  elmo_embedder = ElmoEmbedder()
14
15  # Concatenate the embeddings
16  embedder = ConcatEmbedders([
        word_embedder, char_embedder,
        elmo_embedder])
```

Here we have described one use case, but models for other tasks are built as easily. In a similar way, we have built a similar architecture for the clinical notes parsing task — the ScienceIE task I2B2 NER task.

5 Related Work

Grobid (GRO, 2008–2020) is the closest to a general workbench for scientific document processing. Similarly to SciWING, Grobid also performs document structure classification, reference string parsing, among other tasks. But Grobid is architected in the traditional, manual feature engineering approach, leading to performance losses for many SDP tasks, and difficulties in retrofitting neural models into its framework.

SciSpaCy (Neumann et al., 2019) focuses on biomedical related tasks such as POS-tagging, syntactic parsing and biomedical span extraction. However, SciSpaCy primarily caters for practitioners; it does not easily allow for the development and testing of new models and architectures.

Task- and domain-agnostic frameworks also exist. NCRF++ (Yang and Zhang, 2018) is a tool for performing sequence tagging using Neural Networks and Conditional Random Fields and FLAIR (Akbik et al., 2018) is a framework for general-purpose NLP and mainly provide access to different embeddings and ways to combine them.

6 Conclusion and Future Work

We introduce SciWING, an open-source scholarly document processing (SDP) toolkit, targeted at practitioners and researchers interested in rapid experimentation. It provisions pre-trained models for key SDP tasks that achieve state-of-the-art performance and aids practitioners to deploy models directly on their community's literature.

SciWING's modular design also greatly facilitates SDP researchers in model architecture development, speeding train/test cycles for architecture search, and supporting transfer learning for use cases with limited annotated data. SciWING allows declaration of models, datasets and experiment parameters in a single configuration file.

SciWING is actively being developed. We consider the following improvements in our roadmap:

• SciWING has yet to incorporate natural language generation related models. We would like to consider sequence to sequence neural models which have proven useful for scientific document summarization tasks, among others.

• Scientific document processing involves minimal training data and has found benefits in incorporating document structure, both of which are tackled using multi-task learning. Multi-task learning is thus a future milestone in SciWING.

• We would like SciWING to foster collaboration among the SDP community and encourage assistance with these goals through contributions to our Github repository in the form of models, datasets and improvements to the framework.

References

2008–2020. Grobid. `https://github.com/kermitt2/grobid`.

Alan Akbik, Duncan Blythe, and Roland Vollgraf. 2018. Contextual string embeddings for sequence labeling. In *Proceedings of the 27th International Conference on Computational Linguistics*, pages 1638–1649, Santa Fe, New Mexico, USA. Association for Computational Linguistics.

Waleed Ammar, Dirk Groeneveld, Chandra Bhagavatula, Iz Beltagy, Miles Crawford, Doug Downey, Jason Dunkelberger, Ahmed Elgohary, Sergey Feldman, Vu Ha, Rodney Kinney, Sebastian Kohlmeier, Kyle Lo, Tyler Murray, Hsu-Han Ooi, Matthew Peters, Joanna Power, Sam Skjonsberg, Lucy Wang, Chris Wilhelm, Zheng Yuan, Madeleine van Zuylen, and Oren Etzioni. 2018. Construction of the literature graph in semantic scholar. In *Proceedings of the 2018 Conference of the North American Chapter of the Association for Computational Linguistics: Human Language Technologies, Volume 3 (Industry Papers)*, pages 84–91, New Orleans - Louisiana. Association for Computational Linguistics.

Waleed Ammar, Matthew Peters, Chandra Bhagavatula, and Russell Power. 2017. The AI2 system at SemEval-2017 task 10 (ScienceIE): semi-supervised end-to-end entity and relation extraction. In *Proceedings of the 11th International Workshop on Semantic Evaluation (SemEval-2017)*, pages 592–596, Vancouver, Canada. Association for Computational Linguistics.

Iz Beltagy, Kyle Lo, and Arman Cohan. 2019. SciBERT: A pretrained language model for scientific text. In *Proceedings of the 2019 Conference on Empirical Methods in Natural Language Processing and the 9th International Joint Conference on Natural Language Processing (EMNLP-IJCNLP)*, pages 3615–3620, Hong Kong, China. Association for Computational Linguistics.

C. Clark and S. Divvala. 2016. Pdffigures 2.0: Mining figures from research papers. In *2016 IEEE/ACM Joint Conference on Digital Libraries (JCDL)*, pages 143–152.

Arman Cohan, Waleed Ammar, Madeleine van Zuylen, and Field Cady. 2019. Structural scaffolds for citation intent classification in scientific publications. In *Proceedings of the 2019 Conference of the North American Chapter of the Association for Computational Linguistics: Human Language Technologies, Volume 1 (Long and Short Papers)*, pages 3586–3596, Minneapolis, Minnesota. Association for Computational Linguistics.

Arman Cohan, Franck Dernoncourt, Doo Soon Kim, Trung Bui, Seokhwan Kim, Walter Chang, and Nazli Goharian. 2018. A discourse-aware attention model for abstractive summarization of long documents. In *Proceedings of the 2018 Conference of the North American Chapter of the Association for Computational Linguistics: Human Language Technologies, Volume 2 (Short Papers)*, pages 615–621, New Orleans, Louisiana. Association for Computational Linguistics.

Arman Cohan and Nazli Goharian. 2015. Scientific article summarization using citation-context and article's discourse structure. In *Proceedings of the 2015 Conference on Empirical Methods in Natural Language Processing*, pages 390–400, Lisbon, Portugal. Association for Computational Linguistics.

Arman Cohan and Nazli Goharian. 2018. Scientific document summarization via citation contextualization and scientific discourse. *Int. J. Digit. Libr.*, 19(2–3):287–303.

Jacob Devlin, Ming-Wei Chang, Kenton Lee, and Kristina Toutanova. 2019. BERT: Pre-training of deep bidirectional transformers for language understanding. In *Proceedings of the 2019 Conference of the North American Chapter of the Association for Computational Linguistics: Human Language Technologies, Volume 1 (Long and Short Papers)*, pages 4171–4186, Minneapolis, Minnesota. Association for Computational Linguistics.

Matt Gardner, Joel Grus, Mark Neumann, Oyvind Tafjord, Pradeep Dasigi, Nelson F. Liu, Matthew Peters, Michael Schmitz, and Luke Zettlemoyer. 2018. AllenNLP: A deep semantic natural language processing platform. In *Proceedings of Workshop for NLP Open Source Software (NLP-OSS)*, pages 1–6, Melbourne, Australia. Association for Computational Linguistics.

Guillaume Lample, Miguel Ballesteros, Sandeep Subramanian, Kazuya Kawakami, and Chris Dyer. 2016. Neural architectures for named entity recognition.

In *Proceedings of the 2016 Conference of the North American Chapter of the Association for Computational Linguistics: Human Language Technologies*, pages 260–270, San Diego, California. Association for Computational Linguistics.

Minh-Thang Luong, Thuy Dung Nguyen, and Min-Yen Kan. 2012. Logical structure recovery in scholarly articles with rich document features. In *Multimedia Storage and Retrieval Innovations for Digital Library Systems*, pages 270–292. IGI Global.

Mark Neumann, Daniel King, Iz Beltagy, and Waleed Ammar. 2019. ScispaCy: Fast and robust models for biomedical natural language processing. In *Proceedings of the 18th BioNLP Workshop and Shared Task*, pages 319–327, Florence, Italy. Association for Computational Linguistics.

Jeffrey Pennington, Richard Socher, and Christopher Manning. 2014. GloVe: Global vectors for word representation. In *Proceedings of the 2014 Conference on Empirical Methods in Natural Language Processing (EMNLP)*, pages 1532–1543, Doha, Qatar. Association for Computational Linguistics.

Matthew Peters, Mark Neumann, Mohit Iyyer, Matt Gardner, Christopher Clark, Kenton Lee, and Luke Zettlemoyer. 2018. Deep contextualized word representations. In *Proceedings of the 2018 Conference of the North American Chapter of the Association for Computational Linguistics: Human Language Technologies, Volume 1 (Long Papers)*, pages 2227–2237, New Orleans, Louisiana. Association for Computational Linguistics.

Animesh Prasad, Manpreet Kaur, and Min-Yen Kan. 2018. Neural parscit: A deep learning-based reference string parser. *Int. J. Digit. Libr.*, 19(4):323–337.

Vahed Qazvinian and Dragomir R. Radev. 2008. Scientific paper summarization using citation summary networks. In *Proceedings of the 22nd International Conference on Computational Linguistics (Coling 2008)*, pages 689–696, Manchester, UK. Coling 2008 Organizing Committee.

Vahed Qazvinian, Dragomir R. Radev, Saif M. Mohammad, Bonnie Dorr, David Zajic, Michael Whidby, and Taesun Moon. 2013. Generating extractive summaries of scientific paradigms. *J. Artif. Int. Res.*, 46(1):165–201.

Xuan Su, Animesh Prasad, Min-Yen Kan, and Kazunari Sugiyama. 2019. Neural multi-task learning for citation function and provenance. *2019 ACM/IEEE Joint Conference on Digital Libraries (JCDL)*, pages 394–395.

Dung Thai, Zhiyang Xu, Nicholas Monath, Boris Veytsman, and Andrew McCallum. 2020. Using bibtex to automatically generate labeled data for citation field extraction. In *Automated Knowledge Base Construction*.

Thomas Wolf, Lysandre Debut, Victor Sanh, Julien Chaumond, Clement Delangue, Anthony Moi, Pierric Cistac, Tim Rault, R'emi Louf, Morgan Funtowicz, and Jamie Brew. 2019. Huggingface's transformers: State-of-the-art natural language processing. *ArXiv*, abs/1910.03771.

Jie Yang and Yue Zhang. 2018. NCRF++: An open-source neural sequence labeling toolkit. In *Proceedings of ACL 2018, System Demonstrations*, pages 74–79, Melbourne, Australia. Association for Computational Linguistics.

Zenan Zhai, Dat Quoc Nguyen, Saber Akhondi, Camilo Thorne, Christian Druckenbrodt, Trevor Cohn, Michelle Gregory, and Karin Verspoor. 2019. Improving chemical named entity recognition in patents with contextualized word embeddings. In *Proceedings of the 18th BioNLP Workshop and Shared Task*, pages 328–338, Florence, Italy. Association for Computational Linguistics.

Multi-task Peer-Review Score Prediction

Jiyi Li[1], Ayaka Sato[2], Kazuya Shimura[3] and Fumiyo Fukumoto[4]
University of Yamanashi, Kofu, Japan
{jyli[1],g17tk008[3],fukumoto[4]}@yamanashi.ac.jp,{t15cs027[2]}@gmail.com

Abstract

Automatic prediction of the peer-review aspect scores of academic papers can be a useful assistant tool for both reviewers and authors. To handle the small size of published datasets on the target aspect of scores, we propose a multi-task approach to leverage additional information from other aspects of scores for improving the performance of the target aspect. Because one of the problems of building multi-task models is how to select the proper resources of auxiliary tasks and how to select the proper shared structures, we thus propose a multi-task shared structure encoding approach that automatically selects good shared network structures as well as good auxiliary resources. The experiments based on peer-review datasets show that our approach is effective and has better performance on the target scores than the single-task method and naïve multi-task methods.

1   Introduction

Automatic prediction of the peer-review aspect scores (e.g. "clarity" and "originality") of academic papers can be a useful assistant tool for both reviewers and authors. On the one hand, because the number of submissions to AI-related international conferences has significantly increased in recent years, it is challenging for the review process. Rejecting some papers with evidently low quality can reduce the workload. On the other hand, suggesting the weak aspects to the authors can also help them improve their papers.

There are several existing works related to the paper review which concentrate on the quality of the review (De Silva and Vance, 2017; Langford and Guzdial, 2015). Huang (2018) et al. predicted the acceptance of a paper only based on a paper's visual appearance (Huang, 2018). Automatic essay scoring (Dong and Zhang, 2016; Dong et al., 2017;

Amorim et al., 2018) can be regarded as a related sub-topic that mainly focus on the grammatical and syntactic features in short essays. PeerRead is the first public dataset of scientific peer reviews for research purposes (Kang et al., 2018), which can be used for paper acceptance classification and review aspect score prediction. It provides detailed peer-reviews including the final decisions, the aspect scores such as clarity and originality, and the review contents. It raises two NLP tasks, paper acceptance classification and review aspect score prediction. We focus on the later one in this paper. However, the dataset is relatively small; the set of papers for each review aspect can be different. To improve the performance of aspect score prediction, we propose a solution based on the multi-task learning that can leverage additional rich information from the resources obtained by other aspect scores. We treat the prediction of each aspect as a separate task. The multi-task model for each aspect score has a main-auxiliary manner.

Multi-task methods have been widely utilized in many NLP tasks, such as summarization (Isonuma et al., 2017; Guo et al., 2018), classification (Liu et al., 2017b; Shimura et al., 2019), parsing (Hershcovich et al., 2018), sequence labeling (Lin et al., 2018), and Entity and Relation (Luan et al., 2018). When building a multi-task model, there are two critical issues, i.e., which auxiliary resources (tasks) can be used for sharing useful information and how to share the information among the tasks. In these previous studies, researchers always select specific auxiliary resources, and design handcrafted shared structure in the model for a particular NLP topic.

However, for different datasets and tasks, there may exist other better auxiliary resources and shared structures. We thus propose an approach selecting the shared structures automatically as well as the auxiliary resources that are more beneficial

Proceedings of the First Workshop on Scholarly Document Processing, pages 121–126
Online, November 19, 2020. ©2020 Association for Computational Linguistics
https://doi.org/10.18653/v1/P17

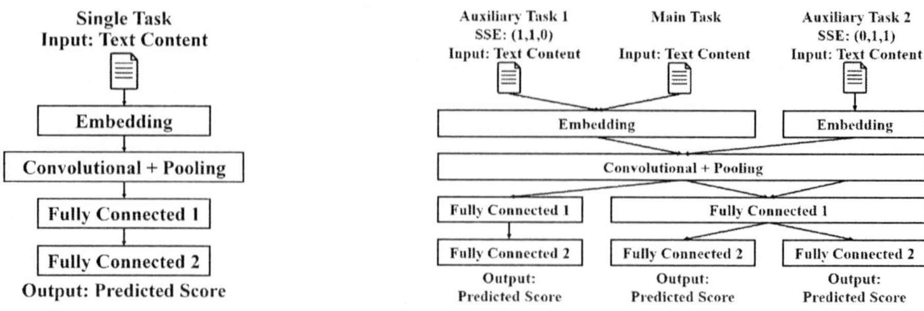

Figure 1: Basic model CNN   Figure 2: Example of Multi-task CNN with Shared Structure Encoding (SSE)

for the main task. There are diverse parameter sharing manners in the multi-task methods for deep neural networks (Ruder, 2017). How to define the exploration space for automatic selection is a problem. Our approach encodes the multi-task shared structures in the manner of hard parameter sharing and defines the exploration space. We also propose a strategy to search the optimal structures and auxiliaries from the candidate models. It is also flexible to add more auxiliary tasks.

Our approach can be integrated with hyperparameter optimization methods (Snoek et al., 2012) or network architecture search methods (Zoph and Le, 2016) for searching. Furthermore, our method is capable for not only review score prediction but also some other NLP tasks such as text classification. Our main contributions can be summarized as follows. (1). We address an application that predicting the peer-review aspect scores of papers which can be a useful assistant tool for both reviewers and authors. (2). We propose a multi-task shared structure encoding method which automatically selects good shared network structures as well as good auxiliary resources. (3). The experiments based on real paper peer-review datasets show that our approach can build a multi-task model with effective structures and auxiliaries which has better performance than the single-task model and naïve multi-task models.

2 Our Approach

2.1 Preliminary

Peer-review aspect score prediction is a regression problem with text data. We can utilize existing text classification methods (Kim, 2014; Liu et al., 2017a) based on deep neural network for this problem by changing the loss function from cross-entropy for classification to mean squared

error for regression. Without loss of generality, we use the basic CNN-based text classification model (Kim, 2014) as the example to facilitate the description of our multi-task approach. Figure 1 shows the architecture of this model for predicting the aspect score. It includes the embedding layer, convolutional and pooling layer, and fully connected layers. The multi-task approach we propose is not limited to be adapted with this model. It can be integrated with similar neural network structures in this example, e.g., XML-CNN (Liu et al., 2017a) and DPCNN (Johnson and Zhang, 2017).

We have n single tasks (i.e., aspect scores) and assume that they have the same network structures with k layers. For each task, we regard it as the main task and search the proper shared structures and auxiliary tasks.

2.2 Multi-task Shared Structures

To automatically search the proper shared structures and auxiliary tasks, we need to define the exploration space. Because it is difficult to mix diverse parameter sharing manners proposed in various multi-task methods (Ruder, 2017), we utilize the typical manner of hard parameter sharing as the starting point to implement our idea. Other manners of parameter sharing will be addressed in future work.

Figure 2 shows an example of the shared structure encoding (SSE) that we propose with three tasks (one main task and two auxiliary tasks). Given a main task t_0, for each auxiliary task t_i, if the jth layer of t_i is shared with t_0, then we encode this shared structure as $l_{ij} = 1$; if the jth layer is not shared, then $l_{ij} = 0$. We do not encode the shared structures among auxiliary tasks to decrease the complexity of the model. It is flexible to add more auxiliary tasks to a model. There are two special cases of this SSE. One is $l_{ij} = 1$ for all auxiliary tasks. The corresponding model is equivalent to one single model for all tasks. Another is $l_{ij} = 0$ for all auxiliary tasks. It is equivalent to a single-task model for the main task. In other words, in the search stage, these models are also included. Lu et al. (2017) adaptively generate the feature sharing structure by splitting the network into branches without merging. Its exploration space is a subset of our approach.

Our multi-task approach utilizes a main-auxiliary manner, rather than a manner which equally treats all tasks. The later manner makes a sum of the weighted losses of all tasks and requires a trade-off among the tasks (Sener and Koltun, 2018), which may not be able to reach optimal results for a specific task. In our approach, we thus use every single task as the main task respectively and other tasks as the candidates for auxiliary tasks. It is flexible for us to define all candidate shared structures in the exploration space and decrease the size of the exploration space.

2.2.1 Shared Structure and Auxiliary Task Search

In our search strategy, we denote the number of auxiliary tasks in a model as m, $m \leq n - 1$. There are $\binom{n-1}{m}$ combinations of the auxiliary tasks. For each combination of auxiliary tasks, we search the shared structures and select the one with minimized loss. For the selection criterion, because the dataset is too small, we use the loss on both the training set and validation set rather than only using the loss of validation set.

After selecting the shared structures for all combinations of the auxiliary tasks, we select the combination of which the average loss of all candidate shared structures is minimum. For a main task, the number of candidate multi-task models is $\mathcal{N}_m = \binom{n-1}{m} \times 2^{km}$. When $m = n - 1$, i.e., using all other tasks as the auxiliary tasks, this number is $\mathcal{N}_{n-1} = 2^{k(n-1)}$. If $m \ll n - 1$, then $\mathcal{N}_m \ll \mathcal{N}_{n-1}$.

If $\mathcal{N}_m$ is small, we can explore all candidates. Otherwise, we need to refer some other methods to search in the exploration space, for example, the hyperparameter optimization methods based on Bayesian optimization (Snoek et al., 2012); the network architecture search (NAS) methods based on reinforcement learning (Zoph and Le, 2016; Zoph et al., 2018; Liu et al., 2018). Random search is also possible to be used.

Dataset	Aspects	Train	Valid	Test
ICLR	Clarity	65	8	6
	Originality	72	11	5
	Correctness	64	6	4
	Comparison	27	6	2
	Substance	38	7	2
	Impact	51	9	4
ACL	All six	137	7	7

Table 1: Statistics of Datasets

Settings	CNN	XMN-CNN
Input word vectors	fastText	fastText
Embedding Dimension	200	200
Stride size	1	2
Filter region size	2	2
Feature maps (m)	64	64
Pooling	max pooling	dynamic max pooling
Activation function	ReLu	ReLu
Hidden layers	1024	512
Batch sizes	8	8
Dropout rate 1	0.25	0.25
Dropout rate 2	0.5	0.5
Optimizer	Adam	Adam
Loss function	MSE	MSE
Epoch	40	40

Table 2: Settings of basic models CNN and XML-CNN: Dropout rate 1 is for the embedding layer, and Dropout rate 2 is for the fully connected layers.

3 Experiments

3.1 Experimental Settings

We use the ICLR and ACL datasets in the Peer-Read Dataset (Kang et al., 2018) because they provide the scores of the peer-review aspects. Table 1 shows the statistics of these datasets. We utilize the papers which have the scores in some of the six aspects ($n = 6$), i.e., Clarity (cla), Originality (ori), Correctness (cor), Comparison (com), Substance (sub) and Impact (imp). The scale of these scores is from 1 to 5. We utilize the dataset splitting provided by PeerRead. Because not all papers contain all six aspects in the ICLR dataset, the number of papers for each aspect are diverse. For the ground truth, we use the mean score of multiple reviews which is the general method of multiple score aggregation without considering the review bias. Analyzing the review bias among different reviewers is out of the scope of this paper.

Note that although PeerRead contains both paper text and review text, we only used the paper text because the purpose of this work is to predict the aspect scores before review progress. Moreover, because in the PeerRead (Kang et al., 2018) article, the authors utilized the first 1,000 tokens because the paper text was extremely long; and we used full paper text with our own text pre-processing in the experiments, the results obtained by our experiments and that reported in PeerRead are thus not exactly comparable.

We remove the stop words and use stemming to the words in the papers. The initial word embeddings in the models are pre-trained by fastText (Bojanowski et al., 2016; Joulin et al., 2016) from each dataset. The hyperparameters of the CNN structures for the approaches refer to the common ones used in exiting work (Shimura et al., 2018). Table 2 shows the parameter settings of CNN and XML-CNN, which are used as basic models of the proposed multi-task approach in the paper.

The baselines are as follows.

Single task model: It is equivalent to the case that SSEs of all auxiliary tasks are "000". It uses one network for one aspect score like the models in (Dong and Zhang, 2016; Dong et al., 2017).

All-in-one (Ain1): It builds a single model that the main task and m auxiliary tasks use same network like the models in the PeerRead (Kang et al., 2018). It is equivalent to treating the prediction of all aspects as one task or as a multi-task that SSEs of all auxiliary tasks are "111".

Average performance of all explored Multi-Task models (AMT): It is equivalent to the expectation of the performance if randomly selecting a multi-task model from all candidates.

We select the aspect of Clarity, which has most test data as the main task for the evaluation in this paper. The evaluation metric is the Root Mean Square Error (RMSE). We first verify our approach by using CNN (Kim, 2014) as the basic model. We set $m \in [1, 2, n-1]$. When $m = n - 1$, the $\mathcal{N}_m = 8^5$ is very huge. We use random search method by exploring 1000 candidate models and evaluate the mean performance of five times.

3.2 Experimental Results

We first verify whether our SSE method can select a good shared structure for a given combination of auxiliary tasks. Table 3.(a) shows the results in the case of $m = 1$. It shows that our method successfully builds a better model than the single task model and the model in which all tasks completely share with each other. The comparison result with AMT shows our method can select a better shared structure from all candidate structures.

Table 3.(b) shows the results in the case of $m = 2$. Our method can select a better shared

Auxiliary	Our (SSE)	AMT	Ain1
ori	*0.801* (001)	0.931	1.027
cor	*0.839* (111)	0.951	0.858
com	*0.792* (100)	0.913	0.908
sub	*0.782* (100)	0.916	0.981
imp	*0.831* (100)	0.924	0.970

(a). $m = 1$

Auxiliaries	Our (SSEs)	AMT	Ain1
ori,cor	*0.881* (001,110)	0.957	1.036
ori,com	*0.946* (111,101)	0.976	1.136
ori,sub	*0.849* (001,101)	0.971	1.211
ori,imp	**0.853** (001,100)	0.977	1.046
cor,com	0.996 (111,101)	*0.965*	1.226
cor,sub	*0.761* (101,001)	0.967	1.143
cor,imp	*0.799* (101,001)	0.965	1.189
com,sub	0.892 (001,001)	0.979	1.243
com,imp	*0.732* (101,101)	0.981	0.918
sub,imp	*0.932* (001,101)	0.969	1.087

(b). $m = 2$

Table 3: Results (Performance and SSEs) of shared structure selection for each combination of auxiliary tasks. Main task: "Clarity"; basic model: CNN; dataset: ICLR; metric: RMSE; performance of single task model: 0.849. **Bold** marks the best performance (including performance of the single task model). *Italic* marks the better one between "Our" and "AMT".

m	$\mathcal{N}'_m$	Our Selected (SSEs)	Our RMSE	AMT
1	40	com (100)	*0.792*	0.927
2	640	ori, imp (101,101)	*0.732*	0.971
5	1000	All (5 times)	*0.841*	1.001

Table 4: Results of selecting both shared structures and auxiliary tasks. Main task: "Clarity"; basic model: CNN; dataset: ICLR; performance of single task model: 0.849. **Bold** marks the best performance. *Italic* marks the better one between "Our" and "AMT".

structure from all candidate structures. But it cannot always be better than the single task model this time. It is because that the corresponding combinations of auxiliaries are not proper. After using our search strategy to select the combinations of auxiliaries, in 2nd row of Table 4, our method can select the auxiliaries and structures with better performance. In addition, in Table 4, the performance for $m = 2$ is better than $m = 1$, it shows that increasing m is possible to improve the performance. However, a large m results in a large $\mathcal{N}_m$. In the case of $m = 5$, although it is possible to obtain a better model than $m = 1$ or 2 if exploring all $\mathcal{N}_5 = 8^5$ candidate models, only exploring a subset ($\mathcal{N}'_5 = 1000$) cannot reach better performance even though $\mathcal{N}'_5$ has been larger than $\mathcal{N}_2$. Without a better search method, using a small m (e.g., $m = 2$) rather than a large m (e.g., $m = 5$, all

Changed Settings	m	Our			AMT	Single
		$\mathcal{N}_m$	Selected (SSEs)	RMSE		
Basic model: XML-CNN	1	40	cor (111)	*0.939*	1.144	0.976
	2	640	ori,cor (100,100)	*0.842*	1.201	
Main Task: Originality	1	40	sub (101)	*0.725*	1.032	1.004
	2	640	com,imp(111,001)	*0.887*	1.017	
Dataset: ACL	1	40	cor (101)	*1.296*	1.414	1.332
	2	640	cor,sub (001,100)	*1.237*	1.455	
Embedding: Wikipedia	1	40	com (101)	*1.151*	1.272	1.241
	2	640	com,sub (101,001)	*0.992*	1.280	

Table 5: Results of selecting both shared structures and auxiliary tasks, by changing four settings respectively

other aspects as auxiliaries) is recommended.

Furthermore, we also respectively change the following four settings while keeping other settings unchanged to verify our approach in different conditions, (1). basic model: one of the SOTA text classification methods XML-CNN (Liu et al., 2017a); (2). main task: Originality, besides the clarity aspect, we also show the results when another aspect is the main task; (3). dataset: ACL. (4). embedding: the pre-trained embeddings by fastText are initialized by the embeddings trained from Wikipedia data.

Table 5 shows that our approach can robustly generate better results in different settings. Table 4 and 5 also show that the selected auxiliary tasks and shared structures are diverse in different settings. It would be better to automatically select them rather than manually decide them. For the underlying characteristics of review aspects in this dataset, there is no apparent observation that one aspect is exactly related to the main aspect and must be the auxiliary. Finally, from the results of "originality" aspect in Table 5, it shows that "substance", "comparison" and "impact" support "originality", the selected aspects by SSEs is reasonable and fit human intuitions.

4 Conclusion

In this paper, we focus on the peer-review score prediction for papers. We propose a multi-task shared structure encoding approach which automatically selects good shared network structures as well as good auxiliary resources. There are some issues in the future work, e.g., trying search methods such as network architecture search and finding evidences of the score predictions.

Acknowledgments

This work was partially supported by KDDI Foundation Research Grant Program.

References

Evelin Amorim, Marcia Cançado, and Adriano Veloso. 2018. Automated essay scoring in the presence of biased ratings. In *Proceedings of the 2018 Conference of the North American Chapter of the Association for Computational Linguistics: Human Language Technologies, Volume 1 (Long Papers)*, pages 229–237, New Orleans, Louisiana. Association for Computational Linguistics.

Piotr Bojanowski, Edouard Grave, Armand Joulin, and Tomas Mikolov. 2016. Enriching word vectors with subword information. *arXiv preprint arXiv:1607.04606*.

Pali UK De Silva and Candace K Vance. 2017. Preserving the quality of scientific research: peer review of research articles. In *Scientific Scholarly Communication*, pages 73–99. Springer.

Fei Dong and Yue Zhang. 2016. Automatic features for essay scoring – an empirical study. In *Proceedings of the 2016 Conference on Empirical Methods in Natural Language Processing*, pages 1072–1077, Austin, Texas. Association for Computational Linguistics.

Fei Dong, Yue Zhang, and Jie Yang. 2017. Attention-based recurrent convolutional neural network for automatic essay scoring. In *Proceedings of the 21st Conference on Computational Natural Language Learning (CoNLL 2017)*, pages 153–162, Vancouver, Canada. Association for Computational Linguistics.

Han Guo, Ramakanth Pasunuru, and Mohit Bansal. 2018. Soft layer-specific multi-task summarization with entailment and question generation. In *Proceedings of the 56th Annual Meeting of the Association for Computational Linguistics (Volume 1: Long Papers)*, pages 687–697, Melbourne, Australia. Association for Computational Linguistics.

Daniel Hershcovich, Omri Abend, and Ari Rappoport. 2018. Multitask parsing across semantic representations. In *Proceedings of the 56th Annual Meeting of the Association for Computational Linguistics (Volume 1: Long Papers)*, pages 373–385, Melbourne, Australia. Association for Computational Linguistics.

Jia-Bin Huang. 2018. Deep paper gestalt. *arXiv preprint arXiv:1812.08775.*

Masaru Isonuma, Toru Fujino, Junichiro Mori, Yutaka Matsuo, and Ichiro Sakata. 2017. Extractive summarization using multi-task learning with document classification. In *Proceedings of the 2017 Conference on Empirical Methods in Natural Language Processing*, pages 2101–2110, Copenhagen, Denmark. Association for Computational Linguistics.

Rie Johnson and Tong Zhang. 2017. Deep pyramid convolutional neural networks for text classification. In *Proceedings of the 55th Annual Meeting of the Association for Computational Linguistics*, pages 562–570, Vancouver, Canada. Association for Computational Linguistics.

Armand Joulin, Edouard Grave, Piotr Bojanowski, and Tomas Mikolov. 2016. Bag of tricks for efficient text classification. *arXiv preprint arXiv:1607.01759.*

Dongyeop Kang, Waleed Ammar, Bhavana Dalvi, Madeleine van Zuylen, Sebastian Kohlmeier, Eduard Hovy, and Roy Schwartz. 2018. A dataset of peer reviews (PeerRead): Collection, insights and NLP applications. In *Proceedings of the 2018 Conference of the North American Chapter of the Association for Computational Linguistics: Human Language Technologies, Volume 1 (Long Papers)*, pages 1647–1661, New Orleans, Louisiana. Association for Computational Linguistics.

Yoon Kim. 2014. Convolutional neural networks for sentence classification. In *Proceedings of the 2014 Conference on Empirical Methods in Natural Language Processing (EMNLP)*, pages 1746–1751, Doha, Qatar. Association for Computational Linguistics.

John Langford and Mark Guzdial. 2015. The arbitrariness of reviews, and advice for school administrators. *Communications of the ACM*, 58(4):12–13.

Ying Lin, Shengqi Yang, Veselin Stoyanov, and Heng Ji. 2018. A multi-lingual multi-task architecture for low-resource sequence labeling. In *Proceedings of the 56th Annual Meeting of the Association for Computational Linguistics (Volume 1: Long Papers)*, pages 799–809, Melbourne, Australia. Association for Computational Linguistics.

Hanxiao Liu, Karen Simonyan, and Yiming Yang. 2018. Darts: Differentiable architecture search. *arXiv preprint arXiv:1806.09055.*

Jingzhou Liu, Wei-Cheng Chang, Yuexin Wu, and Yiming Yang. 2017a. Deep learning for extreme multi-label text classification. In *Proceedings of the 40th International ACM SIGIR Conference on Research and Development in Information Retrieval*, pages 115–124. ACM.

Pengfei Liu, Xipeng Qiu, and Xuanjing Huang. 2017b. Adversarial multi-task learning for text classification. In *Proceedings of the 55th Annual Meeting of the Association for Computational Linguistics (Volume 1: Long Papers)*, pages 1–10, Vancouver, Canada. Association for Computational Linguistics.

Yongxi Lu, Abhishek Kumar, Shuangfei Zhai, Yu Cheng, Tara Javidi, and Rogério Schmidt Feris. 2017. Fully-adaptive feature sharing in multi-task networks with applications in person attribute classification. In *2017 IEEE Conference on Computer Vision and Pattern Recognition, CVPR 2017, Honolulu, HI, USA, July 21-26, 2017*, pages 1131–1140.

Yi Luan, Luheng He, Mari Ostendorf, and Hannaneh Hajishirzi. 2018. Multi-task identification of entities, relations, and coreference for scientific knowledge graph construction. In *Proceedings of the 2018 Conference on Empirical Methods in Natural Language Processing*, pages 3219–3232, Brussels, Belgium. Association for Computational Linguistics.

Sebastian Ruder. 2017. An overview of multi-task learning in deep neural networks. *arXiv preprint arXiv:1706.05098.*

Ozan Sener and Vladlen Koltun. 2018. Multi-task learning as multi-objective optimization. In *Advances in Neural Information Processing Systems*, pages 525–536.

Kazuya Shimura, Jiyi Li, and Fumiyo Fukumoto. 2018. HFT-CNN: Learning hierarchical category structure for multi-label short text categorization. In *Proceedings of the 2018 Conference on Empirical Methods in Natural Language Processing*, pages 811–816, Brussels, Belgium. Association for Computational Linguistics.

Kazuya Shimura, Jiyi Li, and Fumiyo Fukumoto. 2019. Text categorization by learning predominant sense of words as auxiliary task. In *Proceedings of the 57th Annual Meeting of the Association for Computational Linguistics*, pages 1109–1119, Florence, Italy. Association for Computational Linguistics.

Jasper Snoek, Hugo Larochelle, and Ryan P Adams. 2012. Practical bayesian optimization of machine learning algorithms. In *Advances in neural information processing systems*, pages 2951–2959.

Barret Zoph and Quoc V Le. 2016. Neural architecture search with reinforcement learning. *arXiv preprint arXiv:1611.01578.*

Barret Zoph, Vijay Vasudevan, Jonathon Shlens, and Quoc V Le. 2018. Learning transferable architectures for scalable image recognition. In *Proceedings of the IEEE conference on computer vision and pattern recognition*, pages 8697–8710.

ERLKG: Entity Representation Learning and Knowledge Graph based association analysis of COVID-19 through mining of unstructured biomedical corpora

Sayantan Basu [1]   Sinchani Chakraborty [2]   Atif Hassan [3]
Sana Siddique [4]   Ashish Anand [5]

[1,5] Indian Institute of Technology Guwahati
[2,3] Indian Institute of Technology Kharagpur
[4] Eras Lucknow Medical College and Hospital

[1] sayantan18@iitg.ac.in   [2] sinchanichakraborty@gmail.com

Abstract

We introduce a generic, human-out-of-the-loop pipeline, ERLKG, to perform rapid association analysis of any biomedical entity with other existing entities from a corpora of the same domain. Our pipeline consists of a Knowledge Graph (KG) created from the Open Source CORD-19 dataset by fully automating the procedure of information extraction using SciBERT. The best latent entity representations are then found by benchmarking different KG embedding techniques on the task of link prediction using a Graph Convolution Network Auto Encoder (GCN-AE). We demonstrate the utility of ERLKG with respect to COVID-19 through multiple qualitative evaluations. Due to the lack of a gold standard, we propose a relatively large intrinsic evaluation dataset for COVID-19 and use it for validating the top two performing KG embedding techniques. We find TransD to be the best performing KG embedding technique with Pearson and Spearman correlation scores of 0.4348 and 0.4570 respectively. We demonstrate that a considerable number of ERLKG's top protein, chemical and disease predictions are currently in consideration for COVID-19 related research.

1 Introduction

COVID-19 is a global epidemic with a considerable fatality rate and a high transmission rate, affecting millions of people world-wide since its outbreak.[1] The search for treatments and possible cures for the novel Coronavirus (Wang et al., 2020b) has led to an exponential increase in scientific publications, but the challenge lies in effectively processing, integrating and leveraging related sources of information.

Rapid and effective utilization of literature during times of pandemic such as COVID-19 is of utmost importance in combating the disease. In this paper, we introduce a fully automated generic pipeline consisting of an Information Extraction (IE) system followed by Knowledge Graph construction. The IE module uses SciBERT (Beltagy et al., 2019) for performing Named Entity Recognition (NER) and Relationship Extraction (RE). The entire entity extraction procedure is fully automated and no human expertise is used. The major goal is to ensure rapid access of relevant data through a structured representation of free text articles. Following this, we focus on the task of association analysis of essential biomedical entities, namely, proteins, diseases and, chemicals. Such entities are well explored in existing literature and an analysis of their relatedness to COVID-19 is provided by leveraging the CORD-19 Open Research Dataset (Wang et al., 2020a). This can assist the physicians to accelerate knowledge discovery and provide support for clinical decision making. The dataset and related resources of this paper are made public[2].

Due to a lack of gold standard information, we perform extensive qualitative evaluations in order to show that our system does not suffer from redundancy or bias. These evaluations include performance on a link prediction task and intrinsic evaluation. For the former, KG embeddings along with graph adjacency matrix are fed to a GCN-AE (Kipf and Welling, 2016) model to perform link prediction. Average Precision (AP) and ROC scores were used to benchmark different KG embeddings on the generated knowledge graph. For the intrinsic evaluation, we propose a new dataset that has been developed with the help of three physicians and benchmark our embeddings against it. Finally,

---

[1] https://www.who.int/docs/default-source/coronaviruse/situation-reports/20200811-covid-19-sitrep-204.pdf?sfvrsn=1f4383dd_2

[2] https://github.com/sayantanbasu05/ERKLG

Proceedings of the First Workshop on Scholarly Document Processing, pages 127–137
Online, November 19, 2020. ©2020 Association for Computational Linguistics
https://doi.org/10.18653/v1/P17

based on cosine similarity score, the best representation was used to predict top chemicals, proteins and diseases related to COVID-19. The contributions of our approach are as follows :

1. We propose a fully automated, human-out-of-the-loop, end-to-end generic pipeline for rapidly determining association of any biomedical entity of interest with other existing well explored entities.

2. We benchmark multiple KG embedding techniques on the task of link prediction and demonstrate that simple embedding methods provide comparable performance on straightforward structured KGs.

3. We introduce two human gold-standard entity lists, COV19_25 and COV19_729. The former consists of expert ratings for 25 entities predicted by ERLKG while the latter consists of expert ratings for 729 entities sampled from the CORD-19 dataset. The ratings are based on every entity's relatedness with respect to COVID-19.

2   Related Work

We mostly focus on recent works centered around the CORD-19 dataset by discussing about the techniques used for IE and KG generation.

2.1   Entity and Relation Extraction

Most of the recent NLP systems use pretrained language models on unannotated text like ELMo (Peters et al., 2018), BERT (Devlin et al., 2019), and XLNet (Yang et al., 2019). In the biomedical and clinical domains, BERT based architectures pretrained with domain-specific unlabelled text have been used for IE (Lee et al., 2020; Alsentzer et al., 2019). The CORD-19 dataset, curated for the COVID-19 pandemic, integrates related scientific articles for various information retrieval tasks (Roberts et al., 2020). Multiple NLP applications have been developed around CORD-19 like Question Answering (Das et al., 2020), Summarization (Park, 2020), NER (Wang et al., 2020c), etc.

2.2   Knowledge Graph

KGs were immensely used in different fields like Life Science (Chen et al., 2009), Decision Support System (Russell and Norvig, 2010) etc. Using the CORD-19 dataset and many other textual sources,

KGs have been built and used for performing different tasks that aid in knowledge discovery. Chen et al. (2020) performs NER using BioBERT on CORD-19 and PubMed Dataset (Dernoncourt and Lee, 2017) while developing a Coronavirus KG from PubMed KG based on two different methods, namely, cosine similarity and co-occurence frequency to predict plausible drugs. Wang et al. (2020b) construct a KG termed as COVID-KG, by extracting multimodal knowledge from existing scientific literature and ontology followed by a QA system, built on top of this information, with an aim to answer questions related to drug repurposing. Comparatively smaller KGs have been constructed for COVID-19 like (Domingo-Fernández et al., 2020) which covers 145 articles consisting of 3945 nodes and 9484 relations covering 10 entity types. Previously built KGs have also been employed for COVID-19 drug discovery (Richardson et al., 2020). However, the scope of the network built by the last two methods is limited owing to the smaller dataset size. Also, to learn node representations and leverage the structural information of the graph, various techniques are used for Knowledge Graph embeddings. Rossi et al. (2020) conducts extensive survey on 16 KG embedding techniques to perform a comparative analysis. They form a taxonomy of the embedding methods, grouping various methods to tensor decomposition models like DisMult (Yang et al., 2015), Geometric models like TransE (Bordes et al., 2013), TransD (Ji et al., 2015), ComplEx (Trouillon et al., 2016) and Rotate (Sun et al., 2019) and Deep Learning models like ConVE (Dettmers et al., 2018) and CapsE (Nguyen et al., 2019). Shifting from textual source to construct a KG, Ray et al. (2020) uses biological interaction networks like drug-protein and protein-protein networks to predict repurposable drugs for SARS-CoV-2 through link prediction while employing Variational Graph AutoEncoders with features from Node2Vec (Grover and Leskovec, 2016) for entity representation.

3   Dataset

3.1   CORD-19

The CORD-19 corpus (Wang et al., 2020a) was published by Allen AI in association with White House and other organizations. It was made publicly available on the Kaggle [3] platform as a part

---

[3]https://www.kaggle.com/allen-institute-for-ai/CORD-19-research-challenge

of an open research challenge. The data, containing scholarly articles, is collected from sources like PubMed Central (PMC), PubMed, the World Health Organization's COVID-19 Database, and various preprint servers like bioRxiv, medRxiv and arXiv.

CORD-19 corpus (2020-05-12) contains a pool of 1,38,000 scholarly articles with 69,000 full-text articles related to COVID-19, SARS-CoV-2, etc. Each paper is associated with bibliographic metadata such as Title, Author etc, as well as unique identifiers such as a DOI, PubMed Central ID etc. Various sub-tasks have been identified for effective information retrieval, however, it lacks task oriented ground truth data. We merge all the metadata with corresponding full text papers and retain the title, abstract and full text from the corpus.

3.2 Datasets for Fine-tuning SciBERT

For NER, we consider the following three datasets, namely, JNLPBA (Collier and Kim, 2004) corpus which consists of 5 distinct tags: *Protein, DNA, RNA, Cell line and Cell type*, the CHEMDNER (Krallinger et al., 2015) corpus which consists of : *Abbreviation, Family, Formula, Identifiers, Multiple, Systematic and Trivial*, the NCBI Disease Corpus (Dogan et al., 2014) which is used to identify only disease mentions.

For RE, the following datasets are used, namely, CHEMPROT (Kringelum et al., 2016) which consists of 13 different relationship types based on identified positive associations according to : *Inhibitor, Substrate, Indirect-Down regulator, Indirect-Up regulator, Activator, Antagonist, Product-Of, Agonist, Down regulator, Up regulator, Agonist-Activator, Agonist-Inhibitor and Substrator-Product-Of* and BC5CDR (Li et al., 2016) which captures binary relations predicting positive or negative interaction for chemical-induced-disease pairs.

4 ERLKG

In this section we discuss about the entire pipeline and its various components. Figure 1 depicts the pipeline which consists of the following modules : Preprocessing, Named Entity Recognition (NER), Relation Extraction (RE) and Knowledge Graph (KG) construction. The rest part of the Figure 1 depicts the evaluation strategies adopted for a reliable association analysis of various chemical, protein and drug entities from CORD-19 corpus with respect to COVID-19.

4.1 Preprocessing

Each abstract or full text was split into sentences using NLTK (Loper and Bird, 2002) sentence tokenizer and the sentences, in turn, were tokenized using the Spacy (v2.0.10) tokenizer[4]. Following this we removed all the non-functional tokens and attached POS tags to the remaining tokens.

4.2 Named Entity Recognition

Named Entity Recognition (NER) is the task of identifying domain-specific proper nouns in a sentence. In order to gain meaningful insights about the major classes of biomedical entities present in the dataset, it was necessary to tag the entities using an NER module by fine-tuning on various biomedical datasets. Since the CORD-19 dataset is a collection of scientific articles, we use SciBERT for NER extraction. SciBERT is a variant on the BERT (Devlin et al., 2019) model and is pretrained on a scientific corpus of 1.14M articles where 82 percent of the literature comprised of the biomedical domain and the rest was from various computer science domains. In order to extract chemical, protein and disease entities, SciBERT is fine-tuned on different task specific datasets one-by-one, namely, JNLPBA (Collier and Kim, 2004), CHEMDNER (Krallinger et al., 2015) and NCBI Disease Corpus (Dogan et al., 2014) to obtains proteins, chemical and disease annotations respectively.

We use the SciBERT-scivocab-uncased model for NER extraction. The input to the SciBERT model is the pre-processed dataset modified according to the tokenization of BERT. The output of the model consists of the input sentence along with labels according to the BIO scheme where "B" stands for Beginning of an entity tag, "I" stands for Inside of an entity tag and "O" means Outside the entity as can be seen in NER module of Figure 1.

Due to a lack of human gold standard dataset for NER on the CORD-19 data, we do not retain the obtained fine-grained entity annotations. Following the NER tagging, we therefore, tag the Protein, DNA and RNA entities extracted upon fine-tuning the JNLPBA dataset simply as PROTEIN, CHEMDNER as CHEMICAL and NCBI-Disease Corpus as DISEASE. We drop all entities with tags Cell line and Cell type as they could not be merged into any existing categories.

---

[4]https://spacy.io/api/tokenizer

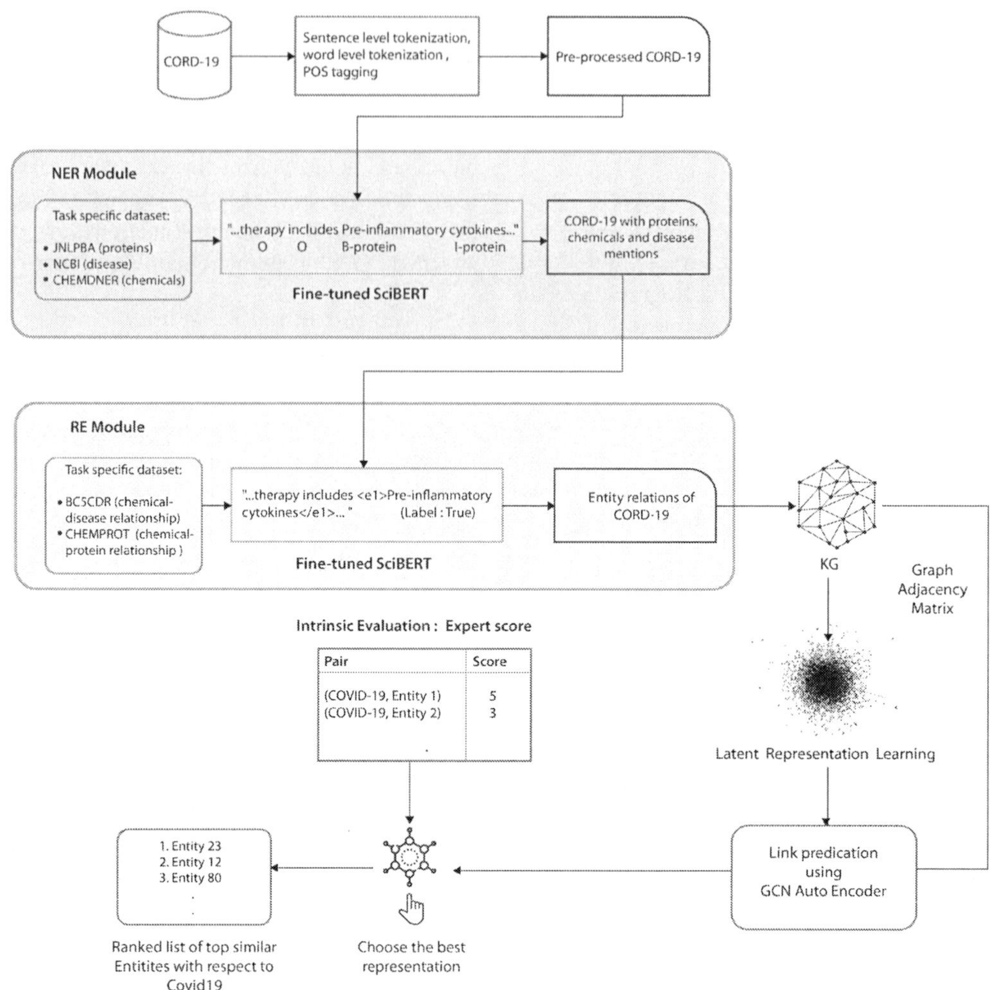

Figure 1: ERLKG Pipeline

4.3 Relation Extraction

From the NER module we obtain an annotated dataset. To further exploit the underlying information present in the running sentences we perform intra sentence Relationship Extraction (RE) which is the task of identifying relationships between any two named entities present within a sentence. Using this RE module we try to identify the relationships that different pairs of entities have at sentence level. The output from the NER module was further processed in order to discover sentences containing more than one entity. For a given set of entities, E, in a sentence, it is split into $\binom{E}{2}$ instances. So, a single sentence, is represented as: $X = \{e_1, e_2, w_1...w_n\}$ where e_1 and e_2 are two tagged entities and w_j is the jth word in the sentence.

An approach similar to the NER module is performed, employing SciBERT for identifying relations from sentences through contextual evidence. We fine tune SciBERT on two datasets, CHEMPROT (Kringelum et al., 2016) and BC5CDR (Li et al., 2016), to capture relations between chemical-protein and chemical-disease pairs.

Following the RE task on the CORD-19 data, we combine the 13 different types of associations obtained upon fine-tuning CHEMPROT as a single relation type called CHEMICAL-PROTEIN. Similarly, only the positive associations obtained upon fine-tuning BC5CDR were retained

Task	Types	# of instances	Total instances
NER Tagged Entities	CHEMICAL	6153	64593
	PROTEIN	42108	
	DISEASE	16332	
Relation Pairs	CHEMICAL -PROTEIN	110485	111916
	CHEMICAL -INDUCED -DISEASE	1431	

Table 1: Statistics of the processed CORD-19 dataset from NER and RE Modules

as CHEMICAL-INDUCED-DISEASE. This ensures that less error is propagated in the absence of gold labels for RE. It also makes sure that the subsequent task of obtaining KG and learning latent entity representations are not misguided during their training phase.

4.4 Knowledge Graph Construction

Statistics of the consolidated set of entity mentions and relation pairs obtained as a result of NER and RE on the CORD-19 dataset can be seen from Table 1. To obtain an overview of the different entities and their association with each other, we generate a KG which is a good association representation of the entire unstructured CORD-19 dataset.

We construct a KG which is defined as $KG = (E, R, G)$, where,

- E: a set of nodes representing disease/ protein/ drug entities

- R: a set of labels representing chemical-protein relation or chemical-disease

- $G \subseteq E \times R \times E$: a set of edges that represent facts connecting entity pairs.

Each fact is a triple $\langle h, r, t \rangle$, where h is the head, r is the relation, and t is the tail of the fact.

4.5 COV19_729

After generating the KG, a list of all entities are supplied to a physician, who clubbed the terms into 3 groups based on their relatedness to COVID-19, i.e., NOT RELATED, PARTIALLY RELATED and HIGHLY RELATED. It was identified that the number of entities in the HIGHLY RELATED group

are much less in comparison to the other two categories. Thus, in order to reduce bias, the physician sampled nearly equal number of entities from each group, resulting in a final dataset comprising of 729 entities named as COV19_729. This dataset was then shuffled and passed on to two independent physicians, who provided ratings to each sample indicating how related an entity is to COVID-19 on a scale of 0 (NOT RELATED) to 5 (HIGHLY RELATED).

The inter-rater agreement score (kappa score) is found to be 0.5116, which lies in the moderate agreement range. We, therefore, average out the ratings and propose a relatively large, intrinsic evaluation dataset called COV19_729 for benchmarking COVID-19 related embedding techniques. Table 4 shows a snapshot of the COV19_729.

5 Experiment and Results

5.1 Implementation Details

To generate the intrinsic evaluation dataset, the total list of 78K entities present in our KG are reduced to 5K by removing all entities having less than 5 indegrees. This is done in order to reduce noise. After experimenting with multiple values, the threshold 5 provided the highest signal to noise ratio. For fine-tuning SciBERT, all hyper-parameters are left at their default values except truncate_long_sequences parameter which is set to false. For training KG embedding, in OpenKE (Han et al., 2018), the dimension is set to 400 and the rest of the parameters are kept as default. In the case of GCN-AE (Kipf and Welling, 2016), for the link prediction task, the learning rate is set to 0.01, epochs to 200, hidden units in the first and second layer as 32 and 16 respectively.

5.2 Link Prediction

Latent entity representation learning of the constructed KG is crucial so that one can effectively analyze associations of any given biomedical entity with respect to COVID-19. Rather than randomly choosing a method, we first evaluate popular KG embedding techniques on a downstream Natural Language Processing task of Link Prediction. We consider Node2Vec (Grover and Leskovec, 2016), Tensor decomposition models like DisMult (Yang et al., 2015) and Geometric models, namely, TransE (Bordes et al., 2013), TransD (Ji et al., 2015), ComplEx (Trouillon et al., 2016) and RotatE (Sun et al., 2019).

The test and validation set is created from the removed edges with the addition of equal number of randomly sampled pairs of false links (nodes that did not have connections in the graph). The test and validation sets have 10 percent and 5 percent of true links, respectively. We use OpenKE (Han et al., 2018) which is an Open-source Framework for Knowledge Embedding techniques. The results are reported based on the model's performance on the test set. The embeddings resulting from these methods are treated as features, along with the graph adjacency matrix and is fed to GCN-AE (Kipf and Welling, 2016). The Average Precision and ROC score of each setting is noted and used to benchmark these embedding types as can be seen in Table 2.

Method	ROC	AP
RotatE (Sun et al., 2019)	0.858	**0.887**
TransD (Ji et al., 2015)	**0.860**	0.883
TransE (Bordes et al., 2013)	0.853	0.877
DistMult (Yang et al., 2015)	0.855	0.883
ComplEx (Trouillon et al., 2016)	0.852	0.881
Node2Vec (Grover and Leskovec, 2016)	0.821	0.849

Table 2: Link Prediction performance of different KG embedding techniques on test set using GCN-AE

From Table 2 in terms of Average Precision, RotatE performs the best among all KG embeddings while in terms of ROC score, TransD outperforms the rest. Models like TransE capture inversion and composition patterns well, whereas models like DisMult capture symmetrical relationships. But in case of RotatE all the different aspects like symmetry, anti-symmetry, inversion and composition are captured. Also, TransD has a similar performance to RotatE. This is because in our setting every relationship pair has the head and tail entity to be of different entity types (either chemical-protein or chemical-disease). The inherent property of TransD to separate the head and tail entity spaces was useful to model this graph structure. Hence, giving comparable results to RotatE.

Node2Vec performs relatively poor since it relies on the internal mechanism of grouping nodes with identical connection patterns which could be less frequent in our KG as it is not raised from an interaction network and is rather constructed from entities and relations obtained from free text.

5.3 Intrinsic Evaluation

We conduct Intrinsic Evalaution where Table 3 shows the performance of TransD and RotatE embedding methods in terms of Pearson and Spearman correlation scores between the ratings and the cosine similarity scores of entities on the COV19_729 dataset. The cosine similarity scores for each entity was generated with respect to the COVID-19 embedding vector obtained from our proposed pipeline. However, most of the top entities generated by two of our best methods, TransD and RotatE (selected on basis of the link prediction task) were not present in COV19_729 since the said dataset was randomly sampled. In our view, these entities require immediate attention and hence, we conduct another round of scoring to evaluate them and in the process, propose COV19_25.

Entity List	Spearman Correlation	Pearson Correlation
COV19_729 (TransD)	**0.2186**	**0.2117**
COV19_729 (RotatE)	0.1933	0.1879
COV19_25 (TransD)	**0.4570**	**0.4348**
COV19_25 (RotatE)	0.4240	0.4105

Table 3: Pearson and Spearman Correlation values between the ratings and the cosine similarity scores of 729 randomly sampled entities and 25 pipeline predicted entities with respect to the COVID-19 vector

5.3.1 COV19_25

The top 100 predicted entities from TransD and RotatE were selected and an intersection of the generated entities was taken, which was then passed on to a physician. The physician recommended a list of 25 relevant entities, out of the provided set. This list was then sent to another physician who rated the entities based on their relatedness to COVID-19. This was named as COV19_25.

It is evident from Table 3 that TransD has the highest Pearson and Spearman score on the COV19_729 and COV19_25 datasets. Hence, we use TransD as the final embedding generation method for ERLKG.

6 Discussion

We exploit the contextual evidence from CORD-19 corpus in finding entities and relations. This is followed by KG construction for determining the relatedness between any biomedical entity with respect to COVID-19. A simple co-occurrence ma-

Entity	Tags	Cosine_with_COVID-19	Rating_by_physician
retinoic acid inducible gene-1	protein	-0.079917936	0
hydroxyprolinol	chemical	-0.018277158	2
acute asthma attacks	disease	0.05297136	1
pc18	chemical	0.153728574	1
s1 domain	protein	0.166142751	2
immunodominant epitopes	protein	0.189406748	2
nsp1	protein	0.202800478	3
hcov whole genomes	protein	0.306899184	1
spike glycoprotein	protein	0.413827424	4
receptor binding domain	protein	0.464432383	5

Table 4: Scores given by Raters on few samples from COV19_729. The cosine similarity scores are generated from TransD embeddings

trix based method is not sufficient to capture the different relationship association types. We, therefore, use state-of-the-art SciBERT for the purpose of entity and relationship extraction. We construct a KG from entity pairs and the relationship among them. Our aim was to utilize this KG for effective association analysis for which identifying the best entity representation was necessary. We therefore conduct link prediction task and evaluate popular KG embedding techniques. Since, our KG consists of a simple bare-bone structure, deep learning based KG embedding methods like ConvE were not explored in this work. This is because such methods lead to an increase in the number of hyperparameters while providing little to no explainability.

We face the challenge of an absence of ground truth data for CORD-19 corpus. Thus, we conduct extensive qualitative evaluations and in the process, introduce two gold-standard, annotated entity lists, COV19_25, and COV19_729. COV19_25 consists of 25 entities predicted by the top two embedding techniques, TransD and RotatE while COV19_729 consists of 729 entities sampled from the processed CORD-19 dataset. The ratings were based on an entity's relatedness to COVID-19. From the correlation scores 3 of our intrinsic evaluation, we observe that our model could provide considerable insight in predicting important associations with respect to COVID-19.

TransD has the highest Pearson and Spearman score on the COV19_729 and COV19_25 datasets. Hence, we use TransD as the final embedding generation method for ERLKG. Figures 2, 3 and 4 show the top related proteins, chemicals and diseases that ERLKG, using TransD embedding, pre-

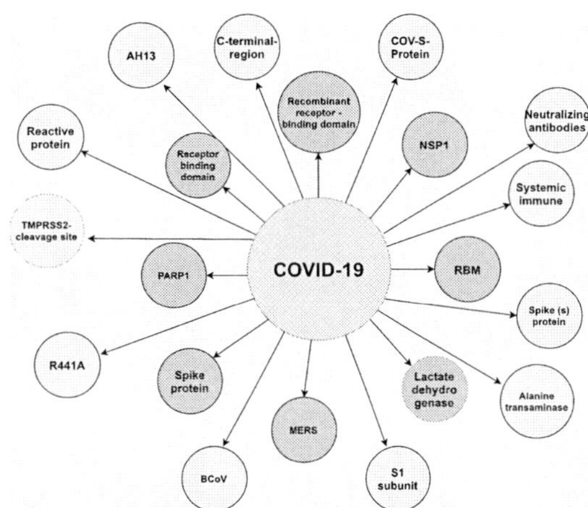

Figure 2: COVID-19 related Proteins based on cosine similarity obtained from ERLKG. Entities color coded Green signify a higher cosine similarity value compared to entities colour coded Yellow.

dicted with respect to COVID-19. Without using any external knowledge resources, our pipeline predicts various chemicals, proteins and diseases that are highly related with COVID-19. These predicted entities could help the biomedical community to get a better understanding of COVID-19. A few top chemicals like Mitoxantrone (Giovannoni et al., 2020), Carfilzomib (Iyer et al., 2020), Flutamide (Cava et al., 2020), Bortezomib (Al Saleh et al., 2020), Lopinavir and Ritonavir (Cao et al., 2020) are being considered as a potential cure for the virus. From the predicted proteins list, entities like PARP1 (Kouhpayeh et al., 2020), Spike protein (Bosch et al., 2003), Lactate Dehydrogenase (Han et al., 2020) and NSP1 (Thoms et al., 2020) have direct relevance with COVID-19. Entities like Ventricular tachycardia (VT) (Wu et al., 2020), Myas-

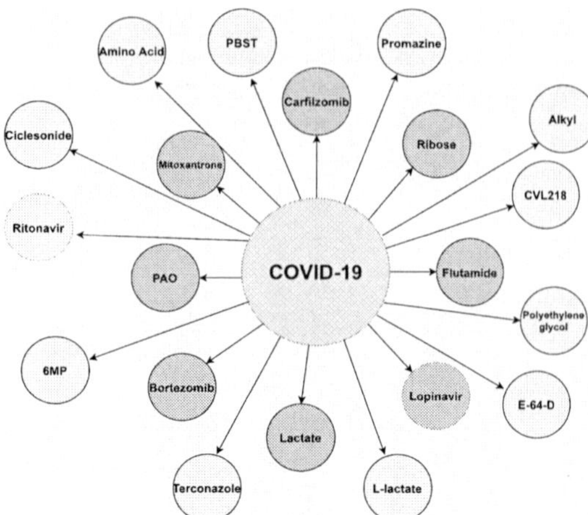

Figure 3: COVID-19 related Chemicals based on cosine similarity obtained from ERLKG. Entities color coded Green signify a higher cosine similarity value compared to entities color coded Yellow.

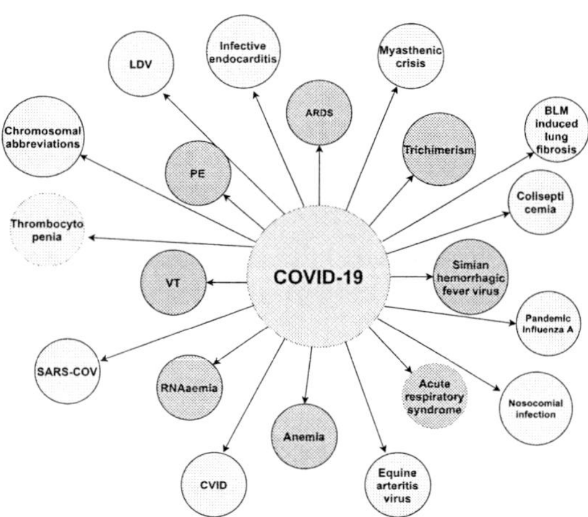

Figure 4: COVID-19 related Diseases based on cosine similarity obtained from ERLKG. Entities color coded Green signify a higher cosine similarity value compared to entities color coded Yellow.

thenic (Delly et al., 2020) crisis, Acute Respiratory Syndrome (Lai et al., 2020), ARDS (Respiratory distress syndrome) (Marini and Gattinoni, 2020) and Thrombocytopenia (Lippi et al., 2020) are a few diseases that are very likely to occur in patients suffering from COVID-19.

7 Conclusion and Future Work

We propose ERLKG, a generic pipeline, for association analysis with respect to a given entity from an unstructured dataset. The part of the pipeline integrating IE and KG construction keeps human-out-of-the-loop. In order to learn the latent representation of the formed KG, we first benchmark various types of KG embedding techniques on the task of Link Prediction. According to our experiments we find TransD and RotatE producing a comparable performance.

In this work our approach is evaluated only on CORD-19 dataset and no additional resources have been employed. However, due to the lack of gold standard data we introduce COV19_729, which is a list of extracted named entities from our pipeline selected randomly and given to physicians for assigning association scores with respect to COVID-19. Owing to random selection most of the entities listed with greater association scores by TransD and RotatE were found to be missing in COV19_729 hence another set was given to physicians from the top entites which we call COV19_25. Finally TransD is used as our best KG embedding technique to predict top entities that are closely associated to COVID-19 from CORD-19 corpus. As a future scope, we plan to implement a normalization and abbreviation expansion module after the detection of entities. The study of these top predicted entities, by the domain experts, can help them understand the different types of associations and relationships they exhibit with respect to COVID-19.

Acknowledgments

The authors acknowledge the Department of Biotechnology, Govt. of India for the financial support for the project BT/COE/34/SP28408/2018. The authors would also like to thank Dr. Shahid Aslam, Department of General Medicine, AMRI Dhakuria Hospitals Kolkata and Dr. Khalid Iqbal, Assistant Professor, Eras Lucknow Medical College and Hospital, for helping with the Intrinsic Evaluation datasets and Sanket Wakade, Department of Design, IIT Guwahati for helping with illustrations. Besides, the authors would like to thank the anonymous reviewers for their valuable comments and feedback.

References

Abdullah S Al Saleh, Taimur Sher, and Morie A Gertz. 2020. Multiple myeloma in the time of covid-19. *Acta haematologica*, pages 1–7.

Emily Alsentzer, John R. Murphy, Willie Boag, Wei-Hung Weng, Di Jin, Tristan Naumann, and Matthew B. A. McDermott. 2019. Publicly available clinical bert embeddings. *ArXiv*, abs/1904.03323.

Iz Beltagy, Kyle Lo, and Arman Cohan. 2019. Scibert: A pretrained language model for scientific text. In *EMNLP/IJCNLP*.

Antoine Bordes, Nicolas Usunier, Alberto García-Durán, Jason Weston, and Oksana Yakhnenko. 2013. Translating embeddings for modeling multi-relational data. In *NIPS*.

Berend Jan Bosch, Ruurd van der Zee, Cornelis A M de Haan, and Peter J. M. Rottier. 2003. The coronavirus spike protein is a class i virus fusion protein: Structural and functional characterization of the fusion core complex. *Journal of Virology*, 77:8801 – 8811.

Bin Cao, Yeming Wang, Danning Wen, Wen Liu, Jingli Wang, Guohui Fan, Lianguo Ruan, Bin Song, Yanping Cai, Ming Wei, et al. 2020. A trial of lopinavir–ritonavir in adults hospitalized with severe covid-19. *New England Journal of Medicine*.

Claudia Cava, Gloria Bertoli, and Isabella Castiglioni. 2020. In silico discovery of candidate drugs against covid-19. *Viruses*, 12.

Bin Chen, Xiao Dong, Dazhi Jiao, Huijun Wang, Qian Zhu, Ying Ding, and David J. Wild. 2009. Chem2bio2rdf: a semantic framework for linking and data mining chemogenomic and systems chemical biology data. *BMC Bioinformatics*, 11:255 – 255.

Chongyan Chen, Islam Akef Ebeid, Yi Bu, and Ying Ding. 2020. Coronavirus knowledge graph: A case study. *ArXiv*, abs/2007.10287.

Nigel Collier and Jin-Dong Kim. 2004. Introduction to the bio-entity recognition task at jnlpba. In *NLPBA/BioNLP*.

Debsmita Das, Shashank Dubey, Aakash Deep Singh, Kushagra Agarwal, Sourojit Bhaduri, Rajesh Kumar Ranjan, Yatin Katyal, and Janu Verma. 2020. Information retrieval and extraction on covid-19 clinical articles using graph community detection and bio-bert embeddings.

Fadi Delly, Maryam Jamil Syed, Robert P. Lisak, and Deepti Zutshi. 2020. Myasthenic crisis in covid-19. *Journal of the Neurological Sciences*, 414:116888 – 116888.

Franck Dernoncourt and J. Lee. 2017. Pubmed 200k rct: a dataset for sequential sentence classification in medical abstracts. In *IJCNLP*.

Tim Dettmers, Pasquale Minervini, Pontus Stenetorp, and Sebastian Riedel. 2018. Convolutional 2d knowledge graph embeddings. *ArXiv*, abs/1707.01476.

Jacob Devlin, Ming-Wei Chang, Kenton Lee, and Kristina Toutanova. 2019. Bert: Pre-training of deep bidirectional transformers for language understanding. In *NAACL-HLT*.

Rezarta Islamaj Dogan, Robert Leaman, and Zhiyong Lu. 2014. Ncbi disease corpus: A resource for disease name recognition and concept normalization. *Journal of biomedical informatics*, 47:1–10.

Daniel Domingo-Fernández, Shounak Baksi, Bruce Schultz, Yojana Gadiya, Reagon Karki, Tamara Raschka, Christian Ebeling, Martin Hofmann-Apitius, and Alpha Tom Kodamullil. 2020. Covid-19 knowledge graph: a computable, multi-modal, cause-and-effect knowledge model of covid-19 pathophysiology. *bioRxiv*.

Gavin Giovannoni, Chris Hawkes, Jeannette Lechner-Scott, Michael Levy, Emmanuelle Waubant, and Julian Gold. 2020. The covid-19 pandemic and the use of ms disease-modifying therapies. *Multiple Sclerosis and Related Disorders*, 39:102073.

Aditya Grover and Jure Leskovec. 2016. node2vec: Scalable feature learning for networks. *Proceedings of the 22nd ACM SIGKDD International Conference on Knowledge Discovery and Data Mining*.

Xu Han, Shulin Cao, Lv Xin, Yankai Lin, Zhiyuan Liu, Maosong Sun, and Juanzi Li. 2018. Openke: An open toolkit for knowledge embedding. In *Proceedings of EMNLP*.

Yi Han, Haidong Zhang, Sucheng Mu, Wei Wei, Chaoyuan Jin, Yuan Xue, Chaoyang Tong, Yunfei Zha, Zhenju Song, and Guorong Gu. 2020. Lactate dehydrogenase, a risk factor of severe covid-19 patients. *medRxiv*.

Mahalaxmi Iyer, Kaavya Jayaramayya, Mohana Devi Subramaniam, Soo Bin Lee, Ahmed Abdal Dayem, Ssang-Goo Cho, and Balachandar Vellingiri. 2020. Covid-19: an update on diagnostic and therapeutic approaches. *BMB reports*, 53(4):191.

Guoliang Ji, Shizhu He, Liheng Xu, Kang Liu, and Jun Zhao. 2015. Knowledge graph embedding via dynamic mapping matrix. In *ACL*.

Thomas Kipf and Max Welling. 2016. Variational graph auto-encoders. *ArXiv*, abs/1611.07308.

Shirin Kouhpayeh, Laleh Shariati, Maryam Boshtam, Ilnaz Rahimmanesh, Mina Mirian, Mehrdad Zeinalian, Azhar Salari-jazi, Negar Khanahmad, Mohammad Sadegh Damavandi, Parisa Sadeghi, et al. 2020. The molecular story of covid-19; nad+ depletion addresses all questions in this infection.

Martin Krallinger, Obdulia Rabal, Florian Leitner, Miguel Vazquez, David Salgado, Zhiyong Lu, Robert Leaman, Yanan Lu, Dong-Hong Ji, Daniel M. Lowe, Roger A. Sayle, Riza Theresa Batista-Navarro, Rafal Rak, Torsten Huber, Tim Rocktäschel, Sérgio Matos, David Campos, Buzhou Tang, Hua Xu, Tsendsuren Munkhdalai, Keun Ho Ryu, S. V. Ramanan, P. Senthil Nathan, Slavko Zitnik, Marko Bajec, Lutz Weber, Matthias Irmer, Saber A. Akhondi, Jan A. Kors, Shuo Xu, Xin An,

Utpal Kumar Sikdar, Asif Ekbal, Masaharu Yoshioka, Thaer M. Dieb, Miji Choi, Karin M. Verspoor, Madian Khabsa, C. Lee Giles, Hongfang Liu, K. E. Ravikumar, Andre Lamurias, Francisco M. Couto, Hong-Jie Dai, Richard Tzong-Han Tsai, Caglar Ata, Tolga Can, Anabel Usie, Rui Alves, Isabel Segura-Bedmar, Paloma Martínez, Julen Oyarzábal, and Alfonso Valencia. 2015. The chemdner corpus of chemicals and drugs and its annotation principles. *Journal of Cheminformatics*, 7:S2 – S2.

Jens Kringelum, Sonny Kim Kjærulff, Søren Brunak, Ole Lund, Tudor I. Oprea, and Olivier Taboureau. 2016. Chemprot-3.0: a global chemical biology diseases mapping. *Database: The Journal of Biological Databases and Curation*, 2016.

Chih-Cheng Lai, Tzu-Ping Shih, Wen-Chien Ko, Hung-Jen Tang, and Po-Ren Hsueh. 2020. Severe acute respiratory syndrome coronavirus 2 (sars-cov-2) and corona virus disease-2019 (covid-19): the epidemic and the challenges. *International journal of antimicrobial agents*, page 105924.

Jinhyuk Lee, Wonjin Yoon, Sungdong Kim, D. Kim, Sunkyu Kim, Chan Ho So, and Jaewoo Kang. 2020. Biobert: a pre-trained biomedical language representation model for biomedical text mining. *Bioinformatics*.

Jiao Li, Yueping Sun, Robin J. Johnson, Daniela Sciaky, Chih-Hsuan Wei, Robert Leaman, Allan Peter Davis, Carolyn J. Mattingly, Thomas C. Wiegers, and Zhiyong Lu. 2016. Biocreative v cdr task corpus: a resource for chemical disease relation extraction. *Database: The Journal of Biological Databases and Curation*, 2016.

Giuseppe Lippi, Mario Plebani, and Brandon Michael Henry. 2020. Thrombocytopenia is associated with severe coronavirus disease 2019 (covid-19) infections: a meta-analysis. *Clinica Chimica Acta*.

Edward Loper and Steven Bird. 2002. Nltk: the natural language toolkit. *arXiv preprint cs/0205028*.

John J Marini and Luciano Gattinoni. 2020. Management of covid-19 respiratory distress. *Jama*.

Dai Quoc Nguyen, Thanh Vu, T. Nguyen, Dat Quoc Nguyen, and Dinh Q. Phung. 2019. A capsule network-based embedding model for knowledge graph completion and search personalization. *ArXiv*, abs/1808.04122.

Jong Won Park. 2020. Continual bert: Continual learning for adaptive extractive summarization of covid-19 literature. *ArXiv*, abs/2007.03405.

Matthew E. Peters, Mark Neumann, Mohit Iyyer, Matt Gardner, Christopher Clark, Kenton Lee, and Luke Zettlemoyer. 2018. Deep contextualized word representations. *ArXiv*, abs/1802.05365.

Sumanta Ray, Snehalika Lall, Anirban Mukhopadhyay, Sanghamitra Bandyopadhyay, and Alexander Schonhuth. 2020. Predicting potential drug targets and repurposable drugs for covid-19 via a deep generative model for graphs.

Peter Richardson, Ivan Griffin, C. Tucker, D. Smith, Olly Oechsle, Anne Phelan, Michael Rawling, Edward Savory, and J. Stebbing. 2020. Baricitinib as potential treatment for 2019-ncov acute respiratory disease. *Lancet (London, England)*, 395:e30 – e31.

Kirk Roberts, Tasmeer Alam, Steven Bedrick, Dina Demner-Fushman, Kyle Lo, Ian Soboroff, Ellen M. Voorhees, Lucy Lu Wang, and William R. Hersh. 2020. Trec-covid: Rationale and structure of an information retrieval shared task for covid-19. *Journal of the American Medical Informatics Association : JAMIA*.

Andrea Rossi, Donatella Firmani, Antonio Matinata, Paolo Merialdo, and Denilson Barbosa. 2020. Knowledge graph embedding for link prediction: A comparative analysis. *ArXiv*, abs/2002.00819.

Stuart J. Russell and Peter Norvig. 2010. Artificial intelligence : a modern approach - 3rd ed.global ed.

Zhiqing Sun, Zhi-Hong Deng, Jian-Yun Nie, and Jian Tang. 2019. Rotate: Knowledge graph embedding by relational rotation in complex space. *ArXiv*, abs/1902.10197.

Matthias Thoms, Robert Buschauer, Michael Ameismeier, Lennart Koepke, Timo Denk, Maximilian Hirschenberger, H. Kratzat, Manuel Hayn, T. Mackens-Kiani, Jingdong Cheng, C. Stürzel, T. Fröhlich, O. Berninghausen, T. Becker, F. Kirchhoff, K. Sparrer, and R. Beckmann. 2020. Structural basis for translational shutdown and immune evasion by the nsp1 protein of sars-cov-2. *bioRxiv*.

Théo Trouillon, Johannes Welbl, Sebastian Riedel, Éric Gaussier, and Guillaume Bouchard. 2016. Complex embeddings for simple link prediction. *ArXiv*, abs/1606.06357.

Lucy Lu Wang, Kyle Lo, Yoganand Chandrasekhar, Russell Reas, Jiangjiang Yang, Darrin Eide, Kathryn Funk, Rodney Michael Kinney, Ziyang Liu, William. Merrill, Paul Mooney, Dewey A. Murdick, Devvret Rishi, Jerry Sheehan, Zhihong Shen, Brandon Stilson, Alex D. Wade, Kuansan Wang, Christopher Wilhelm, Boya Xie, Douglas M. Raymond, Daniel S. Weld, Oren Etzioni, and Sebastian Kohlmeier. 2020a. Cord-19: The covid-19 open research dataset. *ArXiv*.

Qingyun Wang, Manling Li, X. Wang, Nikolaus Nova Parulian, Guangxing Han, Jiawei Ma, Jingxuan Tu, Ying Lin, H. Zhang, Weili Liu, Aabhas Chauhan, Yingjun Guan, Bangzheng Li, Ruisong Li, Xiangchen Song, Huai zhong Ji, Jiawei Han, Shih-Fu Chang, J. Pustejovsky, D. Liem, A. El-Sayed, Martha Palmer, Jasmine Rah, C. Schneider, and

B. Onyshkevych. 2020b. Covid-19 literature knowledge graph construction and drug repurposing report generation. *ArXiv*, abs/2007.00576.

Xuan Wang, Xiangchen Song, Yingjun Guan, Bangzheng Li, and Jiawei Han. 2020c. Comprehensive named entity recognition on cord-19 with distant or weak supervision. *ArXiv*, abs/2003.12218.

Cheng-I Wu, Pieter G Postema, Elena Arbelo, Elijah R Behr, Connie R Bezzina, Carlo Napolitano, Tomas Robyns, Vincent Probst, Eric Schulze-Bahr, Carol Ann Remme, et al. 2020. Sars-cov-2, covid-19 and inherited arrhythmia syndromes. *Heart Rhythm*.

Bishan Yang, Wen tau Yih, Xiaodong He, Jianfeng Gao, and Li Deng. 2015. Embedding entities and relations for learning and inference in knowledge bases. *CoRR*, abs/1412.6575.

Z. Yang, Zihang Dai, Yiming Yang, J. Carbonell, R. Salakhutdinov, and Quoc V. Le. 2019. Xlnet: Generalized autoregressive pretraining for language understanding. In *NeurIPS*.

Towards Grounding of Formulae

Takuto Asakura[1], André Greiner-Petter[2], Akiko Aizawa[3], Yusuke Miyao[4]
The University of Tokyo[1,4], University of Wuppertal[2], National Institute of Informatics[3]
{takuto,yusuke}@is.s.u-tokyo.ac.jp[1,4], andre.greiner-petter@zbmath.org[2],
aizawa@nii.ac.jp[3]

Abstract

A large amount of scientific knowledge is represented within mixed forms of natural language texts and mathematical formulae. Therefore, a collaboration of natural language processing and formula analyses, so-called mathematical language processing, is necessary to enable computers to understand and retrieve information from the documents. However, as we will show in this project, a mathematical notation can change its meaning even within the scope of a single paragraph. This flexibility makes it difficult to extract the exact meaning of a mathematical formula. In this project, we will propose a new task direction for grounding mathematical formulae. Particularly, we are addressing the widespread misconception of various research projects in mathematical information retrieval, which presume that mathematical notations have a fixed meaning within a single document. We manually annotated a long scientific paper to illustrate the task concept. Our high inter-annotator agreement shows that the task is well understood for humans. Our results indicate that it is worthwhile to grow the techniques for the proposed task to contribute to the further progress of mathematical language processing.

1 Introduction

In modern research, scientific progress is often solely shared in digital form. Especially in technical research fields, such as in Science, Technology, Engineering, and Mathematics (STEM), it is a crucial aspect to access data and new results in a quick and uniform way. Nevertheless, mathematical formulae, which transport essential information in scientific documents, often remain semantically unutilized in large databases such as Digital Library of Mathematical Functions (DLMF)[1] (Lozier, 2003) and the pre-print archive arXiv.org[2] (hereafter re-

ferred to as arXiv). By applying Math Information Retrieval (MathIR) techniques based on natural language processing (NLP), we are able to utilize this extra knowledge of mathematical formulae to build scientific knowledge bases (KBs) (Koprucki and Tabelow, 2016), improve mathematical search engines (Aizawa et al., 2013; Davila and Zanibbi, 2017; Ohashi et al., 2016), or even convert entire scientific papers into executable formats (Kohlhase and Iancu, 2014).

Formulae often express key ideas in scientific documents. Consequently, working with STEM documents requires to grasp the meaning and intention of the respective formulae. In other words, grounding of formulae is crucial for processing STEM documents and developing its applications. However, the grounding is not a trivial process because of the flexibility of mathematical notation and the impreciseness of natural languages. First, generally, formulae in documents are not independent content that can be understood separately from surrounding texts. For this reason, some initiative projects, e.g., the mathematical language processing (MLP) project (Pagel and Schubotz, 2014), the Mathcat project (Kristianto et al., 2014), and the Part-of-Math (POM) tagger (Youssef, 2017), have been undertaken to integrate NLP techniques into formula analysis. We also follow this MLP direction. Second, there is a necessity of disambiguation of mathematical notation because a letter or symbol in formulae is not used in a constant single meaning in a document (Greiner-Petter et al., 2020a,b). The usage of notation is highly-flexible and, as we will show in this paper, a notation can be used for several meanings even in a paragraph. This notation flexibility is not a problem for tasks that targeting short fragments of text, e.g., the ARQMath task (Mansouri et al., 2020; Zanibbi et al., 2020) for question posts from a question answering website. However, it is necessary to perform the grounding in consider-

---

[1]https://dlmf.nist.gov/
[2]https://arxiv.org/

Proceedings of the First Workshop on Scholarly Document Processing, pages 138–147
Online, November 19, 2020. ©2020 Association for Computational Linguistics
https://doi.org/10.18653/v1/P17

ation of the flexibility for processing longer STEM literature.

It is difficult to perform such a grounding in the scopes of existing tasks or MLP tools because many of the tools and approaches are not capable of carrying multiple meanings for a single symbol in a document (Greiner-Petter et al., 2020b; Kristianto et al., 2014; Krstovski and Blei, 2018; Yasunaga and Lafferty, 2019; Schubotz et al., 2016). Therefore, we will propose a new task direction of *grounding of formulae* (Figure 1) in order to take the flexibility into account. In short, the grounding is procedures to identify smallest groups of letters and symbols in formulae, i.e., *math words*, that independently refer to a mathematical concept and associate the math words with a corresponding text description or an entry in an external KB. For example in Figure 1, the first and the third y are parts of math words $y(\cdot)$ (where $\cdot$ represents an arbitrary argument) and associated with a description of a function while the second y is an independent math word and associated with a description for an output vector. In our grounding, instead of directly associating each math word to a text description, we put an intermediate procedure: making groups each of which consists of math words referring to an identical mathematical concept. For instance in Figure 1, the first and the third y belong to a group because they both refer to the same function, while the second one is in another group because it refers to a vector. It is notable that the grounding is similar to some established tasks, namely coreference resolution (Sukthanker et al., 2020) and named entity recognition (Bunescu and Pasca, 2006).

In this work, we checked the feasibility of the proposing task direction for the grounding. For this purpose, we made a long annotated scientific paper in which all formulae are annotated with math word spans and text descriptions of the corresponding mathematical concepts. The math words in the annotated paper which refer to the same mathematical concept are tied together in a group. We did the annotation for an entire paper rather than small fragments of texts to disclose the flexibility of math word usage. Through the analysis of our annotated paper, we revealed that the meanings of math words can be changed even within the scope of a single paragraph in actual STEM literature. In addition, we did the annotation by multiple human annotators and calculated the inner-annotator agreements so that to confirm that our task design can be well-understood, at least for human beings, and can be performed without individual differences.

2   Related Work

A few tasks that are similar to our grounding of formulae have been proposed in the community of MathIR. The NTCIR project run several shared tasks in the past (Aizawa et al., 2013, 2014; Zanibbi et al., 2016). The task designs of these shared tasks focuses on applications, namely searching and question-answering, while our grounding focuses rather basic parts and is regarded as preprocess for numerous MLP tasks including formulae searching, question-answering, and conversions to formal languages. Notably, the NTCIR-10 MathIR Test Collection (Aizawa et al., 2013), which is a specific dataset for their shared task, contains textual descriptions for formulae components, and thus the data are similar to our annotated paper. The dataset includes 10 papers chosen from the arXMLiv dataset using a manually annotated description for each formula element. For instance, in the dataset, a formula $\log(x)$ is annotated with a description like "a function that computes the natural logarithm of the value x". Though their purpose is close to ours, we annotated not only descriptions but also a few pieces of additional information, i.e., affix types and group information (what concept the word refer to). In the terms of linguistics, these two can be regarded respectively as word spans and coreference information. Additionally, we did the annotation for a longer document than their target papers with coherency. We were especially interested in longer documents so that we can analyze how diverse meanings of mathematical concepts can be.

The *variable typing* task (Stathopoulos et al., 2018) is also closely relevant to our goal. Their task is simply associating *mathematical type* (technical terms referring to mathematical concepts) to each variable in STEM documents. For example, for a sentence

> Let P be a parabolic subgroup of $GL(n)$ with Levi decomposition $P = MN$, where N is the unipotent radical.   (Stathopoulos et al., 2018)

they assigned the "parabolic subgroup" and "unipotent radical" respectively to variables P and N as their mathematical types. Based on arXMLiv, they introduced their own dataset, which includes 33,524 labeled variables in 7,803 sentences. Their work re-

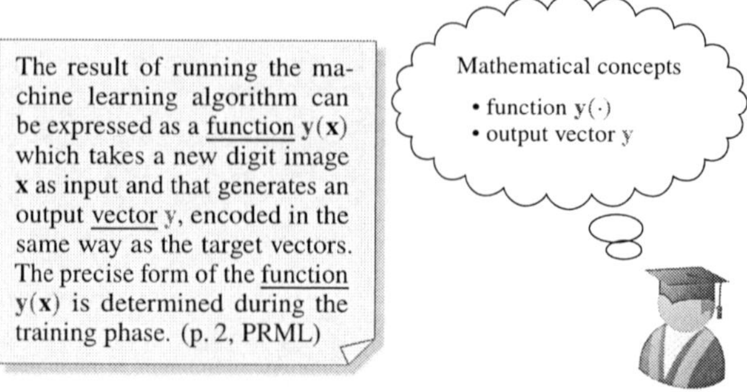

Figure 1: The *grounding of formulae*. It is a 3-step procedure: (1) detecting the span of math words—$y(\cdot)$ is a word for the first and third y, and the sole y is a word for the second y in the above quote (where · can be arbitrary argument), (2) making groups based on the corresponding mathematical description—the first and third y are elements of a group because they both refer to the same function, while the second one is an element of another group because it refers to a vector, (3) associating each group to text description or external knowledge.

sembles ours, but with three major differences. First, they annotated only mathematical types, which are partial components of mathematical concepts. Second, they targeted only those variables appearing as a single token in natural language texts, but we annotated all identifiers including those appearing in complex formulae. Third, they randomly selected sentences in the documents in arXMLiv to create their dataset. They did not attempt to annotate all variables in a full paper.

The POM Tagger (Youssef, 2017) is an initiative for token-level analyses of formulae in documents. The tagger plays the role of formulae akin to Part-of-Speech (POS) taggers in NLP. The tagger is intended to function with multiple scans. The function for the first scan was already implemented. The first scan recognizes lexical math terms (e.g., indexes, functions, left-delimiter, etc.) in formulae. For this tagging process, Youssef built a KB with more than 2,800 entries of symbols (tokens), each of which is associated with typical usage (role and category) and additional information of several kinds, such as the mathematical domain in which the term is used. In the planned following scans (second and third), the tagger will perform disambiguations of various types and extract further semantic information using NLP techniques. Our work is expected to be useful to implement and improve those features.

3 Grounding of Formulae

In order to describe the grounding of formulae precisely, we introduce a few linguistic terms for formulae, roughly borrowing from morphology in natural languages (Nida, 1949):

- A *math morpheme* (also known as *token*) is the smallest unit in formulae. In terms of Presentation MathML (Ausbrooks et al., 2014), this corresponds to an element, i.e., a tag. A morpheme can be a single letter or symbol (e.g., x, θ, $\prime$, $\times$, $=$, and $\sum$) or strings consisting of a few letters (e.g., log and argmax). All characters (both letters and symbols) that appear in formulae must belong to a math morpheme.

- A *math word* is a minimal group of morphemes that refer to a mathematical concept independently. Math words consist of one or more morphemes, typically one or a few morphemes. For instance, x, x', $\stackrel{\text{def}}{=}$, and $\log(\cdot)$ are words. Every word has a *base* morpheme, which reflects a core meaning of the word, and optionally has one or more *affixes*. That is to say, in a word x', x is the base morpheme; $\prime$ is a suffix, which is a type of affix.

Every math word has a corresponding mathematical concept such as the sign function, the set of all natural numbers, and (real) intervals. In the actual data and applications, the math words are associated with textual descriptions. Those descriptions can be taken either from the surrounding text of the formulae or from an external KB. Though some combinations of words, notably an entire formula, also refer to a mathematical concept, we stick to the scope of math words for the grounding. The process of combining the math words and interpreting the constituted concepts will be a subsequent task to our grounding. It is also notable that the concept of math word is close to mathematical objects of interests (MOIs) (Greiner-Petter et al., 2020a), sub expressions in formulae that can be identified as 'important' components, but not exactly the same. While MOIs can contain other MOIs, math words are *minimal* groups of morphemes that can refer to mathematical concepts, so they naturally cannot contain other math words.

With the terms we introduced in the above, we can describe the proposing grounding of formulae as the following 3-step procedure that simulates the processes of understanding formulae by human beings (Figure 1):

1. Identifying spans of *math words*, a minimal group of math morphemes that refer to a mathematical concept. This step is necessary because the morphemes are not always used singly. For instance, in a text "A variable $\hat{x}$", two morphemes x and $\hat{\ }$ do not independently refer to mathematical concepts but refer to a variable as a group.

2. Grouping the math words based on the corresponding mathematical descriptions. As we mentioned, a notation can be used in several meanings in the scope of a single paragraph. With this step, we will obtain the groups each of which consists of math words appearances used in the same meaning. In the example of Figure 1, the first and the third y belongs to a group, each math word of which refers to a function, while the second y is in another group, each of which refers to a vector.

3. Associating the groups with text descriptions or external knowledge. It will be easier to associate all the groups to text descriptions in the same document, but in the actual literature, notations can be used without any description. For instance, π is often used for Archimedes' constant without explicit description. Thus, external knowledge will be required in addition to text descriptions in each document.

Although the grounding is a fundamental step for MLP, the processes, even merely recognizing the word spans, are not easy for computers because of various linguistic phenomena in formulae. The following paragraphs show the two most important phenomena: both make the grounding highly challenging. In short, because of these phenomena, the grounding demands disambiguation of math words. For disambiguation, integration of NLP and analyses for formulae are inescapable. More

phenomena are discussed in detail elsewhere in the literature (Ganesalingam, 2013; Kohlhase and Iancu, 2014). All quotes presented in this section are from a textbook *Pattern Recognition and Machine Learning* (PRML) (Bishop, 2006).

Integration of Formulae and Texts Formulae in scientific documents are generally deeply integrated into narrative texts and inseparable from natural languages. For instance, in the following sentence, the equation is the passive subject in the grammar of English.

> For the case of a single real-value variable x, the Gaussian distribution is defined by
>
> $$\mathcal{N}(x \mid \mu, \sigma^2) = \frac{1}{(2\pi\sigma^2)^{1/2}} \exp\left\{-\frac{1}{2\sigma^2}(x-\mu)^2\right\}$$
>
> which is governed by two parameters: μ, called the *mean*, and σ^2, called the *variance*.　　(p. 24, PRML)

From the viewpoint of the formula, meanings of some math words (x, μ, and σ^2) are described in the surrounding natural language texts. Moreover, natural language texts or their fragments can appear in formulae, as shown in the following:

> Given this definition of likelihood, we can state Beyes' theorem in words
>
> $$\text{posterior} \propto \text{likelihood} \times \text{prior}$$
>
> where all of these quantities are viewed as functions of **w**. (p. 22, PRML)

The natural language parts of the above are just nouns, but they can be sentences, e.g., $\{n \in \mathbb{N} \mid n \text{ is even}\}$.

Because of this integration phenomenon, the grounding cannot be done merely by analyzing formulae. For faithful grounding, one must look into natural language texts to observe information such as the contexts to which formulae belong and to definitions, descriptions, or assumptions for identifiers in formulae.

Ambiguity Various ambiguities arise in formulae. Token-level analyses are responsible for disambiguation (Wang et al., 2016; Youssef, 2017). Different from natural languages, the meanings of words in formulae invariably depend on the context. It is common in STEM documents that a notation has multiple meanings even in a single document. For example, in Figure 1, a letter **y** is used in two meanings. Herein, in the first appearance, **y** is a function, but it is a vector in the second appearance.

We human beings can see that **y** is used in different meanings in these two appearances by the apposition nouns (in this example, the words "function" and "vector" immediately before the formulae) and the usages of the notations. In the first formula, the morpheme **y** is not used alone, but with affixes; it constitutes a word $\mathbf{y}(\cdot)$. However, the second **y** is used as a single word with no affixes. There are also syntactic ambiguities in formulae. For instance, a formula $f(a + b)$ can be interpreted in two ways: it means $f \times (a + b)$ if f is a variable, or applying the value of $a + b$ to a function f. Ambiguities of these types can be resolved by disambiguating the meanings of math words (the meanings of f and the parentheses in this case).

4 Manual Annotation for the Grounding

We performed manual annotation for the proposed grounding task so that to show the feasibility of the task with sufficient reproducibility. Moreover, language resources are indispensable to automate the task to contribute to the development of MLP tools. The annotated document for this work should play an initiative role to develop larger language resources for developing and evaluating the grounding technology. Collections of natural languages and corresponding formal expressions are not enough for this purpose, because it does not directly provide token-level information for each formula in natural language texts. It is still difficult to extract such information from simple parallel translations.

In order to reveal the flexibility of the math word usage, we annotated an entire long paper rather than small fragments of multiple texts. As we described, the grounding can be regarded as a three-step process. Corresponding to the first two steps of the grounding, the reference data should also have two types of information for each math morpheme in documents: (1) which word the morpheme belongs to and (2) which mathematical concept the word is referring to. We annotated these two pieces of information coherently for all formulae in a document. We also annotated text description by an annotator for each group, that is the information corresponding to the result of Step 3, but it is not literally extracted from the paper itself nor from external knowledge bases. These textual description are rather for the convenience for the annotators.

The classification-based annotation made it possible to evaluate the quality of annotated data. Moreover, the annotation is expected to be beneficial for

Table 1: Basic statistics of the paper (Simeone, 2018).

#words in texts	10,616	#<mi> tags	937
#sections	7	#inline math	331
#pages (in PDF)	20	#display math	23

numerous future applications. First, by studying the appearance pattern of mathematical concepts corresponding to formula words in a document, one can obtain linguistic statistics for formulae. For instance, it can help us to infer the form of the *scopes* for variables in documents. Secondly, the annotated information for each mathematical concept group can be extended easily in accordance with applications. We annotated referential descriptions for each math word as well, but these descriptions can be improved at any point.

4.1 Targets

We took the original XHTML documents from the arXMLiv:08.2018 dataset (Ginev, 2018). The XHTML documents in the dataset were generated automatically by converting LaTeX document sources of scientific papers from arXiv with LaTeXML[3] (Ginev et al., 2011; Miller, 2018). In the dataset, we selected a paper *A Very Brief Introduction to Machine Learning With Applications to Communication Systems*[4] (Simeone, 2018) for our annotation because it has suitable numbers of words and formulae. This paper works with the topic with which the authors are familiar. In addition, the paper is easy to read and includes a reasonable number of formulae (Table 1). We annotated the group information to all identifiers in the paper. The analysis for the annotation are described in Section 5.

As the first attempt for performing such an annotation, we narrowed down a target to identifiers, which are one type of math morpheme. An identifier is a letter (e.g., x, **y**, and θ) or a string consisting of a few letters (e.g., sin and log) commonly representing variables, functions, and constants in formulae. We chose identifiers as targets because they are the most major class in standard formulae. In Presentation MathML, an identifier is placed in a <mi> tag, where mi stands for "math identifier".

4.2 Annotation Procedure

Before manual annotation, we preprocessed the target XHTML. First, several inappropriate MathML

---

[3]https://dlmf.nist.gov/LaTeXML/
[4]https://arxiv.org/abs/1808.02342

markups that were originally from unsuitable LaTeX markups by the author of the target paper were fixed to the right markups. This fixing was achieved by simple rule-based replacements, e.g., replacing `<mtext>E</mtext>` (`\text{E}` in the original LaTeX source by the author) to `<mi>E</mi>` (which corresponds to `\mathrm{E}` in LaTeX). Since our targets are only the `<mi>` tags for this time, this replacement was useful to annotate all the tokens that should be grounding manually. For the target document, we defined seven replacement rules. Secondly, lists of two types for annotation were generated by extracting information from the target XHTML file. The first one is a list of identifiers. It had entries for all letters and strings (case-sensitive and typeface-sensitive) with blank description fields. This list played the role of a *dictionary*. In other words, it was an extremely detailed "index to notations" (Table 2). The second list was a simple list of all identifiers' appearances in the document: the list of ids for all `<mi>` tags in the XHTML file. We took this dictionary-based approach to clearly show the groups of math words which are used in the same meaning.

The annotation process was done by manually modifying these two lists. When reading the target paper, the annotator added items to the entries when an identifier is defined or used in a new meaning. As presented in Table 2, each item was given a few fields: a description for the identifier usage, types of affixes in the corresponding words. Then, the annotator associates each identifier's appearance to the corresponding item in the dictionary within the list of identifiers (Figure 2). This task was accomplished efficiently with a GUI application we developed. We associate all identifiers in the document to the items even if the identifier morphemes appeared in a word as an affix.

Our language resource and all programs developed for this project are available with annotation via our repository[5].

5   Analysis on the Annotated Paper

5.1   Agreements and Mismatch Analyses

To verify our annotations, three persons annotated the same target article independently, and the agreements were calculated. First, Annotator 1 performed the whole process of the annotation (Section 4.2). The annotator created both a dictionary

[5]`https://sigmathling.kwarc.info/resources/grounding-dataset/`

and the annotation file, which is a list of identifier appearances associated with the corresponding items in the dictionary. Then the dictionary, that includes all possible mathematical concepts that can be referred to in the paper, was sent to the other two annotators (Annotator 2 is a coauthor of this work. Annotator 3 is not). They performed the step of annotation that associates each identifier's appearance to a dictionary item. They needed about a day to complete the annotation. We shared the common dictionary this time for the ease of annotation work, but all annotators should create their own dictionaries in future work. Table 3 presents results of our experiment. With the given dictionary, the inter-annotator agreements were 96.48% (between Annotator 1 and Annotator 2) and 87.94% (between Annotator 1 and Annotator 3). Of 937 appearances, 132 (14.09%) are identifiers, each of which has a single candidate item. These are included in these agreements. In addition, mismatches of affix types between annotators are important because the numbers of such affix type mismatches reflect disagreements on the *math word spans*. A few examples are explained below. Therefore, we also counted affix mismatches. The numbers are presented in the second column of Table 3.

The two affix type mismatches by Annotator 2 were simply mistakes. The other 31 mismatches were all attributable to a single disagreement on the mathematical concept for $\mathcal{D}$ in the document. In the target paper, the identifier $\mathcal{D}$ refers training datasets for the learning tasks they are discussing, but the assumptions for the dataset (e.g., whether or not the data points follow a true distribution) differ among sections. For example, in §3.1, $\mathcal{D}$ is introduced for the first time as:

> we are given a training set $\mathcal{D}$ of N training points (x_n, t_n), with $n = 1, \ldots, N$, where the variables x_n are the inputs (Simeone, 2018)

Moreover, some times, there is no clear declaration about the assumption, e.g.,

> Under this assumption, the data set $\mathcal{D}$ is not necessary, ... (Simeone, 2018)

and it engenders disagreement. Because the meanings of some identifiers depend on the meanings of others, mismatches might have cascading effects. Results show that we obtained 31 mismatches from a single disagreement of the referring to mathematical concept of a math word.

The agreement of Annotator 3 was lower than

Table 2: Excerpt from the dictionary. In the actual dictionary file, all identifiers appear in the descriptions are also associated to the corresponding items in the same dictionary.

Identifier	Description	Affixes
t (*italic*)	an output of a regression or classification problem in general	(NONE)
	an output of a regression problem, generated by $p(x, t)$	(NONE)
	n-th output in the training set $\mathcal{D}$	subscript
	a predicator which takes an input x and return a predicated value	over, parentheses
	$\vdots$	
t (roman)	a random variable for a test output for regression problem	(NONE)
	$\vdots$	

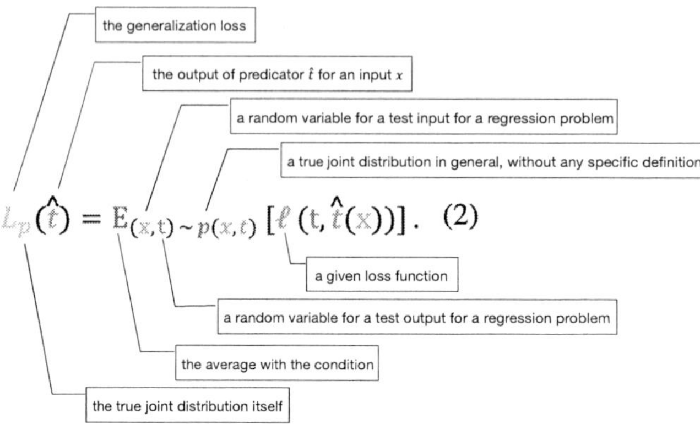

$$L_p(\hat{t}) = \mathrm{E}_{(x,t) \sim p(x,t)} \left[\ell\left(t, \hat{t}(x)\right) \right]. \quad (2)$$

Figure 2: Example of annotated mathematical concepts in a bit complex formula. Due to the space limitation, only the descriptions for some of the identifiers are shown, but all of the identifiers are annotated with mathematical concepts in the actual data. The same letter in the same color is associated with the same mathematical concept.

Table 3: Performances of the annotators. The second column shows the inter-annotator agreements (compared to the golden data created by Annotator 1). The third column shows the number and ratio of identifiers annotated with an item that has different affix types (patterns) out of all disagreements.

	Agreements	Affixes mismatches
Annotator 2	904/937 (96.48%)	2/33 (6.06%)
Annotator 3	824/937 (87.94%)	60/113 (53.10%)

that of Annotator 2. Closer examination of the 113 mismatches reveals many duplications of the mismatch patterns. For example, the annotator marked a word $p(\cdot \mid \cdot, \cdot)$, which refers to "a parameterized predictive distributions" in the correct annotation as $p(\cdot \mid \cdot)$, which refers to "a parameterized true distribution" 19 times. By excluding such duplications, we found that the 113 mismatches can be categorized into 40 patterns, of which 25 patterns were affix type mismatches. Most of them can be distinguished easily by their appearance (e.g., annotating $p(\cdot \mid \cdot, \cdot)$ as $p(\cdot \mid \cdot)$). Apparently, many of these cases are mistakes or are the result of a misunderstanding of the concept of the affix types

for Annotator 3. In the remaining 15 patterns, 10 are exactly the same mismatches made by Annotator 2. This finding indicates that choosing the most suitable mathematical description as an identifier $\mathcal{D}$ was the most difficult for the document.

5.2 Analyses on the Annotation and Notable Phenomena in the Target Document

The dictionary we created for the target document consists of 104 items within 40 entries. We counted items for each entry (identifier) in the dictionary (Figure 3). Herein, 18 entries out of 40 have two or more items. This finding indicates that about half of the identifiers in the documents have ambiguities on their meanings and the readers must disambiguate to perform the grounding of formulae. The entry with the greatest number of items in the document was t in regular font. Concretely, it has 13 meanings in the single document (see Table 2).

Figure 4 portrays a plot of the positions of identifier appearances and annotated items in the dictionary. Biases are readily apparent in the plot. The trends of referred mathematical concepts, which are sort of *scopes*, differ from section to section. For

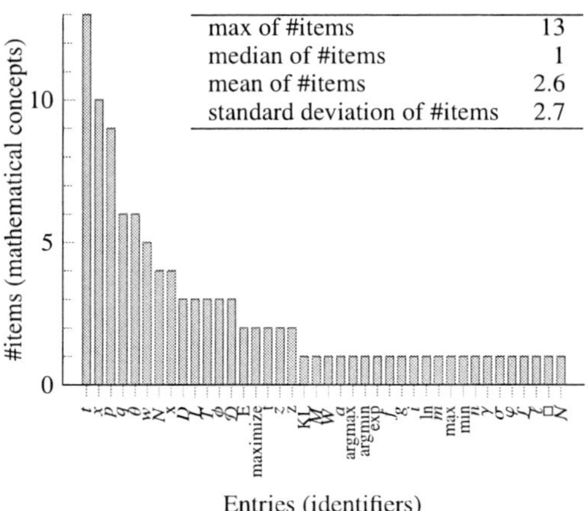

max of #items	13
median of #items	1
mean of #items	2.6
standard deviation of #items	2.7

Figure 3: Number of items for each entry in the dictionary. In the paper, identifier t, x, p are used for 13, 10, 9 meanings respectively.

example, the scope of identifier x changed clearly at the beginnings of §3.2, §3.5, §3.6, and §5.1 in the target document. Moreover, some identifiers are used in the same meaning independent of such trends. The scope for t cannot be seen so clearly compared to x. The mathematical concepts referred by identifier $\mathcal{D}$, which is the most arguable one in the document, switch back and forth several times. Overall, as we mentioned, the usage of a notation is not constant in the paper but in fact so flexible that the meaning can change even in a single paragraph.

Incidentally, the target document includes several noteworthy sentences (Simeone, 2018). In the beginning of the article, the author of the paper states the following:

> Throughout, we use Roman font to denote random variables and the corresponding letter in regular font for realizations. (Simeone, 2018)

This is a meta-declaration about the font usage in formulae throughout the article. The annotators had to keep this declaration in mind to distinguish differences between variables in Roman font and in regular font.

6 Future Work

We made a long annotated paper and show that the flexibility of the mathematical notation is high in actual STEM literature. Moreover, we could check the feasibility of our task direction of the grounding of formulae. The number of annotated papers for the grounding needs to be increased because a single paper is naturally biased. However, the entirely

manual annotation costs too much to enhance the size of the resource in the same way. Therefore, we will work on partial automation of the process first. With the combination of the partial automatic method of the grounding and manual annotation by humans, we will be able to efficiently enlarge the resource. Furthermore, we will develop an entirely automated grounding method, including the third step, i.e., the part of associating the groups with text descriptions or external knowledge, for various MLP applications.

Acknowledgments

This work was supported by the Japan Science and Technology Agency (JST CREST, Grant JP-MJCR1513) and the German Research Foundation (DFG, Grant GI-1259-1).

References

Akiko Aizawa, Michael Kohlhase, and Iadh Ounis. 2013. NTCIR-10 math pilot task overview.

Akiko Aizawa, Michael Kohlhase, and Iadh Ounis. 2014. NTCIR-11 math-2 task overview. page 11.

Ron Ausbrooks, Stephen Buswell, David Carlisle, Giorgi Chavchanidze, Stéphane Dalmas, Stan Devitt, Angel Diaz, Sam Dooley, Roger Hunter, Patrick Ion, and Michael Kohlhase. 2014. *Mathematical Markup Language (MathML) 3.0 Specification.*

Christopher M Bishop. 2006. *Pattern Recognition and Machine Learning.*

Razvan Bunescu and Marius Pasca. 2006. Using encyclopedic knowledge for named entity disambiguation. In *Proceedings of 11th Conference of the European Chapter of the Association for Computational Linguistics (EACL 2006).*

Kenny Davila and Richard Zanibbi. 2017. Layout and semantics: Combining representations for mathematical formula search. In *SIGIR 2017.*

Mohan Ganesalingam. 2013. *The Language of Mathematics: A Linguistic and Philosophical Investigation.*

Deyan Ginev. 2018. arxmliv:08.2018 dataset, an html5 conversion of arxiv.org. SIGMathLing.

Deyan Ginev, Heinrich Stamerjohanns, Bruce R. Miller, and Michael Kohlhase. 2011. The LaTeXML daemon: Editable math on the collaborative web. In *CICM 2011.*

André Greiner-Petter, Moritz Schubotz, Fabian Müller, Corinna Breitinger, Howard S. Cohl, Akiko Aizawa, and Bela Gipp. 2020a. Discovering mathematical objects of interest—a study of mathematical notations. In *WWW 2020.*

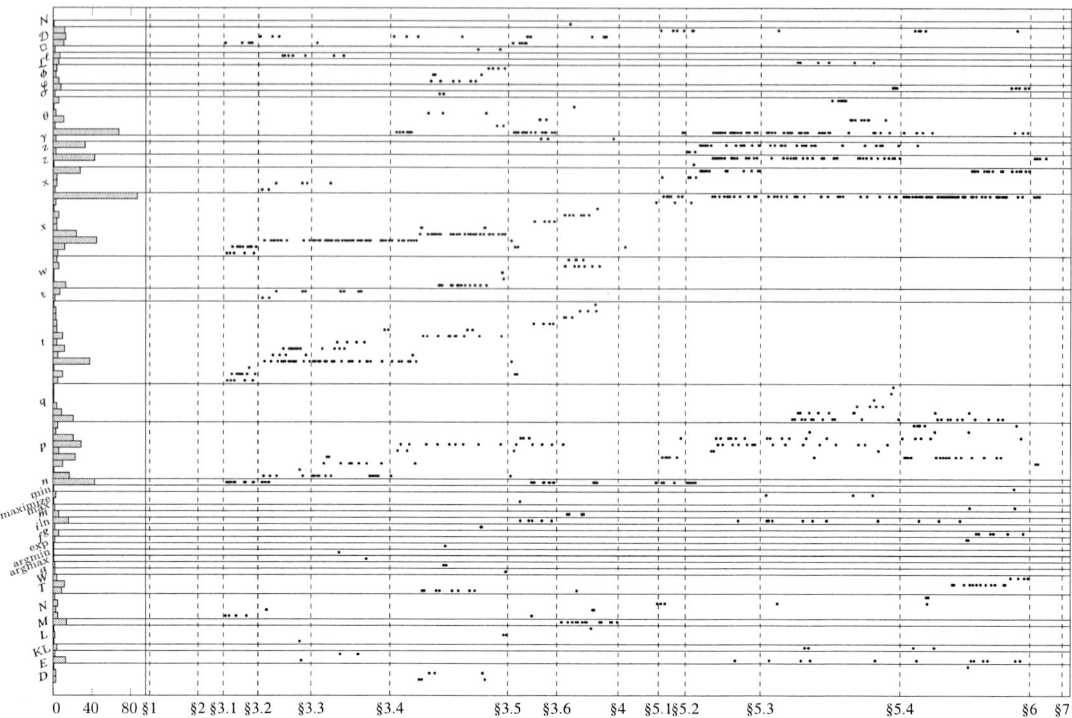

Figure 4: Math words appearances in the target document. The value of a coordinate on the horizontal axis is the position of the corresponding `<mi>` tag in the XHTML document. A notation can be used in several meanings in the document, and the concept that is referred to by each appearance is shown as the position in vertical axis. Between each separator, items are sorted by the positions of their first appearances.

André Greiner-Petter, Abdou Youssef, Terry Ruas, Bruce R. Miller, Moritz Schubotz, Akiko Aizawa, and Bela Gipp. 2020b. Math-word embeddings in math search and semantic extraction. *Scientometrics*.

Michael Kohlhase and Mihnea Iancu. 2014. Co-representing structure and meaning of mathematical documents.

Thomas Koprucki and Karsten Tabelow. 2016. Mathematical models: A research data category? In *Mathematical Software – ICMS 2016*, volume 9725, pages 423–428.

Giovanni Yoko Kristianto, Goran Topic, and Akiko Aizawa. 2014. Exploiting textual descriptions and dependency graph for searching mathematical expressions in scientific papers. In *Ninth International Conference on Digital Information Management (ICDIM 2014)*, pages 110–117.

Kriste Krstovski and David M. Blei. 2018. Equation embeddings. *arXiv*.

Daniel W. Lozier. 2003. Nist digital library of mathematical functions. *Annals of Mathematics and Artificial Intelligence*.

Behrooz Mansouri, Anurag Agarwal, Douglas Oard, and Richard Zanibbi. 2020. Finding old answers to new math questions: The arqmath lab at CLEF 2020. In *Advances in Information Retrieval*, volume 12036, pages 564–571.

Bruce Miller. 2018. *LaTeXML The Manual—A LaTeX to XML/HTML/MathML Converter, Version 0.8.3*.

Eugene A Nida. 1949. *Morphology: The descriptive analysis of words*.

Shunsuke Ohashi, Giovanni Yoko Kristianto, Goran Topic, and Akiko Aizawa. 2016. Efficient algorithm for math formula semantic search. *IEICE Transactions on Information and Systems*.

Robert Pagel and Moritz Schubotz. 2014. Mathematical language processing project. In *Joint Proceedings of the MathUI, OpenMath and ThEdu Workshops and Work in Progress track at CICM*.

Moritz Schubotz, Alexey Grigorev, Marcus Leich, Howard S. Cohl, Norman Meuschke, Bela Gipp, Abdou S. Youssef, and Volker Markl. 2016. Semantification of identifiers in mathematics for better math information retrieval. In *Proceedings of the 39th International ACM SIGIR Conference on Research and Development in Information Retrieval - SIGIR '16*, pages 135–144.

Osvaldo Simeone. 2018. A very brief introduction to machine learning with applications to communication systems. *IEEE Transactions on Cognitive Communications and Networking*.

Yiannos Stathopoulos, Simon Baker, Marek Rei, and Simone Teufel. 2018. Variable typing: Assigning meaning to variables in mathematical text. In *NAACL 2018*.

Rhea Sukthanker, Soujanya Poria, Erik Cambria, and Ramkumar Thirunavukarasu. 2020. Anaphora and coreference resolution: A review. *Information Fusion*, 59:139–162.

Kai Wang, Xinfu Li, and Xuedong Tian. 2016. On ambiguity issues of converting latex mathematical formula to content mathml. In *Collaborative Computing: Networking, Applications, and Worksharing*.

Michihiro Yasunaga and John D. Lafferty. 2019. Topiceq: A joint topic and mathematical equation model for scientific texts. *Proceedings of the AAAI Conference on Artificial Intelligence*, 33:7394–7401.

Abdou Youssef. 2017. Part-of-math tagging and applications. In *CICM 2017*.

Richard Zanibbi, Akiko Aizawa, and Michael Kohlhase. 2016. NTCIR-12 MathIR task overview. page 10.

Richard Zanibbi, Douglas W. Oard, Anurag Agarwal, and Behrooz Mansouri. 2020. Overview of arqmath 2020: Clef lab on answer retrieval for questions on math. In *Experimental IR Meets Multilinguality, Multimodality, and Interaction*, pages 169–193.

SChuBERT: Scholarly Document Chunks with BERT-encoding boost Citation Count Prediction

Thomas van Dongen, Gideon Maillette de Buy Wenniger, and Lambert Schomaker

Bernoulli Institute for Mathematics,Computer Science and Artificial Intelligence

University of Groningen, Groningen, The Netherlands

`t.a.van.dongen AT student.rug.nl`

`gemdbw AT gmail.com   l.r.b.schomaker AT rug.nl`

Abstract

Predicting the number of citations of scholarly documents is an upcoming task in scholarly document processing. Besides the intrinsic merit of this information, it also has a wider use as an imperfect proxy for quality which has the advantage of being cheaply available for large volumes of scholarly documents. Previous work has dealt with number of citations prediction with relatively small training data sets, or larger datasets but with short, incomplete input text. In this work we leverage the open access ACL Anthology collection in combination with the Semantic Scholar bibliometric database to create a large corpus of scholarly documents with associated citation information and we propose a new citation prediction model called SChuBERT. In our experiments we compare SChuBERT with several state-of-the-art citation prediction models and show that it outperforms previous methods by a large margin. We also show the merit of using more training data and longer input for number of citations prediction.

1 Introduction

Predicting the quality of scientific articles is a novel task in the field of deep learning. There are many indicators of quality such as whether a paper was accepted or rejected, meta-information such as the author's h-index(es), and the number of citations. The number of citations, while not a perfect indicator of quality, is available for any paper which makes it suitable for constructing a large dataset. In this work we propose ACL-BiblioMetry, a new dataset consisting of 30000 papers with citation information. We also test several state-of-the deep learning models and propose a new model called SChuBERT which outperforms all other methods.

Using the full text of scholarly documents has the potential to substantially improve the performance of the citation count prediction task. But prohibitive memory costs of applying advanced deep learning models on the full text can be a roadblock. In particular, BERT (Devlin et al., 2018) and its variants have been very successful as building blocks for state-of-the-art natural language processing models for many tasks. Citation count prediction for scholarly documents is a task where BERT has clear potential as well. However, scholarly documents are particularly long texts in general. Since BERT has a time complexity that is quadratic with respect to the input length, it is limited to 512 tokens by default, a limit which can not be increased by much without causing prohibitive computational cost.

Recent models including the Reformer (Kitaev et al., 2020) and Longformer (Beltagy et al., 2020) have sought to overcome the quadratic computational cost of the Transformer model (Vaswani et al., 2017) underlying BERT. While these models are very promising, they do not offer the unsupervised pre-training on large amounts of data that makes BERT so powerful as of yet. Although in principle these models could be applied as a drop-in replacement for BERT, it requires more research to show if and how unsupervised pre-training as done in BERT can be made to work well with very long context. For these reasons, in this work we use BERT as our base building block and find effective ways to overcome its input length limit, leaving experimentation with the aforementioned models for future research.

For dealing with large amounts of training examples containing very long input text we need an approach that: 1) Is able to fit the encoding of the long text into memory, 2) can efficiently process the large amount of training examples when training over many epochs. Both requirements can be fulfilled by chunking the long input text of our examples into parts, and pre-computing BERT embeddings for each of these parts using a pre-trained

Proceedings of the First Workshop on Scholarly Document Processing, pages 148–157

Online, November 19, 2020. ©2020 Association for Computational Linguistics

https://doi.org/10.18653/v1/P17

BERT model. The core of the final model is a sequence-model, in particular a gated recurrent unit (GRU) (Cho et al., 2014), which directly uses the pre-computed chunk embeddings as inputs. This approach simultaneously overcomes the memory problems associated with dealing with very long input texts, as well as achieves high computational efficiency by performing the expensive step of computing BERT embeddings for chunks only once.

While the task of citation count prediction using the contents of a scholarly document is not new, and goes back at least to the work of Fu and Aliferis (2008), work up until now has been limited in: a) the size of the training data, b) the size of the input text. Table 1 gives an overview of data used in earlier work, note that most are restricted by using only the title + abstract as well as a small number of examples, while (Maillette de Buy Wenniger et al., 2020) substantially increase the number of examples but still use only a limited part of body text available from S2ORC (Lo et al., 2019). In this work, we show that both these factors have a large influence on the accuracy of models predicting citation counts. Essentially, state-of-the-art methods cannot be adequately evaluated with too small training data. Therefore, apart from providing state-of-the art results for citation-count-prediction on a data set currently unmatched in terms of number of examples with full length input text, we also provide the code for other researchers to rebuild our dataset and the methodology of citation count prediction using the semantic scholar database to label new collections of scholarly documents.

The rest of the paper is organized as follows: in section 2 we discuss related work, in section 3 we describe the models used for citation count prediction, in section 4 we discuss the dataset construction, in section 5 we present our experiments, in section 6 we show our results and in section 7 we end with conclusions.

2 Related Work

Recently, multiple datasets have been released which are useful for the scientific quality prediction problem. The S2ORC dataset (Lo et al., 2019) has abstract information for 81.1M papers and full-text for 8.1M papers, both with citations.

Other large datasets exist such as unarXive and PubMed Central Open Access Subset, but these datasets span various domains. Given the difficulty of the citation prediction task, we made a new dataset for just the computational linguistics and natural language processing domain, to be used as a benchmark for citation prediction models.

The PeerRead dataset (Kang et al., 2018) is another useful dataset that has accept/reject decisions for 14.7K full-text papers. This is a useful dataset on which more research has been performed (Shen et al., 2019), but the amount of papers in it is fairly limited. For this reason, we propose our new dataset which contains full-text and citations for a large number of papers.

A number of methods have been proposed for the citation prediction problem. (Brody et al., 2006) try to predict future citations of a paper by using web usage statistics, e.g. the number of times the paper was downloaded. (Abrishami and Aliakbary, 2019) use deep learning techniques to predict long-term citations using short-term citations. (Bai et al., 2019) use a measure called Paper Potential Index (PPI) which is based on a combination of features such as the impact of the authors and early citations. The problem with these methods is that information such as short-term citations and web usage statistics are only available after the paper is published. Furthermore, these methods disregard any of the actual papers' content. Because of this reason, our work focuses on predicting the citations using only the textual content. Limited research is available on this topic. One of the first papers which focused on predicting citation count by only using information available at publication is by (Fu and Aliferis, 2008). They use the paper title, abstract and keywords as well as bibliometric information as input data for an SVM. They then predict a binary label (positive or negative) based on whether the paper received at least a set number of citations within 10 years. This work was expanded upon by (Ibáñez et al., 2009). They predict a discrete value (few, some or many citations) using multiple classification models, outperforming the baseline set by (Fu and Aliferis, 2008) using both naive Bayes as well as logistic regression. Both papers use a fairly small dataset (3788 papers for (Fu and Aliferis, 2008) and 2246 papers for (Ibáñez et al., 2009)).

3 Models

In this section we briefly describe our two baseline models: BiLSTM and hierarchical attention networks (HANs). This is followed by a description of the BERT-based SChuBERT model, to the best of our knowledge first applied to the task of citation count prediction in this work.

3.1 BiLSTM Based Prediction

Our BiLSTM baseline model, is a re-implementation of the BiLSTM model introduced in (Shen et al., 2017) . This model was initially used for the task of Wikipedia text quality prediction and applied also in (Shen et al., 2019) for the task of accept/reject prediction on the PeerRead dataset, and finally in (Maillette de Buy Wenniger et al., 2020) for the task of citation count prediction. The name "BiLSTM" is somewhat deceptive as the model contains several other layers in addition to a plain BiLSTM to improve performance:

1. The sentence embeddings in the input are fed to an average pooling layer, to combine them to a single representation per input sentence.

2. Following the BiLSTM is a max-pooling layer followed by a rectified linear hidden layer. These additional layers are added to further improve performance.

The simplicity of the sentence encoding employed by this model yields relatively high computational efficiency, lower memory usage and scalability to longer input text. This makes the model competitive in settings where the amount of training material is limited, such as PeerRead accept/reject prediction (Shen et al., 2019; Maillette de Buy Wenniger et al., 2020). However, as we will show later in this work, there is a clear advantage to using the more advanced SChuBERT model given enough training data is available.

3.2 Hierarchical Attention Networks

The HAN model (Yang et al., 2016), see Figure 1, used in this work is a PyTorch re-implementation of the original model.[1] It is in some ways similar to the BiLSTM model discussed earlier, but creates more advanced sentence-level representations by applying a BiLSTM with attention for encoding these as well as employing a BiLSTM with attention for for converting the sentence-level representations to document-level representations.

We next discuss the more advanced BERT-based model.

3.3 SChuBERT

Our SChuBERT model, shown in fig 2, consists of two parts: a pre-trained BERT (Bidirectional Encoder Representations from Transformers) model (Devlin et al., 2018) to extract features and a deep learning model to learn from the features and predict. The main difference between this model and the other models is the use of contextualized word embeddings instead of context-independent word embeddings such as the Glove embeddings used in the HAN model. These offer a much richer context by not just encoding a word using a static embedding but encoding it based on the context it appears in.

One limitation of transformer-based models such as BERT is that they have a time complexity of $\mathcal{O}(N^2)$ with respect to the input length. For this reason, most of these models are pre-trained on sequences of a maximum length of 512. Since we are dealing with very long sequences, we have to work around this limit. The simplest approach is to truncate the documents to a length of 512 as proposed in (Xie et al., 2019). However, since our documents are so long, this would remove a lot of information. For this reason, we adopt the technique proposed in (Joshi et al., 2019). We split each input into chunks of 512 with an overlap of 50 tokens each to preserve a relation between the chunks.

For pre-trained BERT models for feature extraction, there are two considerations to make. Firstly, since BERT generates an embedding of length 768 for each token in our chunks of (max) 512 tokens, we need to pool over these embeddings to get embeddings of equal length. Note that the CLS (classification) token, which is normally used for classification tasks, is not a good representation without fine-tuning since it only holds useful information for the pre-training tasks when no fine-tuning is performed on the target domain. For this reason, we use mean pooling over our embeddings. Secondly, the different layers in BERT hold different information. The earlier layers are closer to the original word embeddings, which in the case of BERT are WordPiece embeddings (Wu et al., 2016), while the later layers are closer to the pre-training targets. Intuitively, it would make sense that the last layers are too close to the pre-training targets and are thus biased. However, our findings correspond with (Pe-

---

[1] Adapted from https://github.com/cedias/Hierarchical-Sentiment

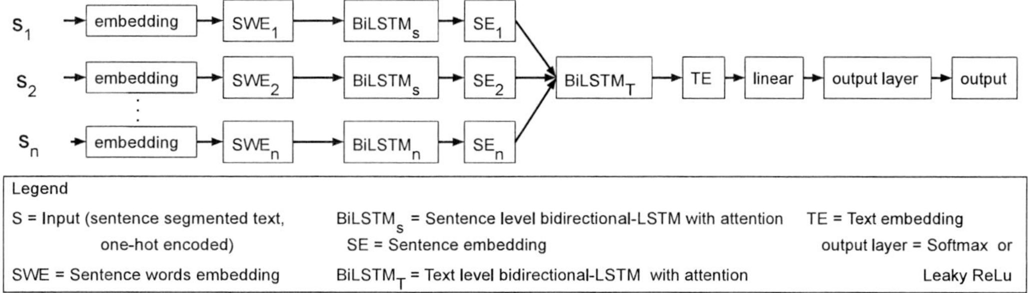

Figure 1: The HAN baseline model used in this work. Adapted from (Maillette de Buy Wenniger et al., 2020) with permission of the authors.

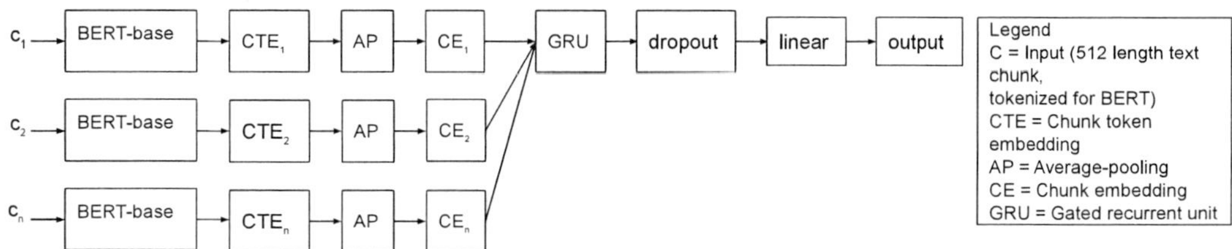

Figure 2: The SChuBERT model proposed in this work.

ters et al., 2019) in which the last layer (layer 12) is found to be the most useful for feature extraction which is why we use this layer.

After extracting the embeddings, they are passed through a fairly simple model to do predictions. We use a GRU, followed by a single dropout layer and a linear layer. We use a simple model since the embeddings already hold a lot of information and are prone to over-fitting when a more complex model is used.

4 Dataset construction

Citation count prediction relies on sufficiently large labeled data, of good quality and preferably with full document text. To obtain such data, we need:

1. A large set of good quality scholarly documents, preferably in the same domain, or a way to collect such a set from the internet.

2. A scalable way to obtain citation counts for papers , and a way to restrict the citation counting to a fixed number of years after a paper's publication, in order to get comparable counts for papers that are published in different years.

To accomplish these, we first discuss a method to collect papers from the ACL Anthology database, yielding a relatively large set of full text documents, of notably good quality and relatively controlled length in comparison to other alternatives such as the arXiv repository which we also considered. The resulting dataset is called ACL-BiblioMetry.[2] We next discuss a method to collect the required citation counts.

4.1 Scraping ACL

For retrieving the data from the ACL Anthology database, we use the method described in Algorithm 1. First, all relevant links are extracted from the ACL Anthology main page. This includes links to all listed venues from all years. The venue as well as the year is saved for each entry as they are used as names for the saved PDF and bib files. Then, for each link, the page source is retrieved. In the page source, all relevant links to PDFs are found. PDF links that correspond to posters, presentations, supplementary materials and notes are ignored. After this, the bib link corresponding to the PDF link is extracted and both are saved using the venue name and year.

4.2 Citations Retrieval

To retrieve the set of papers that cites a given paper, we use the Semantic Scholar database.[3] The

---

[2] Link to scraper code and citation information data: https://github.com/Pringled/ACL-BiblioMetry

[3] The Scholar Database source files are available from https://api.semanticscholar.org/corpus/download/ .

{"entities":[],"journalVolume":"","journalPages":"97-115","pmid":"","fieldsOfStudy":["Computer Science"],
"year":2019,**"outCitations": ["c91f19447f7a72afe58ecf7281033df276b20497",
"bd59f9543127f56074aa2e6adb259099eb333912", "acbd8a36a59b7e27ddf24b64133b6b9cf4c6990c",
"d8c1b48ae4d6e4676d060c06087bb6b1ac81a005", ...,"2671a510c47b7fbe117fa07051829914cd1b4c98"],**
"s2Url":"https://semanticscholar.org/
paper/3958cfb18ce6f32e90bd6ef5473be7ddd5a4e464", "s2PdfUrl":"", **"id":"3958cfb18ce6f32e90bd6ef5473be7ddd5a4e464",**
"authors":[{"name":"Tim van de Kamp","ids":["7401984"]},{"name":"David Stritzl","ids":["146553639"]},{"name":"Willem
Jonker","ids":["6235263"]},{"name":"Andreas Peter","ids":["144253636"]}],"journalName":"",
"paperAbstract":"We propose several functional encryption schemes for set intersection and variants on two or multiple sets.
. . .
"inCitations":["f1a2ab3038bedbdfabd35f8d41103b99f51d0ec7"], "title":"Two-Client and Multi-client Functional Encryption for Set Intersection","doi":"10.1007/978-3-030-21548-4_6","sources":["DBLP"],"doiUrl":"https://doi.org/10.1007/978-3-
030-21548-4_6","venue":"ACISP"}

Figure 3: Example of a JSON paper entry in the Semantic Scholar database source files. The paper id, outCitations, and inCitations are shown in bold, for clarity.

---

scrapeACL
Data: None.
Result: A folder of PDF and corresponding bib
files.
relevant_links ← extractLinks(page)
for *link ∈ relevant_links* **do**
  title ← getVenueAndYear(link);
  page_source ← getPageContent(link);
  for *line ∈ page_source* **do**
    if *in_line("pdf") and not*
    (in_line("poster")
    or in_line("presentation") or
    in_line("supplementary") or
    in_line("notes")) **then**
      pdf_link ← extractPdfLink(line)
      bib_link ← extractBibLink(line)
      downloadPdf(pdf_link)
      downloadBib(bib_link)
return None

Algorithm 1: Algorithm for scraping the ACL anthology database.

findCitationsForArticleFromDatabase
Data: ⟨authors_table, articles_table⟩, ⟨title:
  String, authors: list⟩.
Result: A dictionary of ⟨year,
  citation_ids_list⟩ entries.
for *author ∈ authors* **do**
  article_ids ←
  selectIDsWithAuthor(authors_table,
  author);
  for *article_id ∈ article_ids* **do**
    article ←
    selectArticleWithID(articles_table,
    article_id);
    if *article.title = title* **then**
      return computeYearGroupedCi-
      tations(article)
return None

Algorithm 2: Algorithm for matching an article title and authors list to the database, returning the citations information for the first found article that matches the title and one of the authors.

---

database in its provided form consists of a collection of JSON objects, one per line. Figure 3 shows an example of an entry from the database source-files. Each entry has an *id*, a list of paper *outCitations*: IDs of the papers that the entry paper cites, as well as a list of paper *inCitations*: IDs of papers that are citing the entry paper. For our purposes in this work we are mainly interested in the *inCitations* information. Naively, the raw semantic scholar database entries already provide us with the information of how often a paper is cited. However, in practice this is not very useful, since papers are published in different years. Consequently, more recent papers will have had much less time to "collect" citations. To correct for this, and get comparable citation counts, we need

to count only citations within a fixed window of time from each paper's data of publication. The latter task is slightly more involved to solve, noting that every source file is 1.6 Gigabytes, with 185 source files for a total of 283 Gigabytes of text data at the time of writing.

4.3 SQL database for efficient retrieval

By creating an SQL database that contains all the information in a structured way with proper indices, the task becomes manageable. Specifically we create a database consisting of two tables:

1. Authors table. Fields: [article_id (text, PRIMARY KEY), author_name (text).]
   An index is added to author_name, to facilitate fast lookup of papers that have a certain

computeYearGroupedCitations
Data: ⟨authors_table, articles_table⟩,
    article.
Result: A dictionary of ⟨year,
       citation_ids_list⟩ entries.
result_dict ← dict([]);
for *citing_article_id ∈ article.in_citations*
 do
    citing_article ←
     selectArticleWithID(articles_table,
     citing_article_id);
    if *not(citing_article.year ∈ result_dict)*
    then
     | result_dict[year] ← list([]);
    result_dict[year].
      appcnd(citing_article.article_id);
return result_dict

Algorithm 3: Algorithm for generating a dictionary of ids of citing articles, collected in sub-lists indexed by year.

    author.
2. Articles table. Fields: [article_id (text. PRIMARY KEY), title (text), pages (text), year (text), volume (text), journal (text), inbound_citations (text), outbound_citations (text), doi (text)].

   The fields in the articles table are kept quite minimal, omitting some unnecessary information from the original semantic scholar source files. An index is added to article_id for fast lookup of a paper with a given article_id.

4.3.1 Database creation

After creating the database the two tables are filled by simply looping over the semantic scholar source files and adding a corresponding entry to the articles table for each article entry in the source files. The authors table in addition is filled with an entry for each author of the article entry. The aim of this is that an article can be retrieved based on each of the author's names separately, increasing recall. To further increase recall all the author names are lowercased (in the created database and during retrieval).

4.3.2 Number of citations retrieval

Given an article, the citations of the article are retrieved from the database based on the authors list and title of the paper. This is done in two stages, shown also in Algorithm 2:

1. Paper retrieval: One by one, for each of the authors, all paper ids are retrieved. From these, matching article entries are found from the articles table. The first paper by any of the authors that matches the query title is returned as a positive match.[4] Just as the case for author names, titles are also lowercased to further increase recall.

2. Once the correct article entry is retrieved, the list of paper IDs of inbound citations, can be obtained from this entry. For each of these IDs an article entry is obtained and from that entry the publication year of that article. Finally, the IDs of the citing papers are grouped in a dictionary indexed by year (see Algorithm 3).

4.3.3 Citation scores and year-range uniformity

In our work we follow Maillette de Buy Wenniger et al. (2020) in using citation scores defined as

$$\text{citation\_score} = log(\text{number\_of\_citations} + 1) \quad (1)$$

When computing these (or other) scores, it is critical to use uniform year-ranges, that is a uniform MAX_YEARS: the maximum years after the publication of an article for collecting citations. A secondary question is: what are good values for MAX_YEARS? We believe in principle higher values will reduce the effects of randomness in the scores, and therefore it seems reasonable to allow at least a few years (e.g. setting MAX_YEARS > 3). Taking this into account, we believe that whereas enforcing MAX_YEARS uniformly is important, the value chosen for it is less important: all large enough values will give citation_score distributions such that the citation_score can be used (to some extent) to reflect the relative quality or impact of articles. Therefore, we leave finding an optimal value for future work. Even so, the advantage of the way we collect the citation information is that it is straightforward to experiment with different settings. One practical reason however for not choosing the parameter too large is that it disallows more recent publications to be included. For example, at the time of writing (August 2020) setting MAX_YEARS to 3 means that articles

---

[4]We require only one author name to match, because this significantly increases recall, while the chance of false positives given the full title and one fully matching author name is negligible.

Table 1: Properties of datasets for citation count prediction applied in earlier work.

paper source	# papers (train + validation + test)	# reviews	paper text type
(Fu and Aliferis, 2008)	3788	N/A	title+abstract
(Li et al., 2019)	1739, 384	7171, 1119	title + abstract
(Plank and van Dale, 2019)	3427	12260	title + abstract
(Maillette de Buy Wenniger et al., 2020)	78894 + 4383 + 4382	N/A	title + abstract + partial body
ACL-BiblioMetry dataset (this work)	27853 + 1548 + 1549	N/A	title + abstract + full body

Table 2: Character count per example statistics ACL dataset different settings.

systems	BiLSTM, HAN, SChuBERT	BiLSTM, HAN	SChuBERT		
setting	title + abstract	title + abstract + body text (max 200000 chars)	title + abstract + body text		
			max 5 chunks	max 6 chunks	no limit
#characters (avg, max)	975 , 20000	17293 , 20000	12019 , 19064	14061 , 22643	23787 , 1261656

Table 3: Hyperparameters used in the experiments.

	BiLSTM and HAN	SChuBERT
vocabulary size	10000	
weight initialization		
general	Xavier uniform	
lstm	Xavier normal	
bias	zero	
optimizer, learning rate	Adam, 0.005	Adam, 0.001
epochs	160	30
maximum input characters	20000	no limit
word embeddings	GloVe	N/A
loss function	MAE	MAE
dropout probability	0.5	0.3
BiLSTM/GRU hidden size	192	512
batch size	4, 16	12
word embedding size	50	N/A
BERT sentence embedding size	N/A	768

published up to 2016 can be included, as they have 3 complete years after 2016 (i.e. 2017, 2018, 2019) to "collect" citations. Papers published after 2016 cannot be included with this setting. We used this setting in our experiments, as we believe it to be large enough to give reliable citation_score values, while small enough to allow inclusion of a large number of articles in the data.

Computation

Once MAX_YEARS is chosen, for an article a, and and associated citations dictionary $a\_citations\_dict$ computed by Algorithm 3 selecting included citations is easy. Simply concatenate the lists of year-indexed citations sublists with $year(sublist) \leq a.year + MAX\_YEARS$. Based on the final list of included citations, the citation score or other metrics can then be easily computed.

5 Experiments

In our experiments, we want to assess the usability of the ACL data for number of citations prediction, and generally larger training data for citation prediction, as enabled by the automatic number of citation labeling framework contributed in this work. We also want to test two hypotheses:

1. Longer input text improves performance: using then entire paper text (title + abstract + body text) is substantially better than using only the paper title + abstract.

2. Larger training data substantially improves performance. More specifically, when using training data for number of citation prediction that is n times larger than what has been used for the related task of accept/reject prediction on the PeerRead CL dataset (computation and language domain) yields substantially better results than when using a training set of size comparable to PeerRead CL.

To test these two hypothesis, we perform the following comparisons:

1. Full text input in comparison to abstract only.

2. Full data input in comparison to 50% data input and to 10% data input.

To test our second hypothesis, we take 10% of our dataset to get a dataset which is approximately

Table 4: Results on the full data and with full input.

	BiLSTM	HAN	SChuBERT (5 chunk)	SChuBERT (6 chunk)	SChuBERT
R^2 score	0.319 ± 0.013	0.339 ± 0.013	0.369 ± 0.009	0.380 ± 0.004	$\mathbf{0.398 \pm 0.006}$
MSE	1.110 ± 0.021	1.080 ± 0.021	1.032 ± 0.015	1.013 ± 0.006	$\mathbf{0.985 \pm 0.010}$
MAE	0.824 ± 0.009	0.820 ± 0.009	0.805 ± 0.005	0.798 ± 0.005	$\mathbf{0.789 \pm 0.005}$

Table 5: Results on the full data and with abstract text only.

	BiLSTM	HAN	SChuBERT
R^2 score	0.158 ± 0.006	0.248 ± 0.014	$\mathbf{0.249 \pm 0.002}$
MSE	1.377 ± 0.010	$\mathbf{1.230 \pm 0.023}$	$\mathbf{1.230 \pm 0.004}$
MAE	0.933 ± 0.002	0.885 ± 0.008	$\mathbf{0.884 \pm 0.002}$

Table 6: Results for SChuBERT on a subset of the data and with full input.

	SChuBERT 50% data	SChuBERT 10% data
R^2 score	0.327 ± 0.007	0.205 ± 0.026
MSE	1.058 ± 0.011	1.473 ± 0.048
MAE	0.809 ± 0.005	0.923 ± 0.027

Table 7: Number of trainable parameters for used hidden sizes.

Hidden size	BiLSTM	HAN	SchuBERT
192	1170949	2059525	N/A
256	N/A	N/A	788225
512	N/A	N/A	969665

Table 8: Training time per epoch in seconds.

	BiLSTM	HAN	SchuBERT
Time in seconds	1048	1921	12

Table 9: Results for SChuBERT with hidden size 256 (with full data).

MSE	MAE	R2
0.994 ± 0.013	0.788 ± 0.006	0.392 ± 0.008

the size of PeerRead CL (3000 papers). We then compare this to half our data and full data to show the importance of larger datasets. Lastly, we also test SChuBERT on a portion of the chunks to ensure a fair comparison with BiLSTM and HAN which were capped at 20k characters. Statistics about the number of characters per example in the different settings are shown in Table 2.

5.1 Experimental Settings

Table 3 shows the hyperparameters used for training the models in our experiments. As evaluation metrics, we report the standard metrics of mean squared error (MS) and mean average error (MAE), which are commonly used for regression evaluation, as well as the R^2 score. We repeat each experiment three times to counter false conclusions due to optimizer instability, and report average and standard deviation for each of the metrics.

6 Results

Our results show that SChuBERT is able to outperform both BiLSTM as well as HAN for the citation prediction problem by a significant margin. Table 4 shows a comparison of the three models for full data input and full-text input. While BiLSTM and HAN have a comparable R^2 score, SChuBERT has an R^2 score of almost 0.06 higher, showing the power of contextualized word embeddings. SChuBERT also performs better with 5 chunks (which equates to less total input used than BiLSTM and HAN which were capped at 20k characters) and 6 chunks (which equates to slightly more input used than BiLSTM and HAN). For reference, the average number of chunks was 7.6. In practice, capping the chunks mostly results in extremely long papers being cut off, just like in BiLSTM and HAN.

We also compared how well the different models performed on abstract-only inputs, shown in Table 5. These results show that HAN and SChuBERT have comparable results, which shows that SChuBERT benefits more from longer inputs. In general, the performance of all models is substantially better on full-text inputs when compared to abstract only.

In Table 6 we show the performance of SChuBERT on less data. As expected, the performance decreases substantially with less data, showing the benefit of larger datasets such as the one proposed in this paper. Due to time constraints, we did not test BiLSTM and HAN on less data.

As a final comparison of the systems, we show the number of trainable parameters in Table 7 and the training time in seconds per epoch in Table 8. As can be seen, SChuBERT has a smaller number of trainable parameters even with a larger hidden size for the GRU. Additionally, in Table 9 we show results for SChuBERT when we half the hidden size to 256, which turns out to only give a small drop in performance. The training time in seconds per epoch is also much lower for SChuBERT, which trains approximately 87 faster than BiLSTM and 160 times faster than HAN. However, this is after the embeddings have been generated, which takes relatively long (a little over 7 hours for the full dataset) but only has to be done once. Even when taking this into consideration, training SChuBERT is still much faster given that it converges about 4 times faster than the other systems.

7 Conclusion

In this work, we showed the importance of larger and better curated data for the citation prediction problem. We proposed ACL-BiblioMetry, a new large dataset created with the algorithms we provide in this work. We also proposed SChuBERT, a new model for the citation prediction problem which can deal with large inputs and gets significantly better results than several state-of-the-art models. The model shows the strength of modern language models and contextualized word embeddings and their appliance to the citation prediction problem. Our results showed that both the length of the input as well as the amount of data are important for achieving better results. The current work takes a step forward by using a larger training set of full text examples and leveraging this data with stronger models, in particular the SChuBERT model, without considering the historical publication context and other factors. We leave experimentation with further extended context for the predictive models, as well as other language models and even larger datasets for future work.

Acknowledgments

The Peregrine high performance computing cluster, at the Center for Information Technology of the University (CIT) of Groningen, was used for running part of the experiments in this study. We would like to thank the people at the CIT for their support and access to the cluster. We would also like to thank Charles-Emmanuel Dias for sharing his HAN implementation, which proved to be a solid foundation for the HAN models used in this work.

References

Ali Abrishami and Sadegh Aliakbary. 2019. Predicting citation counts based on deep neural network learning techniques. *Journal of Informetrics*, 13:485–499.

Xiaomei Bai, Fuli Zhang, and Ivan Lee. 2019. Predicting the citations of scholarly paper. *Journal of Informetrics*, 13(1):407 – 418.

Iz Beltagy, Matthew E. Peters, and Arman Cohan. 2020. Longformer: The long-document transformer.

Tim Brody, Stevan Harnad, and Les Carr. 2006. Earlier web usage statistics as predictors of later citation impact. *Journal of the American Association for Information Science and Technology (JASIST)*, 57(8):1060–1072. DOI: 10.1002/asi.20373.

Gideon Maillette de Buy Wenniger, Thomas van Dongen, Eleri Aedmaa, Herbert Teun Kruitbosch, Edwin A. Valentijn, and Lambert Schomaker. 2020. Structure-tags improve text classification for scholarly document quality prediction. In *Proceedings of the the 1st Workshop on Scholarly Document Processing (SDP 2020)*. Association for Computational Linguistics.

Kyunghyun Cho, Bart van Merriënboer, Caglar Gulcehre, Dzmitry Bahdanau, Fethi Bougares, Holger Schwenk, and Yoshua Bengio. 2014. Learning phrase representations using RNN encoder–decoder for statistical machine translation. In *Proceedings of the 2014 Conference on Empirical Methods in Natural Language Processing (EMNLP)*, pages 1724–1734, Doha, Qatar. Association for Computational Linguistics.

Jacob Devlin, Ming-Wei Chang, Kenton Lee, and Kristina Toutanova. 2018. Bert: Pre-training of deep bidirectional transformers for language understanding.

Lawrence Fu and Constantin Aliferis. 2008. Models for predicting and explaining citation count of biomedical articles. *AMIA ... Annual Symposium proceedings / AMIA Symposium. AMIA Symposium*, 6:222–6.

Alfonso Ibáñez, Pedro Larrañaga, and Concha Bielza. 2009. Predicting citation count of Bioinformatics papers within four years of publication. *Bioinformatics*, 25(24):3303–3309.

Mandar Joshi, Omer Levy, Daniel S. Weld, and Luke Zettlemoyer. 2019. Bert for coreference resolution: Baselines and analysis.

Dongyeop Kang, Waleed Ammar, Bhavana Dalvi, Madeleine van Zuylen, Sebastian Kohlmeier, Eduard Hovy, and Roy Schwartz. 2018. A dataset of peer reviews (peerread): Collection, insights and nlp applications.

Nikita Kitaev, Łukasz Kaiser, and Anselm Levskaya. 2020. Reformer: The efficient transformer.

Siqing Li, Wayne Xin Zhao, Eddy Jing Yin, and Ji-Rong Wen. 2019. A neural citation count prediction model based on peer review text. In *Proceedings of the 2019 Conference on Empirical Methods in Natural Language Processing and the 9th International Joint Conference on Natural Language Processing (EMNLP-IJCNLP)*, pages 4914–4924, Hong Kong, China. Association for Computational Linguistics.

Kyle Lo, Lucy Lu Wang, Mark Neumann, Rodney Kinney, and Dan S. Weld. 2019. S2orc: The semantic scholar open research corpus.

Matthew E. Peters, Sebastian Ruder, and Noah A. Smith. 2019. To tune or not to tune? adapting pre-trained representations to diverse tasks.

Barbara Plank and Reinard van Dale. 2019. Cite-tracked: A longitudinal dataset ofpeer reviews and citations. In *Proceedings of the 4th Joint Workshop on Bibliometric-enhanced Information Retrieval and Natural Language Processing for Digital Libraries (BIRNDL 2019)*.

Aili Shen, Jianzhong Qi, and Timothy Baldwin. 2017. A hybrid model for quality assessment of wikipedia articles. In *Proceedings of the Australasian Language Technology Association Workshop 2017*, pages 43–52.

Aili Shen, Bahar Salehi, Timothy Baldwin, and Jianzhong Qi. 2019. A joint model for multimodal document quality assessment.

Ashish Vaswani, Noam Shazeer, Niki Parmar, Jakob Uszkoreit, Llion Jones, Aidan N Gomez, Ł ukasz Kaiser, and Illia Polosukhin. 2017. Attention is all you need. In I. Guyon, U. V. Luxburg, S. Bengio, H. Wallach, R. Fergus, S. Vishwanathan, and R. Garnett, editors, *Advances in Neural Information Processing Systems 30*, pages 5998–6008. Curran Associates, Inc.

Yonghui Wu, Mike Schuster, Zhifeng Chen, Quoc V. Le, Mohammad Norouzi, Wolfgang Macherey, Maxim Krikun, Yuan Cao, Qin Gao, Klaus Macherey, Jeff Klingner, Apurva Shah, Melvin Johnson, Xiaobing Liu, Łukasz Kaiser, Stephan Gouws, Yoshikiyo Kato, Taku Kudo, Hideto Kazawa, Keith Stevens, George Kurian, Nishant Patil, Wei Wang, Cliff Young, Jason Smith, Jason Riesa, Alex Rudnick, Oriol Vinyals, Greg Corrado, Macduff Hughes, and Jeffrey Dean. 2016. Google's neural machine translation system: Bridging the gap between human and machine translation.

Qizhe Xie, Zihang Dai, Eduard Hovy, Minh-Thang Luong, and Quoc V. Le. 2019. Unsupervised data augmentation for consistency training.

Zichao Yang, Diyi Yang, Chris Dyer, Xiaodong He, Alex Smola, and Eduard Hovy. 2016. Hierarchical attention networks for document classification. In *Proceedings of the 2016 Conference of the North American Chapter of the Association for Computational Linguistics: Human Language Technologies*, pages 1480–1489, San Diego, California. Association for Computational Linguistics.

Structure-Tags Improve Text Classification for Scholarly Document Quality Prediction

**Gideon Maillette de Buy Wenniger[†], Thomas van Dongen[†], Eleri Aedmaa[‡],
Herbert Teun Kruitbosch[‡], Edwin A. Valentijn[§], and Lambert Schomaker[†]**

[†]Bernoulli Institute for Mathematics,Computer Science and Artificial Intelligence
University of Groningen, Groningen, The Netherlands

`gemdbw AT gmail.com` `t.a.van.dongen AT student.rug.nl`

[‡]Center for Information Technology, University of Groningen, Groningen, The Netherlands

[§]Kapteyn Astronomical Institute, University of Groningen, Groningen, The Netherlands

Abstract

Training recurrent neural networks on long texts, in particular scholarly documents, causes problems for learning. While hierarchical attention networks (HANs) are effective in solving these problems, they still lose important information about the structure of the text. To tackle these problems, we propose the use of HANs combined with *structure-tags* which mark the role of sentences in the document. Adding tags to sentences, marking them as corresponding to title, abstract or main body text, yields improvements over the state-of-the-art for scholarly document quality prediction. The proposed system is applied to the task of accept/reject prediction on the Peer-Read dataset and compared against a recent BiLSTM-based model and joint textual+visual model as well as against plain HANs. Compared to plain HANs, accuracy increases on all three domains. On the computation and language domain our new model works best overall, and increases accuracy 4.7% over the best literature result. We also obtain improvements when introducing the tags for prediction of the number of citations for 88k scientific publications that we compiled from the Allen AI S2ORC dataset. For our HAN-system with structure-tags we reach 28.5% explained variance, an improvement of 1.8% over our reimplementation of the BiLSTM-based model as well as 1.0% improvement over plain HANs.

1 Introduction

Automatic prediction of the quality of scientific and other texts is a new topic within the field of deep learning. Deep learning has been successfully applied to many natural language processing (NLP) problems including text classification, as well as many computer vision applications including document structure analysis. These successes suggest automatic quality assessment of scientific documents, while still highly ambitious, is feasible for scientific study.

Sequential deep learning models, particularly recurrent neural networks (RNNs), long short-term memories (LSTMs) and their variants, have been particularly successful for applications that require the encoding and/or generation of relatively short sequences of text, typically at most a few sentences. Applications include (short) text classification (Rao and Spasojevic, 2016), entailment (Rocktäschel et al., 2015) and neural machine translation (MT) (Bahdanau et al., 2014; Luong et al., 2015). Newer attention-based models, particularly the transformer model (Vaswani et al., 2017) are even more apt at using all of the possible context when encoding sentences, further improving performance. Transformers are also used to build general sentence embeddings with the BERT model (Devlin et al., 2018). In comparison, the accurate classification of full documents remains challenging. To be effective, a deep learning model for longer text should fulfill the following three criteria:

1. *Trainability*: being trainable on long texts.

2. *Computational efficiency*: efficiency as well as parallelizability, to effectively use GPUs.

3. *Rich context*: having access to rich context at sentence and document level. And avoiding therefore: 1) the assumption that sentences at different locations are independent, 2) the even more crippling assumption of statistical independence of document words.

Plain sequential models such as RNNs and LSTMs model text as unstructured word sequences. This causes problems on longer texts because of the vanishing gradient and exploding gradient problem (Pascanu et al., 2013), which hampers *trainability*. Gradient bounding methods including gradient clipping (Hochreiter, 1998), can help to reduce these problems, but provide no solution for docu-

Proceedings of the First Workshop on Scholarly Document Processing, pages 158–167
Online, November 19, 2020. ©2020 Association for Computational Linguistics
https://doi.org/10.18653/v1/P17

ments with thousands of words. Transformers and BERT are not a good match for long texts either, as these models have a computational cost that grows quadratically with sentence length. Arguably, bag-of-word models, including models performing average pooling over word embeddings accomplish *trainability* and *computational efficiency*. However, their computational cheapness is achieved at the price of making very strong statistical independence assumptions that harm prediction quality.

A group of models does fulfill all three criteria: hierarchical versions of sequential models, in particular hierarchical attention networks (HANs) (Yang et al., 2016). HANs produce hierarchical text encodings using a hierarchical stacking of LSTMs-with attention, for the sentence and text level. This massively increases parallelization while simultaneously reducing the number of steps the gradient signal needs to be back-propagated during training, increasing learnability. HAN text encodings can still take much context into account at every level in the representation, thanks to the use of LSTMs.

While HANs are highly effective in forming adequate representations of longer texts, they are still deficient in the use of *structure information* inherent in the text. The reason is simple: these models have only one ((Bi)LSTM) encoding sub-model per level in the hierarchy. This sub-model is used to encode all the inputs at that level, without access to relevant structure context. In this work we observe that this problem can be tackled by adding XML-like structure-tags at the beginning and end of each input sentence. The effectiveness of our approach is demonstrated on two tasks:

A Paper accept/reject prediction on the Peer-Read dataset (Kang et al., 2018).

B Number of citations prediction for scholarly documents, on a new dataset with 88K articles compiled from the Allen AI S2ORC dataset.

The experiments for both tasks show that using just three tags to mark abstract, title and body text, already provides substantial improvements: A) outperforming all models on the computation and language domain and HAN without tags on all domains, B) outperforming all other models. Larger gains can likely be made by further enriching the tag-set. The proposed tagging approach is particularly useful in the domain of scholarly document understanding, since while these document are typically long, they are also highly structured.

The rest of the paper is structured as follows. In section 2 we discuss the various existing and alternative NLP models for the aforementioned tasks of quality prediction. Section 3 describes the proposed HAN model combined with structure-tags. Section 4 and 5 respectively discuss their use for accept/reject and number of citations prediction.

2 Related Work

Multiple methods have been proposed to estimate the quality of scientific papers. The most common approach is to use the citation counts as a measure of quality, to be predicted by models. Fu and Aliferis (2008) proposed one of the first models which used both the papers content in the form of the paper title, abstract and keywords as well as bibliometric information. Notably they used automated scripts to retrieve bibliometric information, even so their final corpus is still relatively small, containing 3788 papers.

Limited recent research is available on the subject of predicting the quality of papers with deep learning using the textual content. Shen et al. (2019) combine visual and textual content using a CNN and LSTM respectively. The authors make use of the Wikipedia and the arXiv datasets. The authors propose a joint model that classifies the quality of papers. To generate textual embeddings, the authors use a bi-directional LSTM model similar to the one proposed by the same authors in (Shen et al., 2017). The input to the model is the word embeddings of a paper, obtained using GloVe, and the output is a textual embedding.

Some recent work focuses on predicting the number of citations from the paper text augmented with review text. To do so, Li et al. (2019) created a dataset of abstracts and reviews from the ICLR and NIPS conferences: 1739 abstracts with a total of 7171 reviews for ICLR and 384 abstracts with 1119 reviews for NIPS. Plank and van Dale (2019) collect a dataset of 3427 papers with 12260 reviews. Both papers show improvement in the results from using the review information.

Hierarchical sequential models

Hierarchical versions of sequential models have already been pioneered in the literature for a long time in the form of hierarchical RNNs (Hihi and Bengio, 1996). More recently however, use of LSTMs instead of RNNs and use of attention resulted in the now popular HAN model (Yang et al., 2016), which was successfully applied to sentiment

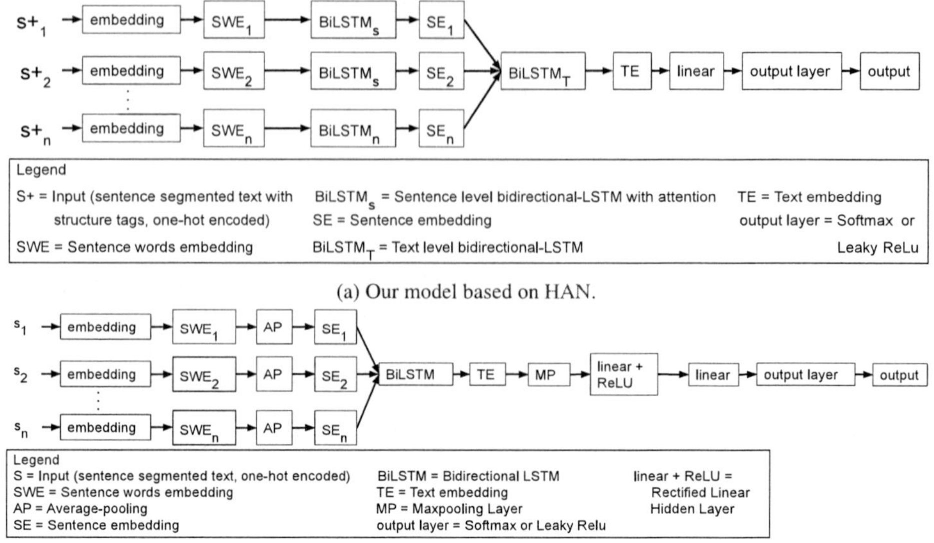

(a) Our model based on HAN.

(b) Model proposed by Shen et al. (2019).

Figure 1: Most important models compared in this work.

analysis and text classification.

Adding structure through additional inputs

Our proposed structure-tag framework resembles the approach that been used for neural MT translating multiple source languages to multiple target languages using a unified model (Johnson et al., 2016), in which a special "command token" is used to indicate which kind of translation is desired. Related also is the idea of using multiple embeddings for different types of information, as introduced in neural MT by Sennrich and Haddow (2016), which was later also exploited in the transformer model (Vaswani et al., 2017). In contrast to the latter approaches which change the embedding layer, like (Johnson et al., 2016) we leave the (HAN) model exactly as is and only change the input.

3 Models

In this work we use and refine state-of-the-art text-based deep learning models for text classification and regression tasks: accept/reject prediction and number of citations prediction respectively. Our contributions focus on HANs,[1] which we show for these tasks to be competitive with models that use a flat BiLSTM encoder at their core (Shen et al., 2019). Figure 1a shows a diagram of our HAN model with structure-tags added to the input, and

---

[1]Our HAN implementation is adapted from https://github.com/cedias/Hierarchical-Sentiment

Figure 1b shows a diagram of the BiLSTM-based model, our baseline for comparison. As can be seen from the diagrams, both models use a BiLSTM at the text level that works on embeddings computed for the sentences of the text. However, while HAN uses the sequential order to compute an embedding, the baseline model averages word vectors, disregarding order, similar to bag-of-word representations. We also use a second baseline model: Average Word Embeddings (AWE), which simply encodes text by the average word embedding.

3.1 Sentence type tags for more structure

The hierarchical structure of text characterized by structure elements such as sections, paragraphs and sentences and labeling elements such as document titles and section titles reveals important information. Models without hierarchy such as plain RNN/LSTM models ignore this structure, which motivated HAN. HAN uses an LSTM with attention to create encodings of each sentence separately and combines this with a second LSTM with attention on top to transform these into an encoding of the entire text. The hierarchical structure of HAN provides several advantages over flat sequential models, i.e. plain RNNs/LSTMs:

1. *Trainability on long texts*: using less steps for back-propagating gradients during training, HAN can process longer texts without running into vanishing/exploding gradient problems.

Figure 2: Example of structure-tags for a paper from in
the PeerRead computation and language arXiv dataset.

HAN preserves high-resolution when forming
sentence-level encodings.

2. *Computational efficiency*: the structure of
   HAN makes computations better paralleliz-
   able, since its sentence encoding LSTMs can
   process their inputs in parallel.

3. *Interpretability of predictions*: visualizing
   HAN attention facilitates some qualitative insight into what inputs are important for making predictions at a sentence and word level.

Despite these large advantages, HAN in its normal application still remains limited in its use of
structure. In particular, while HAN encodes sentences in a hierarchical way, it does so while using
the same LSTM encoder for every sentence without structure context. In this work we introduce
a way to overcome these problems by adding sentence type tags encoding the role of a sentences
or other information, which is then directly available to the BiLSTM when encoding the sentences.
This is illustrated in Figure 2. First the input is
segmented into a list of sentences,[2] as is also done
in preprocessing for regular HAN. Then the role
of each sentence is added at the beginning and
end of each sentence. In our current experiments
the roles are restricted to three options: TITLE,
ABSTRACT, BODY_TEXT, however, the idea is
general enough to include much more specific tags
as well as tags encoding relative or absolute sentence position information; to be explored in future
work. We will refer to this system as hierarchical attention network with structure tags (HAN$_{ST}$). The
advantages of the tag-base approach over other possible solutions, such as using different BiLSTMs
for different types of sentences are simplicity and
scalability. Equally important, using tags allows
the BiLSTM to only specialize its functioning to
specific types of sentences where needed, while
effectively sharing what can be generalized independent of sentence type.

4 Accept/Reject prediction on PeerRead

The first scholarly document quality prediction task
we test our methods on is accept/reject prediction
on arXiv papers from the PeerRead dataset (Kang
et al., 2018). This dataset is chosen because of
the large amount of earlier work in the literature
reporting results on it, allowing comparison against
the state-of-the-art on a well studied task.

The full PeerRead dataset holds 14784 papers
in total, each of which contains implicit or explicit
accept/reject labels. Furthermore, PeerRead contains different subsets of papers. The largest subset
consists of arXiv papers (11778) in three computer-
science sub-domains:[3] machine learning (cs.LG),
computation and language (cs.CL), artificial intelligence (cs.AI), and has only accept/reject labels;
this is the dataset that we use. A part of the papers
also include reviews (3006 papers) and a subset of
the latter also contains aspect scores (586 papers).
However, of these papers with reviews, the large
majority is from NIPS (2420 papers), and those
papers are all accepted. As the arXiv portion is relatively larger, and accept/reject labeled, most work
has focused on the task of accept/reject prediction
for the papers in this set.

Table 1 shows the sizes of the different subsets
of the arXiv PeerRead dataset and their respective
division in number of accept and reject examples.
Note that this division is imbalanced for each of
the three domains, with the least imbalance for the
machine learning subset and the most imbalance for
the artificial intelligence subset, in which around
90% of the examples is rejected. These imbalances
in the number of examples for each of the classes
make learning harder, but can be partly overcome
by using strategies such as re-sampling.

4.1 Experimental Setup

In our experiments we tried to stay close to the experimental setup used by (Shen et al., 2019), while
deviating from their settings when necessary. We
used PyTorch for our code and a single GeForce
RTX 2080 Ti GPU for our experiments. Table 2
gives an overview of the used hyperparameters that
are shared across experiments, as well as the hyperparameters that are specific to the accept/reject

---

[2]We use spaCy for this: https://spacy.io/

[3]Based on arXiv categories within computer science, see:
https://arxiv.org/archive/cs

Table 1: Data sizes and division between the ratio of accepted and rejected papers for the arXiv subsets

	training		validation		testing		total
	num	acc:rej	num	acc:rej	num	acc:rej	
machine learning	4543	36.4% : 63.6%	252	36.5% : 63.5%	253	32.0% : 68.0%	5048
computation & language	2374	24.3% : 75.7%	132	22.0% : 78.0%	132	31.1% : 68.9%	2638
artificial intelligence	3682	10.5% : 89.5%	205	8.3% : 91.7%	205	7.8% : 92.2%	4092

Table 2: Hyperparameters used in the experiments.

	PeerRead	S2ORC
	classification	regression
optimizer, learning rate	Adam, 0.005	
maximum input characters	20000	
vocabulary size	10000	
weight initialization		
general	Xavier uniform	
lstm	Xavier normal	
bias	zero	
word embeddings	GloVe	
loss function	cross entropy	MAE
dropout probability	0.5	0.2
BiLSTM hidden size	256	100
batch size	4	64
embedding size	50	300

Table 3: Total trainable parameters per model.

Task	AWE	BiLSM	HAN/HAN$_{ST}$
PeerRead	500202	1657222	3235206
citation prediction	3000901	3402801	3644801

prediction task. We used Adam (Kingma and Ba, 2014) as optimizer, and Xavier (Glorot) (Glorot and Bengio, 2010) weight initialization. We use a considerably larger learning rate of 0.005, compared to 0.0001 used by (Shen et al., 2019).[4] On PeerRead, we use a small batch size of 4 . This is necessary for HAN as it uses relatively much memory, because it builds rich hierarchical BiLSTM-based representations directly from the word embeddings. We furthermore use re-sampling on the computational language and artificial intelligence subsets, as we find that without it, due to the imbalance in the label frequencies, learning fails. The re-sampling is done for each epoch, by keeping the full subset of examples with the less frequent label, but sub-sampling an equal number of random examples from the more frequent label subset. In our experiments the training of all our models proceeds slower than the number of epochs (60) used by Shen et al. (2019) suggests. This observation holds not only for our models but also for our reimplementation of their model, and in spite of the fact that we are using a higher learning rate. We therefore used a higher number of 360 training epochs.

---

⁴Learning rate 0.0001 gave poor results in our experiments.

Table 4: The effect of the length cutoff policy on the number of words distribution.

	average words per example	median words per example
20000 chars length cutoff	3909 $\pm$ 692	4076
360 sentences length cutoff	**5246 $\pm$ 1717**	5514

In each experiment, we used the highest accuracy score on the validation set to select the best model, using the last epoch that achieves that score in case of ties. We trained plus evaluated every model three times, to control for optimizer instability, reporting mean and standard deviation of the metric scores.

4.1.1 Input cutoff

Using the full text as input is in theory preferred over using only selected text, in order not to lose information prematurely. In practice however, this is not feasible with high resolution deep learning models such as HANs, which take input that starts at the word level. To save memory and computation, models may instead start out from the sentence level, using embeddings directly as inputs. But with simple sentence embeddings, this leads to a substantial loss of input information, which may hamper performance. Even so, (Shen et al., 2019) apply this strategy in a basic way by computing the average word embedding for each sentence, and using a BiLSTM model on top of that. Nevertheless, they still use a limit on the input length, by allowing only a maximum of 350 sentences. With HAN, which uses more memory and computation-intense sentence-level encodings, limiting the input length is even more crucial. However, rather than limiting the number of sentences, we limited the maximum number of characters, set to 20000. We found that with HANs this gives better results, even though on average it corresponds to less words. This is explained by the distribution over the number of words per example for each of the two length cutoff policies, see Table 4. Fixing the number of sentences causes large variance in the number of words per example, likely caused by writing style differences across authors. In contrast, fixing the number of characters by definition assures a con-

Table 5: PeerRead accept/reject prediction accuracy: comparison of HAN_{ST} against state-of-the-art.

arXiv sub-domain dataset	Majority class prediction	Benchmark (Kang et al., 2018)	BiLSTM (Shen et al., 2019)	Joint (Shen et al., 2019)	HAN_{ST}
artificial intelligence	92.2%	92.6%	$91.5 \pm 1.03\%$	$\mathbf{93.4 \pm 1.07}\%$	$89.6 \pm 1.02\%$
computation & language	68.9%	75.7%	$76.2 \pm 1.30\%$	$77.1 \pm 3.10\%$	$\mathbf{81.8 \pm 1.91}\%$
machine learning	68.0%	70.7%	$\mathbf{81.1 \pm 0.83}\%$	$79.9 \pm 2.54\%$	$78.7 \pm 0.69\%$

Table 6: PeerRead accept/reject prediction accuracy and *AUC* (area under ROC curve) scores for our models.

arXiv sub-domain dataset	metric	Majority class prediction	Average Word Embeddings	BiLSTM (re-implemented)	HAN	HAN_{ST}
artificial intelligence	accuracy	92.2%	$74.1 \pm 0.49\%$	$\mathbf{92.4 \pm 1.02}\%$	$88.9 \pm 1.97\%$	$89.6 \pm 1.02\%$
	AUC	0.50	$\mathbf{0.793 \pm 0.0143}$	$\mathbf{0.711 \pm 0.0771}$	0.625 ± 0.042	0.705 ± 0.055
computation & language	accuracy	68.9%	$73.7 \pm 0.87\%$	$80.1 \pm 1.91\%$	$80.3 \pm 2.00\%$	$\mathbf{81.8 \pm 1.91}\%$
	AUC	0.50	0.740 ± 0.010	0.744 ± 0.056	0.712 ± 0.029	$\mathbf{0.745 \pm 0.011}$
machine learning	accuracy	67.9%	$72.9 \pm 0.60\%$	$\mathbf{79.6 \pm 3.19}\%$	$76.7 \pm 2.77\%$	$78.7 \pm 0.69\%$
	AUC	0.50	0.662 ± 0.003	0.743 ± 0.025	0.743 ± 0.019	$\mathbf{0.758 \pm 0.0149}$

stant input length, and hence a more constant number of words (which is proportional to number of characters). We believe this more constant amount of information in the input aides learning.

4.1.2 Results

Table 5 shows our best results on the PeerRead dataset, using HAN_{ST}. The same table also shows the previous literature results of (Shen et al., 2019) and (Kang et al., 2018). Observe that in the computation & language domain, we gain 4.7% accuracy over the best of the these literature models (Joint), while on the machine learning domain and artificial intelligence domain datasets we lose 2.4% and 3.8% respectively in comparison to the best performing of the literature models on these domains (BiLSTM and Joint). In Table 6 we show the results for both our HAN models as well as for the other models. These results show a clear and consistent improvement from HAN_{ST} over plain HAN: 1.5% accuracy for the computation & language domain and 2.1% for the machine learning domain and 0.7% for the machine learning domain. Table 6 also shows results for our own re-implementation of the BiLSTM model described by (Shen et al., 2019). This useful for comparison since we made some changes to the experimental setup, including the use of higher learning rate and use of resampling. We observe better results with our re-implementation of BiLSTM than in the original work for these datasets where re-sampling was helpful, showing its importance for imbalanced datasets. Statistical significance was tested with the exact two-sided McNemar's test.[5] Comparing to the AWE systems: At significance level 0.05, other systems improve significantly over AWE except for HAN on the machine learning domain. At significance level 0.01 improvements over AWE are only significant on the artificial intelligence domain for BiLSTM and HAN_{ST}. Other differences are not statistically significant.

While HAN_{ST} is competitive with the literature models on PeerRead, it benefits from larger training data, as is available for the task of number of citations prediction.

4.1.3 Effects of reducing the label set

To determine the importance of different structure tags, in particular the title marking, we performed ablation experiments in which we reduced the label set. We combined the title and abstract label into one, leaving a structure-tag set with only two tags. Table 7 shows the results. As can be seen, the smaller structure-tag set reduces performance in comparison to HAN with three structure tags on all three domains. In the computation & language domain, the model performs worse also than HAN without structure tags on both accuracy and AUC, and in the artificial intelligence domain it performs equal in terms of accuracy but worse still on AUC. In the machine learning domain the model also loses performance over HAN with three structure tags, but still outperforms plain HAN. The results suggest that the titles of articles contain informa-

<hr>

[5]The scores of the 3 runs for one system are combined at example level by taking the mode/average, i.e. simple voting.

Table 7: Results of the HAN$_{\text{ST}}$ model with a reduced structure-tag set of only two tags.

domain / metric	artificial intelligence	computation & language	machine learning
accuracy	89.6 ± 1.57%	79.3 ± 0.14%	77.2 ± 1.21%
AUC	0.610 ± 0.067	0.727 ± 0.015	0.759 ± 0.017

tion that is relatively important for the model to make correct classification decisions, at least for the accept/reject prediction task with the PeerRead data. We leave study into the effect of extending the structure-tag set for future work.

5 Number of citations prediction

The second task we test our models on is number of citations prediction. A key advantage of this task is that large datasets can be obtained relatively easy by leveraging public sources such as the Semantic Scholar Database. In contrast, obtaining accept/reject labels in large quantities typically requires having an agreement with publishers, and even then because of legal problems, it is hard to obtain and publish such data.[6]

Yet, how useful it is to predict the number of citations? More specifically: is the number of citations of a paper predictive of its quality? Intuitively one would expect this to be the case at least to some extent. Figure 3 shows histograms of the numbers of citations of articles from the PeerRead datasets for accepted and rejected papers.[7] While there are some differences between the two domains, the main trend is the same in both cases: for rejected papers, the counts are peaked around zero citations and quickly decrease to one or zero for high citation counts. In contrast, the number of citations for accepted papers is two to three times higher on average, depending on the domain. Finally, we formally computed correlation in the form of the Spearman rank-order correlation coefficient (ρ) and associated p-value for both domains. For both domains, the value of ρ is high and the p-value extremely close to zero, which indicates significant correlation can be concluded at all p-levels of significance for a two-sided test. These histograms and numbers prove that there is indeed a strong correlation between acceptance/rejection and the number of citations. Therefore it makes sense to consider the number of citations as an imperfect but nonetheless

Table 8: S2ORC dataset size statistics.

data subset	num examples	avg num words
training	78894	839.1 ± 473.7
validation	4383	849.1 ± 477.5
testing	4382	856.4 ± 489.0

useful proxy for the quality of scholarly documents.

5.1 The dataset

Recent works undertake the task of number of citations prediction based on the scholarly document text, but mostly do so while using relatively small datasets. As discussed in related work, some of the recent work adds review text to the input. However, creating models using reviewer comments limits their practical application to after reviewing and reduces available training data. These observations motivated us to rather aim for a relatively large dataset of ⟨paper, number of citations⟩ pairs. We selected a subset of papers in the computer science domain from the S2ORC (Lo et al., 2020) data, for which title, abstract and body text information is present; these are combined as the example text. We did this for papers in the year range 2000–2010, and counted the number of citations of citing papers that are published within 8 years after the publication of a paper. Randomly ordering the papers, from this we compiled a dataset with in total about 88K papers, and statistics as shown in Table 8.[8] Note that to the best of our knowledge, the largest number of articles used for citation prediction in earlier work is described in (Plank and van Dale, 2019), we use more than 23 times the number of articles used in their experiments. While we kept the maximum number of words per example at 20000, during our experiments we have only used the first of the list of text dictionaries for each article in S2ORC , consequently the average number of words is much lower: around 840 words per example.[9] We leave creating examples with the

---

[6]Note that while the PeerRead arXiv accept/reject dataset is relatively large, its labels are based on heuristics.

[7]By restricting citation counting to citing papers published within two years of each paper's publication, we keep citation counts comparable across papers.

[8]The new S2ORC-derived log-citation-count prediction dataset, used in our experiments, is available from: https://github.com/gwenniger/s2orc-cc/

[9]Due to a misunderstanding of the S2ORC data format, which actually does contain longer text when combining all the text dictionaries, which got clarified after submission.

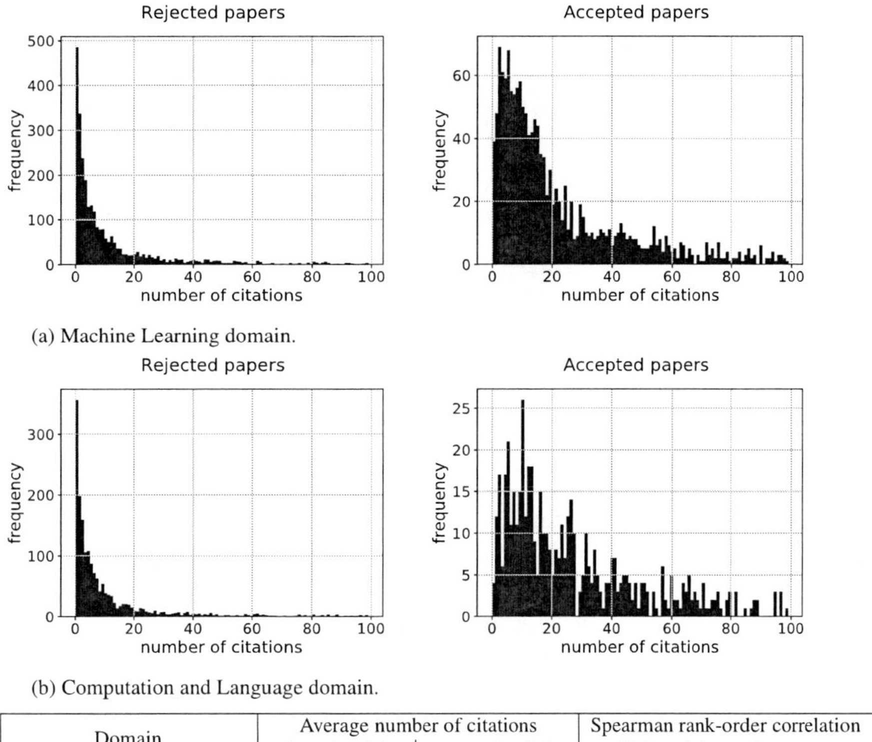

| Domain | Average number of citations | | Spearman rank-order correlation |
	rejected articles	accepted articles	coefficient (ρ), p-value
Machine Learning	24.0 ± 127.3	61.0 ± 232.6	$0.375, 5 \times 10^{-153}$
Computation and Language	14.8 ± 44.3	59.0 ± 105.9	$0.466, 1.6 \times 10^{-128}$

(c) Global statistics.

Figure 3: Histograms and global statistics of number of citations for accepted and rejected papers for the sub-domains of PeerRead. Histograms are truncated on the right at 100 citations. The table in 3c shows the formal correlation measure: average numbers of citations and Spearman rank-order correlation in the different domains

full paper text for future work. The labels added to the examples consist of a function of the number of citations, as explained next.

5.2 Citation-score as a quality proxy

The number of citations follow of scholarly documents follow a Zipfian distribution (Silagadze, 1997). That is, most papers have little citations, but those that obtain more citations tend to get exponentially more. To account for this, we used the log of the number of citations to create a metric that aims to approximates a measure of quality on a linear scale. In practice, we use the function:

$$\text{citation-score} = log_e(n + 1) \qquad (1)$$

adding one to the number of citations n before taking the log, to make sure the function is well-defined even for papers with zero citations.

Comparison to alternative citation scores
What alternatives to our log-based metric have been explored in the literature? Li et al. (2019) map citation counts to the [0,1] range, presumably by simply scaling them after the paper with the maximum and minimum number of citations in a dataset have been determined. But this approach transfers poorly to new data, since as the number of citations follows the Zipfian distribution, still higher citation counts in unseen data are likely. Furthermore, because of the Zipfian nature of the number of citations, this transformation will map the citation score of many papers to a number close to zero, drastically inflating the evaluation scores of predictions for this citation score. A better approach is to discretize the number of citations into a fixed number of ranges. To predict the impact of scientific papers, Plank and van Dale (2019) discretize time-normalized citation statistics into low, medium and high impact papers based on a boxplot and outlier analysis. In comparison however, our approach does not require discretization/binning, which has

Table 9: Test scores for the log number of citations prediction on the S2ORC dataset.

	Average Word Embeddings	BiLSTM (re-implemented)	HAN	HAN$_{\text{struct-tag}}$
R^2 score	0.238 ± 0.0005	0.267 ± 0.007	0.275 ± 0.008	$\mathbf{0.285 \pm 0.002}$
mean squared error	1.261 ± 0.0008	1.214 ± 0.009	1.201 ± 0.007	$\mathbf{1.184 \pm 0.002}$
mean absolute error	0.867 ± 0.0002	0.842 ± 0.001	0.833 ± 0.003	$\mathbf{0.831 \pm 0.001}$

advantages: 1) not committing to a fixed resolution, 2) avoiding problems for papers with a number of citations on the border of two bins, 3) allowing the predicted scores to be deterministically transformed back to a number of citations.

5.3 Loss function and evaluation metrics

The next important question is what loss function we should optimize when training our networks to predict the chosen citation score (1). Whereas *mean-squared-error* (MSE) is the default choice for regression problems, we found this loss function to perform poorly in combination with our score. In contrast, preliminary experiments showed that *mean-absolute-error* (MAE) facilitates effective and relatively stable optimization, so we decided to use this. Another important question is the choice of quality metrics. MSE and MAE are standard metrics for regression evaluation, so we report those. Additionally, we report the R^2 score, denoting the proportion of the variance in the dependent variable that is predictable from the independent variable(s), defined as:

$$R^2 = 1 - \text{FVU} = 1 - \frac{\text{MSE}(Y, Y')}{var[Y]} \qquad (2)$$

With Y' and Y being the predicted and actual labels respectively, MSE being the mean-squared-error and and FVU the fraction of variance unexplained. This explains how the R^2 score normalizes for the relative difficulty for the task, by dividing by the variance of the labels in the test set. Another interpretation is that the R^2 score normalizes by the error obtained when always predicting the average of the test labels. Consequently, a R^2 score larger than 0 means performance better than this baseline, and below 0 means worse. This avoids the need to add scores for this baseline as reference, making the R^2 score more directly interpretable than MSE or MAE. As such, unlike the other metrics the R^2 score is also meaningfully comparable across datasets, which typically differ in test set variance.

5.4 Number of citations prediction results

Table 9 shows the results of our models trained on our new S2ORC number of citations predic-

tion dataset. We observe that the HAN$_{\text{ST}}$ model outperforms the other models. Furthermore, the improvements of HAN$_{\text{ST}}$ over BiLSTM and AWE is statistically significant (wilcoxon signed-rank test), with p-value 0.008 in both cases .

6 Conclusion

This work showed the usefulness of HAN and rich context tags to the processing of scientific documents. Consistent improvements in prediction quality were obtained for both accept/reject estimation and number of citations prediction for HAN when adding structure-tags. A strong and significant correlation between accept/reject labels and number of citations was demonstrated, signaling the usefulness of the latter as a measure of scholarly document quality. With more training data, as available on the citation-score prediction task, HAN with structure-tags outperforms the strong and recently proposed scholarly document quality prediction models that we compared to in this study.

Acknowledgments

This project has been supported by the European Fund for Regional development (EFRO) and the Target Fieldlab. The Peregrine high performance computing cluster, at the Center for Information Technology of the University (CIT) of Groningen, was used for running part of the experiments in this study. We would like to thank the people at the CIT for their support and access to the cluster. We would also like to thank Charles-Emmanuel Dias for sharing his HAN implementation, which proved to be a solid foundation for the HAN-based models used in this work.

References

Dzmitry Bahdanau, Kyunghyun Cho, and Yoshua Bengio. 2014. Neural machine translation by jointly learning to align and translate.

Jacob Devlin, Ming-Wei Chang, Kenton Lee, and Kristina Toutanova. 2018. BERT: pre-training of deep bidirectional transformers for language understanding. *CoRR*, abs/1810.04805.

Lawrence Fu and Constantin Aliferis. 2008. Models for predicting and explaining citation count of biomedical articles. *AMIA ... Annual Symposium proceedings / AMIA Symposium. AMIA Symposium*, 6:222–6.

Xavier Glorot and Yoshua Bengio. 2010. Understanding the difficulty of training deep feedforward neural networks. In *AISTATS*, volume 9 of *JMLR Proceedings*, pages 249–256. JMLR.org.

Salah El Hihi and Yoshua Bengio. 1996. Hierarchical recurrent neural networks for long-term dependencies. In D. S. Touretzky, M. C. Mozer, and M. E. Hasselmo, editors, *Advances in Neural Information Processing Systems 8*, pages 493–499. MIT Press.

Sepp Hochreiter. 1998. The vanishing gradient problem during learning recurrent neural nets and problem solutions. *International Journal of Uncertainty, Fuzziness and Knowledge-Based Systems*, 6(2):107–116.

Melvin Johnson, Mike Schuster, Quoc V. Le, Maxim Krikun, Yonghui Wu, Zhifeng Chen, Nikhil Thorat, Fernanda B. Viégas, Martin Wattenberg, Greg Corrado, Macduff Hughes, and Jeffrey Dean. 2016. Google's multilingual neural machine translation system: Enabling zero-shot translation. *CoRR*, abs/1611.04558.

Dongyeop Kang, Waleed Ammar, Bhavana Dalvi, Madeleine van Zuylen, Sebastian Kohlmeier, Eduard Hovy, and Roy Schwartz. 2018. A dataset of peer reviews (peerread): Collection, insights and nlp applications.

Diederik P. Kingma and Jimmy Ba. 2014. Adam: A method for stochastic optimization. Cite arxiv:1412.6980Comment: Published as a conference paper at the 3rd International Conference for Learning Representations, San Diego, 2015.

Siqing Li, Wayne Xin Zhao, Eddy Jing Yin, and Ji-Rong Wen. 2019. A neural citation count prediction model based on peer review text. In *Proceedings of the 2019 Conference on Empirical Methods in Natural Language Processing and the 9th International Joint Conference on Natural Language Processing (EMNLP-IJCNLP)*, pages 4914–4924, Hong Kong, China. Association for Computational Linguistics.

Kyle Lo, Lucy Lu Wang, Mark Neumann, Rodney Kinney, and Daniel S. Weld. 2020. S2orc: The semantic scholar open research corpus. In *Proceedings of ACL*.

Minh-Thang Luong, Hieu Pham, and Christopher D. Manning. 2015. Effective approaches to attention-based neural machine translation.

Razvan Pascanu, Tomas Mikolov, and Yoshua Bengio. 2013. On the difficulty of training recurrent neural networks. In *ICML (3)*, volume 28 of *JMLR Workshop and Conference Proceedings*, pages 1310–1318. JMLR.org.

Barbara Plank and Reinard van Dale. 2019. Cite-tracked: A longitudinal dataset ofpeer reviews and citations. In *Proceedings of the 4th Joint Workshop on Bibliometric-enhanced Information Retrieval and Natural Language Processing for Digital Libraries (BIRNDL 2019)*.

Adithya Rao and Nemanja Spasojevic. 2016. Actionable and political text classification using word embeddings and lstm.

Tim Rocktäschel, Edward Grefenstette, Karl Moritz Hermann, Tomáš Kočiský, and Phil Blunsom. 2015. Reasoning about entailment with neural attention.

Rico Sennrich and Barry Haddow. 2016. Linguistic input features improve neural machine translation. *CoRR*, abs/1606.02892.

Aili Shen, Jianzhong Qi, and Timothy Baldwin. 2017. A hybrid model for quality assessment of wikipedia articles. In *Proceedings of the Australasian Language Technology Association Workshop 2017*, pages 43–52.

Ali Shen, Bahar Salehi, Timothy Baldwin, and Jianzhong Qi. 2019. A joint model for multimodal document quality assessment. In *JCDL '19: Proceedings of the 18th Joint Conference on Digital Libraries*, pages 107–110.

Z. K. Silagadze. 1997. Citations and the zipf-mandelbrot's law. *Complex Systems*, 11(6):487–499.

Ashish Vaswani, Noam Shazeer, Niki Parmar, Jakob Uszkoreit, Llion Jones, Aidan N. Gomez, Lukasz Kaiser, and Illia Polosukhin. 2017. Attention is all you need. *CoRR*, abs/1706.03762.

Zichao Yang, Diyi Yang, Chris Dyer, Xiaodong He, Alex Smola, and Eduard Hovy. 2016. Hierarchical attention networks for document classification. In *Proceedings of the 2016 Conference of the North American Chapter of the Association for Computational Linguistics: Human Language Technologies*, pages 1480–1489, San Diego, California. Association for Computational Linguistics.

Cydex: Neural Search Infrastructure for the Scholarly Literature

Shane Ding, Edwin Zhang, and **Jimmy Lin**

David R. Cheriton School of Computer Science
University of Waterloo

Abstract

Cydex is a platform that provides neural search infrastructure for domain-specific scholarly literature. The platform represents an abstraction of Covidex, our recently developed full-stack open-source search engine for the COVID-19 Open Research Dataset (CORD-19) from AI2. While Covidex takes advantage of the latest best practices for keyword search using the popular Lucene search library as well as state-of-the-art neural ranking models using T5, parts of the system were hard coded to only work with CORD-19. This paper describes our efforts to generalize Covidex into Cydex, which can be applied to scholarly literature in different domains. By decoupling corpus-specific configurations from the frontend implementation, we are able to demonstrate the generality of Cydex on two very different corpora: the ACL Anthology and a collection of hydrology abstracts. Our platform is entirely open source and available at cydex.ai.

1 Introduction

The ongoing worldwide COVID-19 pandemic has brought about a resurgence of interest in natural language analysis applied to the scientific, particularly biomedical, literature. This has been catalyzed by the availability of corpora, such as the COVID-19 Open Research Dataset (CORD-19) curated by the Allen Institute for AI (Wang et al., 2020), as well as substantial efforts in the creation of evaluation resources, such as the TREC-COVID challenge (Voorhees et al., 2020; Roberts et al., 2020), which has constructed a test collection on information needs related to COVID-19.

Our project builds on Covidex, a full-stack open-source neural search engine for CORD-19 that includes three main capabilities: basic keyword search, neural ranking models, and a faceted search and browsing interface. An early description of our

project can be found in Zhang et al. (2020a) and an updated paper appears in this workshop (Zhang et al., 2020b). Despite the successes of Covidex, parts of the system remain hard-coded to work only with CORD-19. We saw an opportunity to develop our code base into general neural search infrastructure that can be deployed on different corpora of scholarly articles.

The contribution of this work is the execution of this vision: We introduce Cydex, which abstracts Covidex to provide neural search capabilities to scholarly literature in different domains. Throughout this paper, we use the terms "domain" and "corpus" interchangeably, as the most precise way to define a particular domain is by a collection of texts that capture the domain. Our platform is demonstrated on the ACL Anthology and a collection of abstracts in the hydrology domain. All of the components described in this paper are open source.

2 From Covidex to Cydex

This section begins with a description of Covidex, and then describes how we have adapted and generalized each layer in its stack to create Cydex.

2.1 The Covidex Stack

Covidex, which has been available online for searching CORD-19 since late-March 2020, runs a stack comprised of three layers, all of which are open source:

Anserini/Pyserini. Anserini[1] is an information retrieval toolkit (Yang et al., 2018) built on the popular open-source Lucene search library, which is widely deployed in industry to power production search applications. As Lucene is implemented in Java, our tools are designed to run on the Java Virtual Machine (JVM). However, Python is the main language for PyTorch (Paszke et al., 2019) and

---

[1] http://anserini.io/

Proceedings of the First Workshop on Scholarly Document Processing, pages 168–173
Online, November 19, 2020. ©2020 Association for Computational Linguistics
https://doi.org/10.18653/v1/P17

TensorFlow (Abadi et al., 2016), the two most popular neural network toolkits today, and more broadly, Python has emerged as the language of choice for applied machine learning today in part due to its diverse and mature ecosystem. Pyserini (Yilmaz et al., 2020)[2] bridges the gap between the JVM and Python by providing a Python interface to Anserini. Together, Anserini and Pyserini provide basic keyword search capabilities to arbitrary corpora, which include tools to fetch raw document texts as well as utilities to access various term statistics.

PyGaggle. As part of Covidex, Zhang et al. (2020b) built PyGaggle,[3] a Python library for neural text ranking designed to work with Pyserini. Although the application of BERT (Devlin et al., 2019) to text ranking is well known (Nogueira and Cho, 2019), PyGaggle was designed to showcase models that adopt a novel sequence-to-sequence formulation for ranking (Nogueira et al., 2020b), specifically using T5 (Raffel et al., 2020). Deployed as a relevance classifier that reranks BM25 results from Pyserini, the model is fed a query q and each candidate document d in turn. The model is fine-tuned to produce either "true" or "false" depending on whether the document is relevant or not to the query. At inference time, a softmax is applied to the logits of the "true" and "false" tokens, and the resulting probability of the "true" token is used as the relevance score of d. Candidate documents are then reranked using their relevance scores.

Given the lack of COVID-19 training data when the model was initially developed, the T5 ranker was fine-tuned on the popular MS MARCO passage dataset (Bajaj et al., 2018) and directly applied to CORD-19 content. In other words, the ranker was deployed in a zero-shot setting. Additionally, PyGaggle implements an unsupervised sentence highlighting technique using BioBERT (Lee et al., 2020), as described in Zhang et al. (2020a). The key takeaway here is that the current implementation of PyGaggle is completely domain agnostic.

Covidex. To be precise, Covidex is a faceted search and browsing interface built on top of PyGaggle and Anserini/Pyserini, but in this paper, we use it to refer to the entire search engine for convenience. The Covidex layer is comprised of two major components:

The first is a REST API that exposes the keyword search capabilities implemented in Pyserini and the neural ranking capabilities implemented in PyGaggle. This is accomplished by wrapping both into a single API endpoint. Using this endpoint, clients can directly submit search requests containing their queries. The API service is built and deployed using the FastAPI Python web framework, selected for speed and ease of use.[4]

The second of these components is the search and browsing interface itself, which is built with the React JavaScript library[5] to support the use of modular, declarative components and to take advantage of its vast ecosystem. The interface implements a search bar that calls the API service (described above) and renders the results, also providing support for faceted browsing. This feature includes several filters, such as a slider for numeric ranges and a multi-select filter for fields such as the author and publication venue.

2.2 Abstractions for Cydex

At the outset, our goal for Cydex was to minimize the effort required for developers to set up their own Covidex instance on custom corpora.

At the bottom layer, since Anserini/Pyserini was already designed as a general-purpose search toolkit, the only major change required there was the addition of corpus-specific ingesters. For Cydex, after considering a number of options, we settled on an implementation of an ingester that can parse collections of bibtex records to generate Lucene indexes. As it is common to augment bibtex records with abstracts (as is the case with the ACL Anthology), this provides a general-purpose solution that encompasses many scholarly corpora. We specifically decided not to support indexing full text at present for two reasons: (1) due to copyright restrictions, full-text articles are not commonly available, and (2) experimental results from TREC-COVID suggest that abstracts alone achieve reasonable search effectiveness.

The next layer up in the stack, PyGaggle, required no changes at all, since the current neural ranking models are deployed in a zero-shot manner and thus contain no domain-specific knowledge. Of course, there are active research efforts in domain adaptation, both for search tasks (MacAvaney et al., 2020) as well as general NLP tasks (Gururangan et al., 2020), but these efforts are beyond the scope of this paper.

[2] http://pyserini.io/
[3] http://pygaggle.ai/
[4] https://fastapi.tiangolo.com/
[5] https://reactjs.org/

Most of our effort was spent in the top layer of the stack, on the Covidex search and browsing interface itself. In particular, we had to refactor hard-coded values in Covidex into a general configuration framework. To provide a generalized implementation, we abstracted dataset-specific details from all components. Customization is accomplished through two developer-supplied schemas, one ingested by the API service and the other by the interface itself.

The schema for the API service specifies the fields that the system should retrieve from the underlying Lucene index, along with the data type of the field, the default value of the field, and whether the field contains multiple values or not. In addition, since Covidex supports multiple "search verticals" (for example, representing two closely related sub-corpora), the schema also contains a `search_vertical` key, which indicates to Cydex exactly what should be searched. The example below illustrates the API service schema for the ACL Anthology:

```
{
    "document_fields": {
        "abstract_html": {
            "type": "str",
            "default": "None",
            "field_size": "single"
        },
        ...
    },
    "search_vertical": {
        "ACL": "ACL Anthology"
    }
}
```

To enable customization of the actual search and browsing interface, another schema is used to declare the facets, indicating which fields should be filtered and the type of filter that should be applied. The example below is how one such filtering setup may look like for the ACL Anthology:

```
{
    "publish_time": {
        "type": "slider",
        "displayText": "Publish Time"
    },
    "authors": {
        "type": "selection",
        "displayText": "Authors"
    },
    ...
}
```

By implementing the abstraction with schemas, we allow for the dynamic generation of both the service API and user interface components via configurations specified by the developer.

Cydex optionally allows the developer to implement a presentation component to display custom search result layouts. This allows developers to customize how they want to display information about the search results, for example, to specify fonts, font sizes, and the format of the citation. This design allows the developer to focus on rendering, while leaving the configuration and implementation details to Cydex itself.

3 Case Studies

To demonstrate the effectiveness of abstractions within Cydex, we have built and deployed custom instances on two corpora:

- The ACL Anthology, which should already be familiar to readers. The version we used has 57K articles and contains details such as the publication venue and special interest groups (SIGs). We directly index the bibtex files generated as part of the anthology; these records include abstracts, to the extent that they are available.

- A corpus of hydrology abstracts, originally compiled for topic modeling analysis by Rahman et al. (2020). The corpus contains 42K articles from six peer-reviewed hydrology journals such as Hydrology and Earth System Sciences, the Journal of Hydrometeorology, and Water Resources Research. The corpus comprises bibtex records that have been augmented with the abstract texts.

Although Cydex has been verified to work with both corpora, here we focus on the ACL Anthology. A screenshot is shown in Figure 1.

4 Evaluation and Discussion

The focus of our efforts, and the contribution of this work, is search infrastructure to support information access to scholarly literature. However, it is certainly fair to inquire about the quality of the search results produced by Covidex (and Cydex by extension, since there have been no changes to the T5 ranking models in PyGaggle).

We have yet to conduct formal domain-specific evaluations, either in the ACL or hydrology contexts, and can only point to Covidex results based on participation in the multi-round TREC-COVID challenge (Voorhees et al., 2020; Roberts et al., 2020). As detailed in Zhang et al. (2020b), the Covidex team submitted the best automatic runs

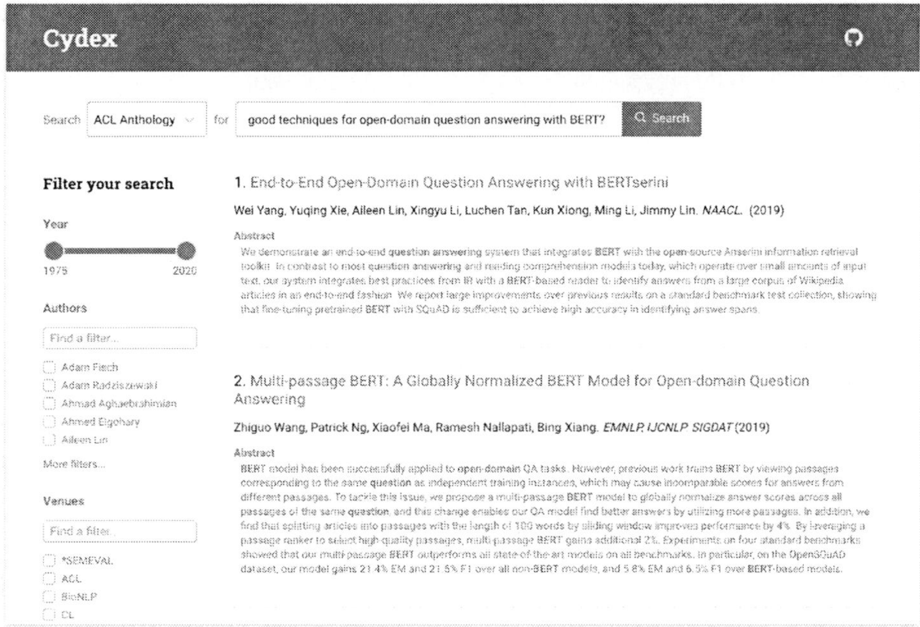

Figure 1: The Cydex search interface on top of the ACL Anthology. On the left, we display all configured facets based on the provided schema, while the right side displays search results using a customizable layout component.

in the final two rounds using a combination of techniques that included ranking with T5. Note that the Covidex ranking model operated in a zero-shot setting, and there is independent evidence that transformer-based ranking models have powerful cross-domain relevance transfer capabilities (Yilmaz et al., 2019; MacAvaney et al., 2020). Thus, we hope that the ranking models would generalize to the NLP and hydrology domains as well.

Despite the lack of domain-specific evaluation data, we performed our own informal evaluation of Cydex on the ACL Anthology. Our evaluation can be characterized as informal "hallway usability testing", primarily as a sanity check. We asked four colleagues (who were not the co-authors) to compare the top five results of five different natural language questions between Cydex and the ACL Anthology's current site-specific Google search. All of our colleagues are familiar with the NLP literature. We came up with the test set of five natural language questions based on our own interests.

Using a standard evaluation methodology, the human assessors were presented side-by-side results (from the two systems) and asked which one (the left system or the right system) they liked better. The identity of the two systems were blinded and randomized, so the assessors had no way to determine the source of the results. All four assessors preferred the results of Cydex for at least three out of the five test questions. Needless to say, there are not enough assessors or questions in this simple evaluation to draw any meaningful conclusions, although these results suggest that our system does not appear to be obviously worse than Google. We consider this to be an encouraging outcome, given that Google presents a high bar in terms of search quality, and we have only begun to build Cydex.

More broadly, however, there are obvious questions worth addressing about the premise of our endeavor: Why do we even need Cydex? Why do we need another search engine to the scholarly literature? Isn't Google Scholar sufficient?

While undoubtedly valuable and certainly the most widely used search engine for the scholarly literature, it would be far-fetched to think that any research project can displace Google Scholar. However, a failure by academic researchers to also engage in the space would be implicitly ceding this important intellectual territory to a commercial search engine that is, at its core, not transparent and controlled by a single entity that may not necessarily act in the best interest of scholars.

Our project does not aspire to be a comprehensive guide to the literature like Google Scholar or AI2's Semantic Scholar. Rather, our niche is domain-specific "verticals" that are manageable

171

from the scale perspective, yet sufficiently large to support interesting analyses. Our two illustrative case studies of the ACL Anthology and hydrology abstracts fit this bill exactly: our software stack can run with only modest resources, and both these corpora are sufficiently rich and self-contained to answer interesting questions—see, for example, recent analyses of the ACL Anthology by Mohammad (2020) and the work by Rahman et al. (2020) on the collection of hydrology abstracts.

5 Ongoing Work and Conclusions

There are two main directions we are currently pursuing as part of ongoing work on Cydex. The first is expansion of the platform to new domains, in particular examining the scalability of our underlying infrastructure. Both the ACL Anthology and the corpus of hydrology abstracts are tiny by modern standards; even CORD-19, with around 300K articles (as of October 2020), is small compared to many information retrieval test collections. A worthwhile target would be the recently released Kaggle arXiv dataset,[6] which contains over 1.7M preprints, in areas ranging from physics to the many subdisciplines of computer science.

The effectiveness of our ranking algorithms is naturally another area of interest, although the development of neural ranking models is orthogonal to the infrastructure that we present here. Our group's latest work on a sequence-to-sequence ranking formulation using T5 is discussed in Nogueira et al. (2020b). While we seek to further improve these core models, in the context of Cydex we are more interested in the end-to-end user experience, where ranking is just one (albeit important) aspect. Beyond features such as faceted browsing and the highlighting of relevant content (already implemented), the platform could benefit from the integration of additional capabilities such as citation recommendation (Bhagavatula et al., 2018; Nogueira et al., 2020a) and related article browsing (Smucker and Allan, 2006; Lin and Wilbur, 2007). These features all contribute to users' perception of system quality and must be evaluated holistically, for example, via user studies.

Cydex represents the starting point of a platform for building information access capabilities for domain-specific scholarly literature, powering our own explorations into scientific literature anal-

ysis. We hope that our open-source approach provides infrastructure that may be useful for other researchers as well.

Acknowledgments

This research was supported in part by the Natural Sciences and Engineering Research Council (NSERC) of Canada.

References

Martín Abadi, Paul Barham, Jianmin Chen, Zhifeng Chen, Andy Davis, Jeffrey Dean, Matthieu Devin, Sanjay Ghemawat, Geoffrey Irving, Michael Isard, Manjunath Kudlur, Josh Levenberg, Rajat Monga, Sherry Moore, Derek G. Murray, Benoit Steiner, Paul Tucker, Vijay Vasudevan, Pete Warden, Martin Wicke, Yuan Yu, and Xiaoqiang Zheng. 2016. TensorFlow: A system for large-scale machine learning. In *12th USENIX Symposium on Operating Systems Design and Implementation (OSDI '16)*, pages 265–283.

Payal Bajaj, Daniel Campos, Nick Craswell, Li Deng, Jianfeng Gao, Xiaodong Liu, Rangan Majumder, Andrew McNamara, Bhaskar Mitra, Tri Nguyen, Mir Rosenberg, Xia Song, Alina Stoica, Saurabh Tiwary, and Tong Wang. 2018. MS MARCO: A Human Generated MAchine Reading COmprehension Dataset. *arXiv:1611.09268v3*.

Chandra Bhagavatula, Sergey Feldman, Russell Power, and Waleed Ammar. 2018. Content-based citation recommendation. In *Proceedings of the 2018 Conference of the North American Chapter of the Association for Computational Linguistics: Human Language Technologies, Volume 1 (Long Papers)*, pages 238–251.

Jacob Devlin, Ming-Wei Chang, Kenton Lee, and Kristina Toutanova. 2019. BERT: Pre-training of deep bidirectional transformers for language understanding. In *Proceedings of the 2019 Conference of the North American Chapter of the Association for Computational Linguistics: Human Language Technologies, Volume 1 (Long and Short Papers)*, pages 4171–4186.

Suchin Gururangan, Ana Marasović, Swabha Swayamdipta, Kyle Lo, Iz Beltagy, Doug Downey, and Noah A. Smith. 2020. Don't stop pretraining: Adapt language models to domains and tasks. In *Proceedings of the 58th Annual Meeting of the Association for Computational Linguistics*, pages 8342–8360.

Jinhyuk Lee, Wonjin Yoon, Sungdong Kim, Donghyeon Kim, Sunkyu Kim, Chan Ho So, and Jaewoo Kang. 2020. BioBERT: A pretrained biomedical language representation model for biomedical text mining. *Bioinformatics*, 36(4):1234–1240.

---

[6]`https://www.kaggle.com/`
`Cornell-University/arxiv`

Jimmy Lin and W. John Wilbur. 2007. PubMed related articles: A probabilistic topic-based model for content similarity. *BMC Bioinformatics*, 8:423.

Sean MacAvaney, Arman Cohan, and Nazli Goharian. 2020. SLEDGE: A simple yet effective baseline for coronavirus scientific knowledge search. *arXiv:2005.02365*.

Saif M. Mohammad. 2020. NLP Scholar: An interactive visual explorer for natural language processing literature. In *Proceedings of the 58th Annual Meeting of the Association for Computational Linguistics: System Demonstrations*, pages 232–255.

Rodrigo Nogueira and Kyunghyun Cho. 2019. Passage re-ranking with BERT. *arXiv:1901.04085*.

Rodrigo Nogueira, Zhiying Jiang, Kyunghyun Cho, and Jimmy Lin. 2020a. Navigation-based candidate expansion and pretrained language models for citation recommendation. *Scientometrics*.

Rodrigo Nogueira, Zhiying Jiang, Ronak Pradeep, and Jimmy Lin. 2020b. Document ranking with a pretrained sequence-to-sequence model. In *Findings of EMNLP*.

Adam Paszke, Sam Gross, Francisco Massa, Adam Lerer, James Bradbury, Gregory Chanan, Trevor Killeen, Zeming Lin, Natalia Gimelshein, Luca Antiga, Alban Desmaison, Andreas Köpf, Edward Yang, Zach DeVito, Martin Raison, Alykhan Tejani, Sasank Chilamkurthy, Benoit Steiner, Lu Fang, Junjie Bai, and Soumith Chintala. 2019. PyTorch: An imperative style, high-performance deep learning library. In *Advances in Neural Information Processing Systems*, pages 8024–8035.

Colin Raffel, Noam Shazeer, Adam Roberts, Katherine Lee, Sharan Narang, Michael Matena, Yanqi Zhou, Wei Li, and Peter J. Liu. 2020. Exploring the limits of transfer learning with a unified text-to-text transformer. *Journal of Machine Learning Research*, 21:1–67.

Mashrekur Rahman, Jonathan M. Frame, Jimmy Lin, and Grey Nearing. 2020. Hidden stories: Topic modeling in hydrology literature. *EarthArXiv*.

Kirk Roberts, Tasmeer Alam, Steven Bedrick, Dina Demner-Fushman, Kyle Lo, Ian Soboroff, Ellen Voorhees, Lucy Lu Wang, and William R. Hersh. 2020. TREC-COVID: rationale and structure of an information retrieval shared task for COVID-19. *Journal of the American Medical Informatics Association*.

Mark D. Smucker and James Allan. 2006. FindSimilar: Similarity browsing as a search tool. In *Proceedings of the 29th Annual International ACM SIGIR Conference on Research and Development in Information Retrieval (SIGIR 2006)*, pages 461–468.

Ellen Voorhees, Tasmeer Alam, Steven Bedrick, Dina Demner-Fushman, William R. Hersh, Kyle Lo, Kirk Roberts, Ian Soboroff, and Lucy Lu Wang. 2020. TREC-COVID: Constructing a pandemic information retrieval test collection. *SIGIR Forum*, 54(1):1–12.

Lucy Lu Wang, Kyle Lo, Yoganand Chandrasekhar, Russell Reas, Jiangjiang Yang, Doug Burdick, Darrin Eide, Kathryn Funk, Yannis Katsis, Rodney Kinney, Yunyao Li, Ziyang Liu, William Merrill, Paul Mooney, Dewey Murdick, Devvret Rishi, Jerry Sheehan, Zhihong Shen, Brandon Stilson, Alex Wade, Kuansan Wang, Nancy Xin Ru Wang, Chris Wilhelm, Boya Xie, Douglas Raymond, Daniel S. Weld, Oren Etzioni, and Sebastian Kohlmeier. 2020. CORD-19: The COVID-19 Open Research Dataset. *arXiv:2004.10706*.

Peilin Yang, Hui Fang, and Jimmy Lin. 2018. Anserini: reproducible ranking baselines using Lucene. *Journal of Data and Information Quality*, 10(4):Article 16.

Zeynep Akkalyoncu Yilmaz, Charles L. A. Clarke, and Jimmy Lin. 2020. A lightweight environment for learning experimental IR research practices. In *Proceedings of the 43rd Annual International ACM SIGIR Conference on Research and Development in Information Retrieval (SIGIR 2020)*, pages 2113–2116.

Zeynep Akkalyoncu Yilmaz, Wei Yang, Haotian Zhang, and Jimmy Lin. 2019. Cross-domain modeling of sentence-level evidence for document retrieval. In *Proceedings of the 2019 Conference on Empirical Methods in Natural Language Processing and the 9th International Joint Conference on Natural Language Processing (EMNLP-IJCNLP)*, pages 3481–3487.

Edwin Zhang, Nikhil Gupta, Rodrigo Nogueira, Kyunghyun Cho, and Jimmy Lin. 2020a. Rapidly deploying a neural search engine for the COVID-19 Open Research Dataset: Preliminary thoughts and lessons learned. *arXiv:2004.05125*.

Edwin Zhang, Nikhil Gupta, Raphael Tang, Xiao Han, Ronak Pradeep, Kuang Lu, Yue Zhang, Rodrigo Nogueira, Kyunghyun Cho, Hui Fang, and Jimmy Lin. 2020b. Covidex: Neural ranking models and keyword search infrastructure for the COVID-19 Open Research Dataset. In *Proceedings of the 1st Workshop on Scholarly Document Processing (SDP 2020)*.

On the Use of Web Search to Improve Scientific Collections

Krutarth Patel, Cornelia Caragea, Sujatha Das Gollapalli

Kansas State University, University of Illinois at Chicago, National University of Singapore

`kipatel@ksu.edu, cornelia@uic.edu, idssdg@nus.edu.sg`

Abstract

Despite the advancements in search engine features, ranking methods, technologies, and the availability of programmable APIs, current-day open-access digital libraries still rely on crawl-based approaches for acquiring their underlying document collections. In this paper, we propose a novel search-driven framework for acquiring documents for such scientific portals. Within our framework, publicly-available research paper titles and author names are used as queries to a Web search engine. We were able to obtain $\approx 267,000$ unique research papers through our fully-automated framework using $\approx 76,000$ queries, resulting in almost $200,000$ more papers than the number of queries. Moreover, through a combination of title and author name search, we were able to recover 78% of the original searched titles.

1 Introduction

Scientific portals such as Google Scholar, Semantic Scholar, ACL Anthology, CiteSeer^x, and Arnet-Miner, provide access to scholarly publications and comprise indispensable resources for researchers who search for literature on specific subject topics. Moreover, many applications such as document and citation recommendation (Bhagavatula et al., 2018; Zhou et al., 2008), expert search (Balog et al., 2007; Gollapalli et al., 2012), topic classification (Caragea et al., 2015; Getoor, 2005), and keyphrase extraction and generation (Meng et al., 2017; Chen et al., 2020) involve Web-scale analysis of up-to-date research collections.

Open-access, autonomous systems such as CiteSeer^x and ArnetMiner acquire and index freely-available research articles from the Web (Li et al., 2006; Tang et al., 2008). Researchers' homepages and paper repository URLs are crawled for maintaining the research collections in these portals,

using focused crawling. Needless to say, the crawl seed lists cannot be comprehensive in the face of the ever changing Scholarly Web. Not only do new authors and publication venues emerge, but also existing researchers may stop publishing or they may change affiliations, resulting in outdated seed URLs. *Given this challenge, how can we automatically augment the document collections in open-access scientific portals?*

To address this question, in this paper, we propose a novel framework (based on Web search) for both automatically acquiring and processing research documents. To motivate our framework, we recall how a Web user typically searches for research papers or authors. As with regular document search, a user typically issues Web search queries comprising of representative keywords or paper titles for finding publications on a topic. Similarly, if the author is known, a "navigational query" (Broder, 2002) may be employed to locate the homepage where the paper is likely to be hosted. To illustrate this process, Figure 1 shows an anecdotal example of a search using Google for the title and authors of a research article. As can be seen from the figure, the intended research paper and the researchers' homepages (highlighted in sets 2 and 3) are accurately retrieved. Moreover, among the top-5 results shown for the title query (set 1), four of the five results are research papers on the same topic (i.e., the first four results). The document at the Springer link is not available for free, whereas the last document corresponds to course slides. The additional three papers are potentially retrieved because scientific paper titles comprise a large fraction of keywords (Chen et al., 2019), and hence, the words in these titles serve as excellent keywords that can retrieve not only the intended paper, but also other relevant documents.

Our framework mimics precisely the above search and scrutinize the approach adopted by

Proceedings of the First Workshop on Scholarly Document Processing, pages 174–183

Online, November 19, 2020. ©2020 Association for Computational Linguistics

https://doi.org/10.18653/v1/P17

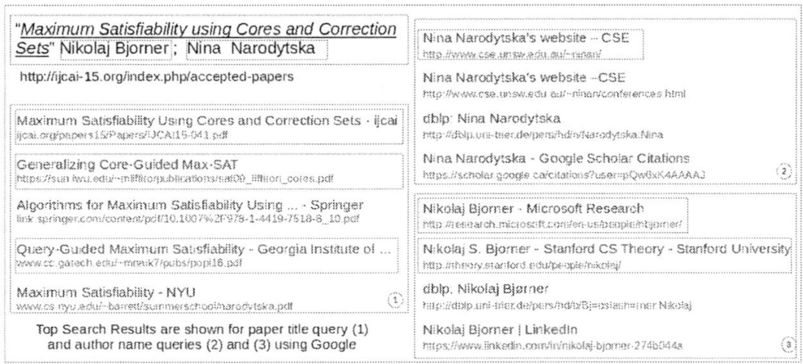

Figure 1: An anecdotal search example for illustration.

Scholarly Web users. Freely-available information from the Web for specific subject disciplines[1] is used to frame title and author name queries in our framework. Our contributions are as follows:

- We propose a novel integrated framework based on search-driven methods to automatically acquire research documents for scientific collections. To our knowledge, we are the first to use "Web Search" based on author names to obtain seed URLs for initiating crawls in an open-access digital library.

- We design a novel homepage identification module and adapt existing research on academic document classification, which are crucial components of our framework. We show experimentally that our homepage identification module and the research paper classifier substantially outperform strong baselines.

- We perform a large-scale, first-of-its-kind experiment using $43,496$ research paper titles and $32,816$ author names from Computer and Information Sciences. We compare our framework with two baselines, a breadth-first search crawler and, to the extent possible, the Microsoft Academic. We discuss that our framework does not substitute these systems, but rather they very well complement each other. As part of our contributions, we will make all the constructed datasets available.

2 Our Framework

Figure 2 shows the control flow paths of our proposed framework to obtain research papers and thus augment existing collections. In **Path 1**, paper titles are used as queries and the PDF documents

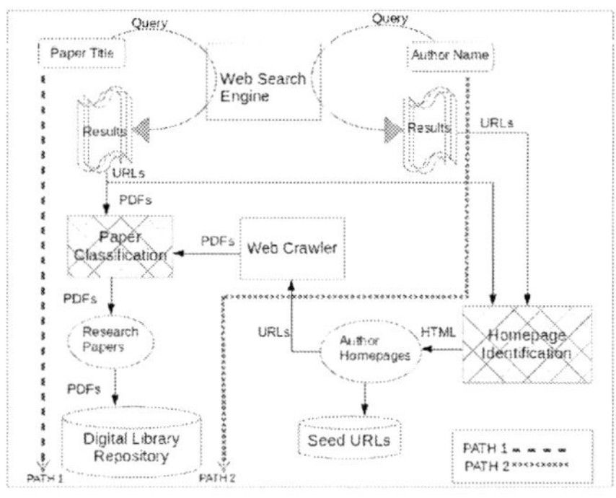

Figure 2: Schematic Diagram of our Framework.

resulting from each title search are classified with a paper classifier based on Random Forest. Author names comprise the queries for Web search in **Path 2**, the results of which are filtered by a homepage identification module trained using RankSVM. The predicted author homepages from **Path 2** serve as seed URLs for the crawler module that obtains all documents up to a depth 2 starting from each seed URL. The paper classification module is once again employed to retain only research papers. Note that we crawl only publicly available and downloadable documents those appear in the search responses of the Web search or from the researcher homepages.

The accuracy and efficiency of our Search/Crawl framework is contingent on the accuracy of two components: (1) the homepage identifier, and (2) the paper/non-paper classifier.

2.1 Homepage Identification

Among the works focusing on researcher homepages, both Tang et al. (2007) and Gollapalli et al. (2015) treated homepage finding as a binary classification and used URL string features and content features (extracted from the entire .html

---

[1] For example, from bibliographic listings such as DBLP or paper metadata available in ACM DL.

page) for classification. However, given our Web search setting, the non-homepages retrieved in response to an author name query can be expected to be diverse with webpages ranging from commercial websites such as LinkedIn, social media websites such as Twitter and Facebook, and several more. To handle this aspect, we frame homepage identification as a supervised ranking problem. Thus, given a set of webpages in response to a query, our objective is to rank homepages higher relative to other types of webpages, capturing our preference among the retrieved webpages. Preference information needed for the ranking can be easily modeled through appropriate objective functions in learning to rank approaches (Liu, 2011). For example, RankSVM (Joachims, 2002) minimizes the Kendalls τ measure based on the preferential ordering information in the training examples.

Note that, unlike classification approaches that independently model both positive (homepage) and negative (non-homepage) classes, we are modeling instances in relation with each other with preferential ordering (Wan et al., 2015). In Section 4, we show that our ranking approach outperforms classification approaches for homepage identification. We design the following feature types for our ranking model, which capture aspects (e.g., snippets) useful for a Web user to find homepages:

1. **URL Features**: Intuitively, the URL strings of academic homepages can be expected to contain (or not) certain tokens. For example, a homepage URL is less likely to be hosted on domains such as "linkedin" and "facebook." On the other hand, terms such as "people" or "home" can be expected to occur in the URL strings of homepages (see examples of homepage URLs in Figure 1). We tokenize the URL strings based on the "slash (/)" separator and the domain-name part of the URL based on the "dot (.)" separator to extract our URL and DOMAIN feature dictionaries.

2. **Term Features**: The current-day search engines display the Web search results as a ranked list, where each webpage is indicated by its HTML title, the URL string as well as a brief summary of the content of the webpage (also known as the "snippet"). We posit that Scholarly Web users are able to identify homepages among the search results based on the term hints in titles and snippets (for example, "professor", "scientist", "student"), and use

words from titles and snippets to extract our TITLE and SNIPPET dictionaries.

3. **Name-match Features**: These features capture the common observation that researchers tend to use parts of their names in the URL strings of their homepages (Tang et al., 2007; Gollapalli et al., 2015). We specify two types of match features: (1) a boolean feature that indicates whether any part of the author name matches a token in the URL string, and (2) a numeric feature that indicates the extent to which name tokens overlap with the (non-domain part of) URL string given by the fraction: $\frac{\#matches}{\#nametokens}$. For the example author name "Soumen Chakrabarti" and the URL string: `www.cse.iitb.ac.in/∼soumen`, the two features have values "true" and 0.5, respectively.

The dictionary sizes for the above feature types based on our training datasets (see Section 3) are listed below:

Feature Type	Size
URL+DOMAIN term features	2025
TITLE term features	19190
SNIPPET term features	25280
NAME match features	2

2.2 Paper/Non-Paper Classification

In order to obtain accurate paper collections, it is important to employ a high-accuracy paper/non-paper classifier. Caragea et al. (2016) studied the classification of academic documents into six classes: Books, Slides, Theses, Papers, CVs, and Others. The authors showed that a small set of 43 structural, text density, and layout features (Str) that are designed to incorporate aspects specific to research documents, are highly indicative of the class of an academic document. Because we are mainly interested in research papers to augment research collections and because binary tasks are considered easier to learn than multi-class tasks (Bishop, 2006), we adapted this prior work on multi-class document type classification (Caragea et al., 2016) and re-trained the classifiers for the two-class setting: paper/non-paper.

3 Datasets

The datasets used in the evaluation of our framework and its components are summarized in Table 1 and are described below:

DBLP Homepages. For evaluating homepage finding using author names, we use the researcher

Dataset		
DBLP Homepages		42,548(T) 4,255(+)
Research Papers	(Train)	960(T) 472(+)
	(Test)	959(T) 461(+)
CiteSeer^x		43,496 (Titles), 32,816 (Authors)

Table 1: Summary of datasets. Total and positive instances are shown using (T) and (+), respectively.

homepages from DBLP. In contrast to previous works that use this dataset to train homepage classifiers on academic websites (Gollapalli et al., 2015), in our Web search scenario, the non-homepages from the search results of an author name query need not be restricted to academic websites. Except the true homepage, all other webpages therefore correspond to negatives. We constructed the DBLP homepages dataset as follows: DBLP provided a set of author homepages along with the authors' names. Using these authors' names as queries, we perform Web search using Bing API and scan the top-10 results (Spink and Jansen, 2004) in response to each query. If the true homepage provided by DBLP is listed among the top-10 search results, this URL and the others in the set of Web results are used as training instances. We were able to locate homepages for $4,255$ authors in the top-10 results for the author homepages listed in DBLP.

Research Papers. To evaluate the paper/non-paper classifier, we used two independent sets of ≈ 1000 documents each, randomly sampled from the crawl data of CiteSeer^x, obtained from Caragea et al. (2016). These sets, called Train and Test, respectively, were manually labeled with six classes: Paper, Book, Thesis, Slides, Resume/CV, and Others. We transform the documents' labels as the binary labels, Paper/Non-paper.

CiteSeer^x. Our third dataset is compiled from the CiteSeer^x digital library. Specifically, we extracted research papers that were published in venues related to machine learning, data mining, information retrieval and computational linguistics. These venues along with the number of papers in each venue are listed in Table 2. Overall, we obtained a set of $43,496$ paper titles and $32,816$ authors (unique names) for the evaluation of our framework at a large scale.

Total # of papers: 43,496, #authors (unique): 32,816
NIPS (5211), IJCAI (4721), ICRA (3883), ICML (2979), ACL (2970), VLDB (2594), CVPR (2373), AAAI (2201), CHI (2030), COLING (1933), KDD (1595), SIGIR (1454), WWW (1451), CIKM (1408), SAC (1191), LREC (1128), SDM (1111), EMNLP (920), ICDM (891), EACL (760), HLT-NAACL (692)

Table 2: Conference venue (#papers) in the CiteSeer^x dataset.

4 Experiments and Results

In this section, we describe our experiments on homepage identification and paper classification along with their performance within the search then crawl then process paper acquisition framework.

Performance measures. We use the standard measures Precision, Recall, and F1 for summarizing the results of author homepage identification and paper classification (Manning et al., 2008). Unlike classification where we consider the true and predicted labels for each instance (webpage), in RankSVM the prediction is per query (Joachims, 2002). That is, the results with respect to a query are assigned ranks based on scores from the RankSVM and the result at rank-1 is chosen as the predicted homepage.

4.1 Author Homepage Identification

We aim to determine how accurate is RankSVM in identifying a homepage for each author name query. Table 3 shows the five-fold cross-validation performance of the homepage identification on the positive class trained using RankSVM compared with various classification algorithms, Naïve Bayes, Maximum Entropy and Support Vector Machines. The results in the table are averaged across all five test sets of cross-validation. Hyperparameter tuning (e.g., C for SVM) was performed on a development set extracted from training.

Method	Precision	Recall	F1
RankSVM	0.8933	0.8933	0.8933
Naïve Bayes	0.4830	0.9239	0.63432
MaxEnt	0.8207	0.8002	0.8102
Binary SVM	0.8353	0.8149	0.8249

Table 3: RankSVM vs. supervised classifiers on DBLP.

As can be seen from the table, RankSVM performs much better compared with the classification approaches, in terms of Precision and F1, although Recall is higher for Naïve Bayes. Hence, RankSVM is able to capture the relative preferential ordering among the search results and performs the best in identifying the correct author homepage in response to a query. A possible reason for the lower performance of the classification approaches such as Binary SVMs, Naïve Bayes, and Maximum Entropy is that they model the positive and negative instances independently and not in relation to one another for a given query. Moreover, the diversity in webpages among the negative class is ignored and they are modeled uniformly as a single class in the classification approaches.

4.2 Research Paper Classification

We compare the performance of classifiers trained using the 43 structural features (Str) with that of classifiers trained using the "bag of words" (BoW), URL-based features (URL), and a Convolutional Neural Network (CNN) model. For BoW and URL, we used the same text processing operations as in Caragea et al. (2016). We experimented with several classifiers: Random Forest (RF), Decision Trees (DT), Naïve Bayes Multinomial (NBM), and Support Vector Machines with a linear kernel (SVM). For CNN, we use the words as a sequence as an input; we first get the word embeddings as a part of the network followed by the CNN filter, max-pooling, concatenation, and the fully connected layer for the classification task, similar to Kim (2014). All models are trained on the "Train" dataset and are evaluated on the "Test" dataset. We tuned model hyper-parameters in 10-fold cross-validation experiments on "Train" (e.g., C for SVM and the number of trees for RF).

Feature/Cls. (Setting)	Precision	Recall	F1
BoW / DT (P-B)	0.860	0.920	0.889
URL / SVM (P-B)	0.729	0.729	0.729
Str / RF (P-B)	0.933	0.967	0.950
CNN (P-B)	0.816	0.890	0.851
Str / RF (A-B)	0.952	0.951	0.951
Str / RF (P-M)	0.918	0.965	0.941
Str / RF (A-M)	0.893	0.902	0.892

Table 4: Performance of paper classifier on "Test". "P" stands for the paper class, while "A" for the average of classes. "B" and "M" stand for binary and multi-class, respectively.

Table 4 shows the performance (Precision, Recall, and F1) for the binary setting on "Test" for each feature type, BoW, URL, and Str, and the CNN, with the classifiers that give the best results for the corresponding feature type or model (first four lines). The results are shown for the "paper" class (P). In the table, we also show the performance on the "paper" class with the multi-class (M) setting and the weighted averages (A) of all measures over all classes for both the settings. As can be seen from the table, the best classification performance is obtained using Random Forest trained on the 43 structural features with the overall performance above 95% being substantially higher in the binary setting compared with the multi-class setting. The reason behind lower performance of the CNN classifier can be the wide variety of documents present in the dataset and the small number of the training examples.

Title Queries
Knowledge-based Knowledge Elicitation. filetype:pdf
Solving Time-Dependent Planning Problems. filetype:pdf

Author Name Queries
Eric T. Baumgartner filetype:html
Nelson Alves filetype:html

Table 5: Example of title and author name queries.

4.3 Large-Scale Experiments

Finally, we evaluate our "search then crawl then process" framework and its components in practice in large scale experiments, using our CiteSeer^x subset. To this end, we evaluate the capability of our framework to obtain large document collections, quantified by the number of research papers it acquires (through both paths). For **Path 1**, we use the $43,496$ paper titles directly as search queries. Structural features extracted from the resulting PDF documents of each search are used to identify research papers with our paper classifier. For **Path 2**, the $32,816$ unique author names are used as queries. The RankSVM-predicted homepages from the results of each author name query are crawled for PDF documents up to a depth of 2, using the wget utility.[2] Again, the paper classifier is employed to identify the papers from the crawled documents. In all experiments, we used the Bing API to perform Web searches. Examples of title and author name queries are provided in Table 5.

4.3.1 Overall Yield

The total numbers of PDFs and research papers found through the two paths in our Search/Crawl/Process framework are shown in Table 6 (the columns labeled as #CrawledPDFs and #PredictedPapers, respectively). Intuitively, the overall yield can be expected to be higher through **Path 2**. This is because once an author homepage is reached, other research papers that are linked from this homepage can be directly obtained. Indeed, as shown in the table, the numbers of PDFs as well as predicted papers are significantly higher along **Path 2**. Crawling the RankSVM-predicted homepages of the $32,816$ authors, we obtain on average ≈ 14 research papers per query ($\frac{452273}{32816} = 13.78$). In contrast, examining only the top-10 search results along **Path 1**, we obtain ≈ 5 papers per query on average ($\frac{213683}{43496} = 4.91$). The high percentage of papers found along **Path 2** is consistent with previous findings that researchers tend to link to their papers via their homepages (Lawrence, 2001; Gol-

[2] https://www.gnu.org/software/wget/

#Queries	#CrawledPDFs	#PredictedPapers	#UniquePapers	#MatchesWithOriginalTitles
43,496 titles (Path 1)	322,029	213,683	91,237	32,565
32,816 names (Path 2)	665,661	452,273	204,014	17,627
Overlap: **Path 1 & Path 2**	-	-	28,374	16,188
Total # of papers: **Path 1 + Path 2**	-	-	266,877	34,004

Table 6: Number of papers obtained through **Path 1** and **Path 2** in our Search/Crawl/Process framework.

lapalli et al., 2015). Note that in all experiments, since the original $43,496$ titles are extracted from CiteSeer[x], for a fair evaluation, we removed all title search results that point to the CiteSeer[x] domain, i.e., http://citeseerx.ist.psu.edu/.

Furthermore, the numbers of unique papers found along each of the two paths are shown in Table 6 (the column labeled as #UniquePapers). We used ParsCit[3] to extract the titles of the research papers obtained from both the paths and then calculated the duplicates from these titles.[4] As can be seen from the table, we are able to obtain $91,237$ and $204,014$ unique papers from **Path 1** and **Path 2**, respectively, which account for ≈ 2 papers per title query on average ($\frac{91237}{43496} = 2.09$) and ≈ 6 papers per author query on average ($\frac{204014}{32816} = 6.21$). However, since our objective is not to use one path or the other, but use a combination of both Path 1 and Path 2, we further expanded our analysis to show the overlap between Path 1 and Path 2 in terms of unique titles.

4.3.2 Overlap between Path 1 and Path 2

Table 6 shows also the overlap in the two sets of unique papers (between **Path 1** and **Path 2**), which is $28,374$. Compared to the overall yields along **Path 1** and **Path 2** ($213,683$ and $452,273$, respectively) and even with the number of unique papers along each path, this small overlap indicates that the two paths are capable of reaching different sections of the Web and play complementary roles in our framework. For example, the top-20 domains of the URLs from which we obtained research papers along **Path 1** are shown in Figure 3. As can be seen from the figure, via Web search, we are able to reach a wide range of domains. This is unlikely in crawl-driven methods without an exhaustive list of seeds since only links up to a specified depth from a given seed are explored (Manning et al., 2008). Interestingly, using a combination of both Path 1 and Path 2, we were able to obtain $266,877$ ($=91,237+204,014-28,374$) unique papers.

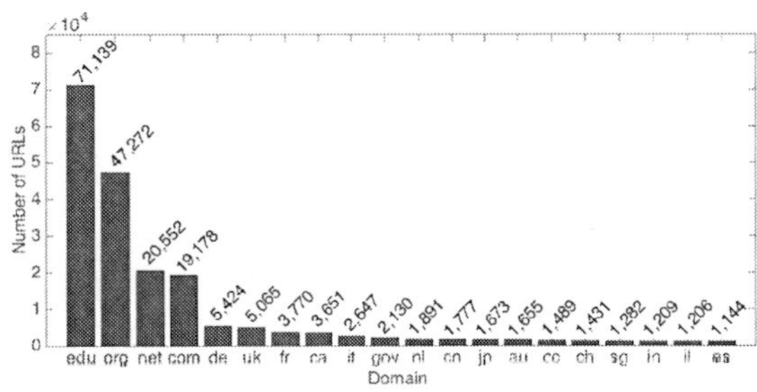

Figure 3: The top-20 domains from which papers were obtained along Path 1 of our framework.

Next, we investigate the recovery power of our framework. Precisely, how many of the original $43,496$ titles were found through each path as well as their combination?

4.3.3 Overlap with the Original Titles

The numbers of papers that we were able to obtain from the original $43,496$ titles through both paths are shown in the last column of Table 6, labeled as #MatchesWithOriginalTitles. To compute these matches, we used the title and author names available in our CiteSeer[x] subset to look up the first page of each PDF document. As can be seen from the table, we were able to recover 75% ($\frac{32565}{43496}$) of the original titles through **Path 1** compared to the 40% ($\frac{17627}{43496}$) through **Path 2**. The total number of matches with the original titles between **Path 1** and **Path 2** was $16,188$. Overall, through a combination of both **Path 1** and **Path 2**, we were able to recover 78% ($\frac{34,004}{43496}$) of the original titles ($34,004=32,565+17,627-16,188$ papers obtained through both paths out of the original titles).

To summarize, using about $76,312$ queries ($43,496 + 32,816$) through **Path 1** and **Path 2**, we are able to build a collection of $665,956$ papers ($213,683 + 452,273$) and $266,877$ unique titles ($91,237 + 204,014 - 28,374$). About 32-33% of the obtained documents are "non-papers" along both paths. Scholarly Web is known to contain a variety of documents including resumes, and presentation slides (Ortega et al., 2006). Some of these documents may include the exact paper titles and may appear in paper search results as well as be

---

[3] http://aye.comp.nus.edu.sg/parsCit/

[4] To find duplicates, we convert the text to lowercase, and remove punctuation and whitespace.

linked from author homepages.

4.3.4 Anecdotal Evidence

Given the size of our CiteSeer[x] dataset and the large number of documents obtained via our framework (as shown in Table 6), it is extremely labor-intensive to manually examine all documents resulting from the large scale experiment. However, since our classifiers and rankers achieve performance above 95% and 89% based on our test datasets compiled specifically for these tasks, we expect them to continue to perform well "in the wild." We show anecdotal evidence to support this claim, i.e., an estimate of how many true papers we are able to obtain via our Search/Crawl/Process framework starting from a small set of titles.

To obtain such an estimate, we randomly selected 10 titles from the CiteSeer[x] dataset. From the corresponding papers of these 10 titles, we extracted 33 unique authors. We manually inspected all PDFs that can be obtained via title search (**Path 1**) as well as the homepages obtained via author name search (**in Path 2**) That is, through **Path 1**, we searched the Web for the 10 selected titles and manually examined and annotated the top-10 resulting PDFs for each title query. The title search resulted in 59 PDFs, of which 33 are true papers and 26 are non-papers. Our paper classifier predicted 32 out of 33 papers correctly and 38 papers overall and achieved a precision and recall of 84% and 97%, respectively.

Similarly, through **Path 2**, we searched for the 33 author names from the Web and manually examined and annotated the top-10 resulting webpages for each author name query. From the author search, manually, we were able to locate 19 correct homepages of the 33 authors. A manual inspection of the predicted homepages revealed that our framework was not able to locate 6 out of the 19 correct homepages. Table 7 shows a few examples where our framework was not able to locate the correct homepages. For example, occasionally, RankSVM ranks university faculty profile or faculty research group at the first rank, which is then predicted as a homepage by RankSVM (e.g., URLs 4 and 6 in Table 7). URL 5 in Table 7 is wrongly predicted by RankSVM as the homepage for the researcher name "David Bell." This is precisely because there is a well known novel writer and also baseball player with the same name, which get ranked higher in the results of the search engine. Note that, interestingly, the actual homepage

Actual homepage
1. http://destrin.smalldata.io/
2. http://www.cs.qub.ac.uk/~D.Bell/dbell.html
3. http://www.ai.sri.com/~yang

Predicted homepage
4. http://research.cens.ucla.edu/people/estrin/
5. http://davidbellnovels.com/
6. http://www.ai.sri.com/people/yang/

Table 7: A few examples where our framework was not able to locate the correct homepage

of David Bell, corresponding to URL 2 was not retrieved in the top 10 search responses of Bing.

4.4 Baseline Comparisons

Breadth-first search crawler. We compare our Search/Crawl/Process framework, through **Path 1**, with a breadth-first search crawler as implemented in CiteSeer[x]. The CiteSeer[x] crawler starts with a list of seed URLs, performs a breadth-first search crawl and saves open-access PDF documents.

For this experiment, we randomly selected 1,000 titles from DBLP. We then searched the Web for these titles and retrieved the top-10 resulting PDFs for each query. Through this search, we obtained a total of 5,793 PDFs, from which we removed 110 documents that were downloaded from CiteSeer[x], since they were obtained as a result of the CiteSeer[x] breadth-first search crawler. Note that there is an overlap of 6 documents, i.e., only located on CiteSeer[x] (and nowhere else on the Web), between the 110 removed documents and the 1000 DBLP initial titles. From the remaining documents, our paper classifier predicted 3,427 documents as papers, out of which 2,797 are unique papers/titles. We searched CiteSeer[x] for these 2,797 titles to determine how many of them are found by the CiteSeer[x] crawler. We found 1,037 titles in CiteSeer[x] by checking if one title string contains the other. Thus, with our framework, we were able to obtain $2,797 - 1,037 = 1,760$ additional papers. Out of the 994 (1000 − 6) DBLP titles, only 121 papers were found by both our framework and the CiteSeer[x] crawler. In addition, our framework found 165 more papers (with a total of 286 out of 994 DBLP titles), whereas the CiteSeer[x] crawler found only 92 more papers (with a total of 213 out of 994 DBLP titles). Moreover, out of the additional yield of our framework, i.e., 2511 (= 2797 − 286) papers, only 552 are found by the CiteSeer[x] crawler (identified by searching for the 2511 titles in the CiteSeer[x] digital library - by exact match). These results are summarized in Figure 4. We note that the two approaches are not substitut-

Figure 4: Comparison of the Search/Crawl framework with the CiteSeer[x] breadth-first search crawler.

ing, but rather complementing each other.

Microsoft Academic. Searching for feeds from publishers (e.g., ACM and IEEE) and using webpages indexed by Bing is also considered by Microsoft Academic (MA) to collect entities such as paper, author, and venue, to be added to the MA graph (Sinha et al., 2015). An edge in the graph is added between two entities if there is a relationship between them, e.g., *publishedIn*. In contrast, in our framework, we collect not only the intended paper for a title search, but also all papers that are found for that search. In addition, we identify author homepages through author name search and, unlike MA, we use them to collect research papers from these homepages. To our knowledge, we are the first to use "Web Search" based on author names to obtain seed URLs for initiating crawls to acquire documents in scientific portals. Both our framework and MA use Bing for searches. Thus, using MA strategy to collect paper entities, $32,565$ papers are recovered out of the $43,496$ original titles. Adding the author search in our framework, we are able to collect an additional $1,439$ (=$34,004 - 32,565$) papers from the original titles and $234,312$ (=$266,877 - 32,565$) overall additional unique papers (see Table 6).

5   Related Work

Web crawling is a well-studied problem in information retrieval, focusing on issues of scalability, effectiveness, efficiency, and freshness (Manning et al., 2008). Despite its simplicity, research has shown that breadth-first search crawling produces high-quality collections in early stages of the crawl (Najork and Wiener, 2001). Focused crawling was introduced by Chakrabarti et al. (1999) to deal with the information overload on the Web in order to build specialized collections focused on specific topics. Since the introduction of focused crawling, many variations have been proposed (Menczer et al., 2004). In contrast to focused crawling, our framework is able to acquire research documents that are not limited to a specific taxonomy.

Prior research has also focused on enhancing digital libraries content to better satisfy the needs of digital library users (Pant et al., 2004; Zhuang et al., 2005; Carmel et al., 2008). Several works studied the coverage in scientific portals such as Microsoft Academic, Google Scholar, Scopus and the Web of Science (Hug and Brändle, 2017; Harzing and Alakangas, 2017). Multiple works focus on better ranking of retrieved documents for a given query (Yang et al., 2017; MacAvaney et al., 2019; Boudin et al., 2020).

Homepage finding and document classification are well-studied in information retrieval. The homepage finding track in TREC 2001 resulted in various machine learning systems for finding homepages (Xi et al., 2002; Upstill et al., 2003; Wang and Oyama, 2006). Tang et al. (2007) and Gollapalli et al. (2015) treated homepage finding as a binary classification task and used various URL and webpage content features for classification. In the context of scientific digital libraries, document classification into classes related to subject-topics (for example, "machine learning," "databases") was studied previously (Getoor, 2005; Caragea et al., 2015). In contrast with existing work, we investigate features from Web search engine results and formulate researcher homepage identification as a learning to rank task. In addition, we are the first to interleave various components of Web search, crawl, and document processing to build an efficient paper acquisition framework.

6   Conclusion and Future Directions

We proposed a framework for automatically acquiring research papers from the Web. We showed the experiments illustrating the state-of-the-art performance for two major modules of our framework: a homepage identifier and a paper classifier. Through an experiment using a large collection of $\approx 76,000$ queries (titles + authors names), our framework was able to automatically acquire an overall collection of $\approx 267,000$ unique research papers and was able to recover 78% of the original searched titles, i.e., $\approx 34,000$ papers from the $43,496$ original searched titles. We also showed that our approach is not meant to replace existing crawling strategies, but can be used in conjunction, to enhance the content of digital libraries.

In the future, it would be interesting to apply our framework to other domains, and study the integration of topic classification.

References

Krisztian Balog, Maarten De Rijke, et al. 2007. Determining expert profiles (with an application to expert finding). In *IJCAI*, volume 7, pages 2657–2662.

Chandra Bhagavatula, Sergey Feldman, Russell Power, and Waleed Ammar. 2018. Content-based citation recommendation. In *Proceedings of the 2018 Conference of the North American Chapter of the Association for Computational Linguistics: Human Language Technologies, Volume 1 (Long Papers)*, pages 238–251, New Orleans, Louisiana. Association for Computational Linguistics.

Christopher M. Bishop. 2006. *Pattern Recognition and Machine Learning (Information Science and Statistics)*. Springer-Verlag New York, Inc.

Florian Boudin, Ygor Gallina, and Akiko Aizawa. 2020. Keyphrase generation for scientific document retrieval. In *Proceedings of the 58th Annual Meeting of the Association for Computational Linguistics (ACL)*.

Andrei Broder. 2002. A taxonomy of web search. In *ACM Sigir forum*, volume 36, pages 3–10. ACM New York, NY, USA.

Cornelia Caragea, Florin Adrian Bulgarov, and Rada Mihalcea. 2015. Co-training for topic classification of scholarly data. In *Proceedings of the 2015 Conference on Empirical Methods in Natural Language Processing, EMNLP 2015, Lisbon, Portugal, September 17-21, 2015*, pages 2357–2366.

Cornelia Caragea, Jian Wu, Sujatha Das Gollapalli, and C Lee Giles. 2016. Document type classification in online digital libraries. In *AAAI*, pages 3997–4002.

David Carmel, Elad Yom-Tov, and Haggai Roitman. 2008. Enhancing digital libraries using missing content analysis. In *Proceedings of the 8th ACM/IEEE-CS Joint Conference on Digital Libraries*, JCDL '08, pages 1–10.

Soumen Chakrabarti, Martin van den Berg, and Byron Dom. 1999. Focused crawling: A new approach to topic-specific web resource discovery. In *Proceedings of the Eighth International Conference on World Wide Web*, WWW '99, pages 1623–1640. Elsevier North-Holland, Inc.

Wang Chen, Hou Pong Chan, Piji Li, and Irwin King. 2020. Exclusive hierarchical decoding for deep keyphrase generation. In *Proceedings of the 58th Annual Meeting of the Association for Computational Linguistics*, pages 1095–1105, Online. Association for Computational Linguistics.

Wang Chen, Yifan Gao, Jiani Zhang, Irwin King, and Michael R. Lyu. 2019. Title-guided encoding for keyphrase generation. In *Proceedings of the AAAI Conference on Artificial Intelligence*, volume 33, pages 6268–6275.

Lise Getoor. 2005. Link-based classification. In *Advanced methods for knowledge discovery from complex data*, pages 189–207. Springer.

Sujatha Das Gollapalli, Cornelia Caragea, Prasenjit Mitra, and C Lee Giles. 2015. Improving researcher homepage classification with unlabeled data. *ACM Transactions on the Web (TWEB)*, 9(4):1–32.

Sujatha Das Gollapalli, Prasenjit Mitra, and C. Lee Giles. 2012. Similar researcher search in academic environments. In *Proceedings of the 12th ACM/IEEE-CS Joint Conference on Digital Libraries, JCDL '12, Washington, DC, USA, June 10-14, 2012*, pages 167–170.

Anne-Wil Harzing and Satu Alakangas. 2017. Microsoft academic: is the phoenix getting wings? *Scientometrics*, 110(1):371–383.

Sven E Hug and Martin P Brändle. 2017. The coverage of microsoft academic: Analyzing the publication output of a university. *Scientometrics*, 113(3):1551–1571.

Thorsten Joachims. 2002. Optimizing search engines using clickthrough data. In *Proceedings of the eighth ACM SIGKDD international conference on Knowledge discovery and data mining*, pages 133–142.

Yoon Kim. 2014. Convolutional neural networks for sentence classification. In *Proceedings of the 2014 Conference on Empirical Methods in Natural Language Processing (EMNLP)*, pages 1746–1751, Doha, Qatar. Association for Computational Linguistics.

Steve Lawrence. 2001. Free online availability substantially increases a paper's impact. In *Nature*, 411 (6837), pages 521–521.

Huajing Li, Isaac G Councill, Levent Bolelli, Ding Zhou, Yang Song, Wang-Chien Lee, Anand Sivasubramaniam, and C Lee Giles. 2006. Citeseerχ: a scalable autonomous scientific digital library. In *Proceedings of the 1st international conference on Scalable information systems*, pages 18–es.

Tie-Yan Liu. 2011. *Learning to rank for information retrieval*. Springer Science & Business Media.

Sean MacAvaney, Andrew Yates, Arman Cohan, and Nazli Goharian. 2019. Cedr: Contextualized embeddings for document ranking. In *Proceedings of the 42nd International ACM SIGIR Conference on Research and Development in Information Retrieval*, pages 1101–1104.

Christopher D Manning, Hinrich Schütze, and Prabhakar Raghavan. 2008. *Introduction to information retrieval*. Cambridge university press.

Filippo Menczer, Gautam Pant, and Padmini Srinivasan. 2004. Topical web crawlers: Evaluating adaptive algorithms. *ACM Trans. Internet Technol.*, 4(4):378–419.

Rui Meng, Sanqiang Zhao, Shuguang Han, Daqing He, Peter Brusilovsky, and Yu Chi. 2017. Deep keyphrase generation. In *Proceedings of the 55th Annual Meeting of the Association for Computational Linguistics (Volume 1: Long Papers)*, pages 582–592. Association for Computational Linguistics.

Marc Najork and Janet L. Wiener. 2001. Breadth-first crawling yields high-quality pages. In *Proceedings of the 10th International Conference on World Wide Web*, WWW '01, pages 114–118.

José Luis Ortega, Isidro Aguillo, and José Antonio Prieto. 2006. Longitudinal study of content and elements in the scientific web environment. *Journal of Information Science*, 32(4):344–351.

Gautam Pant, Kostas Tsioutsiouliklis, Judy Johnson, and C Lee Giles. 2004. Panorama: extending digital libraries with topical crawlers. In *Proceedings of the 4th ACM/IEEE-CS joint conference on Digital libraries*, pages 142–150. ACM.

Arnab Sinha, Zhihong Shen, Yang Song, Hao Ma, Darrin Eide, Bo-june Paul Hsu, and Kuansan Wang. 2015. An overview of microsoft academic service (mas) and applications. In *Proceedings of the 24th international conference on world wide web*, pages 243–246. ACM.

Amanda Spink and Bernard J Jansen. 2004. *Web search: Public searching of the Web*, volume 6. Springer Science & Business Media.

Jie Tang, Duo Zhang, and Limin Yao. 2007. Social network extraction of academic researchers. In *Seventh IEEE International Conference on Data Mining (ICDM 2007)*, pages 292–301. IEEE.

Jie Tang, Jing Zhang, Limin Yao, Juanzi Li, Li Zhang, and Zhong Su. 2008. Arnetminer: extraction and mining of academic social networks. In *Proceedings of the 14th ACM SIGKDD international conference on Knowledge discovery and data mining*, pages 990–998.

Trystan Upstill, Nick Craswell, and David Hawking. 2003. Query-independent evidence in home page finding. *ACM Transactions on Information Systems (TOIS)*, 21(3):286–313.

Ji Wan, Pengcheng Wu, Steven C. H. Hoi, Peilin Zhao, Xingyu Gao, Dayong Wang, Yongdong Zhang, and Jintao Li. 2015. Online learning to rank for content-based image retrieval. In *IJCAI*.

Yuxin Wang and Keizo Oyama. 2006. Web page classification exploiting contents of surrounding pages for building a high-quality homepage collection. In *International Conference on Asian Digital Libraries*, pages 515–518. Springer.

Wensi Xi, Edward Fox, Roy Tan, and Jiang Shu. 2002. Machine learning approach for homepage finding task. In *String Processing and Information Retrieval*, pages 169–174. Springer.

Peilin Yang, Hui Fang, and Jimmy Lin. 2017. Anserini: Enabling the use of lucene for information retrieval research. In *Proceedings of the 40th International ACM SIGIR Conference on Research and Development in Information Retrieval*, pages 1253–1256.

Ding Zhou, Shenghuo Zhu, Kai Yu, Xiaodan Song, Belle L Tseng, Hongyuan Zha, and C Lee Giles. 2008. Learning multiple graphs for document recommendations. In *Proceedings of the 17th international conference on World Wide Web*, pages 141–150.

Ziming Zhuang, Rohit Wagle, and C Lee Giles. 2005. What's there and what's not?: focused crawling for missing documents in digital libraries. In *Digital Libraries, 2005. JCDL'05. Proceedings of the 5th ACM/IEEE-CS Joint Conference on*, pages 301–310. IEEE.

Scaling Systematic Literature Reviews with Machine Learning Pipelines

Seraphina Goldfarb-Tarrant[*] and **Alexander Robertson**[*]
School of Informatics
University of Edinburgh
{s.tarrant,alexander.robertson,jasmina.lazic}@ed.ac.uk

Jasmina Lazic
Bayes Centre
University of Edinburgh

Theodora Tsouloufi and **Louise Donnison** and **Karen Smyth**
Supporting Evidence Based Interventions
Royal (Dick) School of Veterinary Studies
University of Edinburgh
{theodora.tsouloufi,louise.donnison,karen.smyth}@ed.ac.uk

Abstract

Systematic reviews, which entail the extraction of data from large numbers of scientific documents, are an ideal avenue for the application of machine learning. They are vital to many fields of science and philanthropy, but are very time-consuming and require experts. Yet the three main stages of a systematic review are easily done automatically: searching for documents can be done via APIs and scrapers, selection of relevant documents can be done via binary classification, and extraction of data can be done via sequence-labelling classification. Despite the promise of automation for this field, little research exists that examines the various ways to automate each of these tasks. We construct a pipeline that automates each of these aspects, and experiment with many human-time vs. system quality trade-offs. We test the ability of classifiers to work well on small amounts of data and to generalise to data from countries not represented in the training data. We test different types of data extraction with varying difficulty in annotation, and five different neural architectures to do the extraction. We find that we can get surprising accuracy and generalisability of the whole pipeline system with only 2 weeks of human-expert annotation, which is only 15% of the time it takes to do the whole review manually and can be repeated and extended to new data with no additional effort.[1]

1 Introduction

Systematic reviews are part of the field of evidence-based analysis, and are a methodology for conducting literature surveys, where the focus is on comprehensively summarising and synthesising existing research for the purpose of answering research questions (Higgins et al., 2019). The aim of this process is to be very broad coverage to avoid unknown bias creeping into results via the alternative of cherry-picking scientific results (Chalmers et al., 1995). Conducting systematic reviews requires trained researchers with domain knowledge. The stages of the process are time-consuming, but vary in how much physical and mental labour they require (Borah et al., 2017). As a result, systematic reviews suffer from three primary challenges (Allen and Olkin, 1999; Shojania et al., 2007):

1. they are very expensive, as they require many months of expert human labour;

2. they easily become out of date, for the same reason;

3. there is no amortised cost to human time at expanding them; human effort is linear in amount of research reviewed.

So though systematic reviews have been shown to be very effective and less prone to human biases (Mulrow, 1994), these issues often prove prohibitive.

However, these challenges are well suited to Machine Learning solutions, and there has recently been an increase in interest in applying NLP to this process (Marshall and Wallace, 2019). In this paper, we investigate the feasibility of implementing the multi-stage human process of a systematic review as a Machine Learning pipeline. We construct a systematic review pipeline which aims to assist researchers and organisations focusing on livestock health in various African countries who previously performed reviews manually (via a process visualised in Figure 1). The pipeline begins

---

[*] Equal contribution, order determined by coin flip.
[1] Code and links to models available at https://github.com/seraphinatarrant/systematic_reviews

Proceedings of the First Workshop on Scholarly Document Processing, pages 184–195
Online, November 19, 2020. ©2020 Association for Computational Linguistics
https://doi.org/10.18653/v1/P17

with scraping for articles, then classifies them into whether or not to include in the review, then identifies data to extract and outputs a spreadsheet. We discuss the technical options we evaluated at each steps. Pipeline components are evaluated with intrinsic metrics as well as more pragmatic, extrinsic, considerations such as time and effort saved.

While previous work exists surveying the applicability of various Machine Learning methods and toolkits to the systematic review process (Section 6) and a few apply them, there are no extant studies that implement a full system and analyse the trade-offs between different methods of training data creation, different annotation schemas, human expert hours needed to build a system, and final accuracy. We experiment with all of these factors, as well as with a few different architectures, with the aim of informing the planning and implementation of systematic review automation more broadly.

To further this goal, we particularly experiment with low resource scenarios and with generalisability. We investigate different thresholds for training data for the document classifier and different annotation schemas for the data extraction. We additionally test the ability of the system to generalise to documents from new countries.

Key research questions are as follows:

Extraction   Which techniques are best for identifying and extracting the desired information?

Data Requirements   How much labelled training data is needed? Can existing resources be leveraged?

Re-usability   How generalisable is a pipeline to new diseases and countries?

Performance   What is the trade-off between pipeline accuracy and human time savings?

Architecture & Pre-training   How important is model architecture as applied to extraction tasks? How important is embedding pre-training, and how important is pre-training on scientific literature vs. general content (domain match)?

We find that surprisingly little training data (and few human hours) are necessary to get an accurate document classifier, and that it generalises well to unseen African countries (Section 5), which enables systematic reviews to be expanded to new areas with essentially constant time. In our text extraction experiments, we find that both sentence and phrase level extraction models can each play a role in such a pipeline, but that phrase extraction, which has not previously been done for this task, performed better than expected both with baseline CNN models (Yang et al., 2016) and with BERT-based Transformers (Devlin et al., 2019), with Transformers based on scientific pre-training (Beltagy et al., 2019) performing best. We demonstrate how the creation of labelled training data can be sped up through annotation tools, and that consideration should be given to the balance of training examples present within this data, since doing so may require less data overall while still maintaining good performance. Furthermore, besides automatic information extraction, much labour in constructing systematic reviews can be saved through simply automating the process of searching and downloading documents.

We empirically demonstrate that most of the three month pipeline of a systematic review can be automated to require very little human intervention, with acceptable accuracy of results. We release our code, annotation schema, and labelled data to assist in the expansion of systematic reviews via automation.

While we demonstrate this system on one domain, the framework is domain independent and could be applied to other kinds of systematic reviews. New training data and annotation schemes would be necessary to switch to medical or other domains, but our findings on time saving processes for annotation would apply, and confidence thresholds that we implement are adjustable to customise to different levels of accuracy to human time trade-offs that are appropriate to different fields. Our exploration into necessary amounts of training data for accuracy and generalisability are broadly applicable.

2   Background and Motivation

As a case study, we work with the Supporting Evidence Based Interventions team at the Royal (Dick) School of Veterinary Studies at the University of Edinburgh, focusing on putting data and evidence at the centre of livestock decision-making in low and middle-income countries, predominantly in Africa. In these countries, livestock offer a path out of poverty for millions of smallholders, as well as providing vital nutrition for families and communities. While the veterinary technology and techniques required to improve livestock outcomes already exist (and are readily available to large scale commercial concerns worldwide), there is a lack of reliable information on animal health and productivity in these countries, at this scale. This data is needed not only in order to best target interventions, but to select the most efficient intervention in any particular context.

There is very little data in this area for these countries, and it is often out of date. One proxy for direct measurement of livestock health in all herds in a country is the evidence found in veterinary science research publications, which have conducted prevalence studies. Individually, these studies give an indication of the prevalence of a specific disease in a specific region of a country at a specific time, affecting a specific breed of animal. But collectively, they give a much broader understanding of livestock health.

Four strands of data are of key importance: general livestock statistics (herd size and characteristics), health (mortality and disease), production (yields and growth rates) and economics (breeding costs, feeding costs, produce sale values). Here, we focus on health, specifically the prevalence of a wide range of diseases (e.g. brucellosis, foot and mouth disease) that effect ruminants (sheep, goats and cattle), with a focus on countries such as Nigeria, Ethiopia and Tanzania.

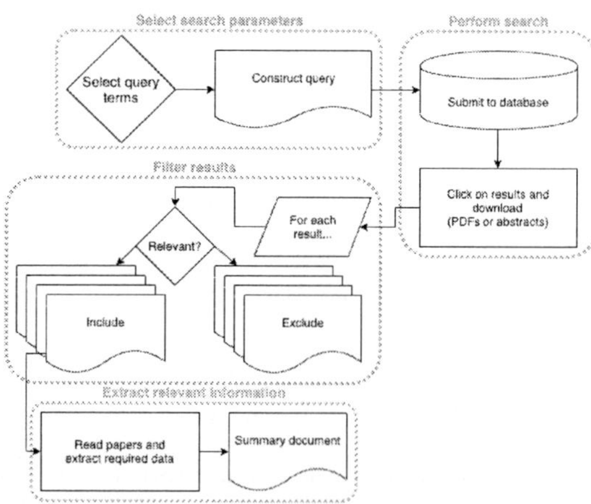

Figure 1: Human-based information extraction systematic review pipeline.

However, collecting and summarising the findings of these studies is time-consuming manual work. For example, searching databases such as Google Scholar, Pubmed and Web of Science for prevalence studies, conducted between 2010 and 2018 on 28 diseases in small ruminants in Ethiopia, returned many thousands of results. Of these, 403 papers were considered relevant and information was extracted by experienced veterinarian researchers. The completely manual process, outlined in Figure 1, produced high quality data but took approximately three months.

The target information consists of dates (the start/end of the study), numerical data (sample size, direct/percentage prevalence numbers, animal age) and small lexical terms. These terms can be veterinary (diagnostic tests used, production systems, study design, statistical analysis performed, species) or geographic (region, ecosystem).[2]

Since this summarisation process isn't abstractive, readers find it easy, if time-consuming, to identify the relevant information in research papers. The current project aimed to automate as much of the process as possible, to allow it to scale to a wider range of diseases (approximately 50) and countries. All but the initial component of Figure 1 can be entirely automated – humans are still required to define search terms.

3 Pipeline Details & Experimental Setup

In the following we detail each stage of the constructed pipeline, how it compares to the human version and the human time saved. In the succeeding Section 4 we detail metrics and evaluation for our targeted experiments with the classification and extraction pipeline components.

3.1 Document Search

The highest return on investment in terms of engineering effort vs. human time-savings was our automation of literature searches. Previously, researchers would construct a list of searches to perform, input these into various databases, then manually download the results they considered relevant. An example search is `(Livestock OR ruminants OR sheep OR goats OR cattle OR cow OR ram OR ewe OR bull) AND (Ethiopia) AND (Anthrax OR "Bacillus anthracis") AND (prevalence OR incidence)`

APIs are available for Scopus, Pubmed and Web of Science, for which we obtained institutional access. Google Scholar has no available API, so we used the SerpApi service[3] which provides paid programmatic access. The pipeline therefore maintains full coverage of paper sources. As the

---

[2] Appendix A contains example target extracted data
[3] https://serpapi.com/

APIs return only links to papers, PDFs still need to be retrieved. Issues to navigate here included links to websites rather than files, which requires additional negotiation through user-agent strings, parsing HTML for links to the PDF or parsing page headers to extract metadata redirecting to a PDF such as `citation_pdf_url`. A generic approach was successful in most cases but site-specific downloaders had to be constructed for 38 domains, based on trial and error.

Time spent on retrieval of potentially relevant documents to include in the systematic reviews were reduced dramatically, with the main limiting factor being rate throttles on APIs. Conducting searches on all four databases for 50 diseases in 3 countries takes approximately one hour on one machine and requires no human input. Parallel downloading of PDFs is even faster. This can be repeated at any interval to keep results up to date. By contrast, this step of the process used to take human experts 83 hours (2 weeks full-time) each time it was done, while covering fewer diseases and only one country.

3.2 Document Classification

Once search results have been collected, retrieved PDFs must be classified for inclusion vs. exclusion in the systematic review. Human reviewers use various criteria to assess inclusion (peer-review, type of study/experiment, subject matter) which, as we observed in user studies, they determine entirely from the title and abstract. We use the PDF DOI or ISSN to retrieve the title and abstract [4] using the Wikimedia Citoid API [5]. We then train an SVM Classifier implemented in Sci-kit Learn (Pedregosa et al., 2011) with concatenated TF-IDF Vectors, which can train in under an hour on a standard Linux machine. The classification process, which previously took a human expert 20 hours for 1000 documents, now generates results in minutes. We additionally implemented human review of documents with low classifier confidence (further details in Section 5) upon consultation with our systematic review experts, as this both increases classifier accuracy and human trust in results.

3.3 PDF to Text Conversion

Relevant PDFs are converted to plain text with the pdfminer.six package [6]. The text data extracted from PDFs can be noisy – tables are especially problematic, headers/footers may end up inside main text, word and line spacing may be inconsistent, fonts may be improperly converted to text. The bulk of this can be overcome through basic pre-processing.

Once converted, the text is split into paper sections (e.g. abstract, introduction, methods) using regular expressions derived from manual inspection of 100 papers. This involves matching spans of text which appear between common section titles. For example, the abstract generally appears between 'abstract' and 'introduction', 'abstract' and 'keywords', 'summary' and 'introduction'.[7]

3.4 Data Extraction

The goal of a systematic review is to output a tabular file where each column stores target information for each paper; this will then later be used to generate visualisations. Manually extracting this information is easy for knowledgeable humans: it isn't abstractive and does not require close reading of the full text. However, it is time-consuming at scale and does require experts, so both performing the process manually and creating training data incurs a significant cost. In addition, the different kinds of target information pose different technical challenges. Consider the sentence *Rose Bengal Plate Test found 1.72% (5/291) of the samples to be sero-positive*, which contains information about the diagnostic test used, the prevalence rate and sample size, all of which we want to capture. The phrase associated with the diagnostic test can be understood out of context but numbers generally cannot. Simply extracting all percentages from a text will be uninformative, rendering rule-based extraction approaches unsuitable. We therefore explored two machine learning approaches to automatic extraction to balance the difficulty in creation of annotated training data with suitability of the extraction approach.

A *sentence-based* classifier can be used to label sentences as containing target information, and has been the method of extraction used in previous work (Marshall et al., 2017; Kiritchenko et al.,

---

[4]PDFs are converted to text in the following step and we could use the title and abstract from extraction, but PDF extraction is noisy and so we chose to rely on reference database lookups where available.

[5]`https://en.wikipedia.org/api/rest_v1`

[6]`https://github.com/pdfminer/pdfminer.six`

[7]PDF processing is documented fully in released code.

2010; Schmidt et al., 2020). But this does not fit in well with the desired tabular output for all target fields: the same information can appear in multiple sentences and the same sentence can contain multiple targets. However, this approach is much easier for a human annotator. It should also work well for numerical targets: the context is preserved in the output and non-relevant numerical targets will be ignored or scored low. Alternatively, a *phrase-based* classifier can apply labels to individual words and phrases within sentences. The extracted information will be more focused and should work well for phrase-based targets. The results will not require rule-based and human post-processing, as with the results of sentence-based extraction, but training data creation is more onerous. So given a fixed amount of human expert hours available, this approach may be less desirable, since it will generate much less training data.

We test the difference between both approaches using CNN-based text classification and named entity recognition models implemented in Prodigy[8]. This tool combines data annotation and model training. We created an annotation schema with 16 labels taken from manually created gold standard systematic review output.[9]

Creating training data for a sentence-based classifier is mechanically simple: the Prodigy annotation tool allows non-technical users to quickly assign labels using an interface with keyboard shortcuts, and we can display one sentence at a time. Prodigy also allows phrase-level labelling, but this is a more involved process as the user must mark the start/end boundaries of a span and then apply the appropriate label. A single veterinarian labelled 4600 items at the sentence level in 56 hours, reporting the process to be easy and straightforward. The same veterinarian labelled 4200 items at the phrase level in 70 hours, reporting it to require much more physical and mental effort.

4   Methodology

We performed detailed evaluation of the different classification and extraction components.

Document Classification   We investigate the trade-off between training data volume and performance, and how generalisable a model is. For training volume, we fix a test set and reduce training data in chunks of 20% of total. We test generalisability by training models on country-specific data and evaluating on unseen data from other countries. We report Accuracy overall, as well as Precision, Recall, and F1 on the *include* label in this binary classification task. Finally, we investigate the effect of thresholding classifier confidence, and sending low confidence documents for manual human review, on both the accuracy of the system and on human time cost.

Data Extraction   We evaluate the sentence classifier and sequence-labelling approach with our CNN models. We also consider the impact of using document representations constructed with embeddings trained entirely on the source data, versus general purpose GloVe embeddings (Pennington et al., 2014) trained on web data, versus general purpose GloVe embeddings fine-tuned on the source data[10]. As the sentence-level classifier is multi-label and multi-class, we report AUC (Area Under Curve).[11] For the phrase-level sequence labelling approach, we report F1 score.

4.1   Training Data Creation

Document Classification   veterinarian experts manually labelled papers as include/exclude: 608 papers from searches for 50 diseases for the countries of Ethiopia, Nigeria and Tanzania. We experimented with labelling 100 test documents: half via a reference manager/document reader[12] and via a simple spreadsheet interface where one column contained the paper title, one contained the paper abstract, and the expert filled in a third column for the include/exclude label.[13] The spreadsheet method was 3 times faster than using a reference manager, enabling experts to complete the 608 papers of training data in 5 hours. Half the data contains country information, so we use only that half for our generalisability experiments.

Data Extraction   52 documents were randomly sampled from the set of documents manually classified for inclusion. The sampled documents covered 13 diseases for studies in Ethiopia, Nigeria and Tanzania. Only abstracts, results and methods sections were annotated.

---

[8]https://prodi.gy/
[9]Annotation schema included in code repository.
[10]Implemented in spacy https://spacy.io/
[11]AUC true positive vs false positive rate over a range of discrimination thresholds
[12]Zotero (zotero.org) was chosen as it is the only service which provides an API
[13]Recall that criteria for inclusion in the study are fully determinable via these fields.

Data	Description	Phrases	Sentences
disease	Animal disease	3307 (31.5%)	778 (31.4%)
species	Species studied	2002 (19.1%)	518 (20.9%)
region	Area within country	1487 (14.2%)	298 (12.0%)
individual_prevalence	Number of infected animals	743 (7.1%)	172 (6.9%)
diagnostic_test	Test used to detect disease	729 (6.9%)	172 (6.9%)
reference	Reference to another study	591 (5.6%)	137 (5.5%)
sample_type	Biological samples used	486 (4.6%)	117 (4.7%)
statistical_analysis	Analysis performed	261 (2.5%)	63 (2.5%)
age	Ages of animals tested	228 (2.2%)	65 (2.6%)
sample_size	Number of animals tested	161 (1.5%)	24 (1.0%)
production_system	Type of farm	141 (1.3%)	43 (1.7%)
ecosystem	Geography of farm	141 (1.3%)	44 (1.8%)
study_design	Type of study used	120 (1.1%)	28 (1.1%)
study_date	Date study was conducted	64 (0.6%)	8 (0.3%)
herd_prevalence	Number of herds infected	28 (0.3%)	7 (0.3%)
mortality	Animals killed by disease	5 (0.0%)	1 (0.0%)

Table 1: Proportion of target items identified during data annotation.

To select a manageable volume of data for annotation, and avoid including noisy data from the PDF extraction process, we applied some restrictions. For the sentence-based task, all sentences of at least 9 words within the abstract were included, along with a random sample of 150 sentences (between 9 and 25 words long) from the results and methods sections. Sentence length was based on the fact that very short/long sentences were generally noisy due to the PDF conversion process. For the phrase-based task, sections were split into chunks of three sentences to preserve some context. The entire abstract was used, plus a random sample of 25 chunks from each of the methods and results sections.

Table 1 briefly describes each item and the breakdown of label frequency in our annotated data. There is a clear imbalance in label frequency — some are not commonly reported in general (e.g. mortality, herd prevalence) while others are reported very few times per paper (e.g. study date).

4.2 Experimental Conditions

Data Volume We trained document classification models using proportions from 20% to 100% of all data.

Generalisability Three document classification models were each trained on two of the three countries, with the final country held out. We included data volume ablations in these experiments as well.

Sentence vs. Phrase Models We trained the CNN-model on sentence labelled vs. phrase labelled data to assess the feasibility of using each annotation approach.

Architecture & Pretraining We experiment with five different architectures for the phrase-based models. We use the Prodigy CNN with randomly-initialised embeddings, the Prodigy CNN with frozen pre-trained embeddings, the Prodigy CNN with pre-trained embeddings fine-tuned on our data, distilBERT (Sanh et al., 2019), and SciBERT (Beltagy et al., 2019). The CNN is easy to implement out of the box, as it is built into the annotation tool, can be trained without access to a GPU, and could potentially be less data-hungry than a transformer - all important considerations in our resource constrained setting. Adding pre-trained embeddings allows us to isolate the effect of pre-training from the effect of architecture. Since the phrase-labelling task is well suited to the masked language modelling objective, we additionally experiment with fine-tuning distilBERT (which is reasonably sized for our small amount of data) and SciBERT, to test whether the domain match of pre-trained data matters.

5 Results

Results for document classification experiments are shown in Figure 2. The upper left quadrant of Figure 2 contains data for 608 documents with an 85-15 train-test split across all 3 countries, showing an expected increase in classifier performance as data increases, but levelling off slightly by 80% of the full training volume. The other quadrants

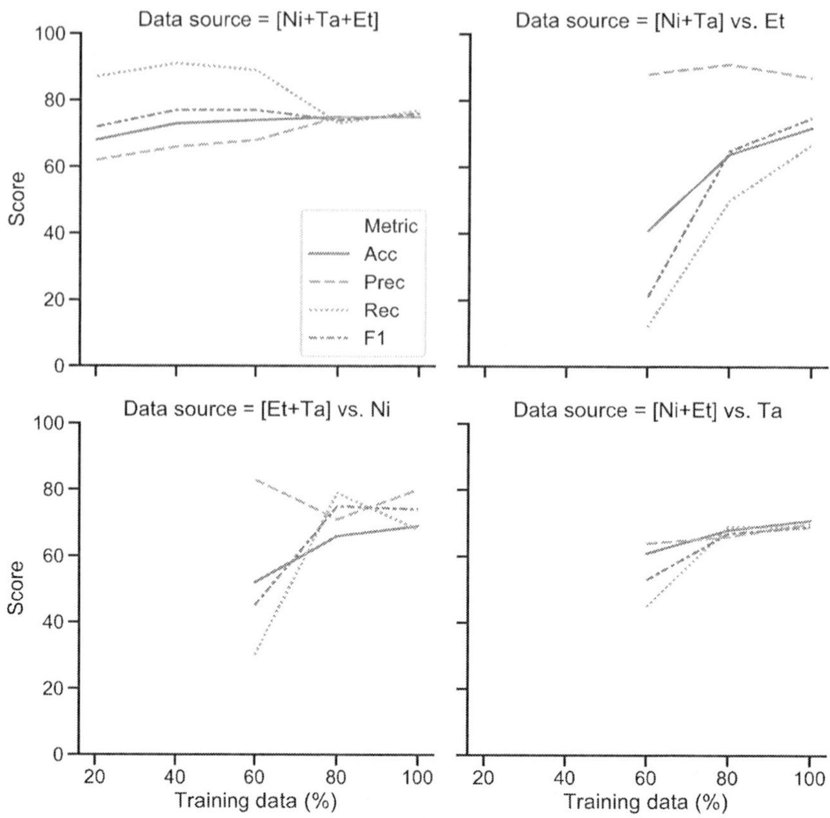

Figure 2: Accuracy, Precision, Recall, and F1 for the document classification model showing performance changes as training data is decreased for the full set of 608 documents (85-15 train-test split), as well as generalisability to held out countries. Et=Ethiopia, Ta=Tanzania, and Ni=Nigeria. Note that country experiments have only 200 train and 100 test documents (100 per country, with test held fixed).

show the same data for 100 documents per country (200 train, 100 test) but with a minimum of 60% of total data, as with less than 100 training samples the model does not converge.

For the data volume studies on the full dataset, a notable trend is that recall is quite high even with very little training data (100 documents), and that what the classifier learns with additional data is predominantly a better precision-recall balance. For the held-out-country generalisability studies, the amount of training data is more important, and recall is no longer high immediately.

This suggests that for a fixed country with a semi-automated system that has resources for a secondary human-filtering, very little training data is necessary. However, extensibility to new countries does require more data. Given that additional more data, performance on unseen countries is equal to that of known countries of equivalent training set volumes. This suggests an important new extensibility opportunity for systematic review systems.

In practice, our experts needed slightly higher accuracy than the best combined accuracy. To address this we implemented confidence-thresholding, such that documents below a user-set threshold are uploaded to a *needs review* folder, which generates a weekly email. 15% of test documents require review at our final confidence threshold, which reduces human time to 20 min per 100 documents classified, but allows for an increased accuracy to 88%. Human reviews are then fed back into classifier training, which should incrementally improve confidence and reduce human labour over time. We leave that longitudinal study for future work.

Results for three CNN-based sentence-level data extraction models are shown in Figure 3a. We report mean AUC score on all labels (with standard deviation shown) with an 80/20 train/test split.

For sentence-level models, fine-tuned web embeddings give better performance overall. Mean

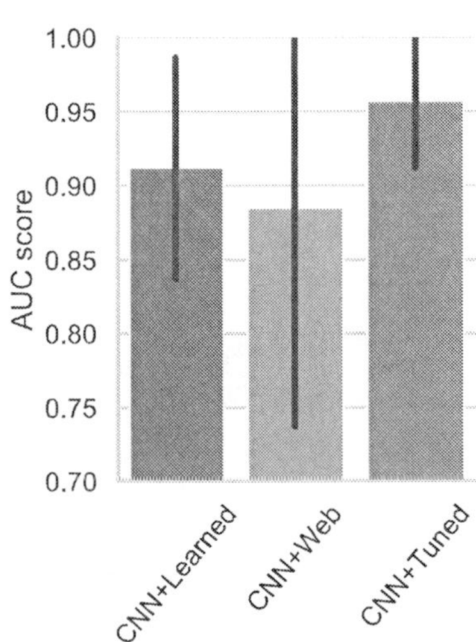
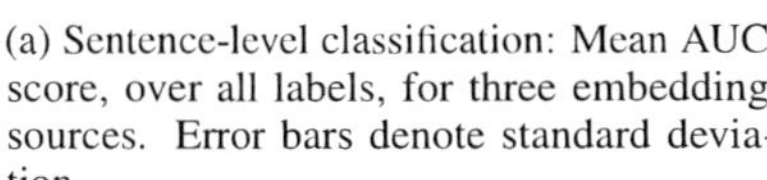

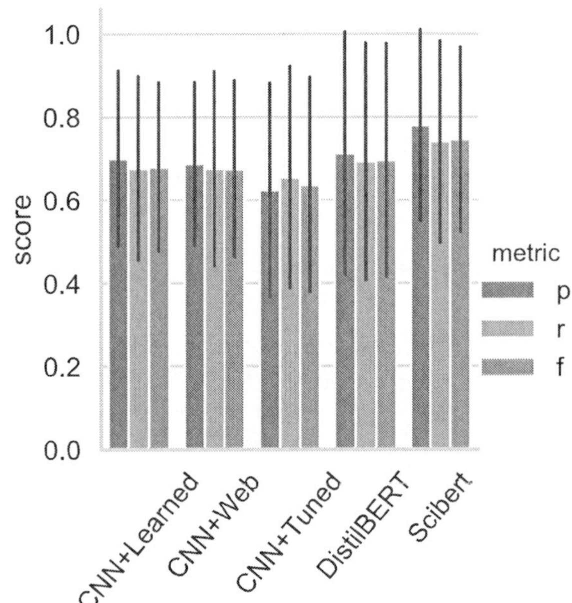

(a) Sentence-level classification: Mean AUC score, over all labels, for three embedding sources. Error bars denote standard deviation.

(b) Phrase-level classification: Mean Precision/Recall/F1, over all labels, for three embedding sources and two Transformer-based models. Error bars denote standard deviation.

AUC score was 0.96 (stdev 0.05) using fine-tuned general purpose web embeddings; 0.91 (stdev 0.08) using learned embeddings; 0.89 (stdev 0.15) using general purpose web embeddings.

For phrase-level models, this is no longer true: mean F1 score was 0.67 (stdev 0.22) using pre-trained general purpose web embeddings; 0.68 (stdev 0.2) using learned embeddings; 0.64 (stdev 0.27) using fine-tuned general purpose web embeddings. Transformer-based models performed more strongly: F1 for DistillBERT was 0.70 (stdev 0.29), SciBERT 0.75 (stdev 0.23).

Focusing on the items considered most important by the veterinarian researchers (disease, species, region, individual prevalence, diagnostic test, sample type, sample size, study date), results in an increase of 0.03 AUC for each sentence-level model. Phrase-based models F1 score increases by 0.10.

These results suggest that pre-training is important for the sentence-based classifier, and that the BERT-based Transformer architecture with the masked language modelling objective can do very well on phrase-level extraction and bring performance high enough to make this approach feasible. However, they show that domain-specific pre-training data has a larger effect than architectural differences. While Transformer-based models for phrase-level labelling out-performed CNN-based

models, it was the SciBERT model trained on academic papers, then fine-tuned on our specific task, which gave the best performance, and a larger performance boost than the initial jump from BERT. The best type of pre-training does vary based on type of extraction: general purpose embeddings perform worst for sentence-level labelling, though are on par with those learned from the training data for phrase-level labelling.

We analyse per-label performance for the SciBERT model to verify phrase-level feasibility, and include this data in Figure 4 in Appendix B. Performance is generally high, even for some low-frequency items. Some of these were uncommon in our training data (due to appearing only once or twice per paper) but naturally appear in *many* academic papers in general, which goes towards accounting for the success of SciBERT on this task. For example, SciBERT was the only model to correctly identify *any* instances of herd prevalence.

6 Related Work

The application of NLP to systematic reviews is relatively new, but has been recently receiving more attention. There is a growing body of work that assesses the potential for automation in systematic reviews, but little that builds systems for the purpose and tests them empirically.

Marshall and Wallace (2019) review available tools that can be used to automate each element of the systematic review pipeline. Marshall et al. (2020) further review opportunities for semi-automation and assess opportunities and risks. Marshall and Brereton (2015); O'Mara-Eves et al. (2015) conduct systematic reviews of automation for systematic reviews. Thomas et al. (2017) analyse the systematic review pipeline to find ways that human-machine collaboration can be applied and improve the speed.

Marshall et al. (2017) create a PDF viewer that humans can use to make the systematic review process easier and faster, by training a CNN to assess risk of bias in a document (an important part of evidence-based analysis in the medical domain, though not for our particular task) and identifies and displays sentences to the user that contain a subset of the information necessary for a systematic review. Kiritchenko et al. (2010) create an extraction system that identifies sentences and then post-processes them to extract data, but operate only on structured HTML & XML. Schmidt et al. (2020) apply fine-tuned BERT-based Transformers to the task of to sentence classification for semi-automated systematic review. Goswami et al. (2019) build a PDF retrieval system for systematic reviews for psychology and use a random forest classifier to identify sentences for extraction.

As far as we are aware, no other work builds a phrase-based system, tests data volume and generalisability, or applies a diverse set of modern architectures to the task.

7 Conclusion & Future Work

We investigated the application of automation to all stages of the systematic review pipeline for our veterinary research case study. We found that with two weeks (80 hours) of human expert annotation we can automate a systematic review that previously took 3 months, and still maintain high levels of accuracy. Our classification system generalises well, enabling it to be applied to new countries for additional systematic reviews with no additional human annotation cost. Sentence-based and phase-based data extraction both perform well, and the creation of phrase-based training data can still fit within a small amount of human annotation hours and avoids the need for extensive post-processing. Fine-tuned BERT-based Transformers perform best at data extraction, with BERT pre-trained on scientific data giving the largest boost in performance, though a baseline CNN still performs surprisingly well. In future work, we plan to test generalisability cross-lingually, expand the generalisability tests to extraction as well as classification, and study the performance improvements of continuous training of classifiers on human corrections of low-confidence output.

References

I Elaine Allen and Ingram Olkin. 1999. Estimating time to conduct a meta-analysis from number of citations retrieved. *Jama*, 282(7):634–635.

Iz Beltagy, Arman Cohan, and Kyle Lo. 2019. Scibert: Pretrained contextualized embeddings for scientific text. *ArXiv*, abs/1903.10676.

Rohit Borah, Andrew W Brown, Patrice L Capers, and Kathryn A Kaiser. 2017. Analysis of the time and workers needed to conduct systematic reviews of medical interventions using data from the prospero registry. *BMJ open*, 7(2):e012545.

Iain Chalmers, Douglas G Altman, et al. 1995. *Systematic reviews*. BMJ Publishing London.

J. Devlin, Ming-Wei Chang, Kenton Lee, and Kristina Toutanova. 2019. Bert: Pre-training of deep bidirectional transformers for language understanding. In *NAACL-HLT*.

Shubhaditya Goswami, Sukanya Pal, Simon Goldsworthy, and Tanmay Basu. 2019. An effective machine learning framework for data elements extraction from the literature of anxiety outcome measures to build systematic review. In *BIS*.

Julian PT Higgins, James Thomas, Jacqueline Chandler, Miranda Cumpston, Tianjing Li, Matthew J Page, and Vivian A Welch. 2019. *Cochrane handbook for systematic reviews of interventions*. John Wiley & Sons.

Svetlana Kiritchenko, Berry de Bruijn, Simona Carini, Joel D. Martin, and Ida Sim. 2010. Exact: automatic extraction of clinical trial characteristics from journal publications. *BMC Medical Informatics and Decision Making*, 10:56 – 56.

Christopher Marshall and Pearl Brereton. 2015. Systematic review toolbox: a catalogue of tools to support systematic reviews. In *Proceedings of the 19th International Conference on Evaluation and Assessment in Software Engineering*, pages 1–6.

Iain Marshall, Joël Kuiper, Edward Banner, and Byron C. Wallace. 2017. Automating biomedical evidence synthesis: RobotReviewer. In *Proceedings of ACL 2017, System Demonstrations*, pages 7–12, Vancouver, Canada. Association for Computational Linguistics.

Iain J Marshall and Byron C Wallace. 2019. Toward systematic review automation: a practical guide to using machine learning tools in research synthesis. *Systematic reviews*, 8(1):163.

Iain James Marshall, Blair T. Johnson, Zigeng Wang, Sanguthevar Rajasekaran, and Byron C. Wallace. 2020. Semi-automated evidence synthesis in health psychology: current methods and future prospects. *Health Psychology Review*, 14:145 – 158.

Cynthia D Mulrow. 1994. Systematic reviews: rationale for systematic reviews. *Bmj*, 309(6954):597–599.

Alison O'Mara-Eves, James Thomas, John McNaught, Makoto Miwa, and Sophia Ananiadou. 2015. Using text mining for study identification in systematic reviews: a systematic review of current approaches. *Systematic reviews*, 4(1):5.

F. Pedregosa, G. Varoquaux, A. Gramfort, V. Michel, B. Thirion, O. Grisel, M. Blondel, P. Prettenhofer, R. Weiss, V. Dubourg, J. Vanderplas, A. Passos, D. Cournapeau, M. Brucher, M. Perrot, and E. Duchesnay. 2011. Scikit-learn: Machine learning in Python. *Journal of Machine Learning Research*, 12:2825–2830.

Jeffrey Pennington, Richard Socher, and Christopher D Manning. 2014. Glove: Global vectors for word representation. In *Proceedings of the 2014 conference on empirical methods in natural language processing (EMNLP)*, pages 1532–1543.

Victor Sanh, Lysandre Debut, Julien Chaumond, and Thomas Wolf. 2019. Distilbert, a distilled version of bert: smaller, faster, cheaper and lighter. *ArXiv*, abs/1910.01108.

Lena Schmidt, Julie Weeds, and Julian P. T. Higgins. 2020. Data mining in clinical trial text: Transformers for classification and question answering tasks. *ArXiv*, abs/2001.11268.

Kaveh G Shojania, Margaret Sampson, Mohammed T Ansari, Jun Ji, Steve Doucette, and David Moher. 2007. How quickly do systematic reviews go out of date? a survival analysis. *Annals of internal medicine*, 147(4):224–233.

James Thomas, Anna Noel-Storr, Iain Marshall, Byron Wallace, Steven McDonald, Chris Mavergames, Paul Glasziou, Ian Shemilt, Anneliese Synnot, Tari Turner, et al. 2017. Living systematic reviews: 2. combining human and machine effort. *Journal of clinical epidemiology*, 91:31–37.

Zichao Yang, Diyi Yang, Chris Dyer, X. He, A. Smola, and E. Hovy. 2016. Hierarchical attention networks for document classification. In *HLT-NAACL*.

A   Target Extracted Data

In Table 2 is the first 15 lines of a sample gold standard target data from a human systematic review (broken into two tables for display) that we use as a template for building our system. Note that some fields are blank because information was not found in or relevant to a given entry.

B   Detailed Analysis of Phrase-level Classification Performance

Displayed in Figure 4 are the per label performance breakdowns for SciBERT, the strongest phrase-level extraction model. Performance remains high across many individual labels, with changes in performance mostly tracking with commonness of the information (and thus, how much training data is available for a fixed set of annotated documents). The exceptions to this trend are the *region* and *sample_size* labels, which have lower performance compared to equivalently common labels

ROW_NUMBER	IDENTIFIER	YEAR_PUBLICATION	REFERENCE	START_DATE_DATA	END_DATE_DATA	STATE	ECOSYSTEM	PRODUCTION_SYSTEM	SPECIES	AGE	AGE_DETAIL
1	Nigussie et al; 2010	2010	Nigussie et al	2007	2008	Oromia		Mixed farming	Cattle		
2	Regassa et al; 2010	2010	Regassa et al	2007	2008	SNNPR			Cattle		
2	Regassa et al; 2010	2010	Regassa et al	2007	2008	SNNPR			Cattle		
3	Regassa et al; 2010	2010	Regassa et al	2007	2008	SNNPR			Cattle		
4	Bekele et al; 2010	2010	Bekele et al	2008	2003	SNNPR			Cattle		
5	Shiferaw et al 2013; 2010	2010	Shiferaw et al 2013	2007	2008	Afar			Cattle		
6	Shiferaw et al 2011; 2010	2010	Shiferaw et al 2011	2007	2008	Afar			Cattle		
7	Shiferaw et al 2010; 2010	2010	Shiferaw et al 2010	2007	2008	Afar			Cattle		
8	Shiferaw et al 2014; 2010	2010	Shiferaw et al 2014	2007	2008	Afar			Cattle		
9	Shiferaw et al 2012; 2010	2010	Shiferaw et al 2012	2007	2008	Afar			Cattle		
10	Kumsa et al; 2010	2010	Kumsa et al	2006	2006	SNNPR			Sheep		
11	Kumsa et al; 2010	2010	Kumsa et al	2006	2006	SNNPR			Sheep		
12	Kumsa et al; 2010	2010	Kumsa et al	2006	2006	SNNPR			Sheep		
14	Amenu et al; 2010	2010	Amenu et al	2007	2007	Oromia		Mixed farming	Cattle		
14	Amenu et al; 2010	2010	Amenu et al	2007	2007	Oromia		Mixed farming	Cattle		

DISEASE	SAMPLE	DIAGNOSTIC_TEST	MEASUREMENT	NUMBER_POSITIVE	NUMBER_TESTED	PERCENTAGE	CALCULATION	COMMENTS	SOURCE
BVD	Serum	i-ELISA	Individual Prevalance	65	567	11.4638447971781	TOTAL	national surveillance/mixed altitudes (midland, highland)/zone&sex splitting/adult>young(<3y)	LITERATURE
Tb	Intraderm test	CIDT	Herd Prevalance	19	39	48.7179487179487	TOTAL	>6 MONTHS	LITERATURE
Tb	Intraderm test	CIDT	Individual Prevalance	48	413	11.6222760290557	TOTAL	>6 MONTHS	LITERATURE
Tb	PM specimen	PM	Individual Prevalance	11	1023	1.0752688172043	TOTAL		LITERATURE
TRYPs	Blood	BC	Individual Prevalance	71	323	22	TOTAL	East African zebus, >1y/T. congolense, vivax&brucei splitting	LITERATURE
FMD		Survey	Individual Mortality			0.73	TOTAL		LITERATURE
Pasteurelloses		Survey	Individual Mortality			1.5	TOTAL		LITERATURE
CBPP		Survey	Individual Mortality			2.5	TOTAL		LITERATURE
Blackleg		Survey	Individual Mortality			0.13			LITERATURE
Anthrax		Survey	Individual Mortality			1.3			LITERATURE
Endoparasites	Faeces	Floatation, Microscopy	Individual Prevalance			6.7	TOTAL	Strongyloides papillosus	LITERATURE
Endoparasites	Faeces	Floatation, Microscopy	Individual Prevalance			15	TOTAL	Trichuris spp	LITERATURE
Endoparasites	Faeces	Floatation, Microscopy	Individual Prevalance			100	TOTAL	Gi parasites/Strongyle eggs	LITERATURE
Tb	Intraderm test	SCIDT	Herd Prevalance			35	TOTAL		LITERATURE
Tb	Intraderm test	SCIDT	Individual Prevalance	27	425	6.35	TOTAL		LITERATURE

Table 2: Example target extracted data from a gold-standard human systematic review

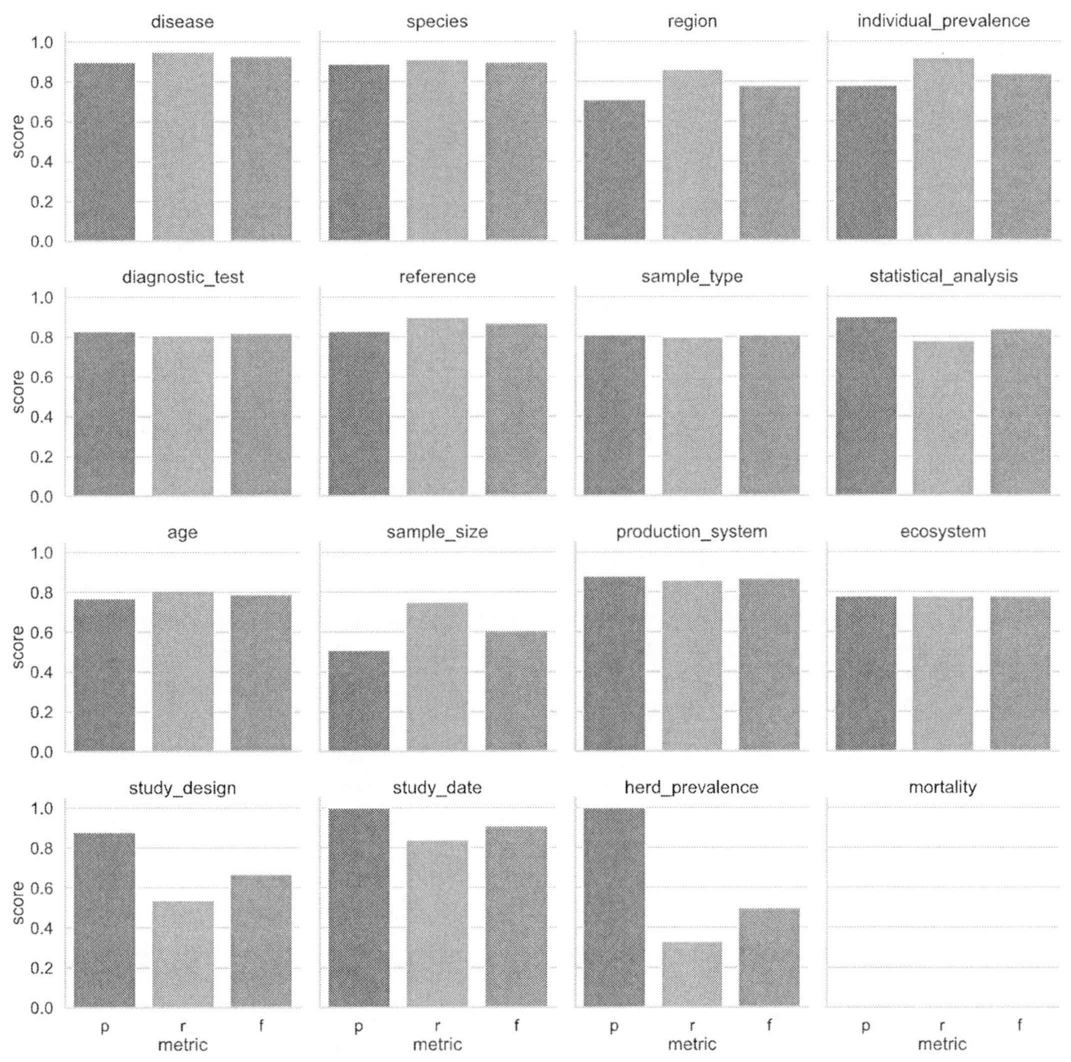

Figure 4: Phrase-level classification: Precision/Recall/F1, per label, for SciBERT. From top left to bottom right: most to fewest examples in training data.

Document-Level Definition Detection in Scholarly Documents: Existing Models, Error Analyses, and Future Directions

Dongyeop Kang[♡]   Andrew Head[♡]   Risham Sidhu[♡]
Kyle Lo[◇]   Daniel S. Weld[◇°]   Marti A. Hearst[♡]

[♡]University of California, Berkeley, [◇]Allen Institute for AI, [°]University of Washington
{dongyeopk,andrewhead,rishamsidhu,hearst}@berkeley.edu
{kylel,danw}@allenai.org

Abstract

The task of definition detection is important for scholarly papers, because papers often make use of technical terminology that may be unfamiliar to readers. Despite prior work on definition detection, current approaches are far from being accurate enough to use in real-world applications.

In this paper, we first perform in-depth error analysis of the current best performing definition detection system and discover major causes of errors. Based on this analysis, we develop a new definition detection system, HEDDEx, that utilizes syntactic features, transformer encoders, and heuristic filters, and evaluate it on a standard sentence-level benchmark. Because current benchmarks evaluate randomly sampled sentences, we propose an alternative evaluation that assesses every sentence within a document. This allows for evaluating recall in addition to precision.

HEDDEx outperforms the leading system on both the sentence-level and the document-level tasks, by 12.7 F1 points and 14.4 F1 points, respectively. We note that performance on the high-recall document-level task is much lower than in the standard evaluation approach, due to the necessity of incorporation of document structure as features. We discuss remaining challenges in document-level definition detection, ideas for improvements, and potential issues for the development of reading aid applications.

1 Introduction

Automatic definition detection is an important task in natural language processing (NLP). Definitions can be used for a variety of downstream tasks, such as ontology matching and construction (Bovi et al., 2015), paraphrasing (Hashimoto et al., 2011), and word sense disambiguation (Banerjee and Pedersen, 2002; Huang et al., 2019). Prior work in au-

Example
s^{task} are softmax-normalized weights and the scalar [...]
Textual entailment is the task of determining whether a "hypothesis" is true, given a "premise".
A biLM combines both a forward and backward LM
[...] a fine grained word sense disambiguation (WSD) task and a POS tagging task.

Table 1: Examples of terms and definitions from Peters et al. (2018). Each row shows a term (e.g., s^{task}) along with its definition (e.g., "softmax-normalized weights").

tomated definition detection has addressed the domain of scholarly articles (Reiplinger et al., 2012; Jin et al., 2013; Espinosa-Anke and Schockaert, 2018; Vanetik et al., 2020; Veyseh et al., 2020). Definition detection is especially important for scholarly papers because they often use unfamiliar technical terms that readers must understand to properly comprehend the article.

In formal terms, definition detection is comprised of two tasks: classifying sentences as containing definitions or not, and identifying which spans within these sentences contain terms and definitions. As the performance of definition extractors continues to improve, these algorithms could pave the way for new types of intelligent assistance for readers of dense technical documents. For example, one could envision future interfaces that reveal definitions of jargon like "biLM" or the symbol "s^{task}" when a reader hovers over the terms in a reading application (Head et al., 2020). Examples of sentences containing terms and definitions are shown in Table 1.

Despite recent advances in definition detection,

Proceedings of the First Workshop on Scholarly Document Processing, pages 196–206
Online, November 19, 2020. ©2020 Association for Computational Linguistics
https://doi.org/10.18653/v1/P17

much work remains to be done before models are capable of extracting definitions with an accuracy appropriate for real-world applications. The first challenge is one of recall: existing systems are typically not trained to identify *all* definitions in a document, but rather to classify individual sentences arbitrarily sampled from a large corpus. The second challenge is one of precision: the state of the art misclassifies upwards of 30% of sentences (Veyseh et al., 2020). This begs the questions of why definition extractors fall short, and how these shortcomings can be overcome.

In this paper, we contribute the following:

- An in-depth error analysis of the current best-performing model. This analysis characterizes the state of the field and illustrates future directions for improvement;

- A new model, Heuristically-Enhanced Deep Definition Extraction (HEDDEx), that extends a state-of-the-art model with improvements designed to address the problems found in the error analysis. An evaluation shows that this improved model outperforms the state of the art by a large margin (+12.7 F1);

- An introduction of the challenging task of full-document definition detection. In this task, models are evaluated based on their ability to identify definitions across an entire document's sentences. We believe this framing of definition detection is critical to preparing future algorithms for real-world use;

- A preliminary analysis of previous models and our model on the document-level definition detection task using a small test set of scholarly papers where every term and definition has been labeled. This analysis shows that HEDDEx outperforms the state of the art, while revealing opportunities for future improvements.

In summary, this paper draws attention to the work yet to be done in addressing the task of document-level definition detection for scholarly documents. We draw attention to the fact that a seemingly straightforward task like definition detection still poses significant challenges to NLP, and that this is an area that needs more focus in the scholarly document processing community.

2 Related Work

Definition detection has been tackled in several ways in prior research. The traditional rule-based systems (Muresan and Klavans, 2002; Westerhout and Monachesi, 2008; Westerhout, 2009a) used hand-written definition patterns (e.g., "is defined as") and linguistic features (e.g., pronoun, verb, punctuation), providing high precision but low recall detection. To address the low recall problem, model-driven approaches (Fahmi and Bouma, 2006; Westerhout, 2009b; Navigli and Velardi, 2010; Reiplinger et al., 2012) were developed using statistical and syntactic features such as bag-of-words, sentence position, part-of-speech (POS) tags, and their combination with hand-written rules. Notably, Jin et al. (2013) used conditional random field (CRF) (Lafferty et al., 2001) to predict tags of each token in a sentence such as TERM for term tokens, DEF for definition tokens, and O for neither. Recently, sophisticated neural models such as convolutional networks (Espinosa-Anke and Schockaert, 2018) and graph convolutional networks (Veyseh et al., 2020) have been applied to obtain better sentence representations in combination with syntactic features. However, our analysis found that the state-of-the-art is still far from solving the problem, achieving an F1 score of only 60 points on a standard test set.

3 Error Analysis of the Leading System

In order to inform our efforts to develop a more advanced system, we performed an in-depth error analysis of the results of the current leading approach to definition and term identification, the joint model by Veyseh et al. (2020). We analyzed the models' predictions on the WOO dataset (Jin et al., 2013) since it matches our target domain of scholarly papers and is the dataset that the joint model was evaluated on. Of the 224 test sentences,[1] the Veyseh et al. (2020) system got 111 correct. The first author annotated the remaining 113 sentences for which the algorithm was partially or fully incorrect to ascertain the root causes of the errors.

We discovered four (for terms) and five (for definitions) major causes for the erroneous predictions, as summarized in Table 3. We illustrate three exam-

---

[1] Note that we use the test set of WOO for manual analysis, which is only 10% of the entire dataset. In our experiment in §4, we didn't use the test set used in this error analysis, but did cross-validation using the train set, following the experimental setup in Veyseh et al. (2020).

Sentences	Cause	Patterns	Solutions
[Equal] is open in something of type collection where that collection is a *[partition of something]* .	• Overgeneralization: technical term bias • description (is)	*(none applicable)*	?
A **[graph - based operator]** defines a transformation on a multi-document graph (MDG) G which preserves *[some of its properties while reducing the number]*...	• Complicated sentence structure	*<term>* defines *<def>*	parsing features
The Inductive Logic Programming learning method that we have developed enables us to automatically extract from a corpus N - V pairs whose elements axe linked by one of the semantic relations defined in the qualia structure ...	• Unfamiliar or unseen vocabulary • Unseen patterns	*<term>* that we have developed enables us to automatically *<def>*	generalize patterns

Table 2: Sample annotations from our analysis of errors produced by Veyseh et al.'s (2020) joint model when extracting definitions from the W00 (Jin et al., 2013) dataset. Each row includes a sentence annotated with gold labels for <u>terms</u> and <u>definitions</u>, and the system's predictions for [**terms**] and {*definitions*} ("Sentences"). Also shown is a class of error ("Cause"), surface patterns that we anticipate could be used to correct the detection of the definition ("Patterns"), and classes of improvements to make to the model ("Solutions"). The first row is an example of a false positive; the second row is a partially-correct prediction; and the third row is a false negative. A transcription error ('axe' instead of 'are') is retained from the dataset.

ples in Table 2. For each example, we also labeled surface patterns between the term and definition (e.g., "*<term>* defines *<def>*"), and potential algorithm improvements to address the underlying problem.

For instance, in the bottom-most example in Table 2, the system did not predict any term or definition, although the sentence includes the term "Inductive Logic Programming Learning method" and the definition "extract from a corpus...". Our conjecture is that the underlying surface pattern is unseen in the training set and too complicated to be generalized; we annotate a potential solution as *pattern generalization*.

Top hypothesized causes of error	(%)
Overgeneralization: technical term bias	48.6%
Unfamiliar or unseen vocabulary	25.7%
Complicated sentence structure	12.9%
Entity detection	4.3%
Overgeneralization: technical term bias	28.9%
Overgeneralization: surface pattern bias	23.3%
Unseen patterns	14.4%
Complicated sentence structure	12.2%
Overgeneralization: description	3.3%

Table 3: Top causes of errors for terms (top) and definitions (bottom)

We rank the causes of errors by frequency and summarize the results in Table 3. For detection of terms, nearly half of the error cases fall into overgeneralization of technical terms: overly predicting words like "equal" and "model" as terms (e.g., the top example in Table 2).

Proposed error correction solution types	(%)
Syntactic (POS, parse tree, entity, acronym)	29.2%
Heuristics	23.6%
Better encoder/tokenizer, UNK	18.0%
Rules (surface patterns)	11.3%
Annotations*	9.4%
Pattern generalization	5.7%
Mathematical symbol detection	1.9%
More context	0.9%

Table 4: Proportions of proposed error correction solution types. Annotations* indicates extremely ambiguous cases even for humans, so additional human annotations are required to disambiguate them.

We again rank the error correction solutions by frequency (Table 4). We predict that 29% of errors can be fixed by informing the system about syntactic features of the sentence such as part-of-speech tags, parse tree annotations, entities, or acronyms for more accurate detection. Surprisingly, simple heuristics (e.g., stitching up discontiguous token spans) seem likely to be highly effective to address the errors in Table 3, such as discarding output that does not successfully predict both a term and a definition. In the next section, we implement the first three solution types on top of the state-of-the-art system and report the resulting performance improvements.

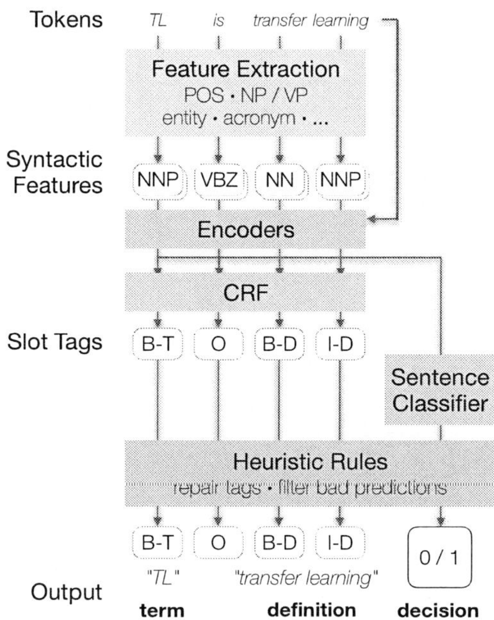

Figure 1: The HEDDEx model. The new modules developed in this work include the incorporation of syntactic features, the addition of pre-trained transformer encoders, and post-processing with heuristics.

4 Definition Sentence Detection Model

To address the errors identified in §3, we designed HEDDEx, a new sentence-level definition detection model. The model incorporates a set of syntactic features, heuristic filters, and encoders. Each of these was designed to address a common class of error revealed in the error analysis. The model achieves superior performance over the state of the art for the task of sentence-level definition detection.

4.1 Proposed Model: Heuristically-Enhanced Deep Definition Extraction (HEDDEx)

HEDDEx extends the joint model proposed by Veyseh et al. (2020). The joint model is comprised of two components. The first component is a CRF-based sequence prediction model for slot tagging. The model assigns each token in a sentence one of five tags: term ("B-TERM", "I-TERM"), definition ("B-DEF","I-DEF"), or other ("O"). The second component is a binary classifier that labels each sentence as containing a definition or not.

HEDDEx has three new modules (Figure 1). First, it encodes input from a transformer encoder

fine-tuned on the task of definition extraction, whereas the joint model encodes input from a combination of a graph convolutional network and a BERT encoder without fine-tuning.[2] We evaluate several state-of-the-art encoders for this task, including BERT (Devlin et al., 2019), RoBERTa (Liu et al., 2019b), and SciBERT (Beltagy et al., 2019).

Second, HEDDEx is provided with additional syntactic features as input. These features include parts of speech, syntactic dependencies, and the token-level labels provided by entity recognizers and abbreviation detectors (Schwartz and Hearst, 2003). The features are extracted using off-the-shelf tools like Spacy[3] and SciSpacy (Neumann et al., 2019).

Third, the output of the CRF and sentence classifier is refined using heuristic rules. The rules clean up the slot tags produced by the CRF, and override predictions made by the sentence classifier. The rules include, among other rules:

- Do not classify a sentence as a definition if it only contains a term without a definition, or a definition without a term.

- Stitch up discontiguous token spans for terms and definitions by assigning all contiguous tokens between two term or definition labels the same label.

These three enhancements developed in HEDDEx were selected specifically to suit the shortcomings of the models identified in the error analysis (§3), leading to significant improvements for definition detection in our experiments.

4.2 Baseline Models

To evaluate the impact of these improvements on the definition detection task, HEDDEx was compared to four baseline systems: (1) DefMiner (Jin et al., 2013), a CRF-based sequence prediction model that makes use of hand-written features; (2) Li et al.'s (2016) model comprised of a CRF with an LSTM encoder; (3) GCDT (Liu et al., 2019a), a global and local context encoder; (4) Veyseh et al.'s (2020) joint model described above. The experimental setup for the models followed the setup described by Veyseh et al. (2020).

---

[2] However, we note that we were unable to replicate the accuracy reported by Veyseh et al. (2020) when using the code provided by the authors.

[3] https://spacy.io/

4.3 Metrics

The models were compared using a set of metrics for both slot tagging and sentence classification on the W00 test set. To evaluate the slot tagger, macro-averaged precision, recall, and F1 score were measured (column "Macro P/R/F" in Table 5). However, the Macro scores do not show performance specific to terms or definitions. Also, macro-averaging over the position tags (B, I) makes it difficult to interpret general performance. Therefore, we measured these three metrics only for term tags ("TERM P/R/F"); B-TERM and I-TERM, and definition tags ("DEF P/R/F"); B-DEF and I-DEF. To evaluate the precision of the bounds of term and definition spans, we also evaluated the degree of overlap between each detected term or definition span and the corresponding span in the gold dataset ("Partial F"). Furthermore, the accuracy of sentence classification was measured (column "Classification"). For each of these metrics, a higher score indicated superior performance. We averaged each score across 10-fold cross validation.

4.4 Setup

Due to computing limitations, we chose the best hyper-parameter set through parameter sweeping with HEDDEx with the BERT encoder only, and use the best hyperparameters for all other models. Here is the ranges of each parameter we tuned: batch sizes in {8, 16, 32}, number of training epochs [30, 50, 100] maximum length of sentences in {80, 256, 512}, learning rates in [{2,5}e-{4,5}].

The other parameters used as defaults in our experiments were as follows: the dropout ratio was 10%, the layer size for POS embeddings was 50, and the hidden size for slot prediction was 512. We follow the default hyper-parameters for each transformer model of each size (base or large) using HuggingFace's transformer libraries.[4]

4.5 Results

Outcomes of the evaluation for all measurements are presented in Table 5. The pre-trained language model encoders (BERT, RoBERTa, SciBERT) achieve comparable performance to more complex neural architectures like the graph convolutional networks used in Veyseh et al.'s (2020). Models that included SciBERT (Beltagy et al., 2019), rather than BERT or ROBERTa, achieved

---

[4]https://github.com/huggingface/
transformers

higher accuracy on most measurements. We attribute this to the domain similarity between the scholarly documents that SciBERT was trained on, and those used in our evaluation.

With SciBERT as the base encoder, the incorporation of syntactic features led to further accuracy gains. Of particular note are the improvements in recall in term spans. During our evaluation, we observed that the gains from syntactic features were more pronounced for encoders with a small mode size (i.e., the "-base" models). We conjecture that this is because the larger encoder models were capable of learning comparable linguistic patterns to those captured by the syntactic features.

The addition of heuristic rules led to significant improvement (+11.8 Macro F1) over the combination of Joint and SciBERT. Given the modest improvement in term and definition tagging, we suspect that much of this improvement can be accounted for by the correction of position markers in the slot tags (i.e., distinguishing between B and I in the tag assignments).

In the following experiments, we call HEDDEx the combination of three components: the encoder (SciBERT or RoBERTa), syntactic features, and heuristic filters.

5 Document-Level Definition Detection

Although HEDDEx attains reasonable performance on individual sentences, it faces new challenges when applied to the scenario of document-level analysis. In this section, we evaluate sentence detection for full papers in two novel ways. First, we assess the *precision* of the HEDDEx model across *all of the sentences* of 50 documents in §5.1. Second, we assess both the *precision* and the *recall* of the algorithm across *all of the sentences* of 2 full documents (§5.2, S5.3).

5.1 Error Analysis on Predicted Definitions

To assess how well HEDDEx works at the document level, we randomly sampled 50 ACL papers from the S2ORC dataset (Lo et al., 2020), a large corpus of 81.1M English-language academic papers spanning many academic disciplines. We ran the pretrained HEDDEx model on every sentence of every document; if the model detected a term/definition pair, the corresponding sentence was output for assessment. (Note that this analysis can estimate precision but not recall, as false negatives are not detected.)

	Macro P/R/F	TERM P/R/F	DEF P/R/F	Partial F	Clsf.
DefMiner (Jin et al., 2013)	52.5 / 49.5 / 50.5	-	-	-	-
LSTM-CRF (Li et al., 2016)	57.1 / 55.9 / 56.2	-	-	-	-
GCDT (Liu et al., 2019a)	57.9 / 56.6 / 57.4	-	-	-	-
Joint (Veyseh et al., 2020)	60.9 / 60.3 / 60.6	-	-	-	-
Joint* (Veyseh et al., 2020)	61.0 / 60.2 / 60.7	-	-	-	70.5
HEDDEx					
Joint* + BERT-base	59.5 / 61.3 / 60.3	66.6 / 70.0 / 68.2	72.1 / 74.0 / 72.8	74.3	83.4
Joint* + BERT-large	60.4 / 61.4 / 60.7	67.5 / 71.0 / 69.0	72.3 / 73.9 / 72.9	74.5	83.2
Joint* + RoBERTa-large	60.3 / 61.6 / 60.7	67.3 / 70.3 / 68.6	72.8 / **74.6** / 73.5	73.2	84.2
Joint* + SciBERT	61.9 / 61.2 / 61.5	**71.1** / 69.1 / 69.9	74.0 / **74.6** / **74.2**	**75.7**	**85.1**
Joint* + SciBERT + Syntactic	61.6 / 61.8 / 61.6	70.7 / 71.3 / **70.9**	73.3 / 72.4 / 72.8	74.3	84.3
Joint* + SciBERT + Syntactic + Heuristic	**72.9** / **74.3** / **73.4**	69.8 / **72.1** / 70.8	**75.4** / 71.8 / 73.3	74.3	84.5

Table 5: Comparison of the accuracy of recent models and the HEDDEx model for the definition detection task. Asterisks (*) indicate that we reimplemented the model from the authors' specification. Models were evaluated on the W00 (Jin et al., 2013) test set. Each score is averaged across 10-fold cross validation. Accuracy measurements include **P**recision, **R**ecall, and **F**1-score. Each of these measurements is macro-averaged.

We replace all citations and references to figures, tables, and sections with corresponding placeholders (e.g., CITATION, FIGURE), but keep raw TeX format of mathematical symbols in order to retain the structure of the equations. From the 50 ACL papers, the model detected 924 definitions out of 13,658 sentences and the average number of definitions per paper is 18.5.

Term (%)		Definition (%)	
Textual term	45.2%	Textual Def.	58.7%
Incorrect term	27.3%	Other: implausible	24.8%
Math symbol term	22.7%	Other: plausible	11.8%
Acronym	3.3%	Short name / Synonym	3.5%
Acronym and text	1.3%	Textual & Formula Def.	0.6%
		Formula Def.	0.4%

Table 6: Analysis of HEDDEx output on 50 ACL papers, ordered by frequency. N = 923.

The third author evaluated the predicted terms and definitions separately by choosing one among the labels shown in Table 6. For terms, the algorithm correctly labeled 72.5%. We subdivide these correctly labeled terms into standard terms (45.2%), math symbols (22.7%), acronyms, acronym (3.3%), or acronym and text (1.3%). Among the correctly labeled definitions (total 63.2% = 58.7%+3.5%+0.6%+0.4%), 92.6% are textual definitions, 5.6% are short names or synonyms, and 1.7% include mathematical symbols. We divided non-definitional text into two types: plausible (24.8%) and implausible (11.8%), which signals an error. The plausible text refers to explanations or secondary information (similar to DEFT (Spala et al., 2019)'s secondary definition, but without sentence crossings).

Term Span (%)		Definition Span (%)	
Correct	83.4%	Correct	89.9%
Too Long (to the right)	10.1%	Cut Off (to the right)	3.4%
Cut Off (to the right)	3.2%	Too Long (to the left)	2.6%
Cut Off (to the left)	1.6%	Cut Off (to the left)	2.4%
Too Long (to the left)	1.4%	Too Long (to the right)	1.3%

Table 7: Analysis of span length of HEDDEx output on 50 ACL papers, ordered by frequency. $N = 923$.

We also measured whether the predicted span length is correct, too long, or cut off (Table 7). These scores are quite high; 83.4% correct for terms and 89.9% for definitions (see Table 10).

5.2 Full Document Definition Annotation

Prior definition annotation collections select unrelated sentences from across a document collection. As mentioned in the introduction, we are interested in annotating full papers, which requires finding *every* definition within a given paper. Therefore, we created a new collection in which we annotate every sentence within a document, allowing assessment of recall as well as precision. Two annotators annotated two full papers using an annotation scheme similar to that used in DEFT (Spala et al., 2019) except for omitting cross-sentence links.

We chose to annotate two award-winning ACL papers: ELMo (Peters et al., 2018) and LISA (Strubell et al., 2018) resulting in 485 total sentences from which we identified 98 definitional and 387 non-definitional sentences. Similar to DEFT (Spala et al., 2019), we measured inter-annotator agreement using Krippendorff's alpha (Krippendorff, 2011) with the MASI distance metric (Passonneau, 2006). We obtained 0.626 for terms and

0.527 for definitions, where the agreement score for terms is lower than those in DEFT annotations (0.80). This may be because our annotations for terms include various types such as textual terms, acronyms, and math symbols, while terms in DEFT are only textual terms. The task was quite difficult: each annotator takes two and half hours to annotate a single paper. Future work will include refining the annotation scheme to ensure more consistency among annotators and to annotate more documents.

5.3 Evaluation on Document-level Definitions

We evaluated document-level performance using the same metrics used in §4.3. All metrics were averaged over scores from 10-fold validation models. The ensemble model aggregates ten system predictions from the 10-fold validation models and choose the final label via majority voting. We use the best single system; HEDDEx but with RoBERTa,[5] for model ensembling.

	Macro	TERM	DEF	Partial	Clf.
Joint model	36.0	30.1	38.1	34.1	86.8
HEDDEx w/ BERT	45.3	32.4	39.0	34.6	89.1
HEDDEx w/ RoBERTa	47.7	36.4	47.2	37.2	88.1
HEDDEx ensemble	**50.4**	**38.7**	**49.5**	**39.0**	**89.8**

Table 8: Document-level evaluation on our annotated documents. F1 score is measured for every metric except for classification (Clf.), which uses accuracy.

Compared to the joint model by Veyseh et al. (2020), HEDDEx showed significant improvements on every evaluation metric, which is slightly larger than that of the sentence-level evaluation (Table 8). With model ensembling, compared to the state-of-the-art system, HEDDEx achieved gains by +14.4 Macro F1 points, +8.7 TERM F1 points, +11.4 DEF F1 points, +4.9 Partial Matching F1 points, and +3.0 classification accuracy scores.

	Precision	Recall	F1
Macro	55.3	46.7	50.4
TERM	44.8	34.0	38.7
DEF	55.6	44.7	49.5

Table 9: Low recall problem in document-level definition detection. We report precision, recall, and f1 scores on three metrics; Macro, TERM, and DEF, using our best system; HEDDEx ensemble.

However, document-level definition detection is

[5]RoBERTa and SciBERT show comparable performance on the document-level definition detection task.

a much harder task than sentence-level detection. Compared to the sentence-level task in Table 5, the document-level task showed relatively lower performance (73.4 Macro F1 in sentence-level versus 50.4 Macro F1 in document-level). In particular, recall is much lower than precision in the document-level task (Table 9), whereas in the sentence-level task, precision and recall are almost the same, indicating the necessity of incorporation of document structure as additional features (See further discussion in §6).

Table 10 shows the predicted terms and definitions as well as annotated gold labels. Acronym patterns (e.g., "biLM," "WSD"), definition of newly-proposed terms (e.g., "LISA"), re-definition of prior work (e.g., "SQuAD," "SRL," Coreference resolution) and some of mathematical symbols were detected well. However, as sentences get more complex, the system made incorrect predictions. Additionally, sub-words or parentheses in abbreviations are sometimes partially predicted (e.g., the beginning of the word "pretrained" is cut off in the definition of "semi-supervised learning" in example 8 of Table 10) .

However, the aforementioned problem of low recall is severe for this task, particularly since the model often fails to detect mathematical symbols or a combination of textual terms and mathematical symbols (e.g., "L-layer biLM"). Moreover, when a sentence contains multiple terms and/or multiple symbols together, the system only ever detects one of them.

6 Discussion

Detecting definitions is a very challenging task, and it is far from solved. Here we discuss remaining challenges and ideas for improvements, and motivate the need for high-precision, high-recall definition detection in an academic document reading aid application.

Outstanding technical challenges include:

- **Poor recognition of mathematical symbols**: As shown in our experiment, our system is less successful at detecting math symbols than textual terms. This is mainly because the lack of coverage of mathematical symbols in our training dataset (`W00`).

- **Contextual disambiguation of symbols**: In our study, we observe that some symbols are used with multiple meanings. For example,

	Predicted definition sentences	Type
1	Our <u>word vectors</u> are learned functions of the internal states of a *{deep bidirectional language model}* (**[biLM]**), which is pre-trained on a large text corpus.	term
2	We use vectors derived from a bidirectional LSTM that is trained with a coupled *{language model}* (**[LM]**) objective on a large text corpus.	term
3	Using intrinsic evaluations, we show that the higher-level **[LSTM states]** capture context-dependent aspects of word meaning (e.g., they can be used without modification to perform well on supervised word sense disambiguation tasks) while lower-level states *{model aspects of syntax}*.	term
4	We first show that they can be easily added to existing models for six diverse and challenging <u>language understanding problems</u> , including textual entailment, question answering and sentiment analysis.	term
5	For tasks where direct comparisons are possible, outperforms **[CoVe]** CITATION, which *{computes contextualized representations using a neural machine translation encoder}*.	term
6	<u>context2vec</u> CITATION uses a bidirectional Long Short Term Memory LSTM ; CITATION to encode the context around a <u>pivot word</u> .	term
7	Unlike most widely used word embeddings CITATION, <u>word representations</u> are functions of the entire input sentence, as described in this section.	term
8	This setup allows us to do **[semi-supervised learning]**, where the biLM is pretr*{ained at a large scale}* (Sec. SECTION) and easily incorporated into a wide range of existing neural NLP architectures (Sec. SECTION).	term
9	Given a sequence of N tokens, $(t_1, t_2, ..., t_N)$, a <u>forward language model</u> computes the probability of the sequence by modeling the probability of token t_k given the history $(t_1, ..., t_{k-1})$:	term
10	A **[backward LM]** is *{similar to a forward LM, except it runs over the sequence in reverse, predicting the previous token given the future context}*:	term
11	A **[biLM]** *{combines both a forward and backward LM}*.	term
12	where $[\boldsymbol{h_{k,0}^{LM}}]$ is *{the token layer}* and $h_{k,j}^{LM} = [\overrightarrow{h}_{k,j}^{LM}; \overleftarrow{h}_{k,j}^{LM}]$, for each biLSTM layer.	symbol
13	In (EQUATION), $[s^{task}]$ are *{softmax-normalized weights}* and the scalar parameter γ^{ask} allows the task model to scale the entire vector.	symbol
14	For each token t_k, a L-layer biLM computes a set of $2L+1$ representations EQUATION where $h_{k,0}^{LM}$ is the token layer and $h_{k,j}^{LM} = [\overrightarrow{h}_{k,j}^{LM}; \overleftarrow{h}_{k,j}^{LM}]$, for each biLSTM layer.	symbol, term
15	In (EQUATION), s^{task} are <u>softmax-normalized weights</u> and the **[scalar parameter γ^{ask}]** *{allows the task model to scale the entire vector}*.	symbol
16	The **[Stanford Question Answering Dataset (SQuAD) CITATION]** *{contains 100K+ crowd sourced question-answer pairs where the answer is a span in a given Wikipedia paragraph}*.	term
17	**[Textual entailment]** is *{the task of determining whether a "hypothesis" is true, given a "premise"}*.	term
18	The **[Stanford Natural Language Inference (SNLI) corpus CITATION]** *{provides approximately 550K hypothesis/premise pairs}*.	term
19	A **[semantic role labeling (SRL) system]** *{models the predicate-argument structure of a sentence}*, and is often described as answering.	term
20	CITATION modeled **[SRL]** *{as a BIO tagging problem and used an 8-layer deep biLSTM with forward and backward directions interleaved}*, following CITATION.	term
21	**[Coreference resolution]** is *{the task of clustering mentions in text that refer to the same underlying real world entities}*.	term
22	The **[CoNLL]** 2003 NER task CITATION *{consists of newswire from the Reuters RCV1 corpus tagged with four different entity types (PER, LOC, ORG, MISC)}*.	term
23	The **[fine-grained sentiment classification]** task in the Stanford Sentiment Treebank SST-5 *{involves selecting one of five labels (from very negative to very positive) to describe a sentence from a movie review}*.	term
24	The sentences contain diverse <u>linguistic phenomena</u> such as <u>idioms</u> and <u>complex syntactic constructions</u> such as <u>negations</u> that are difficult for models to learn.	multi-term
25	Intuitively, the **[biLM]** must be *{disambiguating the meaning of words using their context}*.	term
26	a fine grained *{word sense disambiguation}* (**[WSD]**) task and a POS tagging task.	term

Table 10: All predicted and gold label terms and definitions for the ELMo paper (Peters et al., 2018). Gold labels for <u>terms</u> are <u>underlined</u> and for <u>definitions</u> are <u>dashed</u>. System-predicted **[terms]** are placed in **[boldfaced brackets]** and *{definitions}* are placed in *{italicized braces}*. "CITATION," "SECTION," and "EQUATION" are placeholders inserted for citations, section numbers, and display equations. "Type" means term type.

symbol T in the LISA paper is used for *token representation* as well as *matrix transpose*. Disambiguating terms based on context of use will be an interesting future direction.

- **Description vs Definition**: In our annotation and error analysis, the most difficult distinction was between definitions and descriptions — they have quite similar surface patterns, although they refer to entirely different meanings. For instance, a definition is the exact denotation of a word, while a description is more detailed so it can change from person to person. Training a model that distinguishes these types should lead to better and more useful results.

Potential ideas for improvements of the system include:

- **Annotation of mathematical definitions**: A solution for poor math symbol detection is to annotate math symbols and use them for our training. One option is to add span information to the binary judgements of the math definition collection of Vanetik et al. (2020).
- **Utilization of document-level features**: Document structure and positional information may improve detection. For instance, the section information of a term would be an important feature to recognize whether a term is first introduced or not.
- **Data augmentation or domain-specific fine-tuning for high-recall system**: Existing definition training sets are small (`W00` contains only 731 definitional sentences). To obtain more data, the data can be augmented via seed patterns or fine-tuning with existing language models such as SciBERT.

Lastly, as the performance of definition detection systems increases, these systems can be applied to real-world reading or writing aids. We discuss potential issues of our system in the realistic settings:

- **Metrics for usefulness**: Currently, we measure precision, recall, and F1 scores with the document-level annotations. However, we have not explored the usefulness of the predicted definitions for readability, when they are used in real-world applications like ScholarPhi (Head et al., 2020). Deciding when and where to show definitions based on context and information density still remains an important future direction.

- **Categorization of definitions**: We observe that in fact, terms and definitions can be grouped into multiple categories: short names, acronyms, textual definitions, formula definitions, and more. Automatically categorizing these and showing structured definitions might be helpful for organizing and ranking definitions in a user interface.
- **Repeated definitions and terms within documents**: We observed a pattern in which the same term is referred to multiple times in slightly different ways. Newly proposed terms are especially likely to exhibit this pattern. Grouping and summarizing these in a *glossary table* would be helpful for an academic document reader application.

7 Conclusion

This work sets the stage for bridging the gap between a well-known NLP task; *definition detection*, and real-world applications of the technique that requires both high precision and high recall. To achieve the goal, we proposed a more realistic setup for definition detection task called *document-level definition detection* that requires high recall, mathematical symbol recognition, and document-level feature engineering. Our proposed definition detection system HEDDEx achieved significant gains in both sentence-level and document-level tasks. Yet, the problem is far from being solved. We suggest that better coverage of variability of expression, recognition of mathematical symbols and notation, and other nuances of the task must still be addressed.

Acknowledgements

We like to thank Amir Pouran Ben Veyseh for his help in sharing his code, preprocessed data, and general advice on replication of his work. We also thank Raymond Fok, Vivek Aithal, Hearst lab members at UC Berkeley and anonymous reviewers at SDP 2020 for their helpful comments. This research receives funding from the Alfred P. Sloan Foundation, the Allen Institute for AI, Office of Naval Research grant N00014-15-1-2774, NSF Convergence Accelerator award 1936940, NSF RAPID award 2040196, and the University of Washington Washington Research Foundation/Thomas J. Cable Professorship.

References

Satanjeev Banerjee and Ted Pedersen. 2002. An adapted lesk algorithm for word sense disambiguation using wordnet. In *International conference on intelligent text processing and computational linguistics*, pages 136–145. Springer.

Iz Beltagy, Kyle Lo, and Arman Cohan. 2019. Scibert: A pretrained language model for scientific text. In *Proceedings of the 2019 Conference on Empirical Methods in Natural Language Processing and the 9th International Joint Conference on Natural Language Processing (EMNLP-IJCNLP)*, pages 3606–3611.

Claudio Delli Bovi, Luca Telesca, and Roberto Navigli. 2015. Large-scale information extraction from textual definitions through deep syntactic and semantic analysis. *Transactions of the Association for Computational Linguistics*, 3:529–543.

Jacob Devlin, Ming-Wei Chang, Kenton Lee, and Kristina Toutanova. 2019. BERT: Pre-training of deep bidirectional transformers for language understanding. In *Proceedings of the 2019 Conference of the North American Chapter of the Association for Computational Linguistics: Human Language Technologies, Volume 1 (Long and Short Papers)*, pages 4171–4186, Minneapolis, Minnesota. Association for Computational Linguistics.

Luis Espinosa-Anke and Steven Schockaert. 2018. Syntactically aware neural architectures for definition extraction. In *Proceedings of the 2018 Conference of the North American Chapter of the Association for Computational Linguistics: Human Language Technologies, Volume 2 (Short Papers)*, pages 378–385, New Orleans, Louisiana. Association for Computational Linguistics.

Ismail Fahmi and Gosse Bouma. 2006. Learning to identify definitions using syntactic features. In *Proceedings of the Workshop on Learning Structured Information in Natural Language Applications*.

Chikara Hashimoto, Kentaro Torisawa, Stijn De Saeger, Sadao Kurohashi, et al. 2011. Extracting paraphrases from definition sentences on the web. In *Proceedings of the 49th Annual Meeting of the Association for Computational Linguistics: Human Language Technologies*, pages 1087–1097.

Andrew Head, Kyle Lo, Dongyeop Kang, Raymond Fok, Sam Skjonsberg, Daniel S. Weld, and Marti A. Hearst. 2020. Augmenting scientific papers with just-in-time, position-sensitive definitions of terms and symbols. *arXiv preprint arXiv:2009.14237*.

Luyao Huang, Chi Sun, Xipeng Qiu, and Xuanjing Huang. 2019. GlossBERT: BERT for word sense disambiguation with gloss knowledge. In *Proceedings of the 2019 Conference on Empirical Methods in Natural Language Processing and the 9th International Joint Conference on Natural Language Processing (EMNLP-IJCNLP)*, pages 3509–3514, Hong Kong, China. Association for Computational Linguistics.

Yiping Jin, Min-Yen Kan, Jun-Ping Ng, and Xiangnan He. 2013. Mining scientific terms and their definitions: A study of the ACL anthology. In *Proceedings of the 2013 Conference on Empirical Methods in Natural Language Processing*, pages 780–790, Seattle, Washington, USA. Association for Computational Linguistics.

Klaus Krippendorff. 2011. Computing krippendorff's alpha-reliability. Technical report, University of Pennsylvania. Retrieved from https://repository.upenn.edu/asc_papers/43/.

John D. Lafferty, Andrew McCallum, and Fernando C. N. Pereira. 2001. Conditional random fields: Probabilistic models for segmenting and labeling sequence data. In *Proceedings of the Eighteenth International Conference on Machine Learning*, pages 282–289, San Francisco, CA, USA. Morgan Kaufmann Publishers Inc.

SiLiang Li, Bin Xu, and Tong Lee Chung. 2016. Definition extraction with lstm recurrent neural networks. In *Chinese Computational Linguistics and Natural Language Processing Based on Naturally Annotated Big Data*, pages 177–189. Springer.

Yijin Liu, Fandong Meng, Jinchao Zhang, Jinan Xu, Yufeng Chen, and Jie Zhou. 2019a. GCDT: A global context enhanced deep transition architecture for sequence labeling. In *Proceedings of the 57th Annual Meeting of the Association for Computational Linguistics*, pages 2431–2441, Florence, Italy. Association for Computational Linguistics.

Yinhan Liu, Myle Ott, Naman Goyal, Jingfei Du, Mandar Joshi, Danqi Chen, Omer Levy, Mike Lewis, Luke Zettlemoyer, and Veselin Stoyanov. 2019b. Roberta: A robustly optimized bert pretraining approach. *arXiv preprint arXiv:1907.11692*.

Kyle Lo, Lucy Lu Wang, Mark Neumann, Rodney Kinney, and Daniel Weld. 2020. S2ORC: The semantic scholar open research corpus. In *Proceedings of the 58th Annual Meeting of the Association for Computational Linguistics*, pages 4969–4983, Online. Association for Computational Linguistics.

A Muresan and Judith Klavans. 2002. A method for automatically building and evaluating dictionary resources. In *Proceedings of the Language Resources and Evaluation Conference (LREC*.

Roberto Navigli and Paola Velardi. 2010. Learning word-class lattices for definition and hypernym extraction. In *Proceedings of the 48th Annual Meeting of the Association for Computational Linguistics*, pages 1318–1327, Uppsala, Sweden. Association for Computational Linguistics.

Mark Neumann, Daniel King, Iz Beltagy, and Waleed Ammar. 2019. Scispacy: Fast and robust models for biomedical natural language processing. In *Proceedings of the 18th BioNLP Workshop and Shared Task*, pages 319–327.

Rebecca J Passonneau. 2006. Measuring agreement on set-valued items (masi) for semantic and pragmatic annotation. In *Proceedings of the Fifth International Conference on Language Resources and Evaluation (LREC'06)*.

Matthew Peters, Mark Neumann, Mohit Iyyer, Matt Gardner, Christopher Clark, Kenton Lee, and Luke Zettlemoyer. 2018. Deep contextualized word representations. In *Proceedings of the 2018 Conference of the North American Chapter of the Association for Computational Linguistics: Human Language Technologies, Volume 1 (Long Papers)*, pages 2227–2237.

Melanie Reiplinger, Ulrich Schäfer, and Magdalena Wolska. 2012. Extracting glossary sentences from scholarly articles: A comparative evaluation of pattern bootstrapping and deep analysis. In *Proceedings of the ACL-2012 Special Workshop on Rediscovering 50 Years of Discoveries*, pages 55–65, Jeju Island, Korea. Association for Computational Linguistics.

Ariel S. Schwartz and Marti A. Hearst. 2003. A simple algorithm for identifying abbreviation definitions in biomedical text. *Pacific Symposium on Biocomputing. Pacific Symposium on Biocomputing*, pages 451–62.

Sasha Spala, Nicholas A. Miller, Yiming Yang, Franck Dernoncourt, and Carl Dockhorn. 2019. DEFT: A corpus for definition extraction in free- and semi-structured text. In *Proceedings of the 13th Linguistic Annotation Workshop*, pages 124–131, Florence, Italy. Association for Computational Linguistics.

Emma Strubell, Patrick Verga, Daniel Andor, David Weiss, and Andrew McCallum. 2018. Linguistically-informed self-attention for semantic role labeling. In *Proceedings of the 2018 Conference on Empirical Methods in Natural Language Processing*, pages 5027–5038, Brussels, Belgium. Association for Computational Linguistics.

Natalia Vanetik, Marina Litvak, Sergey Shevchuk, and Lior Reznik. 2020. Automated discovery of mathematical definitions in text. In *Proceedings of The 12th Language Resources and Evaluation Conference*, pages 2086–2094, Marseille, France. European Language Resources Association.

Amir Pouran Ben Veyseh, Franck Dernoncourt, Dejing Dou, and Thien Huu Nguyen. 2020. A joint model for definition extraction with syntactic connection and semantic consistency. In *Thirty-Fourth AAAI Conference on Artificial Intelligence (AAAI-20)*.

Eline Westerhout. 2009a. Definition extraction using linguistic and structural features. In *Proceedings of the 1st Workshop on Definition Extraction*, pages 61–67.

Eline Westerhout. 2009b. Extraction of definitions using grammar-enhanced machine learning. In *Proceedings of the Student Research Workshop at EACL 2009*, pages 88–96, Athens, Greece. Association for Computational Linguistics.

Eline Westerhout and Paola Monachesi. 2008. Creating glossaries using pattern-based and machine learning techniques. In *LREC 2008*.

A New Neural Search and Insights Platform for
Navigating and Organizing AI Research

Marzieh Fadaee[*]   **Olga Gureenkova**[*]   **Fernando Rejon Barrera**[*]
Carsten Schnober[*]   **Wouter Weerkamp**[*]   **Jakub Zavrel**[*]
Zeta Alpha
`{lastname}@zeta-alpha.com`

Abstract

To provide AI researchers with modern tools for dealing with the explosive growth of the research literature in their field, we introduce a new platform, AI Research Navigator, that combines classical keyword search with neural retrieval to discover and organize relevant literature. The system provides search at multiple levels of textual granularity, from sentences to aggregations across documents, both in natural language and through navigation in a domain specific Knowledge Graph. We give an overview of the overall architecture of the system and of the components for document analysis, question answering, search, analytics, expert search, and recommendations.

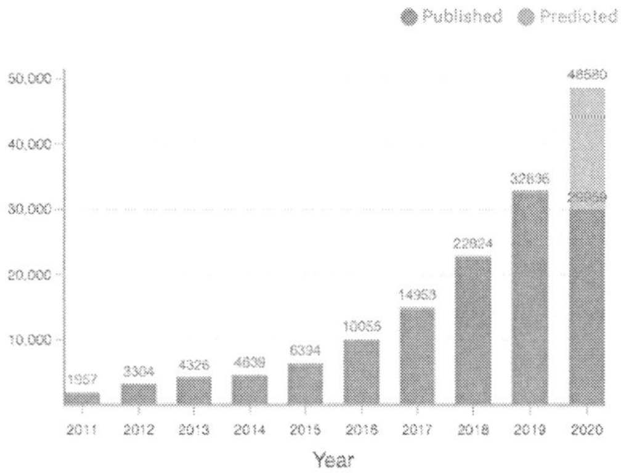

1   Introduction

The growth of publications in AI has been explosive in recent years. A big portion of this growth is happening on platforms outside of traditional publishing venues, for instance arXiv e-print archive (see Figure 1) and blogs. Although this encourages broad access to AI expertise and technology, it makes efficient and effective search, monitoring, and discovery in the AI field increasingly difficult. Most general-purpose academic search engines lack a specialization on AI content and practical know-how, because they focus on classical bibliographic information across all scientific disciplines. At the same time, academic search engines often do not make use of the latest AI technologies in search, as well as natural language processing (NLP) and insights capabilities. The main reason that limits them is the need to operate at a much larger scale and cover a large amount of knowledge.

Recent developments in various NLP tasks are showing fast progress towards an almost human level of language understanding (Devlin et al.,

Figure 1: Growth of AI related documents on arXiv.

2019; Brown et al., 2020). Applying these new technologies to the processing of research and engineering literature bears the promise of accelerating scientific discovery. In addition, providing efficient tools to automate some of the drudgery of human scholarly work by machine understanding of scientific knowledge is extremely valuable. Similar directions are being explored in recent studies (Ammar et al., 2018; Kardas et al., 2020; Zhao and Lee, 2020).

Our system, AI Research Navigator[†], aims to help AI researchers with a simple-to-use semantic search for documents (§4.1), the answering of detailed factual questions (§4.3), the generation of insights via visual analytics (§4.4), combined with recommendations to filter the constant flood of new information in their field (§4.5). These technologies are combined in the platform with both project and task-oriented tools to support a more effective and efficient organization of a researcher's work on multiple projects and topics (§5). This paper presents a short outline of the system.

---

[*]All authors contributed equally.

[†]`search.zeta-alpha.com`

Proceedings of the First Workshop on Scholarly Document Processing, pages 207–213
Online, November 19, 2020. ©2020 Association for Computational Linguistics
https://doi.org/10.18653/v1/P17

2   Document Analysis

A key ingredient to an AI insights platform is the content available to users. We ingest, process, and store documents from a variety of sources, aiming to get broad coverage, as well as detailed views on theoretical and applied AI. At the moment our platform contains approximately 140 thousand scientific papers, collected from `arXiv.org`[*] and `OpenReview.net`, and about 24 thousand posts from data science blogs. Our goal for the near future is to expand this set of sources to include different types of content (e.g., source code, news, tweets). We ingest new content from our sources on a daily basis, offering our users the latest insights. Newly ingested or updated content is fed to our back-end storage system (Section 3) via a distributed processing pipeline that takes the documents through a number of processing and information extraction steps and generates embeddings that capture the intent and meaning of the text. We also extract images from each document to serve as an illustration for the paper in the search engine. We manage the state of each document, as it traverses the pipeline, with a messaging queue platform (Apache Pulsar). This allows us to scale our processing throughput, while keeping certain processing guarantees.

2.1   Parsing and Linking Documents

Scientific publications consist of sections that have varying degrees of informativeness. As an example, the bibliography of a paper is interesting for the citation graph, but does not contain actual new content. In order to process and index only relevant and informative sections, we parse the document structure and extract candidate citation records using ParsCit (Councill et al., 2008). We then sanitize these candidates using a set of heuristics, and link them to our Knowledge Graph (KG, Section 3) using fast approximate string matching.

We make use of domain-specific concepts and their relations to improve the effectiveness of components like Question Answering (QA, Section 4.3), KG population, analytics processing (Section 4.4), and semantic search (Section 4.1). We train a statistical named entity recognizer (NER) using a small manually curated seed set of around a thousand AI related concepts, and run this NER on

every document that we process. We then link the recognized concepts to concepts in our KG using a weighted combination of string and contextual embedding similarity. Finally, those entities that were not linked because they fell below a similarity threshold are considered as new candidates to further populate the KG. Figure 2 shows the domain-specific concept types that are currently in our KG.

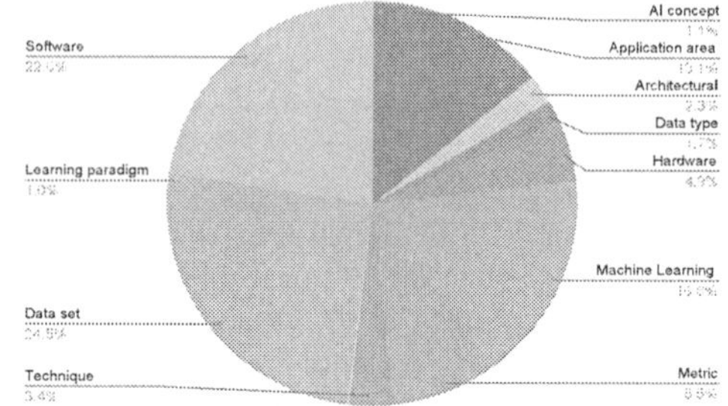

Figure 2: Distribution of KG concept types.

3   Storage Systems

To provide access to the information we obtained from our processing pipeline, we currently store our information in three core systems.

Knowledge Graph.   We store people, content, and concepts in a knowledge graph (stored in Dgraph). The node identifiers are used in the search frontend for navigating content and building queries.

Search Index.   For fast access to documents, we use an open-source search engine (Elasticsearch) in combination with HNSW (Malkov and Yashunin, 2016) for nearest neighbor search. We use three separate indices, one for sentences (31M), one for chunks (approx. 10 consecutive sentences) (4.2M), and one for full documents (160K) and citation records (740K).

Document Representations.   As a result of each processing step, we store new document representations. Most representations are in the form of standoff annotations, linking labels (e.g., a concept ID or vector) to a particular span of characters in the source document.

4   Accessing Information

Processing and storing information is only useful when we can provide meaningful access to it. Our

---

[*]We include all papers from the following AI related categories: cs.AI, cs.LG, cs.CV, cs.IR, CS.NE, cs.CL, and stat.ML.

platform allows information access in a variety of ways. In this section, we discuss content (§4.1) and expert (§4.2) search, QA system (§4.3), analytics component (§4.4), and recommendations system (§4.5).

4.1 Content Search

One of the main methods to access information on our platform is search. We currently support traditional keyword-based search and vector-based (nearest neighbor) search. Both search systems offer valuable information. While keyword-based search is useful in finding documents directly related to the query, vector-based search offers a range of query interpretations and more diversity.

Keyword-based search. Our keyword-based search functionality scores documents for a given user query based on several heuristics. (1) We borrow from Metzler and Croft (2005) the notion of sequential dependencies between query terms, construct term n-grams from the user query, and treat each n-gram as a phrase query. (2) A match of a longer n-gram is more important than the match of a shorter n-gram, which is implemented as a dynamic boost per n-gram query. (3) We combine evidence from multiple document fields (Ogilvie and Callan, 2003) and assign higher weights to metadata fields like author name, title, and abstract, while limiting the weight of the full text field. (4) We use a `dismax` query over fields to determine whether an n-gram refers to an author or to content. (5) Given the limited text length of the metadata fields, we only rely on term presence, and assign a constant field-dependent score. (6) Finally, we assume that highly cited and recent documents are more important to users.

Vector-based. In many cases, keyword searches are hard to use when exploring a new domain. To allow a more meaning-based exploration, fully neural retrieval models can be beneficial. Recent advances in neural language modeling as unsupervised pretraining have achieved significant improvements in a wide variety of NLP tasks (Devlin et al., 2019). However, incorporating them in retrieval systems presents some challenges. Using pretrained language models to jointly encode queries and documents is often not computationally feasible for large-scale retrieval. Recent studies propose various methods to benefit from large neural models. Luan et al. (2020) propose a hybrid method for combining sparse and dense representations that

outperforms baselines in open retrieval. Chang et al. (2020) use a siamese network, initialized with BERT, to encode query and document individually. They propose three self-supervised tasks that capture different aspects of query-document relations.

Inspired by these studies, we use the Sentence-BERT model proposed by Reimers and Gurevych (2019) to generate sentence embeddings for each document and, additionally, we also encode all words in context with SciBERT (Beltagy et al., 2019) embeddings. Finally, we encode sentences, chunks, and full documents into representative vectors, fine-tuned on self-supervised training tasks similar to Chang et al. (2020). In our platform, we encode the query as a vector at search time, and retrieve its N (approximate) nearest neighbor documents in the vector space. This requires the documents and the queries to be encoded in a similar way using the same embedding space. By using HSNW and loading its full graph in memory, we are able to serve nearest neighbor search results in a highly efficient manner.

4.2 Expert Search

In addition to navigating knowledge via natural language search and domain-specific topics from our KG, we also aim to improve navigation by connecting searchers to experts. For this, we follow a document-centric approach to expertise retrieval, along the lines sketched in Balog et al. (2009) and Husain et al. (2019). In the expert search component, we embed user queries and documents using the Sentence-BERT model similar to Section 4.1. This allows the system to retrieve papers that are related to the query. We then derive the experts from the sets of authors of these papers using an approach where each retrieved paper contributes an exponentially weighted vote for an author, with a factor that reduces the bias towards highly prolific authors. Our experiments, described in detail in (Berger et al., 2020) show that these modern Transformer-based contextualized embeddings outperform TF-IDF and LSI-based document representations on this task.

4.3 Question Answering

Our QA module provides an answer to either a concrete user question (e.g., *How many TPUs are needed to train BERT?*) or, alternatively, to a question related to the user's query, which we automatically generate (e.g., *What is a knowledge graph?* for the query *knowledge graph*). To distinguish

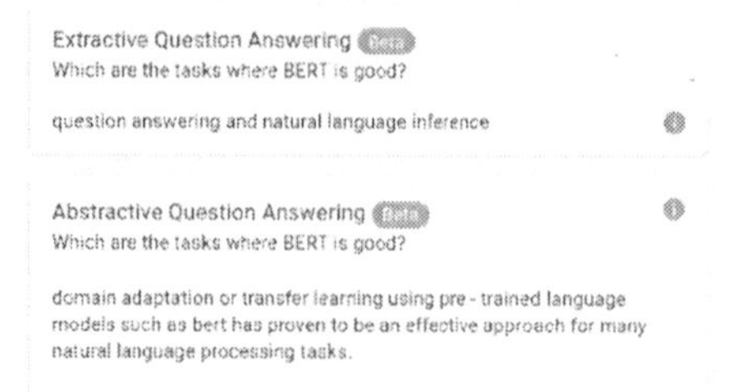

Figure 3: Extractive and abstractive QA components.

between questions and other types of queries, we use a Naive Bayes classifier trained on the NPS Chat Corpus (Forsyth et al., 2006).

We deploy two types of QA deep learning models: extractive QA and abstractive QA (see example in Figure 3). Both models take as input a set of relevant documents, and provide the user with one or more answers. Since an answer is always part of a particular context, we also present this context as a source of explanation of the answer to the user.

Extractive QA. Our extractive QA model is built with an existing BERT-based question answering model from the DeepPavlov library (Burtsev et al., 2018). The model takes as input a pair of question and context and rate their relatedness. At query time, we chunk the input documents and send multiple question-context pairs to the model. We obtain the best answer by filtering the candidates according to the confidence of the model.

Abstractive QA. For the abstractive answers we use a model based on the approach proposed in Nishida et al. (2019), trained on the MS-MARCO data set (Bajaj et al., 2016). Our model and its evaluation in the AI domain are described in detail in Tsiamas (2020). Since this architecture has its own neural retrieval component, at query time the model has access to the question and all input documents. Unlike extractive QA, this model is also capable of answering yes/no questions.

The two QA models complement each other in the types of answers they provide. Although these systems are still experimental (approximately 70% of answers to a benchmark set of in-domain questions were relevant), together with sentence and paragraph retrieval they show potential for discovering interesting information that goes beyond what surface-level single-document-based systems provide.

4.4 Analytics

Rather than reviewing a long list of documents or reading a short answer in response to a query, sometimes users can get to an insight faster by observing a tabular, a summary, or a graph overview over the entire set of relevant documents.

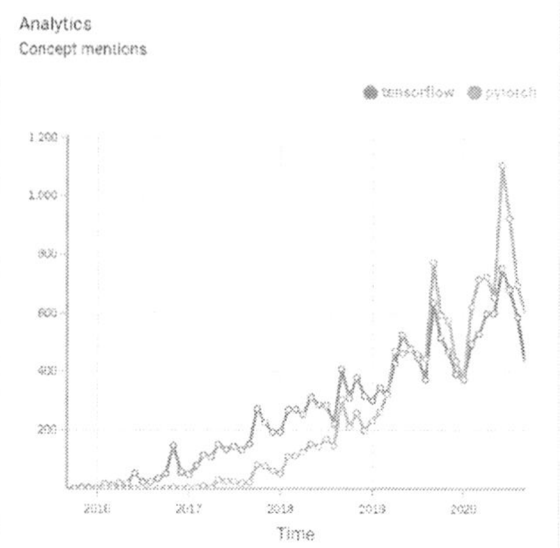

Figure 4: Contrastive popularity analytics.

Our analytics module aims to give users this quick and easy-to-grasp overview over a result set when a query sufficiently matches some pre-defined analytics query templates. For instance, when we detect AI concepts from the KG in a query, or a reference to an abstract concept (e.g., *"Which datasets are used for image classification?"*), we show the contrastive popularity plots for the specific concepts as identified in documents using the NER and linker module. Figure 4 provides an example of a contrastive popularity graph. The graphs provide a global overview and are also clickable so the users can use them to quickly identify patterns and discover specific papers relevant to their interests.

4.5 Recommendations

With the amount of new information available on a daily basis, a recommender system is inevitable to filter and keep track of relevant publications. Users of our platform receive recommendations in notification emails and in the recommendations view (Figure 5).

The relevance of a publication can be decomposed into several factors. We implemented a modular system architecture which allows us to weigh relevance factors on a per-user basis, and to add, remove, modify, and evaluate modules individually. Each module generates recommendations

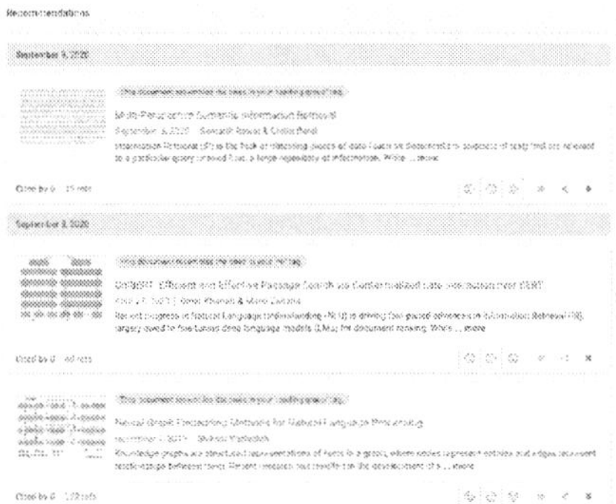

Figure 5: Recommendations on our platform.

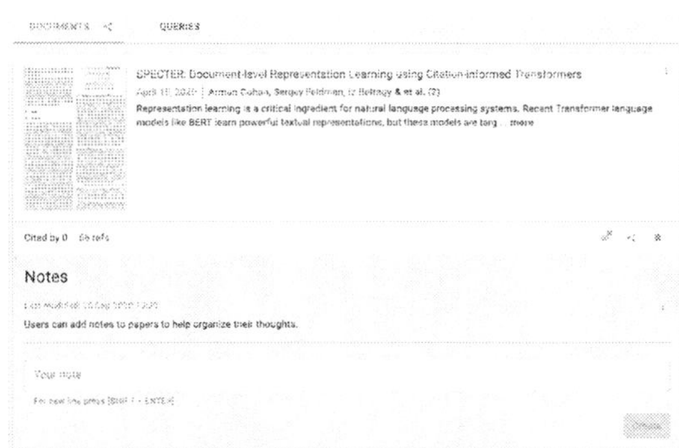

Figure 6: Adding tags and notes to a document.

with (normalized) scores, which are aggregated by the core recommender system, allowing for both global and personalized weights for each module.

Our recommendation architecture is based on hybrid recommender systems (Gomez-Uribe and Hunt, 2016), combining content-based and collaborative filtering. However, since virtually all recommendations are of new papers, we suffer from the cold-start problem and we mostly rely on content-based recommendations. The content-based module generates recommendations based on user-tagged documents: when a user tags a document, it triggers an initial search for related documents. From this point on, recommendations are only generated from the most recent documents.

Our current basic content-based modules are based on similarity metrics derived from our document representations, as described in section 4.1, with score normalization being provided by leave-one-out tuning on the set of documents in a tag.

Apart from these content-based similarity recommendations, we are also experimenting with additional modules that provide similarity scores. **Citation-based** recommendations are based on (indirect) citations to documents stored by the user. **Author-based** recommendations are (co-)authored by authors which are frequently tagged by a user. **Popularity** recommendations are globally "popular" documents, for instance based on the number of views, citation counts, or tag counts.

5 Productivity Tools

Discovering relevant information in an effective way is key to researchers, knowledge workers, and decision makers. Even though an AI-enabled platform like the one described in this paper can be helpful for this purpose, it is only the first step in researching a topic. Organizing and accessing this information is a necessary feature. Users of our platform are also supported to organize information and knowledge without having to rely on external tools for reading lists and notes. Having found a relevant piece of information in our system, users can save this into their own specific project and topic tags. They can also directly write their notes on the papers and projects they are working on in the tool. Tags serve to organize lists of documents, as well as the queries used, and notes taken while working on a project (see Figure 6). The tagging system can also be used to track the status and priority of work. Tag-based lists can easily be shared with others within the platform, on social media, and exported into other tools. As described above, these tags are also the starting point that allows users to be alerted about new results relevant to their interests.

6 Discussion and Next Steps

Having introduced a new platform to discover and organize knowledge for AI researchers, we foresee considerable future research to reach real machine understanding of scientific literature, such as extraction of complex entity relations and more advanced use of neural embeddings to reduce the dependency on manual KG curation. We leverage a mix of state-of-the-art AI components to give researchers transparent access to a body of knowledge from a large volume of heterogeneous and non-reviewed content. As a result, it raises the concern of dealing with fairness, factuality, conflicting opinions, and out-of-date information, which requires deeper investigation. Finally, we are interested to further explore how the productivity tools in our platform can contribute to better collaboration in teams and improving knowledge sharing and discovery.

211

Acknowledgements

We would like to acknowledge the joint effort from Zeta Alpha's team including Shamil Mammadov and Victor Zuanazzi to make this work possible.

References

Waleed Ammar, Dirk Groeneveld, Chandra Bhagavatula, Iz Beltagy, Miles Crawford, Doug Downey, Jason Dunkelberger, Ahmed Elgohary, Sergey Feldman, Vu Ha, et al. 2018. Construction of the literature graph in semantic scholar. *arXiv preprint arXiv:1805.02262.*

Payal Bajaj, Daniel Campos, Nick Craswell, Li Deng, Jianfeng Gao, Xiaodong Liu, Rangan Majumder, Andrew McNamara, Bhaskar Mitra, Tri Nguyen, Mir Rosenberg, Xia Song, Alina Stoica, Saurabh Tiwary, and Tong Wang. 2016. Ms marco: A human generated machine reading comprehension dataset.

Krisztian Balog, Leif Azzopardi, and Maarten de Rijke. 2009. A language modeling framework for expert finding. *Information Processing and Management, 45(1)*, page 1–19.

Iz Beltagy, Kyle Lo, and Arman Cohan. 2019. SciBERT: A pretrained language model for scientific text. In *Proceedings of the 2019 Conference on Empirical Methods in Natural Language Processing and the 9th International Joint Conference on Natural Language Processing (EMNLP-IJCNLP)*, pages 3615–3620, Hong Kong, China. Association for Computational Linguistics.

Mark Berger, Jakub Zavrel, and Paul Groth. 2020. Effective distributed representations for academic expert search. In *First Workshop on Scholarly Document Processing*.

Tom B. Brown, Benjamin Mann, Nick Ryder, Melanie Subbiah, Jared Kaplan, Prafulla Dhariwal, Arvind Neelakantan, Pranav Shyam, Girish Sastry, Amanda Askell, Sandhini Agarwal, Ariel Herbert-Voss, Gretchen Krueger, Tom Henighan, Rewon Child, Aditya Ramesh, Daniel M. Ziegler, Jeffrey Wu, Clemens Winter, Christopher Hesse, Mark Chen, Eric Sigler, Mateusz Litwin, Scott Gray, Benjamin Chess, Jack Clark, Christopher Berner, Sam McCandlish, Alec Radford, Ilya Sutskever, and Dario Amodei. 2020. Language models are few-shot learners. *arXiv preprint arXiv:2005.14165.*

Mikhail Burtsev, Alexander Seliverstov, Rafael Airapetyan, Mikhail Arkhipov, Dilyara Baymurzina, Nickolay Bushkov, Olga Gureenkova, Taras Khakhulin, Yuri Kuratov, Denis Kuznetsov, Alexey Litinsky, Varvara Logacheva, Alexey Lymar, Valentin Malykh, Maxim Petrov, Vadim Polulyakh, Leonid Pugachev, Alexey Sorokin, Maria Vikhreva, and Marat Zaynutdinov. 2018. DeepPavlov: Opensource library for dialogue systems. In *Proceedings of ACL 2018, System Demonstrations*, pages 122–127, Melbourne, Australia. Association for Computational Linguistics.

Wei-Cheng Chang, Felix X. Yu, Yin-Wen Chang, Yiming Yang, and Sanjiv Kumar. 2020. Pre-training tasks for embedding-based large-scale retrieval. In *International Conference on Learning Representations*.

Isaac Councill, C. Lee Giles, and Min-Yen Kan. 2008. ParsCit: an open-source CRF reference string parsing package. In *Proceedings of the Sixth International Conference on Language Resources and Evaluation (LREC'08)*, Marrakech, Morocco. European Language Resources Association (ELRA).

Jacob Devlin, Ming-Wei Chang, Kenton Lee, and Kristina Toutanova. 2019. BERT: Pre-training of deep bidirectional transformers for language understanding. In *Proceedings of the 2019 Conference of the North American Chapter of the Association for Computational Linguistics: Human Language Technologies, Volume 1 (Long and Short Papers)*, pages 4171–4186, Minneapolis, Minnesota. Association for Computational Linguistics.

Eric Forsyth, Jane Lin, and Craig Martell. 2006. The NPS Chat Corpus. Data retrieved from Linguistic Data Consortium, `https://catalog.ldc.upenn.edu/LDC2010T05`.

Carlos A. Gomez-Uribe and Neil Hunt. 2016. The Netflix Recommender System: Algorithms, Business Value, and Innovation. *ACM Trans. Manage. Inf. Syst.*, 6(4):1–19.

Omayma Husain, Naomie Salim, Rose Alinda Alias, Samah Abdelsalam, and Alzubair Hassan. 2019. Expert finding systems: A systematic review. *Applied Sciences (Switzerland)*, 9(20):1–32.

Marcin Kardas, Piotr Czapla, Pontus Stenetorp, Sebastian Ruder, Sebastian Riedel, Ross Taylor, and Robert Stojnic. 2020. Axcell: Automatic extraction of results from machine learning papers. In *2004.14356*.

Yi Luan, Jacob Eisenstein, Kristina Toutanova, and Michael Collins. 2020. Sparse, dense, and attentional representations for text retrieval.

Yury A. Malkov and D. A. Yashunin. 2016. Efficient and robust approximate nearest neighbor search using Hierarchical Navigable Small World graphs. *CoRR*, abs/1603.09320.

Donald Metzler and W. Bruce Croft. 2005. A Markov Random Field Model for Term Dependencies. In *Proceedings of the 28th Annual International ACM SIGIR Conference on Research and Development in Information Retrieval*, page 472–479. ACM.

Kyosuke Nishida, Itsumi Saito, Kosuke Nishida, Kazutoshi Shinoda, Atsushi Otsuka, Hisako Asano, and Junji Tomita. 2019. Multi-style generative reading comprehension.

Paul Ogilvie and Jamie Callan. 2003. Combining Document Representations for Known-Item Search. In *Proceedings of the 26th Annual International ACM SIGIR Conference on Research and Development in Information Retrieval*, page 143–150. ACM.

Nils Reimers and Iryna Gurevych. 2019. Sentence-BERT: Sentence embeddings using Siamese BERT-networks. In *Proceedings of the 2019 Conference on Empirical Methods in Natural Language Processing and the 9th International Joint Conference on Natural Language Processing (EMNLP-IJCNLP)*, pages 3982–3992, Hong Kong, China. Association for Computational Linguistics.

Ioannis Tsiamas. 2020. Complex question answering by pairwise passage ranking and answer style transfer. In *Masters Thesis, University of Amsterdam*.

Tiancheng Zhao and Kyusong Lee. 2020. Talk to papers: Bringing neural question answering to academic search. In *Proceedings of the 58th Annual Meeting of the Association for Computational Linguistics: System Demonstrations*, pages 30–36, Online. Association for Computational Linguistics.

Overview and Insights from the Shared Tasks at Scholarly Document Processing 2020: CL-SciSumm, LaySumm and LongSumm

Muthu Kumar Chandrasekaran
Amazon USA
cmkumar087@gmail.com

Guy Feigenblat
IBM Research AI
guyf@il.ibm.com

Eduard Hovy
Carnegie Mellon University
hovy@cmu.edu

Abhilasha Ravichander
Carnegie Mellon University
aravicha@cs.cmu.edu

Michal Shmueli-Scheuer
IBM Research AI
shmueli@il.ibm.com

Anita de Waard
Elsevier
a.dewaard@elsevier.com

Abstract

We present the results of three Shared Tasks held at the Scholarly Document Processing Workshop at EMNLP2020: CL-SciSumm, LaySumm and LongSumm. We report on each of the tasks, which received 18 submissions in total, with some submissions addressing two or three of the tasks. In summary, the quality and quantity of the submissions show that there is ample interest in scholarly document summarization, and the state of the art in this domain is at a midway point between being an impossible task and one that is fully resolved.

1 Introduction

Scientific documents constitute a rich field for different tasks such as Reference String Parsing, Citation Intent Classification, Summarization and more. The constantly increasing number of scientific publications raises additional issues such as making these publications accessible to non-expert readers, or, on the other hand, to experts who are interested in a deeper understanding of the paper without reading a paper in full.

For this year's Scholarly Document Processing workshop (Chandrasekaran et al., 2020) at EMNLP 2020, we proposed three tasks: *CL-SciSumm, LaySumm* and *LongSumm* to improve the state of the art for different aspects of scientific document summarization.

The *CL-SciSumm* task was introduced in 2014 and aims to explore the summarization of scientific research in the domain of computational linguistics research. It encourages the incorporation of new kinds of information in automatic scientific paper summarization, such as the facets of research information being summarized in the research paper. CL-SciSumm also encourages the use of citing mini-summaries written in other papers, by other scholars, when they refer to the paper.

LaySumm (Lay Summarization) addresses the issue of making research results available to a larger audience by automatically generating 'Lay Summaries', or summaries that explain the science contained within the paper in laymen's terms.

Finally, the *LongSumm* (Long Scientific Document Summarization) task focuses on generating long summaries of scientific text. It is fundamentally different than generating short summaries that mostly aim at teasing the reader. The LongSumm task strives to learn how to cover the salient information conveyed in a given scientific document, taking into account the characteristics and the structure of the text. The motivation for LongSumm was first demonstrated by the IBM Science Summarizer system, (Erera et al., 2019) that retrieves and creates long summaries of scientific documents[1]. While Erera et al. (2019) studied some use-cases and proposed a summarization approach with some human evaluation, the authors stressed the need of a large dataset that will unleash the research in this domain. *LongSumm* aims at filling this gap by providing large dataset of long summaries which are based on blogs written by Machine Learning and NLP experts.

In this paper we present the tasks, datasets, description of the participating systems, and provide their results and insights from shared tasks.

2 CL-SciSumm

2.1 Overview

The CL-SciSumm Shared Task was launched in 2014 as a pilot task aimed at bringing together the summarization community to address challenges in scientific communication summarization. Over time, the Shared Task has spurred the creation

---

[1] https://ibm.biz/sciencesum

Proceedings of the First Workshop on Scholarly Document Processing, pages 214–224
Online, November 19, 2020. ©2020 Association for Computational Linguistics
https://doi.org/10.18653/v1/P17

of new resources (e.g., (Yasunaga et al., 2019)), tools and evaluation frameworks. As a consequence of this wide interest, CL-SciSumm 2020 is jointly organised with the inaugural editions of two other Scientific Summarization shared tasks, all of which were held as part of SDP 2020 workshop at EMNLP[2]) (Chandrasekaran et al., 2020)

A pilot CL-SciSumm task was conducted at TAC 2014, as part of the larger BioMedSumm Task[3]. In 2016, a second CL-Scisumm Shared Task (Jaidka et al., 2018) was held as part of the Joint Workshop on Bibliometric-enhanced Information Retrieval and Natural Language Processing for Digital Libraries (BIRNDL) workshop at the Joint Conference on Digital Libraries (JCDL 2016). From 2017 (Jaidka et al., 2017, 2019) through 2019 (Chandrasekaran et al., 2019) CL-SciSumm was colocated with BIRNDL at the annual ACM Conference on Research and Development in Information Retrieval (ACM SIGIR 2017–2019).

In this section we provide the results and insights from CL-SciSumm 2020.

2.1.1 Corpus

We built the CL-SciSumm corpus by randomly sampling research papers (Reference papers, RPs) from the ACL Anthology corpus and then downloading the citing papers (CPs) for those which had at least ten citations. The prepared dataset then comprised annotated citing sentences for a research paper, mapped to the sentences in the RP which they referenced. Summaries of the RP were also included.

The CL-SciSumm 2020 corpus consisted of 40 annotated RPs and their CPs. These are the same as described in our overview paper in CL-SciSumm 2019 (Chandrasekaran et al., 2019) and 2018. The test set was blind. We reused the blind test we used from CL-SciSumm 2018 and 2019 since we want to have a comparable evaluation CL-SciSumm 2020 systems. After 3 iterations, we now release the gold labels for the 2018 test-set.

For details of the general procedure followed to construct the CL-SciSumm corpus, and changes made to the procedure in CL-SciSumm-2016, please see (Jaidka et al., 2018). In 2017, we made revisions to the corpus to remove citances from passing citations. These are described in (Jaidka et al., 2017).

[2] https://2020.emnlp.org/
[3] http://www.nist.gov/tac/2014

Annotation. Given each RP and its associated CPs, the annotation group was instructed to find citations to the RP in each CP. Specifically, the citation text, citation marker, reference text, and discourse facet were identified for each citation of the RP found in the CP. The corpus has 40 annotated RPs, exclusive of 1000 auto-annotated RPs added in CL-SciSumm 2019. For CL-SciSumm-20 we encourage participants to use out-of-domain data (i.e., scientific document corpora from papers outside of the ACL anthology corpora; e.g., BIGPATENT (Sharma et al., 2019)) to bootstrap training using transfer learning. From 2019 onward, Task 2, training data (summaries) has been augmented with the SciSummNet corpus (Yasunaga et al., 2019).

2.1.2 Task

CL-SciSumm defined two serially dependent tasks that participants could attempt, given a canonical training and testing set of papers.

Given: A topic consists of a Reference Paper (RP) and ten or more Citing Papers (CPs) that all contain citations to the RP. In each CP, the text spans (i.e., citances) have been identified that pertain to a particular citation to the RP. Additionally, the dataset provides three types of summaries for each RP:
- the abstract, written by the authors of the research paper.
- the community summary, collated from the reference spans of its citances.
- a human-written summary, written by the annotators of the CL-SciSumm annotation effort.

Task 1A: For each citance, identify the spans of text (cited text spans) in the RP that most accurately reflect the citance. These are of the granularity of a sentence fragment, a full sentence, or several consecutive sentences (no more than 5).

Task 1B: For each cited text span, identify what facet of the paper it belongs to, from a predefined set of facets.

Task 2: Finally, generate a structured summary of the RP from the cited text spans of the RP. The length of the summary should not exceed 250 words. This was an optional bonus task.

2.1.3 Evaluation

An automatic evaluation script was used to measure system performance for **Task 1A**, in terms of the sentence ID overlaps between the sentences identified in system output, versus the gold standard created by human annotators. The raw number of overlapping sentences were used to calculate the precision, recall and F_1 score for each system. We followed the approach in most SemEval tasks in reporting the overall system performance as its micro-averaged performance over all topics in the blind test set.

Additionally, we calculated lexical overlaps in terms of the ROUGE-2 scores (Lin, 2004) between the system output and the human annotated gold standard reference spans.

We have been reporting ROUGE scoring since CL-SciSumm 17, for Tasks 1a and Task 2.

Task 1B was evaluated as a proportion of the correctly classified discourse facets by the system, contingent on the expected response of Task 1A. As it is a multi-label classification, this task was also scored based on the precision, recall and F_1 scores.

Task 2 was optional, and also evaluated using the ROUGE–2 between the system output and three types of gold standard summaries of the research paper: the reference paper's abstract, a community summary, and a human summary.

We provisioned the evaluation scripts and gold-test-set CL-SciSumm Github repository[4]. For transparency we published all the system runs submitted by the participants. The participants then ran the evaluation and reported the results back to us. We collate and publish these as the CL-SciSumm'20 official result.

2.2 Systems Overview

Following teams submitted systems for evaluation for Task 1a and 1b. Their systems are described in their cited systems papers: NJUST (Zhang et al., 2020), CIST (Li et al., 2020), AUTH (Gidiotis et al., 2020), CiteQA (Umapathy et al., 2020), IITBH-IITP (Reddy et al., 2020), IITP-AI-NLP-ML (Mishra et al., 2020), MLU (Huang and Krylova, 2020), MLUHW (Boltze et al., 2020), UniHD (Aumiller et al., 2020), NLP-PINGAN-TECH (Chai et al., 2020)

Following teams submitted systems for evaluation on Task 2 also which is an optional bonus task: AUTH (Gidiotis et al., 2020), CIST (Li et al., 2020), IITBH-IITP (Reddy et al., 2020), IITP-AI-NLP-ML (Mishra et al., 2020)

Official evaluation results on these systems is presented in the next section.

---

[4] github.com/WING-NUS/scisumm-corpus

2.3 Results

Out of the 11 participants systems, 8 were able complete the final evaluation correctly. We have excluded the rest 3 them from listing in Tables 1 and 2 in the results on the blind test set. However, their systems and results on the development set are published in their respective system papers. We allows teams to submit an unlimited number of runs since this is an offline evaluation with a blind test set. However, we tabulate only the results from the top 5 runs when a large of runs are submitted.

Task 1a. (Table 1)NLP-PINGAN-TECH(Chai et al., 2020) achieve the best result on Task 1a when evaluated using sentence overlaps and ngram overlaps using ROUGE SU4. All top 5 of their runs outperforms other systems. Runs from UniHD's system are a close second.

Task 1b. (Table 2) We note that the runs that perform the best on Task1a are not the same that top performance in Task 1b though Task 1b is evaluated conditioned on Task 1a. CIST (Li et al., 2020)'s systems do consistently well on this task. We note that UniHD's systems, intersection_2_field and intersection_3_field do well on both Task 1a and 1b though they do not top the rankings on either task.

Task 2. Four of the eleven teams also participated in the bonus summarization task. On the summarization task AUTH (Gidiotis et al., 2020) does well when evaluated against both abstract and human written summaries. They score 0.41 on ROUGE-2 on Abstracts which is comparable to the state-of-the-art of general summarization. However, their system does not do well on community summaries, which is dependant on Task 1a. IITBH-IITP (Reddy et al., 2020)'s systems consistently perform better than the rest on community summaries. CIST (Li et al., 2020)'s systems are second and are comparable to the top performing system in this category. Notably CIST's runs do well on both human and community summaries and second only to AUTH on abstracts. This type of systems are the intended goal of the CL-SciSumm shared task.

3 LaySumm

3.1 Task Overview

To improve public understanding of science, researchers are increasingly asked by funders and publishers to outline the scope of their research, described in scientific research articles, by writing a summary for a lay audience. We call this a

System	Task 1A: Sentence Overlap (F_1)	Task 1A: ROUGE-SU4 F_1	System	Task 1B (F_1)
NLP_PINGAN_TECH sembert_scibert_all_top2	**0.17**	**0.15**	CIST run40	**0.41**
NLP_PINGAN_TECH run_scibert_unused_token_top2	**0.17**	**0.15**	CIST run42	**0.41**
NLP_PINGAN_TECH sembert_sembert_scibert_all_top3	0.17	0.11	CIST run41	**0.41**
NLP_PINGAN_TECH run_scibert_all_top3	0.17	0.10	CIST run61	0.39
NLP_PINGAN_TECH run_scibert_all_top2	0.17	0.14	CIST run62	0.39
uniHD intersection_2_field	0.16	0.11	CMU run26	0.31
uniHD intersection_3_field	0.15	0.08	CMU run27	0.31
CMU run110	0.13	0.08	CMU run110	0.30
CMU run12	0.13	0.09	uniHD intersection_3_field	0.29
CMU run13	0.13	0.09	uniHD intersection_2_field	0.29
CMU run32, 33	0.13	0.11	CMU run24, 25	0.29
uniHD negative_only_2_field	0.12	0.06	NLP_PINGAN_TECH run_sembert_scibert_all_top3	0.23
uniHD with_truth_2_field	0.12	0.06	NLP_PINGAN TECH run_scibert_all_top3	0.23
uniHD negative_only_3_field	0.12	0.06	IITBH-IITP variantU	0.23
CIST runs 22-42	0.11	0.05	NLP_PINGAN TECH run_scibert_2_top3	0.21
uniHD with_truth_3_field	0.11	0.05	NLP_PINGAN TECH run_sembert_top3	0.21
CIST runs 43-63	0.11	0.05	NLP_PINGAN TECH run_only_scibert_sp_token_top3	0.21
AUTH run 2	0.10	0.09	AUTH run 1	0.17
IITBH-IITP variantU	0.08	0.03	IITBH-IITP variantF	0.16
IITBH-IITP variantF	0.06	0.03	IITBH-IITP variantA	0.13
CIST runs 1-21	0.05	0.10	IITBH-IITP variantE	0.08
CIST runs 67-72	0.05	0.09	IITBH-IITP variantS	0.06
CIST runs 64-66,73-84	0.05	0.09	IITP-AI-NLP-ML	0.02
IITP-AI-NLP-ML runs 1-10	0.04	0.01	MLU Halle-Wittenberg	0.01
IITBH-IITP variantA	0.03	0.01	IITBH-IITP variantX	0.01
IITBH-IITP variantE	0.02	0.01		
IITBH-IITP variantS	0.02	0.01		
MLU Halle-Wittenberg	0.01	0.02		

Table 1: CL-SciSumm systems' performance in Task 1A and 1B, ordered by their F_1-scores for sentence overlap on Task 1A, Task 1B separately. Each system's rank by their performance on ROUGE on Task 1A is shown in parentheses.

Lay Summary: a text of about 70–100 words intended for a non-technical audience that explains, succinctly and without using technical jargon, the overall scope, goal, and potential impact expressed in a scientific paper. The Lay Summarization task provides data for and evaluates automatically-produced Lay Summaries.

3.1.1 Corpus

The corpus comprised 572 author-generated lay summaries from a multidisciplinary collection of journals in Materials Science, Archaeology, Hepatology and Artificial intelligence, together with their corresponding abstracts and full text articles, provided by Elsevier. A small sample dataset can be found on the GitHub repository[5]). A training corpus of 37 full-text papers and abstracts was made available to enable evaluation.

3.1.2 Task

The Lay Summary Task requires systems to generate a lay summary, given a full-text paper and its abstract. This summary should be representative of the content, comprehensible, and interesting to a lay audience. In addition to their results, system builders were asked to provide an automatically generated lay summary of their own system-description paper. The task was run on CodaLabs[6].

3.1.3 Evaluation

We measured summary quality using the ROUGE measure (Lin, 2004). We used the *Py-Rouge* 0.1.3 package, which is built on the ROUGE 1.5.5 toolkit with its standard parameters setting[7]. We report both Recall and F-Measure for ROUGE-1, ROUGE-2, and ROUGE-L. The evaluation results were displayed on a public leaderboard on Codalab[8]. In addition, a number of automatically

---

[5] https://github.com/WING-NUS/
scisumm-corpus/blob/master/README_
Laysumm.md#sample-dataset

[6] https://competitions.codalab.org/
competitions/25516#learn_the_details

[7] ROUGE-1.5.5.pl -a -c 95 -m -n 2 -2 4 -u -p 0.5

[8] https://competitions.codalab.org/
competitions/25516

System	Abstract	Community	Human
	R–2	R–2	R–2
AUTH run 2 2	**0.41**	0.11	**0.22 (1)**
CIST run43, 46, 49	0.21	0.24(4)	0.18(4)
52, 55, 58, 61			
CIST run22, 25, 28	0.20	0.25(3)	0.20(2)
31, 34, 37, 40			
CIST run 1, 10, 13	0.20	0.22	0.19(3)
16, 19, 4, 7			
IIT-NLP-AI-ML run 4	0.20	0.19	0.17(6)
CIST run 64, 67	0.18	0.23(6)	0.18(4)
70, 73, 76, 79, 82			
IIT-NLP-AI-ML run5	0.16	0.16	0.14
IIT-NLP-AI-ML run6	0.15	0.12	0.14
IITBH-IITP variant A2	0.15	0.14	0.15
E2, F2, S2, U2, X2			
CIST run 11,14	0.14	0.15	0.14
17, 2, 20, 5, 8			
IIT-NLP-AI-ML run2	0.14	0.16	0.12
IIT-NLP-AI-ML run10	0.14	0.16	0.13
CIST run 45, 48, 51	0.12	0.18	0.13
54, 57, 60, 63			
CIST run 24, 27	0.12	0.17	0.16
30, 33, 36, 39, 42			
IIT-NLP-AI-ML run7	0.11	0.18	0.10
IIT-NLP-AI-ML run8	0.11	0.17	0.12
IIT-NLP-AI-ML run9	0.11	0.16	0.10
IITBH-IITP variantU	0.10	**0.27(1)**	0.13
IITBH-IITP variantF	0.09	0.26(2)	0.11
IITBH-IITP variantA	0.07	0.24(4)	0.10
IITBH-IITP variantE	0.09	0.23(6)	0.11
IITBH-IITP variantS	0.13	0.19	0.14
IITBH-IITP variantX	0.06	0.17	0.09

Table 2: CL-SciSumm systems' performance for Task 2 ordered by their ROUGE–2(R–2) F_1-scores. Systems' rank by their performance on the corresponding evaluation is shown in parentheses for the top 5 scores in that category. Winning scores are bolded.

generated lay summaries underwent human evaluation by science journalists and communicators for comprehensiveness, legibility, and interest.

3.2 Systems Overview

We received eight submissions. We briefly describe the approaches taken by the participating teams:
AUTH (Gidiotis et al., 2020) – The authors use a summarization method utilizing PEGASUS (Zhang et al., 2019) to compress and rewrite the abstract of a given article to generate a lay summary. The PEGASUS model is fine-tuned to generate lay summaries, using the article abstract as input and the lay summary as the reference for training the summarization model.
Dimsum (Tiezheng Yu and Fung, 2020) - The system generates a summary by using a joint extractive and abstractive summarization approach, based on the intuition that lay summaries are grounded in sentences that occur within the scientific document. The abstractive summaries are converted to extractive labels, by selecting sentences that maximize the rouge score with the reference summary. The BART encoder (Lewis et al., 2020) is then used to make sentence representations and the model is trained with both extractive and abstractive summarization objectives.
Seungwon (Kim, 2020) - The system built by the team from Georgia Tech primarily uses the PEGASUS model (Zhang et al., 2019) to generate lay summaries, combining this with a BERT-based extractive summarization model. After generating a lay summary using PEGASUS, if the generated summary is shorter than a specified length, the extractive model is used to identify candidate sentences in the document that can be included in the summary. Sentences are only included in the summary by the extractive model if they are judged sufficiently readable, according to a sentence readability metric defined by the authors.
IIITBH-IITP (Reddy et al., 2020) - The authors use an extractive sentence classification method. They develop an unsupervised approach, selecting sentences from the document using variants of the maximum marginal relevance (MMR) metric.
Summaformers (Roy et al., 2020) - This system utilizes the BART model (Lewis et al., 2020) to generate summaries. BART is trained on the CNN/Dailymail summarization dataset (See et al., 2017) and fine-tuned on the Laysumm corpus.
IITP-AI-NLP-ML (Mishra et al., 2020) This method uses a standard encoder-decoder framework for abstractive summarization. The system is based on BERT fine-tuned on the CNN/Dailymail dataset (Liu and Lapata, 2019a), with a decoder consisting of six transformer layers.
DUCS: (no paper submitted) This system uses a two-stage pipeline. In the first phase, extractive summarization is performed, and relevant sentences are selected from the introduction, discussion and conclusion of the article. The abstract, and the extracted sentences from the introduction, discussion and conclusion are summarized using the BART model (Lewis et al., 2020), and the summaries are concatenated.

3.3 Results

Taking these metrics into account, the top 3 systems are: #1 Seungwon Kim, #2 HYTZ, and #3

Table 3: ROUGE Recall and F-Measure evaluation on LaySumm test set

System	Rouge1-F1	Rouge1-Recall	Rouge2-F1	Rouge2-Recall	RougeL-F1	RougeL-Recall
HYTZ	0.4600	0.5013	0.2070	0.2223	0.2876	0.3104
seungwonkim	0.4596	0.4810	0.2146	0.2237	0.2977	0.3105
Summaformers	0.4594	0.4911	0.1902	0.2026	0.2744	0.2923
AUTH	0.4456	0.4298	0.1936	0.1860	0.2772	0.2673
DUCS	0.4253	0.5159	0.1748	0.2102	0.2526	0.3055
IIITBH-IITP	0.4048	0.5414	0.1690	0.2253	0.2244	0.3019
Harita_ramesh_babu	0.3524	0.3865	0.1110	0.1232	0.1995	0.2188
IITP-AI-NLP-ML	0.3132	0.3705	0.0631	0.0746	0.1662	0.1973

Summaformers. Next to the formal ROUGE scores, a subset of documents was evaluated by a team of domain experts. Gratifyingly, this human assessment confirmed this order of the results. Overall, the majority of submitted Lay Summaries was easy to read, though in some cases there were odd errors (e.g., inserted ellipses). The winning systems all produced legible and accessible summaries.

Four of the papers complied with the request that the systems generate a Lay Summary of their own paper, using their own tools. This helps both to explain the concept of a Lay Summary and offers insights into the output of the software; hopefully it also helps explain this work to a non-specialised audience. For examples, please see the Lay Summary Submissions elsewhere in this Anthology.

3.4 Discussion

A comparison of Lay Summaries against typical paper abstracts (Technical Summaries) reveals several systematic differences. These include:

- Lexical specialization: This category includes both domain-based terminological difference (e.g., "renal" vs "kidney" failure, "high-octane" vs "powerful" gasoline) and conceptual specificity / specialization (e.g., "bubblesort" vs "sorting", "kNN" vs "clustering"). Used at even the same level of specificity, the expert uses domain-specialist words. It is well known that experts' Basic Level categories (in the sense of Prototype Theory) (Rosch, 1973) is one level lower/more specific than normal speakers' categories.
- Syntactic complexity: This includes more-complex descriptive NPs vs simpler NPs across more sentences, and longer and deeper sentence parse trees vs shorter and more straightforward ones. Generally an expert author's abstract has no direct verb forms and no personal pronouns, while the lay summary has nothing but. Direct

quotes typically make a lay summary read like journalism.
- Epistemic complexity: Expert text includes more (and more-precise) hedging vs simper, more absolutist claims, and fewer evaluative interjections ("surprising", "lovely", "elegant").
- Content detail: Generally a lay content is more general, wider-ranging, and includes a historically longer but much shallower historical overview compared to the Related Work section of an expert text. Typically there are more examples in the lay text and the examples employ out-of-domain scenarios/entities.
- Author presence: In lay summaries there is generally more explicit 'author foregrounding', leading to the personalization of the knowledge source. The opposite in expert summaries has been argued as suggesting there statement of known facts, a tactic that scientists often use.

As described in the previous section, only a few systems implemented some of these strategies explicitly. Generally the hope was that the training data will allow a sufficiently powerful machine learning model to learn what to do by itself. The results do not really bear out this hope. We believe there is some very interesting and fruitful analysis to be done in order to create machine-learning models that are sufficiently rich to produce truly interesting and readable Lay Summaries.

4 LongSumm

4.1 Task Overview

Existing work on scientific document summarization focuses on generating short, abstract-like summaries. While this might be appropriate when summarizing news articles, such summaries cannot cover all the salient information conveyed in a scientific paper. Writing longer summaries requires deep understanding and domain expertise, as can be found in research blogs. To address this point, the LongSumm task opted to leverage blog posts created by researchers in the NLP and Machine learning communities that summarize scientific articles and use these posts as reference summaries (Boni et al., 2020). The task is, given a scientific document, generate a 600 words summary.

4.1.1 Corpus

The corpus for this task includes a training set that consists of 1705 extractive summaries, and 531 abstractive summaries of NLP and Machine Learning scientific papers. The extractive summaries are based on video talks from associated conferences (Lev et al., 2019), and contain up to 30 sentences. The abstractive summaries are blog posts created by NLP and ML researchers, with length varied between 100-1500 words, an average of 779 (±460) words, and an average of 31 (±18) sentences in a summary. In addition, we created a (blind) test set of 22 abstractive summaries for evaluating the submissions. The corpus can be found on LongSumm GitHub repository[9].

4.1.2 Evaluation

We measured summarization quality using the ROUGE measure (Lin, 2004). The evaluation script utilizes the *rouge-score*[10] python package which is designed to replicate results from the original perl package with its standard parameters. We report both Recall and F-Measure of ROUGE-1, ROUGE-2, and ROUGE-L. The evaluation was executed on a public leaderboard[11], forked from EvalAI (Yadav et al., 2019), an open-source AI challenge hosting platform. In addition, 6 randomly selected summaries are selected from the top performing systems, to undergo human evaluation. The evaluation focuses on informativeness and readability.

4.2 Systems Overview

Nine systems participated in the task, with a total of 100 submissions. We will briefly describe eight of them, that submitted a research report describing their approach.

ARTU (El-Ebshihy et al., 2020) - The system generates an extractive summary which is based on

the papers' abstract. Each sentence from the abstract becomes a query to an index that contains all papers' paragraphs. For each abstract sentence, a cluster that contains the top retrieved paragraphs is created. The final set of sentences is chosen based on the sentences LexRank value, their discourse (based on the section they belong to), and the size of the cluster.

AUTH (Gidiotis et al., 2020) - The authors propose an extractive summarization method that utilizes DANCER, a divide and conquer approach for long document summarization. DANCER (Gidiotis and Tsoumakas, 2020) helps to select key sections in the document to be summarized separately, for that each sentence in the article is classified to a section type. Then using PEGASUS based Transformer (Zhang et al., 2019) they are combined together to form an complete article summary.

CIST_BUPT (Li et al., 2020) - The system supports both an extractive and abstractive summaries using deep-learning architectures. For extractive summaries, they used RNN to compress and represent a sentence, and build a sentences relation graphs which are fed into the Graph Convolutional Network (GCN), and Graph Attention Network (GAN) to create a summary. For abstractive summaries, they used the gap-sentence method in (Zhang et al., 2015) to combine and transform all the data, and then T5 (Raffel et al., 2019), a transformer-liked pre-trained to fine-tune and generation.

GUIR (Sotudeh et al., 2020) - A summarization method that utilizes BERT summarizer (Liu and Lapata, 2019b). The idea is based on multi-task learning heuristic, in which two tasks are optimized. The first is a binary classification task, for sentence selection. The second is section prediction, in which the model predicts section labels associated with input sentences. The extractive network is then trained to optimize both tasks. The authors also propose an abstractive summarizer based on BART (Lewis et al., 2020) transformer that runs after the extractive summarizer.

IIITBH-IITP (Reddy et al., 2020) - The authors propose an extractive sentence classification method. They develop a deep learning architecture utilizing CNN to extract features, followed by Max-Pooling and flattening for sentence representation and classification.

IITP-AI-NLP-ML (Mishra et al., 2020) - An unsupervised summarization technique that is used to extract salient sentences. First, article sentences are

---

[9]https://github.com/guyfe/LongSumm
[10]https://pypi.org/project/rouge-score/
[11]https://aieval.draco.res.ibm.com/challenge/39/

clustered together using various clustering methods
(the authors considered various methods such as
K-means (Lloyd, 1982) and DBScan (Ester et al.,
1996)). Then, each cluster is ranked based on its
centrality. Finally, salient sentences are selected
from each cluster, taking into account cluster score,
until the desired length of the summary.

Monash-Summ (Ju et al., 2020)- The system, inspired by SummPip (Zhao et al., 2020), proposes
an unsupervised approach that leveraging linguistic knowledge to construct sentence graph. The
graph nodes, which represent sentences, are further
clustered. This enables the control of the summary
length. Finally, for each cluster they considered the
key phrases and discourse and created an abstractive sentence.

Summaformers (Roy et al., 2020) - To handle long
documents, each section was allocated with a budget based on its contribution in the training data.
Each section was summarized separately, using
SummaRuNNer (Nallapati et al., 2017), a neural
extractive summarizer.

4.3 Results

Table 4 reports the results of the 9 participating
systems, 8 of them submitted a research report
describing their system[12]. In order to compare
between the systems we considered an average
score of ROUGE-1, ROUGE-2, and ROUGE-L. Although some of the systems developed an abstractive variant, the highest ROUGE scores were obtained by leveraging extractive summarization techniques. The only system that reported abstrative
summarization results, in the official leaderbaord,
is *Monash-Summ*. Most of the systems except
ARTU and *IITP-AI-NLP-ML* employ supervised
learning approaches. The system that achieved the
highest ROUGE average score is *GUIR*, with their
multi-task learning heuristic. Second best is *Summaformers*, with about 3% lower ROUGE score.

In addition, we randomly selected 5 summaries
from the top-3 ranked systems, namely: *GUIR*,
Summaformers and *IIITBH-IITP*, to be evaluated
by experts. We asked them to rank the systems
w.r.t coverage, and readability. For *coverage*, we
asked to take into account how well the summary
contains important, informative information conveyed in the text. For *Readability*, we asked to
take into account fluency, coherence and grammat-

---

[12]Our analysis ignores *Wing* since they did not submit a
system report as required

ical correctness. From coverage perspective, all
experts reported that *GUIR* summaries outperform
the other systems, where the main issue with *Summaformers* and *IIITBH-IITP* is that they mainly
cover the introduction and related works sections.
From readability perspective, the experts pointed
out on several issues such as out of context formulas and reference to tables and figures, sentences
are not sorted by the paper discourse, and footnotes
that are clearly not relevant such as URLs, author's
information, etc.

4.4 Discussion

Scientific documents can be characterized as long,
structured, utilizing technical language (i.e., formulas, tables, definitions, etc.). Analyzing the
summaries and reports of the participated systems
shows that most of them considered the structure
of the document while generating summaries, by
utilizing sections and document discourse. From
a language perspective, some systems utilized language models that were pre-trained on scientific
corpora. However, we believe that more efforts
should be focused on handling mathematical definitions, formulas, tables, and the text surrounding
them. For example, it is not clear whether these
entities should be treated differently than narrative text and whether they should be considered as
atomic units that should not be compressed further.

Moreover, readability should play an important
role in algorithmic design. Due to the nature of scientific documents and LongSumm length requirement, we believe this is even more challenging
compared to traditional summarization tasks. This
should have gotten more attention by the participating systems.

Finally, it was surprising to see that most evaluated systems are extractive and not abstractive.
In the future we plan to extend this corpus, with
the hope that LongSumm will help foster further
research in this domain.

5 Conclusion

The First Scholarly Document Processing workshop (Chandrasekaran et al., 2020) comprise three
summarization tasks, that each aimed to improve
the state-of-the-art of scientific document summarization. In total, we received 18 submissions that
addressed one or more of these tasks. It was a
useful exercise to compare and contrast each of
these summarization tasks, since they allowed re-

Table 4: ROUGE F-Measure and Recall evaluation on the official LongSumm test set. In addition, for each reported result, the Methodology columns indicate whether a reported result employs a Supervised or Unsupervised summarization technique.

System	F-Measure			Recall			F-Measure average	Methodology Supervised/ Unsupervised
	R-1	R-2	R-L	R-1	R-2	R-L		
GUIR	**53.11**	16.77	20.34	**54.60**	**17.28**	**20.90**	**30.07**	S
Wing	50.58	16.62	20.50	51.16	16.75	20.66	29.23	-
Summaformers	49.38	**16.86**	**21.38**	43.90	14.98	18.98	29.21	S
IIITBH-IITP	49.03	15.74	20.46	49.84	16.00	20.80	28.41	S
AUTH	50.11	15.37	19.59	46.93	14.23	18.18	28.36	S
CIST_BUPT	48.99	15.06	20.13	49.74	15.22	20.39	28.06	S
ARTU	48.03	14.76	18.04	46.78	14.28	17.43	26.94	U
IITP-AI-NLP-ML	46.46	14.61	19.58	47.43	14.86	19.95	26.88	U
Monash-Summ	49.16	12.80	18.31	49.35	12.76	18.33	26.76	S

searchers to explore their systems in different contexts, on different corpora, and for different audiences. Overall, what this efforts has shown is that the state of the art of summarizing scientific documents is neither in its nascency, nor a fully solved problem. We are interested in expanding task-based efforts in scholarly document summarization in future workshops, and investigating how scholarly documents differ or are similar to other texts. We are interested in collaborating with others in the NLP and AI-communities to investigate to what degree new technologies can be utilized and developed, to allow for a future where some of the work of tracking the scientific literature can be supported by machines. While CL-SciSumm has run for 6 editions and with the 2020 edition now set up two standard benchmark evaluation datasets for citation based summarization intended for use by researchers to aid in scientific discovery (breadth), LongSumm and LaySumm are inaugural tasks towards building systems that to improve understanding and dissemination of papers (depth).

Acknowledgements

CL-SciSumm would like to Microsoft Research Asia who funded the development of Cl-SciSumm corpus and the shared tasks from 2016 through 2018. We also thank Vasudeva Varma and colleagues at IIIT-Hyderabad, India and University of Hyderabad for their efforts in convening and organizing our annotation workshops in 2016-17. We acknowledge the advice of Min-Yen Kan, Hoa Dang, NIST, Lucy Vanderwende and Anita de Waard from the pilot stage of this task. We would also like to thank Rahul Jha and Dragomir Radev for sharing their software. We are grateful to Kevin B. Cohen and colleagues for their support, and for sharing their annotation schema and tools which have been indispensable for all six editions of CL-SciSumm.

The LongSumm task organizers would like to thank the blog authors Shagun Sodhani, Patrick Emami, Adrian Colyer, Alexander Jung, Joseph Paul Cohen, Hugo Larochelle, Elvis Saravia and to ShortScience.org who generously allowed them to share the content as part of the LongSumm dataset.

The LaySumm task organizers thank Darin McBeath at Elsevier who compiled the test and training data and Ilaria Meliconi, Virgina Prada Lopez and Victor Croes at Elsevier, who acted as domain experts for spot checking the results.

References

Dennis Aumiller, Satya Almasian, Philip Hausner, and Michael Gertz. 2020. UniHD@CL-SciSumm20: Citation Extraction as Search. In *SDP 2020*.

Maik Boltze, Anja Fischer, Artur Jurk Georg, and Keller Lorna Ulbrich. 2020. 1A-Team / Martin-Luther University Halle-Wittenberg@CL-SciSumm20. In *SDP 2020*.

Odellia Boni, Guy Feigenblat, Doron Cohen, Haggai Roitman, and David Konopnicki. 2020. A study of human summaries of scientific articles.

Ling Chai, Guizhen Fu, and Yuan Ni. 2020. NLP-PINGAN-TECH@CLSciSumm-20. In *SDP 2020*.

M. K. Chandrasekaran, G. Feigenblat, D. Freitag, T. Ghosal, Hovy. E., Mayr. P., M. Shmueli-Scheuer, and A De Waard. 2020. Overview of the first workshop on scholarly document processing (sdp). In *Proceedings of the First Workshop on Scholarly Document Processing (SDP 2020)*.

Muthu Kumar Chandrasekaran, Michihiro Yasunaga, Dragomir Radev, Dayne Freitag, and Min-Yen Kan.

2019. Overview and results: CL-scisumm shared task 2019. *arXiv preprint arXiv:1907.09854*.

Alaa El-Ebshihy, Annisa Maulida Ningtyas, Linda Andersson, Florina Piroi, and Andreas Rauber. 2020. ARTU / TU Wien and Artificial Researcher@ LongSumm 20. In *SDP 2020*.

Shai Erera, Michal Shmueli-Scheuer, Guy Feigenblat, Ora Peled Nakash, Odellia Boni, Haggai Roitman, Doron Cohen, Bar Weiner, Yosi Mass, Or Rivlin, Guy Lev, Achiya Jerbi, Jonathan Herzig, Yufang Hou, Charles Jochim, Martin Gleize, Francesca Bonin, Francesca Bonin, and David Konopnicki. 2019. A summarization system for scientific documents. In *Proceedings of the 2019 Conference on Empirical Methods in Natural Language Processing and the 9th International Joint Conference on Natural Language Processing (EMNLP-IJCNLP): System Demonstrations*.

Martin Ester, Hans-Peter Kriegel, Jörg Sander, and Xiaowei Xu. 1996. A density-based algorithm for discovering clusters in large spatial databases with noise. In *Proceedings of the Second International Conference on Knowledge Discovery and Data Mining*, KDD'96, page 226–231. AAAI Press.

Alexios Gidiotis, Stefanos Dimitrios Stefanidis, and Grigorios Tsoumakas. 2020. AUTH@CL-SciSumm20, CL-LaySumm20, LongSumm20. In *SDP 2020*.

Alexios Gidiotis and Grigorios Tsoumakas. 2020. A divide-and-conquer approach to the summarization of academic articles. *arXiv preprint arXiv:2004.06190*.

Rong Huang and Kseniia Krylova. 2020. Team MLU@CL-SciSumm20: Methods for Computational Linguistics Scientific Citation Linkage. In *SDP 2020*.

Kokil Jaidka, Muthu Kumar Chandrasekaran, Devanshu Jain, and Min-Yen Kan. 2017. The cl-scisumm shared task 2017: Results and key insights. In *BIRNDL@ SIGIR (2)*, volume 2002, pages 1–15. CEUR.

Kokil Jaidka, Muthu Kumar Chandrasekaran, Sajal Rustagi, and Min-Yen Kan. 2018. Insights from cl-scisumm 2016: the faceted scientific document summarization shared task. *International Journal on Digital Libraries*, 19(2-3):163–171.

Kokil Jaidka, Michihiro Yasunaga, Muthu Kumar Chandrasekaran, Dragomir Radev, and Min-Yen Kan. 2019. The cl-scisumm shared task 2018: Results and key insights. *arXiv preprint arXiv:1909.00764*.

Jiaxin Ju, Ming Liu, Longxiang Gao, and Shirui Pan. 2020. Monash-Summ@LongSumm 20 SciSummPip: An Unsupervised Scientific Paper Summarization Pipeline. In *SDP 2020*.

Seungwon Kim. 2020. Using Pre-Trained Transformer for a better Lay Summarization. In *SDP 2020*.

Guy Lev, Michal Shmueli-Scheuer, Jonathan Herzig, Achiya Jerbi, and David Konopnicki. 2019. Talksumm: A dataset and scalable annotation method for scientific paper summarization based on conference talks. In *Proceedings of the 57th Conference of the Association for Computational Linguistics, ACL 2019, Florence, Italy, July 28- August 2, 2019, Volume 1: Long Papers*, pages 2125–2131.

Mike Lewis, Yinhan Liu, Naman Goyal, Marjan Ghazvininejad, Abdelrahman Mohamed, Omer Levy, Veselin Stoyanov, and Luke Zettlemoyer. 2020. BART: Denoising sequence-to-sequence pretraining for natural language generation, translation, and comprehension. In *Proceedings of the 58th Annual Meeting of the Association for Computational Linguistics*, pages 7871–7880, Online. Association for Computational Linguistics.

Lei Li, Yang Xie, Wei Liu, Yinan Liu, Yafei Jiang, Siya Qi, and Xingyuan Li. 2020. CIST@CLSciSumm-20, LongSumm 2020: Automatic Scientific Document Summarization. In *SDP 2020*.

Chin-Yew Lin. 2004. Rouge: A package for automatic evaluation of summaries. In *Text summarization branches out: Proceedings of the ACL-04 workshop*, volume 8. Barcelona, Spain.

Yang Liu and Mirella Lapata. 2019a. Text summarization with pretrained encoders. In *Proceedings of the 2019 Conference on Empirical Methods in Natural Language Processing and the 9th International Joint Conference on Natural Language Processing (EMNLP-IJCNLP)*, pages 3730–3740, Hong Kong, China. Association for Computational Linguistics.

Yang Liu and Mirella Lapata. 2019b. Text summarization with pretrained encoders. *arXiv preprint arXiv:1908.08345*.

S. P. Lloyd. 1982. Least squares quantization in pcm. *IEEE Trans. Inf. Theory*, 28:129–136.

Santosh Kumar Mishra, Kundarapu Harshavardhan, Naveen Saini, Sriparna Saha, and Pushpak Bhattacharyya. 2020. IITP-AI-NLP-ML@CLSciSumm-20, CL-LaySumm 2020, LongSumm 2020. In *SDP 2020*.

Ramesh Nallapati, Feifei Zhai, and Bowen Zhou. 2017. Summarunner: A recurrent neural network based sequence model for extractive summarization of documents. In *Proceedings of the Thirty-First AAAI Conference on Artificial Intelligence*, AAAI'17, page 3075–3081. AAAI Press.

Colin Raffel, Noam Shazeer, Adam Roberts, Katherine Lee, Sharan Narang, Michael Matena, Yanqi Zhou, Wei Li, and Peter Liu. 2019. Exploring the limits of transfer learning with a unified text-to-text transformer.

Saichethan Miriyala Reddy, Naveen Sainiand Naveen Saini, Sriparna Saha, and Pushpak Bhattacharyya. 2020. IIITBH-IITP@CL-SciSumm20, CL-LaySumm20, LongSumm20. In *SDP 2020*.

Eleanor H. Rosch. 1973. Natural categories. *Cognitive Psychology*, 4(3):328 – 350.

Sayar Ghosh Roy, Nikhil Pinnaparaju, Risubh Jain, Manish Gupta, and Vasudeva Varma. 2020. Information Retrieval and Extraction Lab, IIIT-H @ LaySumm 20, LongSumm 20. In *SDP 2020*.

Abigail See, Peter J. Liu, and Christopher D. Manning. 2017. Get to the point: Summarization with pointer-generator networks. In *Proceedings of the 55th Annual Meeting of the Association for Computational Linguistics (Volume 1: Long Papers)*, pages 1073–1083, Vancouver, Canada. Association for Computational Linguistics.

Eva Sharma, Chen Li, and Lu Wang. 2019. Bigpatent: A large-scale dataset for abstractive and coherent summarization. *arXiv preprint arXiv:1906.03741*.

Sajad Sotudeh, Arman Cohan, and Nazli Goharian. 2020. GUIR @ LongSumm 2020: Learning to Generate Long Summaries from Scientific Documents. In *SDP 2020*.

Wenliang Dai Tiezheng Yu, Dan Su and Pascale Fung. 2020. Dimsum @LaySumm 20. In *SDP 2020*.

Anjana Umapathy, Karthik Radhakrishnan, Kinjal Jain, and Rahul Singh. 2020. CiteQA@CL-SciSumm20. In *SDP 2020*.

Deshraj Yadav, Rishabh Jain, Harsh Agrawal, Prithvijit Chattopadhyay, Taranjeet Singh, Akash Jain, Shiv Baran Singh, Stefan Lee, and Dhruv Batra. 2019. Evalai: Towards better evaluation systems for ai agents.

Michihiro Yasunaga, Jungo Kasai, Rui Zhang, Alexander R Fabbri, Irene Li, Dan Friedman, and Dragomir R Radev. 2019. Scisummnet: A large annotated corpus and content-impact models for scientific paper summarization with citation networks. In *Proceedings of the AAAI Conference on Artificial Intelligence*, volume 33, pages 7386–7393.

Heng Zhang, Lifan Liu, Ruping Wang, Shaohu Hu, Shutain Ma, and Chengzhi Zhang. 2020. IR&TM-NJUST @ CLSciSumm-20. In *SDP 2020*.

Jingqing Zhang, Yao Zhao, Mohammad Saleh, and Peter J Liu. 2019. Pegasus: Pre-training with extracted gap-sentences for abstractive summarization. *arXiv preprint arXiv:1912.08777*.

Xiang Zhang, Junbo Zhao, and Yann LeCun. 2015. Character-level convolutional networks for text classification. In *Proceedings of the 28th International Conference on Neural Information Processing Systems - Volume 1*, NIPS'15.

Jinming Zhao, Ming Liu, Longxiang Gao, Yuan Jin, Lan Du, He Zhao, He Zhang, and Gholamreza Haffari. 2020. Summpip: Unsupervised multi-document summarization with sentence graph compression. In *Proceedings of the 43rd International ACM SIGIR conference on research and development in Information Retrieval, SIGIR 2020, Virtual Event, China, July 25-30, 2020*, pages 1949–1952.

CIST@CL-SciSumm 2020, LongSumm 2020: Automatic Scientific Document Summarization

Lei Li, Yang Xie, Wei Liu, Yinan Liu, Yafei Jiang, Siya Qi, and Xingyuan Li

Beijing University of Posts and Telecommunications (BUPT)

No.10 Xitucheng Road, Haidian District, Beijing, P.R.China

`{leili,xieyang,thinkwee,lyinan,jiangyafei,qsy,lixingyuan}@bupt.edu.cn`

Abstract

Our system participates in two shared tasks, CL-SciSumm 2020 and LongSumm 2020. In the CL-SciSumm shared task, based on our previous work, we apply more machine learning methods on position features and content features for facet classification in Task1B. And GCN is introduced in Task2 to perform extractive summarization. In the LongSumm shared task, we integrate both the extractive and abstractive summarization ways. Three methods were tested which are T5 Fine-tuning, DPPs Sampling, and GRU-GCN/GAT.

1 Introduction

The increasing scientific documents published on the Internet allow researchers to find more and more documents of interest. However, how to quickly and efficiently obtain the most important facts or ideas of a document is a big challenge. Summarization of scientific documents can mitigate this issue by presenting a brief summary of the whole document to researchers. This year, we participate in two shared tasks of SDP 2020 (Chandrasekaran et al., forthcoming). The CL-SciSumm shared task is the first medium-scale shared task on scientific document summarization in the field of Computational Linguistics and aims to generate a structured summary for the RP (Reference Paper) with the utilization of 10 or more CPs (Citing Papers). The LongSumm shared task opted to leverage blogs created by researchers in the NLP (Natural Language Processing) and Machine learning communities and use these summaries as reference summaries to generate the abstractive and extractive summaries for scientific papers.

In this paper, we will introduce our methods, experiments, and results of two shared tasks. For the CL-SciSumm shared task, based on our previous work (Li et al., 2019), we continue to leverage similarity calculation on multiple features to perform citation linkage in Task1A. In Task1B, we first extract position features and content features of RT (Reference Text) and CT (Citation Text), then apply different machine learning methods to classify the facet. In Task2, we apply DPPs (Determinantal Point Processes) and GCN (Graph Convolutional Network) to perform extractive summarization this time. As for the LongSumm shared task, we retain those extractive methods in the Task2 of the CL-SciSumm shared task as the basis for our summarization system. Furthermore, we also introduce the GAT (Graph Attention Network) and apply an abstractive summarization method based on fine-tuning.

2 Related work

The Task1A of CL-SciSumm is a citation linkage task. The most intuitive method is to calculate and compare the similarity between the CTS (Citation Text Spans) and every text span in RP (Reference Paper), and select the RT with the highest similarity as the result. There are many ways to calculate the similarity, not only traditional IDF and Jaccard similarity, but also Levenshtein distance (Yujian and Bo, 2007). The basic characteristics of words often play an important role in similarity calculating. As the size of the data set continues to grow, neural network language models such as Word2vec (Goldberg and Levy, 2014) and BERT (Devlin et al., 2018) that contain the semantic similarity information in word-level can make a huge improvement. But these word embedding methods will gradually smooth the difference between keywords in the process of calculating, so WMD (Kusner et al., 2015) was proposed to pay attention to the feature mapping between words. In addition to improvement in feature extraction, researchers have also proposed many new algorithms to process features, such as introducing CNN (Kim, 2014) (Dos Santos

Proceedings of the First Workshop on Scholarly Document Processing, pages 225–234

Online, November 19, 2020. ©2020 Association for Computational Linguistics

https://doi.org/10.18653/v1/P17

and Gatti, 2014) into the NLP field to make more complex judgments on feature vectors, or using MatchPyramid (Pang et al., 2016) to process the similarity comparison focusing on the similarity between words.

Task1B of CL-SciSumm is essentially a classification task. Classification methods are mainly divided into two parts: Rule-based methods and supervised machine learning methods. Traditional supervised machine learning methods like LR (Logistic Regression) (Park, 2013), Adaboost (Freund and Schapire, 1997) and XGBoost (Chen and Guestrin, 2016) can be easily applied for this task. Besides, the neural networks, such as TextCNN (Kim, 2014), TextRNN (Liu et al., 2016), TextRCNN (Lai et al., 2015), FastText (Joulin et al., 2016) and CharCNN (Zhang et al., 2015), can work directly on text, and generate dense vectors for classification.

The Task2 of CL-SciSumm and the LongSumm shared task are both summarization task. Recently, the research on automatic summarization tasks has mainly focused on two ways: extractive summarization and abstractive summarization. In the field of extractive summarization, We studied the sampling process used in DPPs (Kulesza and Taskar, 2012) where we calculated the kernel matrix using WMD sentence similarity for further sampling (Li et al., 2018). Zhong et al. (2019) explored how to make the system generate higher quality summaries. They selected three metrics: network architecture, knowledge transfer, and learning mode, and analyzed the impact of the three metrics on the quality of summary generation through experiments.

GCN is a powerful neural network framework processing graph structural data. Defferrard et al. (2016) extended the traditional CNN to non-Euclidean space and introduce local spectral filtering to optimize the propagation process during the training of the standard graph neural network. Kipf and Welling (2017) further studied the application of GCN in semi-supervised classification. GAT (Veličković et al., 2017) allocates different weights on different node neighbors to aggregate information. A document can also be converted into a graph. Yasunaga et al. (2017) introduced GCN in multi-document summarization. The clusters of documents were fed into RNN to obtain intermediate representations. Then GCN continued to extracting features considering the connections of documents clusters. At last, each sentence was

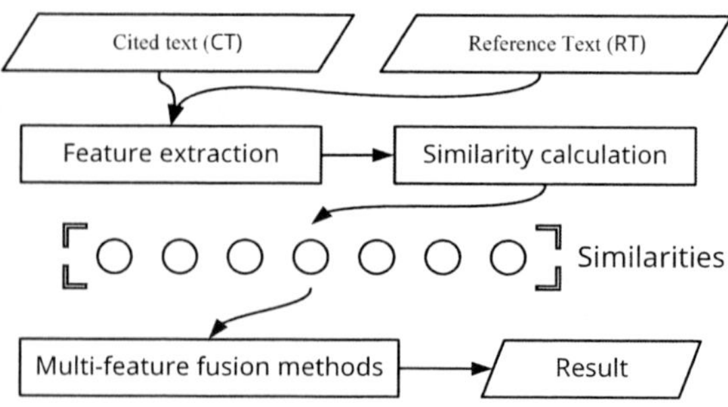

Figure 1: The complete process of Task1A.

scored based on its cluster-aware representations, and sentences with high score were chosen as summaries.

As for abstractive summarization, Rush et al. (2015) introduced an attention mechanism to the Seq2Seq model, which enables the model to focus on words in specific positions in the original text via the weight matrix when generating abstracts, thus avoiding the problem of losing too much information due to long sentences. Since BERT (Devlin et al., 2018) has achieved great success in the field of NLP, the method of pre-training and fine-tuning has become a new paradigm. Researchers began to explore how to apply pre-trained models to natural language generation. At first, researchers tried to replace the encoder with a pre-trained BERT (Liu and Lapata, 2019), then more and more pre-training target functions for the Seq2Seq model were explored like masked generation (Song et al., 2019), denoising (Lewis et al., 2019), text-to-text (Raffel et al., 2019a). Some specially designed tasks for summarization have also been proposed, such as extracting gap-sentences (Zhang et al., 2019). We use the gap-sentence method in (Zhang et al., 2019) to combine and transform all the data, then utilize the T5 model (Lewis et al., 2019) to fine-tune and generate the summary.

3 Method

3.1 CL-SciSumm

3.1.1 Task1A

As shown in Figure 1, the citation linkage task, Task1A of CL-SciSumm, contains two steps: feature extraction and content linkage. In the feature extraction step, we perform similarity calculation based on different feature extraction ways for each RT and every CT (Citation Text) in CTS (Citation Text Spans), where some traditional features will be used, such as IDF similarity and Jaccard simi-

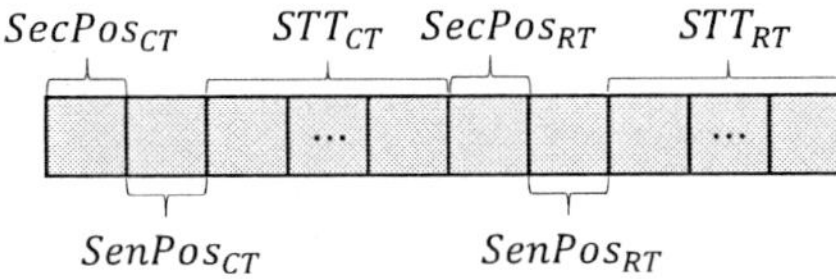

Figure 2: The position feature vector in Task1B.

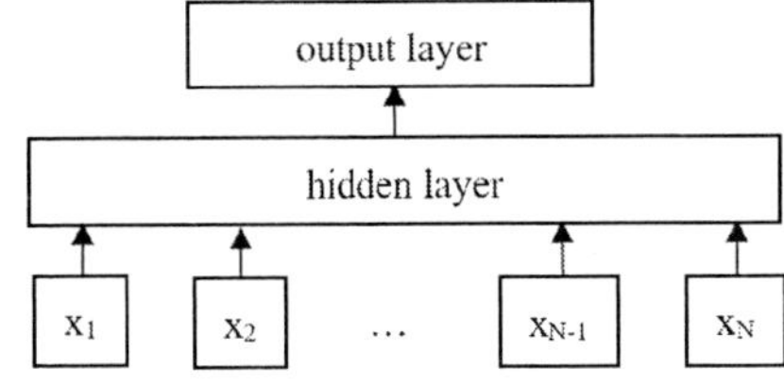

Figure 3: The architecture of FastText in Task 1B.

larity. Additionally sentence context information is used on the basis of these simple features in order to more comprehensively reflect the similarity information of the sentence. Besides, we also use the Lin and Jcn features of WordNet, word-cos, Word vector, and LDA-Jaccard (Li et al., 2019). LDA-Jaccard performs better than LDA on sparse topics, and it pays more attention to the union set of the same topic that both two sentences have. In the content linkage step, we add all the scores that each CT belonging to the same CTS, then sort all RTs by the final scores, and take the first N results as the final answer of Task1A. We use four multi-feature fusion methods: Voting-1.2, Voting-2.1, Jaccard-Focused, and Jaccard-Cascade based on our last year work (Li et al., 2019) by increasing the training set and adjusting the hyper-parameters.

3.1.2   Task1B

Our system applies multiple machine learning methods on multiple features representing different aspects of CT and RT. Since a scientific paper is well-structured and each section represents a different facet of the document, our first motivation is to leverage the position feature of CT and RT to classify which facet the citation belongs to. As shown in Figure 2, the position features are the relative positions of CT and RT, the relative positions of the sections that CT and RT belong to, and the section title text. Suppose the section id is sid, the total amount of sections is $tsid$, the sentence id is $ssid$, and the total amount of sentences is $tssid$. Then, the section relative position($SecPos$) of CT or RT is $sid/tsid$, and the sentence relative position($SenPos$) of CT or RT is $ssid/tssid$. Since the section title text(STT) of CT or RT also implicates the role it plays in the whole paper, we leverage TF-IDF to select the top 189 words as the keywords where each word occurs at least 3 times in the training set, then convert the section title to a one-hot vector. Then we train LR, XGBoost, and Adaboost on the position features.

Next, we focus on the aspect of text content since the texts of CT and RT indicate the content

in detail. First, the texts of CT and RT are preprocessed, such as extracting text from XML file, stop word removal, and word tokenization. Then they are represented by word embeddings and mapped to a dense vector space by FastText. The architecture of FastText is shown in Figure 3 where $x_1, x_2, ..., x_{N-1}, x_N$ represent the n-gram features and each feature is the average of word embeddings. The hidden layer is obtained from the average of $x_1, x_2, ..., x_{N-1}, x_N$. Then the output layer is fully connected to the hidden layer and finally obtain the predicted label by the hierarchical softmax. The reason that we choose FastText as our classifier based on content features is that FastText is relatively lighter than other text classifiers and can avoid overfitting since the training set is small.

3.1.3   Task2

Task2 is a summarization task, and we apply two extractive methods in this paper.

Extractive summarization based on DPPs: This method assumes that each document is a set of sentences, and the process of extracting the summary is to extract the highest quality subset from the set of sentences. To achieve this extraction process, we first represent the document as a matrix L representing the relationship between sentences and then apply the DPPs sampling algorithm to extract candidate sentences. The matrix L is constructed by the Quality-Diversity (QD) model and Sent2Vec (SV) model.

In the Quality-Diversity model, matrix L can be calculated by:

$$L_{ij} = q_i Sim_{ij} q_j$$

where q_i is the quality of each sentence which can be calculated by the features we selected, such as Sentence Length (SL), Sentence Position (SP) and Sentence Coverage (SC). Sim_{ij} represents the similarity between sentences, which can be imple-

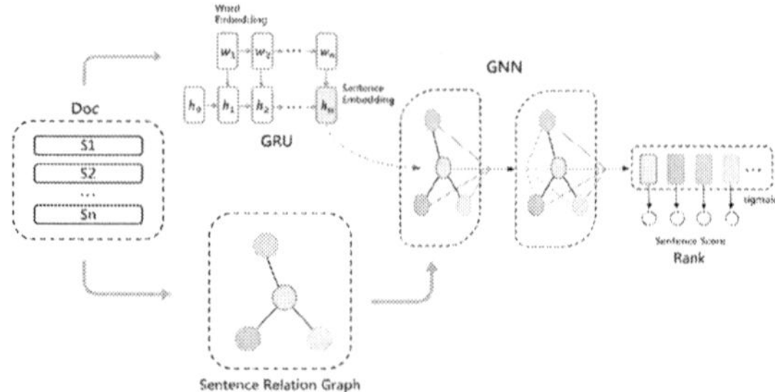

Figure 4: Extractive summarization based on GCN in Task2.

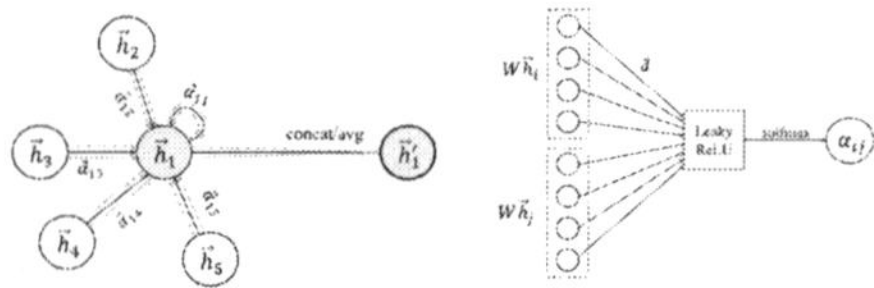

Figure 5: **Left:** Multi-head attention (with 3 heads) computations apply on node 1 and its neighborhood. $\vec{h}_1'$ is obtained by concatenating or averaging from the aggregated features of each head. **Right:** The attention mechanism $a(W\vec{h}_i, W\vec{h}_j)$, and activated by LeakyReLU.

mented as

$$Sim_{ij} = \varphi_i^T \varphi_j \in [0, 1]$$

where φ_i is the diversity vector of a single sentence.

In the Sent2Vec model, we construct matrix L by

$$L_{ij} = B_i^T B_j$$

where B is the sentence vector obtained from the Sent2Vec model.

By constructing matrix L, we can apply the DPPs sampling algorithm to select sentences, the extracted summaries have both high-quality and low-similarity. The details of DPPs can be referred to the work of Kulesza and Taskar (2012).

Extractive summarization based on GNN: We propose an extractive summarization method based on GCN and GAT (Figure 5). As shown in Figure 4, we first build a sentence relation graph based on sentence similarity, calculated by cosine similarity. The similarity graph can objectively reflect the association between sentences, including keywords and sentence similarity information. The graphs and low-level sentence representations compressed by GRU are fed into GCN and GAT. Each node in the undirected graph is a sentence, which is connected to another sentence if their similarity is greater than 0.2, and the origin node feature is the last hidden layer of GRU. Graph convolution can leverage the feature information of the node itself and the structure information of the graph. In the L-layer convolution network, $H^{(l)}$ represents the hidden features of the lth layer, parameterized by a weight matrix $W^{(l)}$. And $\tilde{A}$ is symmetrically normalized from the graph adjacency matrix A. After a non-linear function(ReLU), we obtain advanced representations as the final scoring features.

$$f(H^{(l)}, A) = \sigma(\tilde{A} H^{(l)} W^{(l)})$$

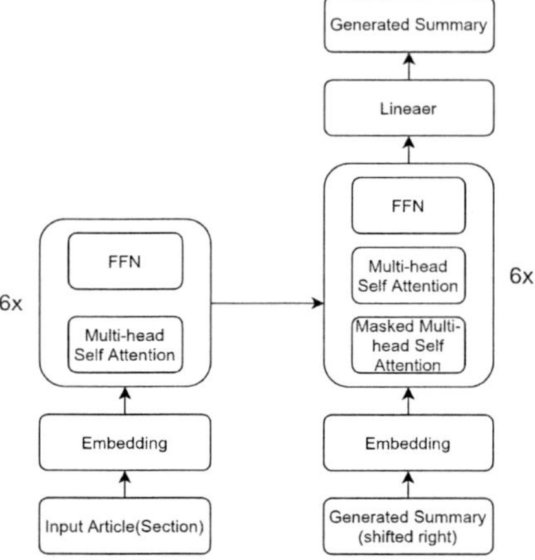

Figure 6: T5 is actually a transformer pretrained on the large corpus. We fine-tuned it for abstractive summarization task.

In the training period, we select the sentences most similar to the community summary from the RP as the summary sentences. The selected sentences are labeled as 1, while the rest sentences are labeled as 0. Then the model is trained as a binary classifier. Finally, we greedily select the highest-scoring sentences from the sentence set.

3.2 LongSumm

For the LongSumm shared task, we use three methods based on our forementioned summarization methods for Task2 of CL-SciSumm in this paper.

3.2.1 T5 Fine-tuning

Although we have divided the dataset into section-wise samples and obtain more than 30000 section-summary pairs, it is still not sufficient to train an abstractive model from scratch. Therefore we use the pre-training and fine-tuning method to deal with this problem. As shown in Figure 6, T5 (Raffel et al., 2019b) is a transformer-liked pre-trained model that has great performance when transfer to a summarization task. It treats every NLP task as a text-to-text task and does both unsupervised pre-training and supervised multi-task pre-training on the large corpus.

3.2.2 DPPs Sampling

This method is based on DPPs sampling, which is similar to the method in Task2 of the CL-SciSumm shared task. We utilize two models to construct matrix L, that is, the Quality-Diversity (QD) model and the Sent2Vec (SV) model. Then DPPs sampling can automatically select the candidate sentences with high quality.

3.2.3 GRU-GCN/GAT

This method contains two parts: an RNN model and a GCN/GAT model. When processing the original text data, we use GRU to compress the sequences. And a similarity graph is constructed for each sentence group as described in 3.1.3, together with the sentence representation as sentence node feature are fed into GCN or GAT. Then we apply the method of supervised training as a reference to the binary classification and select the highest-scored sentences according to the training results.

4 Experiments and Results

4.1 CL-SciSumm

4.1.1 Task1A

In our previous work (Li et al., 2019), we have extracted many kinds of features through various methods. In terms of semantic information, the features are word vector, word-cos, and Lin and Jcn in WordNet. Some traditional features are also used such as IDF and Jaccard similarity, considering that with the increase of the number of topics in the LDA model, the topic vector will gradually become sparse. This time, we abandon LDA and LDA-cos features and introduce the LDA-Jaccard similarity, which can improve the discrimination performance of LDA when the topic vector is sparse and focus on the similarity in the same topic. Based on the original fusion method, there are four new fusion methods by increasing the training set and adjusting the hyper-parameters, which are, Voting-1.2, Voting-2.1, Jaccard-Focused, and Jaccard-Cascade.

LDA model topic size is set to 600, and the pre-training word vector size is set to 300. In the case of high-dimensional LDA, although the word distribution in the topic becomes very sparse, the performance has been improved. Table 4 shows the

Method	Precision	Recall	F1 Score
V1.2	0.0693	**0.2658**	0.1100
V2.1	0.0604	0.2308	0.0958
JF	**0.0698**	0.2650	**0.1105**
JC	0.0605	0.2331	0.0960

Table 1: Task1A experiment results. V1.2, V2.1, JF, JC are Voting-1.2, Voting-2.1, Jaccard-Focused, Jaccard-Cascade respectively.

Facet	Proportion
Aim Citation	0.082
Method Citation	0.718
Hypothesis Citation	0.024
Result Citation	0.138
Implication Citation	0.080
Multi-facet	0.074

Table 2: Facet distribution of the training set in Task1B.

parameter settings of the four multi-feature fusion methods.

As shown in Table 1, the performance of Jaccard-Focused is the best among the four methods. At the same time, there is a big gap between the precision and the recall rate. It is because we manually specify that top-N sentences are answers, so the program finds more sentences in general, so the recall rate is higher than the precision rate.

4.1.2 Task1B

For XGBoost (POS-XGB), we set the learning rate to 0.3, max depth to 1; for Adaboost (POS-ADB), we use the decision tree as the weak learner with max depth 2, learning rate 0.3; for LR (POS-LR), we set the learning rate to 0.3. We also implement a voting method (POS-Vote) based on these base classifiers. As for FastText (CON-CT-FastText and CON-RT-FastText) applied on content features, the CT and RT length are 40 and 50 respectively. The size of word embedding, hidden layer and output layer are 128, 256 and 2 respectively. We use Adam as the optimizer with learning rate 0.0001, and train for 50 iterations. Finally, we combine the classifiers on position features and content features via a voting method (CON-POS-Vote). Both the vote methods mentioned above obey the majority rule.

Since Task1B is a multi-label classification task and the training set is severely imbalanced, as shown in Table 2, we randomly sample an equal number of negative samples for each discourse facet, then train five independent classifiers, respectively. When predicting the test set, we select

Method	Precision	Recall	F1 Score
POS-ADB	0.3088	0.1439	0.1963
POS-LR	0.3685	0.1813	0.2430
POS-Vote	0.4464	0.1831	0.2597
POS-XGB	0.4660	**0.2331**	**0.3108**
CON-CT-FastText	0.4994	0.2047	0.2904
CON-RT-FastText	0.4624	0.1990	0.2783
CON-POS-Vote	**0.5533**	0.1917	0.2847

Table 3: Task1B experiment results.

at most top 2 facets with the highest probability.

Table 3 shows the results of Task1B. We find that CON-POS-Vote has the best Precision, while POS-XGB performs best on Recall and F1 Score. The performance of FastText based on content features is better than most of machine learning methods based on position features. And CTs contain more information indicating the facet than RT.

4.1.3 Task2

In DPPs sampling, Sentence Length (SL), Sentence Position (SP), and Sentence Coverage (SC) are selected as features to calculate the quality of sentences, and the summary compression ratio is set to 20%. For the GCN method, we pick the top 50k words sorted by the frequency from the vocabulary of the original text. We select a sentence subset with the largest ROUGE score as the target for extractive summarization. Based on the greedy algorithm, the sentence with the largest ROUGE score is taken out one by one as a positive sample and added to the extractive summary set until the set cannot increase the score. After cleaning the RP, we rank the sentences by the output score, and then the summaries are generated. Table 5 shows the result on the test set.

From Table5 we can see that GCN based methods perform better than DPPs on various metrics of three different gold summaries. It indicates that end to end supervised learning method can extract better feature than human, even the supervised signals are constructed indirectly (we construct extractive summarization training data from human-write summarization dataset). Although DPPs performs well on improving the diversity of summaries, its ability to evaluate the quality of sentence comes from handcrafted feature, which generalize worse.

4.2 LongSumm

4.2.1 Data preprocessing

The training data set is composed of abstractive parts and extractive parts. The abstractive summarization data are from published papers and blogs which contain around 700 articles with an average of 31.7 sentences per summary and an average of 21.6 words per sentence. The extractive data are from Lev et al. (2019) which have 1705 paper-summary pairs. For each paper, it provides a summary with 30 sentences and 990 words on average. The LongSumm shared task is characterized by long input and output with a high compression ratio. So we choose a mix-and-divide method to deal with it:

1. To make full use of all data samples, we mix abstractive and extractive data.

2. Transform the full paper level summarization into short document summarization by dividing all article-summary pairs into section-summary pairs.

3. Relabel all samples for abstractive models and extractive models.

The first step is easy to understand. The second step is achieved as follows: with PDF parser, we can identify sections in the paper; the highest Jaccard similarity among all pairs between sections sentences and summary sentences is used as section-sentence Jaccard similarity; each summary sentence is allocated to the section which has the highest section-sentence Jaccard similarity with it. Other co-occurrence based metrics like ROUGE (Gidiotis and Tsoumakas, 2020) or BLEU can also be applied but we choose jaccard because of its simplicity(these metrics usually lead to the same allocation). We get 30230 section-summary pairs in total. At last, we build two datasets with different types:

1. For extractive models, sentences in a section that have the highest Jaccard similarity with summary sentences are labeled to be extracted.

2. For abstractive models, there is no need to process abstractive samples. Extractive samples are processed according to Zhang et al. (2019). For the long section, we use textrank to extract some sentences as a summary and exclude these sentences from the section. This preprocessing trick can prevent the abstractive model from learning to copy input. For a short section, we do not exclude summary sentences from the section.

Feature	V1.2		V2.1		JF		JC	
	w	p	w	p	w	p	w	p
Idf similarity	1	12	0.5	5	0.6	16	0.5	16
Idf context similarity			0.8	3	0.5	15	0.4	10
Jaccard similarity	1	5	0.5	6	JS	7		
Jaccard context similarity			0.5	8	0.7	16	0.6	16
Word vector	1	8	0.5	7	0.5	26		
word-cos	1	10	0.7	7	0.5	26	0.5	10
LDA-Jaccard	1	12	0.4	7				
lin			0.5	5				
jcn					0.6	11		

Table 4: Parameters in multi-feature fusion methods in Task1A. V1.2, V2.1, JF, JC are Voting-1.2, Voting-2.1, Jaccard-Focused, Jaccard-Cascade respectively

method	abstract		community		human	
	R2	RSU4	R2	RSU4	R2	RSU4
Jaccard-Cascade_GCN	0.19648	**0.10392**	0.2195	0.14174	0.19117	0.13984
Jaccard-Cascade_QD-DPPs	0.14483	0.09439	0.1492	0.09525	0.13961	0.11623
Jaccard-Cascade_SV-DPPs	0.0981	0.06849	0.17051	0.10209	0.11548	0.09381
Jaccard-Focused_GCN	0.19931	0.09956	**0.24549**	**0.15071**	**0.2042**	**0.14162**
Jaccard-Focused_QD-DPPs	0.12206	0.08266	0.16443	0.09663	0.12376	0.09957
Jaccard-Focused_SV-DPPs	0.12196	0.07936	0.16491	0.09954	0.15772	0.11616
Voting-1.1_GCN	**0.20643**	0.09324	0.24119	0.14578	0.17673	0.11583
Voting-1.1_QD-DPPs	0.1345	0.07303	0.14744	0.09072	0.10559	0.08623
Voting-1.1_SV-DPPs	0.12132	0.06753	0.18003	0.09822	0.13236	0.0937
Voting-2.0_GCN	0.18042	0.07915	0.23088	0.13093	0.17653	0.10737
Voting-2.0_QD-DPPs	0.08908	0.05948	0.17384	0.09739	0.09949	0.07156
Voting-2.0_SV-DPPs	0.14098	0.08039	0.15819	0.09075	0.11406	0.07844

Table 5: Task2 experiment results. JC means Jaccard-Cascade. JF stands for Jaccard-Focused. V1.2 and V2.1 are Voting-1.2 and Voting-2.1 respectively.

We divide the dataset into train/dev/test for comparing different models in this report. ROUGE evaluation is given on the divided test set and we use all 30230 samples for training when inferring on the blind test set.

4.2.2 Result

The result of the LongSumm shared task is illustrated in Table 6.

For model T5, we use the small version which has about 60 million parameters. All input sections are truncated to a maximum of 1024 words. The model is fine-tuned for 5 epochs on the section-wise dataset with a learning rate of 1e-4. The batch size is 32 and we use gradient accumulation to achieve it on a single GPU. Then, we attempt different ways to process the original data, expecting to find the proper input for the model.

1. Construct summary, as mentioned above, all data is transferred to abstractive data.

2. Original summary, as the name suggests, original data are used as input. Because many sections do not have corresponding summaries, there are fewer samples can be utilized, but there are fewer samples can be utilized, but some corresponding summaries are relatively longer.

3. Original+Construct summary, this method merges the original section and the construct section.

In order to generate the summary as long as possible within the limitation of summary length, we design two plans to process the generated summaries. Plan A simply merges the first sentence of summaries that are generated from different sections. Plan B extracts at most three sentences from each summary, for those with fewer words, we can use all sentences. Also, the merged summary is truncated to 600 words if the word count exceeds the limit.

As for DPPs, because the LongSumm task focuses on a long summary, we change the document compression ratio to control the summary length, we set the ratio to 20% and 30%. For the QD method, we select Sentence Length (SL), Sentence Position (SP), and Sentence Coverage (SC) as features and merge them, which can calculate sentence quality.

As for GRU-GCN/GAT, we divide each paper

methods	submission	Description	R1 f	R1 r	R2 f	R2 r	RL f	RL r
Pretrained Language Model Based	0	Construct-A	0.424	0.373	0.120	0.104	0.172	0.149
	1	Original-A	0.487	0.490	0.134	0.136	0.182	0.184
	2	Construct+Original-A	0.417	0.364	0.108	0.094	0.171	0.148
	3	Construct-B	0.489	0.490	0.135	0.136	0.183	0.184
	4	Original-B	0.488	0.494	0.134	0.137	0.183	0.185
	5	Construct+Original-B	0.487	0.487	0.135	0.136	0.183	0.183
GNN Based	6	GRU+GAT-sim	0.479	0.491	0.143	0.146	0.182	0.186
	7	GRU+GCN-sim	**0.490**	**0.497**	**0.151**	**0.152**	**0.201**	**0.204**
DPPs Based	8	QD-DPPs-20	0.448	0.428	0.102	0.097	0.169	0.161
	9	QD-DPPs-30	0.435	0.415	0.103	0.099	0.162	0.154
	10	SV-DPPs-20	0.452	0.427	0.109	0.103	0.165	0.156
	11	SV-DPPs-30	0.451	0.428	0.120	0.114	0.170	0.161

Table 6: LongSumm test set results. ROUGE_f and ROUGE_r are f1 value and recall of ROUGE results.

into sections, since sections are the natural division of paper, and match each section to its gold summaries. For every section, its relation graph is constructed and system summaries are extracted by sentence scores. After we get the section summaries, paper summaries are concatenated by ranking sentences from sections. In our work, GAT has more parameters, thus are more difficult to converge, and the advantage to learn graph structure is weakened since section graphs are rather small, which explains why attention mechanism does not do better than GCN in some way.

The results on the test set show that extractive summarization model using the GCN method performs the best on long summary task and the performance of T5 and DPPs is slightly worse than GCN. Generally speaking, the ROUGE value of abstractive summaries is lower than that of extractive summaries. But as an abstractive summarization model, T5 can compress more semantic information to generate the summary closer to an artificial summary. As for DPPs, as an unsupervised model, it uses hand-constructed features to rank sentences. The sentence quality obtained by this is not accurate. GNN uses RNN to model sentences, and considers sentence diversity in the learning process of neural network. So the ability to measure sentence quality is weaker than GNN. However, DPPs is able to work well under the situation where the training data is lacked.

5 Conclusion and Future Work

In the CL-SciSumm shared task, Jaccard-Focused performs better than other methods in Task1A. In future work, we will try to use the knowledge graph and GNN for better expression of semantic and structure information. In Task1B, POS-XGB performs the best, which shows that the position features contributes more than the content features. In the future, more information can be extracted and fused to obtain richer features, or combined with some hand-craft rules to assist the classification. In Task 2, GCN shows great potential to perform the summarization task. We expect the neural network language models to make contributions to obtain more meaningful semantic representation for sentences against statistical features. In the LongSumm shared task, model T5 and extractive summarization model based on GCN perform well on the official data set, and DPPs still has great potential, we expect to provide more features or modify the sampling processes so as to improve the performance of our models. What's more, in this paper we mainly focus on how to extract/generate section-wise summaries with high quality and diversity, but how to pick and combine these summaries is also an interesting work to be done.

References

M. K. Chandrasekaran, G. Feigenblat, Hovy. E., A. Ravichander, M. Shmueli-Scheuer, and A De Waard. forthcoming. Overview and insights from scientific document summarization shared tasks 2020: CL-SciSumm, LaySumm and LongSumm. In *Proceedings of the First Workshop on Scholarly Document Processing (SDP 2020)*.

Tianqi Chen and Carlos Guestrin. 2016. Xgboost: A scalable tree boosting system. In *Proceedings of the 22nd acm sigkdd international conference on knowledge discovery and data mining*, pages 785–794.

Michaël Defferrard, Xavier Bresson, and Pierre Vandergheynst. 2016. Convolutional neural networks on graphs with fast localized spectral filtering. In D. D. Lee, M. Sugiyama, U. V. Luxburg, I. Guyon, and R. Garnett, editors, *Advances in Neural Information Processing Systems 29*, pages 3844–3852. Curran Associates, Inc.

Jacob Devlin, Ming-Wei Chang, Kenton Lee, and Kristina Toutanova. 2018. Bert: Pre-training of deep bidirectional transformers for language understanding. *arXiv preprint arXiv:1810.04805*.

Cicero Dos Santos and Maira Gatti. 2014. Deep convolutional neural networks for sentiment analysis of short texts. In *Proceedings of COLING 2014, the 25th International Conference on Computational Linguistics: Technical Papers*, pages 69–78.

Yoav Freund and Robert E Schapire. 1997. A decision-theoretic generalization of on-line learning and an application to boosting. *Journal of computer and system sciences*, 55(1):119–139.

Alexios Gidiotis and Grigorios Tsoumakas. 2020. A divide-and-conquer approach to the summarization of academic articles.

Yoav Goldberg and Omer Levy. 2014. word2vec explained: deriving mikolov et al.'s negative-sampling word-embedding method. *arXiv preprint arXiv:1402.3722*.

Armand Joulin, Edouard Grave, Piotr Bojanowski, and Tomas Mikolov. 2016. Bag of tricks for efficient text classification. *arXiv preprint arXiv:1607.01759*.

Yoon Kim. 2014. Convolutional neural networks for sentence classification. *arXiv preprint arXiv:1408.5882*.

Thomas N. Kipf and Max Welling. 2017. Semi-supervised classification with graph convolutional networks. In *International Conference on Learning Representations (ICLR)*.

Alex Kulesza and Ben Taskar. 2012. Determinantal point processes for machine learning. *arXiv preprint arXiv:1207.6083*.

Matt Kusner, Y. Sun, N.I. Kolkin, and Kilian Weinberger. 2015. From word embeddings to document distances. *Proceedings of the 32nd International Conference on Machine Learning (ICML 2015)*, pages 957–966.

Siwei Lai, Liheng Xu, Kang Liu, and Jun Zhao. 2015. Recurrent convolutional neural networks for text classification. In *Twenty-ninth AAAI conference on artificial intelligence*.

Guy Lev, Michal Shmueli-Scheuer, Jonathan Herzig, Achiya Jerbi, and David Konopnicki. 2019. Talk-Summ: A dataset and scalable annotation method for scientific paper summarization based on conference talks. In *Proceedings of the 57th Annual Meeting of the Association for Computational Linguistics*, pages 2125–2131, Florence, Italy. Association for Computational Linguistics.

Mike Lewis, Yinhan Liu, Naman Goyal, Marjan Ghazvininejad, Abdelrahman Mohamed, Omer Levy, Ves Stoyanov, and Luke Zet-tlemoyer. 2019. Bart: Denoising sequence-to-sequence pre-training for natural lan-guage generation, translation, and comprehension. *arXiv preprint arXiv:1910.13461*.

Lei Li, Junqi Chi, Moye Chen, Zuying Huang, Yingqi Zhu, and Xiangling Fu. 2018. Cist@ clscisumm-18: Methods for computational linguistics scientific citation linkage, facet classification and summarization. In *BIRNDL@ SIGIR*.

Lei Li, Yingqi Zhu, Yang Xie, Zuying Huang, Wei Liu, Xingyuan Li, and Yinan Liu. 2019. Cist@ clscisumm-19: Automatic scientific paper summarization with citances and facets. In *BIRNDL@ SIGIR*, pages 196–207.

Pengfei Liu, Xipeng Qiu, and Xuanjing Huang. 2016. Recurrent neural network for text classification with multi-task learning. *arXiv preprint arXiv:1605.05101*.

Yang Liu and Mirella Lapata. 2019. Text summarization with pretrained encoders. *arXiv preprint arXiv:1908.08345*.

Liang Pang, Yanyan Lan, Jiafeng Guo, Jun Xu, Shengxian Wan, and Xueqi Cheng. 2016. Text matching as image recognition. In *AAAI*, volume 16, pages 2793–2799.

Hyeoun-Ae Park. 2013. An introduction to logistic regression: From basic concepts to interpretation with particular attention to nursing domain. *Journal of Korean Academy of Nursing*, 43:154–164.

Colin Raffel, Noam Shazeer, Adam Roberts, Katherine Lee, Sharan Narang, Michael Matena, Yanqi Zhou, Wei Li, and Peter J Liu. 2019a. Exploring the limits of transfer learning with a unified text-to-text transformer. *arXiv preprint arXiv:1910.10683*.

Colin Raffel, Noam Shazeer, Adam Roberts, Katherine Lee, Sharan Narang, Michael Matena, Yanqi Zhou, Wei Li, and Peter J. Liu. 2019b. Exploring the limits of transfer learning with a unified text-to-text transformer. *arXiv e-prints*.

Alexander M. Rush, Sumit Chopra, and Jason Weston. 2015. A neural attention model for abstractive sentence summarization. In *Proceedings of the 2015 Conference on Empirical Methods in Natural Language Processing*, pages 379–389, Lisbon, Portugal. Association for Computational Linguistics.

Kaitao Song, Xu Tan, Tao Qin, Jianfeng Lu, and Tie-Yan Liu. 2019. Mass: Masked sequence to sequence pre-training for language gener-ation. In *International Conference on Machine Learning*, pages 5926–5936.

Petar Veličković, Guillem Cucurull, Arantxa Casanova, Adriana Romero, Pietro Lio, and Yoshua Bengio. 2017. Graph attention networks. *arXiv preprint arXiv:1710.10903*.

Michihiro Yasunaga, Rui Zhang, Kshitijh Meelu, Ayush Pareek, Krishnan Srinivasan, and Dragomir Radev. 2017. Graph-based neural multi-document summarization. In *Proceedings of the 21st Conference on Computational Natural Language Learning (CoNLL 2017)*, pages 452–462, Vancouver, Canada. Association for Computational Linguistics.

Li Yujian and Liu Bo. 2007. A normalized levenshtein distance metric. *IEEE transactions on pattern analysis and machine intelligence*, 29(6):1091–1095.

Jingqing Zhang, Yao Zhao, Mohammad Saleh, and Peter J. Liu. 2019. Pegasus: Pre-training with extracted gap-sentences for abstractive summarization.

Xiang Zhang, Junbo Zhao, and Yann LeCun. 2015. Character-level convolutional networks for text classification. In *Advances in neural information processing systems*, pages 649–657.

Ming Zhong, Pengfei Liu, Danqing Wang, Xipeng Qiu, and Xuanjing Huang. 2019. Searching for effective neural extractive summarization: What works and what's next. *arXiv preprint arXiv:1907.03491*.

NLP-PINGAN-TECH @ CL-SciSumm 2020

Ling Chai, Guizhen Fu, Yuan Ni
PingAn Health Technology, Shenzhen, China
{CHAILING123, FUGUIZHEN037, NIYUAN442}@pingan.com.cn

Abstract

CL-SciSumm Shared Task at EMNLP 2020 Workshop consists of three subtasks about automatic summarization for research papers. This paper introduces the systems of Task 1A and Task 1B submitted by team NLP-PINGAN-TECH. TASK1A is to identify the cited text spans in the reference paper, and Task 1B is to determine the discourse facet of the cited text. Task 1A is regarded as a binary classification task of sentence pairs and the strategies based on language models are proposed. Integration with contextualized embedding with extra information is further explored in this article. For Task 1B, the pre-trained language models are fine-tuned to accomplish a multi-label classification task. The results show that extra information can improve the identification of cited text spans. The end-to-end trained models outperform models trained with two stages, and the averaged prediction of multi-models is more accurate than an individual one.

1 Introduction

With the ever-increasing scientific publications, tracking research status from an extremely huge amount of research papers is getting harder for scholars. To solve this problem, research on automatic summarization provides an efficient way to get the highlights of articles for readers. Citation-based summarization methods leverage information of citing and cited texts to construct the summary of the reference paper (Abu-Jbara, Amjad et al., 1981). Citation texts are considered to contain the most valuable parts for researchers to follow. Moreover, different citing text spans form a relatively complete figure of an article, such as hypothesis, methods, results, and so on. Based on the aforementioned ideas, the CL-SciSumm Shared Tasks propose different tasks about different aspects for scientific publication summarization systems from 2016 to this year (Chandrasekaran, Muthu et al., 2019).

In more detail, the CL-SciSumm 2020 is organized as follows (Chandrasekaran, Muthu et al., 2020).

A set of reference papers (RP) and the citing papers (CPs) that all contain citations to the RP are given. In each CP, the text spans of each particular citation to the RP should be identified. The three subtasks are shown below:

Task 1A: For each citance, identify the spans of text (cited text spans) in the RP that most accurately reflect the citance. These are of the granularity of a sentence fragment.

Task 1B: For each cited text span, identify what facet of the paper it belongs to, from a predefined set of facets.

Task 2 (optional task): Finally, generate a structured summary of the RP from the cited text spans of the RP.

We focus on systems for **Task 1 (Task 1A and Task 1B)** in this paper. Task 1 are evaluated by Sentence Overlap scores and ROUGE-SU4 scores (Chandrasekaran, Muthu et al., 2020).

2 Data Pre-processing

The training sets consist of two datasets: one is 40 manually annotated reference papers and

Proceedings of the First Workshop on Scholarly Document Processing, pages 235–241
Online, November 19, 2020. ©2020 Association for Computational Linguistics
https://doi.org/10.18653/v1/P17

Dataset	Auto-annotated	Manually-annotated
total citance	14903	537
cited sentences(>1)	14885	196
consecutive cited sentence	724	75

Table 1: Distribution of cited text

Dataset	Auto-annotated	Manually-annotated
total cited sentence	19869	522
cited only once	14834	370
cited more than twice	5035	152

Table 2: Cited frequency

their citances, the other is 1000 documents auto-annotated by ScisummNet (Nomoto, T. et al., 2018).

We clean and filter out the noisy sentence using NLTK tools (Bird et al., 2009). We then concatenate the sentences badly segmented, like "this is the first part of a sentence" and "(xx and xx, 2019)". The sentences with less than 4 tokens are eliminated. The citing or cited text spans with more than one sentence have been split into multiple citances. As a result, the processed data are all "sentence-sentence" pairs.

Firstly, we compare the two datasets on the distribution of cited sentences and cited frequency which is shown in Table 1 and Table 2. It is clear that manually-annotated data have less cited text spans with more than one sentence and multiple sentences are more likely consecutive, compared to the auto-annotated data. In the meanwhile, the two datasets have a similar repetition rate of cited sentences. We also tried to train models with the manually-annotated dataset mixed with auto-annotated data, but the results demonstrate that the 1000-document dataset generally has negative effects. Therefore, in the following part, we only describe the systems trained on the 40-document dataset. 32 of 40 reference papers are regarded as train data and the rest 8 papers are development set. To reduce the impact of data imbalance, we randomly select 4 negative sentences for each

piece of citance for the trainset and do nothing on the development set.

3   Method

3.1   TASK 1A

We consider three kinds of approaches for the identification of cited text spans, both based on the concept of identifying sentence relevance between the citing and cited text spans. All the methods for Task1A are binary classification. For the development set, the two or three sentences with the highest scores for one citing sentence are selected as its corresponding cited text spans. We refer to the citing-cited sentences as sentence A and sentence B in the following sections.

BERT-based methods:
For the first approach, we explore the methods based on the BERT framework (Devlin, Jacob et al., 2018). We use the BERT-base-uncased model as the baseline and then find that using domain-specific embedding and extra information utilization can both improve the performance.

Domain-specific embeddings. It has been proven that domain-specific text embedding could better interpret the semantic knowledge of text spans (Beltagy, Iz et al., 2019). To construct embeddings of texts in the scientific research domain, we propose two approaches:

1.   To leverage language model SciBERT (Beltagy, Iz et al., 2019). SciBERT was pre-trained on more than 1,14 million scientific publications (82% on biomedicine and 12% on computer science).

2.   To fine-tune the BERT model with scientific documents. Considering that train data are all computational linguistics scientific documents, we feed ACL anthology reference corpus into the BERT-Large-Uncased model (BERT-large has 24 layers, 1024 hidden size, 16 self-attention heads, which total has 340 million parameters.) and train it by running both Masked Language Model (MLM) and Next Sentence Prediction (NSP) tasks as the

original paper did (Devlin, Jacob et al., 2018). We refer to this model as ACLBERT.

We fine tune the two aforementioned models on our trainset with learning rate of 5e-5 and with 10% training steps as warm up stage. It's worth noting that we feed sentence pairs in the form of "[CLS] sentence A [SEP] sentence B [SEP]" into models, then we also train another model with order the of sentence A and sentence B reversed. The averaged prediction of two models with different sentence orders is better than that of a single model. The final submitted systems SciBERT and ACLBERT in Table 3 are all the averaged predictions of two models as described above.

Extra information utilization. To capture the features at the document level, we try to add the position and section features into the whole model. Position information "sid" and "ssid" (index of the entire document and section, respectively) are already given. With the full text of the reference paper given, we parse the documents and rearrange all section expression to nine categories: title, abstract, introduction, related work, method, experiment, result, conclusion, and none (for texts without sections).

Firstly, we add those three features as the prefixes "[method] [sid=xx] [ssid =xx] " for all sentence B. The section text like "method" and position information like "23" will be treated as normal tokens, and the characters "[" and "]" will be identified to token "[UNK]" but have the effect of isolating each type of information. We name this method SciBERT-fake-token.

We also attempt to add words like "[method]", "[abstract]", "[sid=1]" as special tokens into the dictionary of SciBERT so that the tokenizer would not split them into pieces. We call this method as SciBERT-special-token. The results on the development set of all the strategies based on BERT framework are given in Table 3. The results on the blind test set are shown in Table 7 and Table 8.

SemBERT-based method:
The models based on the BERT framework are not able to leverage other information besides contextualized semantics knowledge. We propose the method based on Semantics-aware BERT for Language Understanding (SemBERT) **(Zhang, Zhuosheng et al., 2020)**. The existing language representation models including ELMo, GPT, and BERT only exploit plain context-sensitive features such as character or word embedding. They rarely consider incorporating structured semantic information which can provide rich semantics for language representation. To promote natural language understanding, Zhang, Zhuosheng et al. proposes to incorporate explicit contextual semantics from pre-trained semantic role labeling and introduces an improved language representation model.

In this work, we use the pre-trained semantic role labeling model, trained on The Stanford Natural Language Inference (SNLI) Corpus, to offline annotate the train and development set. The annotation is an unsupervised process, which makes the annotation task more lightly. Instead of BERT, the language model part is replaced as SciBERT.

With the structured semantic information extracted, we use the sentence pairs and the structured semantic information of every sentence as the input of SemBERT and then select the top-3 candidates as positive pairs. The performance is reported in Table 4, Table 9, and Table 10.

BERT-independent classifier methods:
How to utilize document-level features is still worth discussing. We apply two-stage training methods to combine information from different levels. There are three types of features to be considered in our proposed systems in this part:

Sentence-pair Embeddings. We keep the weights of best fine-tuned SciBERT and ACLBERT models and leverage them as a text encoder in this section. The embedding of token "[CLS]" of the last layer of BERT part is taken as the sentence-pair embedding. Therefore, a vector with the length of 768 or 1024 is gained for a sentence-pair, from SciBERT and ACLBERT, respectively.

Section Embeddings. First of all, we train classification with center loss for nine labels (section categories mentioned in the BERT-based methods part), then take the nine center embedding as fixed embedding for each sections (Qi, Ce et al., 2017). The embedding dimension is set to 32 in our experiments. To illustrate, we also use the 1000 documents in the training process.

Position Features. Three features of position are generated: "sid", "ssid" are directly used as integers. Besides, the value of "sid" over the length of the reference paper is also calculated as the relative position.

We do experiments with different input choices on four classification models without neural network: Random Forest (RF), Logistic Regression (LR), CatBoost (Dorogush, Anna et al., 2018) and LGBM. The systems are shown in Table 5. SciBERT means using all three types of features and the sentence pair embeddings are generated from fine-tuned SciBERT. Similarly, ACLBERT utilizes the sentence pair embeddings from fine-tuned ACLBERT. The sentence pair embeddings used in SciBERT-ACLBERT are the concatenation of the embeddings from two SciBERT and ACLBERT.

The sentence pair embeddings from SciBERT or ACLBERT may weaken the impact of section embeddings and position features due to the high dimension, so that we try to use the scores of the prediction to replace the token embedding. We concatenate the prediction score of the best 4 models (SciBERT and ACLBERT) with section and position features as the input of classifiers. This System is named Four-output in table 5.

The scores on the blind test set are given in Table 11 and Table 12.

3.2 TASK 1B

Task 1B is a task of multi-label classification. The five facet labels are "Implication", "Hypothesis", "Aim", "Results", "Method". In this part, only all cited text spans, and their position and section information are taken into account. We train a multi-label model with the initial weights of SciBERT. To deal with the imbalance of data, we reset the class weights negatively correlated with the sample size for binary cross-entropy loss. And the thresholds of "Implication""Hypothesis" are set less than 0.5 to improve the recall scores. The results are shown in Table 6.

4 Result and Discussion

4.1 TASK 1A

To evaluate the methods, we regard the Sentence Overlap F1 scores of development set as the performance of our proposed methods (Chandrasekaran, Muthu et al., 2020). We sort prediction scores of all candidate sentences for each citing sentence and then keep the top 2 or 3 as the final selection.

The precision, recall, and F1 scores are calculated for every model based on the BERT framework in Table 3. It is noted that the results in table 3 are the assembled results of two best models, so it is likely overfitted on the development set, but these values also make sense to compare the performance of different methods.

Table 3 illustrates that ACLBERT possesses better performance than SciBERT. The use of fake token does make the performance improved, whereas the supplements of special tokens make the F1 score decrease. This is also reasonable because there is not enough data to train tokens that did not appear in pre-training.

Method	TopN	Precision	Recall	F1
SciBERT	N=2	0.1940	0.2949	0.2342
SciBERT-special-token	N=2	0.1606	**0.3653**	0.2231
SciBERT-fake-token	N=2	**0.2038**	0.3077	**0.2452**
ACLBERT	N=2	0.2029	0.3076	0.2446

Table 3: Results of BERT-based methods

Method	TopN	Precision	Recall	F1
SciBERT	N=3	0.1940	0.2949	0.2342

Table 4: Results of SemBERT

Input	RF	LR	CB	LGBM
SciBERT	*0.27*	0.201	0.1959	0.1946
ACLBERT	*0.2392*	*0.2467*	0.2222	0.2239
SciBERT - ACLBERT	*0.2435*	0.2141	*0.2386*	*0.2545*
Four-output	*0.2615*	*0.2612*	0.2357	0.2155

Table 5: Results of BERT-independent classifier

Input	Precision	Recall	F1
Aim	1.0	0.4285	0.6
Hypothesis	0.0727	1.0	0.1355
Implication	0.2603	1.0	0.4131
Method	0.8223	0.9842	0.8960
Results	0.4655	0.9310	0.6206

Table 6: Results of TASK 1B

SciBERT-fake-token is the best strategies based on BERT framework, followed by ACLBERT.

Table 4 shows the result of SemBERT. This result is fairly reliably with minimal over-fitted effect, though the value is lower than those in Table 3. It is noticed that SemBERT gains a considerable recall score, compared to the methods in Table 3.

Table 5 shows the results of the BERT-independent classifier methods. The scores cannot be compared with those in Table 3 and Table 4 because we are based on the most excellent BERT-based models. We choose the systems marked in Italic as the final result for systems based on the BERT-independent classifier framework to submit.

4.2 TASK 1B

We train repeatedly SciBERT models for with different random seeds, then choose the best model for each label, as Table 6. It has to be mentioned that the results of "Aim" and "Hypothesis" are not stable under different random seeds without sufficient training data. "Method" category has the highest score, while "Hypothesis" gains the lowest one.

Method	TopN	Precision	Recall	F1
SciBERT	N=2	0.1178	0.2182	0.1530
SciBERT (5cv)	N=3	0.1043	**0.2901**	0.1534
SciBERT-special-token	N=2	0.1183	0.2224	0.1545
SciBERT-fake-token	N=2	0.1189	0.2238	0.1552
SciBERT-fake-token(5cv)	N=2	**0.1292**	0.2417	**0.1684**
ACLBERT	N=2	0.1143	0.1989	0.1451

Table 7: Sentence Overlap scores of BERT-based methods

Method	TopN	Precision	Recall	F1
SciBERT	N=2	0.2664	0.1063	0.1352
SciBERT (5cv)	N=2	0.2757	0.1044	0.1361
SciBERT-special-token	N=2	0.2820	0.1035	0.1394
SciBERT-fake-token	N=2	0.2741	0.0892	0.1202
SciBERT-fake-token(5cv)	N=2	**0.2950**	**0.1174**	**0.1498**
ACLBERT	N=2	0.2620	0.0924	0.1240

Table 8: ROUGE-SU4 scores of BERT-based methods

Method	TopN	Precision	Recall	F1
SciBERT	N=2	0.1167	0.2155	0.1515

Table 9: Sentence Overlap scores of SemBERT

Method	TopN	Precision	Recall	F1
SciBERT	N=2	0.2634	0.0903	0.1232

Table 10: ROUGE-SU4 scores of SemBERT

5 Submitted Runs

For Task 1A we submit the results of 27 strategies, where each strategy contains two results (top 2 candidates, or top 3 candidates). Among all the submitted runs, the ensemble of SciBERT, SciBERT-fake-token, SciBERT-special-token, and SemBERT based on SciBERT, named "SciBERT_SemBERT" in

Input	RF	LR	CB	LGBM
SciBERT	0.1161	0.1253	0.1303	0.1316
ACLBERT	0.1155	0.1241	0.1335	0.1349
SciBERT-ACLBERT	0.1095	0.1293	**0.1366**	**0.1408**
Four-output	**0.1260**	**0.1440**	/	/

Table 11: Sentence Overlap scores of BERT-independent classifier methods

Input	RF	LR	CB	LGBM
SciBERT	0.0970	0.1097	0.1056	0.1066
ACLBERT	0.0911	0.1109	0.1096	**0.1179**
SciBERT-ACLBERT	0.0922	0.1120	**0.1210**	0.1118
Four-output	**0.1105**	**0.1225**	/	/

Table 12: ROUGE-SU4 scores of BERT-independent classifier methods

Method	TopN	Precision	Recall	F1
SciBERT-ALL	N=3	0.1139	0.3178	0.1677
SciBERT-SemBERT	N=2	0.1318	0.2459	0.1716
SciBer-ACLBERT	N=2	0.1244	0.2265	0.1606

Table 13: Sentence Overlap scores of mixed strategies

Method	TopN	Precision	Recall	F1
SciBERT-ALL	N=2	0.2860	0.1105	0.1433
SciBERT-SemBERT	N=2	0.2976	0.1134	0.1470
SciBer-ACLBERT	N=2	0.2905	0.1029	0.1387

Table 14: ROUGE-SU4 scores of mixed

TASK	Precision	Recall	F1
Task1B	0.1914	0.2899	0.2306

Table 15: Sentence Overlap scores of Task1b

Table 13 and Table 14, wins the highest Sentence Overlap F1 scores (Micro F1: 0.1716, Macro F1: 0.1737). In the meanwhile, the ensemble of SciBERT-fake-token models trained for 5-fold cross-validation gains the highest ROUGE-SU4 F1 score (0.1498), shown in Table 8.

The scores of strategies based on the BERT Framework have been shown in Table 7 and Table 8. Among three single models, SciBERT-fake-token shows the best performance (Sentence Overlap Micro F1: 0.1552), which is consistent with the scores on the development set. SciBERT-special-token gets the highest ROUGE-SU4 F1 score (0.1394). SciBERT-special-token and SciBERT-fake-token perform better, which indicates that the position and section information has a positive effect. Unlike results on the development set, ACLBERT does not perform worse than SciBERT. We submitted the results of two strategies (SciBERT and SciBERT-fake-token) trained for 5-fold cross-validation, with Sentence Overlap Micro F1 0.1534 and 0.1684 respectively. The scores show that the ensemble of models for 5-fold cross-validation outperforms the corresponding individual models.

Table 9 and Table 10 illustrate the performance of SemBERT based on SciBERT of which the Sentence Overlap F1 score is 0.1515 and ROUGE-SU4 F1 score is 0.1232.

The scores of the BERT-independent classifier methods are given in Table 11 and Table 12. The scores are lower than BERT-Based methods and SemBERT-based methods. The figures demonstrate that the end-to-end trained models based on BERT outperform models trained with two independent stages.

We also fuse various strategies and the results are shown in Table 13 and Table 14. Overall, the performance proves better than a single strategy, with all Sentence Overlap F1 scores more than 0.16.

We can be convinced that the ensemble of different models lessens the impact of over fitting, although we only trained on the 40 manually annotated articles.

The evaluation of Task1B is given in Table 15.

6   Conclusions and Future Work

In our systems proposed, the semantic knowledge inside citing sentences and their corresponding cited text spans is encoded by models based on the BERT Framework. Besides, we do the experiments on how to integrate the structured semantic information as well as document-level information. In the result section, we analysis the performance and choose good system of all the proposed models as final systems to submit. The scores on the blind test set indicates position and section information can improve the identification of cited text spans. The end-to-end trained models outperform models trained with two stages, and the averaged prediction of multi-models is more accurate than an individual one. How to learn more extra information should be further explored. The relation between sentences in the same paper is not considered in our methods, which is one of the points we can do in the future work.

References

Abu-Jbara, Amjad & Radev, Dragomir. (2011). Coherent Citation-Based Summarization of Scientific Papers. 500-509.

Chandrasekaran, Muthu & Yasunaga, Michihiro & Radev, Dragomir & Freitag, Dayne & Kan, Min-Yen. (2019). Overview and Results: CL-SciSumm Shared Task 2019.

Chandrasekaran, M. K., Feigenblat, G., Hovy. E., Ravichander, A., Shmueli-Scheuer, M., De Waard, A. (Forthcoming). Overview and Insights from Scientific Document Summarization Shared Tasks 2020: CL-SciSumm, LaySumm and LongSumm. In Proceedings of the First Workshop on Scholarly Document Processing (SDP 2020).

Nomoto, T. (2018). Resolving citation links with neural networks. Frontiers in Research Metrics and Analytics, 3, 31.

Devlin, Jacob & Chang, Ming-Wei & Lee, Kenton & Toutanova, Kristina. (2018). BERT: Pre-training of Deep Bidirectional Transformers for Language Understanding.

Bird, Steven, Edward Loper and Ewan Klein (2009). Natural Language Processing with Python. O'Reilly Media Inc.

Beltagy, Iz & Lo, Kyle & Cohan, Arman. (2019). SciBERT: A Pretrained Language Model for Scientific Text. 3606-3611. 10.18653/v1/D19-1371.

Zhang, Zhuosheng & Wu, Yuwei & Zhao, Hai & Li, Zuchao & Zhang, Shuailiang & Zhou, Xi & Zhou, Xiang. (2020). Semantics-Aware BERT for Language Understanding. Proceedings of the AAAI Conference on Artificial Intelligence. 34. 9628-9635. 10.1609/aaai.v34i05.6510.

Qi, Ce & Su, Fei. (2017). Contrastive-center loss for deep neural networks. 2851-2855. 10.1109/ICIP.2017.8296803.

Dorogush, Anna & Ershov, Vasily & Gulin, Andrey. (2018). CatBoost: gradient boosting with categorical features support.

Wang, Zhiguo & Hamza, Wael & Florian, Radu. (2017). Bilateral Multi-Perspective Matching for Natural Language Sentences. 4144-4150. 10.24963/ijcai.2017/579.

IIITBH-IITP@CL-SciSumm20, CL-LaySumm20, LongSumm20

Saichethan Miriyala Reddy[*], Naveen Saini[†], Sriparna Saha[†], Pushpak Bhattacharyya[†]
[*]Indian Institute of Information Technology, Bhagalpur
[†]Indian Institute of Technology, Patna
miriyala.cse.1725@iiitbh.ac.in, {naveen.pcs16, sriparna, pb}@iitp.ac.in

Abstract

In this paper, we present the IIIT Bhagalpur and IIT Patna team's effort to solve the three shared tasks namely, CL-SciSumm 2020, CL-LaySumm 2020, LongSumm 2020 at SDP 2020. The themes of these tasks are to generate medium-scale, lay and long summaries, respectively, for scientific articles. For the first two tasks, unsupervised systems are developed, while for the third one, we have developed a supervised system. The performances of all the systems are evaluated on the associated datasets with the shared tasks in term of well-known ROUGE metric.

1 Introduction

Due to a lot of research going into the computational linguistic (CL) domain as well as in other domains, the rate of publishing scientific articles has been increased and will continue to expand (Nallapati et al., 2017, 2016; Jaidka et al., 2019). This makes the researchers challenging to update them with the up-to-date advancements. A survey (review) article may help the researcher to have a gist of the recent advancements. But, writing a survey paper is a very laborious and time-consuming task. This challenge demands summarization of scientific articles (Cohan and Goharian, 2018; Conroy and Davis, 2018) by providing their summary in a few words and then prepare the survey article .

But sometimes, for niche practitioners, the published and survey articles may be difficult to understand. To make them relevant for the non-practitioners and to benefit all the researchers, it is indeed a need to outline the contribution of research articles in lay language.

The current paper demonstrates the participation of IIIT Bhagapur and IIT Patna team in three shared tasks namely, *CL-SciSumm 2020, LongSumm 2020 and CL-LaySumm 2020*, at first workshop on Schol-

ary Document Processing[1], 2020 (Chandrasekaran et al., 2020). The theme of these tasks is to generate medium-scale, long and Lay summaries, respectively. Here, Lay summary means a textual summary which is intended for non-technical audience. The scientific articles used for the first and third tasks are related to computational linguistic domain. While, for the second task, scientific articles cover distinct domains: archeology, epilepsy, and materials engineering. In current paper, all these tasks are posed as extractive summarization (Saini et al., 2019) problems where a subset of sentences are selected from scientific articles based on their relevance. For CL-LaySumm and CL-SciSumm, we have developed the system based on the maximal marginal relevance (MMR) (Carbinell and Goldstein, 2017) which considers novelty and informativeness of sentences with respect to what is already included in the summary. And, for LongSumm, our system utilizes neural network based approach. More descriptions about these tasks including datasets and methodology used, are provided in the subsequent sections. The performances of the systems are evaluated in terms of ROUGE (1-gram, 2-gram, and L) metrics on the provided dataset.

2 CL-SciSumm 2020

CL-SciSumm 2020 is the sixth Computational Linguistics Scientific Document Summarization Shared Task which aims to generate summaries of scientific articles not exceeding 250 words. The associated dataset for the task is provided with a Reference Paper (RP) (the paper to be summarized) and 10 or more citing Papers (CPs) containing citations to the RP, which are used to summarise RP. It includes two more sub-tasks: (a) *Task 1(A)*- iden-

---

[1]https://ornlcda.github.io/SDProc/index.html

Proceedings of the First Workshop on Scholarly Document Processing, pages 242–250
Online, November 19, 2020. ©2020 Association for Computational Linguistics
https://doi.org/10.18653/v1/P17

tifying the text-spans in the reference article that mostly reflect the citation contexts (i.e., citances that cite the RP) of the citing articles; (b) *Task 1(B)*- categorizing the identified text-spans into a predefined set of facets. Generation of structured summary for scientific document summmarization using the identified text-spans is covered in *Task 2*.

2.1 Dataset Description

The dataset associated with CL-SciSumm 2020 shared task, consists of 40 annotated scientific articles and their citations for training. In addition to this, a corpus of 1000 documents released as a part of ScicummNet (Yasunaga et al., 2019) dataset for scientific document summarization is readily available for training. For testing, a blind test set of 20 articles used for CL-SciSumm 2018 (Jaidka et al., 2019) and 2019 (Chandrasekaran et al., 2019) shared tasks, is again used for the current shared task.

2.2 Methodology

In this section, we have discussed the system developed for Task 1 and Task 2. The corresponding flowchart is shown in Figure 1.

2.2.1 Task 1(A)

For a given reference paper (RP), in order to identify the reference text-spans using citation context, we have used an unsupervised approach where we have extracted the top 5 sentences by calculating cosine similarity between each citance and sentences of the RP. These 5 sentences are considered as cited/reference text spans. Note that before calculating the similarity, we have converted the text-space into a (numeric) vector-space for which we have utilized different types of sentence embeddings namely, Albert (Beltagy et al., 2019a), ELMO (Peters et al., 2018), fastText (Athiwaratkun et al., 2018), SciBERT (Beltagy et al., 2019a), Universal Sentence Encoder (Cer et al., 2018), XLNET (Yang et al., 2019), which are capable of capturing the semantics of the sentences. Thus, in total, six systems are developed for Task 1(A).

2.2.2 Task 1(B)

For identifying discourse facets (Hypothesis, Implication, Aim, Results and Method) of cited text spans, we have used a voting based method. A supervised multi-class classification model, based on the Gradient Boosting (La Quatra et al., 2019; Li et al., 2008), is trained in order to assign a facet

to each cited text span. Training data statistics are described in Table 1. In our approach, we have extracted top 5 text spans for each citance in Task 1(A). We have used our trained model to identify facet for each cited text span. Later we have used a voting method to finalize facet for each citance.

Section	no. of sentences
Aim	78
Method	823
Hypothesis	23
Implication	91
Results	121
Total	1136

Table 1: Task 1B data statistics

2.2.3 Task 2

For generating structured summary of 250 words, we have used the unique sentences extracted in Task 1(A) (i.e., cited text spans) as the candidate set of sentences. This approach is known as citation-based summarization. For this purpose, a diversity-based unsupervised measure namely, maximal marginal relevance (MMR), inspired from (Carbinell and Goldstein, 2017) which is a linear combination of informativeness (with respect to documents consisting of chosen candidate sentences) and novelty of the sentence (with respect to sentences already included in the summary) is utilized. Mathematically, it is expressed as

$$MMR_1 = \lambda_1 Sim_1(Q, D) - (1 - \lambda_1) Sim_2(Q, d) \tag{1}$$

where, Q is the current sentence, D is the list of extracted sentences in Task 1(A), d is the generated summary till that point of time, Sim_1 is the similarity of a sentence with respect to all other sentences in the document, Sim_2 is the similarity of current sentence with the sentences that are already included in the summary. Note that for representation of sentences into vector form, we have used CountVetorizer[2] which counts the term-frequency of each term in the article.

The authors of the paper (Jaidka et al., 2017) which was on summarizing scientific articles mentioned that system performance using ROUGE mea-

---

[2]https://scikit-learn.org/stable/
modules/generated/sklearn.feature_
extraction.text.CountVectorizer.html

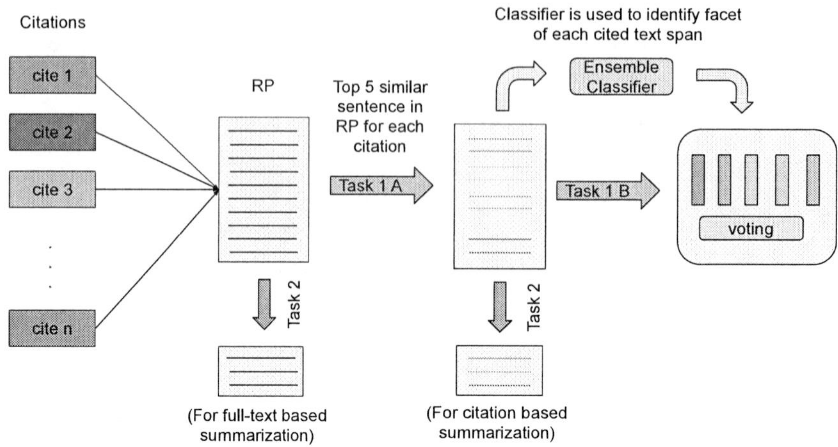

Figure 1: Proposed Architecture for Task 1(A) and Task 1(B) for CL-SciSumm 2020.

sure is not always lenient than sentence overlap F1 scores. They demonstrated how the ROUGE score is biased to prefer shorter sentences over longer ones. Motivated by this, we have proposed a variant of MMR by incorporating length of the sentence and is expressed as

$$MMR_2 = MMR_1 - \frac{\lambda_2}{L} \qquad (2)$$

where, L is the length of the current sentence.

Total twelve systems are developed using the citation-based approach in 6 different semantic spaces (refer to Section 2.2.1), each utilizing MMR_1 and MMR_2 for summary generation. To show the potentiality of citation-based summarization, we have also developed full-text based summarization where we have considered total sentences available in the scientific article as the candidate set of sentences for summary generation and utilized the MMR_2 for summary generation. Thus, in total, 13 systems are submitted in the CL-SciSumm 2020 shared task.

2.3 Discussion of Results

We have submitted a total of 13 system runs out of which 6 runs are for both Task 1(A) and Task 1(B) utilizing different semantic space. Rest of the 7 runs are only for the Task 2. Results obtained by our different runs for Task 1(A) and Task 1(B) are illustrated in Table 2 and Table 3, respectively. For Task 2, we have generated a single summary for each reference paper using MMR_1 and MMR_2 for different embeddings. Out of 13 system runs, 12 are citation-based, and remaining one is full text based. Results obtained are illustrated in Table 4. For task 1A, & 1B, the best results are obtained using universal sentence encoder for sentence embedding. For Task 2, our enhanced diversity based sentence selection approach, i.e., MMR_2, has performed better than existing maximum marginal relevance model (MMR_1). It is important to note that MMR_2 is tested with different embedding space; but all gives the similar results. Therefore, in Table 4, we have mentioned only MMR_2 as representative of those runs. From Table 4, we can also infer that citation based summarization has better sentence overlaps compared to full text based summarization (last row of Table 4). Note: Using MMR_2 we have obtained exact same results irrespective of the embeddings used. So in Table 4, we have added a single entry MMR_2 representative of those 6 systems.

Poor performance of our system for abstract summary can be explained since our approach tries to focus more on coverage, and diversity. Abstract of any scientific article lies in the starting part and since we are not considering position in our pro-

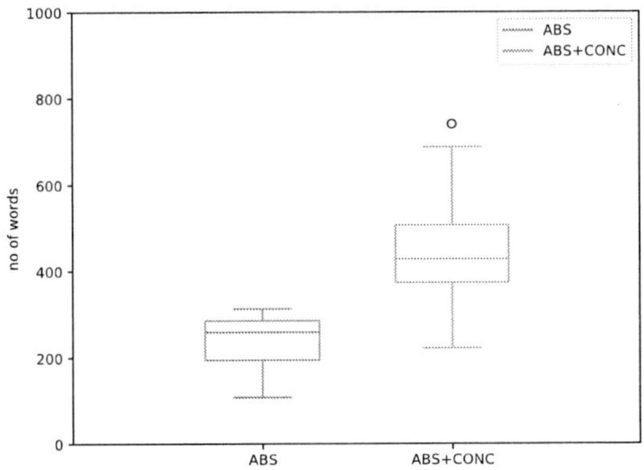

Figure 2: LaySumm test data statistics.

posed approach thus lesser sentence overlaps.

3 CL-LaySumm 2020

The CL-LaySumm 2020, which is the first shared task[3] for Lay summary generation, is for automatic generation of Lay summary in 70-100 words which is readable and easily understandable by the general pubic. In other words, given a full-text paper and its abstract, the task is to generate a Lay Summary of the specified length of that paper.

3.1 Description of Dataset

The dataset is provided with 600 scientific articles with its, abstract, full-text and corresponding lay summary (gold summary) of around 70-100 words. The test data consists of 37 articles (out of 600 articles). Test data statistics in terms of number of words are shown in Figure 2.

3.2 Methodology

In this section, we have discussed the methodology used for Lay summary generation. Similar to CL-SciSumm, we have considered this problem as a sentence selection problem where relevant sentences are selected from the document to generate the summary.

Similar to Cl-SciSumm, here also, we have used both variants of maximum marginal relevance (MMR) mentioned in Eq 1 and Eq 2 for generating summary. As abstract (Let us call it as ABS) conveys the outline of the paper; therefore, we have compared the summary generated using different variants of MMR with the ABS. Other comparisons

[3] https://ornlcda.github.io/SDProc/sharedtasks.html#laysumm

are done with the original Lay summary when using (a) the full-text of the article; (b) abstract (ABS) and conclusion (CON) of the paper.

Note that goal of generating lay summary is to create a human readable summary for non-technical audience. To avoid scientific jargon in the generated summary, we have proposed a three step process (let us call it as **CWR**: Complex Word Removal) where firstly we identify complex words from given sentence, then generate similar words of identified complex words, replace with most suitable word from the generated list. In this paper, we have only identified complex words and removed them, pseudo code for identifying complex words is given in Algorithm 1.

Algorithm 1: CWR

Result: List of Complex Words

set W = set of unique words from generated summary;

set KB = list of words in glove or wordnet;

set len = len(W);

initialize CWR = [];

/*list of complex words*/;

for $i \leftarrow 0$ **to** *len* **do**

    word = W[i];

    cleanWord = clean(word);

    /*remove unwanted symbols*/;

    lemWord = lemmatisation(cleanWord);

    if *lemWord not in KB* **then**

        | CWR.append(word)

    end

end

3.3 Discussion of Results

Results obtained using MMR_1 and, MMR_2 on ABS, FULL-TEXT and ABS+CON, are reported in Table 5. From this Table, it can be observed that by considering length in to the MMR_1, i.e., Eq. (2) and generating summary using the abstract of the article helps in improving the performance of the system in comparison to MMR_1. We have also illustrated how ROUGE-1 F score varied with λ_1 and, λ_2 in Table 6. Note that these parameters play important roles in generating the informative and novel Lay summary and are the parts of Eqs. (1) and (2). The best values of the parameters used in MMR_1 and MMR_2 are highlighted (in bold) in Table 6, i.e., for MMR_1, $\lambda_1 = 0.75$ and for MMR_2, $\lambda_1 = 0.75$, $\lambda_2 = 0.20$, are the best val-

Variant	Task 1A					
	Precision		**Recall**		**F1**	
	Micro	Macro	Micro	Macro	Micro	Macro
ALBERT	0.0202	0.0194	0.0953	0.0937	0.0333	0.0322
ELMO	0.0126	0.0131	0.0594	0.0622	0.0208	0.0216
FastText	0.0357	0.0362	0.1685	0.1727	0.059	0.0598
SciBERT	0.0114	0.0106	0.0539	0.0502	0.0188	0.0175
USE	**0.0469**	**0.0471**	**0.221**	**0.2246**	**0.0773**	**0.0779**
XLNET	0.0029	0.0032	0.0138	0.0146	0.0048	0.0053

Table 2: Performance of different system runs for Task 1A

Variant	Task 1B					
	Precision		**Recall**		**F1**	
	Micro	Macro	Micro	Macro	Micro	Macro
ALBERT	0.4649	0.4102	0.0789	0.0716	0.1349	0.122
ELMO	0.3333	0.2922	0.0461	0.0463	0.0809	0.0799
FastText	0.3882	0.4386	0.0985	0.0991	0.1571	0.1617
SciBERT	0.2644	0.2715	0.0341	0.0311	0.0604	0.0558
USE	**0.4900**	**0.4849**	**0.1469**	**0.1461**	**0.2261**	**0.2245**
XLNET	0.0517	0.0403	0.0044	0.0049	0.0082	0.0088

Table 3: Performance of different system runs for Task 1B

Variant	ABSTRACT		COMMUNITY		HUMAN	
	R-2	**R-SU4**	**R-2**	**R-SU4**	**R-2**	**R-SU4**
ALBERT + MMR_1	0.06548	0.01006	0.24342	0.12235	0.09604	0.01873
ELMO + MMR_1	0.09119	0.01435	0.2328	**0.14525**	0.11379	0.02512
FastText + MMR_1	0.08718	0.01111	0.25724	0.12458	0.10957	0.01945
SciBERT + MMR_1	0.13277	0.01211	0.18978	0.07994	0.14022	0.01846
USE + MMR_1	0.10521	0.01438	**0.27462**	0.13962	0.12955	0.02507
XLNET + MMR_1	0.05816	0.00825	0.17212	0.09749	0.08559	0.0176
MMR_2	**0.15067**	**0.07851**	0.13976	0.07268	**0.15073**	**0.10237**
MMR_2 (full text)	0.03909	0.03708	0.12305	0.06701	0.05206	0.0503

Table 4: Performance (F1 scores) of different system runs for Task 2

ues. Here, λ_1 represents the diversity factor as we increase λ_1, diversity of generated summary decreases. Reader may have in mind that we are using high value of λ_1, i.e., 0.75 and thus, the summary may have less coverage. Since average number of words in ABS are around 250 (Figure 2) and our task is to find lay summary around 100 words; therefore, we have used higher λ_1. Whereas λ_2 tries to maximize Rouge score. As in Table 5, abstract is shown to be good for the summary generation; therefore, we have executed the Algorithm 1 using the same (i.e., ABS). The results attained by CWR using different variants of MMR are shown in Table 7. After observing the results, it is clear that there is not much difference among-st the best

results of Table 5 and 7, or in other words, the results of Table 7 are quite less than those reported in Table 5.

Error analysis of CWR: Some of the common issues associated with identifying complex words are finding lemma. Lemmatization usually refers to performing things properly with the use of a vocabulary and morphological analysis of words, normally aiming to remove inflectional endings only and to return the base or dictionary form of a word, which is known as the lemma. Few common scientific terms which are not present in lexical databases like wordnet (Miller, 1995) can be important and trivial in the context of the paper. For example words like "hepatocellular", "carcinoma"

Variant	Data	F1 Scores		
		R-1	R-2	R-L
MMR_1	ABS	0.4009	0.1679	0.2239
MMR_2	ABS	**0.4048**	**0.1690**	**0.2244**
MMR_1	ABS+CON	0.3837	0.1411	0.2050
MMR_2	ABS+CON	0.3855	0.1394	0.2055
MMR_1	FULL	0.2835	0.0604	0.1609
MMR_2	FULL	0.2875	0.0628	0.1592

Table 5: Results attained using MMR and it's variant for CL-LaySumm 2020. Here, R in second row stands for 'ROUGE'.

λ_1	λ_2	ROUGE 1-F
0.25	0.0	0.3876
0.50	0.0	0.3940
0.75	0.0	**0.4009**
1.00	0.0	0.3971
0.75	0.1	0.4031
0.75	0.2	**0.4048**

Table 6: Study of parameters used in MMR_1 and MMR_2 for Lay Summary generation. Here, we have used only ABSTRACT for generating summary.

Variant	Data	F1 Scores		
		R-1	R-2	R-L
$CWR + MMR_1$	ABS	0.3986	0.1586	0.2187
$CWR + MMR_2$	ABS	**0.4033**	**0.1614**	**0.2209**

Table 7: Results attained by applying CWR on the generated summary using abstract (ABS). Here, R in second row stands for 'ROUGE'.

etc., are trivial for paper (S016882782030009X) but are not present in wordnet vocabulary. Therefore, our result using CWR (Table 7) underperform that by MMR_2 (Table 5), thus demanding more sophisticated model.

4 LongSumm 2020

Most of the existing works on scientific document summarization focus on generating a summary of shorter length (maximum up to 250 words). Such type of length constraint can be sufficient when summarizing news articles, but for scientific articles, the summary requires expertise in the scientific domain to understand it. LongSumm 2020 shared task addresses this issue by generating longer summaries (up to 600 words) of scientific articles.

4.1 Dataset Description

The training corpus for this task includes 1705 extractive summaries, and 531 abstractive summaries of NLP/ML scientific papers. The extractive summaries are based on video talks from associated conferences (Lev et al., 2019), while the abstractive summaries are from blog posts created by NLP and ML researchers. The test set consists of 22 research papers for both extactive and abstractive summarization and task is to generate a summary of 600 words. In the current paper, we have focused only on the extractive summarization of LongSumm.

4.2 Methodology

To solve the LongSumm in an extactive way, we have utilized the neural network based approach, i.e., convolution neural network (Kim, 2014). The sentences which are part of the summary are assigned 1 and remaining sentences are assigned 0. In other words, we have posed this task as a binary classification problem where task is to identify whether the given sentence can be a part of the summary or not. Positional embedding is also used along with sentence embedding. The detailed methodology used in our CNN is described below:

1. **Convolution:** Authors of (Kim, 2014) showed that CNN with one layer of convolution performs remarkably well for sentence classification tasks. Therefore, we have used one dimensional CNN for extracting features from sentences as described below mathematically:

$$c_i = g(W_f^T \dot{X}_{i:i+m-1} + b) \qquad (3)$$

$$c = [c_1, c_2, c_3, ..., c_{n-m+1}] \qquad (4)$$

where b is the bias term, g is a non-linear activation function, W_f, m and X are convolution filter, window size and concatenation vector, respectively.

2. **MaxPooling:** Pooling is a down sampling operation. In max pooling, each pooling operation selects the maximum value of the current view and thus reduces the size yet preserves features as shown below:

$$h_l = max(c) \qquad (5)$$

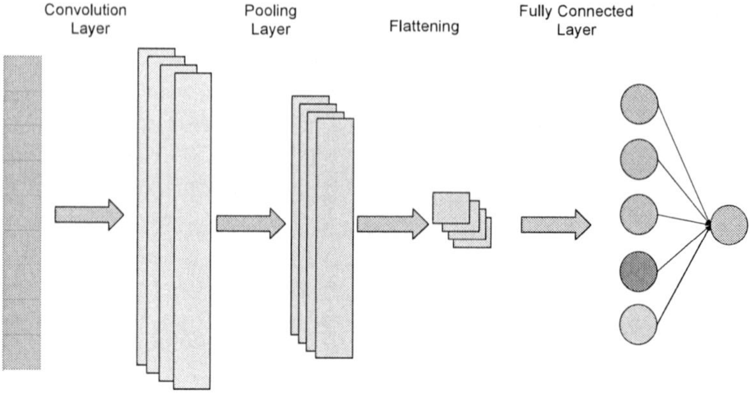

Figure 3: Architecture used for LongSumm2020.

$$h = [h_1, h_2..., h_k]^T \qquad (6)$$

where h is hidden representation of sentence after convolution.

3. **Positional Embedding:**

In any document, regardless of the domain, more relevant sentences can be found in some sections of the document like the leading paragraph of the document (Saini et al., 2019). Particularly scientific articles are structured in a way that sentences at start (abstract) are more informative as represented below.

$$p_i = \frac{1}{1+i} \qquad (7)$$

where p_i is the ith ($0 \leq i < N$) sentence in the article. Higher the score for a sentence, more informative it is. Therefore, positional embedding is also utilized in our CNN framework.

4. **Flattening:** After the max-pooling layer, we obtain the penultimate layer h (Eq. 6), which is the vector representation of the input sentence obtained from CNN. We have also fed sentence position encoding (h_p) as additional feature.

$$h^* = [h, h_p] \qquad (8)$$

where h^* is the semantic representation obtained from CNN and h_p is position encoding represented as

$$h_p = [p_1, p_2..., p_k]^T \qquad (9)$$

To avoid overfitting, we have used regularization as mentioned in Eq 10.

$$\hat{y} = \sigma(w_r(h^* \otimes r) + b_r) \qquad (10)$$

And finally, we have used sigmoid function as per Eq 11 for obtaining probability scores:

$$\sigma(\hat{y}) = \frac{1}{1 + e^{-\hat{y}}} \qquad (11)$$

Note that we have considered sigmoid probability for assigning ranks to sentences and used those for sentence selection to be included in the summary till the length constraint is satisfied.

4.3 Experimental setup

For our experimentation, we have used SciBert (Beltagy et al., 2019b) to get the sentence embeddings as it is trained on a large multi-domain corpus of scientific publications to improve performance on many scientific NLP tasks like summarization (Gabriel et al., 2019) and relation extraction (Sung et al., 2019). For convolution layer, we have used 600 filters, and 3 kernels with ReLU as our activation function. For Pooling, we have used pool size of 2. We train the model for 10 epochs with the Adadelta optimizer.

4.4 Discussion of Results

We have submitted 4 systems for LongSumm shared task. Out of 4, two systems are based on CNN architecture. The key difference between two neural models is essentially the limit of the number of words for summary generation, i.e., the first system (CNN_1) uses a strict 600 words and the second system (CNN_2) maintains on an average of 600 words for generating summaries. For other two systems, we have used MMR_1 and MMR_2 using same hyper parameters as LaySumm (Section 3.3). The results obtained for LongSumm 2020 task are reported in Table 8. From this Table it can be inferred that (a) CNN_2 performs better in term of Rouge-2 and Rouge-L F1-measure, but in terms of Rouge-1 F1-measure, MMR_2 performs the best. Training vs. testing accuracy for the results obtained using CNN_2 are shown in Figure 4.

Model	Rouge 1-F	Rouge 2-F	Rouge L-F
MMR_1	0.4958	0.1415	0.1815
MMR_2	**0.4960**	0.1418	0.1872
CNN_1	0.4840	0.1535	0.1993
CNN_2	0.4903	**0.1574**	**0.2046**

Table 8: Results of our top system runs for LongSumm 2020 shared task

5 Conclusion and Future work

We have investigated the effects of using maximal marginal relevance (MMR) in developing the systems for three shared tasks: CL-SciSumm, CL-LaySumm, and LongSumm 2020. Another variant of MMR is also proposed by incorporating a length-based feature. For LongSumm, we have also investigated the effect of using a convolution neural network. As the goal of LaySumm is to generate Lay summary, which is understandable for a non-technical audience, we have tried a common word removal approach using the lexical database like WordNet, which fails due to non-presence of

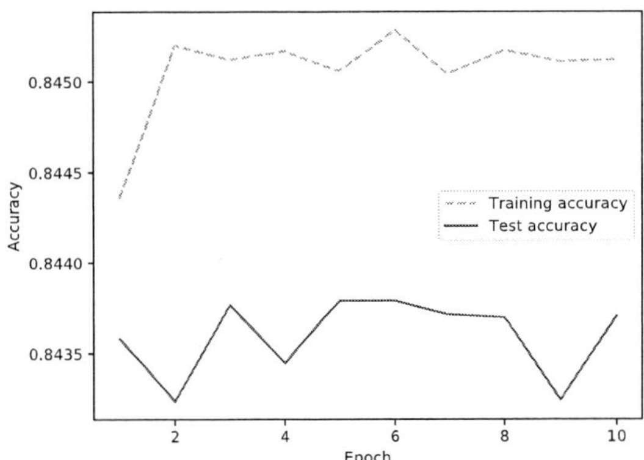

Figure 4: Training vs validation accuracy

scientific terms. In the future, we would like to develop a more sophisticated approach for LaySumm generation.

References

Ben Athiwaratkun, Andrew Gordon Wilson, and Anima Anandkumar. 2018. Probabilistic fasttext for multi-sense word embeddings. *arXiv preprint arXiv:1806.02901.*

Iz Beltagy, Kyle Lo, and Arman Cohan. 2019a. Scibert: A pretrained language model for scientific text. *arXiv preprint arXiv:1903.10676.*

Iz Beltagy, Kyle Lo, and Arman Cohan. 2019b. Scibert: A pretrained language model for scientific text. In *Proceedings of the 2019 Conference on Empirical Methods in Natural Language Processing and the 9th International Joint Conference on Natural Language Processing, EMNLP-IJCNLP 2019, Hong Kong, China, November 3-7, 2019*, pages 3613–3618. Association for Computational Linguistics.

Jaime Carbinell and Jade Goldstein. 2017. The use of mmr, diversity-based reranking for reordering documents and producing summaries. In *ACM SIGIR Forum*, volume 51, pages 209–210. ACM New York, NY, USA.

Daniel Cer, Yinfei Yang, Sheng-yi Kong, Nan Hua, Nicole Limtiaco, Rhomni St John, Noah Constant, Mario Guajardo-Cespedes, Steve Yuan, Chris Tar, et al. 2018. Universal sentence encoder. *arXiv preprint arXiv:1803.11175.*

M. K. Chandrasekaran, G. Feigenblat, Hovy. E., A. Ravichander, M. Shmueli-Scheuer, and A De Waard. 2020. Overview and insights from scientific document summarization shared tasks 2020: CL-SciSumm, LaySumm and LongSumm. In *Proceedings of the First Workshop on Scholarly Document Processing (SDP 2020).*

Muthu Kumar Chandrasekaran, Michihiro Yasunaga, Dragomir Radev, Dayne Freitag, and Min-Yen Kan. 2019. Overview and results: Cl-scisumm shared task 2019. *arXiv preprint arXiv:1907.09854*.

Arman Cohan and Nazli Goharian. 2018. Scientific document summarization via citation contextualization and scientific discourse. *International Journal on Digital Libraries*, 19(2-3):287–303.

John M Conroy and Sashka T Davis. 2018. Section mixture models for scientific document summarization. *International Journal on Digital Libraries*, 19(2-3):305–322.

Saadia Gabriel, Antoine Bosselut, Ari Holtzman, Kyle Lo, Asli Çelikyilmaz, and Yejin Choi. 2019. Co-operative generator-discriminator networks for abstractive summarization with narrative flow. *ArXiv*, abs/1907.01272.

Kokil Jaidka, Muthu Kumar Chandrasekaran, Devanshu Jain, and Min-Yen Kan. 2017. The cl-scisumm shared task 2017: Results and key insights. In *BIRNDL@SIGIR*.

Kokil Jaidka, Michihiro Yasunaga, Muthu Kumar Chandrasekaran, Dragomir Radev, and Min-Yen Kan. 2019. The cl-scisumm shared task 2018: Results and key insights. *arXiv preprint arXiv:1909.00764*.

Yoon Kim. 2014. Convolutional neural networks for sentence classification. In *Proceedings of the 2014 Conference on Empirical Methods in Natural Language Processing (EMNLP)*, pages 1746–1751, Doha, Qatar. Association for Computational Linguistics.

Moreno La Quatra, Luca Cagliero, and Elena Baralis. 2019. Poli2sum@ cl-scisumm-19: Identify, classify, and summarize cited text spans by means of ensembles of supervised models. In *BIRNDL@ SIGIR*, pages 233–246.

Guy Lev, Michal Shmueli-Scheuer, Jonathan Herzig, Achiya Jerbi, and David Konopnicki. 2019. Talksumm: A dataset and scalable annotation method for scientific paper summarization based on conference talks. *arXiv preprint arXiv:1906.01351*.

Ping Li, Qiang Wu, and Christopher J Burges. 2008. Mcrank: Learning to rank using multiple classification and gradient boosting. In *Advances in neural information processing systems*, pages 897–904.

George A Miller. 1995. Wordnet: a lexical database for english. *Communications of the ACM*, 38(11):39–41.

Ramesh Nallapati, Feifei Zhai, and Bowen Zhou. 2017. Summarunner: A recurrent neural network based sequence model for extractive summarization of documents. In *Thirty-First AAAI Conference on Artificial Intelligence*.

Ramesh Nallapati, Bowen Zhou, Caglar Gulcehre, Bing Xiang, et al. 2016. Abstractive text summarization using sequence-to-sequence rnns and beyond. *arXiv preprint arXiv:1602.06023*.

Matthew E Peters, Mark Neumann, Mohit Iyyer, Matt Gardner, Christopher Clark, Kenton Lee, and Luke Zettlemoyer. 2018. Deep contextualized word representations. *arXiv preprint arXiv:1802.05365*.

Naveen Saini, Sriparna Saha, Dhiraj Chakraborty, and Pushpak Bhattacharyya. 2019. Extractive single document summarization using binary differential evolution: Optimization of different sentence quality measures. *PloS one*, 14(11):e0223477.

Chul Sung, Tejas I. Dhamecha, Swarnadeep Saha, Tengfei Ma, V. Pulla Reddy, and Rishi Arora. 2019. Pre-training bert on domain resources for short answer grading. In *EMNLP/IJCNLP*.

Zhilin Yang, Zihang Dai, Yiming Yang, Jaime Carbonell, Russ R Salakhutdinov, and Quoc V Le. 2019. Xlnet: Generalized autoregressive pretraining for language understanding. In *Advances in neural information processing systems*, pages 5753–5763.

Michihiro Yasunaga, Jungo Kasai, Rui Zhang, Alexander R Fabbri, Irene Li, Dan Friedman, and Dragomir R Radev. 2019. Scisummnet: A large annotated corpus and content-impact models for scientific paper summarization with citation networks. In *Proceedings of the AAAI Conference on Artificial Intelligence*, volume 33, pages 7386–7393.

AUTH @ CLSciSumm 20, LaySumm 20, LongSumm 20

Alexios Gidiotis

[1] School of Informatics,
Aristotle University of Thessaloniki,
Thessaloniki, Greece
[2] Atypon Hellas,
Vasilissis Olgas 212,
Thessaloniki, Greece
gidiotis@csd.auth.gr

Stefanos Dimitrios Stefanidis

[1] School of Informatics,
Aristotle University of Thessaloniki,
Thessaloniki, Greece
[2] Atypon Hellas,
Vasilissis Olgas 212,
Thessaloniki, Greece
sstefanidis@atypon.gr

Grigorios Tsoumakas

[1] School of Informatics,
Aristotle University of Thessaloniki,
Thessaloniki, Greece
greg@csd.auth.gr

Abstract

We present the systems we submitted for the shared tasks of the Workshop on Scholarly Document Processing at EMNLP 2020. Our approaches to the tasks are focused on exploiting large Transformer models pre-trained on huge corpora and adapting them to the different shared tasks. For tasks 1A and 1B of CL-SciSumm we are using different variants of the BERT model to tackle the tasks of "cited text span" and "facet" identification. For the summarization tasks 2 of CL-SciSumm, LaySumm and LongSumm we make use of different variants of the PEGASUS model, with and without fine-tuning, adapted to the nuances of each one of those particular tasks.

1 Introduction

For scholars in every scientific domain, the ever growing amount of articles published each year has made the long-lasting challenge of keeping up with the recent literature significantly harder. In addition, there is an increasing need for making research accessible and relevant to the general public and not just a small group of researchers and practitioners. For example, taxpayers want to know where federal money supporting research goes. As a result, there is a need for different types of summaries that can either facilitate scientific research by compressing the key ideas discussed in a scientific paper or make scientific research more relevant for a lay audience.

It is obvious that tasking the author of a paper with writing multiple summaries of her work for different audiences is time-consuming. Consequently, the interest for methods that automatically summarize scientific documents in different styles and variations has increased significantly. Towards this direction, the 1st Scholarly Document Processing Shared Task (SDP 2020) (Chandrasekaran et al., 2020) introduces a number of different tasks that

address these challenges. In addition to the original CL-SciSumm sub-tasks of previous years, the 2020 version includes tasks that are targeting the summarization of complete papers as well as the generation of lay summaries. The different tasks of SDP 2020 can be summarized as follows.

1. **CL-SciSumm:** The original CL-SciSumm challenge includes three sub-tasks. Given a set of reference papers (RP) and the corresponding papers that cite them (CP), task 1A requires for each citance (i.e. a sentence of the CP that references the RP) the identification of the "cited" text spans in the RP. In task 1B participants have to tag each cited span with the appropriate "facets" from a predefined set. Finally, for the optional task 2 a summary of the RP should be generated.

2. **LaySumm:** This task requires participants to generate a short summary for each given paper that accurately represents the content and at the same time is comprehensible and interesting to a lay audience.

3. **LongSumm:** In this task the requirement is to generate an extensive and detailed summary for each of the given scientific papers that sufficiently covers all the salient information.

Exploiting large language models that are pre-trained on huge corpora of unlabelled data and then adapting them to solve NLP problems has proven to be a very successful strategy. This type of approach has yielded state-of-the-art results in a variety of NLP tasks such as question answering, machine translation and summarization and has proven to be especially beneficial when the training data are limited. In this work our main focus is to explore large pre-trained Transformers like BERT (Devlin et al., 2018) and PEGASUS (Zhang et al., 2019)

Proceedings of the First Workshop on Scholarly Document Processing, pages 251–260
Online, November 19, 2020. ©2020 Association for Computational Linguistics
https://doi.org/10.18653/v1/P17

and how they can be effectively used in the context of the SDP 2020 shared task. For CL-SciSumm task 1A we fine-tune a BERT pairwise classifier that is able to identify "cited text spans" of the RP given a number of "citing spans" from multiple CPs. We further improve the efficiency of our system by adding a pre-filtering stage based on TF-IDF that selects good "candidates" for the BERT model. In task 1B we train a simple Logistic Regression classifier that uses embeddings from another pre-trained model, SciBERT (Beltagy et al., 2019), and is able to classify each cited text span into one of five distinct facets. We show that even an algorithm as simple as Logistic Regression can effectively learn a fairly complex task with very few training data when using features from a powerful pre-trained model such as SciBERT.

We approach task 2 of CL-SciSumm as well as LaySumm and LongSumm as abstractive summarization tasks. More specifically, we employ the PEGASUS pre-trained model that has demonstrated very good results in various abstractive summarization benchmarks. We use the pre-trained model without any additional training to generate a comprehensive summary of an article given the abstract as well as the information from the parts of the full text that are cited by other articles for task 2 of CL-SciSumm. For the LaySumm task, we fine-tune the PEGASUS model to compress and re-write the abstract of the given article in order to generate a summary suited for a lay audience. Finally, for the LongSumm task our approach makes use of the Divide-ANd-ConquER (DANCER) (Gidiotis and Tsoumakas, 2020) summarization method in combination with the PEGASUS model aiming to generate an accurate and detailed summary of the article by separately summarizing important sections of the full text.

The rest of this work is structured as follows. In section 2 we very briefly present different summarization approaches focusing on academic articles with emphasis on pre-trained Transformer models. In sections 3 to 5 we describe our approaches to each one of the three tasks and in section 6 we discuss our experiments and results.

2   Related Work

The task of summarizing scientific articles has received increased attention lately. Existing methods usually approach the problem in one of two fundamental ways. Extractive methods (Cohan and Goharian, 2015, 2018; Collins et al., 2017) focus mainly on identifying key sentences of the text and creating a summary by combining the extracted sentences. On the other hand, abstractive methods (Cohan et al., 2018; Subramanian et al., 2019; Zhang et al., 2019) are using language models conditioned on the input text in order to generate a summary.

Both extractive and abstractive methods when applied to scientific articles are typically taking as input the abstract and/or the full text of the article and try to generate an abstract-like summary. In contrast, DANCER (Gidiotis and Tsoumakas, 2020) learns to summarize different sections of the full text separately and combines the individual summaries into a single article summary.

Given the increased popularity and success of large pre-trained Transformer models in various NLP tasks, multiple approaches have decided to use similar models for summarization. Such approaches have either used pre-trained Transformers as encoders combined with a classification decoder that selects sentences in an extractive manner (Subramanian et al., 2019; Liu and Lapata, 2019) or have employed full encoder-decoder models that are pre-trained on various tasks and fine-tuned for abstractive summarization (Song et al., 2019; Dong et al., 2019; Yan et al., 2020).

One notable such model is the Pre-training with Extracted Gap-sentences for Abstractive SUmmarization Sequence-to-sequence (PEGASUS) (Zhang et al., 2019) model. PEGASUS is a Transformer encoder-decoder model pre-trained on massive corpora of documents (Web and news articles) that has demonstrated great potential on various summarization benchmarks. The pre-training of PEGASUS is based on optimizing the Gap Sentence Generation (GSG) objective where whole sentences of the input are masked and the model attempts to generate these gap-sentences from the rest of the input.

A number of summarization approaches we proposed for the CL-SciSumm task B in the previous years of the challenge, including extractive methods based on probabilistic models (Li et al., 2019) and large pre-trained BERT models (Zerva et al., 2019).

3 CL-SciSumm

3.1 Data Processing

The corpus of the CL-SciSumm shared task is split into two separate collections:

1. The manually annotated training set which consists of 40 articles and citing papers. For task 1A, we have multiple citances for each RP and each of these citances corresponds to a specific cited text span. For task 1B we are given the facet annotations for each one of the cited text spans and for task 2 human-written summaries are provided.

2. The ScisummNet corpus (Yasunaga et al., 2019), which consists of 1000 articles that are paired with multiple automatically annotated citing articles.

Out of the 40 articles in the manually annotated dataset, we randomly select 30 articles for the training set and 10 articles for the test set. For task 1A we created "positive" pairs of citing and reference spans as well as "negative" pairs of citing spans and randomly selected sentences from the RP. We also included the whole ScisummNet dataset into the training set of this task. For task 1B we are only able to use the manually annotated data since the ScisummNet dataset does not include facet annotations. One important notice about the task 1B data is the severe class imbalance which can potentially be problematic for the training of machine learning models.

The dataset for task 2 includes multiple human-written summaries for each article of the manually annotated dataset. Those summaries are annotated as "author summary", "community summary" and "human" in the JSON schema. We decided to use the summary labeled "human" as target summary because it was the one out of the three that was present in almost all articles of the dataset. In this task we will not be performing any additional training so we split the 40 articles into 20 for the validation set and 20 for the test set.

3.2 Task 1A

Our approach for task 1A makes use of the pre-trained BERT model (Devlin et al., 2018) and fine tunes it for the task. More specifically, we formulate the task as a sequence classification problem, where we are using the binary classification capabilities of the BERT architecture. Our main fine-tuning objective trains the model to take as input pairs of text spans and tries to predict if the second span is the corresponding span of the RP cited by the first span. We are training using "positive" and "negative" pairs with a 1:1 ratio. We found that creating the same number of negative pairs as the positive pairs yields the best results. The training set for this objective includes both the training part of the manually annotated dataset and the whole ScisummNet dataset.

During the prediction phase, our system evaluates each one of the given citing spans in a pairwise fashion with different sentences from the RP and selects at most two sentences that have the highest probability of being the corresponding cited text. If the probability difference between the top-2 sentences is higher than a threshold $T = 0.015$ then we only keep the first sentence. This way we are able to identify text spans instead of single sentences although we found that most of the time the cited text span is indeed a single sentence. To further improve the predictive power of our model we are providing additional context for the model by extending the both the citing and cited text spans with the previous and next sentence. When making predictions during the test phase we are using the citing span as is and only extend the candidate cited spans with the surrounding sentences.

Based on the findings by (Zerva et al., 2019) we also employed an additional pre-processing step before fine-tuning our model for the task specific objective. In our approach, we further pre-train BERT Base using the MLM objective on the ACL Anthology Reference Corpus (Bird et al., 2008).

In order to increase the computational efficiency of the pairwise evaluation, we are first using TF-IDF similarity to select the top-20 most similar sentences to the citing text span. Then we proceed on evaluating those "candidate" sentences with the pairwise model that we described previously.

3.3 Task 1B

For task 1B we decided to build a classification model that uses as input features contextual embeddings from the pre-trained SciBERT model (Beltagy et al., 2019) in order to classify each cited text into one of the five facets. Previous research has explored the use of contextual embeddings extracted from different layers of Transformer language models such as BERT (Devlin et al., 2018), ELMo (Peters et al., 2018) and GPT (Radford et al., 2019) as features for classification models. Also,

(Ethayarajh, 2019) demonstrates some interesting insights of how the outputs of the different layers compare with each other. Here we decided to use the last layer of SciBERT to get the embeddings, because this model is more relevant to the domain of the task articles and we did not experiment with other model types. The contextual embeddings of each cited text have been obtained from the CLS vector of the last layer of SciBERT.

Although there are some occasions where multiple facets apply to the same span the vast majority of samples had a single facet. For this reason we decided to treat the task as a simple multiclass sequence classification problem. We experimented with multiple classification algorithms like Logistic Regression and Random Forests. We opted for simpler classification models due to the limited amount of training data that were severely limiting our ability to train more sophisticated models.

3.4 Task 2

We approach task 2 as an abstractive summarization problem. It has been suggested by (Yasunaga et al., 2019) that a combination of the abstract and the cited text spans is sufficient content to cover the main aspects and findings of an academic article. We follow this idea and propose a summarization scheme that takes those inputs and tries to generate a comprehensive summary of the article.

More specifically, we are using the PEGASUS model pre-trained on the arXiv dataset in order to generate the summary given the abstract and cited text spans identified from the previous tasks. Given that the combined input sequences are much longer than the maximum input size we can support for PEGASUS (due to GPU memory limitations) we decided to run the PEGASUS model twice, one for the abstract and the second for the cited texts and combine the two individual summaries into the final summary. The combination is a simple concatenation of the abstract summary with the cited text summary. Due to the small size of the manually annotated dataset we cannot expect to sufficiently train a PEGASUS model so we opted to use the model without any additional fine-tuning.

4 LaySumm

4.1 Data Processing

For the LaySumm task, the data are provided in the form of plain text files that have already been parsed from the paper PDFs. For each article in the dataset we are given three text files, one with the full text of the article, one with the abstract and one with the target lay summary. The corpus covers three distinct domains, namely epilepsy, archaeology, and materials engineering and consists of 573 articles in total. We split the dataset in three parts using 338 samples for the training set, 113 samples for the validation set and leaving 114 samples for the test set. We focused our pre-processing on cleaning noise and removing unwanted tokens and artifacts such as equations, tabular elements and references.

The PEGASUS model uses tokenization with the SentencePiece Unigram algorithm (Kudo, 2018) and required us to have all the text lowercased. The particular pre-trained model we are using comes with the Unigram 96k vocabulary that was created during the pre-training of the model. We identified that this vocabulary misses several symbols that appear quite frequently in the LaySumm data (e.g. Greek letters) so we decided to encode those symbols with other "complex" tokens from the vocabulary before tokenization in order for the model to be able to parse them. For example, the Greek letter α is replaced with the complex token "greekalpha" before being tokenized. This allows the model to successfully encode and learn the symbol and gives us the ability to backwards replace it to the original symbol during the decoding phase.

4.2 Lay Summary Generation

Our approach for the LaySumm task focuses on re-writing selected parts of the article in order to make them more relevant and easier to understand for the lay audience. Our main system uses the PEGASUS Large model and fine-tunes it on the task dataset. We are based on the idea that a lot of the key information that we want to include are present in the abstract of the article and we focus our methods to the task of re-writing and compressing the abstract. Our fine-tuning objective involves feeding the abstract as input to the PEGASUS model and using the provided lay summary as target for the summarization training.

We experimented with different variants of the pre-trained PEGASUS model. Those variants include: 1) the pre-trained PEGASUS model, 2) a model fine-tuned on the arXiv dataset and 3) a model fine-tuned on the PubMed dataset. All pre-trained models were open sourced by the authors of the PEGASUS paper. We further fine-tuned the different models on the specific LaySumm task using the provided dataset.

5 LongSumm

5.1 Data Processing

The abstractive dataset for the LongSumm corpus was given in the form of JSON files including article metadata, target summary and URLs to download the article PDFs. We used the provided scripts to download a total of 497 out of the 528 PDFs (we did not have access to the rest) and then extracted the abstract and section text from the downloaded files using Science-Parse[1]. We ended up with a total of 497 JSON files with the combined full text, abstract and target summaries. Out of these articles, 297 were used in the training set, 100 in the validation set and 100 in the test set.

The pre-processing steps followed in this dataset were similar to the ones we have described in the previous section and involve basic cleaning, normalisation and filtering operations. Again we use the same strategy for the tokens that are not supported by the PEGASUS vocabulary.

5.2 Long Article Summarization

Our approach for the LongSumm task is based on the Divide-ANd-ConquER (DANCER) summarization method which processes each section in a distributed way. The method uses text similarities between sentences of the summary and sections of full text in order to create better alignment during training and learns a summarization model that is able to summarize each section of the article separately.

More specifically, our system selects "types" of sections, namely the *introduction,* methods, *results and* conclusion, and uses the PEGASUS model to generate a summary for each section. The corresponding summaries are then concatenated to form the complete summary of the article. When training this system we use as input the full text of the section and as target the part of the summary that is most similar to that particular section.

We first use ROUGE-1 recall as a similarity metric in order to assign each sentence of the summary to one of the selected sections of the full text and then we group all the sentences assigned to each section to form the target summary corresponding

section	keywords
introduction	introduction, case
literature	background, literature, related
methods	method(s), techniques, methodology
results	result(s), experimental, experiment(s)
conclusion	conclusion(s), concluding
acknowledgments	acknowledgments

Table 1: The different section types and the common keywords that are used in order to identify them using heuristics. If the header of a section includes any of the keywords associated with a specific section type it is assigned to that section type. Sections that can't be matched with any section type are ignored.

to this section. The complete system architecture is shown in Figure 1.

5.3 Section Tagger

In order to select the aforementioned types of sections we employ a classification model that classifies each section of a given article into one of six distinct categories (introduction, literature, methods, results, conclusion, acknowledgments). Based on our experiments we found that the combination of introduction, methods, results and conclusion gives us the best summaries overall.

This classifier has a single LSTM (Hochreiter and Schmidhuber, 1997) layer with additive attention (Bahdanau et al., 2015) and takes as input subword level BPEmb embeddings (Heinzerling and Strube, 2019). This model is trained on full text sections from the arXiv dataset. To train this model, we select sections of the corpus where the heading includes specific keywords that are characteristic of the section type. These keywords are shown in Table 1. We skip sections where the heading does not match this pattern. The model is trained to take as input the text of the section (without the heading) and tries to predict the section category.

6 Results and Discussion

6.1 Experimental Setup

In our experiments for task 1A we are using the Tensorflow implementation of BERT *Base* provided by huggingface [2]. After pre-training for 20k steps on the ACL corpus we proceed on fine-tuning for another 4k steps on the pairwise classification objective for task 1A. When we are building the TF-IDF model we are only based on the manually annotated

---

[1]https://github.com/allenai/
science-parse

[2]https://github.com/huggingface/
transformers

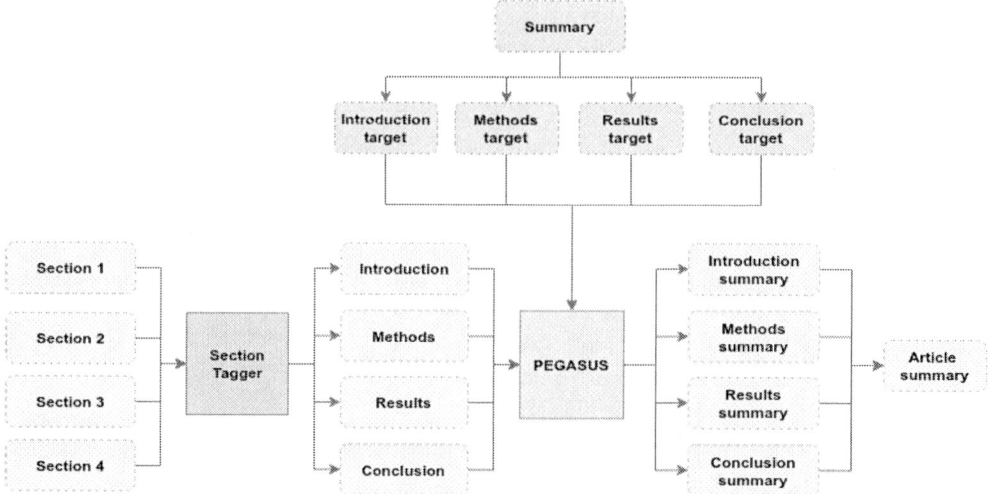

Figure 1: The main DANCER summarization framework combined with PEGASUS and the Section Tagger. During the training phase each section of the full text is paired with a part of the target. During the prediction phase important sections are selected with the help of the section tagger and each one is summarized separately. The individual summaries are then combined to form the article summary.

dataset. For task 1B we are using the SciBERT version open sourced by the authors of the original paper which is similar to the BERT Base model architecture. We are using the SciBERT model to get sentence level embeddings of size 768 which are then used as input to the classifiers.

All of our summarization methods are using the PEGASUS *Large* model which was pre-trained on the C4 and HugeNews dataset and was open sourced by the authors of the original paper. We also used two variations of this model that were fine-tuned for abstractive summarization. The first was fine-tuned for 74k steps on the arXiv dataset and the second for 100k steps on the PubMed dataset.

For task 2 of CL-SciSumm we are using the arXiv version of PEGASUS without any additional fine-tuning. We are running the model twice and generate summaries of up to 256 tokens for the abstract and the cited text spans identified from task 1A.

When fine-tuning our models on the LaySumm task we follow a very basic setup without extensive hyper-parameter tuning. More specifically, we used an input size of 1,024 tokens and an output size of 256 tokens since the evaluation scripts provided by the competition constrained the summary length to 150 words. We fine-tuned for 10k steps and monitor the ROUGE-1 F1 on the validation set in order to avoid overfitting. For the

Model	Macro			Micro		
	P	R	F1	P	R	F1
TF-IDF	14.64	10.45	12.20	15.23	9.30	11.55
BERT	**17.19**	**22.04**	**19.32**	**17.10**	**19.19**	**18.08**

Table 2: Results on our test set for task 1A. TF-IDF uses sentence similarities to select top-3 sentences. BERT is the proposed method.

LongSumm task we are using the arXiv PEGASUS model and we further fine-tune it for 10k steps using the DANCER method on the dataset of the task. The hyper-parameters used are identical to the ones used for the LaySumm model. Detailed hyper parameters can be found in Appendix A.1.

6.2 Results

6.2.1 CL-SciSumm

We are evaluating task 1A on our test set (including only the manually annotated data) and measure the standard micro and macro precision, recall and F1 score. These metrics are shown in Table 2. For reference we are also comparing our method with a simple baseline that uses only TF-IDF to select the top-3 sentences for citing each span.

It can be seen clearly that the BERT based model is definitely superior to the baseline model and is able to correctly retrieve a fair amount of the cited text spans.

For task 1B we are evaluating our methods using 10-fold cross validation on the whole manually

Model	Precision	Recall	F1 score
Random Forest	40.71	34.98	33.84
Logistic Regression	**49.84**	**41.08**	**40.83**

Table 3: 10-fold cross validation results on the development set for task 1B. This results are independent of the outputs of task 1A.

	Macro			Micro		
Task	P	R	F1	P	R	F1
1A	13.47	18.20	15.48	14.03	17.49	15.57
1B	94.72	20.89	34.22	91.89	20.36	33.33

Table 4: Shared evaluation results on our test set using the best performing models for both tasks. Spans that are incorrectly retrieved in the first task are not being scored by the second task.

annotated dataset. In Table 3 we show the macro precision, recall and F1 of our Logistic Regression classifier versus a Random Forest classifier.

These results show that very simple algorithms like Logistic Regression and Random Forests with SciBERT features perform well on this task with very few training examples. On the other hand, training more sophisticated models like neural networks was simply not feasible due to the small size of the dataset and the severe class imbalance. For example when we attempted to train neural networks for the task we ended up with models that only predicted the "methods" facet.

One should keep in mind that the previous results only measure the performance of the task 1B model, assuming that all "cited text spans" have been correctly identified by the task 1A model. We are also evaluating the combination of our best performing methods on our test set using the evaluation scripts provided by the competition. We use the text spans retrieved from task 1A as input for task 1B. The scores from the shared evaluation are shown in Table 4.

Finally, the evaluation of the summarization task 2 is done comparing the generated summary of each article with the "human" summary using ROUGE metrics (Lin, 2004). In Table 5 we present the results of our proposed approach on our test set. Those scores demonstrate the "zero-shot" capabilities of the PEGASUS pre-trained model which is able to perform well on a new task without any additional training.

6.2.2 LaySumm

When evaluating the results we used the official evaluation script provided by the competi-

	F1			Recall		
Model	R-1	R-2	R-L	R-1	R-2	R-L
arXiv	47.93	25.36	31.66	46.13	23.85	30.17

Table 5: ROUGE scores of the proposed method for task 2 on the whole manually annotated dataset.

	F1			Recall		
Model	R-1	R-2	R-L	R-1	R-2	R-L
pre-trained	44.33	20.73	29.73	42.40	19.68	28.25
arXiv	**45.59**	20.68	29.84	**45.38**	20.53	29.59
PubMed	45.29	**21.26**	**30.29**	45.10	**21.03**	**29.92**

Table 6: Method comparison on our hold-out test set of LaySumm. Pre-trained is based on the original PEGASUS model while PubMed and arXiv are first fine-tuned on the PubMed and arXiv dataset respectively before additional fine-tuning on the LaySumm task.

	F1			Recall		
Model	R-1	R-2	R-L	R-1	R-2	R-L
pre-trained	41.14	16.01	25.16	37.75	14.57	23.04
arXiv	**44.56**	19.36	27.72	**42.98**	18.60	26.73
PubMed	44.25	**19.91**	**29.70**	42.06	**18.76**	**28.15**

Table 7: Method comparison on the blind test set of LaySumm.

tion which measures ROUGE-1, ROUGE-2 and ROUGE-L recall and F1-score. The results on our hold-out test set are shown in Table 6.

As expected, both of the fine-tuned models outperform the model without any prior fine-tuning since they are better adapted to summarizing academic articles. However, the differences between the two models are very small with the arXiv model achieving a better ROUGE-1 score while the PubMed one achieving better ROUGE-2 and ROUGE-L F1 scores.

In Table 7 we show the results on the blind test set of the competition. Similarly to the numbers on our own test set, the arXiv model performs slightly better in terms of ROUGE-1 while the PubMed model is better in terms of ROUGE-2 and ROUGE-L. Once again, both models have a clear advantage compared to the model without prior summarization fine-tuning.

6.2.3 LongSumm

Based on the LaySumm results the model fine-tuned on the arXiv dataset had superior performance to both the model without fine-tuning and the model fine-tuned on PubMed so we decided to use this variant for the LongSumm task.

In order to evaluate the impact of the section

Model	F1			Recall		
	R-1	**R-2**	**R-L**	**R-1**	**R-2**	**R-L**
notrain	24.64	6.18	16.29	**33.10**	8.01	**23.12**
arXiv	**25.81**	**8.09**	**18.01**	29.52	**8.91**	21.20
notrain-notag	24.47	4.72	15.07	28.03	7.95	21.48
arXiv-notag	24.26	4.58	15.15	25.53	4.68	16.28

Table 8: Section level comparison between methods on the LongSumm test set. Notrain uses the model fine-tuned on arXiv without additional training. ArXiv is additionally fine-tuned on LongSumm. Notrain-notag and ArXiv-notag are the same models but using heuristics instead of the section tagger for section selection.

Model	F1			Recall		
	R-1	**R-2**	**R-L**	**R-1**	**R-2**	**R-L**
notrain	41.88	10.66	17.46	**45.94**	11.42	**19.79**
arXiv	**43.52**	**12.12**	**18.67**	42.27	**11.59**	18.43
notrain-notag	30.97	6.94	14.45	26.38	5.67	12.49
arXiv-notag	31.36	7.47	15.40	25.75	5.91	13.10

Table 9: Article level comparison between methods on the test set of LongSumm.

tagger model we repeated the same experiments but this time instead of using the section tagger to help us select the appropriate sections we used the section headings and the heuristics described in 5.3.

First, we evaluated the performance at a section level using ROUGE-1, ROUGE-2 and ROUGE-L recall and f1-scores between the input section and the target section summary. Results for this evaluation are shown in Table 8. Second, we evaluate at an article level computing the same metrics between the full generated summary of each article and the full target summary. For this evaluation we use the official evaluation script provided by the competition and the results are shown in Table 9.

Looking at the section level results, we can see that fine-tuning the model with DANCER improves the results in every metric since it is better tuned for section level summarization compared to the model that is trained on whole articles. We should note that in this setup it is hard to have a direct comparison between the systems using the section tagger and the systems that use heuristics because using the section tagger results in a much larger test set.

The article level results can give us a better idea about the performance of the system on the Long-Summ task itself. Here we run our summarization system to generate the section summaries, combine the summaries by concatenation to create the article level summary and compare it with the target

Model	F1			Recall		
	R-1	**R-2**	**R-L**	**R-1**	**R-2**	**R-L**
notrain	49.91	14.23	19.19	**50.04**	**14.29**	**19.24**
arXiv	**50.11**	**15.37**	**19.59**	46.93	14.23	18.18
notrain-notag	38.89	10.65	17.12	31.32	8.54	13.64
arXiv-notag	38.27	9.48	16.93	29.20	7.14	12.79

Table 10: Article level comparison between methods on the blind test set of LongSumm.

article summary. The results on our test set show that once again DANCER training improves performance across the board. It is also clear that the section tagger has a very large effect as it improves both the trained and un-trained system by more than 10 ROUGE-1 points. This is clearly due to the fact that using the section tagger we include in the summary a lot more sections from the text that might not have a heading following the patterns from the heuristic approach.

Results on the test set of the competition are shown in Table 10. Similar to the results from our test set, we can see that the system trained with DANCER combined with the section tagger is clearly superior to all other systems.

7 Conclusion

We have presented the systems we developed for the SDP 2020 shared task. For task 1A we implemented an efficient pairwise classification approach based on the BERT model that tackles the "cited text identification" problem. For task 1B we show how a simple Logistic Regression classifier using pre-trained SciBERT embeddings as features can effectively learn to solve the problem of facet classification.

For the summarization tasks we employ different variants of the PEGASUS model and adapt them to the nuances of each particular task. For task 2 we use of the pre-trained PEGASUS model in a zero-shot setting to generate a summary given the abstract of an article along with the cited text spans. For LaySumm we propose a re-writing strategy based on the PEGASUS model that works on the abstract and generates a lay summary. Finally, we showcase how the PEGASUS model can be used to summarize an academic paper in a distributed way and we demonstrate an end-to-end system that generates a "long" summary by selecting key sections, summarizing each section independently and combining them to form the final summary.

References

Dzmitry Bahdanau, Kyung Hyun Cho, and Yoshua Bengio. 2015. Neural machine translation by jointly learning to align and translate. In *Proceedings of the 2015 International Conference on Learning Representations*.

Iz Beltagy, Kyle Lo, and Arman Cohan. 2019. SCIBERT: A pretrained language model for scientific text. In *Proceedings of the 2019 Conference on Empirical Methods in Natural Language Processing and the 9th International Joint Conference on Natural Language Processing (EMNLP-IJCNLP)*, pages 3606–3611.

Steven Bird, Robert Dale, Bonnie J. Dorr, Bryan Gibson, Mark T. Joseph, Min Yen Kan, Dongwon Lee, Brett Powley, Dragomir R. Radev, and Yee Fan Tan. 2008. The ACL Anthology reference corpus: A reference dataset for bibliographic research in computational linguistics. In *Proceedings of the 2008 International Conference on Language Resources and Evaluation*.

M. K. Chandrasekaran, G. Feigenblat, Hovy. E., A. Ravichander, M. Shmueli-Scheuer, and A De Waard. 2020. Overview and Insights from Scientific Document Summarization Shared Tasks 2020: {CL-SciSumm}, {LaySumm} and {LongSumm}. In *Proceedings of the First Workshop on Scholarly Document Processing (SDP 2020)*.

Annan Cohan and Nazli Goharian. 2015. Scientific Article Summarization Using Citation-Context and Article Discourse Structure. In *Proceedings of the 2015 Conference on Empirical Methods in Natural Language Processing*, pages 390–400, Stroudsburg, PA, USA. Association for Computational Linguistics.

Arman Cohan, Franck Dernoncourt, Doo Soon Kim, Trung Bui, Seokhwan Kim, Walter Chang, and Nazli Goharian. 2018. A Discourse-Aware Attention Model for Abstractive Summarization of Long Documents. In *Proceedings of the 2018 Conference of the North American Chapter of the Association for Computational Linguistics: Human Language Technologies*, pages 615–621.

Arman Cohan and Nazli Goharian. 2018. Scientific document summarization via citation contextualization and scientific discourse. *International Journal on Digital Libraries*, 19(2-3):287–303.

Ed Collins, Isabelle Augenstein, and Sebastian Riedel. 2017. A Supervised Approach to Extractive Summarisation of Scientific Papers. In *Proceedings of the 2017 Conference on Computational Natural Language Learning*, pages 195–205.

Jacob Devlin, Ming-Wei Chang, Kenton Lee, and Kristina Toutanova. 2018. Bert: Pre-training of deep bidirectional transformers for language understanding. *arXiv preprint arXiv:1810.04805*.

Li Dong, Nan Yang, Wenhui Wang, Furu Wei, Xiaodong Liu, Yu Wang, Jianfeng Gao, Ming Zhou, and Hsiao-Wuen Hon. 2019. Unified language model pre-training for natural language understanding and generation. In *Advances in Neural Information Processing Systems*, pages 13042–13054.

Kawin Ethayarajh. 2019. How contextual are contextualized word representations? Comparing the geometry of BERT, ELMO, and GPT-2 embeddings. In *Proceedings of the 2019 Conference on Empirical Methods in Natural Language Processing and the 9th International Joint Conference on Natural Language Processing (EMNLP-IJCNLP)*, pages 55–65.

Alexios Gidiotis and Grigorios Tsoumakas. 2020. A Divide-and-Conquer Approach to the Summarization of Long Documents. *arXiv preprint arXiv:2004.06190*.

Benjamin Heinzerling and Michael Strube. 2019. BPEMB: Tokenization-free pre-trained subword embeddings in 275 languages. In *Proceedings of the 2019 International Conference on Language Resources and Evaluation*.

Sepp Hochreiter and Jürgen Schmidhuber. 1997. Long short-term memory. *Neural computation*, 9(8):1735–1780.

Taku Kudo. 2018. Subword regularization: Improving neural network translation models with multiple subword candidates. In *Proceedings of the 2018 Annual Meeting of the Association for Computational Linguistics*, volume 1, pages 66–75.

Lei Li, Yingqi Zhu, Yang Xie, Zuying Huang, Wei Liu, Xingyuan Li, and Yinan Liu. 2019. CIST@CLSciSumm-19: Automatic scientific paper summarization with citances and facets. In *CEUR Workshop Proceedings*, volume 2414, pages 196–207.

Chin-Yew Lin. 2004. Rouge: A package for automatic evaluation of summaries. In *Proceedings of the 2004 Workshop on Text Summarization Branches Out, Post Conference Workshop of ACL*.

Yang Liu and Mirella Lapata. 2019. Text Summarization with Pretrained Encoders. In *Proceedings of the 2019 Conference on Empirical Methods in Natural Language Processing and the 9th International Joint Conference on Natural Language Processing (EMNLP-IJCNLP)*, pages 3721–3731.

Matthew E. Peters, Mark Neumann, Mohit Iyyer, Matt Gardner, Christopher Clark, Kenton Lee, and Luke Zettlemoyer. 2018. Deep contextualized word representations. In *NAACL HLT 2018 - 2018 Conference of the North American Chapter of the Association for Computational Linguistics: Human Language Technologies - Proceedings of the Conference*, volume 1.

Alec Radford, Jeffrey Wu, Rewon Child, David Luan, Dario Amodei, and Ilya Sutskever. 2019. Language Models are Unsupervised Multitask Learners. *OpenAI Blog*, 1(8).

Kaitao Song, Xu Tan, Tao Qin, Jianfeng Lu, and Tie Yan Liu. 2019. MASS: Masked sequence to sequence pre-training for language generation. In *Proceedings of the 2019 International Conference on Machine Learning*, pages 5926–5936.

Sandeep Subramanian, Raymond Li, Jonathan Pilault, and Christopher Pal. 2019. On Extractive and Abstractive Neural Document Summarizationwith Transformer Language Models. *arXiv preprint arXiv:1909.03186*.

Yu Yan, Weizhen Qi, Yeyun Gong, Dayiheng Liu, Nan Duan, Jiusheng Chen, Ruofei Zhang, and Ming Zhou. 2020. ProphetNet: Predicting Future N-gram for Sequence-to-Sequence Pre-training. *arXiv preprint arXiv:2001.04063*.

Michihiro Yasunaga, Jungo Kasai, Rui Zhang, Alexander R. Fabbri, Irene Li, Dan Friedman, and Dragomir R. Radev. 2019. ScisummNet: A Large Annotated Corpus and Content-Impact Models for Scientific Paper Summarization with Citation Networks. In *Proceedings of the 2019 AAAI Conference on Artificial Intelligence*, pages 7386–7393.

Chrysoula Zerva, Minh Quoc Nghiem, Nhung T.H. Nguyen, and Sophia Ananiadou. 2019. NaCTeM-UoM @ CL-SciSumm 2019. In *CEUR Workshop Proceedings*, volume 2414, pages 167–180.

Jingqing Zhang, Yao Zhao, Mohammad Saleh, and Peter J Liu. 2019. PEGASUS: Pre-training with Extracted Gap-sentences for Abstractive Summarization. *arXiv preprint arXiv:1912.08777*.

A Appendix

A.1 Model Hyper Parameters

Here we report detailed hyper parameters for the used for the training and evaluation of our models. For task 1A we pre-train on the ACL corpus for 20k steps with a batch size of 32 and a learning rate of 0.00003. Then we fine-tune on on the pairwise classification objective for another 4k steps with a batch size of 32 and a learning rate of 0.00001. For task 1B the Logistic Regression classifier was trained for 100 iterations with a C value of 0.1 and L1 regularization. Our Random Forest classifier has 100 estimators and uses the "Gini impurity" criterion.

The PEGASUS model used is an encoder-decoder model based on Transformers and has 16 Transformer blocks for the encoder and decoder with hidden size of 1,024 units, 16 self-attention heads and feed-forward layer size of 4,096 units. The model is pre-trained with MLM and GSG on a combination of the C4 and HugeNews datasets. For the LaySumm task the model is fine-tuned for 10k steps with a learning rate of 0.0001 and a batch size of 6 (mainly due to GPU memory constraints). For the LongSumm task the PEGASUS model is fine-tuned for 10k steps using the DANCER method, batch size of 6 and a learning rate of 0.0001.

A.2 Summarization Examples

In order to demonstrate the quality of the summaries generated by our methods, we present summaries of this paper generated by the arXiv and PubMed DANCER PEGASUS models.

DANCER arXiv: The 1st Scholarly Document Processing shared task (SDP 2020) is a new number of tasks that automatically summarize scientific documents in different styles and variations. In addition to the original CL-SciSumm sub-tasks of previous years, the 2020 version includes additional tasks that are targeting the summarization of complete papers as well as the generation of lay summaries. We present the systems we developed for the SDP 2020 shared task.

DANCER PubMed: For every scientific domain, the ever growing amount of articles published each year has made the long-lasting challenge of keeping up with the recent literature significantly harder. In addition to this, there is an increasing need for making research accessible and relevant to the general public and not just researchers and practitioners. For example, taxpayers want to know where federal money supporting research goes. There is a need for different types of summaries that can either facilitate scientific research compressing the key ideas discussed in a scientific paper or make scientific research relevant for a lay audience. We developed systems for a SDP 2020 shared task that use a pairwise approach to solve the cited text span identification problem, a pre-trained model to solve the problem of facet classification, and models to summarize academic papers.

UniHD@CL-SciSumm 2020: Citation Extraction as Search

Dennis Aumiller*, Satya Almasian*, Philip Hausner*, Michael Gertz
Heidelberg University, Heidelberg, Germany
`{lastname}@informatik.uni-heidelberg.de`

Abstract

This work presents the entry by the team from Heidelberg University in the CL-SciSumm 2020 shared task at the Scholarly Document Processing workshop at EMNLP 2020. As in its previous iterations, the task is to highlight relevant parts in a reference paper, depending on a citance text excerpt from a citing paper.

We participated in tasks 1A (cited text span identification) and 1B (citation context classification). Contrary to most previous works, we frame Task 1A as a search relevance problem, and introduce a 2-step re-ranking approach, which consists of a preselection based on BM25 in addition to positional document features, and a top-k re-ranking with BERT. For Task 1B, we follow previous submissions in applying methods that deal well with low resources and imbalanced classes.

1 Introduction

Scientific papers are among the most important means of communication between researchers that enable scholars to share their knowledge and progress, and provide other scientists with retrospective documentation and starting points for further improvements. A crucial part of this scientific exchange is citations, which refer to prior academic work that helped researchers put their work in the context of a broader scientific vision. The CL-SciSumm Shared Task aims to construct meaningful summarization of this scientific communication by utilizing information extracted from such citations. The key contributions of a paper are identified by investigating which parts of the paper are cited, since citations usually highlight the critical points and main contributions of a paper. Additionally, citations often target several aspects of a paper, and hence, can complement each other (Jaidka et al., 2018a). As a result, a paper's contributions may be outlined by summarizing the parts of the paper that other researchers cited.

Another essential aspect of citations is the manner in which they cite another work: Some may refer to results obtained in previous work, some build on top of the reference paper's methodology or propose modifications, and some debate claims hypothesized in a prior paper (Teufel et al., 2006). Therefore, particular citations of the same paper may refer to different text spans in various sections of the reference paper. If the authors use the cited work as a basis or starting point, they often refer to the methodology section. At the same time, a citation comparing the goals or results with that of prior work mainly refers to the introduction or evaluation of a paper.

Building on the ideas presented above, the CL-SciSumm Shared Tasks (Jaidka et al., 2016, 2017, 2018b; Chandrasekaran et al., 2019, forthcoming) split up the task of scientific summarization into multiple sub-tasks. These sub-tasks are formulated as follows: Given a set of reference papers (RP) and a set of corresponding citing papers (CP) that contain citations to one of the reference papers, and in which text spans (so called citances) have been identified that pertain to a particular citation to the respective RP, participants of the Shared Task have to develop methods to solve the following tasks:

- *Task 1A:* For each text span around a citation (citance), a span in the RP has to be identified that most accurately reflects the citance. Spans may be a sentence fragment, a complete sentence, or up to 5 consecutive sentences.

- *Task 1B:* Each citance has to be classified based on its citation context. The five facet categories are *Aim, Hypothesis, Implication, Method*, and *Results*. Additionally, a cited text span may belong to more than one facet.

---

* These authors contributed equally to this work.

261

Proceedings of the First Workshop on Scholarly Document Processing, pages 261–269
Online, November 19, 2020. ©2020 Association for Computational Linguistics
https://doi.org/10.18653/v1/P17

- *Task* 2: The final task is to generate a summary of the RP, based on the cited text spans, with a word limit of 250. Task 2 is optional.

Our team participated in Tasks 1A and 1B, and hence, we do not construct a final summarization of the respective RPs. As the quality of a pre-selection can significantly improve the results of downstream tasks (Liu and Lapata, 2019), we focus primarily on improving selection results in Tasks 1A and 1B. We formulate Task 1A as a search problem modeled in two steps: First, a set of cited sentences is extracted by employing a search using BM25 in combination with the sentence position in the document. Here, the query term is the citation itself, and each sentence in the reference paper is treated as a single document in the search process. In the second step, a top-k re-ranking is applied that utilizes BERT to extract the most relevant sentences. For Task 1B, we follow previous work by Zerva et al. (Zerva et al., 2019) in implementing one-versus-rest classifiers, but base them on perceptron classifiers instead of random forests or BERT-based models.

2   Related Work

In previous editions of the CL-SciSumm Shared Task, various effective strategies were proposed to solve Task 1 (Chandrasekaran et al., 2019). To find the relevant reference sentence, most systems from 2019 focused on sentence similarity. Similarities are either obtained by methods such as TF-IDF and Jaccard or embedding-based methods to mine more semantic information (Pitarch et al., 2019) or by designing specific features and learning sentence similarities in a supervised manner (Li et al., 2019; Chiruzzo et al., 2019). Task 1A can also be framed as a classification task and solved via a single or ensemble of multiple classifiers. An ensemble of regression and classification models are trained on the reference and citation sentences (Quatra et al., 2019; Ma et al., 2019). The best performing system from 2019 (Zerva et al., 2019) uses a BERT-based model to solve the task in two ways, first by using sentence similarity of BERT vectors trained on citation and reference sentence pairs, and second by using bilateral multi-perspective matching model. The authors also perform extensive data cleaning and mine additional data from the PDF version of the papers to fine-tune their language model. The most similar work to our approach is by (Kim and Ou, 2019), where the authors propose a two-stage similarity-based unsupervised ranking method. In the first stage, they use modified Jaccard similarity to select the top-5 relevant sentences. These top-5 selected sentences are ranked again using a listwise ranking model and the features from the first stage. In contrast, we utilize a variant of BM25 for our original ranking, a larger candidate set of 10 sentences, and a pair-wise ranking for our second stage using BERT. Since neural models pretrained on language modeling such as BERT have achieved impressive results for several NLP tasks, many have applied them to search-related tasks. BERT is used in ad-hoc document ranking (MacAvaney et al., 2019; Yang et al., 2019) and also for multi-stage ranking, where the original ranking is often performed by an efficient method like BM25 and the results are ordered by their relevancy score by single or multiple re-ranking stages (Nogueira and Cho, 2019; Nogueira et al., 2019).

3   Methodology

In our approach, we aim to solve Task 1A and 1B independently. We formulate the citation linkage in Task 1A as a search problem, where the CP sentence is the query, and each sentence in the respective RP is considered a separate "document" in an indexed collection. For Task 1B, we mainly follow existing work to deal with the unbalanced data and a low number of samples. In the following, we explain the framework in more detail.

3.1   Task 1A

The citation linkage module consists of three main stages: 1) Retrieval of the top-k relevant sentence to a given citation from the reference paper by a standard search mechanism, such as BM25. 2) Re-ranking the retrieved sentences using a more computationally expensive model, such as BERT re-ranker (Nogueira and Cho, 2019), and 3) choosing the relevant candidates as answers based on thresholding of re-ranking scores. The full pipeline is shown in Figure 1. In the ranking stage, the reference paper is indexed using Apache Solr, and candidate sentences are generated by querying with the citation sentence. The BERT re-ranker filters the set to only relevant sentences, and the facet classifier predicts the respective facets for them.

3.1.1   Ranking

While submissions to previous iterations of the workshop already considered a wide range of similarity metrics, such as TF-IDF, Word2Vec (Pitarch

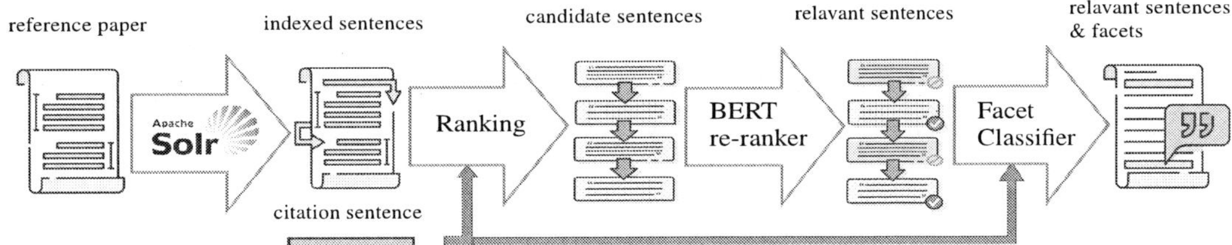

Figure 1: Overview of the proposed pipeline. Documents are indexed in Apache Solr, and a candidate ranking set is formed by querying with the citing span. A BERT-based re-ranking module chooses the relevant sentences based on the candidate set, on which facet prediction is performed.

et al., 2019), or learned similarities (Zerva et al., 2019; Syed et al., 2019), there is only the approach by (Kim and Ou, 2019) that similarly phrases the problem as a 2-step ranking problem. Specifically, we similarly treat each reference paper as a "document collection" of its pre-segmented sentences, and construct a search index using Apache Solr[1]. Per default, Solr implements the Lucene variant of BM25 detailed in (Kamphuis et al., 2020) as its scoring function. BM25 is in our opinion more suitable than related measures, such as TF-IDF, as it considers both sentence lengths, as well as the full input query, instead of single terms. We chose the entire 40 annotated documents from the 2018 training data to tune parameters. Feature selection as well as the indexing step itself is unsupervised, and thus requires no further splitting into training and validation set. Experiments with alternative weighting metrics (we compared TF-IDF, DFR (Amati and van Rijsbergen, 2002), and IBS (Clinchant and Gaussier, 2010)) yielded worse results and were discarded.

Preprocessing   Aside from the scoring function, Solr's indexing modules allow for a custom preprocessing pipeline of both indexed documents and submitted queries. We performed experiments varying the following functions over different search fields: 1) Stopword filtering, 2) keyphrase filtering, 3) lowercasing, 4) porter/Snowball stemmer, 5) synonym filter, 6) word delimiter filter, and 7) shingling. For stopwords, we used the English stopwords provided by Solr. Synonyms were manually generated by comparing citances and references of the 2018 training corpus and consist mostly of spelling variations (e.g., "co-occurrence" and "cooccurrence") or community-specific abbreviations (e.g., "HMM", "Hidden Markov Model").

Additional Document Features   While Li et al. utilized further features such as (relative) section position (Li et al., 2019), we found that the pre-segmented data contained insufficiently accurate section annotations. Instead, we chose to only incorporate the relative sentence position, defined as $\frac{\text{sentence id}}{\#\text{sentences}}$, since it is in theory more tolerant to incorrect segmentations. Specifically, we boost the ranking scores of query results that appear in the first 30% of the document by 1.5 times of their original score. Further features did not improve results in our experiments.

Text/Query Formatting   As the quality of results depends on the quality of the input, rule-based preprocessing was employed to clean both the indexed content and query strings. Mainly, indicators of citations from the citances were deleted, as they do not relate to the sentence content, and results degrade by leaving them in. Furthermore, "math-like" text, such as formulas or vector representations, for both indexed sentences and queries were masked with special tokens <COMPLEXITY>, <PROBABILITY>, <FUNCTION> or <VECTOR>. The masked tokens are protected from tokenization by Solr.

Ensembling   To emphasize the generalization of our ranking module, we finally ensemble several text fields with varying configurations. Aggregation of results is performed by first retrieving the top-k results including their ranking scores for each of the text fields in the ensemble. We merge individual query results by summing up ranking scores, and return the re-ordered top-k results of the aggregated candidate set. These are then handed over to the re-ranking module. Note that in this scenario, a sentence can be deemed relevant if it only appears in a single query result, but with a sufficiently high score. In our experiments, we chose $k = 10$.

---

[1] https://lucene.apache.org/solr/; we used version 8.5.2 in our experiments.

Baseline Approach Since the BERT re-ranker performs the final restriction of candidates, we also wanted to compare to a direct restriction of candidates through Solr only. For this, we return only four results per model in an ensemble. We then employ simple majority voting over the individual model results to return a final set of candidates.

3.1.2 Re-ranking with BERT

The re-ranker module estimates a relevance score of sentence s_i for each pair of candidate passage and query. In our case, the candidate passage is an arbitrary sentence in the reference paper, denoted as rs_i, and the query is the citing sentence, cs_i. The candidate sentences from the reference paper are generated by the ranker described in the previous section. The re-ranker than takes the output of the ranking module and learns which of the top-k results are relevant to the citation sentence. To compute the relevance score we use the BERT re-ranker (Nogueira and Cho, 2019), which uses the pre-trained deep bidirectional language model, BERT (Devlin et al., 2019), to learn relevance patterns. There exist multiple variations of the BERT architecture for re-ranking; However, we chose the simple addition of one linear layer on top of the BERT representation. The simple one layer re-ranker is proven to be most effective in comparison to more complex architectures, where instead of the last layer representation combination of different intermediate layers are used for re-ranking (Qiao et al., 2019). Following the same notation as (Devlin et al., 2019), we feed in the citation sentence, cs_i, as sentence A and reference sentence, rs_i, as sentence B. We truncate the sentence from the reference paper, so that the concatenation of cs_i and rs_i results in at most 512 tokens. We add a classification layer on top of BERT_{BASE} for binary classification and use the [CLS] vector as the input to the classification layer. The [CLS] vector encodes the joint representation of the citation sentence and the reference sentence, and the classification layer computes the relevance probability for each reference sentence independently. The final list of the relevant sentences is obtained by sorting the candidates based on the relevance probability. We fine-tune the pre-trained BERT model using cross-entropy loss as follows:

$$L = \sum_{j \in J_{pos}} log(s_j) - \sum_{j \in J_{neg}} log(1 - s_j) \quad (1)$$

where J_{pos} contains the set of all relevant reference sentences, and J_{neg} are the negative examples, retrieved from the top-10 sentences by BM25. The final set of relevant sentences is computed by thresholding the relevance probability.

We acknowledge the possibility of mixing results with the pre-selection scores returned by BM25, but argue that a recall-optimized tuning of BM25 would likely not improve hard instances that are generally based on semantic similarity, rather than syntactic similarities. Furthermore, we also did not experiment with pair-wise losses, as the query lengths exceed those of traditional IR setups (Nogueira et al., 2019), and subsequently triplets required for training are frequently longer than the 512 token limit of BERT.

3.2 Task 1B

Task 1B aims to extract discourse facets from the given citation spans. We formulated this as a multi-class and multi-label classification task, in which each of the five predefined facets (*Aim, Hypothesis, Implication, Method,* and *Result*) is one class. A first investigation of the given data reveals two challenges relevant to this task. First, the data set consists of only 753 samples, which is a small number of instances to train a machine learning model. Second, there is a significant imbalance in the distribution of labels, as seen in Figure 2. To overcome these challenges, we framed the problem as multiple binary classification tasks by employing five one-vs-rest perceptron classifiers. We then extracted features for the classification as follows:

- First, all words in the citation sentences and the reference sentences predicted in Task 1A are lemmatized, and stop-words are removed using NLTK's stop word list.

- Word-level uni- and bigrams are extracted from all reference and citation sentences. Following this, a bag-of-words model is constructed, and TF-IDF scores are calculated.

While these were the final (and only) features of the constructed classifier, we experimented with the following features as well, which unfortunately did not improve results:

- Since the position of a sentence in the document should be meaningful, we integrated the sentence ID as a feature.

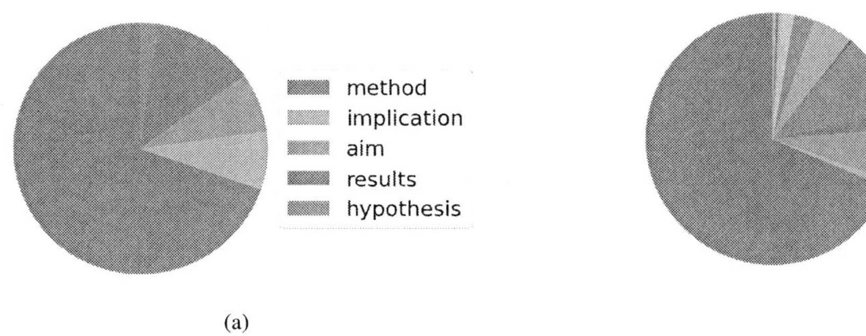

Figure 2: Distribution of discourse facets among the annotated data set when (a) counting all facets independently, and (b) counting combinations of discourse facets as well.

- As a follow-up, multiple common sections within a scientific paper were defined: *Abstract, Introduction, Related Work, Methods, Results, Conclusion, Acknowledgments* while remaining sections were labeled as *Unknown*. We constructed a mapping from the 50 most occurring section titles within the training data set to one of the 7 section types. The section ID then replaced the sentence ID that was used in the previous approach as a feature.

- In another attempt, the imbalance of the data set was targeted by sampling at most 100 samples from each discourse facet class. This experiment resulted in a situation in which the rare discourse facets classification accuracy improved. However, precision and recall for the most common facets (*Method* and *Results* citations) dropped significantly. Hence, this approach was not pursued any further.

4 Experimental Settings and Evaluation

Aside from the pure evaluation of results, we further verified the correctness of the existing training data. For the manually annotated samples from 2018, we were able to identify several citations that were either duplicated or mismatched (differing reference text and reference offset, or similar for the citance). Further, we deleted around 30 empty documents from the Scisummnet corpus (containing non-empty "sentences" for less than 10% of the document). A pull request with several changes is currently awaiting approval for the main shared task repository.

Feature	Field 1	Field 2	Field 3
Tokenizer	Standard	Whitespace	Standard
Lowercase	Yes	Yes	Yes
Word Filters	Possessive	Delimiter	No
Stemming	No	Porter	Snowball
Shingling	Bigram	Bigram	Trigram
Stopwords	Yes	Yes	No
Synonyms	Yes	Yes	Yes

Table 1: Features for the text fields used in the ensembles. Configurations differ significantly to ensure a heterogeneity of results for better generalization.

4.1 Task 1A

As detailed in Section 3.1.1, we experimented with several combinations for our ensemble models. Specifically, we ended up with three different text fields, which we combined into two ensembles. The first ensemble consists of fields 1&2 (*2-field*), and another of all three fields (*3-field*) Specific configurations of the fields are detailed in Table 1. As mentioned previously, the performance is judged by evaluation of the manually annotated documents from the 2018 corpus.

4.1.1 Re-ranking with BERT

To train the BERT re-ranker, we use the combination of manually and automatically annotated data. To make our result comparable to Zerva et al. (Zerva et al., 2019), we held out the same eight articles from the manually annotated articles as a preliminary test set[2]. The training data is provided by the Solr ranker in two formats, resulting in two training strategies. In the first variation, the

---

[2]The ids of the papers used for validation are: C00-2123, C04-1089, I05-5011, J96- 3004, N06-2049, P05-1004, P05-1053, P98-1046

265

top-10 sentences are ranked with Solr, using the 2-field or 3-field ensembles, respectively, and relevant sentences among the retrieved data are marked a positive example. The remaining examples are considered negative examples. One drawback of this approach is that if Solr mistakenly misses one of the relevant sentences, it does not appear in the candidate set for re-ranking in the first place. Therefore, the re-ranker cannot incorporate the missing positive examples in the training process. To overcome this shortcoming, we propose the supervised candidate set, in which we manually added any missing true positive example from the ground truth data to the candidate set. The second approach is denoted by subscript S in the evaluation runs. All models are trained for 3 epochs with a batch size of 52 on two TITAN RTX GPUs, with $24GB$ of RAM. Training takes approximately 3.5 hours. We used Adam as the optimizer for our network with a learning rate of $5e-7$. Moreover, to avoid exploding gradients, we clipped gradients larger than 0.5. The final list of relevant sentences is generated by re-ordering the sentences based on the relevance score and choosing the top-4 sentences. Experiments to return results based on fixed thresholds yielded much lower precision, and indicate that the model may not yet properly normalize scores across samples.

4.1.2   Analysis of Results

Table 2 shows the precision, recall, and F1-score on the held-out preliminary test set, and re-ranking based on BERT degrades the performance. Since the recall could not be improved by re-ranking, our main objective was to obtain better precision. However, BERT fails to learn to improve upon that. We attribute this failure to the limited training data and noisy annotation of the automatically annotated data, as well as a small set of positive vs. negative sentences on which the classifier was trained. Despite the additional re-ranking step, our best performing models are the original Solr ranking top-4. Surprisingly, the models trained on supervised candidate sets have significantly lower precision, indicating that the additional information from the missing examples can be misleading to the final re-ranking. One reason for the weak performance could be the difference in the distribution of the training and test set imposed by adding the additional ground truth values, as these results do not initially show up in our first step ranking procedure. Furthermore, the majority of the seen samples dur-

Model	Precision	Recall	F1
Solr$_2$	0.128	0.217	0.161
Solr$_3$	0.124	0.217	0.158
(Zerva et al., 2019)	0.171	0.334	0.226
BERT$_{S2}$	0.084	0.239	0.124
BERT$_{S3}$	0.077	0.219	0.114
BERT$_2$	0.087	0.248	0.129
BERT$_3$	0.095	0.270	0.141

Table 2: Precision, recall, and F1-score on the preliminary test set used by (Zerva et al., 2019), for which we also report their best-performing model. Subscript numbers describe the number of ensemble fields for ranking. Subscript S indicates the supervised variant, where the ground truth is always added to the pre-selection candidate set.

Discourse Facet	Precision	Recall	F1	#samples
Aim	1.000	0.333	0.500	18
Hypothesis	0.000	0.000	0.000	1
Implication	0.000	0.000	0.000	21
Method	0.742	0.969	0.841	98
Results	0.444	0.800	0.571	15
Micro Average	0.685	0.739	0.711	153
Macro Average	0.437	0.421	0.382	153

Table 3: Precision, recall, F1-score, and number of samples in the validation set for each discourse facet as well as micro and macro average.

ing training time consists of the automatically extracted citation spans by Scisummnet (Yasunaga et al., 2019), which significantly differs from extracted portions on the manually annotated data. Moreover, high-quality results form the ranking step can also influence the effectiveness of our two-stage retrieval. The 3-field ensemble produces a better original ranking and candidate set, resulting in slightly better relevancy scores.

4.2   Task 1B

For evaluation of task 1B, the data set of the 40 manually annotated papers are randomly split into a training set consisting of about 80% of the data, and a validation set consisting of the remaining 20% of annotations. Table 3 shows the results of the trained model. As shown, recall of discourse facets is reasonable for classes *Method* and *Results*. For facets less represented in the data set, however, the model performs poorly. This imbalance in the data set is also observed in the micro and macro average: The micro average indicates a much better performance than the macro average, since the majority of discourse facets in the data set are of type

Model	SO F1	ROUGE F1	1B F1
Solr$_2$	**0.161**	0.113	0.292
Solr$_3$	0.153	0.107	0.294
(Zerva et al., 2019)	0.126	0.075	0.312
(Wang et al., 2018)	0.145	**0.131**	0.262
(Li et al., 2019)	0.106	0.034	**0.389**
(Li et al., 2018)	0.122	0.049	0.381
BERT$_{S2}$	0.122	0.059	-
BERT$_{S3}$	0.110	0.055	-
BERT$_2$	0.122	0.059	-
BERT$_3$	0.118	0.059	-

Table 4: Task 1A Sentence Overlap F1 (SO F1), task 1A ROUGE F1, and task 1B F1 on the official test set. For comparison, we report the best-performing models for Task 1A (based on SO F1) and task 1B from the 2018 and 2019 shared tasks, which were evaluated on the same test set.

method, which is classified correctly more often than the rare occurrences of other classes.

4.3 Official Test Results

Table 4 shows the results of our models on the 2018 test set, used as the official benchmark for this year's iteration as well. Comparing our results to the best-performing models from the past two years, we can see a clear improvement of Sentence Overlap F1. Surprisingly, our model shows a much better generalization to the official test set than Zerva et al., based on their results shown in Table 2. However, despite a better Sentence Overlap F1, our ROUGE is still trailing behind the submission by Wang et al., which leaves open questions regarding the best optimization criterion. For task 1B, our results are significantly lacking behind previous best-performing entries, however, we would be interested how our improved selection of sections would affect their respective predictions.

5 Future Work

As indicated in the results on the different test sets for Task 1A, a high-quality sub-selection of potentially relevant sections can significantly boost the performance of more learning-based methods. Despite some optimization, we still saw relatively low recall values for some citation spans, which can have several causes. We believe that improvements to the initial recall can still significantly boost results, but require measures that do not entirely rely on simple word frequency measures such as BM25 or TF-IDF. While the re-ranker seemed to struggle with the limitations of the current setup, future

exploration with different re-ranking approaches might ultimately yield improvements over the results returned by Solr. We intend to utilize contextualized results, or "snippets" of several sentences within a single result in future submissions to the workshop to increase pre-selection recall. Similarly, for Task 1B, replacing prediction for low-resource classes with rule-based approaches could balance classification scores on the unseen test set.

References

Gianni Amati and C. J. van Rijsbergen. 2002. Probabilistic models of information retrieval based on measuring the divergence from randomness. *ACM Trans. Inf. Syst.*, 20(4):357–389.

M. K. Chandrasekaran, G. Feigenblat, Hovy. E., A. Ravichander, M. Shmueli-Scheuer, and A De Waard. forthcoming. Overview and insights from scientific document summarization shared tasks 2020: CL-SciSumm, LaySumm and LongSumm. In *Proceedings of the First Workshop on Scholarly Document Processing (SDP 2020)*.

Muthu Kumar Chandrasekaran, Michihiro Yasunaga, Dragomir R. Radev, Dayne Freitag, and Min-Yen Kan. 2019. Overview and Results: CL-SciSumm Shared Task 2019. In *Proceedings of the 4th Joint Workshop (BIRNDL) co-located with the 42nd International ACM SIGIR*, volume 2414 of *CEUR Workshop Proceedings*, pages 153–166. CEUR-WS.org.

Luis Chiruzzo, Ahmed AbuRa'ed, Àlex Bravo, and Horacio Saggion. 2019. LaSTUS-TALN+INCO @ CL-SciSumm 2019. In *Proceedings of the 4th Joint Workshop (BIRNDL) co-located with the 42nd International ACM SIGIR*, volume 2414 of *CEUR Workshop Proceedings*, pages 224–232. CEUR-WS.org.

Stéphane Clinchant and Éric Gaussier. 2010. Information-based models for ad hoc IR. In *Proceeding of the 33rd International ACM SIGIR Conference on Research and Development in Information Retrieval*, pages 234–241. ACM.

Jacob Devlin, Ming-Wei Chang, Kenton Lee, and Kristina Toutanova. 2019. BERT: Pre-training of Deep Bidirectional Transformers for Language Understanding. In *Proceedings of the 2019 Conference of the North American Chapter of the Association for Computational Linguistics: Human Language Technologies, NAACL-HLT, Volume 1 (Long and Short Papers)*, pages 4171–4186. Association for Computational Linguistics.

Kokil Jaidka, Muthu Kumar Chandrasekaran, Devanshu Jain, and Min-Yen Kan. 2017. The CL-SciSumm Shared Task 2017: Results and Key Insights. In *Proceedings of the Computational Linguistics Scientific Summarization Shared Task (CL-SciSumm 2017) organized as a part of the 2nd Joint*

Workshop (BIRNDL) and co-located with the 40th International ACM, volume 2002 of CEUR Workshop Proceedings, pages 1–15. CEUR-WS.org.

Kokil Jaidka, Muthu Kumar Chandrasekaran, Sajal Rustagi, and Min-Yen Kan. 2016. Overview of the CL-SciSumm 2016 Shared Task. In Proceedings of the Joint Workshop (BIRNDL) co-located with the Joint Conference on Digital Libraries 2016 (JCDL), volume 1610 of CEUR Workshop Proceedings, pages 93–102. CEUR-WS.org.

Kokil Jaidka, Muthu Kumar Chandrasekaran, Sajal Rustagi, and Min-Yen Kan. 2018a. Insights from CL-SciSumm 2016: the faceted scientific document summarization Shared Task. Int. J. on Digital Libraries, 19(2-3):163–171.

Kokil Jaidka, Michihiro Yasunaga, Muthu Kumar Chandrasekaran, Dragomir R. Radev, and Min-Yen Kan. 2018b. The CL-SciSumm Shared Task 2018: Results and Key Insights. In Proceedings of the 3rd Joint Workshop (BIRNDL) co-located with the 41st International ACM SIGIR Conference on Research and Development in Information Retrieval (SIGIR), volume 2132 of CEUR Workshop Proceedings, pages 74–83. CEUR-WS.org.

Chris Kamphuis, Arjen P. de Vries, Leonid Boytsov, and Jimmy Lin. 2020. Which BM25 Do You Mean? A Large-Scale Reproducibility Study of Scoring Variants. In Advances in Information Retrieval - 42nd European Conference on IR Research, ECIR 2020, Proceedings, Part II, volume 12036 of Lecture Notes in Computer Science, pages 28–34. Springer.

Hyonil Kim and Shiyan Ou. 2019. NJU@CL-SciSumm-19. In Proceedings of the 4th Joint Workshop (BIRNDL) co-located with the 42nd International ACM SIGIR, volume 2414 of CEUR Workshop Proceedings, pages 247–255. CEUR-WS.org.

Lei Li, Junqi Chi, Moye Chen, Zuying Huang, Yingqi Zhu, and Xiangling Fu. 2018. Cist@clscisumm-18: Methods for computational linguistics scientific citation linkage, facet classification and summarization. In Proceedings of the 3rd Joint Workshop on Bibliometric-enhanced Information Retrieval and Natural Language Processing for Digital Libraries (BIRNDL 2018) co-located with the 41st International ACM SIGIR Conference on Research and Development in Information Retrieval (SIGIR 2018), Ann Arbor, USA, July 12, 2018, volume 2132 of CEUR Workshop Proceedings, pages 84–95. CEUR-WS.org.

Lei Li, Yingqi Zhu, Yang Xie, Zuying Huang, Wei Liu, Xingyuan Li, and Yinan Liu. 2019. CIST@CLSciSumm-19: Automatic Scientific Paper Summarization with Citances and Facets. In Proceedings of the 4th Joint Workshop (BIRNDL) co-located with the 42nd International ACM SIGIR, volume 2414 of CEUR Workshop Proceedings, pages 196–207. CEUR-WS.org.

Yang Liu and Mirella Lapata. 2019. Hierarchical Transformers for Multi-Document Summarization. In Proceedings of the 57th Conference of the Association for Computational Linguistics, ACL, Volume 1: Long Papers, pages 5070–5081. Association for Computational Linguistics.

Shutian Ma, Heng Zhang, Tianxiang Xu, Jin Xu, Shaohu Hu, and Chengzhi Zhang. 2019. IR&TM-NJUST @ CLSciSumm-19. In Proceedings of the 4th Joint Workshop (BIRNDL)= co-located with the 42nd International ACM SIGIR, volume 2414 of CEUR Workshop Proceedings, pages 181–195. CEUR-WS.org.

Sean MacAvaney, Andrew Yates, Arman Cohan, and Nazli Goharian. 2019. CEDR: Contextualized Embeddings for Document Ranking. In Proceedings of the 42nd International ACM SIGIR, pages 1101–1104. ACM.

Rodrigo Nogueira and Kyunghyun Cho. 2019. Passage Re-ranking with BERT. CoRR, abs/1901.04085.

Rodrigo Nogueira, Wei Yang, Kyunghyun Cho, and Jimmy Lin. 2019. Multi-Stage Document Ranking with BERT. CoRR, abs/1910.14424.

Yoann Pitarch, Karen Pinel-Sauvagnat, Gilles Hubert, Guillaume Cabanac, and Ophélie Fraisier-Vannier. 2019. IRIT-IRIS at CL-SciSumm 2019: Matching Citances with their Intended Reference Text Spans from the Scientific Literature. In Proceedings of the 4th Joint Workshop (BIRNDL) 2019 co-located with the 42nd International ACM SIGIR), volume 2414 of CEUR Workshop Proceedings, pages 208–213. CEUR-WS.org.

Yifan Qiao, Chenyan Xiong, Zhenghao Liu, and Zhiyuan Liu. 2019. Understanding the Behaviors of BERT in Ranking. CoRR, abs/1904.07531.

Moreno La Quatra, Luca Cagliero, and Elena Baralis. 2019. Poli2Sum@CL-SciSumm-19: Identify, Classify, and Summarize Cited Text Spans by means of Ensembles of Supervised Models. In Proceedings of the 4th Joint Workshop (BIRNDL) co-located with the 42nd International ACM SIGIR, volume 2414 of CEUR Workshop Proceedings, pages 233–246. CEUR-WS.org.

Bakhtiyar Syed, Vijayasaradhi Indurthi, Balaji Vasan Srinivasan, and Vasudeva Varma. 2019. Helium @ CL-SciSumm-19 : Transfer Learning for Effective Scientific Research Comprehension. In Proceedings of the 4th Joint Workshop (BIRNDL) co-located with the 42nd International ACM SIGIR, volume 2414 of CEUR Workshop Proceedings, pages 214–223. CEUR-WS.org.

Simone Teufel, Advaith Siddharthan, and Dan Tidhar. 2006. Automatic classification of citation function. In EMNLP 2006, Proceedings of the 2006 Conference on Empirical Methods in Natural Language Processing, pages 103–110. ACL.

Pancheng Wang, Shasha Li, Ting Wang, Haifang Zhou, and Jintao Tang. 2018. NUDT @ clscisumm-18. In *Proceedings of the 3rd Joint Workshop on Bibliometric-enhanced Information Retrieval and Natural Language Processing for Digital Libraries (BIRNDL 2018) co-located with the 41st International ACM SIGIR Conference on Research and Development in Information Retrieval (SIGIR 2018), Ann Arbor, USA, July 12, 2018,* volume 2132 of *CEUR Workshop Proceedings,* pages 102–113. CEUR-WS.org.

Wei Yang, Haotian Zhang, and Jimmy Lin. 2019. Simple applications of BERT for ad hoc document retrieval. *CoRR,* abs/1903.10972.

Michihiro Yasunaga, Jungo Kasai, Rui Zhang, Alexander R. Fabbri, Irene Li, Dan Friedman, and Dragomir R. Radev. 2019. Scisummnet: A large annotated corpus and content-impact models for scientific paper summarization with citation networks. In *The Thirty-Third AAAI Conference on Artificial Intelligence, The Ninth AAAI Symposium on Educational Advances in Artificial Intelligence, EAAI,* pages 7386–7393. AAAI Press.

Chrysoula Zerva, Minh-Quoc Nghiem, Nhung T. H. Nguyen, and Sophia Ananiadou. 2019. NaCTeM-UoM @ CL-SciSumm 2019. In *Proceedings of the 4th Joint Workshop (BIRNDL) co-located with the 42nd International ACM SIGIR,* volume 2414 of *CEUR Workshop Proceedings,* pages 167–180. CEUR-WS.org.

IITP-AI-NLP-ML@ CL-SciSumm 2020, CL-LaySumm 2020, LongSumm 2020

Santosh Kumar Mishra, Kundarapu Harshavardhan , Naveen Saini, Sriparna Saha and Pushpak Bhattacharyya
Department of Computer Science & Engineering
Indian Institute of Technology Patna
Patna, Bihar, India-801106
{santosh_1821cs03, 1801cs29, naveen.pcs16, sriparna, pb}@iitp.ac.in

Abstract

The publication rate of scientific literature increases rapidly, which poses a challenge for researchers to keep themselves updated with new state-of-the-art. Scientific document summarization solves this problem by summarizing the essential fact and findings of the document. In the current paper, we present the participation of IITP-AI-NLP-ML team in three shared tasks, namely, CL-SciSumm 2020, LaySumm 2020, LongSumm 2020, which aims to generate medium, lay, and long summaries of the scientific articles, respectively. To solve CL-SciSumm 2020 and LongSumm 2020 tasks, three well-known clustering techniques are used, and then various sentence scoring functions, including textual entailment, are used to extract the sentences from each cluster for a summary generation. For LaySumm 2020, an encoder-decoder based deep learning model has been utilized. Performances of our developed systems are evaluated in terms of ROUGE measures on the associated datasets with the shared task.

1 Introduction

Massive amounts of scientific articles are published day by day (Cohan et al., 2015; Cohan and Goharian, 2017, 2018), which impose a big challenge for researchers in various fields to keep themselves up-to-date with the new developments. A bibliometric analyst's study shows that after nine years, the number of published articles will be doubled (Bornmann and Mutz, 2015). The scientific document summarization objective is to provide a summary of the reference paper. This summary should contain all the important facts. Therefore, it reduces the human effort to understand the document.

Challenges of each style of the summary are as follows:

- Objective of CL-SciSumm is to generate a short summary of a paper which must contain all relevant facts and findings. To solve this problem, we have used the extractive summarization technique. We have used unsupervised techniques and explored different features for scientific summarization. These used features help in identifying important sentences of the article using different aspects.

- Objective of LongSumm is to generate a long summary of the scientific article that should be extractive and abstractive. The generated long summary must contain all important facts of the article. To solve the extractive long summarization problem, we have an unsupervised technique similar to CL-SciSumm. To solve the abstractive LongSumm problem, we have used the encoder-decoder based generative model.

- Objective of CL-LaySumm is to generate a lay summary that can be understood by a non-technical reader. The generated summary should not contain any technical words or jargon. We have solved this task using the abstractive summarization technique. Here, Fine-tuned BERT based encoder-decoder architecture is used to solve the problem.

The current paper addresses this issue by participating in the three shared tasks, namely, CL-SciSumm 2020, LaySumm 2020, LongSumm 2020 (Chandrasekaran et al., 2020). These tasks' goals are to generate medium, Lay (understandable for the non-technical audience), and long summaries of the scientific articles. We are using an extractive approach for CL-SciSumm, For LongSumm, an extractive followed by an abstractive approach is utilized, and for LaySumm, an abstractive approach is utilized. The detailed descriptions of these tasks are provided in the subsequent sections.

Proceedings of the First Workshop on Scholarly Document Processing, pages 270–276
Online, November 19, 2020. ©2020 Association for Computational Linguistics
https://doi.org/10.18653/v1/P17

2 CL-SciSumm 2020

It is the sixth shared task on scientific document summarization. In the literature, two approaches have been used to solve this problem. The first one considers abstract as the summary of the paper, but the problem with the approach is it provides only the theme of the paper. The abstract may not convey all the important points of the summary (Yasunaga et al., 2019; Atanassova et al., 2016). Therefore, the second approach has been followed to solve the scientific summarization, which is citation-based summarization (Qazvinian et al., 2013). It utilizes a set of citations referencing to the original article (reference paper to be summarized). Citations are short descriptions that explain the reference paper all its contributions; this text can be termed as citation text or citance.

2.1 Dataset

The dataset contains a blind test set of 20 papers and corresponding citing papers. Each paper belongs to the computation linguistics and natural language processing domain. It can be found at `https://github.com/WING-NUS/scisumm-corpus/tree/master/data/Test-Set-2018`. Training data is also provided. But, as our approach is purely unsupervised; therefore, we are making use of only test data.

2.2 Tasks Descriptions

- **Task-1 (A)** In this task, the objective is to identify the spans of text (cited text spans) in the reference paper (RP) for each citance given the RP and citing papers (CPs).

- **Task-1 (B)** is to classify each cited text span into facets that are predefined (Hypothesis, Aim, Method, Results, and Implication).

- **Task-2** is to produce a summary of the reference paper by utilizing its citation. The generated summary length should be less than or equal to 250 words.

2.3 System Description

In this section, the steps followed in our proposed framework for solving different sub-tasks are elaborated.

Task 1 (A) To find out the cited text span in the reference paper for each citance, we have utilized the word mover's distance (Kusner et al., 2015).

For each citation sentence, WMD is used to identify the most similar sentences from the reference paper. WMD denotes the semantic similarity between sentences. Here we have selected the top five most similar sentences from the reference paper.

Task 1 (B) To classify each cited text span, we have calculated the similarity between the cited text span and all the five facets using word mover's distance (WMD). The cited text span is assigned that facet, which is closest in terms of WMD.

Task 2 To generate a structured summary, we have used the unsupervised technique, i.e., clustering, followed by the sentence extraction from each cluster based on various sentence-scoring functions. The sentence having a high score from each cluster is included in the summary until the desired length of the summary is reached. A series of steps followed are as follows:

1. Grouping of the sentences has been done using the traditional clustering techniques, namely, K-means (Lloyd, 1982), K-medoid (Kaufman et al., 1987), and DB-scan (Ester et al., 1996).

2. We have determined the document center/representative sentence (RS) of the reference paper. It is that sentence in the article which is most similar to the remaining sentences. We can also call it as an article's center. In other words, the sentence having the minimum average WMD with respect to other sentences is called the RS.

3. Clusters are ranked based on their distances from the representative sentence (RS). In other words, the cluster closest to the RS is assigned the highest rank.

4. After ranking the clusters, we have calculated the scores of the sentences within each cluster based on the following features and then selected the highest scored sentence from each cluster considering their rankings. Note that the selection of sentences from the ranked clusters (in a sequence) will continue until we get the desired length of the summary.

   Position of the Sentence (F1): In the literature, it has been shown that important sentences are found in the title and lead sentences of a paragraph. It is expressed as follows

$m_i = \sqrt{\frac{1}{n_i}}$ where n_i is the position of a sentence in the reference paper. The sentence is given the highest priority, which lies at the start of the document (Saini et al., 2019).

Similarity with the title (F2): In any document, the sentence, which is very much similar to the title of the document, can be an important sentence for the summary (Saini et al., 2019) as it represents the theme of the article. Here word mover's distance is used to find the similarity.

Length of the Sentence (F3): In the previous works, it is shown that longer sentences can be relevant for generating a summary for a document describing some news (Mendoza et al., 2014; Saini et al., 2019). The sentence is assigned the highest priority, which has the longest length.

Textual Entailment (F4): Textual entailment (Saini et al., 2020) has been used as an anti-redundancy measure. In a good summary, sentences should not be related to each other to have more coverage. Here, initially, the cluster centers are included in the summary following the ranked order of the clusters. In the next step, those sentences are selected from the ranked clusters and included in the summary, which does not entail any sentence in summary.

2.4 Submitted Run

Details of the submitted systems are provided in Table 1. Here we have used five clusters for K-means and K-medoid, whereas DB-scan decides the number of clusters automatically. In Table 1 each run describes the features used for the selection of sentences within clusters to form the summary. Here, twelve different runs have been used for task-2.

2.5 Result

Results of task-1 (a), task-1 (b) and task-2 are shown in Table 2, Table 3 and Table 4 respectively.

	DB-Scan	K-means	K-medoid
F1	run1	run2	run3
F2	run4	run5	run6
F3	run7	run8	run9
F4	run10	run11	run12

Table 1: Details of submitted runs of CL-SciSumm

3 CL-LaySumm 2020

The motivation of the CL-LaySumm Shared Task is to automatically produce Lay Summaries of technical (scientific research article) texts. A Lay Summary is defined as a textual summary easily understood by a non-technical audience. It is typically produced either by the authors or by a journalist or commentator. The corpus released in shared tasks covers three distinct domains: epilepsy, archeology, and materials engineering.

In a lay summary, there should not be any technical jargon. It should reflect the overall scope, goal, and potential impact of a scientific paper. It is typically less than 150 words in length. The objective is to generate summaries that represent the content, understandable and interesting to a lay audience.

3.1 Dataset

The dataset has a training set of 572 articles having corresponding lay summaries. It contains a blind test set of 37 papers.

3.2 System Description

Neural network based approach formulates abstractive summarization problem as sequence to sequence problem, here encoder is used to read the token of source documents $\mathbf{x} = [x_1, x_2, ...x_n]$ into an intermediate representation $\mathbf{z} = z_1, z_2, ...z_n$. Finally, decoder uses the intermediate representation to generate the final summary $\mathbf{y} = y_1, y_2, ...y_m$ token by token by using conditional probability $p(y_1, ...y_m | x_1, ...x_n)$.

We have used standard encoder-decoder architecture for our lay summarization task. Here the encoder is pre-trained BERTSUM, and it is fine-tuned on CNN daily mail dataset, and the decoder is a six-layer transformer network (as shown in Fig 1). It should be noted that there is a difference between encoder and decoder as the encoder is pre-trained while the decoder has to be trained. This can create an unstable process of fine-tuning, due to which encoder and decoder can have the problem of under-fitting and over-fitting. To resolve this problem, the different optimizers for encoder and decoder have been used.

Here two Adam optimizers are used with $\beta_1 = 0.9$ and $\beta_2 = 0.99$, respectively, along with different learning rate and warm-up states as follows:

$$l_{re} = \tilde{l}_{re}.min(step^{0.5}, step.warmup_\epsilon^{-1.5}) \quad (1)$$

Precision		Recall		F1 score	
micro_avg	macro_avg	micro_avg	macro_avg	micro_avg	macro_avg
0.0222	0.0221	0.1049	0.1058	0.0367	0.0365

Table 2: Scores of Task-1 (a)

Precision		Recall		F1 score	
micro_avg	macro_avg	micro_avg	macro_avg	micro_avg	macro_avg
0.0169	0.0364	0.0148	0.0162	0.0158	0.0224

Table 3: Scores of Task-1 (b)

Runs	Human		Community		Abstract	
	R-2	R-SU4	R-2	R-SU4	R-2	R-SU4
Run 1	0.1028	0.0833	0.1482	0.0899	0.0959	0.0622
Run 2	0.1229	0.0893	0.1561	0.0889	0.1377	0.0669
Run 3	0.1154	0.0888	0.1283	0.0733	0.1206	0.0673
Run 4	**0.1749**	**0.1169**	**0.1897**	**0.1208**	**0.1959**	**0.0962**
Run 5	0.1430	0.1002	0.1624	0.0998	0.1649	0.081
Run6	0.1380	0.1121	0.1245	0.0845	0.1508	0.0856
Run7	0.0997	0.0760	0.1768	0.1013	0.1134	0.0627
Run 8	0.1156	0.0746	0.1658	0.0836	0.1104	0.0610
Run 9	0.0992	0.0732	0.1614	0.0765	0.1187	0.0647
Run 10	0.1251	0.0883	0.1605	0.0989	0.1356	0.0671
Run 11	0.1221	0.0883	0.1602	0.0913	0.1274	0.0703
Run 12	0.1217	0.0938	0.1145	0.0713	0.1194	0.0678

Table 4: Task-2 scores of different runs in terms of rouge scores. Here, R-2 and R-SU4 are denoting rouge-1, rouge-SU4 respectively. All the reported values are f1 scores.

$$l_{rD} = \tilde{l}_{rD}.min(step^{0.5}, step.warmup_D^{-1.5}) \quad (2)$$

where $l_{r\epsilon} = 2e^-3$ and warm-up = 20000 for the encoder whereas $l_{rD} = 0.1$ and warm-up =10000 for decoder. Here the assumption is that the pre-trained encoder must be trained with a lower learning rate and a lower learning rate smoothens the decay. This process helps the encoder in training with a better gradient when the decoder is in stable condition.

We have used a two-stage fine-tuning approach, first is fine-tuning for extractive summarization and then for abstractive summarization. It has been shown in the literature (Li et al., 2018) (Gehrmann et al., 2018) extractive object helps in obtaining a better abstractive summary.

3.3 Result

Our system has the following score (shown in Table 5).

4 LongSumm 2020

In all the previous works of scientific summarization (Cohan and Goharian, 2017, 2018), there is a summary length constraint of a maximum of 250 words. But in the current LongSumm shared task, the generated summary can be the length of between 100-1500 words.

4.1 Dataset

This dataset consists of a training set of 1705 papers associated with extractive summaries and 531 papers associated with abstractive summaries. It has a blind test set of 22 files. It can be found at https://github.com/guyfe/LongSumm.

4.2 System Description

We have used both extractive and abstractive approaches on the blind test set to generate a structured summary. We have used clustering followed by the sentence-scoring and extraction procedure within each cluster based on various features. The sentence having the highest score is included in the

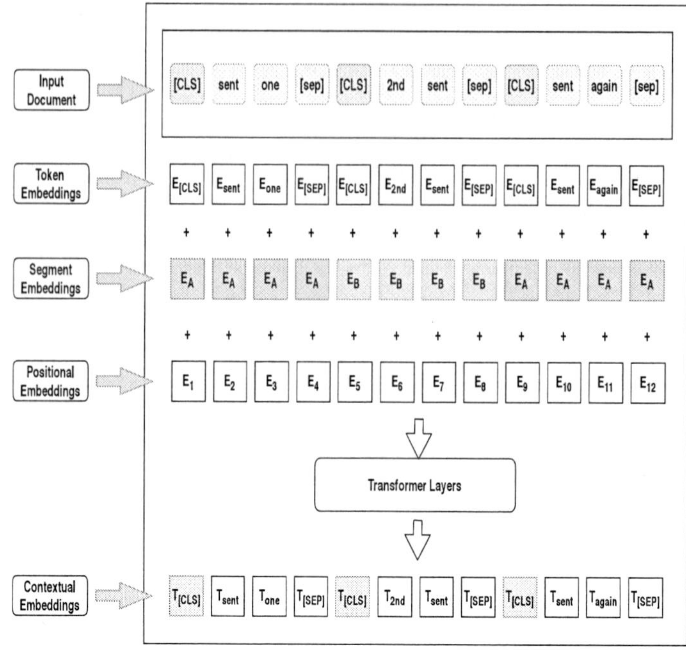

Figure 1: Architecture for Lay Summarization task

R-1 (f)	R-2 (r)	R-2 (f)	R-2 (r)	R-l (f)	R-l (r)
0.3132	0.3705	0.0631	0.0746	0.1662	0.1973

Table 5: Obtained scores on blind set of CL-LaySumm, Here, R-1, R-2, and R-l are denoting rouge-1, rouge-2, and rouge-l, respectively, f and r representing f-1 score and recall, respectively.

summary. Note that for LongSumm extractive summarization, we have used the same methodology as used for CL-SciSumm 2020. A deep learning-based encoder-decoder model is used for LongSumm abstractive summarization.

4.3 Submitted Run:

Details of submitted systems are provided in Table 6. Here we have used five clusters for K-means and K-medoid, whereas DB-scan decides the number of clusters automatically. In Table 6 each run describes the features used for the selection of sentences within the cluster to form the summary.

	DB-Scan	K-means	K-medoid
F1	run1	run2	run3
F2	run4	run5	run6
F3	run7	run8	run9
F4	run10	run11	run12

Table 6: Details of submitted runs of LongSumm

We have used deep learning-based technique as run13, which is as follows:

run13: Proposed model has utilized encoder-decoder based deep learning model. Fine-tuned BERT model has been used for the generation of embedding. We have used same model as used for LaySumm.

4.4 Result

The results of all runs are shown in Table 7, here from run-1 are run-12 are the scores of long summarization using an extractive approach, whereas run-13 is the score of long summarization using the abstractive approach.

5 Conclusion

This paper has presented the results of participation of the IITP-AI-NLP-ML team in three shared tasks, namely, CL-SciSumm 2020, CL-LaySumm 2020, LongSumm 2020, at SDP 2020. For CL-SciSumm, three sub-tasks are there: Task 1(A), Task 1(B), and Task 2. For Task 1 (A), we have utilized WMD

Runs	R-1 (f)	R-1 (r)	R-2 (f)	R-2 (r)	R-l (f)	R-l (r)
Run 1	0.4112	0.4226	0.4112	0.0967	0.1539	0.1581
Run 2	0.4469	0.425	0.4469	0.1128	0.1675	0.1591
Run 3	0.4112	0.4226	0.4112	0.0967	0.1539	0.1581
Run 4	0.3962	0.4062	0.3962	0.094	0.1503	0.1538
Run 5	0.3948	0.3815	0.3948	0.096	0.144	0.1393
Run 6	0.3554	0.3657	0.3554	0.0868	0.1301	0.1337
Run7	0.335	0.3432	0.335	0.0803	0.1283	0.1313
Run 8	0.4485	0.4288	0.4485	0.1099	0.1667	0.1592
Run 9	0.4448	0.4564	0.4448	0.1207	0.1638	0.1677
Run 10	0.4631	0.4723	0.4631	0.1345	0.1749	0.1784
Run 11	0.4597	0.4366	0.4597	0.1368	0.1778	0.1687
Run 12	0.449	0.4603	0.449	0.1385	0.1679	0.1721
Run 13	**0.4646**	**0.4743**	**0.4646**	**0.1486**	**0.1958**	**0.1995**

Table 7: Scores obtained by different runs for LongSumm. Here, R-1, R-2, and R-L are denoting rouge-1, rouge-2, and rouge-l, respectively, f and r representing f-1 score and recall, respectively.

to extract the cited text span from the reference paper; for task 1 (B), the similarity-based measure has been used to identify the facet of each cited text span. Task 2 is based on clustering, followed by sentence extraction from each cluster based on their relevance/score. For LongSumm, we have utilized clustering and deep learning techniques and reported 13 different ways to generate a long summary. For LaySumm, we have proposed a deep learning-based encoder-decoder model that generates the lay summary utilizing the fine-tuned BERT language model's embedding.

Acknowledgments

Special thanks to Mr. Saichethan Miriyala Reddy for helping us at various levels.

References

Iana Atanassova, Marc Bertin, and Vincent Larivière. 2016. On the composition of scientific abstracts. *Journal of Documentation*, 72(4):636–647.

Lutz Bornmann and Rüdiger Mutz. 2015. Growth rates of modern science: A bibliometric analysis based on the number of publications and cited references. *Journal of the Association for Information Science and Technology*, 66(11):2215–2222.

M. K. Chandrasekaran, G. Feigenblat, Hovy. E., A. Ravichander, M. Shmueli-Scheuer, and A De Waard. 2020. Overview and insights from scientific document summarization shared tasks 2020: CL-SciSumm, LaySumm and Long-Summ. In *Proceedings of the First Workshop on Scholarly Document Processing (SDP 2020)*.

Arman Cohan and Nazli Goharian. 2017. Scientific article summarization using citation-context and article's discourse structure. *arXiv preprint arXiv:1704.06619*.

Arman Cohan and Nazli Goharian. 2018. Scientific document summarization via citation contextualization and scientific discourse. *International Journal on Digital Libraries*, 19(2-3):287–303.

Arman Cohan, Luca Soldaini, and Nazli Goharian. 2015. Matching citation text and cited spans in biomedical literature: a search-oriented approach. In *proceedings of the 2015 conference of the North American Chapter of the association for computational linguistics: Human language technologies*, pages 1042–1048.

Martin Ester, Hans-Peter Kriegel, Jörg Sander, Xiaowei Xu, et al. 1996. A density-based algorithm for discovering clusters in large spatial databases with noise. In *Kdd*, volume 96, pages 226–231.

Sebastian Gehrmann, Yuntian Deng, and Alexander M Rush. 2018. Bottom-up abstractive summarization. *arXiv preprint arXiv:1808.10792*.

L Kaufman, PJ Rousseeuw, and Y Dodge. 1987. Clustering by means of medoids in statistical data analysis based on the.

Matt Kusner, Yu Sun, Nicholas Kolkin, and Kilian Weinberger. 2015. From word embeddings to document distances. In *International conference on machine learning*, pages 957–966.

Wei Li, Xinyan Xiao, Yajuan Lyu, and Yuanzhuo Wang. 2018. Improving neural abstractive document summarization with explicit information selection modeling. In *Proceedings of the 2018 Conference on Empirical Methods in Natural Language Processing*, pages 1787–1796.

Stuart Lloyd. 1982. Least squares quantization in pcm. *IEEE transactions on information theory*, 28(2):129–137.

Martha Mendoza, Susana Bonilla, Clara Noguera, Carlos Cobos, and Elizabeth León. 2014. Extractive single-document summarization based on genetic operators and guided local search. *Expert Systems with Applications*, 41(9):4158–4169.

Vahed Qazvinian, Dragomir R Radev, Saif M Mohammad, Bonnie Dorr, David Zajic, Michael Whidby, and Taesun Moon. 2013. Generating extractive summaries of scientific paradigms. *Journal of Artificial Intelligence Research*, 46:165–201.

Naveen Saini, Sriparna Saha, Pushpak Bhattacharyya, and Himanshu Tuteja. 2020. Textual entailment–based figure summarization for biomedical articles. *ACM Transactions on Multimedia Computing, Communications, and Applications (TOMM)*, 16(1s):1–24.

Naveen Saini, Sriparna Saha, Dhiraj Chakraborty, and Pushpak Bhattacharyya. 2019. Extractive single document summarization using binary differential evolution: Optimization of different sentence quality measures. *PloS one*, 14(11).

Michihiro Yasunaga, Jungo Kasai, Rui Zhang, Alexander R Fabbri, Irene Li, Dan Friedman, and Dragomir R Radev. 2019. Scisummnet: A large annotated corpus and content-impact models for scientific paper summarization with citation networks. In *Proceedings of the AAAI Conference on Artificial Intelligence*, volume 33, pages 7386–7393.

1A-Team / Martin-Luther-Universität Halle-Wittenberg@CLSciSumm 20

Maik Boltze   **Anja Fischer**   **Artur Jurk**   **Georg Keller**   **Lorna Ulbrich**

`maik.boltze` `anja.fischer3` `artur.jurk` `georg.keller` `lorna.ulbrich`

`@student.uni-halle.de`

Abstract

This document demonstrates our groups approach to the CL-SciSumm shared task 2020 (Chandrasekaran et al., 2020). There are three tasks in CL-SciSumm 2020. In Task 1a, we apply a Siamese neural network to identify the spans of text in the reference paper best reflecting a citation. In Task 1b, we use a SVM to classify the facet of a citation.

1 Introduction

Task 1 of the CL-SciSumm shared task 2020 contains two sub tasks. The document dataset for the tasks consists of multiple reference papers (RPs) and for each RP a set of citing papers (CPs) that all contain a citation of the original RP. For each of these citations the cited text spans and the belonging facet have been manually annotated.

For task 1a the goal was to predict the cited text span for a given citation and its reference paper.

In task 1b the participants had to identify what facet a cited text span belongs to, from a predefined set of facets.

Our team's approach utilizes a neural network for task 1a to classify pairs of (citation, reference paper sentence) as either matching or not matching.

For task 1b the syntax of reference text in the form of part-of-speech n-grams is used to predict it's facet.

2 Related Work

Citations play a more significant role in the scientific development than one might expect. Fact is, that they help tracking the development of scientific problems and build a foundation for future research. Citations spread information and are a key attribute of determining the impact of a paper or rather its value to science (Hernández-Alvarez and Gomez, 2016).

There are different methods of extracting useful citations. Some utelize supervised Markov Random Fields classifiers (Qazvinian and Radev, 2010), others modeling the link information and the citation texts (Kataria et al., 2010), or sequence labeling with segment classification (Abu-Jbara and Radev, 2012). The main goal of these approaches is to find the sentences or spans of a CP that explain some facets of the RP. Because a way to see citations is as short textual parts describing some facets of the cited work.

However in this document we don't need to generate or extract citations from a cited work. The citances are already given and we need to find a method to determine the sentence or span in a RP corresponding to the given citance. For this purpose it may help analyzing the aim or rethorical status of a citance like in (Hernández-Alvarez and Gomez, 2016). One work presented a classification framework based on lexically and linguistically inspired features for classifying citation functions (Teufel et al., 2006).

A different mind may think about text summarization as a helping feature to find the corresponding textual span to a given citance. Fortunately the field of summerization grew to a well researched subject in the recent decades. There are several approaches to consider. Some of them are topic modeling (Gong and Liu, 2001), supervised models (Chali and Hasan, 2012), graph based models (Mihalcea, 2004) and neural networks (Chopra et al., 2016). For topic modeling a probabilistic framework is used to estimate the distribution of content in the final summary. Supervised models get a selection of sentences relevant for the final summary to learn on, to afterwards be able to seek the right sentences for a final summary. Graph based models focus on finding the most central sentence in a graph of a text, where sentences are nodes and similarities are edges, which represents a summarizing

Proceedings of the First Workshop on Scholarly Document Processing, pages 277–281
Online, November 19, 2020. ©2020 Association for Computational Linguistics
https://doi.org/10.18653/v1/P17

Table 1: Results for Task 1

Task	precision		recall		f1-score	
	micro avg	macro avg	micro avg	macro avg	micro avg	macro avg
1a	0.369	0.403	0.369	0.403	0.369	0.403
1b (POS 5-grams)	0.483	0.482	0.125	0.169	0.199	0.25

Table 2: Structure of input data for task 1a

	citation	original	is_match
0	Another related...	Supersense tagging...	1
1	Another related...	Our approach uses ...	0
2	Another related...	Some specialist to...	0
3	Another related...	Our approach uses ...	0

sentence or to build a summary on.

3 Baseline

Task 1a

As baseline we trained a SVM for each citation and chose the one with the largest tf-idf score as prediction. On the 2018 training set we got an F1-score of 0.09 (micro) and 0.10 (macro).

3.1 Task 1b

The dataset of 2018 consists of a total of 176 citations. 104 citations are labelled as method facet, 9 as implication facet, 34 as result facet, 22 as aim facet and only 7 citations belong to the hypothesis facet. That is why we decided to keep our baseline simple and tagged all citations with the majority label "method". The performance of this simple baseline can be seen in table 4.

4 Approach and Experiment

4.1 Task 1a

Our first preprocessing step is computing the cross product for all citations and every sentence of a reference paper, given annotated citations. The pairs consisting of a citation and its matching reference sentence were labelled as class "1" and all other pairs as class "0". The resulting data matrix, as shown in table 2, contains the citation-sentence pairs and the class labels.

By defining a threshold value of 0.9 we were able to use our NN as a binary classifier. Figure 1 shows the performance of our system when using different thresholds. With our training dataset, a value of 0.9 seemed to be suited best as threshold value.

Our second preprocessing step was mapping each word, which is contained in the word2vec vocabulary (Mikolov et al., 2013b,a) to a unique number in the training data. Based on this, an $|$word2vec vector size$| \times |$vocabulary size$|$ embedding matrix E was constructed as a ground layer for the NN. We used a set pre-trained on the GoogleNewsArchive as a word2vec embedding. Reference sentences and citations are represented as one-hot over the vocabulary. Because of the construction of the training data the class "1" was very much underrepresented. For the NN to be able to handle this, we decided to undersample the huge "0" class. This improved our results by a factor of 30, as shown in table 3.

Our system for task 1a is based on a neuronal network (NN) that utilizes two identical long short-term memory (LSTM) networks, mostly referred to as a "Siamese"[1] neural network. The output of the two networks is computed by the exp negate Manhattan distance function (1) as proposed by (Mueller and Thyagarajan, 2016):

$$e^{-||h^{(left)}-h^{(right)}||_1} \qquad (1)$$

The complete NN architecture is shown in figure 2.

Table 1 shows the evaluation results of our system on 2017 training data. For the experiment we trained the NN with 2016, 2018 and 2019 training data for 50 epochs and a threshold value of 0.9. We used the "adam" function of the keras tensorflow library (Chollet et al., 2015; Kingma and Ba, 2014) as an optimizer.

4.2 Task 1b

Our approach is based on a support vector machine (SVM) which uses part-of-speech (POS) n-grams as features. During the experiment, we tried using different POS n-gram features in SVMs with linear and polynomial kernels and compared their performances. We did not include the results of SVMs with polynomial kernel, because they showed bad performances.

---

[1] A Siamese neural network is characterized by using the same weights while working on two different input vectors in tandem, to compute comparable output vectors.

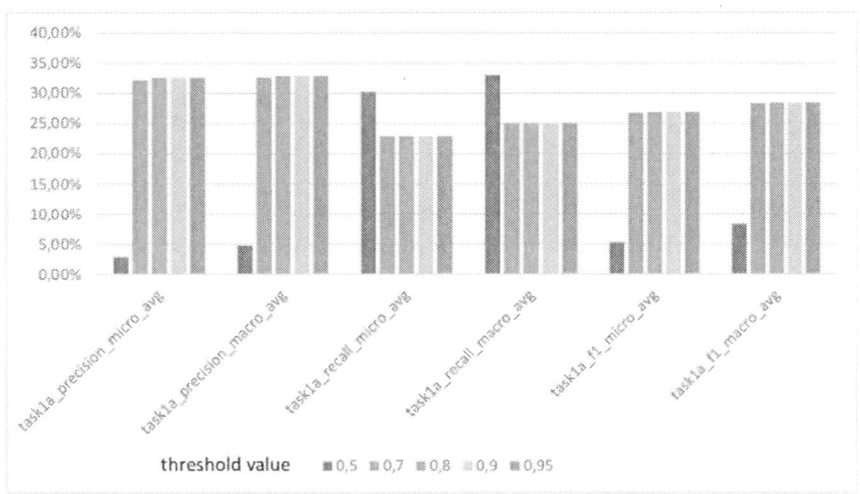

Figure 1: Comparison of threshold values, evaluated on 2017 training data for task 1a

Table 3: Differences between balanced and unbalanced training data for task 1a

	precision		recall		f1-score	
	micro avg	macro avg	micro avg	macro avg	micro avg	macro avg
Without balancing, 25 epochs	0.003	0.003	0.155	0.168	0.005	0.006
With balancing, 25 epochs	0.326	0.329	0.229	0.250	0.269	0.284
With balancing, 50 epochs	0.369	0.403	0.369	0.403	0.369	0.403

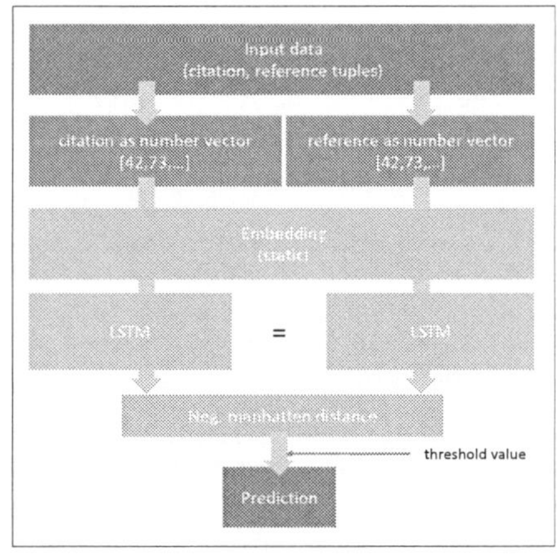

Figure 2: Neural network architecture

Basically, the polynomial kernel considers both the similarity between vectors in the same dimension and the similarities across dimensions. When used in machine learning algorithms, this allows to observe the interaction between different features.

The polynomial kernel with input vectors x , y and kernel degree d is defined as:

$$k(x, y) \;=\; (yx^T y + c_0)^d$$

If $c_0 \;=\; 0$ the kernel is called homogeneous. The linear kernel is a special case of the polynomial kernel where $d = 1$ and $c_0 = 0$. If x, y are column vectors, their linear kernel is described as:

$$k(x, y) \;=\; x^T y$$

In machine learning, kernel methods are a class of algorithms that use a kernel to perform their calculations implicitly in a higher-dimensional space. On one hand we used the function `linear_kernel` which determines the linear kernel. On the other hand we used the function `polynomial_kernel` which determines the degree-d polynomial kernel between two vectors. The polynomial kernel represents the similarity between two vectors.

We tried different degrees with the polynomial kernel, but did not include these in the results of SVMs, because they showed bad performances as well as the results with unbalanced training data. We used the python nltk (Bird et al., 2009) and spaCy (Honnibal and Montani, 2017) libraries for POS tagging and n-gram construction. As shown in table 4 the biggest improvement was gained when increasing n from POS 4-grams to POS 5-grams. Increasing n further seems to deteriorate the results

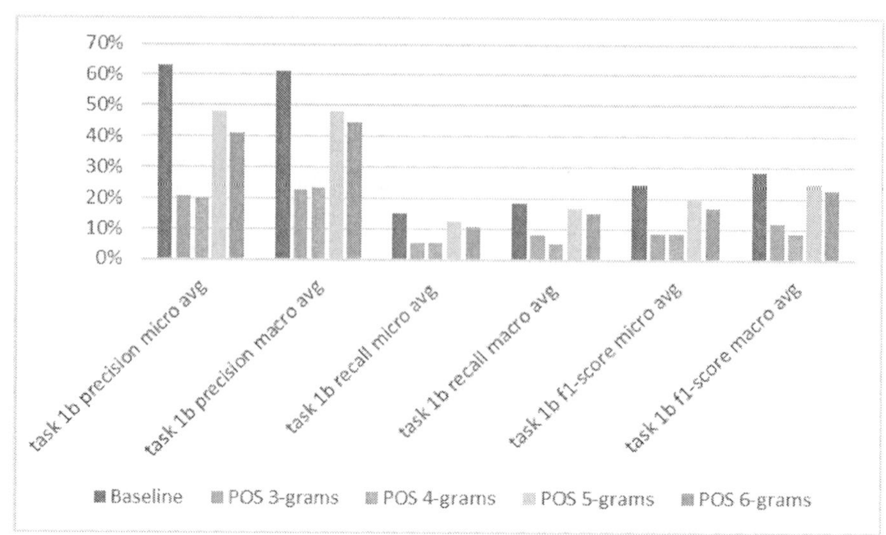

Figure 3: Task 1b results for different POS n-grams

Table 4: Task 1b results for different POS n-grams

	precision		recall		f1-score	
	micro avg	macro avg	micro avg	macro avg	micro avg	macro avg
Baseline	0.63	0.613	0.152	0.186	0.245	0.285
POS 3-grams	0.207	0.226	0.054	0.081	0.085	0.119
POS 4-grams	0.2	0.232	0.054	0.051	0.085	0.084
POS 5-grams	0.483	0.482	0.125	0.169	0.199	0.25
POS 6-grams	0.413	0.446	0.107	0.153	0.17	0.228

again and thus we decided to not test POS n-grams for higher n.

As the results in table 4 and figure 3 show, the best performance was reached using POS 5-grams in combination with a linear kernel SVM.

Conclusion

We could improve upon the solutions of past-year's PolyU approach (Cao et al., 2016) for task 1a. In future works better results may be obtained with more training data as is often the case with neural networks. Moreover the parameters of the neuronal network for task 1a could be tuned.

References

Amjad Abu-Jbara and Dragomir Radev. 2012. Reference scope identification in citing sentences. In *Proceedings of the 2012 Conference of the North American Chapter of the Association for Computational Linguistics: Human Language Technologies*, pages 80–90, Montréal, Canada. Association for Computational Linguistics.

Steven Bird, Ewan Klein, and Edward Loper. 2009. *Natural Language Processing with Python*, 1st edition. O'Reilly Media, Inc.

Ziqiang Cao, Wenjie Li, and Dapeng Wu. 2016. Polyu at cl-scisumm 2016. In *Proceedings of the joint workshop on bibliometric-enhanced information retrieval and natural language processing for digital libraries (BIRNDL)*, pages 132–138.

Yllias Chali and Sadid a. Hasan. 2012. Query-focused multi-document summarization: Automatic data annotations and supervised learning approaches. *Nat. Lang. Eng.*, 18(1):109–145.

M. K. Chandrasekaran, G. Feigenblat, Hovy. E., A. Ravichander, M. Shmueli-Scheuer, and A De Waard. 2020. Overview and insights from scientific document summarization shared tasks 2020: CL-SciSumm, LaySumm and Long-Summ. In *Proceedings of the First Workshop on Scholarly Document Processing (SDP 2020)*.

François Chollet et al. 2015. Keras. `https://keras.io`.

Sumit Chopra, Michael Auli, and Alexander M. Rush. 2016. Abstractive sentence summarization with attentive recurrent neural networks. In *Proceedings of the 2016 Conference of the North American Chapter of the Association for Computational Linguistics:*

Human Language Technologies, pages 93–98, San Diego, California. Association for Computational Linguistics.

Yihong Gong and Xin Liu. 2001. Generic text summarization using relevance measure and latent semantic analysis. In *Proceedings of the 24th Annual International ACM SIGIR Conference on Research and Development in Information Retrieval*, SIGIR '01, page 19–25, New York, NY, USA. Association for Computing Machinery.

Myriam Hernández-Alvarez and José M. Gomez. 2016. Survey about citation context analysis: Tasks, techniques, and resources. *Natural Language Engineering*, 22(3).

Matthew Honnibal and Ines Montani. 2017. spaCy 2: Natural language understanding with Bloom embeddings, convolutional neural networks and incremental parsing. To appear.

Saurabh Kataria, Prasenjit Mitra, and Sumit Bhatia. 2010. Utilizing context in generative bayesian models for linked corpus.

Diederik P. Kingma and Jimmy Ba. 2014. Adam: A method for stochastic optimization.

Rada Mihalcea. 2004. Graph-based ranking algorithms for sentence extraction, applied to text summarization. In *Proceedings of the ACL 2004 on Interactive Poster and Demonstration Sessions*, ACLdemo '04, page 20–es, USA. Association for Computational Linguistics.

Tomas Mikolov, G.s Corrado, Kai Chen, and Jeffrey Dean. 2013a. Efficient estimation of word representations in vector space. pages 1–12.

Tomas Mikolov, Ilya Sutskever, Kai Chen, Greg Corrado, and Jeffrey Dean. 2013b. Distributed representations of words and phrases and their compositionality. In *Proceedings of the 26th International Conference on Neural Information Processing Systems - Volume 2*, NIPS'13, page 3111–3119, Red Hook, NY, USA. Curran Associates Inc.

Jonas Mueller and Aditya Thyagarajan. 2016. Siamese recurrent architectures for learning sentence similarity. In *thirtieth AAAI conference on artificial intelligence*.

Vahed Qazvinian and Dragomir Radev. 2010. Identifying non-explicit citing sentences for citation-based summarization. pages 555–564.

Simone Teufel, Advaith Siddharthan, and Dan Tidhar. 2006. Automatic classification of citation function. In *Proceedings of the 2006 Conference on Empirical Methods in Natural Language Processing*, pages 103–110, Sydney, Australia. Association for Computational Linguistics.

Team MLU@CL-SciSumm20:
Methods for Computational Linguistics Scientific Citation Linkage

Rong Huang, Kseniia Krylova
Martin-Luther-Universität Halle-Wittenberg (MLU)

Abstract

This paper describes our approach to the CL-SciSumm 2020 shared task toward the problem of identifying reference span of the citing article in the referred article. In Task 1a, we apply and compare different methods in combination with similarity scores to identify spans of the reference text for the given citance. In Task 1b, we use a logistic regression to classifying the discourse facets.

1 Introduction

The CL-SciSumm Shared Task focuses on automatic paper summarization in the domain of computational linguistics research. Given a document set with a reference papers and citing papers that all contain citations to the reference paper. In Task 1a we should identify the spans of text (cited text spans) in the reference paper that most accurately reflect the citance. In Task 1b for each cited text span, we should identify what facet of the paper it belongs to, from a predefined set of facets: hypothesis, aim, method, results, and implication. Task 2 is to generate a summary of the reference paper. In this work, we focus on Task 1.

For comparison purposes, we experimented with the following approaches: SVM, logistic regression, decision tree (CART), voting, and calculated a set of similarity metrics between reference spans and citance: tf-idf approach, cosine similarity, Jaccard similarity, WordNet similarity. The best results are obtained by method which combined similarity scores using tf-idf approach, cosine similarity, WordNet similarity, bigram distance and SVM.

We also analyzed a dataset to identify features and highlights, which help us in solving the task. We found that most reference spans contain only one sentence. Also, we conduct a semantic analysis to extract the named entities such as persons, organizations, products or locations. The most common named entities such as organizations and persons can be used for feature extraction.

2 Dataset

The dataset contains 40 topics with citation sentences and human-annotated reference summaries. Each topic is composed of a Reference Paper (RP) and some Citing Papers (CP). We have separate the data into two sets: 30 for training and 10 for testing. For this analysis all uppercase letters in train dataset were transformed into lowercase letters and all words that included non-alphabetical characters were removed. There are 46451 unique words among the reference documents. There are 648 reference sentences and 559 citances. An average number of reference sentences is 1.2, that means, a citation text can be linked to many sentences in the reference paper. The Fig. 1 shows the distribution of the number of sentence in reference spans. The horizontal axis represents the

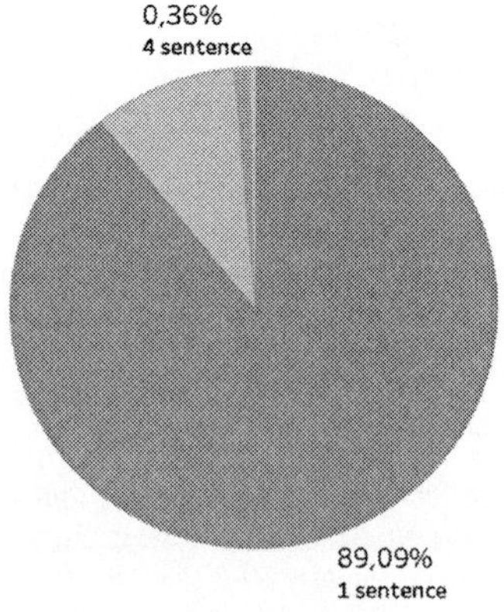

Figure 1 A distribution of the number of sentence in reference spans for train dataset

Proceedings of the First Workshop on Scholarly Document Processing, pages 282–287
Online, November 19, 2020. ©2020 Association for Computational Linguistics
https://doi.org/10.18653/v1/P17

number of sentences in each reference span. The vertical axis shows the frequency. As can be seen, a large proportion of reference spans (about 90%) in train dataset contain only one sentence. We assume to fit our model in such a way it identifies one reference sentence referred to by a given citance.

Citations play an important role in understanding the relationship between scientific works that are related to each other (Iman Tahamtan et al., 2019). Given the citation texts, we find the text spans in the reference article that most closely reflect the citation text.

The noteworthy feature here is that citances have a few peculiarities, such as an abundance of citation markers and proper names. Citations sometimes include the names of the authors, which results in more frequent use of our own proposals. In our work we identify and ignore citation markers such as the author's name, which allows to reduce noise.

We propose syntactic and semantic analysis of citation content that can be used to better analyze the context of research behavior. There are 717 entities for 559 citances. Table 1 shows entity frequency classified by entity types.

We considered the distribution of the following elements: organizations (companies, agencies,

Entity type	Count	Description
ORG	269	Companies, agencies, institutions
PERSON	157	People, including fictional
PRODUCT	41	Objects, vehicles, foods, etc. (Not services.)
GPE	21	Countries, cities, states

Table 1: Entity distribution classified by entity

institutions), persons (people, including fictional), products (objects, vehicles, foods etc.) and locations (countries, cities, states). The total number of tokens in reference spans 9076.

The distribution of entities and percentage are presented in Fig.2. The horizontal axis represents one of entities types, which we are considering. The vertical axis shows the frequency. As can be seen from the figure, the most citied are organizations – 37,52% of the number of citied entities (total 269). It represents 2,96% of the total number of tokens in reference spans. This is followed by persons, which represent 21,9% of the

total number of entities and 1,73% of total number of tokens. Products make up 5,72% of number of citied entities and location represent nearly 3% of total number of citied entities.

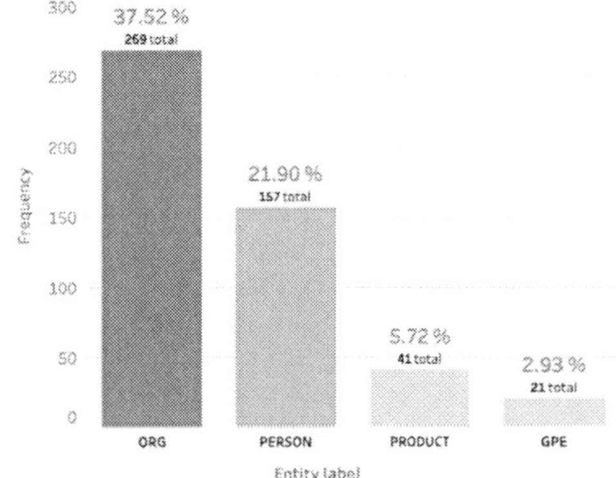

Figure 2: Entity distribution classified by entity types in reference spans in train dataset.

Based on this distribution, we choose first three most common named entities – organizations (ORG), persons (PERSON) and products (PRODUCT) to find a number of matches between named entities in citation and a citation-candidate in a reference text.

3 Approach

3.1 Task 1a

In Task 1a we should identify cited text spans in the reference paper for each citance. Applied methods are highly relevant to the methods of calculating similarity. We propose different approaches that complement each other.

The first approach based on tf-idf cosine similarity between a citance and a reference span in the reference paper. In this approach we transform our work into binary classification problem which is to classify every sentence in the reference paper into relevant or irrelevant. Each reference sentence is assigned a score according to the cosine similarity between tf-idf vectors of itself and the citance. The major feature we use is the threshold, which is manually selected based on analysis of similarity and our experiments.

We consider Task 1a as a classification task, which is to find reference span by a given citance. In this case feature selection plays an important role in identifying citances from reference. It is proposed four categories of features: location-based features, sentence importance-based features, similarity-based features and rule-based features (Qi Zhang et al., 2019). Location-based features contain the information about position of the sentence in the reference paper. Similarity-based features indicate similarity measures between the citance and the reference sentence. Finally, rule-based features refer to identifying citances from reference paper using manual rules. We choose following features:

Sentence Position (SID). We choose the serial number of a citance candidate (sid) in a full reference text as a location-based feature.

Jaccard similarity (JS). Jaccard similarity coefficient is a statistic used for gauging the similarity and diversity of sample sets. It is defined as the size of the intersection divided by the size of the union of two sets. We choose JS as one of the similarity-based features.

Bigram distance (BD). Another similarity-based feature work by converting strings into sets of n-grams. The similarity or distance between the strings is then the similarity or distance between the sets. For this purpose, we used a set class that supports lookup by N-gram string similarity provided by NGram Module.

Count Cosine Similarity (CS). Cosine similarity is a measure of similarity between two non-zero vectors of an inner product space. We use CountVectorizer from scikit-learn to convert sentences into vectors.

Tf-Idf Cosine Similarity (TFIDF). The difference of this method compared to the previous one (CS) is using of TfIdfVectorizer instead of CountVectorizer.

WordNet Similarity (WS). WordNet is a lexical database for the english language (Miller, 1995). Synonymous words are grouped into sets of cognitive synonyms (synsets), each expressing the same concept. Synsents are organized in a structure similar to inheritance tree. More abstract words called hypernyms and more specific are hyponyms. This tree can be used for calculating similarity between two sentences. The closer the two Synsets are in the tree, the more similar they are (Nitin Hardeniya et al., 2016). For this purpose,

we use WordNet provided by NLTK package. This algorithm was proposed by Mihalcea et al. (2006).

Matches Named Entities (ME). We find the number of matches between named entities in citation and a citation-candidate in a reference text. Based on semantic analysis, we choose organizations (ORG), persons (PERSON) and products (PRODUCT).

Matches Named Entities Labels (MEL): We find the number of matches between labels of named entities in citation and a citation-candidate in a reference text. This features are defined and set manually, therefore they are rule-based features.

General Inquirer Category Listings (INQ). General Inquirer Category Listings is a dictionary that contains it about 12 000 words, divided into categories. Each category is a list of words and word senses (Stone, 2006). We indicate whether there are words from General Inquirer Category Listings both in citance and in reference sentence. It is also a rule-based feature.

General Inquirer Category Listings - Sentiment (INQS). There are two large valence categories - 1,915 words of positive outlook and 2,291 words of negative outlook. Each sentence pair is assigned a score by taking scores for each token by using positive or negative labels.

After we defined features, we classify the pairs of citance and reference sentence as relevant or irrelevant.

Logistic regression (LR). We use similarity-based features and rule-based features with logistic regression to classify sentences as being reference spans or not.

Voting (VT). Voting classifier is a machine learning model that trains on a collection of fitted sub-estimators. The predicted output class is a class with the highest majority of votes i.e. the class which had the highest probability of being predicted by each of the classifiers. We defined as sub-estimators logistic regression, SVM and Decision Tree Classifier.

3.2 Task 1b

For Task 1b, we use a logistic regression with bag-of-words as features.

For Task 1, the distribution of examples across the classes is not equal and it makes the problem strongly imbalanced. In our case, class "irrelevant" is present with 15:1 ratio in training set. To solve the problem of imbalance, we use classifier SVM with stochastic gradient descent (SGD) training. For this purpose, we use SGDClassifier provided by scikit-learn, which yield behavior such as that of a SVC with a linear kernel for classes that are unbalanced (Pedregosa et al., 2011).

4 Experiment

The dataset Training-Set-2018 provided by CL-SciSumm Shared Task are training data and test data in our system. The dataset contains 40 topics with citation sentences and human-annotated reference summaries. As described in section "Dataset", we separated data into two sets: 30 for training and 10 for testing. The documents were selected in alphabetical order.

Before we use dataset in our system we preprocessed the dataset to reduce some xml-coding errors. Formatting problems such a missed tags, broken words, non-ascii characters in XML files are some examples of these problems. We manually fixed broken words and automatically removed all non-ascii characters. We also fixed some missed closing tags.

To remove the effect of using words to their different words we used lemmatization. This process is used to return the word to its origin. Stopwords were removed for all configurations.

We have also limited reference sentences by number of words. The average number of words in

sentences is 47, minimal number is 6, maximal 282. In order to reduce noise we consider sentences with more than 10 and less than 70 words.

In our baseline method, first we analyzed results of similarity calculations in order to choose a threshold.

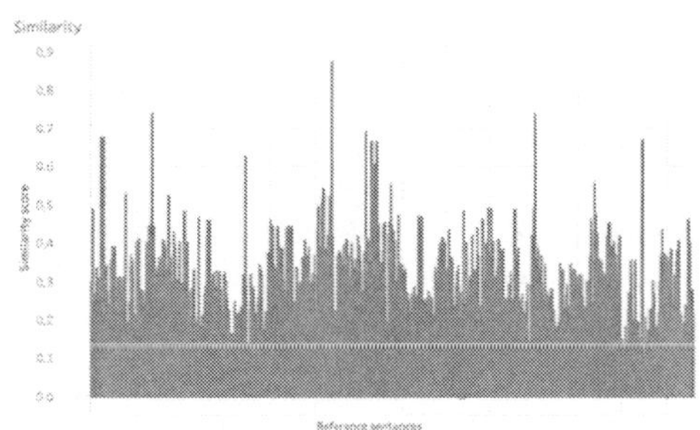

Figure 3: Demonstrates similarity score distribution. The horizontal axis represents reference sentences, the vertical axis represents similarity score. Based on our experimental results we defined threshold 0.14.

In approach method, we train our feature-based classifiers on all the relevant sentences pairs.

5 Results

We implement our system and use official scripts to evaluate the training data. The evaluation of our approaches is done by comparison of several metrics which are presented in tables below.

From Table 2, Table 3 and Table 4, we can find, that SVM method in combination with TF-IDF approach (TFIDF), Bigram Distance (BD), Jaccard Similarity (JS), Count Cosine Similarity (CS) and WordNet Similarity show better performance in our experiments.

The second best score is represented by SVM method in combination with TF-IDF approach (TFIDF), Bigram Distance (BD), Jaccard Similarity (JS), Count Cosine Similarity (CS), WordNet Similarity and Sentence Position (SID).

Method	Precision
TFIDF+Threshold	0.0507
SVM+TFIDF+BD+JS+CS	0.0648
SVM+TFIDF+BD+JS+CS+WS	**0.375**
SVM+SGD+TFIDF+BD+JS+CS+WS	0.5
SVM+SID+TFIDF+BD+JS+CS+WS	0.1389
SVM+SID+TFIDF+BD+JS+CS+WS+INQ+INQS	0.1111
SVM+TFIDF+BD+JS+CS+WS+ME+MEL	0.25
LR+TFIDF+BD+JS+CS	0.0806
LR+TFIDF+BD+JS+CS+WS	0.0694
LR+TFIDF+BD+JS+CS+WS+ME+ MEL	0.0139
DT+TFIDF+BD+JS+CS	0.0745
VT+TFIDF+BD+JS+CS	0.0926
VT+TFIDF+BD+JS+CS+WS	0.0556
VT+TFIDF+SID+BD+JS+CS+WS	0.0388

Table 2: Precision score metric

Our set of experimental results, shown in Figure 4, present the performance of baseline method and approach method with respect to the metrics of precision, recall and F1-score. The vertical axis represent metric values, the horizontal axis represent the evaluation metrics, namely precision, recall and F1-score.

Compares to the baseline, the increases in approach method are 640% (0.3750 vs 0.0507), 85% (0.0783 vs 0.0423) and 180% (0.1295 vs 0.0462) respectively.

However, performance degrades when we take into account data imbalance issue. Figure 5 demonstrates performance comparison for SVM approach method and for improved SVM method with stochastic gradient descent (SGD).

Method	Recall
TFIDF+Threshold	0.0423
SVM+TFIDF+BD+JS+CS	0.0469
SVM+TFIDF+BD+JS+CS+WS	**0.0783**
SVM+SGD+TFIDF+BD+JS+CS+WS	0.0505
SVM+SID+TFIDF+BD+JS+CS+WS	0.0863
SVM+SID+TFIDF+BD+JS+CS+WS+INQ+INQS	0.037
SVM+TFIDF+BD+JS+CS+WS+ME+MEL	0.0227
LR+TFIDF+BD+JS+CS	0.0513
LR+TFIDF+BD+JS+CS+WS	0.0528
LR+TFIDF+BD+JS+CS+WS+ME+ MEL	0.0139
DT+TFIDF+BD+JS+CS	0.0432
VT+TFIDF+BD+JS+CS	0.0570
VT+TFIDF+BD+JS+CS+WS	0.0370
VT+TFIDF+SID+BD+JS+CS+WS	0.0241

Table 3: Recall score metric

Method	F$_1$-score
TFIDF+Threshold	0.0462
SVM+TFIDF+BD+JS+CS	0.0544
SVM+TFIDF+BD+JS+CS+WS	**0.1295**
SVM+SGD+TFIDF+BD+JS+CS+WS	0.0917
SVM+SID+TFIDF+BD+JS+CS+WS	0.1065
SVM+SID+TFIDF+BD+JS+CS+WS+INQ+INQS	0.0556
SVM+TFIDF+BD+JS+CS+WS+ME+MEL	0.0417
LR+TFIDF+BD+JS+CS	0.0627
LR+TFIDF+BD+JS+CS+WS	0.06
LR+TFIDF+BD+JS+CS+WS+ME+ MEL	0.0139
DT+TFIDF+BD+JS+CS	0.0574
VT+TFIDF+BD+JS+CS	0.0706
VT+TFIDF+BD+JS+CS+WS	0.0444
VT+TFIDF+SID+BD+JS+CS+WS	0.0297

Table 4: F1 score metric

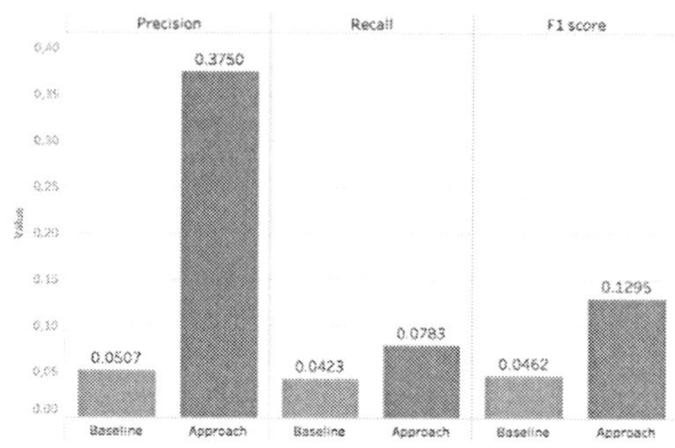

Figure 4: Comparison of performances of baseline method and approach

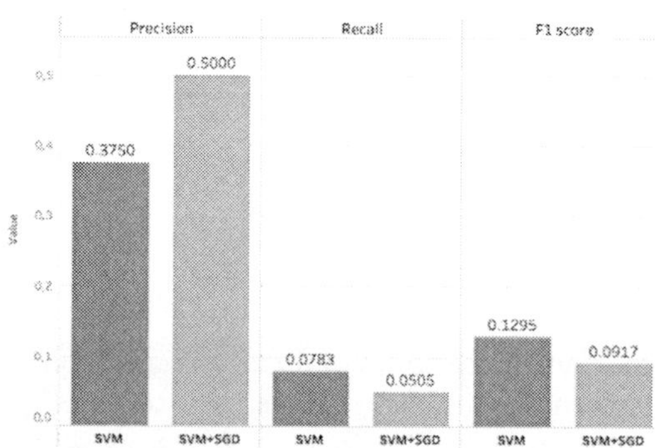

Figure 5: Performance comparison for SVM approach method and SVM approach with stochastic gradient descent (SGD)

6   Conclusion and future work

In this paper, we transform our work into binary classification problem and apply various methods to identify the spans of text in the reference paper reflecting the citance. We compare feature-based classifiers in combination with different features. Although results show an improvement over the baseline, it is important to improve the performance of imbalanced data classification.

Acknowledgements

We are very grateful to Professor Matthias Hagen and Mr. Yamen Ajjour for their guidance on our research work and programming. Thanks to the members of other groups in our university, and thank you for the time of online activities that we discussed and made progress together. We are especially grateful to Mr. Muthu Kumar Chandrasekaran for his patient guidance, forgiving and helping us when we first participated in the event. We thank each other, we have completed this project together, and it still has a lot to improve. We look forward to working together in the future. We are the best partner.

References

Tahamtan, Iman and Bornmann, Lutz. 2019. *What do citation counts measure? An updated review of studies on citations in scientific documents published between 2006 and 2018.* Scientometrics.

Qi Zhang, Xiangwen Liao and Zhaochun Ren. 2019. *Information Retrieval: 25th China Conference, CCIR 2019, Fuzhou, China, September 20–22, 2019, Proceedings.*

George A. Miller. 1995. *WordNet: A Lexical Database for English.* Communications of the ACM Vol. 38, No. 11: 39-41.

Nitin Hardeniya, Jacob Perkins, Deepti Chopra, Nisheeth Joshi, Iti Mathur. 2016. *Natural Language Processing: Python and NLTK.*

Rada Mihalcea and Courtney Corley. 2006. *Corpus-based and Knowledge-based Measures of Text Semantic Similarity.*

Philip Stone. 2006. *General Inquirer Categories.* The Gallup Organization.

Corinna Cortes and Vladimir Vapnik. 1995. *Support-vector networks. Machine Learning,* 20(3):273–297, 1995.

Charu C. Aggarwal. 2014. *Data Classification: Algorithms and Applications.* Chapman & Hall/CRC Data Mining and Knowledge Discovery, Band 35

Scikit-learn: Machine Learning in Python, Pedregosa *et al.*, JMLR 12, pp. 2825-2830, 2011.

IR&TM-NJUST@CLSciSumm 20

Heng Zhang, Lifan Liu, Ruping Wang, Shaohu Hu, Shutian Ma, Chengzhi Zhang*

Department of Information Management, Nanjing University of Science and Technology, Nanjing, China, 210094
zh_heng@njust.edu.cn, liulf@njust.edu.cn, 2935843497@qq.com,
191226105@qq.com, mashutian0608@hotmail.com, zhangcz@njust.edu.cn

Abstract

This paper mainly introduces our methods for Task 1A and Task 1B of CL-SciSumm 2020. Task 1A is to identify reference text in reference paper. Traditional machine learning models and MLP model are used. We evaluate the performances of these models and submit the final results from the optimal model. Compared with previous work, we optimize the ratio of positive to negative examples after data sampling. In order to construct features for classification, we calculate similarities between reference text and candidate sentences based on sentence vectors. Accordingly, nine similarities are used, of which eight are chosen from what we used in CL-SciSumm 2019 and a new sentence similarity based on fastText is added. Task 1B is to classify the facets of reference text. Unlike the methods used in CL-SciSumm 2019, we construct inputs of models based on word vectors and add deep learning models for classification this year.

1 Introduction

The rapid growth of papers has provided scholars with various knowledge and methods, which can offer references for development or innovation of the research. But it makes difficult for researchers to get brief summaries quickly from such massive amount of papers (Radev et al., 2002). Automatic summarization can solve this problem. Researchers express their views on reference paper through citation text. So, citation text can be used to generate summary of paper (Cohan & Goharian, 2018; Qazvinian & Radev, 2008). However, as a result of researchers' different views (citation), the quality of the summary is not guaranteed and the summary cannot fully restore the original information of paper. Therefore, CL-SciSumm proposes to generate summary by the original text corresponding to citation. CL-SciSumm is the first medium-scale shared task on scientific document summarization, with over 500 annotated documents [1]. This competition is organized annually from 2016, and we can view details about CL-SciSumm2020 at the website: https://ornlcda.github.io/SDProc/sharedtasks.html#clscisumm. The introduction of CL-SciSumm2020 is as follows:

Given: A topic consisting of a Reference Paper (RP) and Citing Papers (CPs) that all contain citations to the RP. In each CP, the text spans (i.e., citances) have been identified that pertain to a particular citation to the RP.

Task 1A: For each citance, identify the spans of text (cited text spans) in the RP that most accurately reflect the citance. These are of the granularity of a sentence fragment, a full sentence, or several consecutive sentences (no more than 5).

Task 1B: For each cited text span, identify what facet of the paper it belongs to, from a predefined set of facets.

Task 2 (optional bonus task): Finally, generate a structured summary of the RP from the cited text spans of the RP. The length of the summary should not exceed 250 words.

In Figure 1, The blue text span in the citing paper shows the citation text, and the green text span in the reference paper shows the reference text which most accurately reflects the citance.

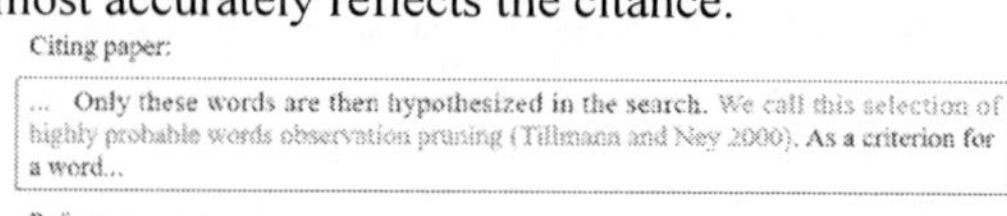

Figure 1: Citation text in citing paper and reference text in reference paper

---

* Corresponding Author.

[1] https://github.com/WING-NUS/scisumm-corpus/

Proceedings of the First Workshop on Scholarly Document Processing, pages 288–296
Online, November 19, 2020. ©2020 Association for Computational Linguistics
https://doi.org/10.18653/v1/P17

Our team has participated in the CL-SciSumm competition in 2017 (Ma et al., 2017), 2018 (Ma, et al., 2018) and 2019 (Ma et al., 2019). For Task 1A, a similarity-based negative sampling strategy is applied to construct the training set. Nine similarity features and sentence vectors are used to represent citation text and candidate sentences. Then we employ traditional machine learning methods and build MLP model to identify the reference text in reference papers. For Task 1B, sentence vectors are generated based on word frequency and word vector. Traditional machine learning models and deep learning models are built to identify the facets. As for Task 2, cosine similarity is calculated between reference sentences and the original abstract based on their sentence vectors. Then sentences are selected to construct summary according to their similarities, and length of the summary does not exceed 250 words.

Compared with previous work, we make changes in following steps. In Task 1A, we optimize ratio of positive to negative examples after negative sampling. The structure and parameters of MLP model are adjusted to get better results. For Task 1B, we first try to use word vector to construct inputs of models. And the result has been improved about 10% at accuracy score.

2 Related works

2.1 Identification of the citation text spans

As for the related work of Task 1A, most previous teams solved it by using classification models, and they constructed different features as input of models. Some researchers used three types of classification features, namely similarity-based features, rule-based features and location-based features (Jaidka et al., 2017). Ma et al. (2017) extracted several features at the words level from the citation text spans in the training set to calculate the corresponding similarities, such as IDF similarity, Jaccard similarity, Dice similarity, Word2Vec similarity and so on.

In recent years, machine learning models are mostly used for the identification of citation text spans. Mei and Zhai (2008) highlighted the importance of citance, and they proposed a method to generate the abstract of the cited document by extracting the most influential sentences in the document. The machine learning models mainly include classification models and ranking models.

Yeh et al. (2017) used classification models, such as SVM (Support Vector Machines), DT (decision trees), KNN (K-Nearest Neighbors) and so on in the identification of citances. Their method performed well with competitive results when it was evaluated using the CL-SciSumm 2016 datasets. In ranking models, sentences were sorted based on the integration of multiple features. Lu et al. (2016) constructed word-level (e.g. TF-IDF similarity and Jaccard similarity) and topic-level features (based on LDA model) separately and used the learning-to-rank algorithm to identify cited text spans. Their results showed that Jaccard similarity achieved better F measures, and the performance of topic similarity features varies slightly among different number of topics. Additionally, Moraes et al. (2016) investigated cosine similarity with multiple incremental modifications and SVMs with a tree kernel. They calculated the similarity not only between reference and citance sentences, but also between the reference spans and the citance sentences.

In summary, the current research about identification of citation text spans mainly includes feature construction and model selection. Most of the researches attempt to construct a huge feature system for model training and learning. As for model selection, most of the works are based on traditional machine learning models or sorting algorithms.

2.2 Identification of the facets of reference text

Task 1B is to identify the facets of reference text. It provides 5 facets in this task. Most teams in previous CL-SciSumm competitions used rule-based methods, because the amounts of different facets of reference text are imbalanced (Ma et al., 2018). In the learning process of the classification algorithms, the result tends to focus on the facets with most samples. This problem will have a huge impact on model training (He & Garcia, 2009). He et al. (2008) reviewed researches about learning from imbalanced data, then they highlighted that the opportunities and challenges to solve this problem would be a new research field in the future research. Ma, et al. (2018) combined the NN algorithm with the SMOTE algorithm to make training data and extend the penalty factor in the processing of imbalanced datasets, and NN algorithm behaved best on testing data.

There are plenty of researches about identifying the facets of reference text, rule-based methods and statistical-based methods are widely used. Wang et al. (2012) proposed an orderly clue phrase matching method and got 62% accuracy and 42% recall. Sándor et al. (2006) presented two natural language processing systems to help researchers rapidly accessing relevant knowledge in text. Agarwal et al. (2011) used two statistical machine learning models, SVM and NB, to classify the facets of reference. And they found that the classification result of SVM was better. Aggarwal and Sharma (2016) determined the facets based on the location of the cited text spans. Li et al. (2019) used the Word2Vec and the CNN model to calculate the sentence similarity, and further apply CNN to classify the facets of reference texts. They indicated that the features of high frequency word and subtitle are important in the identification of facets.

In summary, in the researches about classification of facets, the approaches applied in this task mainly include rule-based methods and statistical-based methods. However, because of the limited experimental dataset and the imbalance in the number of samples in different facets, these two methods are difficult to learn the relevant features of the facets more accurately and efficiently.

3 Methodology

Before introducing the methodology of each task, we define some concepts to avoid ambiguity in the following description.

Table 1: Concepts and their definitions

Concept	Definition
Citation text	It is "Citance" in introduction of Task 1A, and it consists of one or several sentences from citing paper. See blue highlighted span in Figure 1.
Reference text	It is "cited text spans" in introduction of Task 1B, and it consists of one or several sentences from reference paper. See green highlighted span in Figure 1.
Facets	It is the type of reference text, there is a predefined set of facets: "Method_Citation", "Result_Citation", "Aim_Citation", "Implication_Citation", "Hypothesis_Citation".
Candidate sentences	Citation text and candidate sentences as a pair of input to models. And candidate sentences contain reference text as positive samples and sentences selected from reference paper as negative samples.

3.1 Task 1A based on negative sampling

In Task 1A, we are given citation text to find the corresponding sentences in the reference paper. This task can be regarded as a binary classification task. For a citation text, it is need to identify the classification labels of all sentences in the reference paper. There are two classification labels: "1" or "0". If "1", it means that the sentence belongs to the correct reference text. If "0", it means that the sentence is not. Figure 2 shows our research framework of Task 1A. Firstly, preprocessing is conducted for the data extracted from data set. Secondly, training data is constructed by negative sampling. Then, nine similarities are calculated between citation text and candidate sentences, which are used as features to construct input of traditional machine learning models. Additionally, MLP model is built based on sentence vector. Finally, these models are evaluated with Precision (P), Recall (R), and F_1-value (F_1).

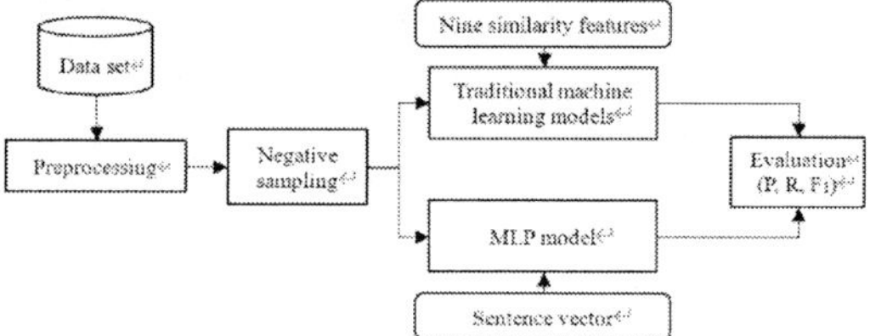

Figure 2: Framework of Task 1A

Negative sampling: 753 pairs of citation text and reference text are extracted from annotation in "Training-Set-2018", and they are used as positive samples (label "1"). Citation text and other arbitrary sentences in reference papers can be regarded as negative samples (label "0"), but the number of negative samples is too huge. In order to balance positive and negative samples, negative sampling based on sentence vector similarity is performed. We calculate the average of all word vectors in the sentence and obtain a new vector to represent the sentence. Then, cosine similarities are calculated between the citation text and all sentences in reference paper (apart from the reference text annotated). Next, sentences are chosen from the highest, lowest, and middle similarity levels to form negative samples. Through comparative experiments, the ratio of the number of positive to negative samples is finally determined as 1:6 (two sentences with the highest similarity, two sentences with the lowest similarity, and two sentences with medium similarity as negative samples).

Using traditional machine learning models to identify reference text: The first idea is to use traditional machine learning methods to solve Task 1A. We calculate multiple similarities between citation text and candidate sentences as features. It is worth noting that candidate sentences contain reference text and 6 negative samples, citation text and reference text are regarded as a whole respectively to calculate their sentence vectors. Nine similarity indicators are selected and they are showed in Table 2. Then several machine learning models are trained for classification. These models contain Support Vector Machine (SVM) (Cortes and Vapnik, 1995), Naive Bayesian (NB) (McCallum et al., 1998), K-Nearest Neighbor (KNN) (Altman, 1992), Decision Tree (DT) (Quinlan, 1987), Random Forest (RF) (Ho, 1995) and ensemble learning tool (Xgboost[2]).

Table 2: Nine similarities as features

Similarity	Description
Jaccard similarity	Segment setence1 and setence2 into set of words, denoted as s_1 and s_2 respectively, and calculate the division of the intersection and union between two sets. Its formulation is as follows: $$J(s_1,s_2)=\frac{len(s_1 \cap s_2)}{len(s_1) + len(s_2) - len(s_1 \cap s_2)}$$
Dice similarity	Segment setence1 and setence2 into sets of words(s_1, s_2). Its formulation is as follows: $$\frac{2 * intersection(s_1, s_2)}{length(s_1) + length(s_2)}$$
Word Overlap	Segment setence1 and setence2 into sets of words, and calculate the number of overlaps between them.
Bigram Overlap	Segment setence1 and setence2 into sets of bigrams, and calculate the number of overlaps between them.
Longest Common Subsequence	Denote setence1 and setence2 as two sets of sequences with words as basic unit, find the longest subsequence (not necessarily consecutive in original sequences) common of them.
Longest Common Substring	Denote setence1 and setence2 as two sets of strings with words as basic units, and find the longest string(s) that is a substring(s) (required to occupy consecutive positions within the original strings) of them.
Levenshtein distance	Calculate the average of Levenshtein distance (the minimum number of single character edits required to change one to the other) for all the words between setence1 and setence2.
Word2Vec similarity	Represent words as low-dimensional and dense distributed representation by Word2Vec algorithm and calculate the average of the similarity between words from two sentences via cosine value.
fastText [3] similarity	Represent words as low-dimensional and dense distributed representation by fastText algorithm and calculate the average of the similarity between words from two sentences via cosine value.

Using MLP model to identify reference text: The second idea is to use deep learning models. Word2Vec(Mikolov et al., 2013) and fastText are used to train word vectors. And we calculate the average of all word vectors in sentence to get sentence vectors. Vector of citation text and vector of candidate sentence are concatenated as input of models. We build MLP model and adjust hidden layers and parameters for optimization.

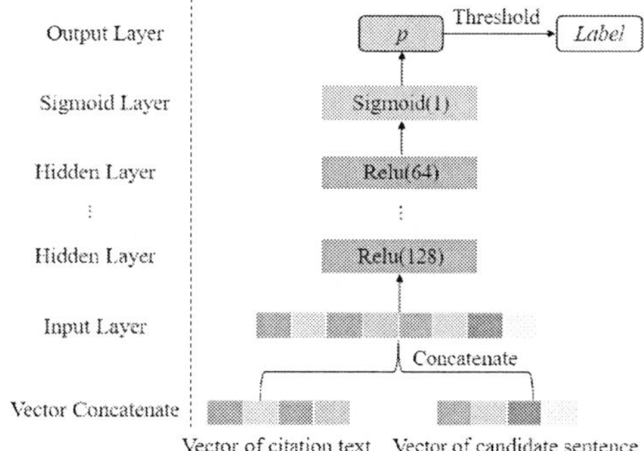

Figure 3: Framework of MLP model in Task 1A

The framework of MLP model is shown in Figure 3. The input of the model is concatenated sentence vector from citation text and reference text. Concatenated sentence vector passes through two hidden layers, and then passes through the sigmoid layer. We get the probability of two labels through the output layer and set a threshold to determine which label the candidate sentence belongs to. It should be noted that the activation

---

[2] https://github.com/dmlc/xgboost

[3] https://github.com/facebookresearch/fastText

function of the hidden layer is Relu, and the number of neural nodes is 128 and 64 respectively. These parameters are finally determined based on comparative experiments.

3.2 Task 1B based on sentence vector and word embedding

In Task 1B, it is a multi-label classification task. There are five labels (facets): "Method_Citation", "Result_Citation", "Aim_Citation", "Implication_Citation", "Hypothesis_Citation". The research framework of Task 1B is shown in Figure 4. Firstly, 753 pairs of citation text and reference text is extracted from data set. Secondly, training set and test set are split from the extracted data by sampling. Then, sentence vectors are generated from word frequency and word vector based on which traditional machine learning models are used to classify the facets. In addition, the word embedding matrix is used as input, and deep learning models are also applied in Task 1B. In order to test the effects of different models, accuracy score is used.

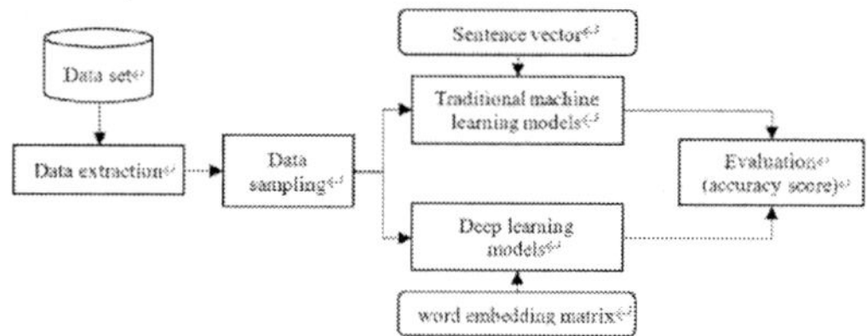

Figure 4: Framework of Task 1B

Data sampling: The number of samples in five facets varies greatly (see Figure 5). Training set and test set should not be divided from all the samples directly. In order to balance all kinds of samples in training set and test set, we randomly select 80% of samples from each label to form training set, and the remaining 20% of the samples are used as test set.

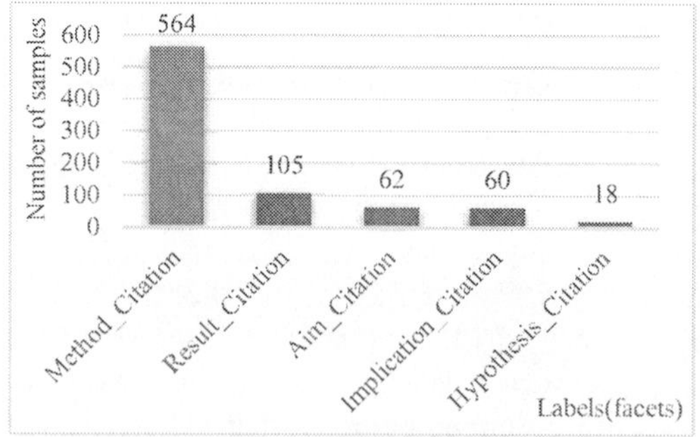

Figure 5: Number of samples in each label

Using traditional machine learning models to identify the facets based on sentence vector: As illustrated in the framework, traditional machine learning models are employed in Task 1B based on the input of sentence vectors. By the way, sentence vectors are generated from word frequency and word vector separately. In the first way, nouns, verbs, adverbs, adjectives are selected after part-of-speech tagging. Then, sentence vectors are generated by One-hot or TF (Term Frequency) based on the selected words. In the second way, fastText and BERT[4] are used to train word vector. And we calculate the average of all word vectors in the sentence to generate the sentence vector. After that, traditional machine learning models introduced in Task 1A are used for the multi-label classification. Besides, we add another ensemble learning tool LightGBM[5]. During testing, if the model cannot assign a label to a sample, we will set the sample's label to "Method_Citation".".

Using deep learning models to identify the facets based on word embedding: We also build deep learning models for the multi-label classification in Task 1B. In this scheme, word embedding matrix is used as input. Long Short-Term Memory (LSTM) (Hochreiter & Schmidhuber, 1997) and Recurrent Neural Network (RNN) (Rumelhart et al., 1986) are applied in the feature selection layer separately. They convert the word embedding matrix into a 128-dimensional vector. Then the vector passes through a hidden layer, and we get the probabilities that the sample belongs to five labels. When the probability is greater than 0.5, we assign the corresponding label to the sample. If the sample fails to obtain a label, we set its label to "Method_Citation".

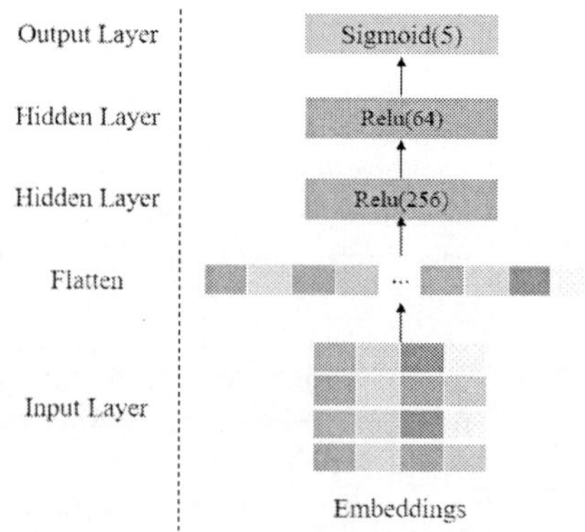

Figure 6: Framework of MLP model in Task 1B

---

[4] https://github.com/google-research/bert

[5] https://github.com/microsoft/LightGBM

In Figure 5, We build an MLP model for Task 1B. The word embedding matrix is flatted into a vector, and the vector pass through two hidden layers. Finally, the model outputs the probabilities that the sample belongs to five labels.

3.3 Task 2 based on sentence similarity

In Task 2, we select sentences from reference text by calculating cosine similarity between the sentence and the original abstract to generate abstract. The steps are as follows:

a. Word vector is trained by fastText.

b. Sentence vectors of reference sentences (identified in Task 1A) and the original abstract are generated by calculating the average of vectors of all words in the sentence.

c. Calculate cosine similarity between reference sentences and the original abstract based on their sentence vectors.

d. Select sentences according to their similarities to generate summary, and length of the summary does not exceed 250 words.

4 Experiments and results analysis

In this section, we report the results of different models in Task 1A and Task 1B.

4.1 Experimental result of Task 1A

For task 1A, we use nine similarities as features and applied traditional machine learning models to identify reference text. MLP model is also employed based on the input of sentence vector. In this section, we report and analysis the results of these models.

Results of traditional machine learning models: Input of sentence vector is generated based on nine similarities. And five classification models in Scikit-learn[6]: Random Forest, Decision Tree, SVM, NB, KNN are applied. In addition, ensemble learning model by Xgboost is employed. Precision, Recall, and F_1-value are used to evaluate their performance. The results of 5-fold cross validation are shown in Table 3.

Table 3: Evaluation results of models

Model	P	R	F_1
Xgboost	0.5124	0.5449	**0.5280**
Random Forest	0.6732	0.4087	0.5084
Decision Tree	0.4680	0.4442	0.4550
SVM	0.6415	0.3168	0.4230
NB	0.2626	0.9430	0.4106
KNN	0.4957	0.3345	0.3987

From Table 3, we can see that ensemble learning method by Xgboost achieves the optimal F_1-value.

Results of MLP model: Word vectors are trained through two tools: Word2Vec and fastText. The training corpus consists of two parts: (1) Full-text of reference papers and citing papers from "Training-Set-2018". (2) Full-text of reference papers from "ScisummNet-2019". The vector dimension is set to 200. Through comparative experiments, we finally determined the optimal parameter settings under these two kinds of word vector, as shown in Table 4.

Table 4: Parameters of MLP models

Model	MLP_FT	MLP_FT
Word vector	fastText	Word2Vec
Optimizer	adam	RMSprop
Loss	binary_cross entropy	mse
Epoch	20	20
Hidden layer	Rule (128) Rule (64)	Rule (128) Rule (64)
Threshold	0.577	0.602

The evaluation results of these two models are shown in Table 5.

Table 5: Evaluation results of MLP models

Model	P	R	F_1
MLP_FT	0.6486	0.6316	**0.6400**
MLP_W2Vs	0.6428	0.5684	0.6034

As surfaced in Table 5, the results based on fastText is better than Word2Vec. F_1-value of the best result is 0.64. Compared with the results of machine learning models, MLP works better.

But when we use the trained models to identify the sentences in reference papers for citation text, the models output far more than 5 sentences. In order to ensure the effect of the final test, we develop a sentence filtering strategy in reference papers:

a. We pick out nouns in citation text and sentences of reference papers.

b. In reference paper, sentences with the same noun as citation text are filtered out.

c. We use trained models to identify the filtered sentences. Because we find that 609 of the 753 pairs of citation text and reference text have the same nouns.

d. When the final test, if there is no sentence with

---

the same noun as citation text in the reference paper, we will test all sentences in the reference paper.

4.2   Experimental results of Task 1B

For Task 1B, sentence vector and word embedding matrix are used as input. Then traditional machine learning models and deep learning models are applied for the multi-label classification. Now, we report and analysis the results of these models.

Accuracy score of traditional machine learning models based on one-hot: Sentence vectors are generated by one-hot in two ways. (1) Nouns, verbs, adverbs and adjectives are only selected in citation text. (2) Nouns, verbs, adverbs and adjectives are selected in both citation text and reference text. Many machine learning models in Scikit-learn and ensemble learning models by Xgboost and LightGBM are applied for classification. Accuracy score is used to evaluate these models. Random Forest and two ensemble models work better, and their accuracy scores are demonstrated in Table 6.

Table 6: Evaluation results of models based on One-hot

Model	citation text	citation text and reference text
Random Forest	0.7580	**0.8025**
Xgboost	0.7134	0.6688
LightGBM	0.7707	0.7962

From Table 6, when sentence vectors are generated by One-hot based on citation text and reference text, Random Forest works better and its accuracy score is 0.8025.

Accuracy score of traditional machine learning models based on TF (Term Frequency): We also use TF to generate vectors in two ways: citation text, citation text and reference text. Evaluation results of Random Forest, Xgboost and LightGBM are shown in Table 7.

Table 7: Evaluation results of models based on TF

Model	citation text	citation text and reference text
Random Forest	0.7580	**0.7962**
Xgboost	0.7134	0.7580
LightGBM	0.6624	**0.7962**

As suggested in Table 7, when sentence vectors are generated by TF based on citation text and reference text, Random Forest and LightGBM achieve higher accuracy score.

Accuracy_score of traditional machine learning models based on fastText: Sentence vectors are generated based on fastText word vector. Sentence vector of citation text is recorded as $v_1 = (x_1, x_2 \ldots x_n)$, and sentence vector of reference text is recorded as $v_2 = (y_1, y_2 \ldots y_n)$. We also calculate $|v_1-v_2| = (|x_1-y_1|, |x_2-y_2| \ldots |x_n-y_n|)$ and $v_1{*}v_2 = (x_1{*}y_1, x_2{*}y_2 \ldots x_n{*}y_n)$. We make four combinations of v_1 and v_2:

a. $(v_1, v_2) = (x_1, x_2 \ldots x_n, y_1, y_2 \ldots y_n)$

b. $(v_1, v_2, |v_1-v_2|) = (x_1, x_2 \ldots x_n, y_1, y_2 \ldots y_n, |x_1-y_1|, |x_2-y_2| \ldots |x_n-y_n|)$

c. $(v_1, v_2, v_1{*}v_2) = (x_1, x_2 \ldots x_n, y_1, y_2 \ldots y_n, x_1{*}y_1, x_2{*}y_2 \ldots x_n{*}y_n)$

d. $(v_1, v_2, |v_1-v_2|, v_1{*}v_2) = (x_1, x_2 \ldots x_n, y_1, y_2 \ldots y_n, |x_1-y_1|, |x_2-y_2| \ldots |x_n-y_n|, x_1{*}y_1, x_2{*}y_2 \ldots x_n{*}y_n)$

In each combination, vectors are concatenated as input of different models. Evaluation results of Random Forest, Xgboost and LightGBM are shown in Figure 7.

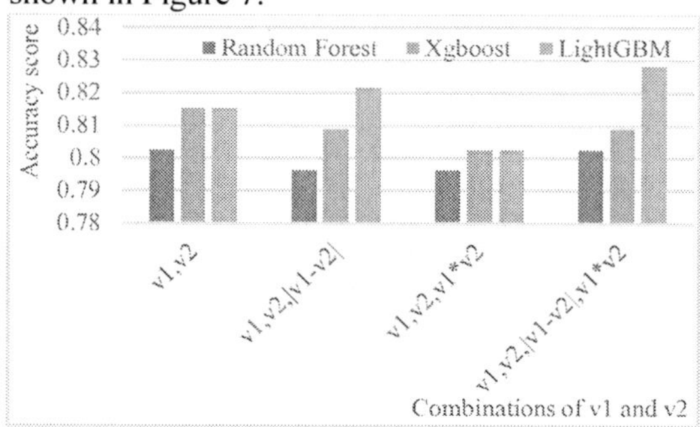

Figure 7: Evaluation results of models based on fastText

As shown in Figure 7, under different conditions, LightGBM performs better than the other two models. When v_1, v_2, $|v_1-v_2|$ and $v_1{*}v_2$ are concatenated as input, LightGBM reaches the highest accuracy score (0.8280).

Accuracy score of traditional machine learning models based on BERT: We train word vector by BERT and calculate sentence vectors. Evaluation results of three models are shown in Figure 8.

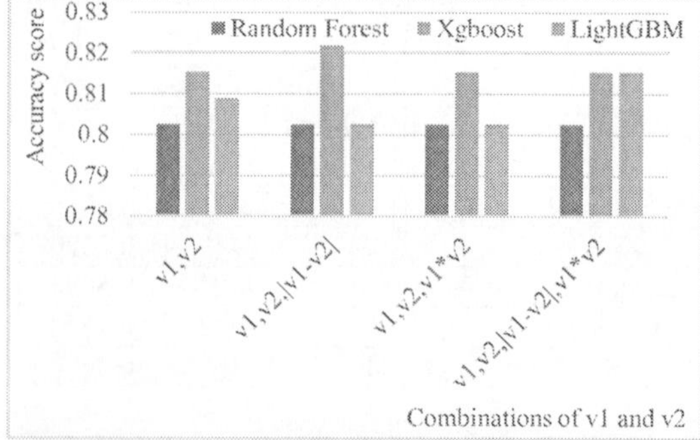

Figure 8: Evaluation results of models based on BERT

As illustrated in Figure 8, under different conditions, Xgboost performs better than the other two models. When v_1, v_2, and $|v_1\text{-}v_2|$ are concatenated as input, Xgboost get the highest accuracy score (0.8217). But its performance is slightly worse than LightGBM with fastText word vectors (see Figure 7).

Accuracy score of deep learning models based on word embedding: Word vectors trained by fastText and BERT are used to construct word embedding matrix of citation text and reference text. Then three deep learning models: LSTM, RNN and MLP are applied with the input of word embedding matrix. Accuracy score of the three models are shown in Figure 9.

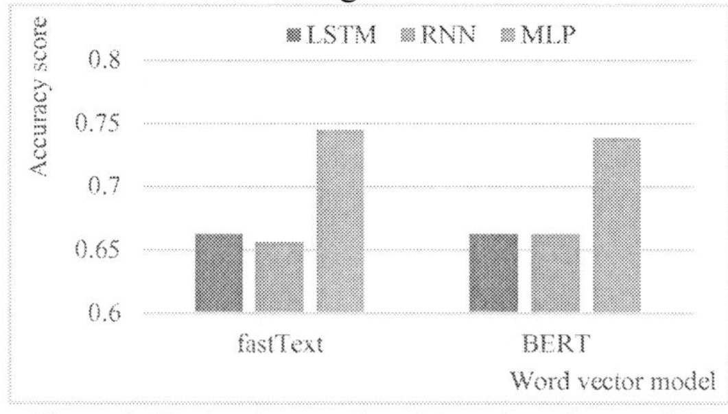

Figure 9: Evaluation results of deep learning models

From Figure 9, we can see that MLP performs best among the three models. But its accuracy score is lower than the previous results of LightGBM and Xgboost (see Figure 7 and Figure 8).

5   Conclusion and future work

In Task 1A, training data and test data are constructed by negative sampling. And the ratio of positive to negative examples has been optimized. Next, we use deep learning model (MLP) with the input of sentence vectors and traditional machine learning models based on nine similarity features to identify the reference text. The effect of MLP is proved to be better than that of traditional machine learning models. As for Task 1B, we calculate different combinations of sentence vectors as input. Traditional machine learning models and deep learning models have been evaluated on classifying the facets of reference text. In this process, the effect of using pre-training model (BERT) to obtain word vector is worse than that of using fastText to train word vector based on training set. And traditional machine models (LightGBM and Xgboost) work better than deep learning models.

Generally, word vectors can reflect more semantic information compared to traditional machine learning features. We create a suitable number of training data by negative sampling in Task 1A, so deep learning model (MLP) works better. While in Task 1B, insufficient training data makes deep learning models inferior to traditional machine learning models.

In future work, we can optimize training set through Data Augmentation Technology and apply other deep learning models for Task 1A. As for Task 1B, its recognition result is affected by the imbalance of data. We will try to expand the training data for the facets with smaller data scale from other data sources, such as structured abstract.

Acknowledgements

This work is supported by National Natural Science Foundation of China (Grant No. 72074113).

Reference

Agarwal, N. K., Xu, Y. (Calvin), & Poo, D. C. C. (2011). A context-based investigation into source use by information seekers. Journal of the American Society for Information Science and Technology, 62(6), 1087‑1104. https://doi.org/10.1002/asi.21513

Aggarwal, P., & Sharma, R. (2016). Lexical and Syntactic cues to identify Reference Scope of Citance. Proceedings of the Joint Workshop on Bibliometric-Enhanced Information Retrieval and Natural Language Processing for Digital Libraries (BIRNDL), 103‑112.

Altman, N. S. (1992). An introduction to kernel and nearest-neighbor nonparametric regression. The American Statistician, 46(3), 175‑185.

Cohan, A., & Goharian, N. (2018). Scientific document summarization via citation contextualization and scientific discourse. International Journal on Digital Libraries, 19(2‑3), 287‑303.

Cortes, C., & Vapnik, V. (1995). Support-vector networks. Machine Learning, 20(3), 273‑297. https://doi.org/10.1007/BF00994018

He, H., & Garcia, E. A. (2009). Learning from Imbalanced Data. IEEE Transactions on Knowledge and Data Engineering, 21(9), 1263‑1284. https://doi.org/10.1109/TKDE.2008.239

He, H., Yang Bai, Garcia, E. A., & Shutao Li. (2008). ADASYN: Adaptive synthetic sampling approach for imbalanced learning. 2008 IEEE International Joint Conference on Neural Networks (IEEE World Congress on Computational Intelligence), 1322-1328. https://doi.org/10.1109/IJCNN.2008.4633969

Ho, T. K. (1995). Random decision forests. Proceedings of 3rd International Conference on Document Analysis and Recognition, 1, 278-282.

Hochreiter, S., & Schmidhuber, J. (1997). Long Short-Term Memory. Neural Comput., 9(8), 1735-1780. https://doi.org/10.1162/neco.1997.9.8.1735

Jaidka, K., Chandrasekaran, M. K., Jain, D., & Kan, M.-Y. (2017). The CL-SciSumm Shared Task 2017: Results and Key Insights. BIRNDL@ SIGIR (2).

Li, L., Zhu, Y., Xie, Y., Huang, Z., Liu, W., Li, X., & Liu, Y. (2019). CIST@ CLSciSumm-19: Automatic Scientific Paper Summarization with Citances and Facets. BIRNDL@ SIGIR, 196-207.

Lu, K., Mao, J., Li, G., & Xu, J. (2016). Recognizing reference spans and classifying their discourse facets. Proceedings of the Joint Workshop on Bibliometric-Enhanced Information Retrieval and Natural Language Processing for Digital Libraries (BIRNDL), 139-145.

Ma, S., Xu, J., Wang, J., & Zhang, C. (2017). NJUST @ CLSciSumm-17. Proceedings of the Joint Workshop on Bibliometric-Enhanced Information Retrieval and Natural Language Processing for Digital Libraries (BIRNDL 2017).

Ma, S., Xu, J., & Zhang, C. (2018). Automatic identification of cited text spans: A multi-classifier approach over imbalanced dataset. Scientometrics, 116(2), 1303-1330. https://doi.org/10.1007/s11192-018-2754-2

Ma, S., Zhang, H., Xu, J., & Zhang, C. (2018). NJUST @ CLSciSumm-18. BIRNDL@ SIGIR.

Ma, S., Zhang, H., Xu, T., Xu, J., Hu, S., & Zhang, C. (2019). IR&TM-NJUST@ CLSciSumm-19. BIRNDL@ SIGIR, 181-195.

McCallum, A., Nigam, K., & others. (1998). A comparison of event models for naive bayes text classification. Proceedings of the AAAI-98 Workshop on Learning for Text Categorization, 752(1), 41-48.

Mei, Q., & Zhai, C. (2008). Generating impact-based summaries for scientific literature. Proceedings of ACL-08: HLT, 816-824.

Mikolov, T., Chen, K., Corrado, G., & Dean, J. (2013). Efficient Estimation of Word Representations in Vector Space. ArXiv:1301.3781 [Cs]. http://arxiv.org/abs/1301.3781

Moraes, L., Baki, S., Verma, R., & Lee, D. (2016). University of Houston at CL-SciSumm 2016: SVMs with tree kernels and Sentence Similarity. Proceedings of the Joint Workshop on Bibliometric-Enhanced Information Retrieval and Natural Language Processing for Digital Libraries (BIRNDL), 113-121.

Qazvinian, V., & Radev, D. R. (2008). Scientific paper summarization using citation summary networks. ArXiv Preprint ArXiv:0807.1560.

Quinlan, J. R. (1987). Simplifying decision trees. International Journal of Man-Machine Studies, 27(3), 221-234.

Radev, D. R., Hovy, E., & McKeown, K. (2002). Introduction to the special issue on summarization. Computational Linguistics, 28(4), 399-408.

Rumelhart, D. E., Hinton, G. E., & Williams, R. J. (1986). Learning representations by back-propagating errors. Nature, 323(6088), 533-536. https://doi.org/10.1038/323533a0

Sándor, Á., Kaplan, A., & Rondeau, G. (2006). Discourse and citation analysis with concept-matching. International Symposium: Discourse and Document (ISDD), 15-16.

Wang, W., Villavicencio, P., & Watanabe, T. (2012). Analysis of reference relationships among research papers, based on citation context. International Journal on Artificial Intelligence Tools, 21(02), 1240004. https://doi.org/10.1142/S0218213012400040

Yeh, J.-Y., Hsu, T.-Y., Tsai, C.-J., & Cheng, P.-C. (2017). Reference Scope Identification for Citances by Classification with Text Similarity Measures. Proceedings of the 6th International Conference on Software and Computer Applications, 87-91. https://doi.org/10.1145/3056662.3056692

CiteQA@CLSciSumm 2020

Anjana Umapathy*   **Karthik Radhakrishnan***   **Kinjal Jain***   **Rahul Singh***

Language Technologies Institute
Carnegie Mellon University
`{aumapath, kradhak2, kinjalj, rahuls2}@cs.cmu.edu`

Abstract

In academic publications, citations are used to build context for a concept by highlighting relevant aspects from reference papers. Automatically identifying referenced snippets can help researchers swiftly isolate principal contributions of scientific works. In this paper, we exploit the underlying structure of scientific articles to predict reference paper spans and facets corresponding to a citation. We propose two methods to detect citation spans - keyphrase overlap, BERT along with structural priors. We fine-tune FastText embeddings and leverage textual, positional features to predict citation facets.

1 Introduction

With the ballooning growth in the number of research papers published every year (Larsen and Von Ins, 2010), being able to automatically identify the main contributions of a paper would be a useful tool to aid the ingestion of academic works. Given that citations are expected to focus on the important or note-worthy aspects of a paper (Nakov et al., 2004), tagging a citation with its corresponding reference paper snippet could help identify the main contributions of the reference paper.

While methodologies to find influential papers exist, there is currently no established method to identify the aspects of a reference paper that make it influential. Uncovering important aspects has a range of downstream applications such as discovering interesting insights about salient, frequently cited concepts or empowering researchers to quickly read and understand a large volume of papers. Ability to quickly sift through a large volume of papers is especially useful during times of crisis to get equipped with the most relevant research in a new area (such as COVID-19). External

to research papers, this tool could also be leveraged by journalists and paralegals as news articles and legal documents follow a similar citation structure.

In this work, we tackle two tasks - citation span detection and facet identification. We utilize the structural characteristics of scientific articles such as section and sentence importance, location of sentences in conjunction with textual features. We present a keyphrase extraction and a BERT model for citation identification and augment sentence embeddings with hand-crafted features to classify the citation onto a set of pre-defined facets[1].

2 Task and Dataset Description

We break down our objective into two sub-tasks: Citation span detection and Facet identification.

A. Span Detection - Given a reference paper (RP), a citing paper (CP), and the citation sentence (citance), identify the spans in the reference paper which most accurately capture the citation.

B. Facet Identification - Given reference and citing papers, perform a multi-label citation classification onto 5 pre-defined facets {METHOD, RESULT, AIM, HYPOTHESIS, IMPLICATION} indicating the type of citation.

For both Task A and Task B, we make use of the dataset released as part of the shared task at CL-SciSumm (Chandrasekaran et al., 3002forthcoming) for EMNLP 2020.

The CL-SciSumm dataset contains a set of 40 reference papers (in the domain of computational linguistics), each paired with up to 35 citing papers, totalling 753 unique citations. The dataset introduces two tasks: 1) Span detection(A) and

---

[1] Our code and models can be found at `https://github.com/karthikradhakrishnan96/CiteQA`

*Equal contribution

Proceedings of the First Workshop on Scholarly Document Processing, pages 297–302
Online, November 19, 2020. ©2020 Association for Computational Linguistics
https://doi.org/10.18653/v1/P17

facet identification(B) , and 2) Summarization. In this work, we focus on task 1. Each citation is tagged with the gold reference spans and one or more facets. There is, however, no inter-annotator agreement or human performance reported on this dataset. An example from our dataset is shown below.

> **Citing Sentence** - Given that close to 95% of the word occurrences in human labeled data are tagged with their most frequent part of speech (Lee et al. , 2010)
>
> **Reference Sentence** - Simply assigning to each word its most frequent associated tag in a corpus achieves 94.6% accuracy on the WSJ portion of the Penn Treebank
>
> **Facet** - RESULT

We also make use of SciSummNet (Yasunaga et al., 2019) and a cleaned version (Lahiri, 2014) of the ACL-ARC corpus (Bird et al., 2008) for pre-training our models. SciSummNet contains over 1000 reference papers auto-annotated with citation spans and ACL-ARC corpus contains over 10K articles from ACL anthology.

We utilize SciSummNet to fine-tune our BERT (Devlin et al., 2019) model to adapt to 'scholarly document' style of text and use ACL-ARC corpus to generate domain-specific word embeddings using FastText (Joulin et al., 2016).

3 Related Work

Prior work on task A can be broadly classified into two categories - text similarity and deep learning based methods. Text similarity methods typically compute similarity scores between each reference sentence and the citing sentence and rank them to predict the reference spans. Similarity can be computed in different ways - Baruah (2018) use a word-embedding cosine similarity while Syed (2019) and Abura'ed (2018) use multiple similarity metrics like Jaccard, BM25, TF-IDF as features to train a classifier to predict the best reference sentence. PolyU (Cao et al., 2016) groups sentences into chunks and performs predictions by using a RankSVM over these chunks.

Deep learning models such as CiteListNet (Kim, 2019) and NacTem-UoM (Zerva et al., 2019) learn textual feature representations for classification.

CiteListNet employs a text-similarity phase followed by a CNN reranker while NacTem-UoM trains BERT to score a reference, citing sentence pair and predicts top-3 reference sentences.

For the facet identification task, Wang (2018) use bag of words in conjunction with some sentence features in multiple facet-specific classifiers, Baruah (2018) use average word2vec embeddings for prediction, and Zerva et al. (2019) use bag of words with random forests.

A common theme across previous works was that they predominantly only utilized the paper text but citations often depend on external factors like section of sentence, position in section etc. We augment our models with these biases to perform a structure aware citation span and facet detection.

4 Proposed Approach

In this section, we briefly describe our data preprocessing and the models used for span and facet identification.

4.1 Data Preprocessing

As noted by previous works (Zerva et al.,2019; Wang,2018) the CL-SciSumm dataset has numerous formatting issues stemming from the Optical Character Recognition (OCR) module used to transcribe the PDF documents. We removed sentences with either over 50% of single-character alphabets or sentences with under 70% of valid words in English dictionary (these sentences usually correspond to tables and figures and annotators do not tag them as gold spans). We replaced common hexadecimal unicode characters with their ascii equivalents and fixed word fragmentation issues occurring in hyphenated words.

We also stripped all citation markers from the reference sentences and removed sentences with over two citations (a reference sentence citing multiple other works is unlikely to be substantial enough to be cited by a different paper). We filtered sentences which were either shorter than 5 or longer than 30 words as these sentences were almost never cited (as measured empirically on the training dataset). Additionally, the marker citing the reference paper was replaced with with a special '##CITATION##' token and all other citations were stripped from the citing sentences.

4.2 Task A

For task A, we incorporate two different methods for span detection - Keyphrase similarity and BERT. We also apply some inductive biases accounting for the underlying writing structure of scientific papers.

4.2.1 Keyphrase similarity

We observed (on over 200 sampled citances) that citing sentences are usually paraphrases of references and tend to reuse the same words from the reference sentence. Though prior works (Wang, 2018) have incorporated word-based similarity methods, they evaluate overlap on complete sentences. We observed (through manual evaluation) that humans focus on important keyphrase similarity as opposed checking similarity over entire sentences. Hence we extract keyphrases from reference and citing sentences through Rapid Automated Keyword Extraction algorithm (Rose et al., 2010) and measure similarity using keyphrase overlap.

4.2.2 BERT for citation identification

Domain-specific BERT models have shown superior language understanding and success on downstream tasks. Though scientific versions of BERT exist (Beltagy et al., 2019), they are trained on the broader domain of scientific text as opposed to just computational linguistics. We make use of the SciSummNet and CL-SciSumm dataset to finetune BERT on in-domain computational linguistics papers. We then frame the citation identification problem as a sentence-pair classification task. Positive samples are gold sentences from our reference paper and 5 negative samples were chosen per positive sample from a combination of 3 random and 2 high-word overlap sentences. The word overlap negative samples were found through Jaccard and included to discriminate similar but wrong spans from the correct ones. We use weighted-cross entropy to account for the imbalance between positive and negative pairs. During inference, we picked the top 3 sentences ranked by the probabilities produced by BERT. Our model architecture is shown in figure 1.

4.2.3 Section Importance Bias

From our preliminary analysis, we observed that the introduction and conclusions are cited more than the others. This is especially apparent when the citing text cites multiple papers along with the reference paper (indicating that the citation is rel-

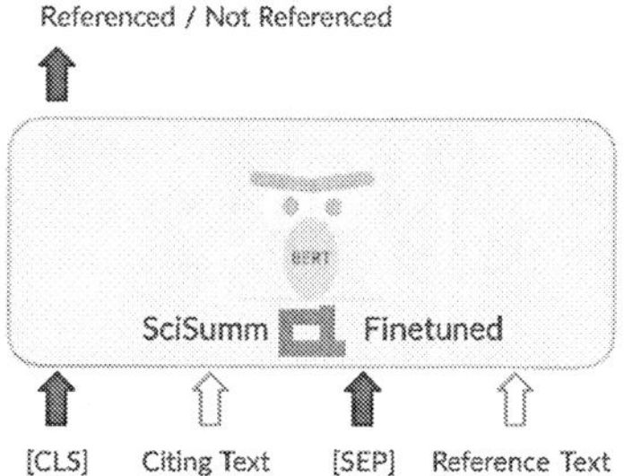

Figure 1: Architecture of our model for Task A. Citing Text is paired with every Reference sentence to predict citation probability

atively generic and is talking about a high-level detail about the reference). To incorporate this, we add an explicit bias to the reference sentences from these sections when the citing sentence has multiple citations, causing them to be weighted higher. More specifically, for sentences from introduction / conclusion sections we add a constant hyperparameter value for every citation present in the citing sentence.

4.2.4 Sentence Importance Bias

Research papers usually have few key contributions and sentences which capture these aspects tend to get cited repeatedly. Beyond relevance to the citing sentence (captured by our model), we propose favoring sentences unequally based on their importance in the reference paper. We incorporate this bias using the TextRank (Mihalcea and Tarau, 2004) score of the reference sentences.

TextRank constructs a weighted graph of sentences based on the keywords present followed by a ranking phase where it assigns a score to each sentence in the graph. This score enables us to incorporate the 'citability' of a reference sentence into our predictions. The TextRank score is linearly interpolated (with the co-efficient as a hyperparameter) with our model score to generate the final score for a reference sentence.

4.3 Task B

For identifying citation facets, we make use of the reference sentences (predicted from our task A model) in conjunction with features capturing facet priors and positional information.

We train FastText on the ACL-ARC corpus to generate domain-specific embeddings for the reference sentences.

While previous works have incorporated rule-based classifiers to include facet priors, we instead compute prior facet probabilities for each word (in the predicted reference sentences) and each section (in the reference paper) from our training data and use them as additional features. We also add a positional feature - reference SID ratio and textual features - presence of floating points or percentages (as they are highly indicative of RESULT facet).

We then train a Multi-Label Logistic Regression classifier over our input vectors (FastText embeddings + facet features) to predict the citation facet.

5 Experimental Setup

We fine-tune BERT$_{\text{BASE}}$ on Masked Language Modeling and Sequence Classification tasks using the Transformers library[2] for 2-6 epochs (with early stopping) on an NVIDIA T4 Tensor Core GPU and optimize our models using Adam (Kingma and Ba, 2019). We use 32 out of 40 papers present in the 2018 training data to fine-tune our model on sentence pair classification, reserving the remaining 8 papers for validation. We chose not to use the automatically annotated 2019 training data as we noticed a drop in performance on the validation set. The section and sentence importance bias coefficients were hyperparameters and were varied across runs. Our code repository contains more details on the exact hyperparameter values.

6 Results

Table 1 shows the performance of our models against various baselines. Our BERT model with biases achieves an F_1 of 0.128, outperforming last year's best model (NacTem-UoM). Our model performs competitively with other baseline models on the facet identification task as shown in Table 2.

7 Error Analysis

7.1 Facet Disparity

Our model achieved better performance on identifying citation spans when the underlying facet was METHOD or AIM while it was unable to identify RESULT effectively. This is because the citing and reference sentences are not similar when results are cited. A potential solution would be to identify the facet first and apply facet-specific models for span detection but we would have to ensure that such hard decisions do not cascade errors.

---

[2]https://huggingface.co/transformers/

Dataset	Model	Micro F_1	Macro F_1
2016-Test	PolyU	0.10	-
	Keyphrase (KP)	0.122	-
	KP + Biases	0.137	0.147
	BERT + Biases	**0.139**	0.117
Test	CiteListNet	0.124	-
	NacTem-UoM	0.126	-
	BUPT	0.087	-
	KP + Biases	0.123	0.127
	BERT + Biases	**0.128**	0.128

'-' → scores not available

Table 1: Performance of different models on Task A. 2016-Test refers to our held-out set and Test refers to the official CL-SciSumm results

Dataset	Model	Micro F_1	Macro F_1
2016-Test	PolyU	0.214	-
	KP + FT	0.285	0.295
	BERT + FT	**0.34**	0.265
Test	NacTem-UoM	0.312	-
	BUPT	**0.389**	-
	KP + FT	0.310	0.315
	BERT + FT	0.299	0.302

'-' → scores not available, FT → FastText

Table 2: Performance of different models on Task B

7.2 Unsolvable examples

Upon an initial manual annotation on a small subset of papers, we noticed that though our predictions seemed perfectly reasonable, gold annotations were often completely different sentences, highlighting the inherent ambiguity of this task and potentially explaining the low performance of all models. An example is shown below.

Citing Sentence - In the large-scale HPSG-based spoken Japanese analysis system developed at ATR, sometimes 98 percent of the elapsed time is devoted to graph unification (Kogure, 1990)

Gold Reference - Furthermore, structure sharing increases the portion of token identical substructures of FSs which makes it efficient to keep unification results of substructures of FSs and reuse them.

Our prediction - Japanese analysis system based on llPSG[Kogure 89] uses 90% - 98% of the elapsed time in FS unification.

Furthermore, we noticed some noisy annotations (P08-1102_sweta.csv contains different reference paper IDs), some papers with 0 sentences (probably owing to OCR errors), and XML formatting issues.

8 Conclusion

In this work, we show that application of biases exploiting the underlying structure of scientific texts is useful on the tasks of citation span and facet identification. In the future, we hope to incorporate these biases into the training process instead of interpolating them during evaluation.

9 Acknowledgement

We would like to thank Dr. Eric Nyberg and Dr. Teruko Mitamura for their valuable suggestions and guidance through the course of this work. We would also like to thank the task organizers and our anonymous peer reviewers for their valuable feedback on our work.

References

Bravo A. Chiruzzo L. Saggion1 H. Abura'ed, A. 2018. LaSTUS/TALN+INCO @ CL-SciSumm 2018 - Using Regression and Convolutions for Cross-document Semantic Linking and Summarization of Scholarly Literature. In *3rd Joint Workshop on Bibliometric-enhanced Information Retrieval and Natural Language Processing for Digital Libraries (BIRNDL2018)*.

Kolla M. Baruah, G. 2018. Klick Labs at CL-SciSumm 2018. In *3rd Joint Workshop on Bibliometric-enhanced Information Retrieval and Natural Language Processing for Digital Libraries (BIRNDL2018)*.

Iz Beltagy, Kyle Lo, and Arman Cohan. 2019. SciBERT: A pretrained language model for scientific text. *arXiv preprint arXiv:1903.10676*.

Steven Bird, Robert Dale, Bonnie J. Dorr, Bryan Gibson, Mark T. Joseph, Min-Yen Kan, Dongwon Lee, Brett Powley, Dragomir R. Radev, and Yee Fan Tan. 2008. The ACL Anthology Reference Corpus: A Reference Dataset for Bibliographic Research in Computational Linguistics. In *Proc. of the 6th International Conference on Language Resources and Evaluation Conference (LREC'08)*, pages 1755–1759.

Ziqiang Cao, Wenjie Li, and Dapeng Wu. 2016. Polyu at cl-scisumm 2016. In *Proceedings of the joint workshop on bibliometric-enhanced information retrieval and natural language processing for digital libraries (BIRNDL)*, pages 132–138.

M. K. Chandrasekaran, G. Feigenblat, Hovy. E., A. Ravichander, M. Shmueli-Scheuer, and A De Waard. 3002forthcoming. Overview and Insights from Scientific Document Summarization Shared Tasks 2020: CL-SciSumm, LaySumm and LongSumm. In *Proceedings of the First Workshop on Scholarly Document Processing (SDP 2020)*.

Jacob Devlin, Ming-Wei Chang, Kenton Lee, and Kristina Toutanova. 2019. BERT: Pre-training of Deep Bidirectional Transformers for Language Understanding. In *NAACL-HLT*.

Armand Joulin, Edouard Grave, Piotr Bojanowski, Matthijs Douze, Hérve Jégou, and Tomas Mikolov. 2016. Fasttext.zip: Compressing text classification models. *arXiv preprint arXiv:1612.03651*.

Ou S. Kim, H. 2019. Ranking-based Identification of Cited Text with Deep Learning. In *3rd Joint Workshop on Bibliometric-enhanced Information Retrieval and Natural Language Processing for Digital Libraries (BIRNDL2019)*.

Diederik P Kingma and J Adam Ba. 2019. A method for stochastic optimization. arXiv 2014. *arXiv preprint arXiv:1412.6980*, 434.

Shibamouli Lahiri. 2014. ACL ARC Style Browser. http://ec2-54-186-204-149.us-west-2.compute.amazonaws.com/acl_arc_style_browser/.

Peder Larsen and Markus Von Ins. 2010. The rate of growth in scientific publication and the decline in coverage provided by Science Citation Index. *Scientometrics*, 84(3):575–603.

Rada Mihalcea and Paul Tarau. 2004. Textrank: Bringing order into text. In *Proceedings of the 2004 conference on empirical methods in natural language processing*, pages 404–411.

Preslav I Nakov, Ariel S Schwartz, and Marti Hearst. 2004. Citances: Citation sentences for semantic analysis of bioscience text. In *Proceedings of the SIGIR*, volume 4, pages 81–88. Citeseer.

Stuart Rose, Dave Engel, Nick Cramer, and Wendy Cowley. 2010. *Automatic Keyword Extraction from Individual Documents*, pages 1 – 20.

Indurthi V. Srinivasan B.V. Varma V. Syed, B. 2019. Transfer learning for effective scientific research comprehension. In *3rd Joint Workshop on Bibliometric-enhanced Information Retrieval and Natural Language Processing for Digital Libraries (BIRNDL2019)*.

Li S. Wang T. Zhou H. Tang J. Wang, P. 2018. NUDT @ CLSciSumm-18. In *3rd Joint Workshop on Bibliometric-enhanced Information Retrieval and Natural Language Processing for Digital Libraries (BIRNDL2018)*.

Michihiro Yasunaga, Jungo Kasai, Rui Zhang, Alexander R Fabbri, Irene Li, Dan Friedman, and Dragomir R Radev. 2019. Scisummnet: A large annotated corpus and content-impact models for scientific paper summarization with citation networks. In *Proceedings of the AAAI Conference on Artificial Intelligence*, volume 33, pages 7386–7393.

Chrysoula Zerva, Minh-Quoc Nghiem, Nhung T. H. Nguyen, and Sophia Ananiadou. 2019. NaCTeM-UoM @ CL-SciSumm 2019. In *BIRNDL@SIGIR*.

Dimsum @LaySumm 20: BART-based Approach for Scientific Document Summarization

Tiezheng Yu[1], Dan Su[1,2], Wenliang Dai[1], Pascale Fung[1,2]
[1]Center for Artificial Intelligence Research (CAiRE)
The Hong Kong University of Science and Technology, Clear Water Bay, Hong Kong
[2]EMOS Technologies Inc.
{tyuah,dsu,wdaiai}@connect.ust.hk,
pascale@ece.ust.hk

Abstract

Lay summarization aims to generate lay summaries of scientific papers automatically. It is an essential task that can increase the relevance of science for all of society. In this paper, we build a lay summary generation system based on the BART model. We leverage sentence labels as extra supervision signals to improve the performance of lay summarization. In the CL-LaySumm 2020 shared task, our model achieves 46.00% Rouge1-F1 score.

1 Introduction

Nowadays, researchers have been increasingly tasked by funders and publishers to outline their research for the public by writing a lay summary. Therefore, it is essential to automatically generate lay summaries to reduce the workload for researchers as well as build a bridge between the public and science. Previous studies have investigated scientific article summarization especially for papers (Cohan et al., 2018; Lev et al., 2019; Yasunaga et al., 2019). However, less work has been done to generate lay summaries.

Recently, the First Workshop on Scholarly Document Processing (Chandrasekaran, 2020), Lay Summary Task[1] (LaySumm 2020) first proposed the task of Lay Summary Generation. The task aims to generate summaries that are representative of the content, comprehensible and interesting to a lay audience. After checking the dataset that the task provides, we observe that lots of the sentences in lay summaries have corresponding sentences in original papers. Inspiring by this observation, we think that making binary sentence labels for extractive summarization and utilize them as extra supervision signals can help model generate better summaries. Therefore, we conduct BART (Lewis

et al., 2019) encoder to make sentence representations and train extractive summarization together with abstractive summarization.

Experimental results show that leveraging sentence labels can improve the Lay summary generation performance. In the Laysumm 2020 competition, our model achieves 46.00% Rouge1-F1 score. The code will be released on Github [2].

2 Related Work

Text Summarization Text summarization aims to produce a condensed representation of input text that captures the core meaning of the original text. Recently, neural network-based approaches have reached remarkable performance for news articles summarization (See et al., 2017; Liu and Lapata, 2019; Zhang et al., 2019). Comparing with news articles, scientific papers are typically longer and contain more complex concepts and technical terms.

Scientific Paper Summarization Existing approaches for scientific paper summarization include extractive models that perform sentence selection (Qazvinian et al., 2013; Cohan and Goharian, 2017, 2018) and hybrid models that select the salient text first and then summarize it (Subramanian et al., 2019). Besides, Cohan et al. (2018) built the first model for abstractive summarization of single, longer-form documents (e.g., research papers).

In order to train neural models for this task, several datasets have been introduced. The arXiv and PubMed datasets (Cohan et al., 2018) were created using open access articles from the corresponding popular repositories. Yasunaga et al. (2019) developed and released the first large-scale manually-annotated corpus for scientific papers (on computational linguistics).

---

[1]https://ornlcda.github.io/SDProc/index.html

[2]https://github.com/TysonYu/Laysumm

Proceedings of the First Workshop on Scholarly Document Processing, pages 303–309
Online, November 19, 2020. ©2020 Association for Computational Linguistics
https://doi.org/10.18653/v1/P17

Large Pre-trained Language Model Large pre-trained language models, such as BERT (Devlin et al., 2018), UniLM (Dong et al., 2019) and BART (Lewis et al., 2019) have shown great performance on a variety of downstream tasks including summarization. For example, BART achieved state-of-the-art performance on CNN/DM (Hermann et al., 2015) news summarization dataset.

3   Datasets

We use two datasets for this work, which are the dataset of CL-LaySumm 2020 and ScisummNet (Yasunaga et al., 2019). In this section, we introduce the details of them and the pre-processing method we used.

3.1   CL-LaySumm 2020 Dataset

The CL-LaySumm 2020 Dataset is released by the CL-LaySumm Shared Task that aims to produce lay summaries of scientific texts. A lay summary refers to a textual summary intended for a non-technical audience. There are 572 samples in the dataset for training and each sample contains a full-text paper with a lay summary. To test the summarization model, we need to generate lay summaries for 37 papers within 150 words.

Since the original papers are very long and the task requires us to generate relatively short summaries, it is crucial to extract important parts of papers first before feeding them to large pre-trained models. Given our own experience of how papers are written, we start with the assumption that the Abstract, Introduction and Conclusion are most likely to convey the topic and the contributions of the paper. So, we make different combinations of these three sections as input to our model.

3.2   ScisummNet Dataset

The ScisummNet is the first large-scale, human-annotated Scisumm dataset. The dataset provides 1009 papers with their citation networks as well as their manual summaries. The gold summaries are written by annotators based on the abstract and selected citation sentences that also convey the contributions of papers. We take the abstract and annotators selected citation sentences as our models' input.

3.3   Data Pre-processing

As mentioned above, we first represent the document using the sentences in its Abstract, Introduc-

tion and Conclusion. Then we use two approaches to pre-process the text.

The first pre-processing approach is removing tags and outliers. The original text of the Laysumm dataset has lots of tags such as TITLE, SECTION and PARAGRAPH. We remove all different kinds of tags. Besides, some samples of the Laysumm dataset do not contain an Abstract or Introduction. We regard these samples as outliers and delete them while training the model. The total number of outliers is 23. Then, we truncate all input text to a max length of 1024 tokens due to the carrying capacity of the BART model.

4   Methodology

4.1   Baseline

We use BART, a denoising autoencoder for pre-training sequence-to-sequence models (Lewis et al., 2019) as our baseline.

BART is based on the standard Transformer model (Vaswani et al., 2017), which can be regarded as generalizing BERT (due to the bidirectional encoder), GPT (with the left-to-right decoder). It is pre-trained on the same corpus as RoBERTa (Liu et al., 2019) with two tasks: text infilling and sentence permutation. For text infilling, 30% of tokens in each document are masked and the model is trained to recover them at the output. For the sentence permutation, all sentences are permuted as input and the model is supposed to generate the output sentences with the correct order.

BART obtains great performance on the summarization task. We use the BART fine-tuned on CNN/DailyMail dataset (Hermann et al., 2015) to initialize our model.

4.2   Multi-Label Summarization Model

There are two canonical strategies for summarization: extractive summarization, which concatenates sentences into the summary and abstractive summarization, which generate novel sentences for the summary. Inspired by the observation that lots of the sentences in human written lay summaries have corresponding sentences in original papers, we use an unsupervised approach to convert the abstractive summaries to extractive labels and train abstractive summarization together with extractive summarization.

To make the ground truth sentence-level binary labels for extractive summarization, which we call

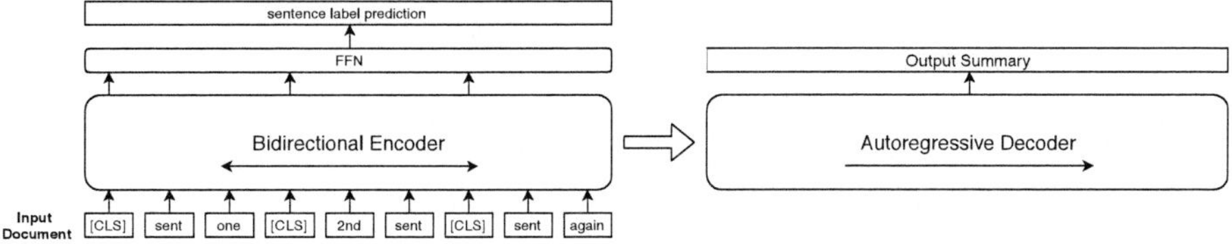

Figure 1: Multi-label summarization model. The left part is based on a bidirectional encoder and the right part is an autoregressive decoder.

Model	Rouge1-F1	Rouge1-Recall	Rouge2-F1	Rouge2-Recall	RougeL-F1	RougeL-Recall
BART (Abs)	0.4350	0.4697	0.1807	0.1968	0.2722	0.2934
BART (Abs+Intro)	0.4518	0.4923	0.1977	0.2135	0.2820	0.3061
BART (Abs+Intro$_{all}$)	0.4443	0.4816	0.1991	0.2142	0.2825	0.3040
BART (Abs+Intro+Con)	0.4536	**0.5171**	0.2016	**0.2271**	0.2864	**0.3243**
BART (Data augmentation)	0.4490	0.4887	0.1972	0.2136	0.2895	0.3139
BART + Two-stage	0.4529	0.4882	0.2067	0.2224	**0.2929**	0.3140
BART + Multi-label	**0.4600**	0.5013	**0.2070**	0.2223	0.2876	0.3104

Table 1: Our results on CL-LaySumm 2020 shared task.

ORACLE, we use a greedy algorithm introduced by (Nallapati et al., 2017). The approach is based on the idea that the selected sentences from the input should be the ones that maximize the Rouge score (Lin and Hovy, 2003) with the respect gold summary.

The architecture of our model is shown in Figure 1, which follows the BART model's structure. The input document is fed into the bidirectional encoder, then the contextual embeddings of the ith [CLS] symbol are used as the sentence representations. After a feedforward neural network, these sentence representations produce a binary distribution about whether they belong to the extractive summary. As for the abstractive summary, it is generated by the autoregressive decoder. The overall loss L is calculated by $L = w_e L_e + L_a$. Here L_e and L_a refer to the Cross-Entropy loss of extractive and abstractive summary respectively.

4.3 Data Augmentation

Data augmentation has been an effective technique to create new training instances when the training data is not enough, as demonstrated in computer vision as well as for many NLP tasks (Chen et al., 2017; Yang et al., 2019; Yuan et al., 2017).

Existing data augmentation approaches in NLP tasks can be categorized into retrieval-based methods (Chen et al., 2017; Yang et al., 2019) and generation-based methods (Yuan et al., 2017; Buck et al., 2017). However, none of these suits our situation, since external sources or auxiliary training data are still required. So we adopted a similar method from (Nema et al., 2017). A pre-defined

vocabulary of 24,822 words was used where each word had been associated with a synonym. Then for each training instance, certain ratios (in our case, 1/9) in each document were randomly selected (except stop words and numerical values) and then replaced with their synonyms found in the vocabulary. If a selected word was not found in the vocabulary, it was added there with the most similar word found based on cosine similarity in the GloVe (Pennington et al., 2014) vocabulary. For each training instance, this process is repeated 9 times to create 9 new documents. But the same summary of the original instance was used in the newly generated instances.

4.4 Two-Stage Fine-tuning

To make use of the ScisummNet dataset, we conduct a two-stage fine-tuning method. In the first stage, we fine-tune the pre-trained BART model on the ScisummNet dataset. We use the Abstract and annotators selected citation sentences as the input and the gold summary as the output. The model is fine-tuned with 20000 iterations before saved. As for the second stage, we use the same settings as we directly fine-tune on the CL-LaySumm 2020 dataset.

5 Experiments

During the training phase, we randomly select 90% of the CL-LaySumm 2020 Dataset for training and 10% for validation. If a data sample doesn't contain an Abstract or Introduction, we don't include it in training or validation. To find the optimal architecture for this task within the models we have, we set up seven different experiments.

BART (Abs): We only use the Abstract as the input to the BART model.

BART (Abs+Intro): We use the Abstract and the first paragraph of the Introduction as the input to the BART model.

BART (Abs+Intro$_{all}$): We use the Abstract and the whole Introduction as the input to the BART model.

BART (Abs+Intro+Con): We use the Abstract, the first paragraph of the Introduction, and the Conclusion (if the paper has) as the input to the BART model.

BART (Data augmentation): We use the same data as BART (Abs+Intro+Con). For each training sample, we create 9 new input documents by synonym data augmentation.

BART + Two-stage: We use the same data as BART (Abs+Intro+Con) to the BART model. The two-stage fine-tuning method is introduced in Section 4.4

BART + Multi-label: We use the same data as BART (Abs+Intro+Con). In addition, for each sentence in the input, we add [CLS] token at the beginning.

As for the hyperparameters, we use a dynamic learning rate, warm up 1000 iterations, and decay afterward. We set the batch size to 1 because of the limitation of GPU memory. The gradient will accumulate every ten iterations and we train all models for 6000 iterations on 1 GPU (GTX 1080 Ti). We save the best model that has the highest Rouge1-F1 score based on the validation set. For the BART model, we use the implementation from the huggingface[3]. We use the BART large model pre-trained on CNN/DailyMail dataset.

6 Result Analysis

The results are shown in Table 1 and we analyze them from three aspects. Besides, we also generate a Lay Summary of our paper, which is presented in the appendix A.

Different inputs to the model. The experiment results of BART (Abs), BART (Abs+Intro), and BART (Abs+Intro+Con) show by adding the Introduction and Conclusion to the input, the models' performance improves consistently. However, comparing with the results from BART (Abs+Intro) and BART (Abs+Intro$_{all}$), using the whole Introduction

rather than the first paragraph of the Introduction decreases the performance on Rouge1 score. We think it is because the CL-LaySumm 2020 task requires to make a relatively short summary, less than 150 words. If the input is too long, it makes the model harder to summarize because longer input contains more noisy data. Since the CL-LaySumm 2020 dataset is also small, the model doesn't have enough samples to learn the task.

Two-stage fine-tuning and Data Augmentation. The experimental results show that two-stage fine-tuning doesn't help to improve the model's performance. After checking the details of ScisummNet, we find the corpus comes from ACL Anthology Network (AAN) (Radev et al., 2013), which means all data relates to computational linguistics. In contrast, the CL-LaySumm 2020 dataset use papers from a variety of domains including biology and medicine. The Statistical differences between these two datasets make the model hard to learn prior knowledge that can be utilized in CL-LaySumm 2020 task.

As for the Data Augmentation, the model performance also doesn't increase as we expected, which contradicts the results from the original paper (Nema et al., 2017). However, the same method also fails in (Laskar et al., 2020), which also adopted a large pre-trained model as a startpoint for fine-tuning. So we think the possible reason might be that large pre-trained models are less robust to noisy input. Our synonyms replacement method is too simple as well as unsupervised. On one hand, it can increase the vocabulary diversity of the training data without changing the semantic meaning a lot, but on the other hand, the quality especially the grammar of the generated instances can not be guaranteed to be correct. Thus, some noise might be introduced and decreases the model performance when we augment the data.

Multi-label summarization. Comparing with BART (Abs+Intro+Con) and BART + Multi-label models, we find that with multi labels, the Rouge1-F1 score is better but the Recall score is lower, which means that the precision increase a lot. We think that with the extra supervision of sentence labels, the model can learn a better sentence understanding. As a result, the model is able to extract important content from the input which helps upper the F1 and Precision scores.

---

[3]https://github.com/huggingface/transformers

7 Conclusion

In this paper, we showcased how different inputs, data augmentation, training strategy, and sentence labels influence the lay summarization task. We introduce a new method to utilize sentence labels as another supervision signal while training BART based model. Experimental results show our models can generate better summaries evaluated by the Rouge1-F1 score.

References

Christian Buck, Jannis Bulian, Massimiliano Ciaramita, Wojciech Gajewski, Andrea Gesmundo, Neil Houlsby, and Wei Wang. 2017. Ask the right questions: Active question reformulation with reinforcement learning. *arXiv preprint arXiv:1705.07830*.

Feigenblat G. Hovy. E. Ravichander A. Shmueli-Scheuer M. De Waard A. Chandrasekaran, M. K. 2020. Overview and insights from scientific document summarization shared tasks 2020: Clscisumm, laysumm and longsumm. In *In Proceedings of the First Workshop on Scholarly Document Processing (SDP 2020)*.

Danqi Chen, Adam Fisch, Jason Weston, and Antoine Bordes. 2017. Reading wikipedia to answer open-domain questions. *arXiv preprint arXiv:1704.00051*.

Arman Cohan, Franck Dernoncourt, Doo Soon Kim, Trung Bui, Seokhwan Kim, Walter Chang, and Nazli Goharian. 2018. A discourse-aware attention model for abstractive summarization of long documents. *arXiv preprint arXiv:1804.05685*.

Arman Cohan and Nazli Goharian. 2017. Scientific article summarization using citation-context and article's discourse structure. *arXiv preprint arXiv:1704.06619*.

Arman Cohan and Nazli Goharian. 2018. Scientific document summarization via citation contextualization and scientific discourse. *International Journal on Digital Libraries*, 19(2-3):287–303.

Jacob Devlin, Ming-Wei Chang, Kenton Lee, and Kristina Toutanova. 2018. Bert: Pre-training of deep bidirectional transformers for language understanding. *arXiv preprint arXiv:1810.04805*.

Li Dong, Nan Yang, Wenhui Wang, Furu Wei, Xiaodong Liu, Yu Wang, Jianfeng Gao, Ming Zhou, and Hsiao-Wuen Hon. 2019. Unified language model pre-training for natural language understanding and generation. In *Advances in Neural Information Processing Systems*, pages 13063–13075.

Karl Moritz Hermann, Tomas Kocisky, Edward Grefenstette, Lasse Espeholt, Will Kay, Mustafa Suleyman, and Phil Blunsom. 2015. Teaching machines to read and comprehend. In *Advances in neural information processing systems*, pages 1693–1701.

Md Tahmid Rahman Laskar, Enamul Hoque, and Jimmy Huang. 2020. Query focused abstractive summarization via incorporating query relevance and transfer learning with transformer models. In *Canadian Conference on Artificial Intelligence*, pages 342–348. Springer.

Guy Lev, Michal Shmueli-Scheuer, Jonathan Herzig, Achiya Jerbi, and David Konopnicki. 2019. Talksumm: A dataset and scalable annotation method for scientific paper summarization based on conference talks. *arXiv preprint arXiv:1906.01351*.

Mike Lewis, Yinhan Liu, Naman Goyal, Marjan Ghazvininejad, Abdelrahman Mohamed, Omer Levy, Ves Stoyanov, and Luke Zettlemoyer. 2019. Bart: Denoising sequence-to-sequence pre-training for natural language generation, translation, and comprehension. *arXiv preprint arXiv:1910.13461*.

Chin-Yew Lin and Eduard Hovy. 2003. Automatic evaluation of summaries using n-gram cooccurrence statistics. In *Proceedings of the 2003 Human Language Technology Conference of the North American Chapter of the Association for Computational Linguistics*, pages 150–157.

Yang Liu and Mirella Lapata. 2019. Text summarization with pretrained encoders. *arXiv preprint arXiv:1908.08345*.

Yinhan Liu, Myle Ott, Naman Goyal, Jingfei Du, Mandar Joshi, Danqi Chen, Omer Levy, Mike Lewis, Luke Zettlemoyer, and Veselin Stoyanov. 2019. Roberta: A robustly optimized bert pretraining approach. *arXiv preprint arXiv:1907.11692*.

Ramesh Nallapati, Feifei Zhai, and Bowen Zhou. 2017. Summarunner: A recurrent neural network based sequence model for extractive summarization of documents. In *Thirty-First AAAI Conference on Artificial Intelligence*.

Preksha Nema, Mitesh Khapra, Anirban Laha, and Balaraman Ravindran. 2017. Diversity driven attention model for query-based abstractive summarization. *arXiv preprint arXiv:1704.08300*.

Jeffrey Pennington, Richard Socher, and Christopher D Manning. 2014. Glove: Global vectors for word representation. In *Proceedings of the 2014 conference on empirical methods in natural language processing (EMNLP)*, pages 1532–1543.

Vahed Qazvinian, Dragomir R Radev, Saif M Mohammad, Bonnie Dorr, David Zajic, Michael Whidby, and Taesun Moon. 2013. Generating extractive summaries of scientific paradigms. *Journal of Artificial Intelligence Research*, 46:165–201.

Dragomir R Radev, Pradeep Muthukrishnan, Vahed Qazvinian, and Amjad Abu-Jbara. 2013. The acl anthology network corpus. *Language Resources and Evaluation*, 47(4):919–944.

Abigail See, Peter J Liu, and Christopher D Manning. 2017. Get to the point: Summarization with pointer-generator networks. *arXiv preprint arXiv:1704.04368*.

Sandeep Subramanian, Raymond Li, Jonathan Pilault, and Christopher Pal. 2019. On extractive and abstractive neural document summarization with transformer language models. *arXiv preprint arXiv:1909.03186*.

Ashish Vaswani, Noam Shazeer, Niki Parmar, Jakob Uszkoreit, Llion Jones, Aidan N Gomez, Łukasz Kaiser, and Illia Polosukhin. 2017. Attention is all you need. In *Advances in neural information processing systems*, pages 5998–6008.

Wei Yang, Yuqing Xie, Luchen Tan, Kun Xiong, Ming Li, and Jimmy Lin. 2019. Data augmentation for bert fine-tuning in open-domain question answering. *arXiv preprint arXiv:1904.06652*.

Michihiro Yasunaga, Jungo Kasai, Rui Zhang, Alexander R Fabbri, Irene Li, Dan Friedman, and Dragomir R Radev. 2019. Scisummnet: A large annotated corpus and content-impact models for scientific paper summarization with citation networks. In *Proceedings of the AAAI Conference on Artificial Intelligence*, volume 33, pages 7386–7393.

Xingdi Yuan, Tong Wang, Caglar Gulcehre, Alessandro Sordoni, Philip Bachman, Sandeep Subramanian, Saizheng Zhang, and Adam Trischler. 2017. Machine comprehension by text-to-text neural question generation. *arXiv preprint arXiv:1705.02012*.

Jingqing Zhang, Yao Zhao, Mohammad Saleh, and Peter J Liu. 2019. Pegasus: Pre-training with extracted gap-sentences for abstractive summarization. *arXiv preprint arXiv:1912.08777*.

A Case Study

A.1 The Lay Summary of this Paper

In the CL-LaySumm 2020 shared task, our model achieves 46.00% Rouge1-F1 score. In this paper, we build a lay summary generation system based on the BART model. We leverage sentence labels as extra supervision signals to improve the performance of lay summarization. Experimental results show that leveraging sentence labels can improve the Lay summary generation performance. The code will be released on Github.

A.2 Observation

The summary above is generated by our own system with Abstract, Introduction and Conclusion from this paper. Although many sentences are copied from the original text, they are well organized and coherent. Besides, the content of the summary also conveys the topic and the contribution of this paper. In conclusion, our system can produce accurate and readable summaries.

ARTU / TU Wien and Artificial Researcher@ LongSumm 20

Alaa El-Ebshihy
TU Wien / Vienna, Austria
alaa.el-ebshihy@tuwien.ac.at

Annisa Maulida Ningtyas
TU Wien / Vienna, Austria
annisa.ningtyas@student.tuwien.ac.at

Linda Andersson
Artificial Researcher IT GmbH / Vienna, Austria
linda.andersson@artificialresearcher.com

Florina Piroi
TU Wien / Vienna, Austria
florina.piroi@tuwien.ac.at

Andreas Rauber
TU Wien / Vienna, Austria
andreas.rauber@tuwien.ac.at

Abstract

In this paper, we present our approach to solve the LongSumm 2020 Shared Task, at the 1st Workshop on Scholarly Document Processing. The objective of the long summaries task is to generate long summaries that cover salient information in scientific articles. The task is to generate abstractive and extractive summaries of a given scientific article. In the proposed approach, we are inspired by the concept of Argumentative Zoning (AZ) that defines the main rhetorical structure in scientific articles. We define two aspects that should be covered in scientific paper summary, namely *Claim/Method* and *Conclusion/Result* aspects. We use Solr index to expand the sentences of the paper abstract. We formulate each abstract sentence in a given publication as query to retrieve similar sentences from the text body of the document itself. We utilize a sentence selection algorithm described in previous literature to select sentences for the final summary that covers the two aforementioned aspects.

1 Introduction

Scientific publications differ in structure, format, and style when compared with other text works (e.g. news articles). As a result, summarizing scientific articles is a challenging task since exploiting known summarization techniques, like those employed by the MEAD system (Radev et al., 2004), that work well for general texts, cannot work well when applied to scientific articles.

Summarization of texts, scientific of not, has been of interest to researchers since the 1950s, when Peter Luhn published his paper "The automatic creation of literature abstracts". One of the most notable approaches to the summarization of scientific papers introduces the concept of *Argumentative Zoning* (Teufel et al., 1999) which refers to the examination of the argumentative status of sentences in scientific articles and their assignment to specific argumentative categories (i.e. zones). Building on this work, further research has been done to design automatic techniques for argumentative zoning (Teufel and Moens, 2002; Teufel et al., 2009; Liu, 2017).

A different and more recent approach to summarization makes use of citations to construct a summary of the main concepts and contributions in scientific articles (Qazvinian and Radev, 2008, 2010; Abu-Jbara and Radev, 2011). Starting from this research, since 2014, a series of pilot and shared tasks on summarization have been organized with some regularity. The CL-SciSumm Shared tasks (Jaidka et al., 2014, 2016, 2019; Chandrasekaran et al., 2019) require task participants to map citation sentences from a given scientific publication to reference sentences in the original articles, and generate a summary from those sentences using predefined facets.

This year, 2020, the CL-SciSumm Shared Task has introduced LongSumm as a new challenge (Chandrasekaran et al., 2020). In this challenge, given a scientific paper, it is required to generate the extractive and the abstractive summaries of the paper.

In this paper, we report on our approach to solving the LongSumm challenge of the CL-SciSumm Shared Task. We are proposing a summarization technique that builds on the concept of Argumentative Zoning (Teufel et al., 1999) and uses a Solr

Proceedings of the First Workshop on Scholarly Document Processing, pages 310–317
Online, November 19, 2020. ©2020 Association for Computational Linguistics
https://doi.org/10.18653/v1/P17

index to expand the abstract of a scientific article to obtain a summary of it. In this approach we extract the main aspects of the scientific articles into a summary by defining zones of interest in the article: claims, methods, results and conclusions. From our own experience we have observed that these aspects are best to form an informative summary for the researcher.

The rest of the paper is organized as follows: Section 2 discusses the components of the processing pipeline that constitute our approach in more detail. In Section 3 we describe our experimental settings and evaluation results for individual components of our pipeline. Finally, we discuss the conclusion and potential direction of future work in Section 4.

2 Approach

In a nutshell, our approach to solve the LongSumm Shared Task is to extract an article summary by expanding its abstract. That is, for each sentence in the article's abstract we extract relevant paragraphs from the same article employing a combination of Language Model-based retrieval and then classification to find similar paragraphs out of which, in a final step, we select certain sentences to be part of the article summary.

Figure 1 shows an overview of our proposed approach. In a first phase, we convert the PDF papers to an XML format using the GROBID[1] PDF parser (the box marked with 1 in figure 1). The output of this step is split into the abstract of the article and the article body. The latter is processed by a rule-based annotation module (2) which will assign specific category labels to the individual paragraphs. The paragraphs and their category annotations are fed into a Solr[2] index (3). The abstract sentences are classified into two categories, *Claim/Method* and *Conclusion/Result* (block 5a in Figure 1).

In the next phase, the abstract sentences are sent as queries to the Solr index in order to find paragraphs that are similar to them (4). We note that the abstract sentence annotations are not used in this phase. These annotations will be used later in the last phase of our summarization process. The $\langle sentence, paragraph \rangle$ pairs that are the output of the Solr retrieval step are now passed to a classifier which will decide if the two are similar to each other or not (5b). Pairs that are classified as similar

are used to extract the final paper summary by applying the sentence selection algorithm mentioned in (Abu-Jbara and Radev, 2011) (6).

The details for each module are discussed in the following subsections.

2.1 PDF Parsing with GROBID

In order to process scientific publications stored as PDF files, we need to convert them to a representation to which we can later apply further text processing methods. We have explored various PDF parsers and we settled to use GROBID[3] as a tool to process scientific articles. GROBID takes as input the PDF file and outputs its extracted content in an XML format. We have chosen GROBID for several reasons: i) it divides the paper to paragraphs; ii) it sorts out special, non-visible characters (e.g. line breaks "\n"); and iii) it identifies figures and tables and places information about their occurrence in the PDF file in special XML tags.

The XML output of the GROBID module (box 1 in Figure 1) differentiates between the abstract text and the text in the article's body, which will be treated separately in the next steps of our pipeline (see the next sections).

2.2 Rule-Based Annotation

Taking from the previous step the XML representation of the article body, we want to assign different discourse categories to its paragraphs. We define five categories, or discourse sections: *Introduction, Background, Method, Conclusion* and *Result*. Each paragraph in the article body will be assigned to one of these discourse sections. The category assignment is done by employing a rule-based annotation module (box 2 in Figure 1), where the rules were manually created by the authors of this paper. At the end of this processing step, the paragraphs of the article body will each have a discourse section label attached to it, in addition to the paragraph meta-data delivered by the GROBID tool. Figure 2 shows a sample of the rule-based annotation step output, where the paragraph is categorized as "Method" with the $\langle discourse\_section \rangle$ XML element.

The paragraphs annotated by this module are now fed into a Solr index (box 3), together with meta-data provided by the GROBID tool.

---

[1]https://grobid.readthedocs.io
[2]https://lucene.apache.org/solr/

[3]In our implementation, we use GROBID as a tool for PDF parsing to convert PDF articles to an XML format

311

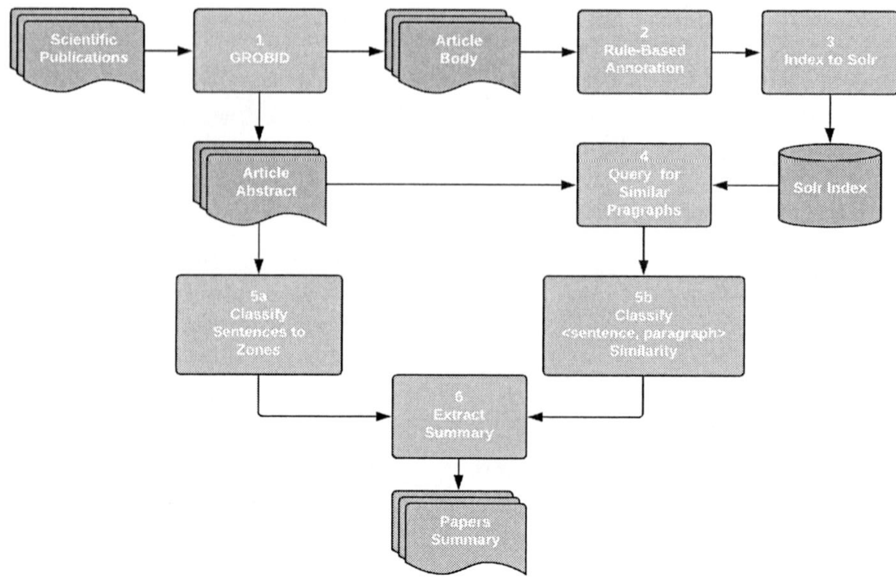

Figure 1: Overview of the ARTU/TU Wien approach to the LongSumm challenge.

```
<field paragraph_id="16">
 <annotation>
  <citations>
   <citation target="#b7"/>
  </citations>
  <discourse_section section_id="METHOD" section_name="Previous Work"/>
  <lexicon entity="['Figure 1']"/>
 </annotation>
 <text>
  Thus, these definitions only allow histories that would occur in a system using long/short read/write item/
  predicate locks. Since locking serializes transactions by preventing certain situations (e.g., two concurrent
  transactions both  modifying the same object), we refer to this approach as the preventative approach. Figure 1
  summarizes the isolation levels as defined in [8] and relates them to a lock-based implementation. Thus the READ
  UNCOMMITTED level proscribes P0; READ COM-MITTED proscribes P0 and P1; the REPEATABLE READ level proscribes P0
  -P2; and SERIALIZABLE proscribes P0 -P3.
 </text>
</field>
```

Figure 2: Output sample of the rule-based annotation module.

2.3 Classification of *Abstract Sentence, Paragraph Text* Pairs

One of the key ideas of our approach is to find a summary of an article by expanding on the abstract sentences. To this end, we have to first find the paragraphs in the article body that are related to the sentences in the abstract. Therefore, we use the sentences in the abstract to formulate queries and send them to the Solr index to get paragraphs similar to the abstract sentence (box 4 in Figure 1). To further filter out paragraphs in the article body that may not be useful in extracting the final article summary, we send the obtained pairs of $\langle abstract\_sentence, paragraph \rangle$ to a classifier (box 5 in Figure 1) that will decide whether the two pair components are relevant to each other or not (box 5*b*).

To train the classifier used in this phase we created a training set by sampling 330 pairs of abstract sentences and retrieved paragraphs, and by manually annotating them as *relevant* or *not relevant*. The annotation made use of a simple GUI implemented by us (see Figure 3) where the annotator could compare the abstract sentence to the paragraph text part of its pair and decide whether the paragraph is relevant to the abstract sentence or not. Using this manually annotated set, we train a Random Forest classifier to build the classification model. Important features of this classifier are the similarity score between the abstract sentences and paragraph texts given by Solr, as well as the discourse sections annotations (see Section 2.2).

The evaluation of this classification module is presented later, in Section 3.3.

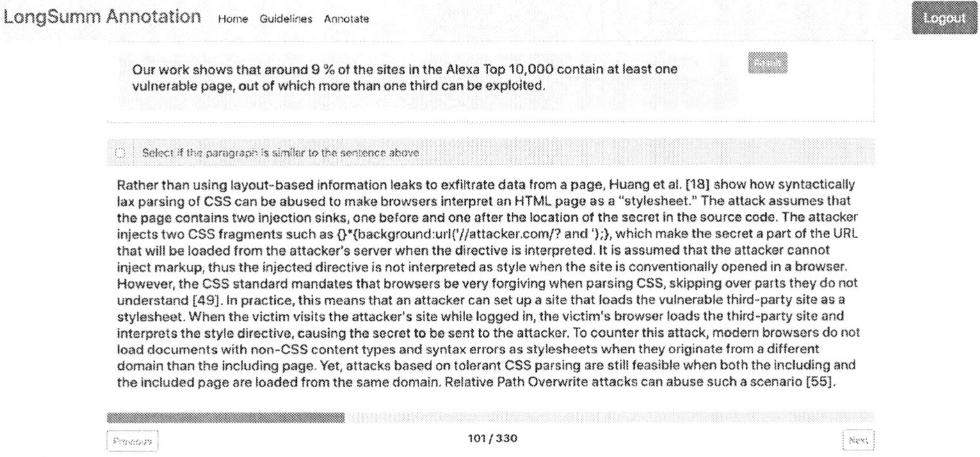

Figure 3: Paragraph to sentence relevance annotation sample.

2.4 Abstract sentences Classification

To make sure that a summary of the article equally covers the discourse sections defined in Section 2.2, we have to attach the same categories to the abstract sentences.

For this phase we decided, again, to use a classification model that would annotate the abstract sentences with one of the discourse sections chosen by us (box $5a$ in Figure 1). The training data to build this classification model has been collected by running an annotation task where we sampled 50 abstracts from the LongSumm data set and split them by sentences. The annotators had to decide which discourse category each abstract sentence falls into. For this task, the annotators had to select one of four categories: *Claim, Method, Conclusion* and *Result*. The *Introduction* category was left out as we consider it not to be relevant when constructing a summary of a scientific article using our approach. We used the BRAT tool (Stenetorp et al., 2012) to collect the annotations (see Figure 4). Because the inter-annotator agreement score turned out to be unsatisfactory, we have analyzed in more detail the labels assigned by the annotators to find a reason for the low score. We have found that there were disagreements between the *Claim* and the *Method* categories and between the *Conclusion* and the *Result* categories as the annotators could not clearly differentiate, for example, whether a sentence should be considered part of the *Conclusion* discourse or of the *Result* discourse. Therefore we took the decision to combine the *Claim* and the *Method* categories into one category, *Claim/Method*, and the *Conclusion* and the *Result* categories into the *Conclusion/Result* category.

From the sentences manually classified into one of these latter two categories, we extract key phrases and build a lexicon, where each phrase in the lexicon has two weights attached to it, one for each of the two categories. These weights are based on the key phrase occurrence frequency in the two categories.

The classifier trained with the manually annotated data just described will assign categories to abstract sentences by summing the weights of the lexicon key phrases that are part of the sentence, and choosing the category with the highest sum. In case of a tie, the sentence is classified as a *Method/Claim* sentence.

2.5 Summary Extractor

Having completed the parsing, indexing, and classifying paragraphs and sentences, we are now in the position of creating an article sumary (box 6 in Figure 1). The implementation of this module follows the methodology described in (Abu-Jbara and Radev, 2011) where, in our implementation, we consider the abstract sentences to be the target paper sentences, and the sentences similar to the abstract sentences (as per Section 2.3) to be the implicit citation sentences.

In our final processing step, we first split the paragraphs similar to the abstract sentences into single sentences. Then, we define a cluster for each abstract sentence which collects all single sentences split from all paragraphs similar to the abstract sentence. Lastly, for each sentence in the cluster, we calculate its LexRank score (Erkan and

313

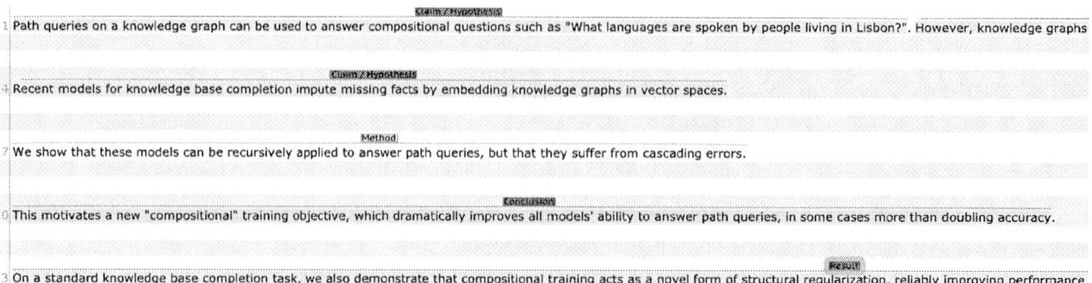

Figure 4: Abstract sentences annotation sample.

Radev, 2004).

To construct the final summary, similarly to (Abu-Jbara and Radev, 2011), sentences are added to the summary in the order of their category, the size of their clusters, then their LexRank values. The first category in our order is *Claim/Method*. Clusters within the same category are ordered by their size (i.e. the number of sentences in each cluster) and finally the sentences in each cluster are ordered by their LexRank values in descending order.

According to the task description, the maximum summary size allowed is 600 words. We extract the sentences from the clusters in a round-robin sequence. In other words, we extract the first ranked sentence in the largest cluster in the *Claim/Method* category then the first ranked sentence in the largest cluster in the *Result/Conclusion* category then the first ranked sentence in the second largest cluster in the *Claim/Method* category and so on. This process continues until either the maximum size of the summary is reached or we run out of sentences in the clusters.

3 Experiments and Result

In this section, we discuss the experimental setup and the evaluation results for the annotation tasks and the classification modules described in the previous section. We close the section with an evaluation of the final summarization step in our approach.

3.1 Abstract Sentence Annotation

Two annotators have provided the category labels for the abstract sentence annotation task discussed earlier in section 2.4. To measure the effectiveness of the annotation task, we computed Cohen's kappa coefficient of agreement between annotators, (κ) (Cohen, 1960). For this specific annotation task, the coefficient (κ) was **0.613**. We considered this

agreement value to be acceptable for this task.

3.2 Abstract Sentence Classification

As described in section 2.4, we use a lexicon based approach to assign one category to each sentence in the abstract. To evaluate this module, we have measured the Precision, Recall, F-measure and the Accuracy of our approach on the annotated data set from previous step. Table 1, shows the evaluation results of Precision, Recall and F-measure for each category. The Accuracy of the this approach is **81.5%**.

	Claim /Method	**Conclusion /Result**	**Average**
Precision	0.875	0.613	0.744
Recall	0.883	0.597	0.739
F-measure	0.879	0.605	0.742

Table 1: Abstract sentences classification evaluation results.

3.3 *Abstract Sentence, Paragraph Text* **Pair Annotation**

Two annotators have participated in the annotation task described in section 2.3. The value of the inter annotation agreement, using the Cohen's kappa coefficient (κ) (Cohen, 1960), is **0.361**. We notice that the inter annotation agreement is rather low. Therefore, as a future work, we plan to analyze the reasons for low agreement and design a second annotation round after clarifying the task.

3.4 *Abstract Sentence, Paragraph Text* **Pair Classification**

We use the data generated from the annotation task, as discussed earlier in section 2.3, to build a classification model that determines whether, for an abstract sentence the paired paragraph text is relevant or not. We split the training data into 70%

training and 30% validation sets to determine the best classification model and its parameters.

We have tested different classification models including: linear SVM, Logistic Regression and Random Forest algorithms. We decided to use the model given by the Random Forest algorithm since it gives the best evaluation results (see Table 2).

	Similar	**Not Similar**	**Average**
Precision	0.755	0.474	0.624
Recall	0.861	0.333	0.597
F-measure	0.815	0.391	0.604

Table 2: Abstract sentence paragraph random forest classification evaluation results.

3.5 Final Summary Evaluation

Our main goal was to develop an extractive summarizer algorithm that starts from abstract sentences pre-labeled as *Method/Claims* and *Result/Conclusions*, and thereafter extracts relevant sentences from the remainder of a given publication. In order to quickly give the user the essence of the paper, a secondary interest of our work was to see if this method is applicable to abstractive summarization as well. We compared the summaries obtained by our approach with both the extractive and the abstractive summaries available in the task repository[4]. We used the provided evaluation script (Chandrasekaran et al., 2020) to evaluate the summaries given by our approach. As seen in Table 3 the method is more adapted to be extractive summarization.

In Table 4, we compare our method with the other submitted runs in the 2020 Longsumm task. We see that our team (ARTU) holds the place 7-9 depending on the descending order of different rouge measurements.

4 Conclusion and Future work

We have presented an approach to solve the LongSumm'20 Shared Task. Our aim was to extract the essence of a scientific paper in order to give the reader a quick overview of its central aspects: the authors' hypothesis (the claim), the method used test the hypothesis and the outcome of the experiment.

In (Saggion and Lapalme, 2002), the authors propose to create Indicative-Informative summaries by observing how professional abstractors generated scientific summaries, and thereafter manually align the professional abstract with the source data. An Indicative Abstract is composed of the topic of the document, i.e. the essence of the paper. Since we did not have access to professional abstractors, we have decided to use different approach to derive the essence of a paper. We assumed that the existing abstract is a very short summary focusing on the *why*, the *how*, and on the general outcome of a scientific work, which we organize into *Claims*, *Methods*, *Results* and *Conclusions* using the Argumentative Zoning schema.

In a first run we asked students to label abstract sentences with these four categories. In order to align the labeled abstract sentences with the body text of an article, we have used a Language Model where each abstract sentence is converted into a query and the system retrieves similar sentences from the body text of the same article. In a second annotation task we have asked students to assess if the retrieved sentence is relevant to the abstract, and if it could be considered to be assigned to same category as the abstract sentence.

Finally, we utilize the sentence selection method described by (Abu-Jbara and Radev, 2011) to form the final summary.

We have not yet explored the full potential of the algorithm due to two main factors:

- Limited training data.

- Ambiguous annotation due to the low inter annotator agreement score in the second annotation task.

As future work, we plan to address these these issues by clarifying the annotation guidelines and test the anotators' performance accross different scientific fields. Other future work is to investigate how changes in the round-robin sentence selection algorithm may impact the quality of the extracted summaries. More specifically, we may look at recomputing the scores of the sentences in the clusters after each sentence selection, where scores could reflect not only relevance to the abstract sentence, but also novelty compared to the other sentences in the same cluster, as well as the clusters of other abstract sentences of the same category.

---

[4]https://github.com/guyfe/LongSumm#training-data
Maximum summary size for an article was of 600 words.

	rouge1_f	rouge1_r	rouge2_f	rouge2_r	rougeL_f	rougeL_r
Abstractive summaries	0.411	0.484	0.108	0.125	0.159	0.198
Extractive summaries	0.548	0.529	0.275	0.265	0.230	0.221

Table 3: The evaluation results of the proposed approach using rouge metrics against the abstractive and extractive data sets.

Participant Team	rouge1_f	rouge1_r	rouge2_f	rouge2_r	rougeL_f	rougeL_r
Summaformers	0.4938	0.439	0.1686	0.1498	0.2138	0.1898
GUIR	0.5311	0.546	0.1677	0.1728	0.2034	0.209
wing	0.5058	0.5116	0.1662	0.1675	0.205	0.2066
IIITBH-IITP	0.4903	0.4984	0.1574	0.16	0.2046	0.208
Auth-Team	0.5011	0.4693	0.1537	0.1423	0.1959	0.1818
CIST_BUPT	0.4899	0.4974	0.1506	0.1522	0.2013	0.2039
ARTU	**0.4803**	**0.4678**	**0.1476**	**0.1428**	**0.1804**	**0.1743**
IITP-AI-NLP-ML	0.4646	0.4743	0.1461	0.1486	0.1958	0.1995
Monash-Summ	0.4916	0.4935	0.128	0.1276	0.1831	0.1833
mummert	0.1232	0.0683	0.063	0.0349	0.0989	0.0549

Table 4: Submission results of all participating teams from the Longsumm 2020 leaderboard. Our team is **ARTU**.

References

Amjad Abu-Jbara and Dragomir Radev. 2011. Coherent citation-based summarization of scientific papers. In *Proceedings of the 49th annual meeting of the association for computational linguistics: Human language technologies*, pages 500–509.

Muthu Kumar Chandrasekaran, Guy Feigenblat, Eduard Hovy, Abhilasha Ravichander, Michal Shmueli-Scheuer, and Anita De Waard. 2020. Overview and insights from scientific document summarization shared tasks 2020: Cl-scisumm, laysumm and longsumm. In *Proceedings of the First Workshop on Scholarly Document Processing (SDP 2020)*.

Muthu Kumar Chandrasekaran, Michihiro Yasunaga, Dragomir Radev, Dayne Freitag, and Min-Yen Kan. 2019. Overview and results: Cl-scisumm shared task 2019. *arXiv preprint arXiv:1907.09854*.

Jacob Cohen. 1960. A coefficient of agreement for nominal scales. *Educational and psychological measurement*, 20(1):37–46.

Günes Erkan and Dragomir R Radev. 2004. Lexrank: Graph-based lexical centrality as salience in text summarization. *Journal of artificial intelligence research*, 22:457–479.

Kokil Jaidka, Muthu Kumar Chandrasekaran, Beatriz Fisas Elizalde, Rahul Jha, Christopher Jones, Min-Yen Kan, Ankur Khanna, Diego Molla-Aliod, Dragomir R Radev, Francesco Ronzano, et al. 2014. The computational linguistics summarization pilot task. In *Proceedings of Text Ananlysis Conference, Gaithersburg, USA*.

Kokil Jaidka, Muthu Kumar Chandrasekaran, Sajal Rustagi, and Min-Yen Kan. 2016. Overview of the cl-scisumm 2016 shared task. In *Proceedings of the joint workshop on bibliometric-enhanced information retrieval and natural language processing for digital libraries (BIRNDL)*, pages 93–102.

Kokil Jaidka, Michihiro Yasunaga, Muthu Kumar Chandrasekaran, Dragomir Radev, and Min-Yen Kan. 2019. The cl-scisumm shared task 2018: Results and key insights. *arXiv preprint arXiv:1909.00764*.

Haixia Liu. 2017. Automatic argumentative-zoning using word2vec. *CoRR*, abs/1703.10152.

Vahed Qazvinian and Dragomir Radev. 2010. Identifying non-explicit citing sentences for citation-based summarization. In *Proceedings of the 48th annual meeting of the association for computational linguistics*, pages 555–564.

Vahed Qazvinian and Dragomir R Radev. 2008. Scientific paper summarization using citation summary networks. *arXiv preprint arXiv:0807.1560*.

Dragomir R. Radev, T. Allison, Sasha Blair-Goldensohn, John Blitzer, A. elebi, S. Dimitrov, E. Drábek, A. Hakim, W. Lam, D. Liu, Jahna Otterbacher, H. Qi, Horacio Saggion, S. Teufel, M. Topper, Adam Winkel, and Zhu Zhang. 2004. MEAD - A Platform for Multidocument Multilingual Text Summarization. In *LREC*.

Horacio Saggion and Guy Lapalme. 2002. Generating indicative-informative summaries with SumUM. *Computational Linguistics*, 28(4):497–526.

Pontus Stenetorp, Sampo Pyysalo, Goran Topić, Tomoko Ohta, Sophia Ananiadou, and Junichi Tsujii. 2012. Brat: a web-based tool for nlp-assisted text annotation. In *Proceedings of the Demonstrations at the 13th Conference of the European Chapter of the Association for Computational Linguistics*, pages 102–107.

Simone Teufel and Marc Moens. 2002. Summarizing scientific articles: experiments with relevance and rhetorical status. *Computational linguistics*, 28(4):409–445.

Simone Teufel, Advaith Siddharthan, and Colin Batchelor. 2009. Towards domain-independent argumentative zoning: Evidence from chemistry and computational linguistics. In *Proceedings of the 2009 conference on empirical methods in natural language processing*, pages 1493–1502.

Simone Teufel et al. 1999. *Argumentative zoning: Information extraction from scientific text*. Ph.D. thesis, Citeseer.

SciSummPip: An Unsupervised Scientific Paper Summarization Pipeline

Jiaxin Ju[1], Ming Liu [2], Longxiang Gao[2], and Shirui Pan[1]

[1]Faculty of Information Technology, Monash University, Australia, VIC 3800
[2]School of Information Technology, Deakin University, Australia, VIC 3217
`jjuu0002@student.monash.edu`
`{m.liu, longxiang.gao}@deakin.edu.au`
`shirui.pan@monash.edu`

Abstract

The Scholarly Document Processing (SDP) workshop is to encourage more efforts on natural language understanding of scientific task. It contains three shared tasks and we participate in the LongSumm shared task. In this paper, we describe our text summarization system, SciSummPip, inspired by SummPip (Zhao et al., 2020) that is an unsupervised text summarization system for multi-document in news domain. Our SciSummPip includes a transformer-based language model SciBERT (Beltagy et al., 2019) for contextual sentence representation, content selection with PageRank (Page et al., 1999), sentence graph construction with both deep and linguistic information, sentence graph clustering and within-graph summary generation. Our work differs from previous method in that content selection and a summary length constraint is applied to adapt to the scientific domain. The experiment results on both training dataset and blind test dataset show the effectiveness of our method, and we empirically verify the robustness of modules used in SciSummPip with BERTScore (Zhang et al., 2019a).

1 Introduction

Text summarization aims at automatically generating a fluent and coherent summary that mainly contains the salient information from the source document(s). Two main categories are typically involved in the text summarization task, one is extractive approach (Luo et al., 2019; Xu and Durrett, 2019) which directly extracts salient sentences from the input text as the summary, and the other is abstractive approach (Sutskever et al., 2014; See et al., 2017; Sharma et al., 2019) which imitates human behaviour to produce new sentences based on the extracted information from the given document.

In order to meet the requirements of modern data-driven methods, several large datasets have been presented. The majority of those datasets are for generic domain, but few available corpora from other task-specific domains. Most of existing state-the-art summarization systems (Liu and Lapata, 2019; Zhou et al., 2020; Wang et al., 2020) target news or simple documents, and they are less adequate for summarizing scientific work due to the length and complexity. Those summarization systems cannot provide sufficient information conveyed in the scientific paper.

The general domain have been paid enough attention, whereas the attention in scientific domain is far from enough. To address this point, the Scholarly Document Processing (SDP) workshop (Chandrasekaran et al., 2020) is held to accelerate scientific discovery in research community, they appeal to researchers for designing a summarization system that can generate a relatively long summary for scientific work.

Since the release of Transformer (Vaswani et al., 2017) and BERT (Devlin et al., 2018), much research has been carried out on involving them in their system. Liu (2019) modified the input sequence embedding and built several summarization-specific layers for extractive summarization. Similarly, Liu and Lapata (2019) present a novel document-level encoder based on BERT (Devlin et al., 2018) for both extractive summarization and abstractive summarization. In their model structure, the lower transformer represents adjacent sentences and the higher layer with self-attention mechanism represents the multi-sentence discourse. These works leverage the advantage of deep neural network, not taking into account the linguistic information. In contrast, Zhao et al. (2020)[1] construct semantic clusters and sentence graphs for multi-document summarization, which involves linguistic information and discourse markers. In this paper,

---

[1]https://github.com/mingzi151/SummPip

Proceedings of the First Workshop on Scholarly Document Processing, pages 318–327
Online, November 19, 2020. ©2020 Association for Computational Linguistics
https://doi.org/10.18653/v1/P17

we followed the framework of Zhao et al. (2020) to construct our own unsupervised text summarization system. However, our model is different from the previous work: we modify the pipeline structure of multi-document summarization in the field of news to the single-document summarizer for summarizing scholarly documents, and we introduce two new steps to control the length of generated summary and to remove irrelevant sentences.

Our contributions in this work can be summarized in the following aspects:

- We highlight the importance of sentence embedding for scientific work. A variety of works focus on facilitating the process of obtaining sentence representation from a pretrained language model on generic domain, while less attention is paid on other task-specific domains.

- We compare the performances between PageRank (Page et al., 1999) and the Maximal Marginal Relevance (MMR) (Carbonell and Goldstein, 1998) in the content selection module. To our knowledge, no previous work compares their performances on scientific long document summarization task with deep neural representation.

- We experimentally verify that the effectiveness of the proposed model. We achieve better ROUGE results than original model on both training dataset and blind test dataset. Besides, our model is also evaluated on the BERTScore metric (Zhang et al., 2019a) and the results indicate that our model is more robust to generate high quality summary.

2   Related Work

Text Summarization System   Most of recent text summarization systems leverage the advantages of deep neural networks, their encoder-decoder structures use either recurrent neural networks (Cheng and Lapata, 2016; Nallapati et al., 2016) or Transformer encoders (Zhang et al., 2019b; Khandelwal et al., 2019). Benefit of the sequence-to-sequence structure, a great progress in both extractive and abstractive document summarization is achieved. Though abstractive summarization has more potentials to generate interpretations in a human-like fashion, it has been found that sometimes repeatedly produces the same phrase or

sentence (Suzuki and Nagata, 2016), which greatly reduces the comprehensibility and readability. In contrast, extractive summarization performs better in fluency aspect and it can grammatical and accurately represent the source text. One potential issue in extractive summarization is that not all of information from the extracted sentence is important, which leads more redundancy in the generated summary.

In the work of Zhao et al. (2020), they apply graph structure and consider the discourse relationship between sentences rather than using encoder-decoder structure, and text compression is implemented in the final stage to reduce the redundancy in the generated sentences. However, their model is designed for multi-document summarization in the news domain, we extend their SummPip to single-document settings for scientific long articles.

Sentence Embedding Method   Term frequency–inverse document frequency (TF-IDF) is widely used in traditional NLP, but it cannot capture the semantic information and contextual relationship between sentences. Word2Vec (Mikolov et al., 2013) is used in SummPip (Zhao et al., 2020) to capture contextualized relationship, but this embedding method cannot solve the polysemous problem. More recently, BERT (Devlin et al., 2018) has achieved better performance in many NLP downstream tasks, but it is difficult to derive sentence embeddings. To solve this limitation, single sentences are passed to the BERT and two common ways to extract sentence representation are widely used: averaging the outputs and using the output of the [CLS] token (May et al., 2019; Zhang et al., 2019a).

Xiao (2018) develops a repository, bert-as-a-service[2], which accelerates the process of extracting token and sentence embeddings from BERT (Devlin et al., 2018). Lately, in order to find a better way to derive semantically similar sentence from language models, Reimers and Gurevych (2019) present SBERT. However, above works help facilitate workload in generic domain rather than task-specific domain.

Content Selection   Graph is an intuitive structure for utilizing the relation information between sentences. Some work (Mihalcea and Tarau, 2004; Erkan and Radev, 2004) focuses on selecting salient sentences by leveraging graph-based rank-

---

[2]https://github.com/hanxiao/bert-as-service/

Characteristics	Extractive		Abstractive		Test dataset
	Sci_P	Ref_S	Sci_P	Ref_S	Sci_P
Range of corpus size (sentences)	[37,629]	[9,48]	[24,792]	[1,87]	[119,345]
Median value of corpus size (sentences)	186	31	201	31	219
Range of sentence length (words)	[12,51]	[15,48]	[10,44]	[0.5,54]	[18,27]
Median value of sentence length (words)	26	27	26	21	22

Table 1: Elementary data statistics for the LongSumm shared task of the Scholarly Document Processing @ EMNLP 2020. Sci_P and Ref_S represent scientific paper and reference summary, respectively.

ing methods. Inspired by PageRank algorithm (Page et al., 1999), they consider the document as a graph where sentences are vertices and edges represent the relations between two sentences. Shortly thereafter, some researchers (Carbonell and Goldstein, 1998; Kurmi and Jain, 2014; Mao et al., 2020) involved a query-biased strategy, the Maximal Marginal Relevance (MMR) (Carbonell and Goldstein, 1998), in their summarizers. MMR tries to balance the relevance and diversity by controlling the trade-off parameter λ. The first part of the formula controls query relevance and the second part controls diversity.

$$MMR = \operatorname*{argmax}_{S_i \in \mathcal{C}} \lambda Sim_1(S_i, Q)$$
$$- (1 - \lambda) \operatorname*{argmax}_{S_j \in \mathcal{S}} Sim_2(S_i, S_j)$$

Where C is the set of candidate sentences, S is the set of extracted sentences, Q is the query embedding, S_i, S_j are sentence embeddings of candidate sentences i and j, respectively. Sim indicates the cosine similarity between two embeddings.

Though this approach have been proved that it outperforms generic summarization approaches in the information retrieval task, to our knowledge, there is no previous work compared it with PageRank algorithm on scientific long document summarization task. Our work incorporates deep neural representations into both PageRank algorithm and MMR strategy and shows the comparison between these two methods in the field of scientific work for both extractive and abstractive summarization.

3 Dataset Pre-processing

The training dataset provided by the LongSumm shared task consists of 2236 scientific papers, of which 1705 are for extractive method and 531 are for abstractive method. The reference extractive summaries are generated by TalkSumm (Lev et al., 2019) that extracts sentences appeared in associated conference videos, while the abstractive summaries are collected from blogs written by researchers.

Download paper We download the training corpus from the given URLs (for abstractive) and the script (for extractive).

Paper Parsing All of papers are parsed from PDF form into JSON structure by using Science-Parse[3]. It outputs a JSON file for each PDF, which contains the title, abstract text, metadata, and the text of each section in the paper.

Text processing We concatenate each section text as the paper text. Then sentences are segmented by using the NLTK library, and each sentence is tokenized as well. Table 1 reports the result of the statistics analysis for both training dataset and test dataset, and we can see that the number of sentences in some reference summaries is far less than required length of generated summary, 600 words, which may lead a bias in the evaluation.

4 System overview

We adopt the SummPip (Zhao et al., 2020) as our baseline model, and we modify the pipeline architecture for summarizing scholarly documents. Two new steps are introduce for adapting scientific domain, one is to remove irrelevant sentences and the other is to control the length of generated summary. In the following subsections, we will specify each component in the SciSummPip.

4.1 Embedding Method

Pretrained language model In this paper, we apply a publicly available large-scale language model, SciBERT (Beltagy et al., 2019), which is pretrained based on BERT (Devlin et al., 2018) and extends the idea of word embeddings by learning

---

[3]https://github.com/allenai/science-parse

contextual representations from large-scale scientific corpora. This is implemented in Pytorch using Transformers established by Wolf et al. (2019)[4].

Sentence embedding Using more accurate sentence embeddings can improve the performance of summarization system in language understanding. In SciSummPip, we average the output of SciBERT from the second layer to the last layer. In addition, we also experiment with other embedding methods and the the results show that this is a more accurate way to represent scientific sentences.

4.2 Sentence Graph Construction

Content selection Not all of sentences should be involved in the summary, so we include content selection step before constructing sentence graph. We build a matrix to store the similarity between each two sentences, then PageRank (Page et al., 1999) algorithm is implemented to rank all of sentences. Sentences with lower score will be deleted from the candidate list, here we introduce a new step to control the ratio of removed sentences.

Graph construction We construct the sentence graph, where each node represents a sentence, and nodes are connected if they meet the linguistic requirements. To identify this structure, we borrow the components from the previous work (Zhao et al., 2020). Specifically, this pipeline consists of discovering deverbal noun reference, finding the same entity continuation, recognizing discourse markers, and calculating sentence similarity by taking the cosine similarity.

4.3 Text Generation

Spectral clustering After identifying pairwise sentence connection, we involve a new step for determining the number of clusters. This is to control the length of generated summary so that the summary varies with the length of the original paper.

Multi-sentences compression This module (Boudin and Morin, 2013) is to generate a single summary sentence from each sentence cluster. Sentences with similar semantic information will be compressed by building a word graph. Considering the key phrases and discourse structure, so that the reconstructed sentence will have higher score. Select the sentence with the highest score as the summary sentence, and then combine all

reconstructed summary sentences as the generated summary.

5 Experiment Setup

5.1 Implementation Details

Extractive summarization Task We use SciBERT for sentence embedding in our pipeline, so for extractive text summarization task we directly use Scibert-summarizer[5] with the fixed length range (from 60 to 600 words).

Abstractive summarization Task We implement our pipeline, SciSummPip, in abstractive summarization task, and we compare the performances of PageRank algorithm and of MMR strategy in the content selection module. For PageRank algorithm, we set a cutoff ratio that is a new introduced parameter for removing irrelevant sentences and the empirical results show that setting it as 0.25 achieves better performance. For the MMR strategy, we set 0.2, 0.5, 0.8 for the trade-off parameter in the experiment, respectively. To control the generated summary length, we introduce another new parameter, extended ratio, to modify the number of clusters based on the number of ranking sentences. In our pipeline,we set it as 0.3.

5.2 Comparison Systems

For extractive task, we compare our model with the following unsupervised summarization models:

TextRank (Barrios et al., 2016) TextRank (Mihalcea and Tarau, 2004) applies a variation of PageRank algorithm (Page et al., 1999) over a graph-based structure, and it produces a list of ranked elements in the graph without the need of a training corpus. TextRank implemented in this paper is produced by Barrios et al. (2016), they change the similarity function to Okapi BM25 so that the performance is better than the original texTRank model. We set the output summary with the fixed length 600 words.

LexRank (Erkan and Radev, 2004) Similar with textRank (Mihalcea and Tarau, 2004), LexRank also applies PageRank algorithm and leverages a graph structure for summarization. Differently, textRank calculate the similarity based on the number of words two sentences have in common, while LexRank uses cosine similarity of TF-IDF vectors.

---

[4]https://github.com/huggingface/transformers

[5]bert-extractive-summarizer: https://pypi.org/project/bert-extractive-summarizer/

	R1_F	R1_R	R2_F	R2_R	RL_F	RL_R
Extractive dataset						
Scibert-summarizer	**58.13**	**57.53**	**27.20**	**26.82**	**28.65**	**28.29**
TextRank	57.42	57.31	26.38	26.48	28.48	27.59
LextRank	46.23	36.38	20.71	16.33	21.34	16.76
$\text{MMR}_{Sci}(\lambda{=}0.5)$	55.24	55.48	23.74	23.85	21.00	21.11
Abstractive dataset						
SummPip_{+PR}	36.17	32.73	8.36	7.27	14.80	13.83
SciSummPip_{PR}	**40.90**	**43.09**	**9.52**	**9.83**	**15.47**	**17.26**
$\text{SciSummPip}_{MMR0.2}$	32.34	28.31	6.54	5.48	13.60	12.37
$\text{SciSummPip}_{MMR0.5}$	30.69	25.63	6.64	5.32	13.37	11.56
$\text{SciSummPip}_{MMR0.8}$	33.06	27.88	7.58	6.17	14.18	12.39
Blind Test Dataset						
Scibert-summarizer	**49.16**	**49.35**	**12.80**	**12.76**	**18.31**	**18.33**
SciSummPip	47.37	40.89	13.35	11.40	17.54	15.02
SummPip	38.62	30.16	9.01	6.95	15.15	11.74

Table 2: ROUGE scores reported on the training dataset and the blind test dataset. Best results are in **boldface**. The reference extractive summary and abstractive summary are generated by TalkSumm (Lev et al., 2019) and collected from online blogs, respectively. MMR_{Sci} indicates we implement MMR algorithm with sentence embeddings derived from SciBERT(Beltagy et al., 2019). $SciSummPip_{PR}$ and $SciSummPip_{MMR}$ are our model with different content selection modules, and the number follow the MMR is the setting for trade-off parameter λ. As SummPip cannot effectively run on large scale corpora of long document, we add content selection module and shown as SummPip_{+PR}.

MMR (Carbonell and Goldstein, 1998) MMR is a query-biased summarization approach, it tries to balance the relevance and diversity by controlling the trade-off parameter λ. In the previous works, the similarity usually calculate based on TF-IDF, but in our implementation we use sentence embeddings derived from the output of SciBERT (Beltagy et al., 2019). In addition, we set the document title as the query and the fixed length of generated summary is set as 600 words.

For abstractive task, we apply different sentence embedding methods in SciSummPip:

- SciBERT (Beltagy et al., 2019): We implement two common strategies for sentence embeddings derived from SciBERT model: averaging the output from the second to the last layer and using [CLS] token embedding.

- SummPip (Zhao et al., 2020): We use the same embedding method with the original pipeline to compare the performance.

- SBERT (Reimers and Gurevych, 2019): This is a modification of the BERT network using siamese and triplet networks in order to find semantically similar sentences in vector space. Their empirical results indicate that

their method is better than those two common embedding strategies, so we incorporate it into SciSummPip as a comparison.

6 Evaluation and Results

6.1 Experiment result on training dataset

Extractive summaries The training dataset for extractive method consists of 1705 papers, of which one paper cannot be parsed. Thus, we evaluate 1704 papers with the ROUGE metric(Lin and Hovy, 2003) in our experiments.

As displayed in Table 2, the Scibert-summarizer achieves better ROUGE scores than all other compared systems. We implement MMR algorithm with sentence embedding derived from averaging SciBERT (Beltagy et al., 2019) output, and we can see it performs better than LexRank (Erkan and Radev, 2004) but worse than the textRank model (Barrios et al., 2016) with the Okapi BM25 similarity function. Therefore, we can verify that PageRank ranking algorithm performers better than MMR strategy in extractive task.

Abstractive summaries For abstractive experiments, we collect 530 summaries in total as one paper cannot be parsed by Science-parse.

Sentence Embedding	R1_F	R2_F	RL_F
Avg. SciBERT embeddings	40.90	9.52	15.47
Special token embedding	39.27	8.81	15.09
Word2Vec	36.17	8.36	14.80
SBERT	39.75	9.41	15.27

Table 3: ROUGE F1 scores for SciSummPip with different sentence embedding methods. Special token embedding method is extracting [CLS] token embedding from SciBERT (Beltagy et al., 2019) output.

Sentence Embedding	R1_R	R2_R	RL_R
Avg. SciBERT embeddings	43.09	9.83	17.26
Special token embedding	39.99	8.75	16.13
Word2Vec	32.73	7.27	13.83
SBERT	41.53	9.56	16.73

Table 4: ROUGE Recall results for SciSummPip with different sentence embedding methods.

We implement SciSummPip with different parameter settings to find out the best one. The number of words in each sentence is set from 15 to 29, then we observe that the summary with 26 words in each sentence achieves the best performance. We incorporate PageRank algorithm (Page et al., 1999) and MMR algorithm (Carbonell and Goldstein, 1998) into SciSummPip content selection module, respectively. As displayed in Table 2, it is not surprising to see SciSummPip with PageRank algorithm outperforms all of settings for SciSummPip with MMR algorithm, because the performance of textRank is better than that of MMR in the extractive task.

6.2 Experiment result on test dataset

The blind test dataset consists of 22 scientific papers[6]. It does not declare the blind test data is for extractive summarizer or abstractive summarizer, so we implement both Scibert-summarizer and SciSummPip on it. Comparing with the SummPip (Zhao et al., 2020), the experiment results verify that our new pipeline architecture significantly improve the performance. In addition, we try different number of words generated in each sentence and we find that setting it closes to the median value of that in scientific papers would gain higher score. Besides, although extractive model gains the highest ROUGE score, we still can see our SciSummPip is competitive.

---

[6]Test dataset: https://github.com/guyfe/LongSumm

	Precision	Recall	F1-Score
SciSummPip	**0.807**	0.800	**0.815**
SciSummPip$_{MMR}$	0.806	0.810	0.808
SummPip$_{+PR}$	0.794	0.813	0.806
SBERT	0.795	**0.814**	0.804

Table 5: BERTScore reported on abstractive training dataset to investigate text generation ability of our model. SBERT means we use use SBERT sentence embedding method in SciSummPip.

6.3 Different Sentence Embedding Methods

To find out a more accurate method for representing scientific sentences, we incorporate different embedding strategies into SciSummPip. Performances reported in Table 3 and Table 4 indicate that our model ranks highest with averaging the output of SciBERT (Beltagy et al., 2019) method. SBERT (Reimers and Gurevych, 2019) shows competitive performance even though it is designed for generic domain. In fact, utilizing SBERT significantly reduce the workload of extracting sentence embedding, but it is not sufficient enough for representing scientific sentence.

6.4 BERTScore Evaluation

We evaluate models on BERTScore (Zhang et al., 2019a), an automatic evaluation metric for text generation, to investigate the ability of writing abstractive summary. BERTScore calculates a similarity score for each token in the candidate sentence with each token in the reference sentence by leveraging contextual embeddings. As can be seen in Table 5, SciSummPip achieves highest precision and F1-score while SBERT gains the highest recall. This proves that the summary generated by our model is more informative and representative. Since BERTScore utilizes Bert (Devlin et al., 2018) to calculate similarity score, the max length of input sequence is 512 tokens, which limits the performance of relatively long summary.

We further investigate the distribution of F1-score from BERTScore evaluation. As shown in figure 1, although these models achieve similar performance, the F1-score distribution of SciSummPip obviously more stable than others. SciSummPip achieve the highest frequency in the range of 0.80-0.82, which means near 140 generated summaries gain around 0.81 F1-score. Therefore, we can say that our model is more robust for summarizing scientific work in abstractive task.

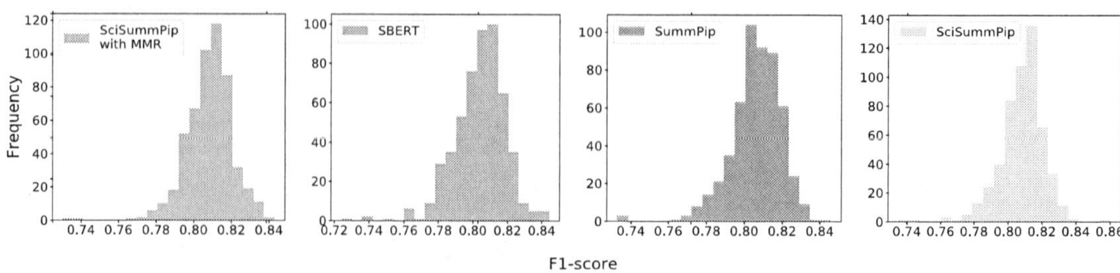

Figure 1: The histogram distribution of F1-score evaluated by BERTScore metric for each model reported in Table 5. X-axis indicates data range of F1-score and Y-axis indicates the frequency of the data in each bin. In order to ensure the bin data range for each distribution is same, we set the data range of each bin as 0.005 so that the parameter, bins, is set as $int(data\ range\ of\ F1 - score/0.005)$.

Extractive Reference Summary:
The analysis of emotions in texts is an important task in NLP. Traditional studies treat this task as a pipeline of two separated sub-tasks: emotion classification and emotion cause detection. The former identifies the category of an emotion and the latter detects the cause of an emotion. This separated framework makes each sub-task more flexible to deal with, but it neglects the relevance between the two sub-tasks. In this paper, we use the human-labeled emotion corpus provided by Cheng et al. (2017) as our experimental data (namely Cheng emotion corpus). Cheng emotion corpus can be considered as a collection of subtweets. For each emotion in a subtweet, all emotion keywords expressing the emotion are selected, and then the class and the cause of the emotion are annotated. (...)

Scibert-summarizer:
The analysis of emotions in texts is an important task in NLP. Cheng emotion corpus can be considered as a collection of subtweets. Given an instance which is a pair of <an emotion keyword, a clause in the subtweet>, ECause assigns a binary label to the instance to indicates the presence of a causal relation. The input text of an ECause instance also has three sequences of words: the emotion keyword (i.e. EmoKW), the current clause (i.e. CauseCL) and the context between EmoKW and CauseCL. The BiLSTM layer focuses on the extraction of sequence features, and the attention layer focuses on the learning of word importance (weights). (...)

Table 6: Example of the generated extractive summary compared with reference summary that is generated by TalkSumm (Lev et al., 2019). Text in the same color indicates the content they describe is the same. Due to the length constraint, we omit part of the generated summary and shown as (...).

6.5 Human Analysis

We further manually inspect the generated summary to explore if our model can capture the salient information from given document. Table 6 and Table 7 display an example of generated summary compared with the corresponding reference summary in the training dataset. The abstractive ref-

---

Abstractive Reference Summary:
The paper proposes a two-stage synthesis network that can perform transfer learning for the task of machine comprehension. The problem is the following: We have a domain DS for which we have labelled dataset of question-answer pairs and another domain DT for which we do not have any labelled dataset. We use the data for domain DS to train SynNet and use that to generate synthetic question-answer pairs for domain DT. Now we can train a machine comprehension model M on DS and finetune using the synthetic data for DT. SynNet Works in two stages: Answer Synthesis - Given a text paragraph, generate an answer. (...) After the word vector, append a '1' if the word was part of the candidate answer else append a '0'. Feed to a Bi-LSTM network (encoder-decoder) where the decoder conditions on the representation generated by the encoder as well as the question tokens generated so far. (...)

SciSummPip:
the ability to quickly use a mc model trained on one domain to answer questions over paragraphs from another with no annotated data. recent work generated synthetic data generated questions leads to improved performance, we use a model where the answer synthesis and question types. we generate the answer first because answers are usually key semantic concepts, while questions can transfer a mc model trained on another domain. when we ensemble a bidaf model fs we use the two-stage synnet to generate data tuples to directly boost performance boost. (...) however, unlike machine translation , for tasks like mc, we need to synthesize both the question and answers given the context paragraph. (...) the first stage of the model, an answer synthesis module , uses a Bi-directional LSTM to predict iob tags on the input paragraph, which mark out key semantic concepts that are likely answers.(...)

Table 7: Example of the generated abstractive summary compared with reference summary that is collected from researcher's blog. Text in the same color indicates the content they describe is similar. Due to the length constraint, we omit part of the generated summary and shown as (...).

erence summary is collected from the online blog written by the researcher, so it is more difficult to capture the similar description in the generated summary. However, As shown in table 7, our model successfully write some similar context in the final output. Notwithstanding, we have to say the readability and grammatically of the generated summary still need to be improved.

For blind test dataset, we also inspect the extractive summary and abstractive summary for the same paper. We find that the Scibert-summarizer tends to extract the sentence appeared in the early part of the paper, and the generated summary usually lack of logicality and consistency. In contrast, the summary produced by SciSummPip is more logical and contains more salient information about the methodology and the experiment. Although Scibert-summarizer gains higher ROUGE score on the blind test dataset, the summary generated by our model is more consistent with the purpose of the LongSumm Shared Task.

7 Conclusion and Limitation

In this paper, we have presented the modified unsupervised pipeline architecture, SciSummPip, that leverages a transformer-based language model for summarizing scientific papers. We add content selection module and two steps to remove irrelevant sentences and to control the length of generated summary. After that, the linguistic knowledge will be incorporated into the process of multi-sentences compression for summarizing scientific work. The experiment results of automatic evaluation prove that our new pipeline significantly improves the overall performance on both training and blind test dataset. Besides, through manual inspection we find that our model indeed capture the salient information from the given source document. However, we have to admit that the readability of generated summary needs to be improved.

We incorporated deep neural representation into both MMR (Carbonell and Goldstein, 1998) strategy and PageRank (Page et al., 1999) algorithm. Even though MMR strategy performs better in information retrieval task, we empirically verified that it is not sufficient for our model to summarize scientific work. MMR is a query-biased approach and we chose the title as query in our implementation, thus the potential reason for worse performance may be the query we chose is not effective enough.

To investigate a sentence embedding method for sufficiently summarizing scholarly document, we compared the performances among several embedding strategies and we also evaluated their performances on both ROUGE metric and BERTScore metric. Although averaging the output of SciBERT (Beltagy et al., 2019) achieves better performance, the workload of using it to extract sentence embeddings is heavier than that of directly using SBERT (Reimers and Gurevych, 2019). There is enough work for generic domain while the attention paid for task-specific domain is far from enough, therefore we appeal to researchers for making more efforts on task-specific domain in their further research.

8 Future work

As the future, we will evaluate our pipeline on larger scientific datasets to show the effectiveness and robustness, and we also would like to conduct a analysis on the faithfulness and the level of abstraction for the generated summary.

Acknowledgments

We would like to thank the anonymous reviewer(s) for helpful comments and suggestions.

References

Federico Barrios, Federico López, Luis Argerich, and Rosa Wachenchauzer. 2016. Variations of the similarity function of textrank for automated summarization. *arXiv preprint arXiv:1602.03606*.

Iz Beltagy, Arman Cohan, and Kyle Lo. 2019. Scibert: Pretrained contextualized embeddings for scientific text. *arXiv preprint arXiv:1903.10676*.

Florian Boudin and Emmanuel Morin. 2013. Keyphrase extraction for n-best reranking in multi-sentence compression.

Jaime Carbonell and Jade Goldstein. 1998. The use of mmr, diversity-based reranking for reordering documents and producing summaries. In *Proceedings of the 21st annual international ACM SIGIR conference on Research and development in information retrieval*, pages 335–336.

Maroli Krishnayya Chandrasekaran, Guy Feigenblat, Hovy. Eduard, Anirudh Ravichander, Michal. Shmueli-Scheuer, and Anita De Waard. 2020. Overview and insights from scientific document summarization shared tasks 2020: Cl-scisumm, laysumm and longsumm. In *In Proceedings of the First Workshop on Scholarly Document Processing (SDP 2020)*.

Jianpeng Cheng and Mirella Lapata. 2016. Neural summarization by extracting sentences and words. *arXiv preprint arXiv:1603.07252*.

Jacob Devlin, Ming-Wei Chang, Kenton Lee, and Kristina Toutanova. 2018. Bert: Pre-training of deep bidirectional transformers for language understanding. *arXiv preprint arXiv:1810.04805*.

Günes Erkan and Dragomir R Radev. 2004. Lexrank: Graph-based lexical centrality as salience in text summarization. *Journal of artificial intelligence research*, 22:457–479.

Urvashi Khandelwal, Kevin Clark, Dan Jurafsky, and Lukasz Kaiser. 2019. Sample efficient text summarization using a single pre-trained transformer. *arXiv preprint arXiv:1905.08836*.

Rashmi Kurmi and Pranita Jain. 2014. Text summarization using enhanced mmr technique. In *2014 International Conference on Computer Communication and Informatics*, pages 1–5. IEEE.

Guy Lev, Michal Shmueli-Scheuer, Jonathan Herzig, Achiya Jerbi, and David Konopnicki. 2019. Talksumm: A dataset and scalable annotation method for scientific paper summarization based on conference talks. *arXiv preprint arXiv:1906.01351*.

Chin-Yew Lin and Eduard Hovy. 2003. Automatic evaluation of summaries using n-gram co-occurrence statistics. In *Proceedings of the 2003 Human Language Technology Conference of the North American Chapter of the Association for Computational Linguistics*, pages 150–157.

Yang Liu. 2019. Fine-tune bert for extractive summarization. *arXiv preprint arXiv:1903.10318*.

Yang Liu and Mirella Lapata. 2019. Text summarization with pretrained encoders. *arXiv preprint arXiv:1908.08345*.

Ling Luo, Xiang Ao, Yan Song, Feiyang Pan, Min Yang, and Qing He. 2019. Reading like her: Human reading inspired extractive summarization. In *Proceedings of the 2019 Conference on Empirical Methods in Natural Language Processing and the 9th International Joint Conference on Natural Language Processing (EMNLP-IJCNLP)*, pages 3024–3034.

Yuning Mao, Yanru Qu, Yiqing Xie, Xiang Ren, and Jiawei Han. 2020. Multi-document summarization with maximal marginal relevance-guided reinforcement learning. *arXiv preprint arXiv:2010.00117*.

Chandler May, Alex Wang, Shikha Bordia, Samuel R Bowman, and Rachel Rudinger. 2019. On measuring social biases in sentence encoders. *arXiv preprint arXiv:1903.10561*.

Rada Mihalcea and Paul Tarau. 2004. Textrank: Bringing order into text. In *Proceedings of the 2004 conference on empirical methods in natural language processing*, pages 404–411.

Tomas Mikolov, Ilya Sutskever, Kai Chen, Greg S Corrado, and Jeff Dean. 2013. Distributed representations of words and phrases and their compositionality. In *Advances in neural information processing systems*, pages 3111–3119.

Ramesh Nallapati, Bowen Zhou, Caglar Gulcehre, Bing Xiang, et al. 2016. Abstractive text summarization using sequence-to-sequence rnns and beyond. *arXiv preprint arXiv:1602.06023*.

Lawrence Page, Sergey Brin, Rajeev Motwani, and Terry Winograd. 1999. The pagerank citation ranking: Bringing order to the web. Technical report, Stanford InfoLab.

Nils Reimers and Iryna Gurevych. 2019. Sentence-bert: Sentence embeddings using siamese bert-networks. *arXiv preprint arXiv:1908.10084*.

Abigail See, Peter J Liu, and Christopher D Manning. 2017. Get to the point: Summarization with pointer-generator networks. *arXiv preprint arXiv:1704.04368*.

Eva Sharma, Luyang Huang, Zhe Hu, and Lu Wang. 2019. An entity-driven framework for abstractive summarization. *arXiv preprint arXiv:1909.02059*.

Ilya Sutskever, Oriol Vinyals, and Quoc V Le. 2014. Sequence to sequence learning with neural networks. In *Advances in neural information processing systems*, pages 3104–3112.

Jun Suzuki and Masaaki Nagata. 2016. Cutting-off redundant repeating generations for neural abstractive summarization. *arXiv preprint arXiv:1701.00138*.

Ashish Vaswani, Noam Shazeer, Niki Parmar, Jakob Uszkoreit, Llion Jones, Aidan N Gomez, Łukasz Kaiser, and Illia Polosukhin. 2017. Attention is all you need. In *Advances in neural information processing systems*, pages 5998–6008.

Danqing Wang, Pengfei Liu, Yining Zheng, Xipeng Qiu, and Xuanjing Huang. 2020. Heterogeneous graph neural networks for extractive document summarization. *arXiv preprint arXiv:2004.12393*.

Thomas Wolf, Lysandre Debut, Victor Sanh, Julien Chaumond, Clement Delangue, Anthony Moi, Pierric Cistac, Tim Rault, Rémi Louf, Morgan Funtowicz, Joe Davison, Sam Shleifer, Patrick von Platen, Clara Ma, Yacine Jernite, Julien Plu, Canwen Xu, Teven Le Scao, Sylvain Gugger, Mariama Drame, Quentin Lhoest, and Alexander M. Rush. 2019. Huggingface's transformers: State-of-the-art natural language processing. *ArXiv*, abs/1910.03771.

Han Xiao. 2018. bert-as-service. https://github.com/hanxiao/bert-as-service.

Jiacheng Xu and Greg Durrett. 2019. Neural extractive text summarization with syntactic compression. *arXiv preprint arXiv:1902.00863*.

Tianyi Zhang, Varsha Kishore, Felix Wu, Kilian Q Weinberger, and Yoav Artzi. 2019a. Bertscore: Evaluating text generation with bert. *arXiv preprint arXiv:1904.09675*.

Xingxing Zhang, Furu Wei, and Ming Zhou. 2019b. Hibert: Document level pre-training of hierarchical bidirectional transformers for document summarization. *arXiv preprint arXiv:1905.06566*.

Jinming Zhao, Ming Liu, Longxiang Gao, Yuan Jin, Lan Du, He Zhao, He Zhang, and Gholamreza Haffari. 2020. Summpip: Unsupervised multi-document summarization with sentence graph compression. In *Proceedings of the 43rd International ACM SIGIR Conference on Research and Development in Information Retrieval*, pages 1949–1952.

Qingyu Zhou, Furu Wei, and Ming Zhou. 2020. At which level should we extract? an empirical study on extractive document summarization. *arXiv preprint arXiv:2004.02664*.

Using Pre-Trained Transformer for Better Lay Summarization

Seungwon Kim
Incheon Airport Corporation, Georgia Institute of Technology
skim3222@gatech.edu

Abstract

In this paper, we tack lay summarization tasks, which aim to automatically produce lay summaries for scientific papers, to participate in the first CL-LaySumm 2020 in SDP workshop at EMNLP 2020. We present our approach of using Pre-training with Extracted Gap-sentences for Abstractive Summarization (PEGASUS; Zhang et al., 2019b) to produce the lay summary and combining those with the extractive summarization model using Bidirectional Encoder Representations from Transformers (BERT; Devlin et al., 2019) and readability metrics that measure the readability of the sentence to further improve the quality of the summary. Our model achieves a remarkable performance on ROUGE metrics, demonstrating the produced summary is more readable while it summarizes the main points of the document.

1 Introduction

Recent summarization techniques have greatly benefitted from the advancement of language models and successfully produced plausible summaries for both general news articles in real-life and technical scholarly documents in the expert domain. An informative but concise summary can help people to reduce the search time and boost the decision making by expeditiously providing more relevant documents (Mani et al., 2002; Roussinov and Chen, 2001; Maña-López et al., 2004; McKeown et al., 2005). For processing scholarly documents, automatic summarization is promising since it can benefit researchers to cope with the pace of the exponentially growing number of publications (Bornmann and Mutz, 2015).

Despite the recent advancement in automatic summarization literature, summarization for scholarly documents has been less explored compared to the works regarding summarization for ordinary news articles due to the absence of large-scale datasets. Developing human-written lay summaries

for scholarly documents is challenging since it involves expert knowledge to understand the technical jargon and the complex structure of scientific documents. Because of these inherent challenges, existing summarization techniques for scientific documents is limited in a sense, which the produced summary is either too concise to provide important information (Vasilyev et al., 2019; Cachola et al., 2020) or aiming to directly extract the content from abstract or citation sentences (Yasunaga et al., 2019), which mostly resembles the abstract, making it hard for the public and researchers from outside of the particular domain to understand the main points of the scientific papers. Although the readability of the abstracts in scientific papers had continuously decreased due to the increase in the use of technical jargon (Plavén-Sigray et al., 2017), the summarization of scientific papers for the public and researchers from outside of the certain field has been remained elusive.

To provide a better summary for the public and researchers, we participated in the first Computational Linguistics Lay Summary Challenge (CL-LaySumm 2020) Shared task (Chandrasekaran et al., (Forthcoming) and developed a summarization system that automatically produces lay summaries for scholarly documents. The main task of CL-LaySumm is producing a corresponding lay summary given the full-text and abstract of the research paper. We employed the dataset from the CL-LaySumm 2020 committee and performed experiments using recent summarization models including Pre-training with Extracted Gap-sentences for Abstractive Summarization (PEGASUS; Zhang et al., 2019b), extractive summarization with Bidirectional Encoder Representations from Transformers (BERT; Devlin et al., 2019), and a new evaluation protocol that measures the readability of the sentence in the summary. We showcase how PEGASUS, BERT, and readability metric improve the summarization system and demonstrate that

Proceedings of the First Workshop on Scholarly Document Processing, pages 328–335
Online, November 19, 2020. ©2020 Association for Computational Linguistics
https://doi.org/10.18653/v1/P17

the produced summary is more readable while it summarizes the main ideas of the documents.

2 Related Work

The type of recent benchmark datasets that are widely utilized for evaluating the performance of the summarization system can be categorized into two themes: news articles and scientific documents.

Summarization of news articles have been more actively explored since it is relatively easy to develop human-written summaries. Woodsend and Lapata (2010) and Cheng and Lapata (2016) created a large-scale dataset that contains 200K news articles with manually written gold summaries. Owing to the large-scale dataset and relatively simple structure of the articles, neural abstractive summarization using sequence models such as Long Term Short Memory (LSTM, Hochreiter and Schmidhuber, 1997) with attention mechanism (Bahdanau et al., 2014) has been actively used in abstractive summarization for news articles. The attention-based encoder-decoder network has been improved by others. See et al. (2017) used LSTM with two different networks: pointer-generator network that produces accurate expression by pointing each word in the source and coverage network that avoids repetition. Paulus et al. (2017) incorporated reinforcement learning (RL) into sequence models for summarization tasks and Celikyilmaz et al. (2018) developed multi-agent encoders that communicate with each other by sharing outputs for each layer in the encoder network.

After the advent of pre-trained language models such as Transformer, BERT, and Bidirectional and Auto-Regressive Transformers (BART), the summarization literature benefits from these pre-trained language models that provide more contextual word representation (Vaswani et al., 2017; Devlin et al., 2019; Lewis et al., 2020). Liu and Lapata (2019) used BERT model as an encoder, Zhang et al. (2019a) applied BERT to both encoder and decoder networks, Scialom et al. (2020) constructed generative adversarial networks using BERT models, and Yoon et al. (2020) appended semantic similarity layers on top of the pre-trained BART. While neural sequence models have been successfully applied to the summarization for news articles, applying the same techniques to scientific documents would be challenging since the scholarly documents are far longer than ordinary news articles and have a complicated structure. Our work is different from

the described works as we tackle summarization for scientific documents.

Although summarization for scientific texts is less explored, Cohan et al. (2018) proposed hierarchical encoder-decoder network to address the long scholarly documents for constructing abstract summary, Yasunaga et al. (2019) suggested summarization using abstract and citation sentences with graph convolutional networks (Kipf and Welling, 2016) and LSTM, and released the medium-scale dataset that contains 1000 scientific papers in the computational linguistic domain with human-written summaries and citation sentences for each paper. Cachola et al. (2020) implemented an extreme summarization system, which is TLDR (Too Long; Don't Read) summarization, for scientific documents using multi-task learning with headline generation models (Vasilyev et al., 2019). Zhang et al. (2019b) proposed PEGASUS by masking important sentences in the input document with a Transformer-based encoder-decoder network to force the model to summarize main points of the contents given the remainder of the text. PEGASUS tackled summarization for both news articles and scholarly documents but it only aimed to produce the abstract. In contrast, our work is distinct from the previous approaches as we aim to produce lay summaries for scientific documents rather than generating extremely short sentences or summaries that contain technical words which makes it difficult for lay audiences to understand.

To facilitate scholarly document processing, there have been annual workshops regarding data mining, natural language processing (NLP), information retrieval for scientific publications: BIRNDL (Bibliometric-enhanced Information Retrieval and Natural Language Processing for Digital Libraries), WOSP (Workshop on Mining Scientific Publications), TAC (Text Analytics Conference). In particular, the annual CL-SciSumm (Jaidka et al., 2016, 2018; Chandrasekaran et al., 2019) encouraged participants to research on scientific documents summarization. Our work is closely related to the CL-LaySumm 2020, which is the first lay summary challenge shared task. We employed the LaySumm dataset provided by the workshop organizing committee and performed experiments using a variety of recent summarization models to develop the lay summarization system.

3 Data Analysis

3.1 Overview

Laysumm dataset consists of around 600 scientific papers in epilepsy, archeology, and materials engineering domain, including full-text, abstract and corresponding lay summaries written by authors and journalists. The task for CL-LaySumm 2020 is creating a lay summary with less than 150 words given the full-text and the abstract of the paper. For evaluation, a test set which contains 37 scientific papers without ground truth lay summary is given. The below table shows the average number of words and sentences for each document. Here Spacy (Honnibal and Johnson, 2015) is used for word tokenization.

-	Train		Test	
	words	sentences	words	sentences
Full-text	4915.31	254.41	5696.57	306.36
Abstract	271.96	13.27	264.28	12.51
Laysum	109.07	3.82	—	—

Table 1: Average word, sentence length of dataset.

3.2 Sentence similarity

Before developing a specific summarization model, we measured the sentence similarity to determine which type of summarization is suitable for lay summarization. There are two types of summarization: extractive summarization and abstractive summarization. The extractive summarization scores the importance of sentences in the source and directly extracts the sentences based on the score. In contrast, the abstractive summarization generates the summary from scratch while it maintains the representative content of the source. We assumed that this resembles the way humans summarize the contents and the lay summarization can be categorized into the abstractive summarization. However, if the sentences in the lay summary exist in the abstract or full-text of the paper, extractive summarization is more promising. Table 2 shows the average number of overlapping sentences between the sentences in the lay summary and the abstract and full-text for the training set.

—	# overlapping sentences
Full-text	0.01
Abstract	0.12

Table 2: Average number of overlapping sentences.

As shown in Table 2, the lay summaries were written from scratch rather than directly using the

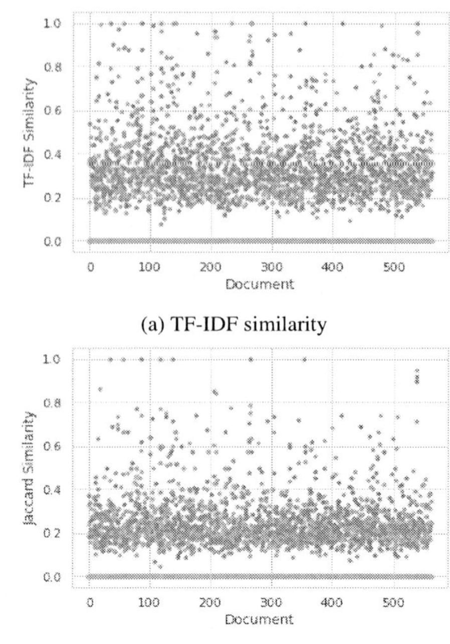

(a) TF-IDF similarity

(b) Jaccard similarity

Figure 1: Sentence similarity between the sentences in the lay summary and sentences in the full-text.

sentences from the abstract or full-text of the paper. We observed that overlapping occurs only 7% of the training set (40 of 572) and if any sentence in the lay summary exists in the abstract, there are 1.73 overlapping sentences in the abstract on average.

We also measured the similarity between the sentences in the lay summary and the sentences in the full-text. For this task, Term Frequency–Inverse Document Frequency (TF-IDF) and Jaccard similarity are used (Sammut and Webb, 2010; Hamers et al., 1989). Figure 1 shows the maximum value of similarity for each sentence in the lay summary in terms of TF-IDF and Jaccard similarity. As shown in the figures, the similarity is below 0.4 on average for TF-IDF and it becomes lower for Jaccard similarity. From the results of the analysis, we excluded full-text and aimed to produce the lay summary solely with the abstract.

4 Method

There are two main summarization models used in our system to generate the lay summary. We tried to use PEGASUS which is an abstractive summarization model and Presumm (Liu and Lapata, 2019) for extractive summarization to produce the summary. We trained the summarization model on the lay summary dataset in a supervised way by pairing the abstract and the corresponding lay summary of the paper. After producing the lay summary using PEGASUS, we improved the quality of the produced summary by appending important sentences to the summary of which the number of words is under a certain threshold. For example, if the number of the lay summary generated by the abstractive model was under 90, we added the sentences from the corresponding summry geneated by extractive model up to this threshold. When appending the sentences to the produced summary, we prioritized the sentences in the abstract based on the score predicted by Presumm model and readability metric and applied Tri-gram blocking to avoid repetition (Paulus et al., 2017). Detailed descriptions of each summarization model and the readability metric are presented in the following sections.

4.1 PEGASUS

We used PEGASUS that is trained on large text corpus of news text from the web pages to produce abstractive summaries (Zhang et al., 2019b). The architecture of PEGASUS model is Transformer-based encoder-decoder network and the model targets to output the important sentences by masking principal sentences or greedily selected sentences based on the ROUGE (Nallapati et al., 2016) in the input text during the training process. We used the official implementation and the checkpoint of the pre-trained PEGASUS model without any modification and trained this model directly on the lay summary dataset.

4.2 PreSumm

For extractive summarization, we used the Presumm model (Liu and Lapata, 2019) which uses BERT, a pre-trained language model, for news article summarization without any modification. Presumm model uses BERT as a pre-trained encoder. The authors added [CLS] token between the sentences as the input of BERT to obtain sentence representation. This token is used to calculate the score to determine whether each sentence is included in the lay summary.

For training this summarization model, we assumed that the model needs a large-scale dataset that contains thousands of instances to train over one hundred million of parameters. Since the lay summary dataset only consists of 600 documents, we used the CNN/DM dataset that consists of 300K news articles for the pre-training stage before train-ing the lay summary dataset. CNN/DM dataset is a common benchmark used in the summarization literature and the target summary for this dataset is somewhat extractive rather than abstractive, thus we considered this dataset seemed suitable for the extractive summarization. After training the model on the CNN/DM dataset for a few iterations, we switched the dataset with the lay summary dataset.

4.3 Readability of the Sentence

The evaluation metric that is widely used in the summarization literature is ROUGE, which reflects the ratio of overlapping vocabulary between the produced summary and the ground-truth summary. However, ROUGE only focuses on counting the overlapping words and it is unable to determine whether the sentence is difficult or not to understand. We believe the produced lay summary has to be more readable for the lay audience, thus we adopted the readability of the sentence as an additional metric and we combine this metric with extractive summarization. Specifically, we combine this metric with extractive summarization. When we produced the extractive summary based on the important score predicted by Presumm model, we pruned the sentence of which readability score is under a certain threshold.

The readability of the sentence is measured by considering the ratio of jargon. We used the corpus of words developed by Rakedzon et al. (2017). The authors collected 900 million words published on the BBC site and classifying the word as easy, medium, and rare (jargon) based on the frequency of words used on the BBC site. The dictionary contains around 500K words which were the most frequently used. To measure the readability of the sentence, we followed the authors as shown in equation (1) with different constant factors (c_1, c_2, c_3) in front of each ratio (r_1 : medium, r_2 : rare, r_3 : out of dictionary). We used $10, 20, 30$ as constant factors in front of each ratio.

$$Score = 100 - (c_1 r_1 + c_2 r_2 + c_3 r_3) \quad (1)$$

Using this metric, we measured the average sentence readability of the abstract and the lay summary in the Laysumm dataset. As shown in table 3, the lay summary achieves high readability than the abstract since it avoids using technical words. In the next section, we present the readability of the produced summary with ROUGE metric to show whether the summarization model can achieve a high score in both ROUGE and readability metrics.

—	# Average Sentence Readability
Abstract	92.25
Laysumm	96.18

Table 3: Average sentence readability.

5 Experiments

5.1 Dataset and Evaluation

We evaluated the performance of the model on the lay summary dataset. The lay summary dataset is divided into the train, validation, and test set (8/1/1 split). Evaluation metrics are ROUGE recall and F1 score in terms of unigram, bigram, and the longest common subsequence overlap.

5.2 Implementation Details

We mainly used the official implementation of the PEGASUS, Presumm, and pre-trained checkpoints provided by the authors. We did not modify any network architecture and for Presumm model, the dataset was switched from CNN/DM to lay summary data after sufficient training steps. After switching the dataset, all the trainable parameters are gradually fine-tuned with a lower learning rate.

Presumm extractive models were trained on dual GPUs (NVIDIA RTX 2080ti) with gradient accumulating every 4 steps. The model was trained for 50,000 steps for the pre-training stage and 10,000 steps after switching the data into the Laysumm dataset. We saved the checkpoints of the model every 200 steps after switching the dataset and performed validation by choosing the top three checkpoints, which have the lowest validation loss, to evaluate the model on the test set. To generate the extractive summary, we selected the sentence from the highest score only if the readability score is over 85 until the number of words in the produced summary is over 150. Trigram Blocking (Paulus et al., 2017) is applied when generating the summary to reduce the redundancy.

PEGASUS model was trained for 20,000 steps on a single GPU (NVIDIA RTX 2080ti) with hyperparameters provided by the authors except for batch size and learning rate. Due to the memory constraints, we decreased batch size to 1 with a decreased learning rate at 0.0001. We saved the checkpoints of the model every 1000 steps and performed the same validation done in the extractive summarization and chose beam search at size 10 to encourage the model not to generate short sentences.

5.3 Results

The best results were achieved by submitting different checkpoints from the validation and test stage for each model. The performance of extractive and abstractive models are summarized in table 4. EXT and ABS indicate Presumm extractive model and PEGASUS abstractive model respectively. ABSEXT means sentences produced by the extractive model are appended to the abstractive summary until the number of words is over 90. As reported in the table 4, the hybrid approach outperforms a solely extractive or abstractive model. Hybrid model benefits from high recall in the extractive model and high precision in the abstractive model.

Model	ROUGE-F1(1/2/L)			ROUGE-R(1/2/L)		
EXT	42.96	17.85	23.38	45.85	18.92	25.02
ABS	43.61	20.51	28.98	43.16	20.35	28.59
ABSEXT	**45.96**	**21.46**	**29.77**	**48.10**	**22.37**	**31.05**

Table 4: Best ROUGE F1, Recall results on test set.

5.4 Analysis of Threshold

In this section, we investigate how the number of words in the produced lay summary affects the performance of the summarization model. We first produced lay summaries using PEGASUS(ABS) and measured the number of words for each summary. Then, we set a standard threshold and appended sentences from the extractive summary produced by PRESUMM(EXT) if the number of words in the abstractive summary is below that limit. Table 5 shows the ROUGE F1 score with respect to different threshold values and the average number of words of lay summaries after appending sentences. ABSEXT with a threshold at 90 performs best and it shows appending sentences from the extractive model to the abstractive summary consistently improves the performance. This makes sense as the abstractive model(ABS) tends to produce short summaries: the average number of words in abstractive summary is 82, whereas the average number of words in the ground-truth lay summaries in the Laysumm dataset is around 110.

5.5 Readability of Summary

We provide ROUGE-F1 and readability scores for each model. As shown in Table 6, for the extractive summary, EXT performs better than EXT W/O R, demonstrating excluding hard sentences improves the performance on both ROUGE and readability metrics. When the extractive summary is combined

Threshold	# of words	ROUGE-F1 (1/2/L)		
—	82.54	43.61	20.51	28.98
70	85.92	44.12	20.33	29.12
90	95.19	**45.96**	**21.46**	**29.77**
115	105.78	45.19	21.00	29.02
135	114.54	45.17	20.95	28.22

Table 5: F1 with different threshold on test set. The first row indicates the abstractive model without being embedded with sentences from the extractive summary.

with abstractive summary (ABSEXT W/O R, AB-SEXT), readability constraints slightly improves the performance on both ROUGE-F1 and readability metric. Overall, we observed that our models successfully produce lay summaries that are more readable than the abstract.

Model(dataset)	Readability	ROUGE-F1 (1/2/L)		
EXT w/o R	93.09	42.35	17.66	23.37
EXT	93.39	42.69	17.85	23.38
ABSEXT w/o R	93.83	45.86	21.46	29.76
ABSEXT	**93.85**	**45.96**	**21.46**	**29.77**
(Abstract)	92.25	—	—	—
(LaySumm)	96.18	—	—	—

Table 6: ROUGE-F1 and readability score on test set. EXT W/O R means PRESUMM extractive summarization model without readability constraints, whereas EXT model involves pruning sentences whose readability is under 85 from the produced summary. ABS + EXT W/O R and ABS + EXT indicate sentences from EXT W/O R and EXT W/O R are embedded to abstractive summary respectively. (Abstract) and (Lay summary) are the abstract and the lay summary of Laysumm dataset.

6 Discussion and Future work

We applied transfer learning to mitigate the absence of large-scale datasets to tackle the lay summarization task. While we demonstrated that transfer learning can result in a good performance, it can create a bottleneck for the model due to the discrepancy between the distributions of datasets, resulting in sub-optimal solutions. Our summarization model also excludes the full-text of the paper and tries to produce the summary solely based on the abstract. Although the model achieves good performance, there might exist important points in the body of the paper. It is obvious for humans to utilize the full-text of the paper to write a better lay summary. Creating a large-scale lay summary dataset that handles scholarly documents and considering important sentences from the body text can be a promising direction to address these issues.

The readability score might be usefully utilized for constructing the large-scale dataset since it is necessary to pair the difficult sentences and a more readable lay summary.

Secondly, in the optimization process during training the model, we only focused on predicting the only ground truth lay summary. This might limit the capability of the summarization model. Applying the readability score as an additional feature in the training stage would make the model more creative and help the system to summarize the contents while it selectively chooses easier words.

References

Dzmitry Bahdanau, Kyunghyun Cho, and Yoshua Bengio. 2014. Neural machine translation by jointly learning to align and translate. *arXiv preprint arXiv:1409.0473*.

Lutz Bornmann and Rüdiger Mutz. 2015. Growth rates of modern science: A bibliometric analysis based on the number of publications and cited references. *Journal of the Association for Information Science and Technology*, 66(11):2215–2222.

Isabel Cachola, Kyle Lo, Arman Cohan, and Daniel S Weld. 2020. Tldr: Extreme summarization of scientific documents. *arXiv preprint arXiv:2004.15011*.

Asli Celikyilmaz, Antoine Bosselut, Xiaodong He, and Yejin Choi. 2018. Deep communicating agents for abstractive summarization. In *Proceedings of the 2018 Conference of the North American Chapter of the Association for Computational Linguistics: Human Language Technologies, Volume 1 (Long Papers)*, pages 1662–1675, New Orleans, Louisiana. Association for Computational Linguistics.

M. K. Chandrasekaran, G. Feigenblat, E. Hovy, A. Ravichander, M. Shmueli-Scheuer, and A. De Waard. (Forthcoming). Overview and insights from scientific document summarization shared tasks 2020: Cl-scisumm, laysumm and longsumm. *In Proceedings of the First Workshop on Scholarly Document Processing (SDP 2020)*.

Muthu Kumar Chandrasekaran, Michihiro Yasunaga, Dragomir Radev, Dayne Freitag, and Min-Yen Kan. 2019. Overview and results: Cl-scisumm shared task 2019. *arXiv preprint arXiv:1907.09854*.

Jianpeng Cheng and Mirella Lapata. 2016. Neural summarization by extracting sentences and words. In *Proceedings of the 54th Annual Meeting of the Association for Computational Linguistics (Volume 1: Long Papers)*, pages 484–494, Berlin, Germany. Association for Computational Linguistics.

Arman Cohan, Franck Dernoncourt, Doo Soon Kim, Trung Bui, Seokhwan Kim, Walter Chang, and Nazli Goharian. 2018. A discourse-aware attention model for abstractive summarization of long documents. In *Proceedings of the 2018 Conference of the North American Chapter of the Association for Computational Linguistics: Human Language Technologies, Volume 2 (Short Papers)*, pages 615–621, New Orleans, Louisiana. Association for Computational Linguistics.

Jacob Devlin, Ming-Wei Chang, Kenton Lee, and Kristina Toutanova. 2019. BERT: Pre-training of deep bidirectional transformers for language understanding. In *Proceedings of the 2019 Conference of the North American Chapter of the Association for Computational Linguistics: Human Language Technologies, Volume 1 (Long and Short Papers)*, pages 4171–4186, Minneapolis, Minnesota. Association for Computational Linguistics.

Lieve Hamers et al. 1989. Similarity measures in scientometric research: The jaccard index versus salton's cosine formula. *Information Processing and Management*, 25(3):315–18.

Sepp Hochreiter and Jürgen Schmidhuber. 1997. Long short-term memory. *Neural computation*, 9(8):1735–1780.

Matthew Honnibal and Mark Johnson. 2015. An improved non-monotonic transition system for dependency parsing. In *Proceedings of the 2015 Conference on Empirical Methods in Natural Language Processing*, pages 1373–1378, Lisbon, Portugal. Association for Computational Linguistics.

Kokil Jaidka, Niyati Chhaya, and Lyle Ungar. 2018. Diachronic degradation of language models: Insights from social media. In *Proceedings of the 56th Annual Meeting of the Association for Computational Linguistics (Volume 2: Short Papers)*, pages 195–200, Melbourne, Australia. Association for Computational Linguistics.

Kokil Jaidka, Muthu Kumar Chandrasekaran, Sajal Rustagi, and Min-Yen Kan. 2016. Overview of the CL-SciSumm 2016 shared task. In *Proceedings of the Joint Workshop on Bibliometric-enhanced Information Retrieval and Natural Language Processing for Digital Libraries (BIRNDL)*, pages 93–102.

Thomas N Kipf and Max Welling. 2016. Semi-supervised classification with graph convolutional networks. *arXiv preprint arXiv:1609.02907*.

Mike Lewis, Yinhan Liu, Naman Goyal, Marjan Ghazvininejad, Abdelrahman Mohamed, Omer Levy, Veselin Stoyanov, and Luke Zettlemoyer. 2020. BART: Denoising sequence-to-sequence pretraining for natural language generation, translation, and comprehension. In *Proceedings of the 58th Annual Meeting of the Association for Computational Linguistics*, pages 7871–7880, Online. Association for Computational Linguistics.

Yang Liu and Mirella Lapata. 2019. Text summarization with pretrained encoders. In *Proceedings of the 2019 Conference on Empirical Methods in Natural Language Processing and the 9th International Joint Conference on Natural Language Processing (EMNLP-IJCNLP)*, pages 3730–3740, Hong Kong, China. Association for Computational Linguistics.

Manuel J Maña-López, Manuel De Buenaga, and José M Gómez-Hidalgo. 2004. Multidocument summarization: An added value to clustering in interactive retrieval. *ACM Transactions on Information Systems (TOIS)*, 22(2):215–241.

Inderjeet Mani, Gary Klein, David House, Lynette Hirschman, Therese Firmin, and Beth Sundheim. 2002. Summac: a text summarization evaluation. *Natural Language Engineering*, 8(1):43–68.

Kathleen McKeown, Rebecca J Passonneau, David K Elson, Ani Nenkova, and Julia Hirschberg. 2005. Do summaries help? In *Proceedings of the 28th annual international ACM SIGIR conference on Research and development in information retrieval*, pages 210–217.

Ramesh Nallapati, Feifei Zhai, and Bowen Zhou. 2016. Summarunner: A recurrent neural network based sequence model for extractive summarization of documents. *arXiv preprint arXiv:1611.04230*.

Romain Paulus, Caiming Xiong, and Richard Socher. 2017. A deep reinforced model for abstractive summarization. *arXiv preprint arXiv:1705.04304*.

Pontus Plavén-Sigray, Granville James Matheson, Björn Christian Schiffler, and William Hedley Thompson. 2017. The readability of scientific texts is decreasing over time. *Elife*, 6:e27725.

Tzipora Rakedzon, Elad Segev, Noam Chapnik, Roy Yosef, and Ayelet Baram-Tsabari. 2017. Automatic jargon identifier for scientists engaging with the public and science communication educators. *PloS one*, 12(8):e0181742.

Dmitri G Roussinov and Hsinchun Chen. 2001. Information navigation on the web by clustering and summarizing query results. *Information Processing & Management*, 37(6):789–816.

Claude Sammut and Geoffrey I Webb. 2010. Tf–idf.

Thomas Scialom, Paul-Alexis Dray, Sylvain Lamprier, Benjamin Piwowarski, and Jacopo Staiano. 2020. Discriminative adversarial search for abstractive summarization. *arXiv preprint arXiv:2002.10375*.

Abigail See, Peter J. Liu, and Christopher D. Manning. 2017. Get to the point: Summarization with pointer-generator networks. In *Proceedings of the 55th Annual Meeting of the Association for Computational Linguistics (Volume 1: Long Papers)*, pages 1073–1083, Vancouver, Canada. Association for Computational Linguistics.

Oleg Vasilyev, Tom Grek, and John Bohannon. 2019. Headline generation: Learning from decomposable document titles. *arXiv preprint arXiv:1904.08455*.

Ashish Vaswani, Noam Shazeer, Niki Parmar, Jakob Uszkoreit, Llion Jones, Aidan N Gomez, Łukasz Kaiser, and Illia Polosukhin. 2017. Attention is all you need. In *Advances in neural information processing systems*, pages 5998–6008.

Kristian Woodsend and Mirella Lapata. 2010. Automatic generation of story highlights. In *Proceedings of the 48th Annual Meeting of the Association for Computational Linguistics*, pages 565–574, Uppsala, Sweden. Association for Computational Linguistics.

Michihiro Yasunaga, Jungo Kasai, Rui Zhang, Alexander R Fabbri, Irene Li, Dan Friedman, and Dragomir R Radev. 2019. Scisummnet: A large annotated corpus and content-impact models for scientific paper summarization with citation networks. In *Proceedings of the AAAI Conference on Artificial Intelligence*, volume 33, pages 7386–7393.

Wonjin Yoon, Yoon Sun Yeo, Minbyul Jeong, Bong-Jun Yi, and Jaewoo Kang. 2020. Learning by semantic similarity makes abstractive summarization better. *arXiv preprint arXiv:2002.07767*.

Haoyu Zhang, Jingjing Cai, Jianjun Xu, and Ji Wang. 2019a. Pretraining-based natural language generation for text summarization. In *Proceedings of the 23rd Conference on Computational Natural Language Learning (CoNLL)*, pages 789–797, Hong Kong, China. Association for Computational Linguistics.

Jingqing Zhang, Yao Zhao, Mohammad Saleh, and Peter J Liu. 2019b. Pegasus: Pre-training with extracted gap-sentences for abstractive summarization. *arXiv preprint arXiv:1912.08777*.

A Lay Summary Example

We present our approach of using Pre-training with Extracted Gap-sentences for Abstractive Summarization (PEGASUS; Zhang et al., 2019b) to produce the lay summary and combining those with the extractive summarization model using Bidirectional Encoder Representations from Transformers (BERT; Devlin et al., 2019) and readability metrics that measure the readability of the sentence to further improve the quality of the summary. Our model achieves a remarkable performance on ROUGE metrics, demonstrating the produced summary is more readable while it summarizes the main points of the document.

Table 7: An example of a lay summary generated by ABSEXT model. The model only considers the abstract to produce the lay summary.

Scientific Document Summarization for LaySumm '20 and LongSumm '20

Sayar Ghosh Roy, Nikhil Pinnaparaju, Risubh Jain, Manish Gupta*** and Vasudeva Varma**

Information Retrieval and Extraction Lab
International Institute of Information Technology, Hyderabad, India

{sayar.ghosh, nikhil.pinnaparaju}@research.iiit.ac.in,
risubh.jain@students.iiit.ac.in, {manish.gupta, vv}@iiit.ac.in

Abstract

Automatic text summarization has been widely studied as an important task in natural language processing. Traditionally, various feature engineering and machine learning based systems have been proposed for extractive as well as abstractive text summarization. Recently, deep learning based, specifically Transformer-based systems have been immensely popular. Summarization is a cognitively challenging task – extracting summary worthy sentences is laborious, and expressing semantics in brief when doing abstractive summarization is complicated. In this paper, we specifically look at the problem of summarizing scientific research papers from multiple domains. We differentiate between two types of summaries, namely, (a) LaySumm: A very short summary that captures the essence of the research paper in layman terms restricting overtly specific technical jargon and (b) LongSumm: A much longer detailed summary aimed at providing specific insights into various ideas touched upon in the paper. While leveraging latest Transformer-based models, our systems are simple, intuitive and based on how specific paper sections contribute to human summaries of the two types described above. Evaluations against gold standard summaries using ROUGE (Lin, 2004) metrics prove the effectiveness of our approach. On blind test corpora, our system ranks first and third for the LongSumm and LaySumm tasks respectively.

1 Introduction

Popularity of data science in recent years has led to a massive growth in the number of published papers online. This has generated an epochal change in the way we retrieve, analyze and consume information from these papers. Also wider interest in data science implies even lay persons (readers outside

---

*The author also works as a researcher at Microsoft

the data science community) are significantly interested in keeping up with the latest developments. The readers have access to a huge amount of such research papers on the web. For a human, understanding large documents and assimilating crucial information out of them is often a laborious and time-consuming task. Motivation to make a concise representation of huge text while retaining the core meaning of the original text has led to the development of various automated summarization systems. These systems provide users filtered, high-quality and concise content to work with at an unprecedented scale and speed. Summarization methods are mainly classified into two categories: *extractive* and *abstractive*. Extractive methods aim to select salient phrases, sentences or elements from the text while abstractive techniques focus on generating summaries from scratch without the constraint of reusing phrases from the original text.

Scientific papers are large, complex documents that tend to be geared towards a particular audience. This is a very small percentage of the population while majority of individuals are unable to fully comprehend the contents of long scientific documents. Even among the people who are able to understand the material, the length of such documents often spanning several pages demand a great deal of time and attention. Hence, tasks like layman summarization (LaySumm) and long-form summarization (LongSumm) are of great importance in today's world.

Typically scientific research papers are fairly structured documents containing standard sections like abstract, introduction, background, related work, experiments, results, discussion, conclusion and acknowledgments. Thus, summarization of such documents should be aware of such sectional structure. An intuitive way is to pick a few sentences from each of the sections to be a part of the summary. But how do we decide how many sentences to pick from each section? Also, which

Proceedings of the First Workshop on Scholarly Document Processing, pages 336–343
Online, November 19, 2020. ©2020 Association for Computational Linguistics
https://doi.org/10.18653/v1/P17

sentences to pick? Can we rewrite sentences so as to obtain a concise abstractive summary? We investigate answers to these questions in this paper.

Multiple survey papers have provided a detailed overview of the automatic text summarization task (Tas and Kiyani, 2007; Nenkova and McKeown, 2012; Allahyari et al., 2017). Most of the practically usable summarization systems are extractive in nature. Also, most summarization studies have focused on summarization of news articles. In this work, we mainly focus on two interesting aspects of text summarization: (1) summarization of *scientific research papers*, and (2) summarization for *laymen*.

Cohan et al. (2018) propose that section level processing of scientific documents is useful. Further, Collins et al. (2017) conclude that not all sections are equally useful. Also, recent papers have observed that a hierarchical summarization of scientific documents is highly effective where at the first level, an extractive summary of each section is independently generated and at the second level, the sectional output is abstracted into a brief summary (Subramanian et al., 2019; Erera et al., 2019). (Xiao and Carenini, 2019) observe that while summarizing, local context is useful, but global is not. Thus, in our approach at the sectional level, we use extracted information from only within the section text to obtain a section's extractive summary, ignoring the remaining text of the entire paper.

For the LaySumm task, we observe that abstract is the most relevant section of a scientific paper from a layman perspective. We therefore feed the abstract to a Transformer-based model and generate an abstractive summary for the LaySumm task. For the LongSumm task, we first perform extractive summarization for each section and choose a selected number of sentences from each section into the final summary.

On blind test corpora of 37 and 22 papers for the LaySumm and LongSumm tasks, our proposed system leads to a ROUGE R1 of 45.94 and 49.46 respectively. These results helped us bag the top positions on the leaderboards for the two tasks.

2   Related Work

In this section, we discuss related areas including text summarization and style transfer.

2.1   Automatic Text Summarization

Text summarization focuses on summarizing a given document and obtaining its key information bits. There are two types of text summarization methods: Extractive Summarization and Abstractive Summarization.

2.1.1   Extractive Summarization

Extractive Summarization deals with extracting pieces of text directly from the input document. Extractive Summarization can also be seen as a text classification task where we try to predict whether a given sentence will be part of the summary or not (Liu, 2019). Most papers in this area focus on the summarization of news articles. But several others focus on specific domains like summarization of medical documents, legal documents, scientific documents, etc. Summarization can also be performed in a query-sensitive manner or a user-centric manner. Sentence-scoring methods include graph-based methods like LexRank (Erkan and Radev, 2004) or TextRank (Mihalcea and Tarau, 2004), machine learning or deep learning techniques and position-based methods. Recently, various deep learning architectures such as HIBERT (Zhang et al., 2019), BERTSUM (Liu and Lapata, 2019), SummaRuNNer (Nallapati et al., 2016), CSTI (Singh et al., 2018) and Hybrid MemNet (Singh et al., 2017) have been proposed for extractive summarization.

2.1.2   Abstractive Summarization

In abstractive summarization, the model tries to generate the summary instead of extracting sentences or keywords. As compared to extractive summarization, this is more challenging and requires strong language modeling schemes to achieve good results. Traditionally, abstractive summarization techniques have focused on generating short text such as headlines or titles. But more recently, there have been efforts on generation of longer summaries. Older methods have depended on tree transduction rules (Cohn and Lapata, 2008) and quasi-synchronous grammar approaches (Woodsend and Lapata, 2011) for effective abstractive summarization. Recently, neural summarization approaches have been found to be more effective. Effective neural representative language models are very important for text generation tasks. With the recent breakthrough of Transformer-based (Vaswani et al., 2017) architectures like BERT (Devlin et al., 2018), T5 (Raffel

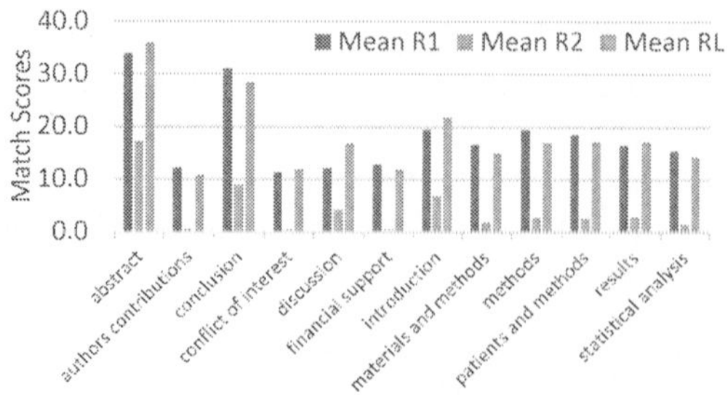

Figure 1: ROUGE-1, ROUGE-2 and ROUGE-L overlaps between paper sections and LaySumm summary

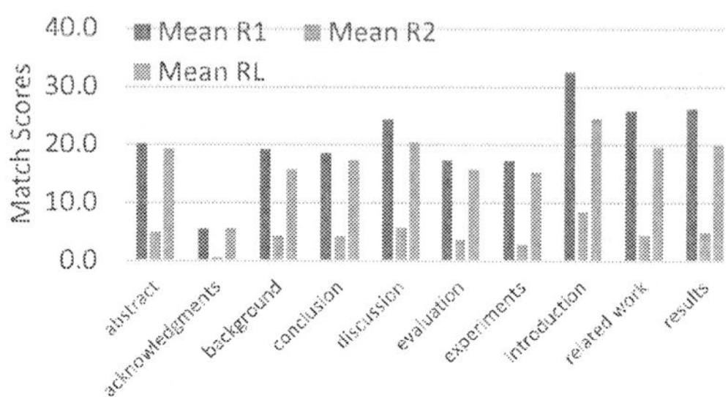

Figure 2: ROUGE-1, ROUGE-2 and ROUGE-L overlaps between paper sections and LongSumm summary

et al., 2019) and BART (Lewis et al., 2019), utilizing these types of models is crucial for obtaining good textual representations on the target side for neural abstractive summarization.

2.2 Text Style Transfer

Neural text style transfer is yet another related area of work where the document in style A is converted to style B without any loss of content or semantics (Syed et al., 2020; Vadapalli et al., 2018). This work leverages Transformer encoder-decoder models. The text-encoder is used to obtain robust latent representations while the decoder generates text with a particular target style.

3 Datasets

We first describe the datasets which were provided by the organizers of the 'Workshop on Scholarly Document Processing @EMNLP 2020'[1].

3.1 LaySumm Dataset

A dataset of 572 research papers and corresponding gold standard lay-summaries were available for training, 84 tokens being the average length of a

summary. A set of 37 research papers were provided as the blind test data. The LaySumm dataset comprises of full-text papers with lay summaries, in a variety of domains (epilepsy, archeology, and materials engineering), and from a number of journals. Elsevier made available a collection of lay summaries from a multidisciplinary collection of journals, as well as their abstracts and full-texts. For a small sample dataset, look at LaySumm's official GitHub repository[2].

3.2 LongSumm Dataset

The corpus for this task includes a training set that consists of 1705 extractive summaries, and 531 abstractive summaries of scientific papers in the domains of Natural Language Processing and Machine Learning. The extractive summaries are based on video talks from associated conferences (Lev et al., 2019) while the abstractive summaries are blog posts created by NLP and ML researchers. The average gold summary length was 767 tokens. The research papers were parsed using the science-parse[3] library. A collection of pdfs of 22 research papers served as the blind test set. The LongSumm train and test datasets are publicly accessible on LongSumm's official GitHub repository[4].

4 System Overview

In this section, we present an overview of the proposed systems for the LaySumm and LongSumm tasks.

4.1 System Overview for LaySumm

We observed that the LaySumm summaries in the train set were highly abstractive in nature with a length limit of 150 words. In Fig. 1, we analyze how information from each paper section contributes to the final lay-summary by evaluating the ROUGE overlap between a paper section and the available gold summary. This analysis is performed for the entire dataset. Fig. 1 shows that the 'abstract' was the most significant section followed by the 'conclusion'. Moreover, a relatively high ROUGE-L overlap indicates some degree of verbatim copying from the abstract onto

---

[1] https://ornlcda.github.io/SDProc/
sharedtasks.html

[2] https://github.com/WING-NUS/
scisumm-corpus/blob/master/README_
Laysumm.md

[3] https://github.com/allenai/
science-parse

[4] https://github.com/guyfe/LongSumm

the lay-summary. In addition to providing a high ROUGE overlap, the conclusion section was relatively shorter in length. This indicates that the conclusion section contains a great degree of useful information in a more condensed fashion.

Note that we picked the paper sections directly from the paper text without performing any elaborate conflation on section headers. Conflation in general should not hurt the performance of our models since a particular paper will contain only one form of the section heading, e.g., it will contain either "materials and methods" or "methods". However, we plan to explore deeper section-wise analysis using improved conflation as part of future work.

We leveraged pretrained Transformer models for conditional generation given a set of individual sections. Our results indicate that using abstract as the only sequence for conditional generation is a better choice as compared to utilizing more sections. Therefore, the problem at hand is one of capturing salient information as one would expect from a summarization task, with the additional flavor of text style transfer.

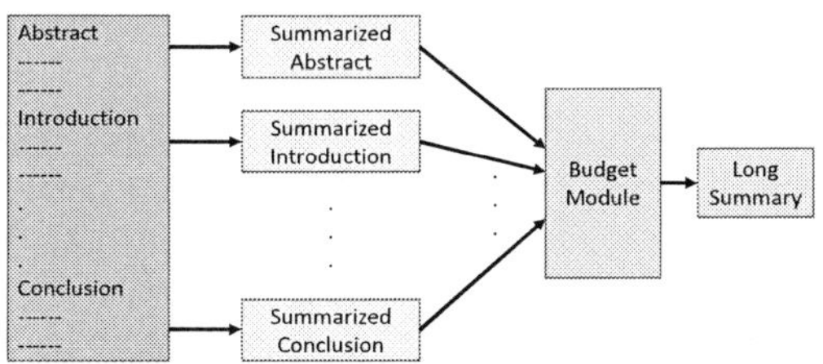

Figure 3: System Architecture for LongSumm

4.2 System Overview for LongSumm

We performed a similar section-contribution evaluation and considered section headings which appeared in at least 5% of all papers in our training set for the LongSumm task. Fig. 2 shows that the 'introduction' is the most important section when it comes to creating summaries followed by 'related work' and 'results'.

For our summary generation architecture, we considered one section at a time without the global context. As discussed earlier, this was guided by existing scientific evidence from (Xiao and Carenini, 2019) which showed that not considering the global context and focusing purely on the section at hand is marginally better than doing otherwise. Based on section-contribution evaluations, we constructed a budget module to calculate how much weight to assign to a section for the purpose of combining section summaries into the final long-summary. Fig. 3 illustrates the broad architecture of our proposed system.

For summarizing each individual section, we used SummaRuNNer (Nallapati et al., 2016), a simple neural extractive summarizer. We pre-trained SummaRuNNer on the PubMed (Cohan et al., 2018) dataset to generate paper abstracts from various paper sections. We show results using variations in our budget module, setting various cutoff thresholds for ROUGE-1 overlap in order for a section to be considered for the summary, i.e., we ignore a section if overlap is less than the threshold value. The system performance indicates that even with a fairly simple neural summarizer at the base, our architecture is capable of achieving superior results on a blind test dataset.

5 Experimental Settings

We used Hugging Face's[5] implementation of T5 and BART. We experimented with various length settings for training and generation. We found that minimum and maximum sequence lengths of 120 and 140 respectively for generation gave us the best results. We used Adam optimizer with an initial learning rate of 5e-5 with learn rate scheduling based on ROUGE-1 values calculated on the validation split. In the hyper-parameter tuning phase, a repetition penalty of 1.8 while generating lay summaries provided the most optimal results.

We used hpzhao's implementation of SummaRuNNer[6] with default hyper-parameter values. The 'topk' parameter was dynamically adjusted to set the summary length of each section based on the section-specific budget.

6 Results

Our system (with the team name: Summaformers) ranks first and third for the LongSumm[7] and LaySumm[8] tasks respectively. Further details on these tasks can be found in the shared tasks overview paper (Chandrasekaran et al., 2020). In this section, we present detailed results.

---

[5] https://huggingface.co/
[6] https://github.com/hpzhao/SummaRuNNer
[7] https://aieval.draco.res.ibm.com/challenge/39/leaderboard/39
[8] https://competitions.codalab.org/competitions/25516

Method	R-1 F1	R-2 F1	R-L F1	R-1 recall	R-2 recall	R-L recall
Lead-150 baseline	40.85	17.40	25.01	**54.77**	**22.96**	**33.34**
(abs)+SummaRuNNer	39.89	16.30	24.44	51.73	20.89	31.62
(abs)+T5-base	40.74	15.29	24.13	40.32	14.93	23.74
(abs+conc)+T5-base	40.99	15.21	23.72	40.44	14.82	23.28
(abs+conc+intro)+T5-base	40.94	15.32	23.49	40.36	14.92	23.06
(SummaRuNNer)+BART$_L$	40.87	14.72	24.31	43.36	15.46	25.77
(small abs)+BART$_L$	44.81	18.76	26.71	47.61	19.78	28.31
(abs+conc)+BART$_L$	45.45	**19.22**	27.24	49.56	20.83	29.61
(abs+conc+intro)+BART$_L$	45.69	19.07	27.17	50.17	20.90	29.78
(abs+conc+intro+methods)+BART$_L$	45.61	18.95	27.05	50.50	20.95	29.93
(abs)+BART$_L$	**45.94**	19.01	**27.43**	49.11	20.26	29.23

Table 1: LaySumm Results (Best results are highlighted in bold)

Method	R-1 F1	R-2 F1	R-L F1	R-1 recall	R-2 recall	R-L recall
Section cutoff at R-1=10.0	47.18	14.10	18.37	43.15	12.93	16.80
Section cutoff at R-1=17.5	49.20	16.49	21.03	44.67	15.00	19.07
Section cutoff at R-1=20.0	48.93	16.57	21.07	**44.99**	**15.23**	**19.36**
Section cutoff at R-1=20.0 + Post-Proc	**49.46**	**16.86**	**21.42**	43.87	14.94	18.98

Table 2: LongSumm Results (Best results are highlighted in bold)

6.1 Lay Summary Generation

We experimented with the BART-large-CNN model which is pre-trained on the CNN/Dailymail summarization dataset and with T5-base in summarization mode. We fine-tuned the conditional generation architectures of these models using the available LaySumm train corpus of 572 documents which we split into training and validation splits in a 4:1 ratio. Our initial results proved the superiority of BART-large-CNN (BART$_L$) over T5. We experimented with various generative sources such as abstract only, abstract + conclusion, abstract + conclusion + introduction, abstract + conclusion + introduction + methods. Furthermore, owing to the structure of the abstract itself, we considered the first, second and final paragraphs of the abstract (also referred to as "small abs") as the source. Our results (Table 1) show that using the complete abstract as input to BART$_L$ is the best performing setting for LaySumm. Since the papers in the dataset were published in various scientific journals, the original abstracts contain highly domain-specific technical jargon. The BART$_L$ model captures the salient points from the abstract in a short 150-word budget while transferring the text style from scientific to a layman style.

After hyper-parameter tuning on the generation end, we achieved a ROUGE-1 score of 45.94 on the blind-test corpus. Our generated summaries are coherent in addition to being highly abstractive in nature.

For comparison, we also present results for a naïve "Lead-150" baseline which outputs the first 150 tokens of the abstract as the summary. As shown in Table 1, surprisingly, this simple baseline leads to impressive results especially on recall metrics. Running SummaRuNNer on the abstract leads to results which are worse than the Lead-150 baseline.

6.2 Long Summary Generation

We used the SummaRuNNer (Nallapati et al., 2016) neural extractive summarization system as our base section summarizer. We pretrained this on the training set of the publicly available PubMed dataset (using GloVe (Pennington et al., 2014) 6B 100D word embeddings) to generate the paper abstract as closely as possible from any given section. This grounds the network in a setting where it can easily capture salient points. We plan to explore pretraining with other datasets as part of future work.

This was further finetuned using the LongSumm train set as follows. The given LongSumm training dataset was divided into train and validation splits in a 9:1 ratio. We used the same previous settings to finetune on documents in the LongSumm train split. Now, the pretrained SummaRuNNer model was conditioned to extract sentences which maximize the ROUGE-1 overlap with the provided gold standard long summaries.

Finally, based on our budget module, we assign a weight to each available section and generate section summaries of computed lengths which are further concatenated to generate the final summary. We experiment with various settings in the weight assignment based on specified overlap cutoffs in the budget module as shown in Table 2. The best performing setting corresponds to selecting sections whose ROUGE-1 overlap with the long summary is greater than 20.0. Intuitively, this prunes out irrelevant sections such as 'abbreviations' and 'acknowledgements'. The remaining sections were assigned weights based on the ROUGE-1 overlap with the provided long summary. The generated long summaries are extractive and capture the most salient pieces of information from the given research papers. The results improve slightly when we perform ad hoc post-processing using heuristics like removing paper citations within brackets, removing non-English Unicode characters and mathematical notation symbols.

6.3 Case Studies

In the following, we present two cases of lay summaries generated by our system. As we can see, the generated summaries are highly abstractive and coherent. They also capture the important aspects of the paper.

For the article at this URL[9], the generated lay summary was as follows: 'This paper proposes a novel approach to support the transformation of bioinformatics data into Linked Open Data (LOD). It defines competency questions that drive not only the definition of transformation rules, but also the data transformation and exploration afterwards. The paper also presents a support toolset and describes the successful application of the proposed approach in the functional genomics domain. According to this approach, a set of competency criteria drive the transformation process. This paper presents a framework for the development of an open data management system that can be easily adapted to different data types.'

For the article at this URL[10], the generated lay summary was as follows: 'To foster interaction, autonomous robots need to understand the environment in which they operate. One of the main challenges is semantic segmentation, together with the recognition of important objects, which can aid robots during exploration, as well as when planning new actions and interacting with the environment. In this study, we extend a multi-view semantic segmentations system based on 3D Entangled Forests (3DEF) by integrating and refining two object detectors, Mask R-CNN and You Only Look Once (YOLO), with Bayesian fusion and iterated graph cuts. The new system takes the best of its components, successfully exploiting both 2D and 3D data.'

Finally, the following lay summary was generated by our model for this very paper: 'In this paper, we develop a novel system for summarizing scientific research papers from multiple domains. We differentiate between two types of summaries, namely, (a) LaySumm : a very short summary that captures the essence of the research paper in layman terms restricting overtly specific technical jargon and (b) LongSumm a much longer detailed summary aimed at providing specific insights into various ideas touched upon in the paper. While leveraging latest Transformer-based models, our systems are simple, intuitive and based on how specific paper sections contribute to human summaries of the two types described above.'

7 Conclusions

In this paper, we studied two scientific document summarization tasks: LaySumm and LongSumm. We experimented with popular text neural models in a section-aware manner. Our results indicate that modeling of the document structure with strong focus on which parts of a research paper to attend to while composing a summary gives a significant boost to the quality of the resultant output. On blind test corpora, our system ranks first and third for the LongSumm and LaySumm tasks respectively.

References

Mehdi Allahyari, Seyedamin Pouriyeh, Mehdi Assefi, Saeid Safaei, Elizabeth D Trippe, Juan B Gutierrez, and Krys Kochut. 2017. Text summarization techniques: a brief survey. *arXiv preprint arXiv:1707.02268*.

M. K. Chandrasekaran, G. Feigenblat, Hovy. E., A. Ravichander, M. Shmueli-Scheuer, and

---

[9]https://doi.org/10.1016/j.engappai.2020.103495
[10]https://doi.org/10.1016/j.engappai.2019.103467

A. De Waard. 2020. Overview and insights from scientific document summarization shared tasks 2020: Cl-scisumm, laysumm and longsumm. In *Proceedings of the First Workshop on Scholarly Document Processing (SDP)*, page "Forthcoming".

Arman Cohan, Franck Dernoncourt, Doo Soon Kim, Trung Bui, Seokhwan Kim, Walter Chang, and Nazli Goharian. 2018. A discourse-aware attention model for abstractive summarization of long documents. *arXiv preprint arXiv:1804.05685*.

Trevor Cohn and Mirella Lapata. 2008. Sentence compression beyond word deletion. In *Proceedings of the 22nd International Conference on Computational Linguistics (Coling 2008)*, pages 137–144.

Ed Collins, Isabelle Augenstein, and Sebastian Riedel. 2017. A supervised approach to extractive summarisation of scientific papers. *arXiv preprint arXiv:1706.03946*.

Jacob Devlin, Ming-Wei Chang, Kenton Lee, and Kristina Toutanova. 2018. Bert: Pre-training of deep bidirectional transformers for language understanding. *arXiv preprint arXiv:1810.04805*.

Shai Erera, Michal Shmueli-Scheuer, Guy Feigenblat, Ora Peled Nakash, Odellia Boni, Haggai Roitman, Doron Cohen, Bar Weiner, Yosi Mass, Or Rivlin, et al. 2019. A summarization system for scientific documents. *arXiv preprint arXiv:1908.11152*.

Günes Erkan and Dragomir R Radev. 2004. Lexrank: Graph-based lexical centrality as salience in text summarization. *Journal of artificial intelligence research*, 22:457–479.

Guy Lev, Michal Shmueli-Scheuer, Jonathan Herzig, Achiya Jerbi, and David Konopnicki. 2019. Talksumm: A dataset and scalable annotation method for scientific paper summarization based on conference talks. *arXiv preprint arXiv:1906.01351*.

Mike Lewis, Yinhan Liu, Naman Goyal, Marjan Ghazvininejad, Abdelrahman Mohamed, Omer Levy, Ves Stoyanov, and Luke Zettlemoyer. 2019. Bart: Denoising sequence-to-sequence pre-training for natural language generation, translation, and comprehension. *arXiv preprint arXiv:1910.13461*.

Chin-Yew Lin. 2004. Rouge: A package for automatic evaluation of summaries. page 10.

Yang Liu. 2019. Fine-tune bert for extractive summarization. *arXiv preprint arXiv:1903.10318*.

Yang Liu and Mirella Lapata. 2019. Text summarization with pretrained encoders. In *Proceedings of the 2019 Conference on Empirical Methods in Natural Language Processing and the 9th International Joint Conference on Natural Language Processing (EMNLP-IJCNLP)*, pages 3721–3731.

Rada Mihalcea and Paul Tarau. 2004. Textrank: Bringing order into text. In *Proceedings of the 2004 conference on empirical methods in natural language processing*, pages 404–411.

Ramesh Nallapati, Feifei Zhai, and Bowen Zhou. 2016. Summarunner: A recurrent neural network based sequence model for extractive summarization of documents. *arXiv preprint arXiv:1611.04230*.

Ani Nenkova and Kathleen McKeown. 2012. A survey of text summarization techniques. In *Mining text data*, pages 43–76. Springer.

Jeffrey Pennington, Richard Socher, and Christopher D Manning. 2014. Glove: Global vectors for word representation. In *Proceedings of the 2014 conference on empirical methods in natural language processing (EMNLP)*, pages 1532–1543.

Colin Raffel, Noam Shazeer, Adam Roberts, Katherine Lee, Sharan Narang, Michael Matena, Yanqi Zhou, Wei Li, and Peter J Liu. 2019. Exploring the limits of transfer learning with a unified text-to-text transformer. *arXiv preprint arXiv:1910.10683*.

Abhishek Kumar Singh, Manish Gupta, and Vasudeva Varma. 2017. Hybrid memnet for extractive summarization. In *Proceedings of the 2017 ACM on Conference on Information and Knowledge Management*, pages 2303–2306.

Abhishek Kumar Singh, Manish Gupta, and Vasudeva Varma. 2018. Unity in diversity: Learning distributed heterogeneous sentence representation for extractive summarization. In *AAAI*.

Sandeep Subramanian, Raymond Li, Jonathan Pilault, and Christopher Pal. 2019. On extractive and abstractive neural document summarization with transformer language models. *arXiv preprint arXiv:1909.03186*.

Bakhtiyar Syed, Gaurav Verma, Balaji Vasan Srinivasan, Anandhavelu Natarajan, and Vasudeva Varma. 2020. Adapting language models for non-parallel author-stylized rewriting. In *AAAI*, pages 9008–9015.

Oguzhan Tas and Farzad Kiyani. 2007. A survey automatic text summarization. *PressAcademia Procedia*, 5(1):205–213.

Raghuram Vadapalli, Bakhtiyar Syed, Nishant Prabhu, Balaji Vasan Srinivasan, and Vasudeva Varma. 2018. When science journalism meets artificial intelligence: An interactive demonstration. In *Proceedings of the 2018 Conference on Empirical Methods in Natural Language Processing: System Demonstrations*, pages 163–168.

Ashish Vaswani, Noam Shazeer, Niki Parmar, Jakob Uszkoreit, Llion Jones, Aidan N Gomez, Łukasz Kaiser, and Illia Polosukhin. 2017. Attention is all you need. In *Advances in neural information processing systems*, pages 5998–6008.

Kristian Woodsend and Mirella Lapata. 2011. Learning to simplify sentences with quasi-synchronous grammar and integer programming. In *Proceedings of the 2011 Conference on Empirical Methods in Natural Language Processing*, pages 409–420.

Wen Xiao and Giuseppe Carenini. 2019. Extractive summarization of long documents by combining global and local context. *arXiv preprint arXiv:1909.08089*.

Xingxing Zhang, Furu Wei, and Ming Zhou. 2019. Hibert: Document level pre-training of hierarchical bidirectional transformers for document summarization. In *Proceedings of the 57th Annual Meeting of the Association for Computational Linguistics*, pages 5059–5069.

Divide and Conquer: From Complexity to Simplicity for Lay Summarization

Rochana Chaturvedi[1], Saachi[2*], Jaspreet Singh Dhani[2*], Anurag Joshi[2*],
Ankush Khanna[2*], Neha Tomar[2*], Swagata Duari[2], Alka Khurana[2] and
Vasudha Bhatnagar[2]

[1]Keshav Mahavidyalaya, University of Delhi
[2]Department of Computer Science, University of Delhi

{*rochana.chaturvedi, saachi.mcs19.du, jaspreet.mcs19.du,
anuragjoshi.mca19.du, ankush.mcs19.du, neha.mcs19.du*}@gmail.com,
{*sduari, akhurana, vbhatnagar*}@cs.du.ac.in

Abstract

We describe our approach for the 1st Computational Linguistics Lay Summary Shared Task CL-LaySumm20. The task is to produce non-technical summaries of scholarly documents. The summary should be within easy grasp of a layman who may not be well versed with the domain of the research article. We propose a two step *divide-and-conquer* approach. First, we judiciously select segments of the documents that are not overly pedantic and are likely to be of interest to the laity, and over-extract sentences from each segment using an unsupervised network based method. Next, we perform abstractive summarization on these extractions and systematically merge the abstractions. We run ablation studies to establish that each step in our pipeline is critical for improvement in the quality of lay summary. Our approach leverages state-of-the-art pre-trained deep neural network based models as zero-shot learners to achieve high scores on the task.

1 Introduction

Acceptance of science by society is accelerated by sharing scientific knowledge and engaging with the public at large. Scientifically backed information, when suitably summarized and conveyed to the common man, spurs empowerment to combat the spread of misinformation. Lay summary of a scientific scholarly text, targeted for the general public, captures the broad scientific idea and its potential impact with minimal technical jargon. Funding agencies, scientists within and outside the field,

and science journalists also benefit from lay summaries (Kuehne and Olden, 2015).

CL-LaySumm20 shared task aims to develop NLP methods to bridge the gap between advances made by the scientific community and non-specialist audience, by summarizing scholarly scientific articles in language understandable by lay persons. Evaluation for the task is done on the basis of Recall and F1-scores of ROUGE-1, -2, and -L metrics (Lin, 2004). Additionally, selective summaries are evaluated by science journalists and communicators for ease of comprehension as well as for interestingness. Chandrasekaran et al. (Forthcoming) document the results and insights from the shared task.

1.1 Abstractive Vs. Extractive Summarization

Automatic summarization of generic documents is accomplished by either using *Extractive* or *Abstractive* approach. *Extractive* summarization algorithms rank salient sentences in the input text, and subsequently select top ranked sentences for inclusion in summary. These algorithms effectively identify sentences containing important facts, but often suffer from weak coherence. An extractive summary, which is more like bullet points, does not compare favourably with human written summary, which is a cohesive piece of text generally written after paraphrasing and fusing different sentences or phrases from the text. Overall coherence between sentences in an extractive summary depreciates because of severe loss of context and several dangling anaphora (Antunes et al., 2018).

With rapid and remarkable developments in neu-

---

*These authors have equal contribution to this work.

Proceedings of the First Workshop on Scholarly Document Processing, pages 344–355
Online, November 19, 2020. ©2020 Association for Computational Linguistics
https://doi.org/10.18653/v1/P17

ral language models, *Abstractive* summarization algorithms have gained traction. These models are trained on sequence to sequence text generation (Sutskever et al., 2014) and are able to generate high quality natural language texts. They are competent to abstract long sentences into short and meaningful sentences, and are germane enough to introduce novel expressions and paraphrases while maintaining almost human-like quality. The current state-of-the-art neural abstractive summarizers are based on transformers (Vaswani et al., 2017), which use self-attention mechanism to allow contextual encoding of input sequence.

A major shortcoming of transformer based models is that their memory requirement and computational cost depends quadratically on the length of input sequence. A two stage extractive-abstractive pipeline is usually proposed to alleviate this shortcoming including in the prominent works of Chen and Bansal (2018), Gehrmann et al. (2018) and Zhao et al. (2020). Extractive step before abstraction has also been deemed important to improve the content selection in abstractive summaries (Liu and Liu, 2009; Mehdad et al., 2014).

1.2   Lay Summarization

Dubé and Lapane (2014) provide a checklist for manually writing lay summary for specified audience, which serves as a desiderata for designing algorithms for lay summarization. Manually translating complex research ideas into lay language incurs extensive patience, time, subject knowledge and effort. This has motivated research in the area of automatic *lay summarization*, which aims at condensing core ideas of scientific research and transforming them in accessible language for lay audiences, while remaining true to science.

Extractive summarization is insufficient for the task of lay summarization because of two reasons. First, when the sentences are selected for inclusion in summary they carry the burden of scientific jargon along with them, which degrades readability and comprehension for lay audience. Second, loss of contextual information and the consequent lack of coherence seriously detriments the purpose of lay summary.

As discussed earlier, state-of-the-art transformer based neural abstractive summarizers do not scale well for documents exceeding 1000 sequence tokens (Zhao et al., 2020). As scholarly articles are usually much longer, abstractive summarizers

cannot be effectively used standalone for the CL-Laysum20 task.

Lay Summarization can benefit from tactfully exploiting the strengths of extractive and abstractive summarization, while renouncing their respective caveats. Distilling important sentences conveying core scientific ideas from the paper using extractive summarization, and feeding it to state-of-the-art abstractive summarizer has potential to yield desired non-technical summary of the scientific article in simple and understandable language.

1.3   Our Approach

We propose a two step approach that *divides* the scientific scholarly text into segments to *conquer* the *complexity* before generating *simple* lay summary. Following the heuristic advanced by Collins et al. (2017a) that certain sections of the document are more pertinent from the summarization viewpoint, we exploit the structure of scientific scholarly text to select information rich segments. We discerningly combine state-of-the-art extractive and abstractive summarization methods, to first extract important sentences from the selected segments, and then compress and paraphrase these sentences via abstractive summarizer. Subsequently, we combine the summaries in a rule based manner to obtain the final lay summary. We report systematic ablation studies to demonstrate the benefit of (i) using abstraction after extraction, and (ii) focusing on specific sections for lay summarization.

2   Background and Related Work

Earlier works on summarization of scientific articles aim to automatically produce the summary for researchers from multiple perspectives that complement each other. These cover automatic creation of abstract (Luhn, 1958; Lloret et al., 2013), extraction of keywords (Duari and Bhatnagar, 2019; Campos et al., 2020), title generation (Putra and Khodra, 2017), extraction of highlights (Collins et al., 2017b; Cagliero and La Quatra, 2020), query-focused summarization (Erera et al., 2019) and citation based summarization of articles (Cohan and Goharian, 2018; Yasunaga et al., 2019).

Various supervised and unsupervised techniques have been used so far for accomplishing distinctive tasks pertinent to scientific articles (Altmami and Menai, 2020). Recently, Miller (2019) propose to leverage the state-of-the-art BERT model (Devlin et al., 2018) for extractive summarization of lectures. In this approach, K-means clustering is performed on sentence embeddings obtained from BERT, and the sentences that are closest to cluster centroids are extracted to create the summary. Among non-neural models, a popular approach is to capture relations between sentences or word phrases via a weighted graph. Gupta et al. (2014, 2019) model the sentences of the document as nodes of a weighted directed graph and compute idf based entailment scores between sentence pairs. They use weighted minimum vertex cover to extract most salient sentences.

Most recent neural abstractive summarizers are trained on masked language modeling task where random sequences of inputs are masked and the model learns to reproduce the masked portions of text. One such model that has achieved state-of-the-art results on abstractive summarization datasets is BART (Lewis et al., 2019). BART is an autoencoder which is pretrained to reproduce the original input after it has been corrupted with arbitrary noise. BART uses transformer (Vaswani et al., 2017) based architecture that employs self-attention mechanism to allow contextual encoding of input sequence.

3   Data

The organizers provide training and validation corpora for CL-LaySumm20 task, named Laysumm2 (215 documents) and Batch3 (357 documents). These documents comprise abstracts and full texts of scholarly articles from epilepsy, archaeology, and materials engineering domains. Each document in the two corpora is accompanied with a gold-standard lay summary. The test set contains 37 documents (abstracts and full texts). Table 1 presents basic statistics for the training, validation, and test datasets.

Stats	Dataset				
	Fulltext + Abstract			Gold-Summary	
	Laysumm2	Batch3	Test	Laysumm2	Batch3
N_{avg}	5493	4803	6125	116	93
NS_{avg}	230	109	272	5	3
S_{avg}	24	46	23	23	31

Table 1: Descriptive statistics for complete text and gold-standard summaries of training and test corpora. N_{avg}: average document length in words, NS_{avg}: average number of sentences in documents, and S_{avg}: average sentence length in words.

4   Methodology

Our approach is based on the premise that not all sections of scientific scholarly text are equally comprehensible to non-experts. Gist of the scientific ideas and the important findings are concentrated in *Abstract* and *Conclusion* sections, while most of the technical details of the research are liberally spread in sections describing methodology and experimentation. *Introduction* and *Discussion* sections lie somewhere in between the spectrum.

Based on the intuition that *Abstract, Introduction and Conclusion* sections in scientific scholarly text are information rich, Kavila and Radhika (2015) construct summaries sourced from these sections. Collins et al. (2017a) argue that the *Abstract*, being an author generated summary is most important section in a paper. Using corpus of 10K computer science research papers, they empirically compare the overlap between different sections and paper highlights. It is reported that among *Abstract, Conclusion, Discussion* and *Introduction* sections (ACDI), *Introduction* section shows least overlap. The authors attribute low importance of *Introduction* section to its longer length.

We empirically test this conjecture for lay summaries. We divide the scientific document in two parts - (i) combined ACDI text, and (ii) rest of the document and compute the ROUGE scores of the two parts[1] with respect to the gold standard summary. Table 2 shows the result of the experiment for both corpora, affirming the observations documented by Collins et al. (2017a). For both corpora the combined ACDI sections, despite being shorter, boast of higher ROUGE scores compared to the remaining text. The results confirm that ACDI sections are apposite for generating summaries from layman perspective.

	Section	N_{avg}	1F	1R	2F	2R	LF	LR
L	ACDI	1581	**12.92**	**90.57**	**7.98**	**57.32**	**9.07**	**65.08**
	Rest	3720	9.85	82.02	3.52	36.19	5.75	53.04
B	ACDI	1901	**8.35**	**91.66**	**4.63**	**54.13**	**5.76**	**65.23**
	Rest	2406	6.30	83.17	2.49	35.55	4.11	56.44

Table 2: Average ROUGE scores of combined ACDI sections vs rest of the text for Laysumm2 (L) and Batch3 (B) datasets.

4.1   Section-wise Analysis

We further study the relative importance of each of these four sections from lay summary perspective

---

[1]We use pre-processed text for this analysis.

and present our results in Table 3. Note that all research papers in the corpora are not structured uniformly and there is a variation in the sections present in a paper. Column N_{Doc} shows the number of documents that contain the particular section. All ROUGE scores are computed over the *existing* sections in the documents.

For Laysumm2 corpus, *Abstract* consistently exhibits high ROUGE scores, except for slightly better ROUGE-recall of *Introduction*. Length of the *Introduction* section, which is almost four times that of abstract, possibly begets this advantage. *Discussion* and *Introduction* sections, which have similar average lengths score comparably. *Conclusion*, the shortest section, displays relatively higher F-score for its length. Its low recall score is clearly due to its short length.

Documents in Batch3 corpus evince different trend in ROUGE scores due to difference in the lengths of the sections. *Discussion* section is strikingly longer compared to others, gaining higher recall scores. Interestingly, the gain due to length is annulled by F scores, which are the lowest among the four sections. *Abstract* consistently earns second highest score, despite short length.

	Section	N_{Doc}	N_{avg}	1F	1R	2F	2R	LF	LR
L	A	205	210	**49.33**	69.91	**29.20**	**41.71**	**36.74**	**52.12**
	C	175	326	31.78	56.94	10.10	18.66	17.53	31.40
	D	129	816	19.89	66.91	5.93	21.79	10.98	37.99
	I	206	**852**	22.24	**71.44**	8.48	28.90	13.06	42.74
B	A	357	302	30.55	68.89	**13.68**	31.57	19.62	44.78
	C	24	113	**33.89**	42.21	11.25	12.80	**20.13**	24.24
	D	356	**1298**	10.79	**81.16**	4.50	**35.50**	6.97	**54.12**
	I	355	505	21.81	73.24	7.95	27.24	12.45	42.55

Table 3: Average ROUGE scores for *Abstract* (A), *Conclusion*(C), *Discussion*(D), *Introduction*(I) sections wrt gold standard lay summaries for Laysumm2 (L) and Batch3 (B) datasets. The averages are taken by considering only the cases where these sections are present in the document. N_{Doc}: is the number of documents in which a particular section appears.

The experiment leads to conclusion not different from (Collins et al., 2017a), and forms the basis of rules we use for generation of lay summary (described in the following subsection).

4.2 Lay Summarization Framework

The complete pipeline of our system is shown in Figure 1. We reconstruct the input for summarization by extricating *Abstract, Conclusion, Discussion* and *Introduction* sections from the preprocessed text. Recognizing the richness and simplicity of the information contained in *Abstract*, supported by high ROUGE scores, we choose not

to perform extractive summarization over it. We over-determine important sentences from each of the remaining three sections using a common extractive summarization method. The four segments, viz. *Abstract* and *Conclusion, Discussion* and *Introduction*, are further condensed using an abstractive summarizer to obtain corresponding simplified texts. Finally, the four abstractive summaries are concatenated one by one in the ACDI order until the desired *Lay summary* length is achieved. We observe from Table 3 that some sections might be missing in some documents. We simply move on to the next most important section (as per ACDI order) in such cases.

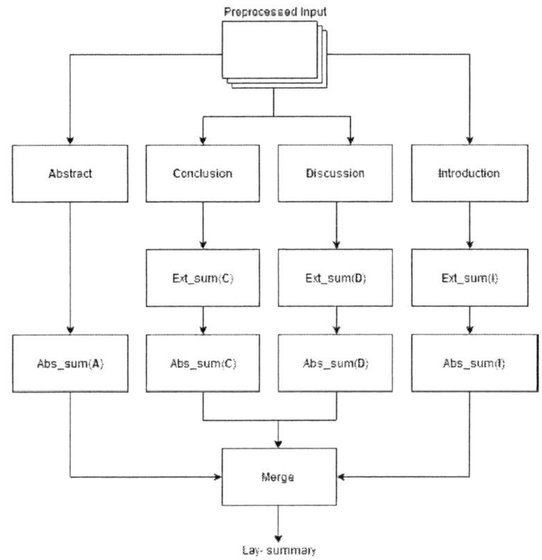

Figure 1: Pipeline of our Methodology. Ext-sum: Extractive summarization step, Abs-sum: Abstractive summarization step.

5 Experimental Setting

In this section we describe the choices we made for implementing the lay summarization framework. All the source code is made publicly available on Github [2].

5.1 Data Pre-processing

We pre-process the input text by removing redundant whitespaces, hyperlinks, and references. Based on the intuition that sentences containing relatively more mathematical symbols and non-English characters might not be comprehensible to lay readers, we completely remove the sentences which are comprised of more than one fifth special

---

[2] github.com/anuragjoshi3519/laysumm20

characters. We also remove any single character or numeral preceded by a period, since this character will constitute beginning of a valid sentence only if it was upper case and was preceded by a period and single whitespace- for instance, 'ab.c' is replaced with 'ab c'. We also replace common acronyms with their full forms. Finally, we remove all punctuation symbols except periods, question marks and exclamation marks which constitute end of sentence markers for effective sentence tokenization.

5.2 Extractive Summarization

We experiment with two extractive summarization methods belonging to different genres with the objective of comparing the cost and benefit. We choose a pretrained supervised neural model BioBERT with k-means clustering (BioBERT_SUM), and a frugal, unsupervised network based summarization algorithm. The two methods are briefly described below.

(i) Supervised: BioBERT_SUM - Motivated by the approach proposed in Miller (2019), we apply k-means clustering on BioBERT embeddings. BioBERT (Lee et al., 2020) is initialized with weights from BERT (Devlin et al., 2018) model pretrained on general domain corpora followed by further training on scholarly text specific to Biomedical domain, which is one of the specified domains of our input corpora. Thus, we expect it to perform well with both general domain as well as biological domain inputs. We use the fine tuned version (BioBERT-NLI[3]) of BioBERT with the bert-extractive-summarizer package[4] for extractive summarization.

(ii) Unsupervised: Entailment based Weighted Minimum Vertex Cover (wMVC) is an unsupervised network based approach proposed by Gupta et al. (2014). The sentences are modelled as vertices of the graph, and Inverse Document Frequency (IDF) based entailment is employed to link sentences Gupta et al. (2019). The algorithm considers those sentences important, which entail many sentences. The extent to which a sentence A entails another sentence B is captured by the weight of directed edge (A, B) defined as:

$$E_{A,B} = \frac{\sum_{w \in A \cap B} idf_w}{\sum_{w \in B} idf_w}$$

where, the idf score of a word w is computed as:

$$idf_w = \log \frac{N}{n_i}$$

n_i = number of sentences containing w, N = Total number of sentences in a document

The connectivity score $Conn_u$ of the vertex determines the importance of the corresponding sentence:

$$Conn_u = \sum_{u \neq v} E_{u,v}$$

In a vertex pruning step, all vertices having connectivity score below a threshold are removed. Finally, minimum number of sentences that encapsulate the essence of document are identified using weighted minimum vertex cover. The aim is to prefer vertices with high connectivity score therefore the vertex weights are inverted for reduction to weighted minimum vertex cover. Highest scoring k sentences are extracted from the solution. These sentences are then re-ordered as per original document ordering. We implement wMVC using Python 3.8 and NetworkX (Hagberg et al., 2008) package.

5.3 Abstractive Summarization

We noticed through manual checks that the gold summaries provided for the task are abstractive in nature. Therefore we extract a longer than required length summary using extractive summarizer and compress them using BART abstractive summarizer. We use the transformers library provided by Wolf et al. (2019) and weights from pretrained model facebook/bart-large-cnn[5] for experiments. We run the BART and BioBERT_SUM on Google Colaboratory with GPU setting while wMVC experiments are run on a CPU.

5.4 Experimental Design

We design experiments to answer three research questions.

I. How does unsupervised wMVC method compare with BioBERT_SUM for extractive summarization?

II. Does staging of extractive and abstractive summarization bring in improvement in the quality of lay summaries?

III. Does *divide-and-conquer* approach for generating lay summaries pay-off?

---

[3] https://huggingface.co/gsarti/biobert-nli

[4] https://pypi.org/project/bert-extractive-summarizer/0.4.2/

[5] https://huggingface.co/facebook/bart-large-cnn

To answer questions (I) and (II), we extract summaries from the full text using BioBERT_SUM and wMVC. Next we feed the extracted summaries to BART for comparison. The findings are described in Section 6.1. To answer question (III), we compare lay summaries generated by combining ACDI as single unit and those generated by the framework. The observations are discussed in Section 6.2.

6 Results

6.1 Experiment I and II

We compare the performances of wMVC and BioBERT based summarizers by extracting 100 word summaries from the full text of the given documents and computing their respective ROUGE scores (Section (i) of Table 4). Macro-averaged scores for both datasets are higher for wMVC summaries, indicating that wMVC yields better quality summary for the two corpora.

In order to test effectiveness of staging extractive and abstractive summarization, we extract 200 word (twice the length of stipulated summaries) summaries from the full text using the two extractive summarizers, and feed these to BART abstractive summarizer to obtain two sets of lay summaries. Final average summary length is 103 words for Laysumm2 and 93 for Batch3 documents, meeting the stipulated length restriction. ROUGE scores of the summaries are recorded in Section (ii) of Table 4.

It is observed that abstraction distinctly improves ROUGE scores in all cases for all metrics. Interestingly, the quantum of improvement is apparently more for BioBERT based summaries, which makes it winner for lay summaries of Batch3 documents. The conclusion is not confirmatory, however. We plan to investigate deeper using statistical tests.

This experiment indicates that performance of abstractive summarizers for generating lay summaries can be leveraged by feeding them focused and quality content obtained by extractive summarizer. However, the quantum of boost is not predictable and depends on the input. It is noteworthy that staging of pretrained extractive and abstractive summarizers for inference is less data and resource intensive than training a model end to end.

6.2 Experiment III

Next we describe our experiment to test our conjecture of *divide-and-conquer*. We generate lay summaries using the *Abstract, Conclusion, Discussion* and *Introduction* sections as single unit, and compare with those obtained by the proposed framework.

We extract 200 word summaries after combining *Abstract, Introduction, Discussion* and *Conclusion* sections in document order and abstract using BART which delivers lay summaries of average length 113. Next, based on the framework (Figure 1), we generate 150-170 length extractive summaries from the *Conclusion, Discussion* and *Introduction* sections. If any section has length less than 250 words, it is not subjected to extractive summarization. Section-wise lay summaries for each of the four sections are obtained, which are finally assembled by appending in order of ACDI till desired length of lay summary is achieved (90-110 words). Note that in case any section is missing from the paper, the framework quietly ignores it. We present the results in Table 5.

All ROUGE scores for both data sets show significant improvement over the scores obtained for lay summaries of full text (Part (ii) of Table 4 and part (i) of Table 5). It is abundantly clear that *Abstract, Introduction, Discussion* and *Conclusion* sections are most useful for generating lay summaries. Part (ii) of Table 5, further reveals that summary generation from individual sections and their subsequent merging in ACDI order results in higher scoring lay summaries than those generated from combined text of ACDI.

This validates the *divide-and-conquer* approach of focussing on limited segments of scholarly scientific documents, extracting the gist and abstracting it to make it comprehensible. The insight available from this result may help in designing better lay summarizers.

We report the evaluation results of summaries produced from our final experiment ACDI Incremental on the test set in Table 6. In the first variant,

	Data	Model	1F	1R	2F	2R	LF	LR
(i)	L	BioBERT_SUM	35.88	36.77	8.50	8.67	18.88	19.37
		wMVC	**37.52**	**37.96**	**10.88**	**10.97**	**20.70**	**20.93**
	B	BioBERT_SUM	29.87	35.01	6.04	7.09	16.48	19.41
		wMVC	**32.22**	**38.70**	**8.69**	**10.52**	**18.51**	**22.43**
(ii)	L	BART_BioBERT_SUM	37.09	37.95	10.92	11.04	20.85	21.29
		BART_wMVC	**38.54**	**39.60**	**11.68**	**11.97**	**21.29**	**21.88**
	B	BART_BioBERT_SUM	**34.72**	**39.68**	**10.16**	**11.64**	**20.20**	**23.19**
		BART_wMVC	33.13	38.21	8.90	10.30	18.46	21.38

Table 4: Evaluation scores on training (L) and validation (B) datasets for complete text (i) Extractive only (ii) Extractive + Abstractive: Abstracting after extracting 200 word summaries using BART.

Data	Model	1F	1R	2F	2R	LF	LR
(i) L	BART_BioBERT_SUM	41.93	45.07	15.56	16.70	25.01	26.85
	BART_wMVC	**43.29**	**46.82**	**16.34**	**17.68**	**24.91**	**26.97**
(i) B	BART_BioBERT_SUM	**36.92**	**46.70**	**12.10**	**15.47**	**21.56**	**27.45**
	BART_wMVC	36.56	46.48	11.73	15.06	20.63	26.45
(ii) L	BART_BioBERT_SUM	**47.04**	52.97	**21.66**	**24.37**	**28.74**	**32.33**
	BART_wMVC	46.93	**52.99**	21.00	23.66	28.45	32.08
(ii) B	BART_BioBERT_SUM	**38.33**	**51.93**	**13.90**	**18.98**	**22.28**	**30.46**
	BART_wMVC	36.74	49.95	12.77	17.45	21.11	28.87

Table 5: Evaluation scores for experiments on partial input text for both training (L) and validation (B) sets. (i) ACDI Combined. (ii) ACDI Incremental.

BioBERT_SUM is used for extractive summarization and summary lengths are 90 words on an average while in the next two rows, wMVC is used for extractive step and summary lengths are 100 and 110 words respectively. Our final results submitted towards shared task are from BART_wMVC_110 variant. [6]

System Variant	1F	1R	2F	2R	LF	LR
BART_BioBERT_SUM_90	42.43	49.53	17.30	20.19	24.84	29.03
BART_wMVC_100	**42.76**	50.32	17.23	20.13	**25.28**	29.68
BART_wMVC_110*	42.53	**51.59**	**17.48**	**21.02**	25.26	**30.55**

Table 6: Results on the Test corpus. BART_wMVC_110 is submitted towards evaluation for the competition.

It is noteworthy that the quality of generated lay summary is sensitive to the order of the sections. In case the abstract is simple and long enough, there is a possibility that the lay summary might be a condensed form of abstract only. Lay summary of this paper is shown in A.

7 Discussion

We present two sample system summaries along with the gold standard summaries in appendix B in Tables 8 and 9. We can observe that Table 8 has remarkably high overlap (highlighted) with the gold summary. In Table 9, we observe that some technical terms (highlighted) do find their way into lay summary. Use of appropriate ontologies and substituting these terms with their synonyms or entity classes can possibly make the meaning clearer to laity. At times, some sentences (example highlighted in Table 9) end up being extracted that are loosely coupled with the rest of the summary and are not even important from the viewpoint of a layman. Such sentences may increase the ROUGE score, but deteriorate the overall readability.

---

[6]The evaluation scores for test set are retrieved from codalab- https://competitions.codalab.org/competitions/25516#results.

Manual inspection by authors for few other system summaries indicates that we need to improve pre-processing and sentence tokenization. For example, one of the summaries contains confidence interval values which may not be comprehensible to laity. Certain inconsistencies in the input format, confuse our parsing algorithms leading to inaccurate segmentation of sections in a few cases. Moreover, we notice that in few scenarios, BART leaves out incomplete sentences towards the end, which degrades the quality of lay summary. An astute post-processing check is desirable to address this problem.

Dependence on abstractive summarizer for the quality of lay summary is the main caveat of the proposed framework. Anticipating constant improvement in the state-of-the-art in NLG, we expect the framework to yield high quality lay summaries.

8 Conclusion

We propose a framework for generating *Lay Summaries* of scientific scholarly documents. The framework is based on the core idea of extractive-abstractive pipeline to generate lay summaries. We *divide* the text into segments and focus on information rich segments to extract important sentences. These extracts are fed to the state-of-the-art abstractive summarizer for further compression which improves readability of the summary. This strategy improves the quality of lay summary, while cutting down on the training data requirement as well as computational resources. The proposed framework is frugal in terms of both types of resources. We show that reusing pre-trained publicly available models can be favoured over devising new training architectures. Thereby, reaping advantages of transfer learning for specialized tasks.

Acknowledgments

We thank the anonymous reviewers for helpful feedback. We also thank Google Colaboratory for GPU access.

References

Nouf Ibrahim Altmami and Mohamed El Bachir Menai. 2020. Automatic summarization of scientific articles: A survey. *Journal of King Saud University-Computer and Information Sciences*.

Jamilson Antunes, Rafael Dueire Lins, Rinaldo Lima, Hilario Oliveira, Marcelo Riss, and Steven J Simske. 2018. Automatic cohesive summarization with pronominal anaphora resolution. *Computer Speech & Language*, 52:141–164.

Luca Cagliero and Moreno La Quatra. 2020. Extracting highlights of scientific articles: A supervised summarization approach. *Expert Systems with Applications*, 160:113659.

Ricardo Campos, Vítor Mangaravite, Arian Pasquali, Alípio Jorge, Célia Nunes, and Adam Jatowt. 2020. Yake! keyword extraction from single documents using multiple local features. *Information Sciences*, 509:257–289.

M. K. Chandrasekaran, G. Feigenblat, Ravichander A. Hovy. E., Shmueli-Scheuerand M., and A. De Waard. Forthcoming. Overview and insights from scientific document summarization shared tasks 2020: Cl-scisumm, laysumm and longsumm. In *Proceedings of the First Workshop on Scholarly Document Processing (SDP 2020)*.

Yen-Chun Chen and Mohit Bansal. 2018. Fast abstractive summarization with reinforce-selected sentence rewriting. *arXiv preprint arXiv:1805.11080*.

Arman Cohan and Nazli Goharian. 2018. Scientific document summarization via citation contextualization and scientific discourse. *International Journal on Digital Libraries*, 19(2-3):287–303.

Ed Collins, Isabelle Augenstein, and Sebastian Riedel. 2017a. A supervised approach to extractive summarisation of scientific papers. *arXiv preprint arXiv:1706.03946*.

Ed Collins, Isabelle Augenstein, and Sebastian Riedel. 2017b. A supervised approach to extractive summarisation of scientific papers. *arXiv preprint arXiv:1706.03946*.

Jacob Devlin, Ming-Wei Chang, Kenton Lee, and Kristina Toutanova. 2018. Bert: Pre-training of deep bidirectional transformers for language understanding. *arXiv preprint arXiv:1810.04805*.

Swagata Duari and Vasudha Bhatnagar. 2019. scake: semantic connectivity aware keyword extraction. *Information Sciences*, 477:100–117.

Catherine E Dubé and Kate L Lapane. 2014. Lay abstracts and summaries: Writing advice for scientists. *Journal of Cancer Education*, 29(3):577–579.

Shai Erera, Michal Shmueli-Scheuer, Guy Feigenblat, Ora Peled Nakash, Odellia Boni, Haggai Roitman, Doron Cohen, Bar Weiner, Yosi Mass, Or Rivlin, et al. 2019. A summarization system for scientific documents. *arXiv preprint arXiv:1908.11152*.

Sebastian Gehrmann, Yuntian Deng, and Alexander M Rush. 2018. Bottom-up abstractive summarization. *arXiv preprint arXiv:1808.10792*.

Anand Gupta, Manpreet Kaur, Ahsaas Bajaj, and Ansh Khanna. 2019. Entailment and spectral clustering based single and multiple document summarization. *International Journal of Intelligent Systems and Applications*, 11(4):39.

Anand Gupta, Manpreet Kaur, Shachar Mirkin, Adarsh Singh, and Aseem Goyal. 2014. Text summarization through entailment-based minimum vertex cover. In *Proceedings of the Third Joint Conference on Lexical and Computational Semantics (* SEM 2014)*, pages 75–80.

Aric A. Hagberg, Daniel A. Schult, and Pieter J. Swart. 2008. Exploring network structure, dynamics, and function using networkx. In *Proceedings of the 7th Python in Science Conference*, pages 11 – 15, Pasadena, CA USA.

Selvani Deepthi Kavila and Y Radhika. 2015. Extractive text summarization using modified weighing and sentence symmetric feature methods. *International Journal of Modern Education and Computer Science*, 7(10):33.

Lauren M Kuehne and Julian D Olden. 2015. Opinion: Lay summaries needed to enhance science communication. *Proceedings of the National Academy of Sciences*, 112(12):3585–3586.

Jinhyuk Lee, Wonjin Yoon, Sungdong Kim, Donghyeon Kim, Sunkyu Kim, Chan Ho So, and Jaewoo Kang. 2020. Biobert: a pre-trained biomedical language representation model for biomedical text mining. *Bioinformatics*, 36(4):1234–1240.

Mike Lewis, Yinhan Liu, Naman Goyal, Marjan Ghazvininejad, Abdelrahman Mohamed, Omer Levy, Ves Stoyanov, and Luke Zettlemoyer. 2019. Bart: Denoising sequence-to-sequence pre-training for natural language generation, translation, and comprehension. *arXiv preprint arXiv:1910.13461*.

Chin-Yew Lin. 2004. Rouge: A package for automatic evaluation of summaries. In *Text summarization branches out*, pages 74–81.

Fei Liu and Yang Liu. 2009. From extractive to abstractive meeting summaries: Can it be done by sentence compression? In *Proceedings of the ACL-IJCNLP 2009 Conference Short Papers*, pages 261–264.

Elena Lloret, María Teresa Romá-Ferri, and Manuel Palomar. 2013. Compendium: A text summarization system for generating abstracts of research papers. *Data & Knowledge Engineering*, 88:164–175.

Hans Peter Luhn. 1958. The automatic creation of literature abstracts. *IBM Journal of research and development*, 2(2):159–165.

Yashar Mehdad, Giuseppe Carenini, and Raymond Ng. 2014. Abstractive summarization of spoken and written conversations based on phrasal queries. In *Proceedings of the 52nd Annual Meeting of the Association for Computational Linguistics (Volume 1: Long Papers)*, pages 1220–1230.

Derek Miller. 2019. Leveraging bert for extractive text summarization on lectures. *arXiv preprint arXiv:1906.04165*.

Jan Wira Gotama Putra and Masayu Leylia Khodra. 2017. Automatic title generation in scientific articles for authorship assistance: a summarization approach. *Journal of ICT Research and Applications*, 11(3):253–267.

Ilya Sutskever, Oriol Vinyals, and Quoc V. Le. 2014. Sequence to sequence learning with neural networks.

Ashish Vaswani, Noam Shazeer, Niki Parmar, Jakob Uszkoreit, Llion Jones, Aidan N. Gomez, Lukasz Kaiser, and Illia Polosukhin. 2017. Attention is all you need.

Thomas Wolf, Lysandre Debut, Victor Sanh, Julien Chaumond, Clement Delangue, Anthony Moi, Pierric Cistac, Tim Rault, R'emi Louf, Morgan Funtowicz, and Jamie Brew. 2019. Huggingface's transformers: State-of-the-art natural language processing. *ArXiv*, abs/1910.03771.

Michihiro Yasunaga, Jungo Kasai, Rui Zhang, Alexander R Fabbri, Irene Li, Dan Friedman, and Dragomir R Radev. 2019. Scisummnet: A large annotated corpus and content-impact models for scientific paper summarization with citation networks. In *Proceedings of the AAAI Conference on Artificial Intelligence*, volume 33, pages 7386–7393.

Yao Zhao, Mohammad Saleh, and Peter J. Liu. 2020. Seal: Segment-wise extractive-abstractive long-form text summarization.

A Lay Summary of Present Paper

Title: Divide and Conquer: From Complexity to Simplicity for LaySummarization
Summary
The task is to produce non technical summaries of scholarly documents. The summary should be within easy grasp of a layman who may not be well versed with the domain of the research article. We propose a two step divide and conquer approach. We judiciously select segments of the documents that are not overly pedantic and are likely to be of interest to the laity. We over extract sentences from each segment using an unsupervised network based method. We perform abstractive summarization on these extractions and systematically merge the abstractions. We run ablation studies to establish that each step in our pipeline is critical for improvement in the quality of lay summary.

Table 7: Lay Summary of the paper. The length of the *Abstract* is about 140 words, and it contains few technical terms. Due to the length restriction of 100 words the lay summary is an abstraction of *Abstract* only.

B   Sample System Summaries vs Gold Summaries

Summaries Corresponding to Paper ID : S2352409X18305169	
Title	GIS modeling of agricultural suitability in the highlands of the Jornada branch of the Mogollon culture of southcentral New Mexico
Gold Standard	Measures of site location in relation to agricultural potential are an important tool for identifying relative shifts in the importance of agriculture in prehistoric economies over time. We examine GIS modeling of agricultural potential based on soil characteristics, topography, and proximity to drainage in the highlands of the Mogollon culture of southcentral New Mexico. We describe methods, limitations, and advantages of this approach. Preliminary results support other evidence of strong agricultural reliance in the pithouse period, substantially greater than in the Archaic; the pueblo period may be slightly more linked to optimal agricultural land, though the latter conclusion is uncertain.
BART_wMVC	Measures of site location in relation to agricultural potential are an important tool for identifying relative shifts in the importance of agriculture over time within a given region. We examine the application of GIS modeling of agricultural potential based on soil characteristics, topography, and proximity to drainage in the highlands of the Jornada branch of the Mogollon culture of southcentral New Mexico. Our results support other evidence of strong agricultural reliance in the pithouse period, substantially greater than in the Archaic the pueblo period occupation may be slightly more tightly linked to optimal agricultural land, though the latter conclusion is uncertain. Our results have potential implications for both the interpretation of Formative period settlement in the Sierra Blanca Capitan Mountain highlands, and for further methodological approaches to settlement analysis.

Table 8: Gold standard and System Summaries for document scoring highest in ROUGE-1F (79.48). Highlighted sentences appear in gold standard lay summary.

	Summaries Corresponding to Paper ID:S2352409X18303663
Title	An evaluation of classical morphologic and morphometric parameters reported to distinguish wolves and dogs
Gold Standard	Visual traits and measurements that support distinguishing dog and wolf skeletal remains have been long-used, but insufficiently researched. We evaluated 14 of these, including dental abnormalities; mandible shape; orbital angle; hard palate; snout dimensions; and skull dimensions. We found only a few reliable measures, including skull height, very small or large orbital angle, snout width index, and specific measures of the 1st molar and 4th premolar teeth. Thus, much earlier research now must be re-considered toward use of combined visual, measured, and genetic traits for accurate archaeological identifications.
BART_wMVC	Morphological and morphometric differences between wolves and dogs are often overlooked. This article shows how these differences can be used to better understand the history of wolf-dog relations. The study also shows that the differences between the two species are not as large as previously thought. The results of the study were published in the Journal of Archaeology and Ethnology, a journal of the American Museum of Natural History and the American Academy of Arts and Sciences. Traditional morphometric identification of potential early domesticated dogs largely has been based on low numbers of specimens, as well as unverified diagnostic methods and variables. We propose the use of much larger canid reference groups to explore whether variation identified as signs of domestication in these specimens actually reflects natural variation that will be seen more easily within larger sample groups.

Table 9: Gold standard and System Summaries for document scoring lowest in ROUGE-1F (20.96). Highlighted terms and sentences are poor choices for lay audience.

GUIR @ LongSumm 2020:
Learning to Generate Long Summaries from Scientific Documents

Sajad Sotudeh[1], Arman Cohan[2] and **Nazli Goharian[1]**

[1]IR Lab, Georgetown University, Washington DC, USA
{sajad, nazli}@ir.cs.georgetown.edu

[2]Allen Institute for AI, Seattle, WA, USA
armanc@allenai.org

Abstract

This paper presents our methods for the Long-Summ 2020: Shared Task on Generating Long Summaries for Scientific Documents, where the task is to generate *long summaries* given a set of scientific papers provided by the organizers. We explore 3 main approaches for this task: 1. An extractive approach using a BERT-based summarization model; 2. A two stage model that additionally includes an abstraction step using BART; and 3. A new multi-tasking approach on incorporating document structure into the summarizer. We found that our new multi-tasking approach outperforms the two other methods by large margins. Among 9 participants in the shared task, our best model ranks top according to ROUGE-1 score (53.11%) while staying competitive in terms of ROUGE-2.

1 Introduction

The task of document summarization aims at generating a short-form (summary) of a longer sequence of text (source) conveying the key points of the input text. This task can be generally performed in two ways: 1) Extractive: where the system finds the salient sentences within the source and concatenates them to form the summary (Zhou et al., 2018; Dong et al., 2018; Zhang et al., 2018; Narayan et al., 2018; Liu and Lapata, 2019; Xu et al., 2020); and 2) Abstractive: where the model conducts text generation, paraphrasing, and produces novel words that are not necessarily present in the source text (See et al., 2017; Çelikyilmaz et al., 2018; MacAvaney et al., 2019; Zhang et al., 2019; Raffel et al., 2019; Sotudeh et al., 2020a; Lewis et al., 2020).

Over the recent years, the task of summarizing scientific papers has attracted researchers' attention. This is due to linguistic challenges inherent to scientific domain and the longer length of the documents (i.e., scientific papers) in comparison with the documents in other domains such as news.

Most prior works in scientific summarization have focused on producing short-form summaries which are around 200 tokens per summary (Collins et al., 2017; Cohan et al., 2018; Xiao and Carenini, 2019) , rather than long-form summaries. Producing the summary at such length might be adequate when the source document is also of shorter form such as those in the news domain. Nevertheless, when summarizing longer documents such as scientific papers, producing short-length summary (i.e., abstract-like) more favors a high-level view of the source document, rather than covering all the salient information within a given source text. Producing such long summaries requires a deep and comprehensive understanding of specific scientific domain. Generating long summaries of the paper is helpful for researchers who might want to learn more about the paper beyond abstract-level information, without the need to read the entire paper.

The LongSumm 2020 shared task [1] aims to encourage the research at generating longer-form summaries for scientific papers, and we progress this challenge by our participation in this challenge, utilizing pre-trained transformer encoders for summarization task.

In our experiments, we explore three different methods for the challenge including 1) Experimenting with different versions of pre-trained transformer encoders finetuned for summarization task as an extractive method (Liu and Lapata, 2019); 2) A two-stage method where an abstarctive summarizer is added to the extractive summarizer to produce abstractive summaries; and 3) A novel multi-task learning model which aims at jointly incorporating documents' discourse structure into the extractive summarizer. This is inspired by the fact that having close attention to the scientific paper's

---

[1]https://ornlcda.github.io/SDProc/
sharedtasks.html

Proceedings of the First Workshop on Scholarly Document Processing, pages 356–361
Online, November 19, 2020. ©2020 Association for Computational Linguistics
https://doi.org/10.18653/v1/P17

discourse information would result in improved summaries (Cohan et al., 2018). We report comptetive results of our model, which achieves ROUGE scores of 53.11%, 16.17%, and 20.34% for RG-1, RG-2, and RG-L, respectively. With the obtained results, our system ranks 1st (RG-1), 2nd (RG-2), and 4th (RG-L) in terms of evaluation metrics.

2 Related Work

2.1 Scientific document summarization

Summarizing scientific papers has garnished vast attention from research communities during recent years, although it has been studied for decades. The characteristics of scientific papers, namely the length, writing style,and discourse structure, lends itself to some model considerations to tackle the challenging task of summarization. Researchers have utilized different approaches to address these challenges. For example, Cohan and Goharian (2015) utilized a citation-based approach, denoting how the paper is cited in the reference papers, to form the summary. Among the first large-scale datasets, Collins et al. (2017) introduced CSPubSum dataset, with the highlights of the paper (4-5 sentences) as the gold summaries. Cohan et al. (2018) introduced large-scale datasets of arXiv and PubMed, and used a hierarchical encoder to model the discourse structure of a paper, and then used an attentive decoder to generate the summary. More recently, Xiao and Carenini (2019) proposed a sequence-to-sequence model which incorporates both the global context of the entire document, and local context within the specified section. Yasunaga et al. (2019) introduced the first large-scale manually created scientific dataset, and proposed a hybrid method to integrate abstract and citations to form comprehensive summaries. Inspired by the fact that discourse information is of high importance when dealing with long documents (Conroy and Davis, 2017; Collins et al., 2017; Cohan et al., 2018) in scientific research papers, in this work, we step on utilizing such structure in summarization of scientific papers.

2.2 Pre-trained transformer networks

Due to the recent success of Transformer models such as BERT (Devlin et al., 2019), researchers have been motivated to fine-tune them on a variety of downstream NLP tasks such as text summarization. Liu and Lapata (2019) were the first to fine-tune BERT on summarization task. In their pro-posed model, they noted that since BERT outputs token-level vectors, it is not suitable for the extractive summarization task where the model often deals with sentences instead of tokens. To alleviate this problem, they appended a special [CLS] token to the start of each sentence to capture sentence-level representation, fulfilling the bases for extractive summarization task. Their model achieved the state-of-the-art on news domain. Later, BART (Lewis et al., 2020) was proposed which is an encoder-decoder pretrained Transformer model. For pretraining purposes, BART is trained by adding noise to the text, and then reconstruct the text by learning a model. In our model, we extend the BERTSUM model (Liu and Lapata, 2019) by adding a section predictor level that is jointly learned along with the sentence predictor layer (i.e., extractive summarizer).

3 Dataset

The dataset provided for this challenge consists of two types of summaries:

- Extractive summaries: these summaries are based on TalkSumm dataset (Lev et al., 2019), containing 1705 extractive summaries of scientific papers according to their video talks in associated conferences (i.e., ACL, NAACL, and etc.). Each summary within this corpus is formed by appending top 30 sentences of the paper. The average length of summaries in this corpus is around 990 words.

- Abstractive summaries: As an add-on dataset, the organizers have provided 531 abstractive summaries from different domains of CS such as Machine Learning, NLP, and AI, that are written by NLP and ML researchers on their blogs. The summaries' length in this dataset ranges from 100-1500 words per paper.

In our experiments, we use the extractive set along with 50% of abstracitve set as our training set, containing 1969 papers; and the other half of abstractive set is used as validation and test datasets. It has to be mentioned that the official test set (blind) also contains 22 abstractive papers.

4 Methodology

In this section, we discuss our methods with different configurations submitted to the shared task.

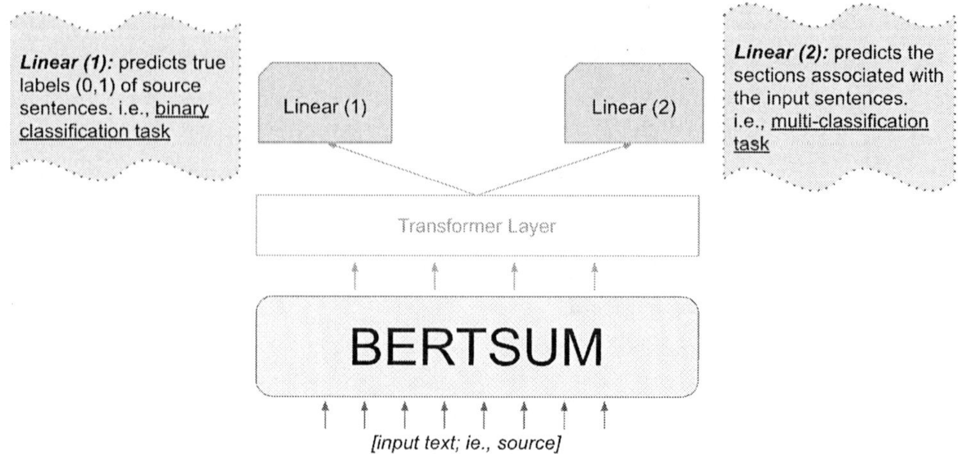

Figure 1: The overview of the proposed BERTSUMEXTMULTI model.

4.1 Pre-trained Transformers

While BERT has been shown to be effective on many natural language processing tasks, its application has not been straightforward for the text summarization task. This is due to the fact that BERT is trained with the objective of masked-language model, thus it results in token-level output vectors instead of sentence-level representations. This is particularly important since in the extractive summarization setting, the model needs to pick up sentences that are salient (Liu and Lapata, 2019). In our experiments, we utilize BERTSUM to obtain the BERT encoding for each sentence within the source document.

4.2 Extractive Summarization

As mentioned earlier, extractive summarization system aims at extracting top and salient sentences that are worthy to be included in summary. Let P show a scientific paper containing sentences $[s_1, s_2, s_3, ..., s_m]$, with m being the count of the sentences of input paper, and s_i denoting the i-th sentence in the document. The extractive summarization is then defined as the task of assigning a binary label ($\hat{y}_i \in \{0, 1\}$) to each sentence s_i in the input, deciding whether the sentence should be included in the summary or not.

BERTSUM is able to produce output vector t_i which is the representation of the i-th sentence within the input document. Afterwards, several inter-sentence Transformer layers are stacked upon top of BERTSUM outputs to collect document-level features for extractive summarization. The final output layer is a linear classifier with sigmoid activation function to decide whether the sentence should be included or not. In our experiments, we use this model to extract salient sentences (i.e., those with the positive label) to form the summary. We call this model as BERTSUMEXT.

4.3 Abstractive Summarizaiton

As the official test set provided for the challenge resembles more of abstractive type, rather than extractive, we aim at utilizing an abstractive model to produce abstractive summaries. After training the extractive model, we run the learned model through the entire papers in the dataset to extract salient sentences for each paper [2], resulting in a minimized input space for the abstractive summarizer. We then use BART, which is a denoising autoencoder for pretraining sequence-to-sequence model (Lewis et al., 2020), as the abstractive summarizer. In our experiments, we denote this model as BERTSUMBARTABS.

4.4 Section-aware Summarization

Inspired by few prior works that have studied the effect of document discourse structure in summarization task (Conroy and Davis, 2017; Cohan et al., 2018), we define a section prediction task, aiming at predicting section(s) that the sentences within the input documents belong to. Specifically, we add an additional linear output layer with sigmoid activation function that outputs scores for a set of pre-defined sections that a sentence can be assigned to. The entire extractive network is then trained to

---

[2]We used a threshold of 70 top sentences.

optimize both tasks (i.e, sentence prediction and section prediction) in a multi-task setting. For constructing training data for section prediction task, we take the approach and dataset introduced by Cohan et al. (2019) and run it over the sentences of the papers within the provided dataset to generate ground-truth labels. The overview of this model is shown in Fig. 1. This model is called BERTSUMEXTMULTI in our experiments.

4.5 Domain-tuned Summarization

Prior works have denoted the importance of fine-tuning language models on domain-related task and data (Gururangan et al., 2020; Sotudeh et al., 2020b). Following this paradigm, herein we experiment with fine-tuning summarization models on a sample of a larger dataset (i.e., arXiv (Cohan et al., 2018)) and an additional step of fine-tuning on the dataset provided in the LongSumm challenge. We use this scheme for both extractive and abstractive models (i.e., BERTSUM, and BART) with different settings. We call this model BERTSUMEXTMULTI-ARXIV.

5   Experimental Setup

As the initial parameters of the BERTSUM, and BART, we used the default hyper-parameters as denoted in the original papers (Lewis et al., 2020; Liu and Lapata, 2019). We used HuggingFace's Transformers library for working with BART [3], and also the open implementation for experimenting with BERTSUM [4]. In order to provide ground-truth labels for the task of section prediction, we utilized the external sequential-sentence package[5] by Cohan et al. (2019). It has to be mentioned that we classified the *Abstract* and *Conclusion* sections [6] into the same section without having their sentences labeled by the external package. For the joint model, we used loss weighting of 0.5 for two losses associated with each task as it resulted the highest scores in our experiments. For domain-tuned summarization, we used 50,000 samples of training set of arXiv dataset, and 2,000 papers samples from the validation set. In all our models, we pick the checkpoint that achieves the best RG-L

score on the validation during training as our best model for inference. For submission purposes, we did a 5-fold cross validation on the second half of abstractive set, and report the average results of test sets over 5 different folds.

6   Results

In this section, we present the performance of our submissions to the challenge, along with the scores achieved by the other participants. We then show the results of our systems over our internal test set that were constructed on the basis of abstractive set of summaries. Note that the reported scores are the average scores over the 5 folds of cross validation sets. To this end, we report the summarization systems' performance in terms of RG-1 (F1), RG-2 (F1), and RG-L (F1) metrics.

Table 1 shows the performance of our submitted systems to the challenge. For comparison, we also show results for the top 5 systems. As expected, our BERTSUMEXTMULTI model outperforms the other two models in terms of RG-1 and RG-L metrics. Comparing our best system's performance, we observe that our system outperform the other participants' system in RG-1 by large margin. While it lags behind the best submitted system by 0.9 point on RG-2 (i.e., comparable performance), and 1.04 point in RG-L.

Since the official test set is small, we also conducted analysis between variants of our model using the validation and an additional internal test set. We see in Table 2 that the Section predictor model performs fairly well over the model without section prediction module. This is particularly important finding since it characterizes the importance of document structure when summarizing a scientific dataset. Interestingly, having BART as the second stage does not yield to improvement in compared to the extractive setting. The most likely explanation of this gap is since the training set is biased toward extractive summaries, the BART model has difficulty figuring out how to produce right abstractive summaries (the number of abstractive summaries are limited in the training set), and in fact, the model learns to extract sentences, rather than producing novel words. We also trained BART on a portion of abstractive set as training set, but the performance was deteriorative, compared to the other settings. On the other hand, and interestingly, having summarization models fine-tuned on the external arXiv dataset does not

---

[3] https://github.com/huggingface/transformers
[4] https://github.com/nlpyang/PreSumm
[5] https://github.com/allenai/sequential_sentence_classification
[6] We used the title text matching to identify such sentences within Abstract and Conclusion.

	RG-1	RG-2	RG-L
Other systems			
Summaformers	49.38	**16.86**	**21.38**
Wing	50.58	16.62	20.50
IIITBH-IITP	49.03	15.74	20.46
Auth-Team	50.11	15.37	19.59
CIST_BUPT	48.99	15.06	20.13
This work			
BERTSUMBARTABS	51.02	14.38	19.32
BERTSUMEXTMULTI-ARXIV	52.67	16.82	19.90
BERTSUMEXTMULTI	**53.11**	16.77	20.34

Table 1: ROUGE (F1) results of our submissions (bottom part of the table) to the challenge (official test set), along with the performance of other participants' systems. We only show top 5 participants in this table. Description of the other systems are not available at the time of submission. Please refer to the overview paper (Chandrasekaran et al., 2020) for details on each system.

Model	Validation			Test		
	RG-1(%)	RG-2(%)	RG-L(%)	RG-1(%)	RG-2(%)	RG-L(%)
BERTSUMEXT	45.39	12.41	17.81	45.34	12.42	17.82
BERTSUMEXTMULTI	**45.61**	**12.96**	**18.23**	45.55	**12.99**	**18.29**
BERTSUMEXTMULTI-ARXIV	45.44	12.95	17.99	**45.56**	12.77	18.06
BERTSUMBARTABS	44.88	11.78	17.63	44.44	11.51	17.26

Table 2: ROUGE (F1) results on abstractive set of LongSumm dataset (internal test set). The results are averaged over 5-fold cross validation.

yield much of improvement on this challenge. This might be due to the fact that the task defined on arXiv is for short summarization, not long which is our target task. For the section prediction task, BERTSUMEXTMULTI model achieves 92.3%, and 86.4% of accuracy in the validation and test sets, respectively.

section associated with the sentence. While fine-tuning summarization model on external dataset does not yield promising results on this shared task, our best model is the one that jointly incorporates the section information into the extractive summarizer.

7 Conclusion

In this paper, we approached the problem of generating long summaries given a scientific dataset of extractive and abstractive summaries. Our approaches explored using methods including 1) Pre-trained transformer encoders for the extractive summarization task using BERTSUM; and 2) An abstractive summarizer (i.e., BART) which runs over the outputs of extractive summarizer at the first stage, to produce abstractive summaries; and 3) Our proposed novel multi-task learner where a section prediciton task is added to the extractive network, trying to jointly learn the sentence importance to be included in the summary, and the

References

M. K. Chandrasekaran, G. Feigenblat, Hovy. E., A. Ravichander, M. Shmueli-Scheuer, and A. De Waard. 2020. Overview and insights from scientific document summarization shared tasks 2020: Cl-scisumm, laysumm and longsumm. *In Proceedings of the First Workshop on Scholarly Document Processing (SDP 2020).*

Arman Cohan, Iz Beltagy, Daniel King, Bhavana Dalvi, and Daniel S. Weld. 2019. Pretrained language models for sequential sentence classification. In *EMNLP/IJCNLP.*

Arman Cohan, Franck Dernoncourt, Doo Soon Kim, Trung Bui, Seokhwan Kim, W. Chang, and Nazli Goharian. 2018. A discourse-aware attention model for abstractive summarization of long documents. In *NAACL-HLT*.

Arman Cohan and Nazli Goharian. 2015. Scientific article summarization using citation-context and article's discourse structure. In *EMNLP*.

Ed Collins, Isabelle Augenstein, and Sebastian Riedel. 2017. A supervised approach to extractive summarisation of scientific papers. In *Proceedings of the 21st Conference on Computational Natural Language Learning (CoNLL 2017)*, pages 195–205, Vancouver, Canada. Association for Computational Linguistics.

John M. Conroy and Sashka Davis. 2017. Section mixture models for scientific document summarization. *International Journal on Digital Libraries*, 19:305–322.

J. Devlin, Ming-Wei Chang, Kenton Lee, and Kristina Toutanova. 2019. Bert: Pre-training of deep bidirectional transformers for language understanding. In *NAACL-HLT*.

Yue Dong, Yikang Shen, E. Crawford, H. V. Hoof, and J. Cheung. 2018. Banditsum: Extractive summarization as a contextual bandit. In *EMNLP*.

Suchin Gururangan, Ana Marasović, Swabha Swayamdipta, Kyle Lo, Iz Beltagy, Doug Downey, and Noah A. Smith. 2020. Don't stop pretraining: Adapt language models to domains and tasks. In *Proceedings of the 58th Annual Meeting of the Association for Computational Linguistics*, pages 8342–8360, Online. Association for Computational Linguistics.

Guy Lev, Michal Shmueli-Scheuer, Jonathan Herzig, Achiya Jerbi, and David Konopnicki. 2019. Talksumm: A dataset and scalable annotation method for scientific paper summarization based on conference talks. *ACL*.

M. Lewis, Yinhan Liu, Naman Goyal, Marjan Ghazvininejad, A. Mohamed, Omer Levy, V. Stoyanov, and Luke Zettlemoyer. 2020. Bart: Denoising sequence-to-sequence pre-training for natural language generation, translation, and comprehension. *ACL*.

Yang Liu and Mirella Lapata. 2019. Text summarization with pretrained encoders. In *EMNLP/IJCNLP*.

Sean MacAvaney, Sajad Sotudeh, Arman Cohan, Nazli Goharian, Ish Talati, and Ross W. Filice. 2019. Ontology-aware clinical abstractive summarization. In *Proceedings of the 42nd International ACM SIGIR Conference on Research and Development in Information Retrieval*, SIGIR'19, page 1013–1016, New York, NY, USA. Association for Computing Machinery.

Shashi Narayan, Shay B. Cohen, and Mirella Lapata. 2018. Ranking sentences for extractive summarization with reinforcement learning. In *NAACL-HLT*.

Colin Raffel, Noam Shazeer, Adam Roberts, Katherine Lee, Sharan Narang, Michael Matena, Yanqi Zhou, Wei Li, and Peter J. Liu. 2019. Exploring the limits of transfer learning with a unified text-to-text transformer. *arXiv e-prints*.

A. See, Peter J. Liu, and Christopher D. Manning. 2017. Get to the point: Summarization with pointer-generator networks. In *ACL*.

Sajad Sotudeh, Nazli Goharian, and R. Filice. 2020a. Attend to medical ontologies: Content selection for clinical abstractive summarization. In *ACL*.

Sajad Sotudeh, Tong Xiang, Hao-Ren Yao, Sean MacAvaney, Eugene Yang, Nazli Goharian, and Ophir Frieder. 2020b. Guir at semeval-2020 task 12: Domain-tuned contextualized models for offensive language detection. *SemEval2020*, abs/2007.14477.

Wen Xiao and Giuseppe Carenini. 2019. Extractive summarization of long documents by combining global and local context. *ArXiv*, abs/1909.08089.

Jiacheng Xu, Zhe Gan, Y. Cheng, and Jing jing Liu. 2020. Discourse-aware neural extractive text summarization. In *ACL*.

Michihiro Yasunaga, Jungo Kasai, Rui Zhang, Alexander Richard Fabbri, Irene Li, Dan Friedman, and Dragomir R. Radev. 2019. Scisummnet: A large annotated corpus and content-impact models for scientific paper summarization with citation networks. In *AAAI*.

Jingqing Zhang, Yao Zhao, Mohammad Saleh, and Peter J. Liu. 2019. Pegasus: Pre-training with extracted gap-sentences for abstractive summarization.

Xingxing Zhang, Mirella Lapata, Furu Wei, and M. Zhou. 2018. Neural latent extractive document summarization. *ArXiv*, abs/1808.07187.

Qingyu Zhou, Nan Yang, Furu Wei, Shaohan Huang, M. Zhou, and T. Zhao. 2018. Neural document summarization by jointly learning to score and select sentences. In *ACL*.

Asli Çelikyilmaz, Antoine Bosselut, Xiaodong He, and Yejin Choi. 2018. Deep communicating agents for abstractive summarization. In *NAACL-HLT*.

Association for Computational Linguistics
209 N. Eighth Street
Stroudsburg, Pennsylvania 18360

ISBN 978-1-7138-1987-5